Clerical Office Procedures

Sixth Edition

William R. Pasewark
Professor
Texas Tech University

Mary Ellen Oliverio
Formerly Professor of Education
Teachers College
Columbia University

K38   Published by
SOUTH-WESTERN PUBLISHING CO.
CINCINNATI   WEST CHICAGO, ILL.   DALLAS   PELHAM MANOR, N.Y.   PALO ALTO, CALIF.

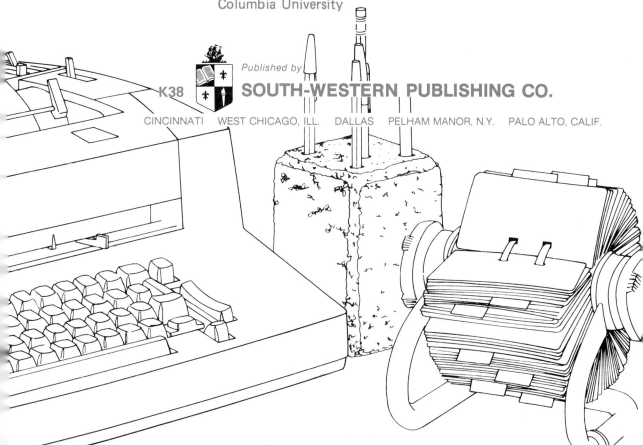

ISBN: 0-538-11380-4

Library of Congress Catalog Card Number: 77-75631

1 2 3 4 5 6 7 K 4 3 2 1 0 9 8

Printed in the United States of America

Preface

Office careers provide more opportunities for employment of young people than any other type of career. There are more office jobs than there are in any other occupational classification according to Bureau of Labor statistics.

The major objective of CLERICAL OFFICE PROCEDURES is to develop the competencies students need to be employed in a wide range of entry-level office jobs. CLERICAL OFFICE PROCEDURES is designed to contribute to students'

1. Mastery of basic office duties that have not been developed in earlier courses, such as handling the mail, filing, duplicating, performing financial tasks, and meeting the public.
2. Development of fully marketable skills in practical tasks such as typewriting, proofreading, and handling correspondence.
3. Command of realistic job demands by providing experience with practical problems and job-like assignments in simulated office situations.
4. Self-confidence and maturity through attention to personal qualities that are esteemed in the world of work.
5. Understanding of the nature of the office and its importance in the business world.
6. Ability to work harmoniously with employers, co-workers, and customers.
7. Awareness of employment opportunities in the business world for beginning positions and future careers.

CLERICAL OFFICE PROCEDURES can be used as the primary or supplementary text in a variety of clerical education programs: battery, rotation, simulated, cooperative, block, intensified, and modular.

The content of the text includes discussions of modern office procedures such as: reprographics, word processing, and micrographics. The emphasis on office job opportunities for all citizens regardless of sex, race, nationality, and religion is reflected in the content, wording, and illustrations of this book.

Activity-oriented exercises at the end of each Part include:

REVIEWING IMPORTANT POINTS — Questions that reinforce information presented in the text.

MAKING IMPORTANT DECISIONS — Office situation case studies that give students experience in identifying correct procedures and making judgments.

LEARNING TO WORK WITH OTHERS — Office situation case studies that give students experience with human relations problems.

IMPROVING LANGUAGE SKILLS — Exercises to strengthen students' skills in English usage.

IMPROVING ARITHMETIC SKILLS — Exercises to strengthen students' arithmetical skills.

DEMONSTRATING OFFICE SKILLS — Tasks that give students opportunities to apply office skills and knowledge.

IMPROVING OFFICE SKILLS (Optional) — Additional tasks which are more complex than those in Demonstrating Office Skills. (At the end of each Unit only.)

Students will apply what they have learned in a realistic setting as they assume a beginning office position in the simulated *All-Star Sporting Goods Company*. The materials needed to complete the simulation are contained in a separate *Supplies Inventory* available from the publisher. The *Supplies Inventory* also includes business forms and papers the students may use to complete exercises at the end of each Part. One test for each Unit and two comprehensive tests are also available from the publisher.

The *Teacher's Manual* provides specific suggestions for teaching each Unit. Course schedules, rotation plans, and grading suggestions explain how to organize a course that includes office procedures and/or office machines. Transparency masters that highlight important concepts and procedures are provided. Dictation keyed to each Unit is provided for those classes where the development of transcribing machine skill is an important vocational goal.

To prepare an attractive, realistic, up-to-date, and instructive textbook requires the blending of thoughts from people in business and in education. Experienced office supervisors, clerical workers, and executives provided information, suggestions, and actual office materials for this edition. The reactions of many teachers and students were utilized in preparing CLERICAL OFFICE PROCEDURES so that it will be effective in preparing students for meaningful office careers. We acknowledge, with thanks, all of these contributions.

William R. Pasewark
Mary Ellen Oliverio

To the Student

Office jobs are available in businesses and organizations throughout the country. Thousands of openings occur each year in many different types of office positions such as typist, clerk-typist, file clerk, office machine operator, administrative assistant, word processing transcriber, and office manager.

Working in a modern office has become more and more interesting. Executives know that the office is a vital part of every business because it is where information is systematically processed and stored. Moreover, almost every individual in a company is involved to some extent with office work, whether that person is an accountant, a sales representative, a typist, a stockroom clerk, or the president of the company.

CLERICAL OFFICE PROCEDURES is designed to prepare you for many of the jobs available to beginning office workers. Each Part starts off with a sketch about an actual office experience. The text and illustrations explain the wide variety of procedures and tasks that make up office work. At the end of each Part, brief questions will reinforce key points presented. In addition, office case studies will help you to develop the ability to make judgments and work with others. And finally, you will handle typical office tasks using business letterhead paper and forms contained in the *Supplies Inventory*. You will also have the opportunity to assume a position in the *All-Star Sporting Goods Company* where you will organize and complete office assignments similar to those done on an actual job.

CLERICAL OFFICE PROCEDURES has been planned to help you learn about office work and acquire the skills, information, and attitudes that will prepare you for a successful, happy office career.

William R. Pasewark
Mary Ellen Oliverio

Contents

The Modern Office and Career Opportunities

Part 1. Office Employees at Work

Part 2. Qualifications for the Modern Office

Part 1

Office Employees at Work

Mr. Brian Norris works for Michigan's Department of the Treasury. As a clerk in the computer department, he handles a variety of tasks including checking computer printouts, sending information through the computer terminals, and checking the coding of the information for computer programs. Brian completed courses in typewriting, data processing, and clerical procedures while in high school. He began working for the State of Michigan shortly after his graduation from high school about a year ago. Brian likes his work because he has the opportunity to learn about the newest developments in computers. He is now enrolled in an advanced course in data processing at a nearby community college.

Ms. Lisa Carpenter is a clerk/typist in the office of the manager of a large hotel in Miami, Florida. Lisa, like Brian, studied typewriting and clerical procedures while in high school. She began working part-time for the hotel when she was a junior in high school. When she graduated she accepted a full-time position. Her tasks are varied, but mainly she types letters and reports, answers the telephone, and files. She works with three other members of the manager's staff. She and her co-workers try to keep the office an efficient and pleasant place for all who come there to transact business.

transmitting:
sending

facilitate:
assist in; make easier

Brian and Lisa are just two of the more than thirteen million persons who are working in clerical jobs in the United States. The business activities of all types of organizations, including business firms, schools, colleges, governmental agencies, hospitals, and legal offices, depend on the services of clerical workers. Clerical workers are responsible for transmitting information, maintaining files, and handling a variety of other tasks that facilitate decision making.

The Changing Office in Modern Society

You are learning the tasks of the office at a time when many changes are taking place in the way office work is performed. Persons who have studied developments in the office ever since the introduction of the type-writer in the 1870s believe that the office of 1990 will be very different from most offices of today. Some even predict, for instance, that record handling will be completely electronic, that correspondence will be read from TV-display terminals, and that communications among executives in different companies will require no paper! These predictions may be a little far-fetched, but advancements in technology are continually chang-ing office procedures and activities. You should be prepared to accept new ways of doing office jobs after you find employment.

Illus. 1-1

Computers, like this display terminal, have become a way of life in today's office.

Photo courtesy of Incoterm Corporation

You may be asking: "What will I have to know to get a good job?" or "What do I need to learn now that will help me when I go to work if there are likely to be changes in the way the work is done?" These are natural questions. Writers who develop materials for courses that pre-pare you for business employment ask similar questions. What you will learn in your course in clerical procedures are basic procedures and un-derstandings which will prepare you for your first job and which will be a foundation from which you can make changes when you have to learn new ways of doing your work. Organizations plan for change. When new equipment is purchased, for example, a training program is usually provided for those employees whose work will be **modified** by using the

modified: changed in a minor or major way

new equipment. Companies know that, with proper training, employees who have done a satisfactory job using present procedures will be competent with the new procedures.

The Modern Office Function

Organizations are complex. Executives make the policies for providing goods and services of the company. To carry out these policies requires the careful attention of many office workers. The basic function of the office is to make it easier to reach the goals established by the top management of the organization.

In some large companies, there is a *manager of administrative services* who oversees all office activities throughout the company. In a small company the individual with overall responsibility for office tasks is often called an *office manager*.

One manager of administrative services for a large manufacturing company commented:

> Our company has offices all over the world. There are more than 3,000 employees in our office headquarters here in New York City. My job is to see that all our executives have the office assistance they need to carry out their responsibilities. In my department we spend time analyzing office services. We raise questions such as: "Are there more efficient ways of communicating with officers in foreign countries?" "Do we handle reports as efficiently as we could?" "Would our typists be more productive if they had the use of more advanced machines?"
>
> By answering these questions, we hope to improve office services to meet our company's goals more efficiently.

Key Competencies for Office Workers

A look at what present-day office workers do and what tasks they are likely to do in the future shows that there are some basic competencies that all well-prepared office workers have. This course will give you an opportunity to develop the basic competencies described briefly in the following paragraphs. As you proceed through this course, you will learn more about the skills and techniques needed to become competent in each major area of office work.

Typewriting

The ability to type is a necessary skill in nearly every office job. Some positions require typewriting most of the time. These positions include the typist, clerk/typist, and statistical typist. Other positions, such as the receptionist, the file clerk, and the general clerk, do not require as much typewriting.

Illus. 1-2

Nearly every office job calls for typewriting ability.

Adequate typing skill means a reasonable speed in producing letters, manuscripts, and reports that are free of errors. To handle typewriting tasks effectively, you will want to know how to arrange the common types of business communications, how to spell, and how to punctuate.

adequate: satisfactory

Data Processing

Data processing refers to the preparing of facts and figures so that they can be used to make decisions. Data processing tasks in the office include the computing of charges and payments for monthly billing statements and the figuring of total sales amounts for purchase orders.

Clerical workers who process data often work with special equipment. Calculating machine operators, keypunch operators, computer operators, and financial clerks are just some of the positions for persons who are skilled in processing data. Data processing duties and skills include understanding the special language of numbers and symbols, recording information quickly in readily usable form, and preparing reports that summarize the organized data.

Mail Processing

Efficient handling of mail is critical in modern business. Mail clerks and messengers must become acquainted with the flow of mail in their organizations. They must also know postal rates and postal schedules.

Illus. 1-3

Mail clerks sort, distribute, and collect the daily mail.

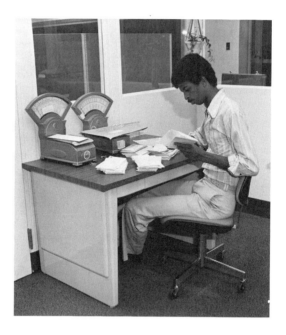

Filing

retrieved: found and brough forth

systematically: following a set of rules or steps carefully

Maintaining records in an orderly fashion so that they can be retrieved quickly is an important office responsibility. Filing clerks and general clerks must have a thorough understanding of filing rules and procedures, they must be able to work quickly and systematically, and they must be alert to detail.

Meeting the Public

Some office workers spend a great deal of their time talking to customers and callers. Those who spend most of their time doing this are usually called receptionists; some are called receptionist/typists. Office workers who meet the public need to be able to talk to others with ease and courtesy. They must learn a great deal about their own organizations so that they can provide the needed information; furthermore, they must clearly understand the needs of those who call on their organization.

Telephoning

Telephones provide a means of rapid communication throughout the world. The modern office worker needs to know how to answer the telephone, how to place a call, and how to record complete and accurate messages.

Illus. 1-4

Using the telephone efficiently is an important office skill.

Making Copies

Seldom is a single copy of a business paper enough. Most of the time several copies are needed; often hundreds of copies are required. Office workers must know how to prepare copies of business papers. Office workers with the basic skills for preparing masters and stencils and for handling copying machines will quickly learn to operate new copying and duplicating equipment.

Preparing Reports

In every office much time is spent preparing reports of various types. Reports are needed because they explain what is happening within an organization. Tasks involved in the preparation of reports include: using library resources, taking notes, preparing rough draft copy, and typing final copy.

Purchasing, Selling, and Controlling Inventories

Regardless of the nature of the organization, the office will have the responsibility for purchasing, selling, and maintaining inventories. After manufacturing firms purchase raw materials, inventories must be kept of the raw materials, goods partially completed, and finished products. They, of course, sell the finished products. Service organizations, such as insurance companies, utility companies, and publishing companies, sell policies, units of electricity or telephone service, and subscriptions to magazines or newspapers. They buy a wide variety of supplies and equipment to facilitate their work and they record and maintain inventories of these purchases.

Illus. 1-5

This stockroom clerk for a book publishing company fills an order from stock.

W. R. Grace & Co.

Every office worker needs to know the basic technical language associated with these tasks, and to be familiar with the basic procedures used in handling the tasks.

Handling Financial Duties

Some office workers spend all their time working with financial records such as payrolls, accounts receivable, or budgets. Others may have only a few financial tasks. All office workers find it valuable to have an understanding of the key financial tasks in an organization.

Office Workers in the American Labor Force

In the United States Department of Labor, the Bureau of Labor Statistics keeps records on the number of workers in various occupations. One of the major categories is "Office Occupations." Below are listed some specific office positions with employment figures for 1976:

Occupation	Annual Average Employment for 1976[1]
Bookkeeping workers	1,688,000
Cashiers	1,256,000
Computer Operating Personnel	563,000
File Clerks	269,000
Hotel front office clerks	62,000*
Office machine operators	726,000
Postal clerks	287,000
Receptionists	502,000
Shipping and receiving clerks	440,000
Statistical clerks	337,000
Stock clerks and storekeepers	492,000
Typists	983,000

*An estimate provided by the Bureau of Labor Statistics in Washington, DC.

The Bureau of Labor Statistics predicts that there will be approximately 33 percent more clerical workers in 1985 than there were in 1975.[2]

What the Clerical Worker Is Expected to Accomplish on the Job

Every organization is concerned about the productivity of each employee, including the clerical worker. How much you are able to do during a normal day's work depends on a number of factors including:

productivity: ability to produce

1. Your basic skill level for each task.
   Example: How many letters you are able to type during a work day will depend, to some degree, on your basic typing speed and your accuracy.
2. The extent to which procedures are well defined.
   Example: How quickly you are able to organize correspondence for filing will depend, to some degree, on how clearly your supervisor or your job training manual outlines the procedure.

[1]From U.S. Department of Labor, Bureau of Labor Statistics, *Employment and Earnings* (January, 1977), pp. 9–10.
[2]U.S. Department of Labor, Bureau of Labor Statistics, *Occupational Outlook Handbook in Brief*, 1976–1977 Edition.

3. The quality and quantity of the equipment and supplies that are available.

Example: How well your typewritten products turn out will depend, to some degree, on how well your typewriter is working and on the quality of the paper and other supplies that you use.

4. The thoroughness of your understanding of the tasks you perform.

Example: If you fail to refer to a manual to check a special procedure or to review a regular one, you will not work as effectively as you could.

standards:
measures of quality

Modern organizations usually try to determine how much work each employee should be able to do during a normal work day. For some clerical tasks, there are established standards, such as the number of letters a typist should complete each day or the number of lines that should be typed during an hour. Because conditions of work vary considerably from company to company, there are few standards that can be used everywhere. In some organizations, supervisors use their judgment to determine whether employees are sufficiently productive.

judgment:
opinion or estimate
formed thoughtfully

You will find that if your basic skills are good and if you are well acquainted with the work you do, your productivity will be satisfactory.

What You Can Expect from a Clerical Position

There are many rewards for working in an office. When clerical workers are asked why they chose their work, they generally mention the rewards described in the following paragraphs.

Nature of Work

interrelatedness:
condition where each
part depends on the
others

Clerical workers like what they do. They enjoy following through on tasks systematically. They like having all their equipment and supplies in order. They like the responsibility they have for tasks assigned to them. They like the interrelatedness of all the work in the organization. They like working with others in order to meet the overall goals of the organization. Here is the way a receptionist in a large insurance company described the rewards of that job:

> I love my job. I feel I am at the heart of the company. My desk is a busy place throughout the day. I need to know where *everyone* is in order to help each person who comes into our building. I keep a detailed schedule of everything going on. It is my goal *never* to have to say to anyone: "I'm sorry, but I don't know."

Illus. 1-6

Some assignments will require consultation with your supervisor.

The **universal** need for clerical workers is also **appealing** to many young office workers. No type of organization can function long without the assistance of persons who can handle telephones, prepare reports and correspondence, and maintain records. Clerical workers know that wherever they choose to live, they are likely to find job opportunities.

universal:
found everywhere

appealing:
interesting; attractive

Working Conditions

Clerical workers take pleasure in the attractive and comfortable surroundings in which they work. In many offices, furnishings and lighting have been selected and combined to create a comfortable environment for the workers. Offices are air-conditioned so that there is no unusual **fatigue** during warm weather. Walls are treated and floors carpeted so that noise from equipment is **minimized**.

Most office employees work from 35 to 40 hours per week. If overtime hours are required, there is additional pay.

fatigue:
tiredness

minimized:
lessened

Salaries and Fringe Benefits

Salaries for clerical occupations vary considerably in different parts of the country. Salaries are determined by a number of factors, including the supply and demand for workers at a given time, the cost of living, and the nature and size of the organization.

Illus. 1-7

Ample lighting, carpeting, and partitions, which create semi-private work areas, make this clerical department a comfortable place to work.

In addition to a basic weekly salary, a beginning clerical worker may find that an employer provides additional benefits. Among the most common benefits are: vacations with pay, allowance for absences due to illness, health and hospital insurance, and educational opportunities (both within the organization and at local schools and colleges).

REVIEWING IMPORTANT POINTS

1. What kinds of organizations need the assistance of clerical workers?
2. What kinds of tasks do clerical workers perform?
3. Is the nature of work in the office changing? Discuss briefly.
4. How should the clerical worker face changes in the office?
5. What is the general overall responsibility of a manager of administrative services?
6. Is typewriting a very important skill for a clerical worker? Discuss briefly.
7. Name three of the most common clerical jobs in the United States.
8. Describe how a clerical worker who is productive functions in an office.
9. How could poor quality paper and supplies affect your productivity?
10. How do experienced clerical workers describe the satisfactions of their work?

MAKING IMPORTANT DECISIONS

David Wolff, who is enrolled in a clerical procedures class, was talking with Jane Francis, another student, one evening after school. Jane said: "Really, David, I don't understand why you are taking a clerical procedures class. I'm learning to type and I know that typing is an important skill for the office. I think if I can type I can get a good job. I don't see why I should take a course in clerical procedures." What do you think David should say in responding to Jane's comment?

LEARNING TO WORK WITH OTHERS

Sherri Eraso is the receptionist in a large public agency in Boston. She is new to her job and she realizes that she does not know much about the reports prepared by the agency. When people who have read about the reports in the newspaper come to her desk with questions about the reports, she must confess that she knows nothing about them. She finally decided to call the office where the reports are prepared. She talked with Gail Hayes, a clerical worker in that office, who said in response to her inquiry: "This office is responsible only for seeing that the reports are prepared; it isn't our job to worry about who gets them. I can't help you."

What do you think Gail should have said? How should she have handled the question from Sherri?

IMPROVING LANGUAGE SKILLS

Nouns are
A. Names of persons:
   Examples: James, typist, porter, waitress

B. Names of places:
   Examples: Seattle, Denmark, cafeteria, mailroom

C. Names of things:
   Examples: file, book, calculator, copier, desk

D. Names of conditions or relations:
   Examples: initiative, courtesy, responsibility, happiness, equality

Copy the following sentences on a separate sheet of paper and underline all the nouns.

1. The statistical typists in our office produce volumes of work every day.
2. There are many clerical workers in every large organization.
3. The elevators in the new office building travel rapidly from the first floor to the twentieth floor.

4. Do you understand why courtesy is considered an important quality in an office?
5. The U.S. Department of Labor collects statistics on office workers.
6. Every worker in this company gets four weeks of vacation during the summer months.
7. Is it possible to complete this job before the afternoon mail is taken to the post office?
8. The messenger comes by our office every morning at ten.
9. The four executives in this department work cooperatively.
10. There is to be a training course for all typists who will be transferred to the new Word Processing Center.

IMPROVING ARITHMETIC SKILLS

Perform each of the operations indicated in the following problems. Write the problems on a separate paper and show all your calculations.

1. $3 + 4 + 7 =$
2. $11 + 14 + 17 =$
3. $241 + 436 + 468 =$
4. $45.3 + 123.15 + 23.1 =$
5. $567.43 - 34.5 =$
6. $456 - 321 =$
7. $10.3 - .7 =$
8. $45 - 13 =$
9. $14 \times 12 =$
10. $351 \times 61 =$
11. $45 \times 20 =$
12. $145.3 \times 1.5 =$
13. $196 \div 14 =$
14. $567 \div 3 =$
15. $156.78 \div 1.2 =$
16. $456.32 \div 14 =$

DEMONSTRATING OFFICE SKILLS

1. You have learned in this Part about common clerical tasks performed in modern offices and for which you will receive instruction during this course. Prepare an outline with these tasks as the major headings. Under each major heading, indicate the skills and abilities you hope to develop.
   Example: WHAT I WOULD LIKE TO LEARN THIS YEAR.
   I. Typewriting
      A. Typing with fewer errors
      B. Arranging letters and reports
2. Below are four questions related to clerical work. Answer one of the four questions expressing your own opinion.
   1. How should clerical workers react to changes made in the way they are to do their work?
   2. What must a clerical worker do in order to be a productive worker?
   3. Where are there opportunities for clerical workers in the United States?
   4. What are some common rewards of clerical work?

Part 2

Qualifications for the Modern Office

Shortly after she graduated from the local high school, Ms. Barbara Garrett applied for a job with a large furniture manufacturing company in North Carolina. She was hired as a clerk/typist and was assigned to the purchasing office. After she had been on the job for six months, Barbara was called to her supervisor's office. Ms. Sacks, her supervisor, asked her if she was satisfied with her assignment. Barbara felt that Ms. Sacks was really interested in her response, so she said: "Ms. Sacks, I like my job very much. I've learned a great deal since I began working here. But I wonder if some of our assignments couldn't be better organized. I believe all of us could work more productively if we had some well-defined procedures, written down in some form, that we could refer to time after time." Ms. Sacks responded: "I appreciate your suggestion, Ms. Garrett. Maybe we should plan a meeting of all members of the staff and discuss ways of working more effectively. I'll think about this matter immediately." The conversation continued for about 15 minutes. When Barbara left, she felt that she was working for a company that cared about constructive comments from its employees; she was glad for the opportunity to talk about her first six months on the job.

Interests and Abilities Necessary for Effective Office Work

Each occupational field has basic requirements that are unique to that particular occupation. Those who want to be successful in that occupation carefully prepare to meet such requirements. In the following paragraphs you will learn about the basic requirements for clerical positions.

unique:
special, one of a kind

An Interest in Working Cooperatively

Few office employees work completely alone. The activities of the typical office require that employees cooperate with each other. You will find that you must understand the instructions others give you. You must provide information to co-workers in a form that is easily understood. At times, you must work in groups in order to accomplish a task. Edward, a young file clerk in a large filing department, commented:

> We have a team in our section of the filing department. The five of us know our work inside-out, and we work together to improve the procedures we use. We take pride in being able to handle any question that comes up. We have a cooperative group because we really like to work together. We are interested in our work and we care about doing a good job.

Illus. 1-8

Office workers who are cooperative know they can rely on each other.

An Interest in the Business of the Organization

You have already learned that office workers are needed in all types of organizations. Therefore, you can choose to work in an organization which has goals in which you have an interest. You will want to know the purpose of your work. The purpose will be meaningful to you if you continue to have an interest in the company's efforts. Peggy, a new office worker in a mail-order hobby company, commented:

I think I am lucky to work in this company. I've always had many hobbies, and I am interested in the hobbies of other people. Here I work in the order department where we receive all kinds of letters from people around the world. Yes, we get orders on the regular order forms, but we also get questions from people who need materials and equipment that are hard to find. When the supervisor realized that I take an interest in every letter I open, I was given the job of keeping track of requests that we can't fill. Then, for each request I write a short report that will be reviewed by those in management who develop new ideas and find manufacturers who can produce the equipment or materials we need.

An Ability to be Accurate

Mistakes are costly in offices. Only information that is error-free is useful. Office workers, therefore, must give constant attention to the quality of work they do. A good office worker is one who makes few errors. Such an office worker has developed a careful, systematic way of paying attention to *each* detail of every task. In addition to making few mistakes, the good office worker is able to recognize a mistake made and

Illus. 1-9

Accuracy is especially important for efficient typing.

correct it in the most efficient way. An office manager commented on the importance of accuracy:

> I think I would place accuracy at the top of the list of requirements for the typists in this office. There would be no efficient way for me to check all the work of every typist. We must have typists who have a consistent record for accurate work. Of course typists make mistakes, but we find that good typists make few mistakes. When they make mistakes, they sense them immediately and correct them. Furthermore, they know how to proofread. We keep records of errors in the work we produce. That record, fortunately, is brief. We expect to add few entries to that record with this fine group of workers.

An Ability to Work with Reasonable Speed

Competent office workers are able to complete tasks in reasonable periods of time. There is little free time in an office. Often tasks must be completed according to an established schedule, so the flow of work cannot be interrupted. Slow workers are costly because they accomplish less than expected during a working day. Workers who realize that they must "catch up," for example, often try to work speedily, but often they fail to do a task properly because they are only concerned with getting the job done. A reasonable speed is one that results in high quality work that is completed according to a schedule that does not put excessive pressure on the person doing the work. A supervisor in a large insurance company commented:

excessive:
more than what is
normal or proper

> We do the same set of tasks over and over again in this office when transactions are checked. We have established standards for our workers. After a period of training, we expect new workers to meet these standards in their daily work. The rate at which our clerks are expected to work was established by noting the work of competent clerks. This doesn't mean that the worker must dash from task to task. It merely requires a steady, even pace with no unusual pressure.

An Ability to Use Standard Procedures

The methods used to perform the work of the modern office are constantly changing and improving. Many of these changes are the result of suggestions made by alert office employees. However, most offices have standard procedures that are followed in doing the majority of tasks.

majority:
greater part or share

For example, in one large firm the mail is received at 9:30 in the morning. It is opened and separated by department. It is then delivered to the various departments according to a regular schedule.

Statements to customers of a department store with last names *A* through *G* are mailed on the afternoon of the 16th of each month. If the

16th falls on a nonworking day, then the statements must be mailed on the afternoon nearest the 16th. These are just two illustrations of standard procedures.

Consider another example. Let's say that you are a file clerk in the central filing department of a large corporation and that all the file clerks follow the same procedure when answering the telephone.

1. You are at the desk when the telephone rings, and you answer it immediately.
2. Before lifting the telephone, you pick up a pencil from your desk and place a message pad in position for taking notes.
3. You answer the telephone by saying, "Central Files, (your full name) speaking."
4. Generally the calls are from other departments in the company that are requesting files. Record the name of the file requested the first time it is stated by the calling party. If there is any doubt about the name, request the spelling. Begin writing as soon as the name is spelled.
5. If you are busy with another task, drop this latest request into the proper tray for immediate pickup by the first clerk free for another assignment.

Standard procedures provide a means of working in the same way time after time so that errors are unlikely to occur.

Systems specialists are employed by many organizations to determine the most efficient procedures to use. Office workers must be willing to follow the instructions that apply to the tasks they perform.

Basic Skills That Have Applications in the Office

As you already know, the basic skills of reading, writing, and arithmetic are constantly used in your personal life. These skills are considered fundamental in the office. This is the way the insurance business stresses the importance of basic skills to young people:

fundamental: basic; essential

"Whatever job you get, you will need the three basic skills: reading, writing, and arithmetic. Many life and health companies have training manuals to tell you about your job and what you have to know to do it well. Being able to read those manuals and other written materials is essential.

essential: of great importance; necessary

"Equally essential is writing legibly. One life insurance personnel executive tells of an enormous problem that grew out of an employee not writing clearly. His company has two million customers called policyholders. One day, one of them wrote in and gave a change of address. The clerk who got the letter put the change of address down on a card but wrote the street number illegibly. The card went to another

illegibly: in unreadable form

clerk to type the change for the computer that contains all the addresses of policyholders. That person, because of the illegible writing, copied the address incorrectly. The error went into the computer and for months the policyholder's premium notices and other communications from the company went to the wrong address. No great damage was done but the policyholder was understandably irritated with the company and put to a great deal of trouble to get the error corrected. The company spent time and money in finding and correcting the error — all because of illegible writing and careless work.

"Much of the business of life and health insurance companies involves numbers and entails correspondence with customers. This is true of many businesses. The basic skills of working carefully with numbers and being able to express yourself clearly and gracefully are important in nearly any job.

"If you are not proficient in reading, writing, and arithmetic, you will be handicapped in your career, no matter what field you enter. Now is the time to improve these basic skills."[1]

What the Institute of Life Insurance is saying about basic skills is exactly what all types of organizations say when they think of fully competent workers. Fortunately, it is never too late to make up for weaknesses you may have in these basic skills. In fact, during your study of clerical office procedures, you will have many opportunities to develop your skills and to apply them to office work.

Illus. 1-10

Writing clearly is an essential skill for office work.

Pitney-Bowes, Inc.

[1]*It's Up to You — A Guide to a Career in Life and Health Insurance* (New York: Institute of Life Insurance, Educational Division, 1971), pp. 8–10.

Behavior and Appearance in the Office

The office is a place where work is done. To complete your work in a pleasant, comfortable way, you will want to follow certain standards concerning your behavior and appearance.

Behavior

Consideration for others is a basic quality required to become a valuable member of an office staff. "Consideration for others" determines how kind and thoughtful you are as you work with others. Below are some rules that you will want to consider as you prepare for working in an office:

1. Greet your co-workers pleasantly. People at work appreciate courteous greetings. Pleasant interaction with the people around you is one of the continuing rewards of working in an office.

Illus. 1-11

Say "Good morning" to your co-workers at the beginning of the day.

2. Give full attention to a co-worker who is talking to you. Listen carefully and patiently, and respond to any question or comment in an **appropriate** manner. Show your interest in what is being discussed.

appropriate: suitable or proper

3. Speak softly to others so as not to disturb persons who are working within hearing range. Many offices have wide, open spaces where persons doing related tasks work together. There are times, however, when only two or three of the people in the area need to talk together. If such a group talks loudly, with no thought for others who are working alone at their desks, it will create a distraction that keeps others from being able to concentrate on their work.

4. Introduce co-workers and visitors to others to whom they have occasion to talk. You will want to know how to introduce persons simply and politely. Workers who become friends find their work more interesting. Your efforts to help people get to know each other will be appreciated.
5. Treat others with courtesy when you meet them on the stairs, in conference rooms, in the elevator, or in the cafeteria. The office worker who helps a stranger trying to find his or her way, who apologizes in a friendly way for bumping into a co-worker on the stairs, who gives up a seat in a crowded conference room to an older person, is conveying a respect and concern for others.

Appearance

Standards for appearance vary considerably from one organization to another and from one area of the country to another. The following two sections contain some general suggestions.

Personal Grooming. Below are some basic rules for personal care that you will want to follow. Most of these rules are common sense, but as you read through them, think of why they are particularly important in the business office:

1. Take a bath or shower at least once each day.
2. Use an antiperspirant or deodorant daily.
3. Brush your teeth at least twice each day.
4. Wash your face thoroughly twice each day.
5. Keep your fingernails clean and trimmed.
6. Wash your hair regularly.
7. Wear clean clothing.

Clothing. There is no standard dress for all offices. However, some companies do state what type of clothing employees are expected to wear. Companies where employees meet with the public regularly are often concerned that employees reflect an efficient organization. Employees may be expected to wear clothes that are conservative in style. Some companies, such as airlines offices and banks, provide standard clothes for their employees. Such standard clothing often bears the emblem of the organization.

If you are employed in a company that does not have a dress code, you should note carefully the clothing worn by the other office workers there. From your own observations you will be able to determine what dress is appropriate.

emblem:
symbol used to identify something

observations:
what you have seen or sensed

General Expectations

Organizations want to achieve their goals with as little waste of valuable human resources as possible. Everyone employed in an organization is considered to be capable of making a contribution to that organization and is thus important. Organizations want to be successful but they also want to provide job satisfaction and rewards for all employees. Organizations need new workers; they look to young high school graduates for the skills and talents needed to keep operating effectively.

human resources:
the skills and abilities of employed people

REVIEWING IMPORTANT POINTS

1. Why should office workers be interested in working cooperatively?
2. How will a person who is interested in the work of her or his company behave?
3. Why is accuracy important in an office?
4. How would you define "reasonable speed"?
5. In what way is a standard procedure useful in an office?
6. What does it mean to pay attention to another person?
7. How does a courteous person behave in the office?
8. What aspects of personal grooming should an office worker never overlook?
9. How may an office worker determine what clothing will be appropriate in an office where he or she has just been hired?
10. What are two general expectations of an organization?

MAKING IMPORTANT DECISIONS

Ken Calmers graduates from high school next month. He has been interviewed for clerical jobs in four companies in his home town and was offered jobs in all four. He is having difficulty deciding which job to take. All four jobs are good jobs, but his interest in fishing made him wonder if he should take the position with a new wholesale fishing equipment company. This position in the wholesale fishing equipment company pays less than the other three jobs. The company is new in town while the other three are old, established firms. The other companies have clear-cut procedures for promotions. They seemed to be better organized, he felt, as he reviewed his experiences during his visits to the personnel offices. Yet, he likes the fishing equipment company. If you were in Ken's situation, what choice would you make? Why?

LEARNING TO WORK WITH OTHERS

Roselie was a competent typist. She did her work with speed and accuracy. She was given additional responsibilities in the office because the supervisor believed she could handle them. One of her additional tasks was handling telephone inquiries, which come mostly from other offices in the company. Roselie believed that she should type as much as possible, so every time the telephone rang, she felt that she was being interrupted. Often she didn't know the answer to a question. Assuming that someone else in the office had the answer, she would ask the caller to wait a minute, and say: "Is there anyone here who has the answer?" If a co-worker knew the answer she would ask, "Would you come and take care of this?" If no one knew, she would tell the caller to try another office. If there was no one else in the office when the telephone rang, Roselie just let it ring so that she wouldn't have to waste her time.

How would you evaluate Roselie's attitude? What might be done to improve it?

IMPROVING LANGUAGE SKILLS

On a separate sheet of paper write a sentence using each of the following verbs in the past tense.

Example: choose

He *chose* to complete the job before he went to lunch.

1. become	11. let
2. bind	12. lose
3. bring	13. make
4. buy	14. mistake
5. foresee	15. pay
6. go	16. sell
7. keep	17. send
8. learn	18. speak
9. leave	19. stand
10. lend	20. take

IMPROVING ARITHMETIC SKILLS

Perform the basic operation required in each of these questions. Show your calculations on a separate sheet of paper.

1. Bob Young purchased the following items at a local office stationery store: 10 large envelopes at 17 cents each, three felt-tipped pens at 69 cents each, a small notebook at $1.59, and a box of paper clips at 79 cents. What was the total cost of his purchases?
2. If there was a sales tax of 7 percent on the purchases Bob made (question 1) how much tax must he pay? What is the total amount he must give the clerk in the stationery store?
3. Office typing chairs are available at $97 each, or in lots of ten for $690. What is the price of each chair if purchased in lots of ten? What is the saving per chair if purchased in a lot of ten?
4. Heidi Oberman worked overtime every evening for four days. Her extra hours were: Monday, 3½; Tuesday, 4; Wednesday, 4¼; and Thursday 2½. How many hours extra did Heidi work during those four days?
5. If Heidi (question 4) earns $3.40 per hour, but gets time-and-a-half for overtime hours, what will be her overtime pay?
6. You are asked to compute the amount of a check to be mailed with an order for a small printing calculator. The cost of the calculator is $79, plus 8 percent tax, plus $1.75 for shipping charges.
7. Eight persons in the office paid Gail $2.75 for a special luncheon that is being planned to honor one of the typists who is moving to London. How much money should Gail have?
8. A large office furniture store is open from 8 a.m. to 5 p.m., Monday through Friday, and from 9 a.m. to 4 p.m. on Saturdays. How many hours a week is this store open?
9. The regular fare for an airline ticket is $179.50, but there is a 25 percent reduction for flights made in midweek. What should be the price of the special midweek flight?

DEMONSTRATING OFFICE SKILLS

1. For each of the interests and abilities discussed in this Part, think of your present attitude and level of ability. Then write in outline form what you believe you must give attention to during this course in order to be better prepared for a full-time job.
2. Write brief descriptions of several instances of what you believe would be inappropriate behavior in the office. (Hint: Think of the situations opposite to those described in the section in this Part headed "Behavior.")

IMPROVING OFFICE SKILLS (Optional)

Make a list of five organizations found in your community. Write a brief description of what you believe are the main goals of each of these organizations. Then, write what you believe is your present interest in working as a clerical worker in each of these organizations.

2

Applying Basic Skills

Part 1. Skillful Reading and Listening
Part 2. Handwriting in the Office
Part 3. Handling Computations
in the Office

Part 1

Skillful Reading and Listening

Miss Rachel Sheehy has been a clerk/typist since her graduation from high school about four months ago. One afternoon as she thought about what she needed to know in order to fulfill her responsibilities, she realized that she was constantly using the basic skills of reading and listening which had been taught to her throughout her school years. She knew that every day she received written instructions that she needed to understand well in order to follow through on various tasks. She also realized that many times each day a co-worker or her supervisor talked with her about her tasks, and she needed to listen carefully in order to understand exactly what was said and how it applied to her own work.

Reading

Every office job requires reading ability. Your employer will expect you to be skillful in several kinds of reading. You must be able to read the information sent you from time to time about your job with the company and about the personnel policies that affect your hours of work, your salary, your vacations, and your insurance **benefits**. You must be able to read instructions about particular tasks you are asked to do. You will also need to know how to read a wide variety of references which you will consult when you need specific information about prices, regulations, schedules, and other details related to your work. Don Jacobs commented about the importance of reading skill in his work:

benefits: protections; coverage

> I have learned to scan and read quickly for the information I must give to the inquiring customer. You see, as a telephone clerk in a central utilities company, I have to listen to callers who have problems with their statements. After I learn the customer's name and number, I enter the appropriate code in my computer keyboard and instantly the customer's record appears on the screen. I am very careful to read accurately, but I also want to read quickly so that I can respond to each customer promptly.

Illus. 2-1

Reading is an ever important skill even with the widespread use of computers.

Courtesy of
Harris Corporation

Reading for Understanding

You will learn a great deal about your job through reading. You must be able to comprehend what you read — that is, to read with understanding — so that you will be able to make what you read a part of your knowledge. When Barbara was employed as an office worker in a large insurance company, she was given a brochure that described her work and responsibilities. Here is part of the brochure:

brochure:
pamphlet; booklet

Your Desk Is Your **Domain**. The desk to which you have been assigned is yours to maintain in an orderly manner so that you can work efficiently. Please remember that papers should be on your desk only **temporarily**. You should process them quickly and accurately and then forward them to the proper office.

domain:
place under control of
one person

temporarily:
for a short while; not
permanently

The drawers of your desk are sufficient for the stock of supplies that you should have available for your work. Do not use the top of your desk as a storage area. Materials that belong in the files should be in the files. Papers temporarily taken from files should be kept in a tray or drawer where they can be located easily when needed. Your desk surface and drawers should be neatly arranged to provide immediate **access** to pens, pencils, and other supplies.

access:
condition of being
easy to reach

How should such a passage be read so that you understand it well? Here are some suggestions:

1. *Determine the general topic of the text.* Ask yourself questions such as these before you begin to read:
   (a) Since the heading is, "Your Desk Is Your Domain," then what is likely to be discussed?
   (b) Why is it important that this message be understood?
2. *Read through the text quickly to get an overview.* Your understanding will be greater if you skim the text to get a *general* idea of what it contains first.
3. *Read through the text a second time.* During this reading give attention to the details so that you have a thorough understanding of the ideas presented. If you read "Your Desk Is Your Domain" carefully, the ideas listed here should now be part of your knowledge.
   (a) You alone will be using your desk.
   (b) To work well, you must keep your desk orderly.
   (c) The desk surface is your work area, and it should not be cluttered with papers and supplies.
   (d) The papers that come to your desk are to be handled quickly and accurately and then sent to the next location.
   (e) Papers that cannot be handled immediately should be filed or kept in a drawer or tray.
   (f) The drawers of the desk have enough space for all the supplies that should keep at your desk.
4. *After you have completed reading the message, ask yourself questions to see if you really understand what you have read.*
   (a) What are the main points of the message?
   (b) What do you understand now about your responsibilities for keeping an orderly desk that you did not understand before you read the passage?

Reading for Specific Information

Frequently you must get information from some printed source in order to complete a task you have underway. Learning efficient ways of using such sources is important in your preparation for office work.

precise:
exact

To use reference sources efficiently, you must have a clear understanding of what you are trying to find. Next, you must get the correct reference source and locate the precise information. You must read it accurately and record it immediately. Illus. 2-2 shows a portion of a Federal Income Tax Withholding Table for Single Persons — Semimonthly Payroll Period. This is the table to use in determining the tax to be withheld for a particular employee who is single and is paid twice each month. The same reference source lists taxes for married persons and for pay periods ranging from daily to monthly.

SEMIMONTHLY Payroll Period—Employee NOT MARRIED

And the wages are-		And the number of withholding allowances claimed is—										
At least	But less than	0	1	2	3	4	5	6	7	8	9	10 or more
		The amount of income tax to be withheld shall be—										
$400	$420	$63.50	$56.30	$49.40	$42.50	$36.70	$31.10	$25.40	$19.80	$14.30	$9.30	$4.30
420	440	68.30	60.80	53.80	46.90	40.30	34.70	29.00	23.40	17.80	12.50	7.50
440	460	73.10	65.60	58.20	51.30	44.50	38.30	32.60	27.00	21.40	15.80	10.70
460	480	77.90	70.40	62.90	55.70	48.90	42.00	36.20	30.60	25.00	19.40	13.90
480	500	83.20	75.20	67.70	60.20	53.30	46.40	39.80	34.20	28.60	23.00	17.30
500	520	88.80	80.10	72.50	65.00	57.70	50.80	43.90	37.80	32.20	26.60	20.90
520	540	94.40	85.70	77.30	69.80	62.30	55.20	48.30	41.40	35.80	30.20	24.50
540	560	100.00	91.30	82.50	74.60	67.10	59.60	52.70	45.80	39.40	33.80	28.10
560	580	105.60	96.90	88.10	79.40	71.90	64.40	57.10	50.20	43.40	37.40	31.70
580	600	111.20	102.50	93.70	85.00	76.70	69.20	61.70	54.60	47.80	41.00	35.30
600	620	116.80	108.10	99.30	90.60	81.80	74.00	66.50	59.00	52.20	45.30	38.90
620	640	122.40	113.70	104.90	96.20	87.40	78.80	71.30	63.80	56.60	49.70	42.80
640	660	128.30	119.30	110.50	101.80	93.00	84.30	76.10	68.60	61.10	54.10	47.20
660	680	134.70	124.90	116.10	107.40	98.60	89.90	81.10	73.40	65.90	58.50	51.60
680	700	141.10	131.10	121.70	113.00	104.20	95.50	86.70	78.20	70.70	63.20	56.00

Illus. 2-2

Reading Instructions. There are many ways of completing tasks, and the careful office worker checks the instructions before beginning a new task. Here is in an example of instructions that were given to typists in a billing department of a small appliance center.

> INSTRUCTIONS: This form is to be prepared in triplicate. The final copy is for your files. Be sure to list unit price as well as extension. Indicate handling and shipping charges for out-of-city orders.

triplicate:
three copies

extension:
total price after the unit price is multiplied by the number of units ordered

Illus. 2-3

Be sure to read any written instructions from your employer before beginning an assignment.

The typist knew to make three copies; however, only the original and one carbon copy would be forwarded. The final carbon copy would be kept in the files. The typist also knew to indicate the price of each unit; that is, if the customer purchased two table lamps at $19.95 each, then it was necessary to indicate that each lamp was $19.95 and the two were $39.90. Furthermore, since this purchase was for delivery within the city, there were no handling and shipping charges.

bibliography:
list of sources referred to or consulted

Another typist was asked to prepare a **bibliography** with these instructions:

> Please type a rough draft of the attached card bibliography. Entries are to be listed alphabetically by author, and then by title. Make two copies.

The typist, immediately realizing that the cards were not necessarily in correct alphabetic order, first put them in order. If one author had two or more references, the titles were placed in alphabetic order. An original plus one carbon copy would be needed.

Sometimes instructions are far more complicated than in the previous examples. Frequently the office worker must inform the executive about details. Below are the instructions for filling in a Travel Expense Report. Read the instructions carefully. Then, check your **comprehension** by answering the questions on page 33 that you might be asked if you were the clerk responsible for preparing expense reports for a group of traveling executives.

comprehension:
understanding

INSTRUCTIONS

1. Travel Expense Reports are to be typewritten or written legibly in ink.
2. Fill in name of city in "FROM" and "TO" columns on date of travel. If entire day is spent in ONE place, the name of the city should appear in the "TO" column.
3. Attach passenger copy of ticket or other receipted bills for transportation cost. Receipted bills must be attached to substantiate lodging expense.
4. All entertainment expense must be fully explained in order to receive reimbursement.
5. Approved travel expense reports must be forwarded promptly to PLANT or CONSOLIDATED OFFICE — CASHIER or Travel Advance Section — Greenwich. Check is to be attached to face of report for all amounts due Company.
6. Include all ADVANCES RECEIVED during the month; except ADVANCES RECEIVED towards the end of a month to be used for a trip that extends into, or to be made in the following month.

INTERNAL REVENUE — All expense reports are subject to review by INTERNAL REVENUE AGENTS. They will consider treating as taxable income to each employee any expenditures which are not accounted for in detail to the Company.
ANY EXPENDITURE OF $25.00 OR MORE MUST BE SUBSTANTIATED BY A RECEIPTED BILL.

Questions asked by executives of the clerk/typist who prepares the Travel Expense Reports:

1. Is my own note enough proof of the transportation costs?
2. Do you need to know only the first and last stops on my trip?
3. Is an advance for the next month to be included with this month's report?
4. I have only a note about lunch for two last week in Chicago. The bill was $14.50. Do I need a receipt for this bill?
5. Will I be repaid for all entertainment expenses?

Reading a Dictionary. Office workers find that one of their most useful references is a general dictionary of the English language. There are many different types of dictionaries. Persons who want a complete reference to all words find that a large, **unabridged** dictionary is the best source of information about general vocabulary. In offices, it is more common to find desk dictionaries, which have a more limited **vocabulary** than standard unabridged dictionaries. A desk dictionary provides enough information in most instances; for office use, you will want a desk dictionary with a very recent publication date. Language is constantly changing, particularly the language of business.

unabridged:
not shortened or condensed

vocabulary:
collection of words

Illus. 2-4

An unabridged dictionary is the most complete word reference.

There are many specialized dictionaries. If you are working in a technically specialized field, you may find that there is a specialized dictionary available that will help you with technical words and phrases.

You can get acquainted with a desk dictionary by examining the entries below, which are from E. L. Thorndike and Clarence Barnhart. *High School Dictionary* (5th ed.; Glenview, Ill.: Scott, Foresman and Company, 1968).

en roll ment or **en rol ment** (en rōl'mənt), *n.* **1.** an enroll- ⓵
ing. **2.** number enrolled: *The school has an enrollment of 200 students.*
en route (än rüt'), on the way: *He is en route to Califor-* ⓺
nia by way of the Panama Canal. [< F]
Ens., Ensign.

i ni ti ate (*v.* i nish'ē āt; *n., adj.* i nish'ē it or i nish'ē āt, ⓶
v., **-at ed, -at ing,** *n., adj.* —*v.* **1.** be the first one to
start; begin. **2.** admit (a person) by special forms or
ceremonies (into mysteries, secret knowledge, or a society). **3.** introduce into the knowledge of some art or
subject: *initiate a person into business methods.* —*n.*
person who is initiated. —*adj.* initiated. [< L *initiare*
< *initium* beginning < *inire* begin. See INITIAL.] —
i ni 'ti a'tor, *n.* —**Syn.** *v.* **1.** commence, originate. **2.** ⓻
install, induct.
i ni ti a tion (i nish'ē ā'shən), *n.* **1.** an initiating. **2.** a ⓷
being initiated. **3.** formal admission into a group or society. **4.** ceremonies by which one is admitted to a
group or society.

su per vene (sü'pər vēn'), *v.,* **-vened, -ven ing.** come as
something additional or interrupting. [< L *supervenire*
< *super-* upon + *venire* come]
su per ven tion (sü'pər ven'shən), *n.* a supervening.
su per vise (sü'pər vīz), *v.,* **-vised, -vis ing.** look after and ⓸
direct (work or workers, a process, etc.); oversee; su-
perintend; manage: *Study halls are supervised by*
teachers. [< Med.L *supervisus* < L *super-* over + *vi-* ⓹
dere see]
su per vi sion (sü'pər vizh'ən), *n.* management; direction;
oversight: *The house was built under the careful super-*
vision of an architect.
su per vi sor (sü'pər vī-zər), *n.* person who supervises:
The music supervisor had charge of the school band
and orchestra.

alternate:
other

1. *Spelling.* The correct spelling is provided. If more than one spelling is acceptable, the **alternate** spellings are indicated. When there are two spellings, the preferred spelling is listed first.
2. *Pronunciation.* The way in which the word is pronounced when spoken is indicated. A guide to the pronunciation symbols is found in the introductory pages of the dictionary.
3. *Part of Speech.* Some words are always used as one part of speech only; others have several uses. The dictionary will show the parts of speech as well as any meanings peculiar to each part.

4. *Variations in form of word.* Dictionaries generally include only the plural, past tense, and gerund forms of the base word that are considered irregular. For example, plurals which are formed by the normal way of adding an "s" would not be shown. However, for a word such as index, you will find in-dex•es *or* in-di•ces.
5. *The sources of words.* The origin of a word is indicated. This information is primarily of historical interest.
6. *Definitions.* The various meanings of each word are given. Meanings that are no longer in use are sometimes shown as archaic. Meanings that are colloquial are so indicated.
7. *Synonyms and Antonyms.* A desk dictionary will in some cases show *synonyms* (words that have the same meaning) or *antonyms* (words that have the opposite meaning).

archaic:
old fashioned

colloquial:
conversational, not formal

Listening

Oral communications are essential in the business office. You will discuss common tasks with co-workers, and your supervisor will talk with you about special instructions for a particular task. Telephone callers will give you information that you must use or transmit to others. If you are to listen efficiently and effectively, you will want to follow the recommendations for good listening in the following paragraphs.

Attention to the Speaker

How well do you listen? If you are always alert when someone is talking to you and you remember exactly what has been said, you are a good listener. To listen well requires that you give your *full attention* to the speaker. This means that you are *mentally* following what is being said. You are not merely *hearing* the speaker's words. Your mind is not elsewhere. You are not, for example, thinking about what you would like to say as soon as the speaker stops talking or what you will do when the day's work ends. Learning to concentrate on what is being said to you will insure your understanding of the many oral communications that will be a part of your working day.

Thoughts Being Conveyed

The message the speaker is trying to communicate to you is more than a collection of words; the message requires an understanding of facts in relation to a particular situation.

Illus. 2-5

When you listen, concentrate on what the speaker is saying.

Paula's supervisor came to her desk with a handwritten report and said, "I've just completed a first draft of a report that must be mailed by the end of the week. I would like to see what it looks like in type, and then I can make changes and additions. Please type this as a rough draft, using triple spacing. Could I have it shortly?"

What thoughts did Paula's supervisor convey to her if she were listening? Among them were these:

1. This is the first draft of a report.
2. A speedy job of typewriting is desired.
3. The copy is to be triple-spaced. It is not necessary that this be an attractive job.

If Paula had *not* been listening for thoughts, she may not have realized that this was a rough draft. She may have taken time to correct errors in the copy and typed the report as a final copy.

The Value of Summarizing

Summarizing is actually done along with the preceding step of listening for thoughts. As you listen for key thoughts, you will want to organize them so that at the end of the conversation you know exactly what was said.

The Usefulness of a Review

Since it is possible to hear something at the moment it is told to you and then quickly forget, you may want to think through what you have just heard. If you have pencil and pad at hand, make notes to be sure that you have the correct information. Reviewing this way will reinforce the message in your memory.

reinforce:
make stronger

REVIEWING IMPORTANT POINTS

1. What points should you keep in mind when you are reading for understanding?
2. What value is there in getting a general overview of what you are to read for understanding?
3. In general, how would you search for specific information in a table or listing?
4. Why is it important to read instructions carefully the first time you read them?
5. What type of dictionary are you likely to find in an office?
6. What types of information about a word can you obtain from a dictionary?
7. Give some illustrations of the use of oral communications in the business office?
8. What is the value of listening with attention?
9. How does the listener gain a full comprehension of the thoughts being conveyed by a speaker?
10. What is the value of reviewing what you have heard?

MAKING IMPORTANT DECISIONS

1. Ellie works as a clerk/typist in a large office of an elevator manufacturing company. One day she was given a new form to be filled in with information provided. Attached to the form was a note saying that she was to refer to the company manual for specific instructions for preparing the form. Since Ellie felt she had had experience in filling in other forms, she didn't think she should waste time reading the instructions in the company manual. She was sure that two copies would be sufficient and that the rules for typewriting this form would be the same as for others. What do you think of Ellie's decision?
2. Ms. Helena Wells asked Ms. Jan Zanger, the receptionist in the office, to make a flight reservation for her for Boston on Saturday afternoon. Ms. Wells was scheduled to attend a professional dinner at 6:30 p.m. and wanted to leave her office at the latest possible

time; but she did want to be at the dinner by 6:30. It will take one hour to get to the meeting place from the airport in Boston. Which flight do you think Ms. Zanger should select from the schedule?

To: **BOSTON (EST)**				
Departure	Arrival	Flight	Type of Aircraft	Schedule
12:30p L	1:14p	82	727	Ex Sat
1:30p L	2:18p	314	727	Daily
2:30p L	3:18p	94	727	Daily
3:30p L	4:18p	690	727	Ex Sat
4:00p L	5:02p	164	707	Daily
4:30p L	5:20p	578	727	Ex Sat
5:30p L	6:20p	366	727	Daily
6:30p L	7:21p	228	727	Ex Sat
7:30p L	8:18p	296	727	Daily
11:50p L	12:33a	502	727	Ex Sat

LEARNING TO WORK WITH OTHERS

Becky works with Kent in a word processing center. Each work station is provided with several reference books including an up-to-date desk dictionary. Becky, however, never uses her dictionary. When she isn't sure about how a word should be divided or how to spell the plural of the word, she just calls across to Kent with a question, such as: "Kent, how do you spell appendices?" Kent doesn't want to be uncooperative, but he thinks that he gets too many unnecessary interruptions from Becky. What do you think Kent should do?

IMPROVING LANGUAGE SKILLS

Pronouns are substitutes for nouns. They agree with the nouns for which they stand (antecedents) in person, number, and gender.

Examples: Connie just placed the first draft of the report in *her* in-progress desk tray. *Connie* (third person, singular number, feminine gender) is the antecedent of *her*, which is also third person, singular number, and feminine gender.

Ms. Hill gave a manual to Mr. Bill Enderman, *who* needed to read instructions for *his* new assignment. *Mr. Bill Enderman* is the antecedent of *who*, the relative pronoun used to refer to a person. *Mr. Bill Enderman* is also the antecedent of *his*.

Type the sentences below, selecting the correct pronouns.

1. Chester and David will get (his, their) new typewriters within a week.
2. Mr. Armstrong, the supervisor, as well as the file clerks, begins (his, their) work day promptly at 8:45.
3. Valerie did not know what (she, her) assignment was for the next day.
4. The committee passed (its, their) resolution after several hours of discussion.
5. Mr. Howland believes that it is Ms. Richards (which, who) is contributing the major suggestions for the redecoration of the office.
6. The students brought (their, his, her) notebooks with them.
7. Miss Wilson approved of the letterheads and envelopes and placed an order for (it, them) yesterday.
8. Our consultants will give (his, her, their) reports on Friday.
9. Members of the commission expressed (its, their) reactions to the proposal in writing.
10. Tom gave (his, her, their) recommendations to the committee.

IMPROVING ARITHMETIC SKILLS

On a separate sheet of paper perform the computation required in each instance.

1.	367 +143	2.	500 +391	3.	790 +299	4.	902 +935	5.	653 + 19
6.	836 +769	7.	186 +436	8.	235 +777	9.	794 −254	10.	654 −235
11.	970 −456	12.	835 −105	13.	439 −389	14.	785 −364	15.	432 −413
16.	902 − 78	17.	230 × 12	18.	689 × 23	19.	814 × 79	20.	935 × 46

DEMONSTRATING OFFICE SKILLS

1. The United States Postal Service has issued the following recommendations for typing addresses on envelopes:

   (a) Addresses should be single-spaced.

   (b) The bottom line of the address must contain the names of the city and state and the ZIP Code. The ZIP Code is usually typed one space after the state.

   (c) The state name should be abbreviated according to the two-letter ZIP Code abbreviation or typed in full if the ZIP Code is not known.

   (d) The next to the last line of the address (including the apartment number) should be reserved for the street address or the Post Office box number.

   (e) A building name (including suite number), if used, should appear on the line above the street address.

   Type each of the following names and addresses on an envelope (or pieces of paper cut to the size of a small envelope, 6½" × 3⅝"). Follow the recommendations of the U.S. Postal Services.

   Mrs. F. T. Neville
   157 Watts Boulevard
   Greenwood Terrace Apartments
   San Diego, California 92108

   Ms. Athea Murray
   472 Wayne Avenue
   Carbondale, Illinois 62183

   Mr. Daniel McDow
   174-14th Street
   Atlanta, Georgia 30330

   Mrs. Ivan F. Oshinsky
   Oak Towers
   17 Greenview Rd.
   Little Rock, Arkansas 72201

2. You have been asked to set up a card file of customers to whom persons in your office frequently send letters and memorandums. Type each of the names and addresses below on a 5" × 3" card (or pieces of paper cut to this size). Each name should be typed in this order: Last name, first name, middle name, or initial. Use the two-letter state abbreviations noted on page 696 in Appendix D instead of the full state name. Arrange in alphabetical order.

   Frank W. White
   568 Dogwood Drive
   Little Rock, Arkansas 72201

   Leland T. Thompson
   570 Midwood Road
   Muncie, Indiana 47301

   Ruth N. Rothenberg
   1454 - 54th Street
   Chicago, Illinois 60604

   Antonio W. Tesori
   7581 Spring Avenue
   Bridgeport, Connecticut 06601

   Thomas O. Tobias
   690 Beulah Road
   Wilmington, Delaware 19809

   Charlotte M. Ross
   5702 Carleton Drive
   Fresno, California 93705

Part 2

Handwriting in the Office

Ms. Wendy Paterson is the receptionist in a small law office. She handles all incoming telephone calls and takes messages for the six lawyers when they are away from their desks. She is constantly recording messages that contain telephone numbers, specific references, and other details that need to be written clearly. She is very careful about her handwriting, because she knows that much time can be lost in trying to read a message written illegibly.

You might think that handwriting is an out-of-date skill because there are so many typewriters, calculators, and computers in modern offices. But this isn't the case. In fact, there are many instances in the office when handwriting is required. To be an efficient office worker you will want to have a clear handwriting style. You should be able to write rapidly, but without **distorting** the letters and numbers of your written messages. Others should be able to read what you have written as easily as if your writing were typewriting!

distorting:
making unclear

Acceptable Styles of Handwriting

Your handwriting is acceptable if it can be read by anyone who knows the English language and understands Arabic numerals. Various styles of handwriting are considered adequate. Look at these two samples of penmanship at the top of page 42. One is a vertical style. The other is slanted. Both are acceptable.

Note that these handwriting samples meet these requirements:

1. Letters are all slanted in the same direction.
2. The spacing between letters is approximately equal.
3. Words are separated from each other by approximately the same amount of space.
4. Capital letters are about twice as large as small letters, and letters are in proper proportion.

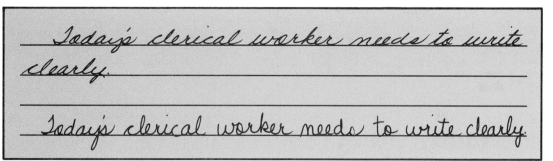

Illus. 2-6

confusion:
uncertainty; difficulty

5. Letters that cause confusion if written improperly, such as *a*'s, *e*'s, *c*'s and *o*'s, are clearly different.
6. All *t*'s are crossed, and all *i*'s are dotted.
7. Rounded and pointed parts of *m*'s, *n*'s, *u*'s, and *v*'s are clear.

How To Improve Your Handwriting

How would you rate your own handwriting? Is it acceptable when evaluated by the standards listed? On a piece of lined paper write the following two paragraphs in your natural handwriting.

Illus 2-7

> Handwriting is a skill that can be improved. Attention to the formation of each letter and number can result in a clearer, more readable style of handwriting.
>
> Modern office tasks often require the use of handwriting. To handle such tasks every office worker needs to write rapidly and, at the same time, legibly.

specimen:
sample

Now, look at the specimen of your handwriting that you have just completed and notice if it meets the requirements listed on pages 41–42.

Unit 2 • Applying Basic Skills

If you are satisfied that your writing is legible and attractive, you may want to see if you can improve your rate of writing without causing your writing to become illegible.

If your writing is not as good as it should be, review your manner of writing. Check the following points about your writing techniques:

1. Do you give yourself enough space in which to write easily? You should have **sufficient** desk space so that your arms can rest comfortably on the desk. There should be enough room so that your arms are free to move away from the body slightly. Your desk should be sufficiently clear of books and papers to allow you to arrange your writing paper conveniently.

sufficient: enough

2. Do you use a hand position that makes it easy to produce clear, complete letters?
   (a) Do you hold your pen comfortably and in a manner that gives you full control over the letters that you are making? (A standard procedure for holding the pen or pencil is to hold it about an inch above the point, between the thumb, the index finger, and the side of the middle finger, near the base of the fingernail.)
   (b) Are you writing in a manner that prevents your hand or arm from becoming tired?
3. Do you give attention to completing each letter before you move on to the next letter?

Printing

There are times when office workers need to use printing because it is normally easier to read than writing. Business firms frequently specify that certain information requested on their business forms, usually names and addresses, be printed or typed to insure legibility.

You can learn to print neatly and attractively if you follow these simple rules:

1. Use a vertical position for the main part of each letter.

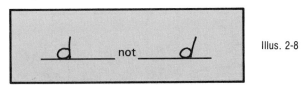

Illus. 2-8

2. Maintain a uniform size for all alphabetic forms.

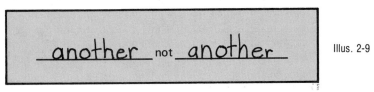

Illus. 2-9

3. Use a consistent style for printing; that is, do not mix capital letters with lower case letters.

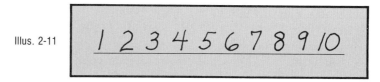

able to meet all the not *able to meet all the*

Illus. 2-10

Writing Numbers

Numbers are an important part of daily business life. They must show exact amounts of money, correct telephone numbers, quantities desired. Numbers must be written clearly so that they can be read quickly and accurately. These numbers are legible:

Illus. 2-11

1 2 3 4 5 6 7 8 9 10

1. Notice that all the numbers are of the same height.
2. Notice that the 6, 8, 9, and 0 are *closed*.
3. Notice that only 4 and 5 require more than a single stroke.

Numbers in Columns

Often numbers are recorded in columns and must be written to fit into prelined spaces. The numbers you write in columns must be written within the space allowed for each digit, or else the values of the numbers may be confused by the reader. Notice the difference between the two illustrations:

Illus. 2-12

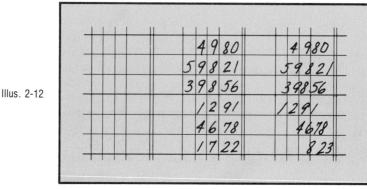

Unit 2 • Applying Basic Skills

Reading Handwriting

Office workers spend much time reading the handwriting of others. Instructions are often handwritten, copy to be typewritten is sometimes handwritten, and signatures often must be deciphered so that the response can be written to the proper person. Here are some aids to help you read writing that is not legible.

deciphered: figured out; made clear

1. Note carefully how the same number or letter is written in places where you are certain of the number or letter. For example, how are letters written in simple words, such as *the, and, but, sales,* etc.? How are the numbers written in the date or in an amount that you already know, such as the amount of the invoice that was sent to the person whose handwriting you are now trying to decipher?
2. Print those parts of a word that you are certain of; it may give you a clue as to rest of the word.

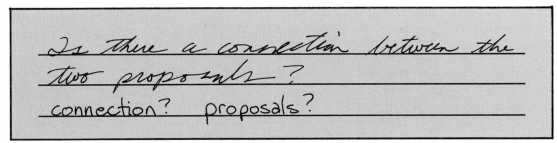

Illus. 2-13

3. Record the numbers that are clear and then attempt to determine what the remaining numbers must be. For example, if a dress manufacturer is identifying one of your products, knowing the nature of the writer's business may indicate which product is being ordered.

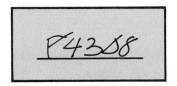

Illus. 2-14

Is this F4308? F4368? P4368? A dress manufacturer is not likely to be ordering F4308, which is a heavy zipper for mattress covers, or P4368, which is a snap for children's pants. The item must be F4368, which is a a lightweight zipper for jersey fabrics.

Learning to read the handwriting of others is a type of detective work and will require your following through a wide variety of clues.

REVIEWING IMPORTANT POINTS

1. Is handwriting an out-of-date skill? Explain.
2. What is an acceptable style of handwriting?
3. What are some letters that cause confusion when written by hand?
4. What are ways of improving your own handwriting?
5. How much space do you need in order to write easily?
6. What is the hand position that is considered most comfortable for writing?
7. What is meant by "using a vertical position" for the main part of each letter when printing?
8. How should numbers in columns be written?
9. When is printing used in the office?
10. How would you attempt to read handwriting which was partially illegible to you?

MAKING IMPORTANT DECISIONS

1. Pam knows that her handwriting isn't always legible, so she avoids giving anyone a written message. After she takes a message from a telephone caller in handwriting, she types a copy of the message which she puts on the desk of the executive. In this way, she is assured that the executive has a clearly readable message. What do you think of Pam's procedure?
2. Les is the receptionist in a chemical manufacturing company. He takes many messages each day. He leaves the messages on the desks of the executives. One day he realized that the secretaries to the executives were asking him again and again to read the telephone numbers he had recorded. What would you suggest to Les to reduce the number of questions he receives from the readers of his messages?

LEARNING TO WORK WITH OTHERS

A new assistant to Mrs. Gales collected statistics and wrote reports that were to be typed by Miss Nancy Sills. The assistant wrote his reports on yellow pads in longhand. He gave his pages to Miss Sills and expected her to prepare a final copy on her first typewriting of his handwritten material. Miss Sills found, however, that she could hardly read a line of his handwriting without being puzzled over at least one word because it was so illegible. She asked one of her co-workers to figure out a few words that she had circled and she found that the co-worker had as much difficulty as she did. She was using too much time figuring out what she should type; minutes would go by without any success in deciphering the puzzling words. After about two weeks of difficulty, Miss Sills felt she had to do something about the problem. What do you think Miss Sills should do?

IMPROVING LANGUAGE SKILLS

Verbs are words that express action or a state of being. They are closely related to subjects and must agree with their subjects in person and in number.

Examples: The *supervisor reads* all personnel bulletins received.
The *file clerks read* all instructions sent to them.

On a separate sheet of paper copy the following sentences, using the correct verb in each case.

1. The two new receptionists (is, are) meeting with the personnel manager today.
2. Every typist in this office (is, are) assigned jobs that must be carefully proofread with a co-worker.
3. Every clerk here (want, wants) his or her handwriting to be easily readable.
4. Don (organize, organized) his desk last week.
5. When you take these letters to the mailroom this afternoon, the mailclerk (weigh, weighs) each for you.
6. Jerry and Philip (go, goes) to lunch at one o'clock each day.
7. The mail was (distribute, distributed) by noon yesterday.
8. The receptionist (receives, received) three long-distance calls last Friday.
9. The general clerk (files, filed) the correspondence each Monday.
10. Will the messenger (take, takes) this package to the downtown office tomorrow morning?

IMPROVING ARITHMETIC SKILLS

1. Richard works in the slipcover and upholstery department of a large downtown department store. Among his jobs is measuring the end pieces of the bolts of fabric and putting prices on each. Here are some sizes and prices per yard of some remnants cut one afternoon. Determine the price for each piece.

3 yards at $4.50 =	2 yards at $6.25 =
2½ yards at $2.75 =	3 yards at $3.50 =
1 yard at $6.59 =	2½ yards at $3.95 =
1¼ yards at $7.50 =	1¾ yards at $5.25 =

2. Wanda maintained a record of the supplies she received from the Central Supply Department. At the end of the month she worked

out the total cost of the supplies she had used during the past month. Below is her record for October.

Supplies, October, 19—

1 box (500) of envelopes at ....$3.25 a box
1 box (500 of envelopes (Kraft) at.............. 4.05 a box
4 reams of letterhead paper at.................. 2.30 a ream
1 gallon of Ditto fluid at .... 2.50 a gallon
6 dozen pencils at .... .60 a dozen
2 rolls of Scotch tape at.......................... .94 a roll
2 boxes of stencils at .... 3.90 a box
1 can of ink liquid at............................... 2.84 a can
1 box (100 sheets) of carbon paper at .... 4.40 a box
2 typewriter ribbons at........................... 1.96 each

Record these amounts on a separate sheet of paper and find the total.

DEMONSTRATING OFFICE SKILLS

1. Cora works as a receptionist/clerk in the audiovisual department for a school district. One of her frequent tasks is taking requests for film loops, 8mm film, and filmstrips from teachers by telephone. She records the information in handwriting directly on a form so there is no need to recopy. Assume that she has received the following requests by telephone. Record each on the forms provided in the *Supplies Inventory* or draw a form similar to the one below.

Date of request _____

Teacher_____

School_____

Room_____

Item(s) requested_____

_____

_____

_____

Date needed_____

_____
Receptionist/Clerk

All these requests were received on September 17, 19––.

Ms. Jane Taylor
Middle School No. 4
Room 213
Aesop's Fables—all 4 filmstrips
for September 27, a.m.

Mr. Lewis Unger
J.H. No. 3
Room 31
The Constitution of the United States for September 28, all day

Mrs. Ruth Westford
Central High School
Room 245
Using Maps—Measuring Distance
The Language of Maps
for September 26, all day

Ms. Maria Perez
Western Regional High School
Room 370
Un Viaje a Mejico
for September 27, all day

2. Bill is a clerk in the subscription office of a regional weekly magazine. Often subscriptions are taken by telephone. Bill must print the names and addresses clearly so that the mailing department has no problems in setting up the new subscription lists. Here are four subscriptions taken by telephone. Print each on the forms given in the *Supplies Inventory* or draw up a form similar to the one below.

Mrs. T. E. Schmidt
369 Hope Avenue
Plainview, New York 11803

Ms. Sally Hecht
435 East 68 Street
New York, NY 10021

Mr. and Mrs. W. Vann
14 Quaker Path
Setauket, New York 11733

Mr. T. E. Del Toro
809 Bartow Avenue
New York, NY 10465

New Subscription

Subscriber _____

Address _____

_____

_____

_____

Clerk _____

3. Below are some examples of the handwriting of high school students. What improvements would you suggest for each of the persons whose handwriting is illustrated.

I need more of a challenge in the work that I did. I need more responsibilities.

That I had to learn, for myself, if I enjoyed the kind of world I entered

Knowing what its like to go to work I have the responsibility for many things.

I think I have been much more grown-up.

My attitude towards work now is that I am more confident in what I do.

Part 3

Handling Computations in the Office

> Mr. Frank Gomez works in the billing department of a large office supplies company in a downtown financial district. Because many of the transactions are paid through credit cards, the salesclerks must fill out sales slips in detail. One of the tasks that Mr. Gomez handles daily is checking the computations of the clerks. He must determine if the correct tax was charged and if all the extensions, as well as totals, are correct. He has recently learned, however, that a new computer system for handling sales will eliminate the need for his checking. He knows, though, that there will continue to be many instances each day when his skill in handling numbers will be required.

Numbers — and how they are used — are not new to you. In fact, you began to learn about numbers when you entered elementary school. In practically every office, there is constant need for workers who understand basic **computations**. It is true that there are many machines to aid the office worker in quickly determining a total, a product, or a percentage. These machines range from **miniature** calculators to giant computers. However, even with these machines, you will find that you can do your work with more **assurance** if you have a thorough mastery of the basic arithmetic operations.

computations: number problems

miniature: very small

assurance: certainty; confidence

Finding a Total — Addition

What is the cost of those five office supplies? How many hours did the typist spend on that project? How much were sales of Bulletin 54 last month? These are examples of common questions often heard in modern offices. All these questions require a *total* — the sum you get when you *add* numbers. To *add* is to combine so that you have one amount. You can add all items of one *set*. A *set*, as you will recall, is a number of things of the same kind that belong together or are used together. The numbers which are to be added are called *addends*. When numbers contain decimals, they should be recorded so that the decimals are aligned.

Addition is a commonly used skill in a business office. On the following pages are some examples.

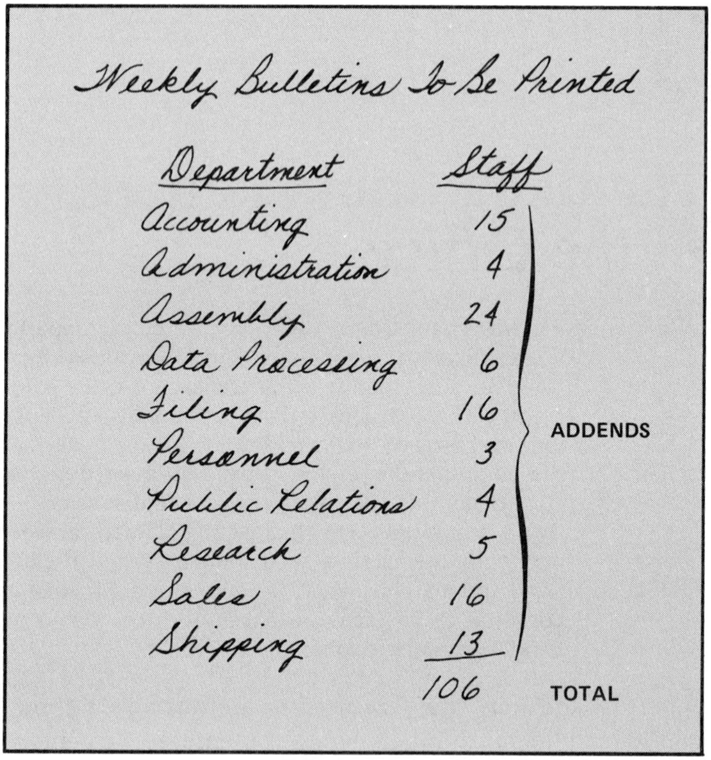

Illus. 2-15

Weekly Bulletins To Be Printed

Department	Staff	
Accounting	15	
Administration	4	
Assembly	24	
Data Processing	6	
Filing	16	ADDENDS
Personnel	3	
Public Relations	4	
Research	5	
Sales	16	
Shipping	13	
	106	TOTAL

You will note that the numbers are clearly written and are in line. The numbers are added in groups of two or more.

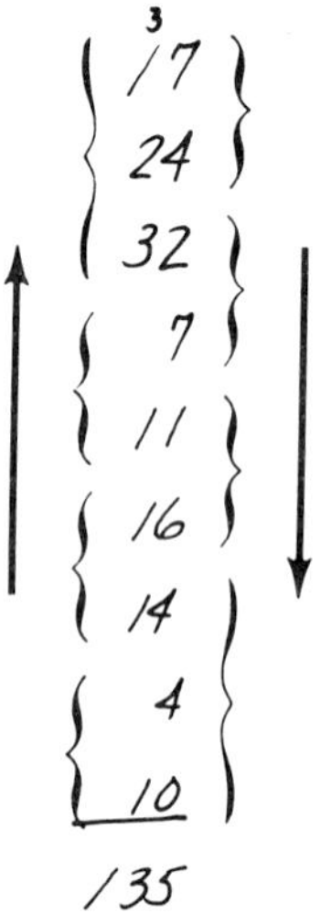

Illus. 2-16

$$
\begin{array}{c}
17 \\
24 \\
32 \\
7 \\
11 \\
16 \\
14 \\
4 \\
10 \\
\hline
135
\end{array}
$$

The total can be double-checked by adding in the opposite direction.

Unit 2 • Applying Basic Skills

At the end of each week, the general office clerk in a small insurance office checked the petty cash fund. During the week receipts showing the payments from petty cash were placed in an envelope. On Friday afternoon the receipts were totaled. Below are the receipts for the week of September 20.

Illus. 2-17

Petty cash receipts

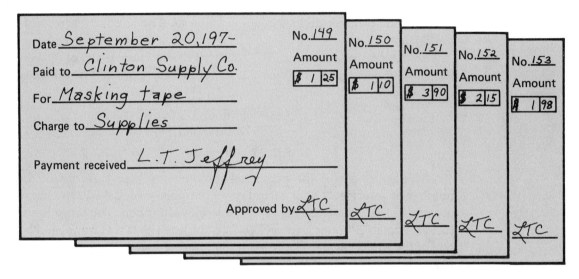

A receptionist in a large company was asked to keep a record of the number of daily callers for a period of one week. To make this task easier, a tally sheet was kept as shown below. Notice how quickly the receptionist was able to determine the number of calls, since the tallies are recorded in groups of five.

Illus. 2-18

Tally sheet of incoming telephone calls

CALLERS, April 18-22			
DAY	MORNING	AFTERNOON	TOTAL
Monday	ⅢⅢ Ⅲ II	ⅢⅢ ⅢⅢ ⅢⅢ I	28
Tuesday	ⅢⅢ ⅢⅢ ⅢⅢ	ⅢⅢ ⅢⅢ IIII	29
Wednesday	ⅢⅢ ⅢⅢ ⅢⅢ III	ⅢⅢ ⅢⅢ ⅢⅢ I	34
Thursday	ⅢⅢ IIII	ⅢⅢ ⅢⅢ III	22
Friday	ⅢⅢ ⅢⅢ ⅢⅢ ⅢⅢ I	ⅢⅢ ⅢⅢ III	34
	75	72	147

Finding a Difference — Subtraction

As you know, subtraction is the opposite of addition. It is the process of taking one number from another number.

The number from which another number is subtracted is called the *minuend*; the number deducted, the *subtrahend*. The subtraction result is the *difference*.

At the end of the week, the total payments from petty cash were $12.85. The petty cash fund was $25.00. How much was left in the petty cash fund?

$25.00 Minuend
−12.85 Subtrahend
$12.15 Difference

A receptionist for the personnel interviewers kept a record of the number of interviews held each day. One interviewer asked how many interviews were yet to be held on a particular afternoon. The receptionist had scheduled 28 interviews and checked off each as it was completed by one of the interviewers. The receptionist, noting that 17 were completed, was quickly able to tell the interviewer how many were still to be completed by subtracting 17 from 28.

28
−17
11 Interviews yet to be completed

To check the accuracy of a subtraction problem, add the subtrahend to the difference and the total should equal the minuend.

$12.15	11
+12.85	+17
$25.00	28

Finding the Product — Multiplication

Multiplication, finding a product, is a short-cut method of repeated addition. There are many office tasks that require multiplication. Some examples are:

If there were six rows of chairs in a conference room and there were 5 chairs in each row, how would you determine how many chairs were in the conference room?

You can add each row of chairs to the next row and get a total of 30. Or you can *multiply* 6 (number of rows) times 5 (number of chairs in each row) which will give you a *product* of 30.

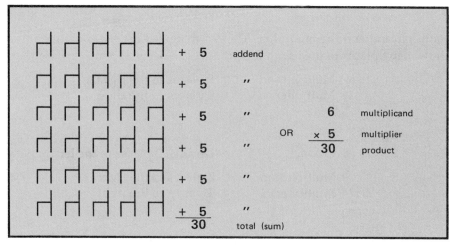

		+ 5	addend	
		+ 5	"	
		+ 5	"	6 multiplicand
	OR			x 5 multiplier
		+ 5	"	30 product
		+ 5	"	
		+ 5	"	
		30	total (sum)	

Illus. 2-19

Stan must type envelopes for a long list of names of addresses. He counts the addresses on each page and multiplies this number (25) by the number of pages in the list (43). He realizes that he will need 1075 envelopes.

Jessie uses a calculator to figure the extensions on the invoices she prepares for customers. A sample of an invoice is shown below:

Illus. 2-20

Tenacity Stationery & Office Supplies   SALES INVOICE

484 TORCH STREET   FARMINGTON, MI   48024

Date: July 12, 19--
Our Invoice No.: 20502
Your Invoice No.: 20883
Shipped By: Truck
Terms: 2/10 net 30

Sold To: Boswell Supply Company
3964 Ambrose Avenue
Indianapolis, IN 46222

QUANTITY	DESCRIPTIONS	CAT. NO.	UNIT PRICE	AMOUNT
36 rolls	Masking Tape, 3/4" x 2160"	MT-242	.89	32.04
36 rolls	Masking Tape, 1" x 2160"	MT-245	1.19	42.84
12 rolls	Scotch Tape, 1/2" x 1296"	ST-600	.56	6.72
12 rolls	Dymo Tape--Plastic, 1/2"			
	(Blue)	DY-149	1.10	13.20
				94.80

Decimal Point Placement

To determine where the decimal point is placed in the product, you must count the numbers to the right of the decimal point in both the multiplicand and the multiplier. These two figures are *added* to determine how many places to the left in the product the decimal point is placed.

$	15.67	Multiplicand	2 places to the right
	×14	Multiplier	0 places to the right

6268
1567

| $ | 219.38 | Product | Decimal 2 places to the left |

| $ | 195.00 | Multiplicand | 2 places to the right |
| | ×.0125 | Multiplier | 4 places to the right |

97500
39000
19500

| $2.437500 | Product | Decimal 6 places to the left |

Rounding Numbers

In the preceding example, the product is $2.437500. Amounts of money are generally rounded to the nearest cent. In this instance .4375 is nearest to .44; therefore, the product would be considered $2.44.

A simple rule to follow is this: If the first digit to the right of the cents position is 5 or more, add 1 to the cents digit; if it is less than 5, disregard it. Therefore:

$15.353 becomes $15.35
1.456 becomes 1.46
10.455 becomes 10.46

disregard:
pay no attention to

Estimating the Product

A good office worker is always aware of the importance of numbers, and the habit of estimating is a measure of this awareness. To estimate the product, you should look at the multiplicand and round it to the nearest whole number and then do the same with the multiplier. Estimating gives you an idea of *about* what the product should be.

estimating:
making a judgment
about how many

As an example, if you had to order 11 reams of paper at $1.98 each, what would be the approximate cost? To estimate, consider the $1.98 as $2.00 and the 11 as 10. The exact answer should be *near* $20.00. The exact answer *is* $21.78. If you had estimated the answer, you would not have accepted an exact answer of $2.17 or $217.80.

Multiplying by 10, 100, 1,000 . . . .

To multiply by 10, 100, 1,000 or by higher powers of 10, you merely add as many zeros to the multiplicand as there are zeros in the multiplier to get the product.

$$167 \times 10 = 1,670$$
$$186 \times 100 = 18,600$$
$$146 \times 1,000 = 146,000$$

If there is a decimal point in the multiplicand, then you must move the decimal point in the product *to the right* for as many digits as there are zeros in the multiplier.

$$45.85 \times 100 = 4585.00 \text{ or } 4,585$$
$$.125 \times 1,000 = 125.000 \text{ or } 125$$

Finding a Quotient — Division

Division and multiplication are opposite operations. In division, you separate into parts.

Multiplication	*Division*
There are 5 rows of chairs with 4 chairs in each row. How many chairs are there altogether?	There are twenty chairs and they are to be arranged in 5 rows. How must the chairs be separated to have 5 rows?

$$5 \times 4 = 20$$

$$20 \div 5 = 4 \longleftarrow \text{Quotient}$$

Dividend   Divisor

To check the accuracy of the computation, multiply the quotient by the divisor (4×5). The product, 20, is the same as the dividend.

There are many occasions in the office when you will need to determine a quotient. An example is:

Brian wanted to determine the cost of a single stencil. He knew that 24 stencils cost $3.12. Therefore he was able to find the cost per stencil by dividing 3.12 by 24:

```
           .13 per stencil
     24) 3.12
         2 4
         ───
          72
          72
         ───
```

Decimal Point Placement

In those cases where there is a decimal point in the dividend and the divisor is a whole number, the decimal point in the quotient is aligned with the decimal in the dividend.

$$
\begin{array}{r}
1.3 \\
15)\overline{19.5} \\
15 \\
\hline
45 \\
45 \\
\hline
\end{array}
$$

Since division can be done with only a whole number divisor, move the decimal point in the divisor all the way to the right. Then move the decimal in the dividend the same number of places to the right, and place the quotient decimal point directly above this. It may be necessary to add zeros to the dividend to have enough places.

$$
\begin{array}{r}
12. \\
15.135)\overline{181.620} \\
151\ 35 \\
\hline
30\ 270 \\
30\ 270 \\
\hline
\end{array}
$$

Dividing by 10, 100, 1,000 . . . .

To divide by 10 or 100 or 1,000 or a higher power of 10, you move the decimal point *to the left* in the dividend for as many places as there are zeros in the divisor. The dividend then becomes the quotient. This is a very useful division shortcut.

$$
\begin{aligned}
156 \div 10 &= 15.6 \\
4567 \div 100 &= 45.67 \\
15.3 \div 1000 &= .0153
\end{aligned}
$$

Remember that when you have a whole number, the decimal point follows the last digit:

156 is the same as 156.

Figuring with Fractions

Many computations in the business office require the use of parts of whole numbers, which are called *fractions*. A fraction is a representation of one number divided by another — ¾, ½. The number above the line is called the *numerator*; the number below is called the *denominator*. From

Unit 2 • Applying Basic Skills

your earlier study of arithmetic you will recall these basic operations when using fractions.

Addition — To add fractions, you must have a common denominator. The least common multiple of the denominators, that is, the smallest number that is evenly divisible by each denominator, is called the *least common denominator*.

divisible:
able to be divided

Example: 1/2 + 2/3 = ?

If you multiply 2 × 3, your product is 6; this is the smallest possible denominator since there is no number smaller that is evenly divisible by both 2 and 3.

$$1/2 = 3/6$$
$$+2/3 = 4/6$$
$$\overline{ 7/6} = 1\ 1/6$$

Remember that the product of the two denominators will always give you a common denominator, but this number is not always the *least* common denominator, which you want to find since it allows you to work with the smallest numbers possible in computing the solution. What is the common denominator found when you multiply the denominators of these two fractions?

$$1/4 + 5/6 = ?$$

Is the common denominator the *least* common denominator? (*No*) What is the least common denominator? (*12*)

Subtraction — In subtracting fractions you must find the least common denominator just as you did when adding. Only the final operation differs:

Example: 5/6 − 1/4 = ?

The least common denominator is 12

$$5/6 = 10/12$$
$$-1/4 = \ \ 3/12$$
$$\overline{ 7/12}$$

Multiplication — To multiply fractions, you merely find the product of the numerators and denominators.

Example: $\dfrac{3}{4} \times \dfrac{2}{3} = ?$

3 × 2 = 6 (product of numerators)
4 × 3 = 12 (product of denominators)
Product for the two fractions is 6/12, which can be reduced to 1/2.

Division — To divide one fraction by another,

1. **Invert** the divisor
2. Proceed as though you were multiplying

Example: 3/4 ÷ 1/3 = 3/4 × 3/1 = 9/4 = 2 1/4

Conversion to decimals — All fractions can be converted to decimal equivalents. The decimal equivalents of fractions are generally used in the office because operations on adding and calculating machines are simpler with decimals.

To convert a fraction to a decimal, you divide the numerator (which becomes the dividend) by the denominator (which becomes the divisor).

Example: 2/3 = .6667

$$\begin{array}{r} .6667 \\ 3\overline{)2.0000} \\ \underline{1\ 8} \\ 20 \\ \underline{18} \\ 20 \\ \underline{18} \\ 2 \end{array}$$

since 2/3 is more than 1/2, the next 6 is rounded up to 7

Office workers who deal with numbers usually know from memory the decimal equivalents of the common fractions. Below is a list of frequently used fractions and their decimal equivalents.

Fraction	Decimal	Fraction	Decimal
1/2	.5	4/5	.8
1/3	.3333	1/6	.16667
2/3	.6667	5/6	.83333
1/4	.25	1/8	.125
3/4	.75	3/8	.375
1/5	.2	5/8	.625
2/5	.4	7/8	.875
3/5	.6		

Handling Percentages

There are many times when it is necessary to determine the relationship of one number to another:

What is the relationship of weekly savings to weekly salary?
What is the relationship of the amount saved to the amount owed on an invoice if the invoice is paid within 10 days?

What is the relationship of the time spent filing to the full working day?

What is the relationship of the number of secretaries to the number of executives?

To find the answer to each of the above questions, you would need to determine a *percentage*. *Percentage* means *per hundred* or *of the hundred*. A percentage is a part of the whole expressed in hundredths. In decimal form:

$$15/100 = 15 \text{ percent} = .15$$

If Fay saves $10 per week from her weekly salary of $140, you can determine the relationship between the two — savings and earnings —by figuring what percentage of the weekly salary is saved. The salary, $140 equals 100 percent. What percentage of $140 is $10?

$$\$140. = 100\%$$
$$10. = \ ?\ \%$$

$$
\begin{array}{r}
.071 = 7.1\% \\
140)\overline{10.000} \\
9\ 80 \\
\hline
200 \\
140 \\
\hline
60
\end{array}
$$

If two hours are spent in filing during a 7 hour day, the percentage of time used for filing can be determined in this manner:

$$7 \text{ hours} = 100\%$$
$$2 \text{ hours} = \ ?\ \%$$

$$
\begin{array}{r}
.285 = 28.5\% \\
7)\overline{2.000} \\
1\ 4 \\
\hline
60 \\
56 \\
\hline
40 \\
35 \\
\hline
5
\end{array}
$$

A *discount* is a reduction on an amount owed. Discounts are allowed for prompt payment of invoices as well as for quantity purchases. For example, an invoice totaling $1,345.00 allows for a 2% discount if payment is made within 10 days.

Two percent of $1,345 = ?
.02 × 1,345 = $26.90 (Discount)

$$
\begin{array}{r}
\$1,345.00 \\
-\ 26.90 \\
\hline
\$1,318.10 \text{ (Payment)}
\end{array}
$$

Metric Measuring

The common method of measurement in the United States has been the English, or imperial, system. It includes these units of measurement: inch, foot, yard, mile, ounce, pound, pint, quart, etc. While this system is still in use in the United States, there is a gradual shift underway to the *metric system*, which includes these units of measurement: centimeter, meter, kilometer, gram, kilogram, liter, etc. The metric system is the most widely accepted system of measurement in the world. With the increase in international trade, it is important that there be a standard for measurements that is in use throughout the world. Such a standard makes it possible for parts produced in one country to be used in another country. For example, a part for a sewing machine produced in Italy may be 3 centimeters wide, while one produced in the United States is 1 inch wide. An inch is equivalent to 2.540 centimeters, which means that the part produced in Italy would be too large for the American produced machine.

Some employees understand both systems thoroughly and can measure with one is easily as with the other. Jay is a clerk in an international shipping company and must know both systems. As he said:

> I can think in pounds as easily as I think in kilograms, because we use both many times each day. Our containers and trucks show weight in both systems. For example, our trucks which are used for domestic deliveries have painted on them:
>
> | | |
> |---|---|
> | TARE | 3,800 Kg. |
> | | 8,380 lbs. |
> | GR. WEIGHT | 30,480 Kg. |
> | | 67,200 lbs. |

The basic unit in the metric system is the meter and all units are based on the decimal system. This means that the division of a meter into ten parts gives you a new unit, the decimeter, which is a decimal part (1/10) of a meter. A division of a meter into a hundred parts gives you still another unit, the centimeter.

You will find more details on the metric system in Appendix G.

REVIEWING IMPORTANT POINTS

1. How do you determine the *total* of a group of expenditures?
2. How does subtraction differ from addition?
3. How would you check to see if you subtracted correctly?
4. Why are tallies recorded in groups of five?

5. Explain the relationship of multiplication to addition?
6. What does it mean to *estimate*?
7. What is the *approximate* cost of 73 items priced at 97 cents each?
8. What are you actually doing when you are dividing?
9. How do you determine a common denominator when you are adding fractions?
10. What is the value of a measurement that is used throughout the world?

MAKING IMPORTANT DECISIONS

1. Jennie feels that she is very good at computing. She always does her computing with pencil and paper. One afternoon, however, her supervisor said she had a small pocket calculator for her to use. The supervisor said that she would be able to work much faster with a calculator. Jennie made no comment, but she thought: "No machine is better than I am. I'll just put the machine in my desk. I want to figure problems in my own way." What do you think of Jennie's judgment?
2. Garth checks the supply cabinet to determine which additional supplies he needs. This is what he finds:

   ¼ box of envelopes (each box holds 500)
   4 packages of large envelopes (each package has 25)
   ¼ ream of letterhead (a ream has 500 sheets)
   2 packages of carbon paper (each package has 100 sheets)
   ½ ream of second sheets (a ream has 500 sheets)

   What is the quantity of each item that is available?

LEARNING TO WORK WITH OTHERS

Candy Maiers was hired as a new clerk in a large accounting department of a manufacturing company. She wasn't sure why she was placed in this department, because she didn't feel confident in handling numbers. However, she felt she should say nothing and simply try to learn as much as she could. Shortly after beginning her new job, the supervisor asked her to help another clerk determine standard prices for some new products being developed. As she looked at the worksheets, she realized that she needed to determine percentages as well as unit prices. The supervisor suggested that she use the calculator for her work. Candy didn't know how to use the calculator. Should she ask the supervisor to help her? Should she just pretend she could do the job on the machine, but actually do it by hand? What would you suggest that Candy do?

IMPROVING LANGUAGE SKILLS

Below are pairs of words that are often confused in both oral and written communication.

accept — to receive
except — to leave out

affect — to influence
effect — the result of

all ready — completely prepared
already — previous to some specified time

beside — next to (position)
besides — in addition to

can — denotes ability
may — denotes permission

farther — indicates distance
further — additional, more, to a greater degree or extent

good — desirable, right, virtuous
well — in a good or proper manner; healthy

On a separate sheet of paper write each of the following sentences choosing the word which correctly completes the sentence:
1. The photocopies were (all ready, already) by noon yesterday.
2. Do you recognize the man who is (beside, besides) the moderator?
3. The supervisor said that Greg (can, may) attend the word processing seminar.
4. Stewart said that he would give (farther, further) attention to the report today.
5. The job was done (good, well) by the three typists.
6. What is the (affect, effect) of a coffee break on our productivity?
7. The supervisor praised the (good, well) job that Betsy did yesterday.
8. How much (farther, further) must we travel to get to the convention site?
9. Everyone is in favor of the change in layout (except, accept) Paul.
10. Did the memorandum we received yesterday (affect, effect) your holiday plans?

IMPROVING ARITHMETIC SKILLS

Copy the following problems on a sheet of paper and perform the operations indicated:

1. $14.56
   3.56
   8.12
   + 29.17

2. $54.67
   13.20
   1.97
   +   .39

3. $3,197.50
   359.21
   1,100.01
   +   97.85

4. $5,901.49
   349.20
   987.65
   +   342.25

5. $689.20
   320.90
   40.95
   + 11.59

6. $3,190.35
   −   294.29

7. $456.78
   − 135.09

8. $543.21
   − 432.98

9. $687.65
   − 123.23

10. $8,769.31
    − 3,642.28

11. $389.46 × 15% =

12. $39.59 × 12½% =

13. $598.76 × 6% =

14. $679.98 × 7.75 % =

15. 398.43 × 5% =

16. $396.46 ÷ 15 =

17. $3,945.25 ÷ 25 =

18. $2,134.50 ÷ 14 =

19. 1/2 = ?%

20. 7/8 = ?%

DEMONSTRATING OFFICE SKILLS

1. You are a clerk in the department of facilities management for a large office building. The Department Head, Ms. Stella Sterns, asked you to prepare a brief memorandum on the cost of carpeting for an office that is being renovated. Prepare the memo on a half sheet of plain paper based on these yardages and prices:

   66¼ yards at 14.99 per yard
   66¼ yards of padding at 2.29 per yard
   Removal of worn out carpeting costs .59 per yard.

2. You were asked to take an inventory of the cotton fabrics on the selling floor of the fabric shop in which you work as a clerk. These are the figures you recorded:

	Extension		Extension
23½ yards at 1.69 = _____		17 yards at 4.29 = _____
17 yards at 1.98 = _____		7 yards at 4.29 = _____
14 yards at 2.49 = _____		3½ yards at 4.29 = _____
7 yards at 2.39 = _____		21½ yards at 1.59 = _____
25 yards at 3.95 = _____		11 yards at 2.29 = _____
15 yards at 1.98 = _____		21 yards at 2.29 = _____
11 yards at 1.98 = _____		19 yards at 2.29 = _____

   Compute the extensions for each item.

IMPROVING OFFICE SKILLS (Optional)

The supervisor of your department has asked you to type the following Table of Occupancy Statistics at the four major hotels in the chain your company is considering buying. Use plain paper and make a carbon copy.

OCCUPANCY STATISTICS

Hotel	Available Rooms	Average Daily Occupancy		
		Year 1	Year 2	Year 3
Lake Blue Hotel	23,826	15,450	14,500	17,690
Paradiso Hotel	21,832	15,121	14,000	16,500
Grand Hotel	20,750	11,453	12,150	17,150
Dante's Hotel	15,111	9,540	11,850	12,200

Unit 2 • Applying Basic Skills

Preparing Mailable Letters

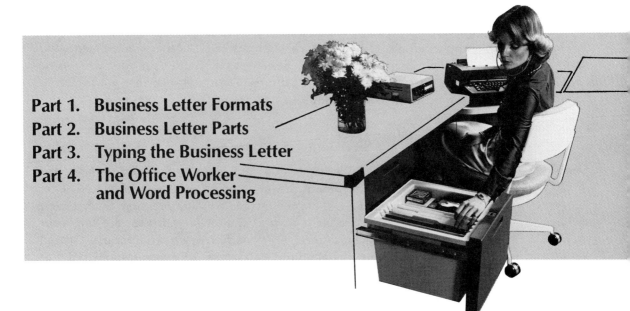

Part 1. Business Letter Formats
Part 2. Business Letter Parts
Part 3. Typing the Business Letter
Part 4. The Office Worker
and Word Processing

Part 1

Business Letter Formats

Melody Cartwright works in the Loan Department of a large bank. She is one of three stenographers who take dictation from the seven loan officers. Melody types all letters in the block style with open punctuation. This is the style that her department has chosen in an effort to be consistent. Melody types many letters which go out to customers concerning the status of their accounts. She makes sure that each letter looks attractive, because she realizes that her letters are, in a sense, advertisements for the bank. Melody also sends messages to other departments in the bank. For this purpose, she uses interoffice memorandums. In all of her typing, Melody takes special pride in doing a good job. She knows that producing a business letter is expensive and she wants to do her part in helping her company cut office costs.

Cost of a Letter

The Dartnell Corporation recently reported that the average cost of a business letter is about $4. This includes the cost of the time spent to dictate and type the letter, the cost of the paper, envelopes, and other supplies. It also includes office overhead, such as space, equipment, and lighting. Since letters do cost money, it will be to your advantage to be thoroughly familiar with the different letter styles so that you can type them accurately and quickly.

overhead: general expense

The First Impression

The recipient of a letter sees the total letter on the sheet of paper and forms an impression before the message is read. A well-placed letter with clean, even type will make a favorable first impression. Such a letter will encourage the recipient to read the letter with the care that your company would like it to receive. A poorly typewritten, carelessly placed letter may fail to get the attention it deserves. It is your responsibility as

recipient: receiver

the typist to judge each letter you type with this question in mind: How will this letter look to the receiver?

A letter gives a good first impression if:

1. Margins, indentations, and spacing are pleasing to the eye.
2. Each part of the letter is correctly placed according to the style selected.
3. There are no obvious erasures and no strikeovers.
4. It is clean — has no smudges or fingerprints.
5. Type is even and clear.

Letter Styles

Letter style refers to the placement of the parts of the letter (see Part 2 of this Unit, pages 77–88). The most popular styles are the modified block, block, and simplified. Many companies use the same style in all their offices, while other companies permit each office or each person to decide which letter style to use. Your employer will tell you which letter style you should use.

Modified Block Style

The modified block style is the letter style used most often in the office. The following parts are typed starting at the **horizontal** center of the page: date, complimentary close, typed name, and official title. For parts of the letter see Illus. 3-4, page 78.

horizontal: parallel to a base line; across

The first line of each paragraph in a modified block style may be indented (Letter A on page 70) or may be blocked (Letter B).

Block Style

In the block style, you begin typing all lines of the letter at the left margin. This style, of course, is one of the easiest to type because you don't use the tabulating key. It is a modern style (Letter C on page 70) and is gaining popularity in many offices.

Simplified Style

The simplified style was introduced by the Administrative Management Society and is sometimes called the AMS Style. It is the easiest letter style to type and the Administrative Management Society reports that the use of this style results in a cost savings of 10.7 percent.

NATIONAL STEEL COMPANY
BUFFALO, N.Y. 14214   716-321-7841

November 18, 19--

Mr. Lloyd Fischer
Standard Steel Products
132 Keller Ave.
Reno, NV 89503

Dear Mr. Fischer:

Thank you for your order for 12 steel racks of
commercial heavy weight, size 12" x 36 " x 75". We
are pleased to have this order from you

A large shipment of these racks is on its way
from our factory. It should reach us within a few
days. We are, therefore, holding your order until
our shipment arrives. Unless we hear from you to
the contrary, we shall assume that this action is
satisfactory. We shall ship the racks as soon as
they arrive.

The enclosed booklet on steel shelving may be
of interest to you. Let us know if we can serve
you further.

Sincerely yours,

George P. Burns

George P. Burns, Manager
Order Department

ra

Enclosure

Letter A
Modified block style, mixed
punctuation, indented paragraphs

Office of Samuel H. Hall
Attorney at Law
663 BLUE ASH TOWER   CINCINNATI, OHIO 45222   513-261-3883

January 28, 19--

Miss Jane Porter
President, Business Club
Kenton High School
Cincinnati, Ohio 45224

Dear Jane

I am glad to accept your invitation to meet with the
Thomas Jefferson High School Business Club. Thank
you very much for giving me a choice of three dates.
I would prefer to be with you on March 20 at 2:30 p.m.

I understand from what you told me over the telephone
that you would like me to speak on office procedures
and practices. I shall be very happy to do so. Within
the next week or ten days I shall send you the exact
title of my remarks so that you will be able to include
that item of information in your program.

May I suggest that I talk for approximately twenty
minutes so that about half of the time will be available
for the question and answer period that you would like
to have.

It will be good to return to the school where I
received my own training. I am looking forward with
pleasure to your meeting of March 20.

Very truly yours

Samuel H. Hall

Samuel H. Hall

da

Letter B
Modified block style, open
punctuation, blocked paragraphs

AMERICAN METALS PRODUCTS, INC.
5223 Riley Avenue   Portland, OR 97202   503-333-6419

May 26, 19--

King & King, Inc.
225 Lucerne Avenue
Nashville, TN 37215

Ladies and Gentlemen

This letter will confirm our telephone conversation
of yesterday afternoon. We shall appreciate your
sending us information on surplus raw materials for
electronics that you have available for sale.

We are particularly interested right now in cold
rolled steel and pretinned nickel and silver. We are
interested, also, in coils of extra tough hard copper.

Keep us in mind when additional lots of materials
for electronics become available. We are suppliers
for South American outlets and are in constant need
of all types of electronic materials.

Yours very truly

Stanley Cooper

Stanley Cooper, Manager
Purchasing Department

jm

Letter C
Block style, open punctuation

Administrative
Management
Society
8221 Sydney Avenue   Kansas City, MO 64131
816-922-0984

September 20, 19--

Mr. Scott Chambers
Arrow Collection Services
243 Euclid Avenue
Tampa, FL 33609

AMS SIMPLIFIED LETTER

This letter is written in the style recommended by
the Administrative Management Society. The formal
salutation and complimentary close are omitted. These
are not the only changes that have been made, however.
Other improvements are given below:

1.   The extreme left block format is used.

2.   A subject heading is used and should be typed
     in capitals a triple space below the address.

3.   Paragraphs are blocked (no indentations).

4.   The writer's name and title are typed in cap-
     itals at the left margin at least three blank
     lines below the body of the letter.

5.   The initials of the typist are typed at the
     left a double space below the writer's name.

Please show this letter to the correspondents in your
company. You will find that its use reduces your
letter-writing costs.

David S. Henry

David S. Henry, President

tm

Letter D
Simplified style

Illus. 3-1   Four business letter styles

In the simplified style, begin all lines at the left margin and omit the salutation and the complimentary close. Type a subject line in all capital letters on the third line below the inside address. Begin the body of the letter on the third line below the subject line. Type your employer's name and title in all capital letters on the fourth line below the last line of the letter (Letter D on page 70).

omit:
leave out

Letter Punctuation

Letter punctuation refers to the use of punctuation marks after the salutation and complimentary close of a letter. The most frequently used styles of punctuation are open and mixed.

frequently:
often; repeatedly

Open Style

In the open style, you do not type any mark of punctuation after the salutation and complimentary close (Letters B and C). This style is gaining in popularity because it takes less time to type.

Mixed Style

If your employer would like you to use the mixed style of punctuation, you would type a colon after the salutation and a comma after the complimentary close (Letter A).

There are several ways of combining letter styles and punctuation styles. For example, you could type a letter in modified block style with open punctuation, in modified block style with mixed punctuation, in block style with open punctuation, or in block style with mixed punctuation. The punctuation styles do not apply to simplified letters because you do not type a salutation or complimentary close.

Simplifying the Typewriting of Letters

Many office managers attempt to reduce the cost of letters in one or more of these ways:

1. *Using open punctuation.* Eliminating marks of punctuation after the salutation and complimentary close is a timesaving feature.

eliminating:
getting rid of

2. *Omitting names that appear in the letterhead.* For example, there is no need to typewrite the name of the company below the complimentary close if it appears in the letterhead. Also, the typewritten name and title of the dictator need not appear in the closing lines if they are in the letterhead.

3. *Typewriting letters in block or simplified style.* These letters can be typed faster than other letter styles because every line is started at the left margin and the tabular key is not used. In addition, in the simplified letter the salutation and complimentary close are omitted.

4. *Using a standard line length for all letters.* When the length of letters varies, a typist can save time by establishing a standard line length and varying the distance between the letterhead and the date and between the complimentary close and the typed signature. Some offices use a six-inch line for all letters, and the skillful typist can make each letter attractive with this standard feature.

Interoffice Memorandums

In the office in which you will be employed, you may type many short business notes or reports on forms called interoffice memorandums. These memorandums are sent within the organization. They are brief and to the point because their only purpose is to communicate a message to other members of the organization quickly and clearly. The chief advantage of these forms is that they can be typed quickly. Titles (*Mr., Ms., Mrs., Dr.,* etc.), the salutation, the complimentary close, and the formal signature are usually omitted.

Illus. 3-2

ACME CORPORATION   Interoffice Memorandum

    TO: Robert Turner   DATE: October 21, 19--

FROM: Wayne Mims   SUBJECT: Interoffice Memos

Start the interoffice memo two blank lines below the typewritten heading material and block it at the left margin.

Since the writer's name is in the heading there is no need to type it at the end of the message. The typist's initials are placed a double space below the message. All end-of-letter notations such as the typist's initials and carbon copy information are typed as they are in letters.

cm

cc Joan Wilson

```
THE PRUETT COMPANY          INTEROFFICE MEMORANDUM


    TO:  Sam Conrad                 DATE:  September 12, 19--
         Melvin Stuart
         Joe Conley             SUBJECT:  Departmental Meeting

    FROM:  Ralph Sanders


    Because of recent large increases in the cost of almost all
    office supplies, a meeting of department heads is called for
    this Friday, September 16, at 3 p.m., in the Board Room.

    Will you please come to this meeting prepared with suggestions
    we can use to conserve office supplies.

    h
```

Illus. 3-3

The forms, with the heading *Interoffice Memorandum*, may be printed on half sheets or whole sheets of paper, generally on less expensive paper than the company letterhead. The printed words *To, From, Date,* and *Subject,* with enough writing space after each of them, may be included in the heading of the form. Usually the company name also appears on the interoffice memorandum.

You should leave two blank lines after the last line of the heading and the first line of the message. Short messages of not more than five lines may be double spaced; longer messages should be single spaced. Reference initials should be typed at the left margin one blank line below the last line of the message. When enclosures are sent with a memorandum, the enclosure notation should be typed one blank line below the reference initials.

An interoffice memorandum is often sent to a number of people within the organization. In such cases carbon copies or photocopies may be used. The names of all who are to receive copies, however, should be listed on the original and on all copies as shown above. Another practice is to type the original and one carbon file copy with the names of the recipients. The original, with any special enclosures, is sent to the first person on the list. When the first person is finished with it, a line is drawn through that person's name and the memorandum is sent along to the next person on the list. This is repeated until all of the interested persons have seen it. This practice is most satisfactory when there is an enclosure or an attachment with the interoffice memorandum that is either too long or too difficult to reproduce.

REVIEWING IMPORTANT POINTS

1. What expenses must you consider to determine the cost of a business letter?
2. Why is it so important that a letter give a good first impression?
3. What does letter style refer to?
4. Which are the most frequently used letter styles?
5. Can you indent paragraphs in the modified block style?
6. Why is the block style letter easy to type?
7. How does the modified block style differ from the block style?
8. How would you type a simplified style letter?
9. How would you type a letter with open style punctuation?
10. What is the major advantage of writing a short business note or report in the form of an interoffice memorandum?

MAKING IMPORTANT DECISIONS

As Mr. Carlson's assistant, you type all of his letters in the modified block style with indented paragraphs and mixed punctuation. One afternoon Mr. Carlson asks you to type a letter which he would like to mail on his way home. After you finish typing the letter, you realize that you forgot to indent one of the paragraphs. What should you do about this mistake?

LEARNING TO WORK WITH OTHERS

Gus Bigham works in the office of Blakely Machine Company. Sally, another office employee, informed Gus that Mr. Blakely wants all his letters typed in the modified block style. Gus had typed the block style letter in high school and felt it was much easier and faster to type. Should Gus try to persuade Mr. Blakely to change to block style?

IMPROVING LANGUAGE SKILLS

There are three degrees of adjective comparison: positive, comparative, and superlative. Comparison is used to indicate increasing and decreasing quality or quantity.
    (a) Most adjectives of one syllable are compared by adding *er* or *est* to the word.

(b) Most adjectives of more than one syllable are compared by using the words *more, most, less,* or *least* before the adjective.

(c) Other adjectives are compared irregularly.

Examples:

Positive	Comparative	Superlative
(a) light	lighter	lightest
(b) expensive	more expensive	most expensive
(c) good	better	best

On a separate sheet of paper type three columns with the headings, *Positive, Comparative,* and *Superlative* and write the forms of comparison for the following adjectives.

1. tall	6. far	11. difficult
2. fast	7. good	12. strong
3. bad	8. useful	13. pretty
4. little	9. happy	14. high
5. warm	10. late	15. satisfactory

IMPROVING ARITHMETIC SKILLS

It is estimated that the cost of an average letter is as follows:

Cost Factor	Average Costs
Dictator's Time	$ .95
Typist's Time	1.19
Nonproductive Labor	.32
Fixed Charges	1.07
Materials Cost	.15
Mailing Cost	.28
Filing Cost	.21
	$4.17

1. What would the total cost of the letter be if costs could be decreased to the following: Dictator's Time, $.84; Typist's Time, $1.05; Nonproductive Labor, $.21; Fixed Charges, $.91; Materials Cost, $.15; Mailing Cost, $.21; Filing Cost, $.20?

2. If you can reduce costs to those described in Item 1:
   (a) How much money can your company save on each letter?
   (b) What will be the percentage of savings?

DEMONSTRATING OFFICE SKILLS

1. Make a collection of five business letters. For each letter, describe briefly what might be done to make the letter more attractive.

2. Using plain paper, type the letter below in modified block style with block paragraphs. Use open punctuation. Type one carbon copy.

Mrs. Fran Wilcox, Ames Employment Service, 1416 Glendora Avenue, Dayton, OH 45409
Dear Mrs. Wilcox (¶1)Thank you for taking the time to discuss office employment opportunities at Ames Employment Service with me last Wednesday afternoon. I deeply appreciate your interest. The suggestions you made during the interview will help me qualify for the office position I really want. (¶2) I plan to take office education courses at Dayton Community College next semester. They will be offered during evening hours in the Continuing Education Program. I have already found part-time employment as a clerk/typist in the Placement Office of the College. The day-to-day work in the Placement Office should give me valuable office experience. (¶3) After I have completed the courses in the program and have acquired the office experience you consider essential, I hope you will grant me another interview. Sincerely yours Valerie Milton

3. Compose a brief letter in which you describe the block form. Type the letter in block style with open punctuation. Address it to your teacher.

4. Using the letterhead from the *Supplies Inventory* or plain paper, type the following letter in simplified style. Type one carbon copy.

Miss Cathy Baker, 2600 Lafayette Boulevard, Detroit, MI 48216
CREDIT CARD (¶1) Your excellent credit record enables you to receive our nationwide credit card for your personal use. Miss Baker, the charge card that is enclosed will enable you to purchase almost any kind of merchandise you might want anywhere in the United States. (¶2) On the first of each month you will receive an itemized statement of all purchases for the preceding month. No interest charge is made if we receive your payment by the 10th of the month. (¶3) We know that you will enjoy using your new credit card and look forward to getting to know you better. Melissa Fields, CREDIT MANAGER Enclosure

Part 2

Business Letter Parts

Paul Hooper works for Mrs. Graham, the Personnel Director of a large data processing company. Paul spends some of his time typing correspondence from a transcribing machine. Since the letters he types contain a variety of letter parts, Paul knows that it is his responsibility to use the proper letter parts and to arrange them correctly on the page. Paul types quickly and accurately from the transcribing machine. Paul never has to be reminded to add any notations that are mentioned in the letters because he makes notations to himself as he transcribes. He knows the different letter parts and their correct placement by memory. He also knows all of the notations that go on the envelope. This knowledge saves Paul time and allows him to concentrate on the content of the letters.

Parts of the Letter

To understand the business letter, you should know the parts of a letter and why each part is needed. You will not use all parts of a letter on every letter you type. Some parts, however, such as the date and signature, are always included in a letter. You will need to use your judgment and the preference of your employer to decide which parts should be included in each letter. The parts of a letter listed below are illustrated on page 78 and discussed on pages 79–88.

preference: choice

1. Printed letterhead
2. Date
3. Mailing notation
4. Inside address
5. Attention line
6. Salutation
7. Subject line
8. Body
9. Complimentary close
10. Signature
11. Typed name
12. Title
13. Reference initials
14. Enclosure notation
15. Separate cover notation
16. Carbon copy notation
17. Postscript

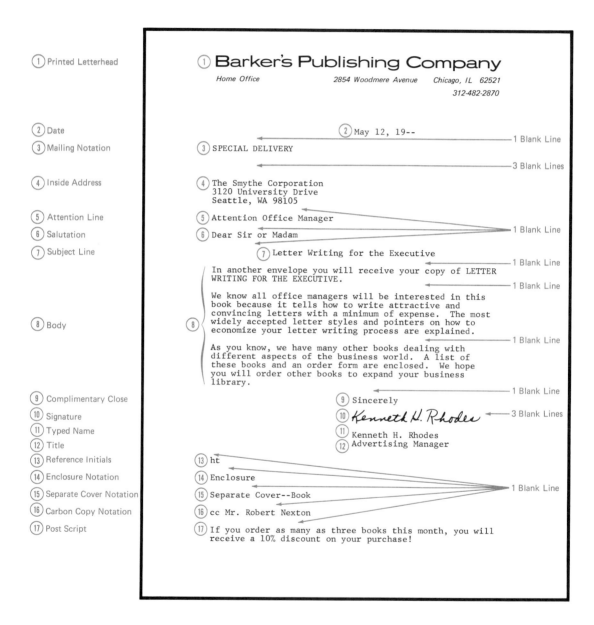

① Printed Letterhead

② Date
③ Mailing Notation

④ Inside Address

⑤ Attention Line
⑥ Salutation
⑦ Subject Line

⑧ Body

⑨ Complimentary Close
⑩ Signature
⑪ Typed Name
⑫ Title
⑬ Reference Initials
⑭ Enclosure Notation
⑮ Separate Cover Notation
⑯ Carbon Copy Notation
⑰ Post Script

① **Barker's Publishing Company**

Home Office   2854 Woodmere Avenue   Chicago, IL 62521
                                                          312-482-2870

② May 12, 19--   1 Blank Line
③ SPECIAL DELIVERY
                                                          3 Blank Lines
④ The Smythe Corporation
    3120 University Drive
    Seattle, WA 98105

⑤ Attention Office Manager   1 Blank Line
⑥ Dear Sir or Madam
⑦ Letter Writing for the Executive   1 Blank Line

In another envelope you will receive your copy of LETTER
WRITING FOR THE EXECUTIVE.   1 Blank Line

We know all office managers will be interested in this
book because it tells how to write attractive and
convincing letters with a minimum of expense. The most
widely accepted letter styles and pointers on how to
economize your letter writing process are explained.   1 Blank Line

As you know, we have many other books dealing with
different aspects of the business world. A list of
these books and an order form are enclosed. We hope
you will order other books to expand your business
library.   1 Blank Line

⑨ Sincerely   3 Blank Lines
⑩ Kenneth H. Rhodes
⑪ Kenneth H. Rhodes
⑫ Advertising Manager

⑬ ht
⑭ Enclosure   1 Blank Line
⑮ Separate Cover--Book
⑯ cc Mr. Robert Nexton
⑰ If you order as many as three books this month, you will
    receive a 10% discount on your purchase!

Model Letter, Modified Block Style, Open Punctuation, Block Paragraphs

Illus. 3-4

Letterhead (1)

The letterhead on a firm's stationery is usually made up of the firm's name, address, and telephone number. The letterhead can be used to identify the nature of the firm's business by including a slogan, picture, or symbol of the firm.

Since the letterhead is the first part of a letter a recipient notices, it should be attractive, easy to read, and representative of the firm. You will want to take the letterhead into consideration when you type the letter so the letter looks attractive and balanced on the page.

representative: descriptive; giving an accurate impression

Date (2)

The date on a letter is very important because it tells the sender and the recipient when the letter was typed. It helps the sender and the recipient identify a particular letter if several letters have been written by the sender to the same person. You must date every letter you typewrite. The dateline contains the name of the month written in full, the date, and the year. Abbreviated forms of the date, such as 11/13/-- or 11—13——–, should never be used in letters.

Type the date anywhere from 12 to 20 blank lines from the top of the page. The exact line on which to type the date is determined by the length of the letter as described in column 4 of the Letter Placement Table on page 93.

In the modified block style letter the date is typed at the horizontal center of the page, and for the block style the date is typed starting at the left margin.

Mailing Notation (3)

When your employer wants to use a special postal service, such as registered mail or special delivery, you should include a mailing notation on the letter. Type the mailing notation even with the left margin midway between the date and the first line of the inside address. Type the mailing notation in all capital letters.

Some companies type the mailing notation only on the carbon copy, but placing it on the original letter helps to remind you that it should go by registered mail or special delivery, and it indicates to the recipient that the letter is important.

Inside Address (4)

The inside address is typed three blank lines below the date at the left margin. If a mailing notation is used, the inside address is typed below it. The inside address is a guide for filing the carbon copy in your office. It also gives complete information as to whom the letter is directed at the recipient company, since often the envelope with the address on it is thrown away when the letter is opened. The inside address should contain the name, title (when appropriate), and the complete address of the person or the company to whom the letter is to be sent.

Abbreviations should be used sparingly because they give a somewhat careless appearance to the letter and because they can increase the difficulty of reading. When you type the inside address, try to make the lines as uniform in length as possible.

Name and Company Lines. The name of the person and the company should be typed to conform exactly with the style used by the person and the company receiving the letter. For example, if you were typing a letter to a man who writes his name *Edward R. Voiers*, you would not type his name *E. R. Voiers*. If an incoming letter does not show whether a woman is to be addressed by *Miss* or *Mrs.*, the modern practice is to use the title *Ms.*

Official Titles. When a person's official title is included in the address, it may be placed on either the first or second line (see example on page 81). If the title is placed on the first line, it is separated from the person's name by a comma. Since either placement is correct, you should choose the one that will give better balance to the length of the lines in the address.

Street Address Line. When the name of the street is a number from one to ten inclusive, the street name is spelled out (367 Second Avenue or 381 Tenth Street); figures are used for street names that are numbers above ten. When a street is identified by figures, the house number is separated from the street number by a hyphen with a space on either side, 157 - 179 Street. If the street number is preceded by *East*, *West*, *North*, or *South*, however, the hyphen is not necessary; for example, 589 South 117 Street.

City, State, and ZIP Code Line. The name of the city is separated from the name of the state by a comma. The Zip Code number should be typed on the same line as the city and state with one space after the state. No mark of punctuation is used between the state and ZIP Code number.

The United States Postal Service has designated two-letter abbreviations for states to be used with the ZIP (Zone Improvement Plan) Code. A list of two-letter state abbreviations can be found on page 696 in Appendix D. These approved abbreviations are written in all capital letters and without periods. Use of the ZIP Code reduces costs and speeds deliveries because automated equipment can be used for sorting and processing the mail.

sparingly:
infrequently

uniform:
not varying

conform:
agree

inclusive:
including

designated:
chosen or specified

Forms for addresses are:

```
Mr. Randolph G. Ludin, President
The American Duplicating Company
4646 Broad Street
Philadelphia, Pa 19140

Mr. Issac A. Steinfeld
President, Investors Consultants
465 Avenue of the Americas
New York, NY 10011
```

Attention Line (5)

The attention line directs a letter to a specific person or department for action even though the letter is addressed to the company. Some feel there is little value in an attention line, and that if attention should be given by a particular person, that person should be named in the address. However, most companies hesitate to open letters in a central office if they are addressed to an individual. If that person is not available at the time, the letter may remain unopened or unattended to until that person returns to the office. An attention line allows a letter to be opened in a central office and then directed to a specific person or department for action. If the person named in the attention line is not available, the letter can be directed to someone else for action.

An attention line is typed one blank line below the inside address. When an attention line is used and the inside address contains a company name, the salutation for the message is *Ladies and Gentlemen, Dear Sir or Madam*, or any other salutation appropriate for a corporation or business firm.

specific:
particular

With Attention Line *Directed to a Person*	*With Attention Line* *Directed to a Position*

```Acme Paper Company```
```4116 San Ramon Way```
```Sacramento, CA 95825```
	```Acme Paper Company```
	```4116 San Ramon Way```
	```Sacramento, CA 95825```

```Attention Mr. B. A. Smith```	```Attention Sales Manager```
	```Dear Sir or Madam```

With No Attention Line

```
Acme Paper Company
4116 San Ramon Way
Sacramento, CA 95825

Ladies and Gentlemen
```

Salutation (6)

The salutation is a greeting to the addressee, the person to whom the letter is written. It is typed one blank line below the address or attention line. The body of the letter begins one blank line below the salutation. A salutation may be as informal as *Dear Joe* or as formal as *Sir*.

The salutations shown below are arranged from the least formal to the most formal. Notice the capitalization used in each.

For Men	*For Women*
Dear Ken	Dear Sharon
My dear Ken	My dear Sharon
Dear Mr. Washington	Dear Miss (Mrs., Ms.) Simon
My dear Mr. Washington	My dear Miss (Mrs., Ms.) Simon
Dear Sir	Dear Madam
Sir	Madam

Illus. 3-5

Clean, well-placed letters create a positive impression.

Facit-Addo, Inc.

Subject Line (7)

emphasize: call attention to; stress

The writer of a letter may wish to use a subject line to emphasize the key topic of the letter. When a subject line is used, type it one blank line below the salutation. Leave one blank line after the subject line. The topic may be **preceded** by the word *Subject*, although there is a trend away from this. The subject line may be typed even with the left margin or centered on the page.

preceded:
came before

Body (8)

One blank line follows the salutation or subject line before you begin the body of the letter. Single spacing is always used for the body of the letter except for very short messages. Be sure to paragraph the body of the letter so that it will be easy to read. Leave one blank line between paragraphs to give the letter a more attractive appearance.

Keep the right margin as even as possible and about as wide as the left margin. You can do this by setting the right margin stop from five to eight spaces beyond the point where you want the line to end, so that the bell will ring just before the space where the line ends. You will still have space to complete a short word or add a hyphen for a word that must be hyphenated before the carriage is stopped by the right margin.

Complimentary Close (9)

The complimentary close, which is typed one blank line below the body of the letter, is the *good-bye* of the letter. The complimentary close and the date start at the same horizontal point on the page. In the block style (see Letter C, page 70), the date and complimentary close begin at the left margin. In the modified block style (see letter A, page 70), they begin at the horizontal center of the page. Only the first word of the complimentary close is capitalized. Some complimentary closings are shown below.

Business Letters

Yours truly	Yours sincerely
Yours very truly	Sincerely yours
Very truly yours	Very sincerely yours

Formal Letters

Respectfully yours   Yours respectfully

Friendly Letters

Cordially yours	Yours sincerely
Yours cordially	Sincerely yours

Signature, Typed Name, and Title (10, 11, 12)

The letter is signed between the complimentary close and the typed name. The typed name overcomes problems caused by a poorly written signature. Your employer's name is typed three to five blank lines below the complimentary close.

Yours truly

D. R. Dunlap

D. R. Dunlap, Vice-President

Sometimes the name of the company is typed as part of the signature. There is little justification for this practice if the company name is in the letterhead. If the company name is used, it is typed in all capital letters one blank line below the complimentary close. The name of your employer is typed three to five blank lines below the company name. When your employer's name and official title are used, the title may be typed on the same line as the typed name or on the line below the typed name.

Very truly yours

NORTHEASTERN SHIPPING ENTERPRISE

Marshall P. Barrington

Marshall P. Barrington
Purchasing Agent

A man's personal title, such as *Mr.* or *Dr.*, should not be shown before the signature or typed name. A woman's personal title, such as *Miss*, *Mrs.*, *Ms.*, or *Dr.*, may be shown before either the signature or the typed name. If it is shown before the signature, the title should be enclosed in parentheses. If it is shown before the typed name, the title is not enclosed in parentheses. A married woman should show her legal name — her own first name, middle initial, and married last name if she uses her husband's surname in business.

Signature of an Unmarried Woman

Yours sincerely

Ann Bagley

Miss Ann Bagley

Yours sincerely

(Miss) Ann Bagley

Ann Bagley

Signature of a Married Woman or Widow

Yours sincerely

Jane L. Hart

Mrs. Jane L. Hart

Yours sincerely

(Mrs.) Jane L. Hart

Jane L. Hart

Some women, whether married or unmarried, prefer to use Ms. as their title.

Signature of a Married or
Unmarried Woman

Yours sincerely

Carolyn Rackler

Ms. Carolyn Rackler

If a woman wants to be known by her married name by using her husband's first name and middle initial (for example, Mrs. John B. Williamson), she can sign her legal name and place her married name below in parentheses.

Signature of a Married Woman

Very truly yours

Alma A. Williamson
(Mrs. John B. Williamson)

Mrs. Alma A. Williamson

Your employer may not be available to sign a letter that must be mailed. You may be asked to sign your employer's name and mail the letter. If you are requested to do this, be sure to initial the signature.

Very truly yours,

Robert E. Bailey
vmh

Robert E. Bailey

You must be sure that each letter is signed, either by your employer or yourself, before you fold it and insert it in an envelope for mailing.

Reference Initials (13)

To indicate who typed the letter, place your initials in lowercase letters one blank line below the typed name even with the left margin.

Sometimes you will see the initials of the dictator before the typist's initials; but this is unnecessary, since the reader knows who dictated the letter from the typed name below the signature.

Enclosure Notations (14)

An enclosure is anything placed in the envelope along with the letter. Any enclosure you send should be noted at the end of the letter. This is a reminder to you to be sure to include the enclosure. It is also a service to the addressee who can quickly check to see if the material is included in the envelope. The enclosure notation should be typed at the left margin one blank line below the reference initials. One enclosure is indicated by the word *Enclosure*. More than one enclosure may also be indicated by the word *Enclosures* typed on one line, followed by a list of the enclosures, each enclosure being listed on a separate line and indented five spaces from the left margin. Typical enclosure notations follow.

```
Enclosure
Enclosures 2
Enclosures
     Price List
     Circular
     Sample X-14
```

Separate Cover Notation (15)

When your employer sends an item to the person addressed in the letter but it is too large to go in the envelope with the letter, you should indicate this by a separate cover notation. Type the separate cover notation at the left margin two blank lines below the last notation.

If you are sending only one item under separate cover, you may merely type the words *Separate Cover*. If you are sending two or more items, you may type the words *Separate Cover* followed by the number of items you are sending.

```
Separate Cover 2
```

Your employer may also want to indicate the means of transportation used for sending the separate cover material.

```
Separate Cover--Express
```

You may also list the items to be sent under separate cover.

```
Separate Cover--Third-Class Mail
     Sample C-12
```

Carbon Copy Notation (16)

When your employer wants to send carbon copies of a letter to other people, you should indicate this on the letter by typing *cc* followed by the names of those who are to receive copies. The carbon copy notation is typed at the left margin one blank line below the reference initials if there is no enclosure. If there is an enclosure notation, the carbon copy notation is typed two lines below the enclosure notation.

```
              Enclosures 2

              cc Lori Howard
```

If carbon copies are sent to several people you list their names.

```
              cc Gayle Johnson
                 Ralph Peters
                 Donald McGregor
```

If your employer does not want the person to whom the letter is addressed to know that a carbon copy has been sent to someone else, you may type a *blind carbon copy* notation. You should type *bcc* or *bc* and the name of the person who is to receive the carbon copy on the carbon copy but *not* on the original letter. The notation on the *carbon copies* would appear as:

```
              bcc Miss Cheryl Byers
```

To type a blind carbon copy notation, you simply place a card or heavy piece of paper over the notation position on the original copy, type the notation, and remove the card. Another way to type a blind carbon copy notation is to release the paper release lever and remove only the original and first carbon sheet from your typewriter. Then turn the remaining sheets and carbon back to the normal position for a carbon copy notation and type the blind carbon copy notation even with the left margin. Using either of these methods, the blind carbon copy notation will be on the carbon copies but not on the original.

The carbon copies of a letter are sent to the individuals listed in the carbon copy notation; therefore, you must type an envelope for each person listed. You may have to get their addresses from a card file of frequently contacted individuals or from previous correspondence. Check each recipient's name with a check mark after you have typed the envelope for the individual recipient.

Postscript (17)

Sometimes your employer may want to add a postscript to a letter. A postscript is a short message that is typed one blank line below all other notations. The postscript is often used to emphasize a special point by setting it apart from the rest of the letter. You may use the abbreviation *PS* before the message, although it is not necessary.

Indent the first line of the postscript if you indented the paragraphs in the body of the letter; block the first line of the postscript if you blocked the paragraphs in the body of the paragraph.

REVIEWING IMPORTANT POINTS

1. Will you use all parts of a letter on every letter you type? How do you decide which parts should be included?
2. Where are two possible places on a horizontal line for typewriting the date?
3. Why is the date important?
4. In what two ways can the official title of a person be typed in the inside address on a letter?
5. Where does the body of a letter begin?
6. Where are two places on a horizontal line for typing the complimentary close?
7. Where do you type the reference initials? Should you include your employer's initials as well as your own?
8. Why should there be a notation for enclosures?
9. Where is a carbon copy notation typed?
10. When is a postscript used?

MAKING IMPORTANT DECISIONS

One morning before leaving for a meeting, your employer reminds you that an important letter from a branch office in another city should arrive in the day's mail. The letter should contain a copy of a report needed by your employer for a special presentation tomorrow afternoon. When the letter arrives, you see the enclosure notation indicating that a copy of the report should be enclosed, but you find no report. How should you handle this situation?

LEARNING TO WORK WITH OTHERS

Deborah Nix, an office worker at the Wilson Insurance Company, often signs letters for her employer, Mr. Gerard. She always signs Mr. Gerard's name and puts her initials below his name. Sue, another office worker, also frequently signs letters for her employer, Mr. Oxford, but she never puts her initials after the signature. Sue said to Deborah, "Why should I put my initials on the letter? It just tells whoever receives the letter that I signed the letter. I want people to think that Mr. Oxford signs all his letters himself." Do you think that Sue's reason for not initialing the letters to which she signs her employer's name is correct? Can you give at least one good reason for adding your initials when you sign your employer's name? Do you think it is a good practice? Why or why not?

IMPROVING LANGUAGE SKILLS

The following adverbs are often used incorrectly. After reading the definitions below, on a separate sheet of paper type each of the sentences and insert the adverb that is correct.

too — an adverb, meaning also or more than enough.
to — a preposition, indicating movement, direction or purpose
well — an adverb, except when you are speaking of health; when referring to health, well is an adjective.
good — an adjective in most cases; sometimes it is used as a noun.
very — an adverb expressing degree.
real — an adjective of quality.

1. Are you feeling (well, good) today?
2. He, (to, too), always included the ZIP Code on his letters.
3. There was a (real, very) difference in the quality of the two letters.
4. Although he is a beginning typist, he types (well, good).
5. She is a good worker; she read her letters (well, good).
6. Although the inside address was (very, real) clearly written, Lorna typed the wrong address.
7. He sent the (real, very) important letter by Special Delivery.
8. She, (too, to), went to work for the Alpine Equipment Company.
9. Do you think he did (well, good) on his typing exam?
10. Although Joe had a sprained ankle, he performed his job (very, real) well.

IMPROVING ARITHMETIC SKILLS

The Johnson Restaurant Equipment and Servicing Company has just opened for business, and your employer decides to send some brochures containing advertisements to prospective customers. The brochures will be sent as enclosure items in letters introducing the company's line of products. Four different brochures will be used, and more than one brochure may be sent to each of the prospective customers. Your employer, Ms. Kincaid, gives you the following list and asks you to determine how many of each brochure will be needed. She classifies the brochures as A, B, C, and D.

The Steakhouse	A, C
Baker's Inn	B, D
The Chinese Palace	A, B, C
Cantu's Cafeteria	D
Southlawn Inn	B, C
The Sirloin Stop	A, D
The La Fiesta Restaurant	B
Muller's Country Kitchen	C, D
Royal King's Restaurant	A, B
Eastside Restaurant	C
Colonial Restaurant	D
Country Cooking Restaurant	B
Seaside Inn	C, D
DeLeo's Italian Restaurant	A, C
The Cambridge Inn	B, C

After you have determined the total number of each brochure needed, your employer asks you to figure the cost of ordering the brochures, based on the following information:

Brochure A — $ .75 per brochure
Brochure B — $1.15 per brochure
Brochure C — $ .80 per brochure
Brochure D — $1.00 per brochure

DEMONSTRATING OFFICE SKILLS

1. In most offices, you will type the standard parts of a letter many times a day. So that you will become familiar with the standard parts of a letter, type the letter in the illustration on page 78 exactly as it appears; however, do not type the colored explanations in the margin. Notice where each part of the letter is placed on the page.

2. Type the appropriate salutation for each of the following letters addressed to:
   (a) Mr. Carl Knight, a good friend of your employer.
   (b) Mrs. Jean Lowry, a real estate broker from whom your employer is buying some property.
   (c) Beauty World Cosmetics, a firm you must write to about an error in a monthly statement; no attention line used.
   (d) Fountain Office Supplies, Inc., a corporation with which you frequently correspond. You will use an attention line to the Personnel Director.
   (e) Miss Jackie and Mrs. Roy Becker, owners of a small business from which you purchase supplies.

3. You are typing a letter which contains these notations: P.S. Hurry now and receive a 15% discount; Separate Cover — Pamphlet; cc

Mr. Larry Weeks; Enclosures — Price List, Circular. Type these notations in correct form in the order in which they would appear.

4. Your employer, Mr. Max Ashcraft, is writing to:
   (a) Melton's Insulation Company, 1234 Beale, Harrisburg, PA, 17113. He wants the letter to go to Mr. Arnold Richmond. Type an appropriate inside address, attention line, and salutation.
   (b) Petree Camera Shop, 2415 Woodtop Drive, Lakeland, FL 32211. This letter is to go to Ms. Barbara Scoggins. Type an appropriate inside address and salutation when you do not use an attention line.

5. You are typing a letter for your employer, Mr. Cyrus Carver, President of Hewlett and Associate Designers, to a prospective customer and are enclosing ten colored layouts for a reception room. On separate lines, type in order and with proper spacing between each item an appropriate complimentary close, typewritten company name, your employer's name and title, reference initials, and enclosure notation for the letter.

Part 3

Typing the Business Letter

Mr. Emmett Nee learned how to type neat, attractive letters without errors in his business courses in high school, but he never realized how vital letters are in business until he took his first full-time job as a clerk/typist. During his first day at work for the Haney Furniture Store, Mr. Nee's supervisor, Mrs. Whitten, showed Mr. Nee two letters and asked him to comment on their appearance. The first letter was perfect as far as he could see. It was properly placed on the page and there were no errors or poor corrections. The second letter, however, was positioned too low on the page, had carbon smears, and he spotted several poor corrections. "Now," Mrs. Whitten asked, "if these two letters were from two different companies wanting your business, with which company would you want to do business?" Mr. Nee knew the answer. He would want to do business with the company whose letters were neat and attractive. Mr. Nee promised himself that each letter he typed would be of high quality so it would make a good first impression on the reader and help promote his company.

Estimating the Placement of a Letter

Placing a letter attractively on a page is a skill that you will develop with experience. To place letters attractively on the page, you must be able to judge whether a letter is short, medium or long.

Your letters will look well balanced on the page if the side margins are even and the bottom margin is slightly wider than the side margins. Until you have developed the skill to place the letters on the page, you may use a Letter Placement Table (illustrated on page 93) to estimate the spacing for your letters. For example, if you are typing a short letter (that is, the letter contains 100 or fewer words), leave two-inch side margins and type the date on Line 20. If you are typing a letter with from 101 to 300 words in it, the side margins are 1½ inches but the line on which you type the date varies (see Column 5 on the Letter Placement Table).

Letter placement table

Letter Classification		5-Stroke Words in Letter Body	Side Margins	Margin Settings Elite	Pica	Dateline Position (From Top Edge of Paper)
Short		Up to 100	2″	24 – 83	20 – 70	Line 20
Average	1	101 – 150	1 1/2″	18 – 89	15 – 75	18
	2	151 – 200	1 1/2″	18 – 89	15 – 75	16
	3	201 – 250	1 1/2″	18 – 89	15 – 75	14
	4	251 – 300	1 1/2″	18 – 89	15 – 75	12
Long		301 – 350	1″	12 – 95	10 – 80	12
Two-page		More than 350	1″	12 – 95	10 – 80	12
Standard 6″ line for all letters*		As above for all letters	1 1/4″	15 – 92	12 – 77	As above for all letters

Illus. 3-6

*Use only when so directed. Some business firms use the standard 6″ line for all letters.

After you have typed several letters, you will be able to judge whether the letter is short, medium, or long and will no longer have to refer to the Letter Placement Table.

Your employer may prefer that you keep the typing line the same length for all letters you type regardless of their length. If this is the case, you can balance the letter on the page by varying the space between the letterhead and the date line and/or between the complimentary close and the typed signature. If the letter is long, leave less space in these parts; if the letter is short, leave more space.

Typing the Second Page

Some letters you will type may take more than one page. As you can see from the Letter Placement Table, you type the two-page letter with one-inch side margins. When you type the second page, you will keep the same one-inch margins.

When you are typing a two-page letter, you must type a heading on the second page. This heading will include

1. The name of the person to whom the letter is written, as it appears in the inside address
2. The page number
3. The date

Either the spread form or the block form is considered correct.

Illus. 3-7

Spread
form of
heading

I plan to arrive in Chicago at 10:06 on TWA Flight 348.
If possible, I would like to meet with you before noon
to discuss last minute plans for the conference. My

Ms. Anna Phillips
Page 2

Illus. 3-8   May 29, 19--

Block
form of
heading

I plan to arrive in Chicago at 10:06 on TWA Flight 348.
If possible, I would like to meet with you before noon
to discuss last minute plans for the conference. My

The block form is the easier to type since you do not have to center the page number or backspace for the date.

Leave at least an inch (six blank lines) at the top of the page before you begin typing the heading and leave two blank lines after the heading. You should try to finish a paragraph on the first page so that you can start a new paragraph on the second page. If you can't do this, you must leave at least two lines of the paragraph at the bottom of the first page and carry over at least two lines of the paragraph to the top of the second page.

succeeding:
following

Always use bond paper of the same quality as the letterhead for the second and succeeding pages of a letter. Do not use letterhead paper for any page but the first.

Making Carbon Copies

When you are working in an office, you will almost always make a carbon copy of the correspondence you type; so you must learn how to make attractive, clean carbon copies.

Assembling Carbon Packs

assemble:
put together

A *carbon pack* is a collection of materials that includes a letterhead, carbon sheets, and copy paper. The quickest way to assemble a carbon pack is to arrange all the materials you will need in your desk drawer so that you can pick up the paper easily and quickly. If your desk drawer has sloping dividers for your stationery, fill three of the dividers with letterheads, carbon paper and copy paper — in that order, from top to bottom. (See Illus. 3-9). If you do not have a desk drawer with dividers, label file folders with the headings, *Letterhead, Carbon, Copy Paper,* and insert the correct paper in each folder. In either case arrange the papers in the order shown in the illustration below. Pull the paper in the folders forward so that you can easily pick up the paper from each folder.

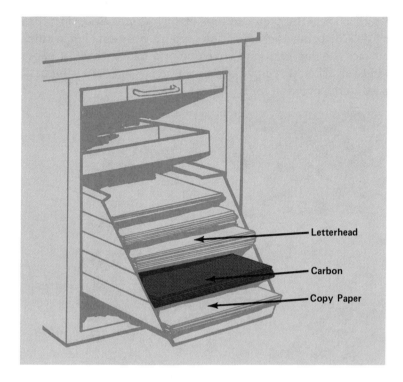

Illus. 3-9

Desk drawer carbon pack assembly

To assemble a carbon pack, take a sheet of letterhead paper and pull it toward the carbon paper in the next slot. Pick up a sheet of carbon paper and pull both sheets toward the copy paper slot and pick up a sheet of copy paper. Take out all three sheets and jog them on the desk to align them. If you need more than one carbon copy, go through the above procedure once and then pick up as many sheets of carbon and copy paper as you need but do not use more than one letterhead.

align:
line up; make even

Some office workers like to assemble carbon packs in a different way:

1. Arrange the letterhead and second sheets and slip them behind the cylinder. Be sure they are inserted just enough to be firmly anchored.
2. Flip the pack forward over the front of the typewriter.
3. Separate the first sheet (the letterhead) and second sheet and insert a piece of carbon, shiny side facing you; repeat this between second sheets until all carbons have been inserted.
4. Turn the cylinder knob, so that all the papers roll into typing position.

Inserting a Carbon Pack in the Typewriter

To insert the carbon pack in the typewriter, you should use the paper release lever, slip the pack into the machine with the shiny side of the carbon facing you, snap the paper release lever into position, and turn the cylinder knob to bring the paper into typing position. For a thick carbon pack, place the flap of a long envelope or a folded sheet of paper over the top of the pack and remove the envelope or paper after the pack has been turned to the position for typing.

Illus. 3-10

Learning how to assemble a carbon pack quickly will improve your productivity.

Using Preassembled Carbon Packs

preassembled:
put together in
advance

Some offices use preassembled carbon packs. These carbon packs have copy paper already assembled in the correct order with carbon sheets attached. They are easy to use and make good carbon copies. Fingerprints and smudges are eliminated because your fingers never touch the carbon.

Handling Carbon Copies

The following steps will insure attractive, clean carbon copies:

1. Handle the carbon paper carefully so that the carbon is not transferred to your fingers where it can smudge the original and the carbon copies.

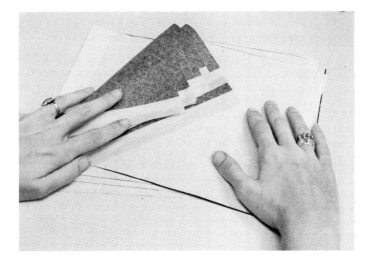

2. Never squeeze the assembled sheets together too hard. A thumb print or fingernail scratch on a sheet of carbon paper may spoil the appearance of the carbon copy.
3. If there are marks on the copy paper from the paper-bail rolls, use carbon paper with a hard finish or have the paper-bail rolls adjusted by a repairer.
4. To make many carbon copies, use lightweight carbon paper and lightweight paper. When you are making only two or three carbon copies, you may use a medium-weight carbon paper.
5. Use a medium-finish carbon paper for regular work, and a soft-finish carbon paper when you are making eight or ten copies.
6. Never use a wrinkled sheet of carbon paper because it will cause a carbon smudge on the copy sheet.
7. Always keep carbon paper in a flat folder or box away from dust, moisture, and heat.
8. Always replace the carbon paper you are using before the copies become too light to read.

By using carbon paper which is one-half inch longer than your letterhead paper, you can easily remove carbon without smudging the copies because you can take hold of the edge of the carbon that extends from the bottom of the pack.

Making Corrections

Making corrections that cannot be noticed is a skill which you will want to develop so that your typed letters will always be attractive and neat. Strikeovers give your work an untidy, careless appearance, and you should never give a letter containing a strikeover to your employer for a signature. Corrections can be made by one of the following methods:

1. *Correction tape or paper.* Small rolls or slips of paper with a white, transferable surface can be used to block out the incorrect letter or letters. To block out the incorrect letters it is necessary to type them once again with the white surface of the correction tape against the incorrect letters. It is then a simple procedure to backspace and insert the correct letters.

2. *Correction fluid.* A white fluid can be used to block out the incorrect letter or letters. You must be careful to use the minimum quantity of correction fluid possible because you don't want a residue of fluid to detract from the attractiveness of your page.

3. *Eraser.* There are several types of erasers used to make corrections in typed copy. Personal preference determines the choice of eraser but the procedure for making corrections is the same for all types.

    a. Move the typewriter carriage to the right or left to prevent erasure particles from clogging the mechanism.

    b. Insert a solid metal or plastic shield or a 5″ × 3″ card directly behind the error in the original. Make certain that it is placed between the original and the first sheet of carbon paper. This protects the carbon copies from smudges.

    c. Place a plastic or metal shield with cutouts over the material to be erased. Using the cutout shield will enable you to erase a single letter of single-spaced copy without smearing other letters or lines. Erase in a circular movement for more than one letter; use up and down motions for one letter.

    d. Insert the solid shield behind the first carbon copy at the point of the error and erase that copy, using the cutout shield.

    e. Continue erasing *all* carbon copies in the pack, moving from front to back of the pack.

    f. Check the alignment to be sure you will be typing on the same line as before.

    g. Strike the correct key or keys lightly, repeating the stroking until the desired darkness is achieved.

There are times when the correction of an error requires that an extra letter be inserted. A letter may be added if the letters are typed in such a way that each one occupies less space than it did before. On some machines, this is done by striking the first letter, then holding the backspacer down slightly and striking the second letter, and continuing in

---

transferable:
capable of being moved from one plac to another

residue:
remaining portion; surplus

particles:
small bits and pieces

Unit 3 • Preparing Mailable Letters

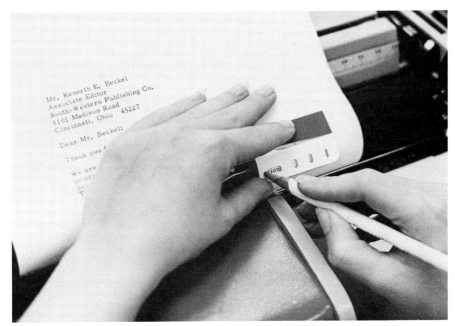

Illus. 3-12

Move the carriage to the side before erasing so that filings do not fall into the mechanism. Use a shield to protect copy that is not to be erased.

this manner until the complete word has been typed. You may want to practice this skill, called *squeezing* , if you have not as yet perfected it.

At other times, the correction of an error requires that a letter be omitted. A letter may be omitted without spoiling the appearance of the page if the remaining letters are typed in such a way that each one occupies more space than it did before. This is done by striking the first letter, striking the space bar, then depressing the backspacer slightly and holding it in that position while striking the second letter, and continuing this operation until the complete word has been typed. This is called *spreading*.

If you are using an electric typewriter, you may have to use slightly different procedures for spreading and squeezing. On some electric typewriters, you will have to hold the carriage by hand while you type the letters in the correct places. On other electric machines, you will find a half-space key that will aid you in proper placement.

Some typewriters have a special mechanism that will obliterate errors. If you discover an error while typing, you simply backspace to the error with the correction key and type the incorrect letter or letters again. The correction key either covers up the letter or completely removes the letter from the paper. You then backspace and type the correction. The special correction key saves time because the typist does not have to pick up an eraser, insert correction paper, or apply correction fluid.

obliterate: remove; erase

Typing an Envelope

After you have typed the letter, you should immediately type the envelope. Place the envelope face up with the flap over the top of the letter and enclosures, if any. This will prevent you from putting a letter into the wrong envelope.

There are two sizes of standard envelopes that are used more than others: large (9½″ × 4⅛″), also called No. 10, or legal; and small (6½″ × 3⅝″), also called No. 6¾, or commercial.

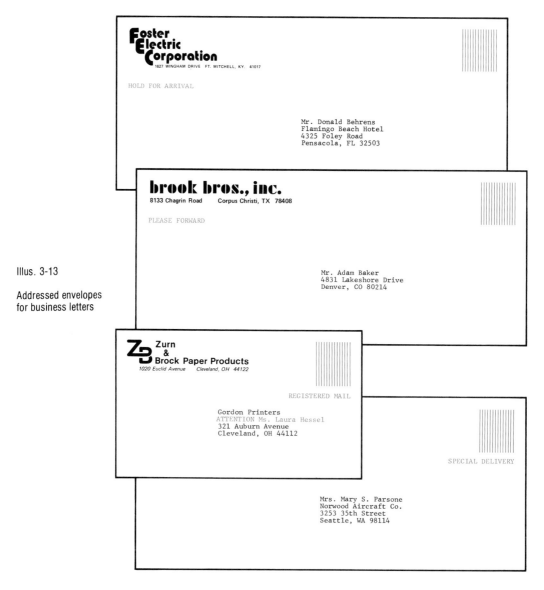

Illus. 3-13

Addressed envelopes for business letters

You should use a large No. 10 envelope (9½" × 4⅛") if the letter is regular business size, has one or two pages, and if you have enclosures. A small No. 6¾ envelope (6½" × 3⅝") is used for half-size letterheads, statements, and some one-page letters.

On a small envelope type the address 2 inches from the top and 2½ inches from the left edge of the envelope. When typing on a large envelope, leave a 2½-inch top margin and a 4-inch left margin.

Illustration 3-13 shows several correctly typed envelopes. The address is typed single spaced exactly as it appeared in the inside address of the letter.

1. Type *mailing notations*, such as REGISTERED MAIL or SPECIAL DELIVERY, in capital letters under the stamp.
2. Type *special notations*, such as HOLD FOR ARRIVAL or PLEASE FORWARD, in all capital letters a triple space below the return address.
3. Type an *attention line*, immediately below the name of the company in the address.

Window Envelopes

Window envelopes are used in business because they eliminate the need to address envelopes. The address on the letter, invoice, or other message, shows through the window. Window envelopes not only save time but prevent letters from being put into wrong envelopes.

The address must be written so that it can be seen through the window after the letter or bill is folded. Some businesses may have a mark printed on their stationery that shows the location for the address. The

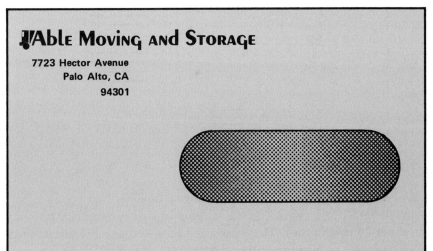

Illus. 3-14

Window envelope

first few letters should be checked to see if they are correctly folded to show through the envelope window. The method of folding the letter or bill for the window envelope is different from the method of folding used for an ordinary envelope. Methods of folding letters are described in Unit 9, Part 2, under "Handling Outgoing Mail."

Business Reply Envelopes and Cards

Your company can get a business reply permit from the post office. This lets you enclose a special business reply envelope or card that the addressee may return without paying postage. The post office collects postage from your company when it receives the returned envelopes and cards.

Such envelopes and cards are frequently used when a firm is sending out correspondence to which replies are invited such as sales literature inviting inquiries from prospective customers. The amount collected for a business reply envelope or card is more than the ordinary postage. A business reply envelope that is enclosed in a No. 6¾ envelope should be of slightly smaller size, such as No. 6¼. Likewise, a No. 9 business reply envelope should be used for an enclosure in a No. 10 envelope.

prospective:
likely; potential

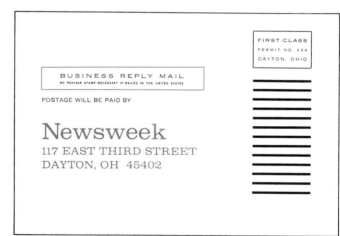

Illus. 3-15

Business reply card

FIRST CLASS
PERMIT NO. 436
DAYTON, OHIO

BUSINESS REPLY MAIL
NO POSTAGE STAMP NECESSARY IF MAILED IN THE UNITED STATES

POSTAGE WILL BE PAID BY

Newsweek
117 EAST THIRD STREET
DAYTON, OH 45402

Interoffice Envelopes

When mail is sent within the company, a business may use interoffice envelopes. These envelopes are economical since they can be used from about 20 to 48 times. They also save time because the addressee's name is simply handwritten, rather than typed, on the envelope.

economical:
avoiding waste; thrifty

INTEROFFICE CORRESPONDENCE

TO	DEPT.	TO	DEPT.	TO	DEPT.
	●		●		●
	●		●		●

Illus. 3-16   Interoffice envelope

REVIEWING IMPORTANT POINTS

1. If your letters are to look balanced, how should your side and bottom margins appear?
2. What are the two types of headings you can type on the second page of a two-page letter?
3. If you cannot finish a paragraph on the first page of a letter, how should the paragraph be carried over to the second page?
4. What kind of paper should you use for the second page of a two-page letter?
5. How many sheets of letterhead paper do you need if you are typing a letter with four carbon copies?
6. If you have a thick carbon pack, what item can you use to help you insert the pack in the typewriter?
7. What are some advantages of preassembled carbon packs?
8. What ways are there to make corrections on typewritten work other than erasing?
9. What are two reasons for using window envelopes?
10. Why are interoffice envelopes economical?

MAKING IMPORTANT DECISIONS

You work as a typist for an advertising agency, and you realize how important it is for your letters to be attractive. One afternoon you type several letters and forget to change the margin settings for the different letter lengths. One letter to a prospective customer looks particularly unbalanced on the page. Other than this, however, the letter looks perfect. Do you think it would be necessary to retype this letter? Why or why not?

LEARNING TO WORK WITH OTHERS

Lloyd and Tina are typists for the Highland Products Company. Lloyd has worked for this company for three years. Tina joined the company just two weeks ago. Lloyd has noticed that although Tina is a very good typist, she always seems to get carbon smears on her hands and even on her letters and envelopes. Tina tries to erase the smears on her letters and envelopes, but this sometimes makes them look even worse. How can Lloyd give Tina some pointers on using carbon paper without hurting her feelings or spoiling a good working relationship?

IMPROVING LANGUAGE SKILLS

On a separate sheet of paper complete the following sentences by choosing the correctly spelled word.

1. They installed shatter-proof glass in the windows to insure the (safty, safety) of the workers.
2. The (activities, activeties) of the club are very interesting.
3. Mrs. Hersley was (sincerely, sincerily) sorry to see Tom leave his job.
4. Although Carla needed a helper, she could not find an (assistance, assistant).
5. It is sometimes hard to (maintain, maintian) a B average.
6. We have not found very many persons who have (sufficient, suficient) background for the job.
7. (Generaly, Generally) we go to a movie on Saturday night.
8. Although we won the game, we must (continue, cuntinue) to improve.
9. The (immediate, immedeate) outcome is unknown.
10. Each person's (training, traning) is extremely important to his or her success.

IMPROVING ARITHMETIC SKILLS

Your employer has asked you to estimate how much stationery you use during a month. You know that you type about twelve letters a day and that you make at least one carbon copy for each letter. Half of the letters require one extra carbon copy. Of course, you type an envelope for each letter. You estimate that you have to retype one letter and one envelope a day. You use about four sheets of carbon paper a week.

Figure the total number of sheets of letterhead paper, copy paper, carbon paper, and envelopes you use in a month (4 weeks) working five days a week.

DEMONSTRATING OFFICE SKILLS

1. For the following letters of different lengths, give the width of the side margins and the line on which you would type the date.

  (a) A letter with 80 words in the body of the letter.
  (b) A letter with 123 words in the body of the letter.
  (c) A two-page letter with 360 words in the body of the letter.
  (d) A letter with 184 words in the body of the letter.

2. Using the letterhead from the *Supplies Inventory* or plain paper, type the following two-page letter in modified block style with blocked paragraphs and open punctuation. Use the block form of second page heading. The sign (¶) means paragraph.

August 17, 19––, Mr. William R. Fritz, Manager, Whiteside Manufacturing Company, 928 Harrison Building, 1258 Columbus Drive, Los Angeles, California 90012.

Dear Mr. Fritz Irritated customers . . . lost orders . . . tied-up lines . . . delays and misunderstandings . . . garbled messages . . . excessive phone bills . . . wasted sales effort. These are some of the costly results of the poor telephone practices so common today in business. (¶) But they don't have to be common in *your* business. You can make sure *all* your calls — incoming and outgoing — are handled courteously, efficiently, and economically by using our unique training program, BETTER BUSINESS BY TELEPHONE. (¶) And right now, as a new subscriber, you will receive a free bonus portfolio of past issues describing correct telephone techniques such as

— The 15 rules of telephone courtesy that *everyone* in business should follow.
— Why no secretary should *ever* have to use the blunt question "Who's calling?"
— How to build sales and goodwill when taking telephone orders.
— What to say — and what *not* to say — in handling complaint calls.
— Why so many executives now make and take their own telephone calls.
— The six ways to save time — and money — on all telephone calls.
— Why *new employees* need telephone training — and how to give it.
— How to handle the caller who doesn't want to give his or her name.

— *Why* and *how* to use the telephone to collect on past due accounts.

— How to turn more of your telephone *inquiries* into actual *sales*.

(¶) BETTER BUSINESS BY TELEPHONE has already helped more than 16,000 companies, of every size and type, make more effective use of their telephones. Included are small businesses — and such companies as Du Pont, American Airlines, Ford, Sears Roebuck, General Electric, *The Wall Street Journal*, etc. (¶) BETTER BUSINESS BY TELEPHONE will help you with every phase of your telephone operation, from handling routine calls to planning a complete telephone sales campaign. (¶) Regular twice monthly bulletins bring you the latest in tested telephone techniques . . . case histories showing how other progressive companies are solving telephone problems and making the most of telephone opportunities . . . hints on time- and money-saving procedures . . . ideas that spark your own thinking on how you can make your company's telephone contacts a sales and public relations *asset* rather than a liability. (¶) Along with the bulletins for management, you get regular biweekly *Fone-Talks* for employees . . . all *Special Reports* and *Supplements* as issued . . . easy access to past issues that may help you . . . and unlimited use of our *free mail consultation service* on your individual telephone problems. And your subscription starts with a "Telephone Improvement Kit" which shows you exactly how to make the best possible use of our material. (¶) As a BETTER BUSINESS BY TELEPHONE subscriber, you'll have everything you need to make your company's handling of the telephone as good as that of any company in the country . . . and to *keep* it that way. And you'll quickly see why we receive such comments as this from Helen C. Wood, President, H. C. Wood, Inc., Lansdowne, Pa.: "I feel you are rendering a splendid service to those business people who want to use the telephone effectively and efficiently." (¶) You'll find full information on rates on the enclosed order form. Just tell us how many copies of each bulletin you will need to cover your department heads and key employees. We'll do the rest. Sincerely yours, Madelyn Dell, Manager, Customer Service.

Part 4

The Office Worker and Word Processing

Clare Snyder works as a machine transcriber in the word processing center of a large legal firm in Los Angeles. She transcribes letters and legal documents which have been dictated by various lawyers. Clare knows that the dictating machines are a great convenience for the lawyers because they can dictate letters from their offices, at home, or when they travel. Clare is learning about the legal profession by being a machine transcriber and she enjoys producing accurate work.

Word Processing

Because the amount of paper work in business continues to increase and the cost of this work continues to rise, more and more businesses are seeking ways to improve the processing of paper work. They want to increase efficiency by decreasing the amount of time, effort, and material it takes to process words. This will decrease expenses and increase profits, and a company cannot **thrive** unless it makes a profit.

thrive: grow, make progress

Recording the executive's thoughts in typewritten form, in a report or a letter, is an expensive office activity. As you recall, the cost of an average business letter is now about $4. One way of reducing costs is through *word processing*, which means simply the **converting** of words in the mind of a dictator into typewritten words on paper.

converting: changing from one form into another

Advantages of Word Processing Equipment

Modern companies provide a variety of ways of recording messages their executives want to transmit. While the stenographer in many offices continues to take dictation directly in shorthand, that same stenographer may from time to time have the task of transcribing from dictation equipment. More and more companies are realizing the advantages of using this equipment.

Dictating equipment permits executives to dictate whenever they wish. Instead of waiting to dictate to a person who can take shorthand, the executive merely picks up the microphone and dictates. Instructions to the transcriber can be dictated along with the correspondence itself.

Using dictating and transcribing machines is less time-consuming than other methods of recording information. When dictation is given to a stenographer, the time of both the dictator and the stenographer is used just to record the information. An employer could write the message in longhand and then have it typed. Dictating a message, given a competent dictator, is much faster than writing it in longhand.

Your employer can take a portable machine along on trips and send the recordings back to the office to be transcribed. When your employer returns to the office, the letters are ready to be signed.

Types of Equipment

Whether a portable unit, a standard unit, or a remote control network system is used for dictation in a particular business will depend upon the operations of the company.

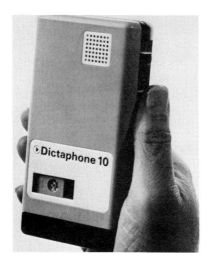

Dictaphone Corporation

Standard Dictating Unit

Portable dictating unit   Illus. 3-17

Portable Units

The small transistorized units provide an executive with the equipment to dictate in comfort at home, in a car, or on a trip. In fact, several airlines provide portable machines for business people who desire to dictate while on a flight. There is also a service that provides a dictating

Unit 3 • Preparing Mailable Letters

machine at the departure point of a flight or at a hotel. The recording which the executive has dictated can be transcribed at a local branch office of the company or it can be mailed back to the home office for transcription there.

Illus. 3-18

Small portable dictating equipment enables the executive to dictate anywhere, anytime.

Dictataphone Corporation

Standard Units

Separate desk-top units for dictation and transcription are available with a variety of features and with different types of recording devices. The executive has one machine for dictating, and the transcriber has a different machine for transcribing. Combination units are also available and are popular in offices where limited use is made of such equipment. A combination unit is used both for dictating and transcribing. Because only one person can use such a unit at one time, the work must be carefully planned so that a transcriber is not using the machine to transcribe when the executive needs it to dictate.

Remote Control Systems

A remote control system means that the belt, disc, or tape on which the message is recorded is not located near the dictator. The dictator could be several floors or many miles away from the recording machine. When the dictator speaks into a special telephone handset, a light appears on the transcribing unit as a signal to the transcriber that dictation is taking place. The transcriber can begin transcribing even before the dictator completes dictating.

Remote recording systems allow executives to dictate over long distances. By dialing a special number on a regular, office telephone, the executive is connected to a dictating machine that is ready to record. With this type of system, an executive at a branch office can call into the home office in another city and record on the dictating machine there. Any regular outside telephone can also be used to call in dictation.

Illus. 3-19

An executive can use any regular outside telephone to call into the office where dictating machines are ready to record.

Remote control systems are useful even when executives are not far removed from the dictating machines. A network of dictating and transcribing equipment permits many executives throughout a company to use the services of a word processing center. An executive dictates into a microphone or into a telephone which is connected to a centralized dictating machine in a word processing center. The word processing center is composed of several transcribers. A supervisor generally coordinates their work and helps them with any special problems they may have.

In a company where a network system has been installed, executives tend to use this service as a supplement to that provided by their own

coordinates:
organizes for smooth
operation

supplement:
addition

office workers. When the workload of regular transcribers is unusually heavy, executives use the word processing center. Typists in the word processing center prepare the transcription which is then returned to the executives' offices for signing.

Word Processing Systems

Some companies use **sophisticated** word processing systems which help to increase efficiency of transforming the spoken word into printed letters, memos, reports, etc. The procedure for one type of word processing system is described below.

sophisticated: improved and refined to a high level

Dictation and Transcription

1. The executive dictates a message into any kind of dictating machine, being careful not to leave the recorder on when simply thinking. The typist can transcribe much faster if there is no wasted recording space.
2. The typist at a word processing station transcribes at the typewriter on a sheet of paper called a *hard copy*. At the same time the information is recorded on a magnetic card, sometimes called a *Mag Card*, or on a reel of magnetic tape. The term

Illus. 3-20

A transcriber inserts a magnetic card into the console of a Magnetic Card Selectric Typewriter

Westinghouse Electric Corporation

MT/ST is often used when the recording is on magnetic tape and it means *Magnetic Tape/Selectric Typewriter*. The Mag Card or the tape is called the *magnetic copy*.

3. The hard copy is really a rough draft copy, and it tells the typist what is stored on the magnetic copy in the console unit. Since the hard copy is to be a rough draft, the typist can transcribe at a rate much faster than if she or he were transcribing final copy. If an error is made, the typist merely strikes over the mistake and the magnetic copy is automatically corrected.

Proofreading and Corrections

1. The dictator reads the rough draft hard copy and makes necessary corrections.
2. The typist places the rough draft in the typewriter and types corrections on the rough draft copy. The corrections are automatically made on the magnetic copy.

Playback

1. The rough draft copy is replaced in the typewriter with letterhead paper.
2. Several control knobs and keys on the console are set and a start button is pushed.
3. The typewriter, instructed by the magnetic tape or card, types out the final copy at about 175 words a minute without a single error.
4. Information on the magnetic copy can be stored indefinitely, and the same letter can be typed over and over if it is being used as a form letter.

Form Letters

In many offices some kinds of letters are written over and over again and it is, therefore, economical to compose letters that can be used in response to similar requests. Companies often build their own files of form letters and organize a coding system so that they can quickly locate

optional:
involving a choice; not
automatically included

an appropriate letter. Often form letters are written with optional paragraphs so that the typist can select the paragraph that is most appropriate for a particular recipient.

Letters acknowledging orders, sending out requested information, requesting references for prospective employees, and thanking companies or individuals for references are just a few of the instances where form letters are used. Illustrations of paragraph inserts for form letters follow.

Prospective Customer

1.   It was a pleasure to talk with you when you visited our booth at the recent _____ Convention. The material that we promised to mail you is enclosed.

2.   Mr. _____, our sales representative in your city, is ready to help you. He will be calling you to arrange an appointment at your convenience.

3.   Would you like additional information? Our representative in your area is _____ at _____, telephone _____. Your questions will receive prompt attention.

Requesting Reference

_____ has applied for a position with our company and has given your name as a reference. We would appreciate your completing the attached form and returning it in the enclosed self-addressed stamped envelope. There is space for any additional comments you may wish to make.

Thank you for your courtesy in responding to this request.

Form letters are prepared in several ways. Sometimes each form letter is typed with an inside address and a salutation so that it looks exactly like a personal letter. There are other times when form letters are prepared in quantity and the specific details for a particular recipient are added on the typewriter. The recipient is aware that the letter is a form letter, for copying processes are not able to duplicate exactly the nature of typed copy. Increasingly, form letters and form paragraphs are prepared on a master tape, which is used on an automatic typewriter that produces a personal-looking letter very quickly.

Dictating

Most dictating machines are operated by controls on a hand microphone. Keys or buttons are used to (1) start and stop dictation, (2) backspace for repeating a few words of the dictation, (3) indicate corrections, and (4) show the length of each dictated letter. If corrections or special instructions must be made, they can be dictated along with the message.

After the dictation is completed, the recording is removed from the machine and transcribed.

Transcribing

Transcribing machines are equipped with ear pieces or headsets that either fit into the ears or rest gently against the ears. You insert the dictated recording in the transcribing machine, then place the indicator slip (a strip of scaled paper which shows corrections, length of letters, and other instructions) in the slot provided for it. Adjust the speed, volume, and tone to suit your particular needs.

Illus. 3-21

Transcribing equipment is timesaving. The operator can adjust speed control, volume control, and tone control.

Westinghouse Electric
Corporation

When you first learn to transcribe, listen for a few words, a phrase, or a sentence, stop the machine, typewrite the words, start the machine again, listen for a few more words, and repeat this until the dictation has been transcribed. As your skill increases, you should be able to stop and start the transcribing machine without pausing in your typing. Also you will not have to backspace so often to relisten to the dictation.

Special instructions to the transcriber may be dictated along with the regular dictation. A system of marks is used on the indicator slip to show the beginning and end of each letter and where special instructions are given on the recording. These marks aid you in judging the length of the letter and in planning its placement on the letterhead. You should listen to the corrections and special instructions before beginning to type from the recording.

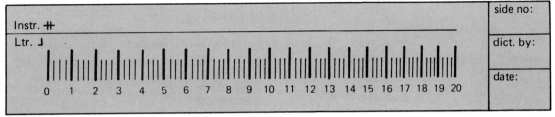

Illus. 3-22

Indicator slip

If you work for a large company you will probably have an office manual which will tell you the style of letter to use and the procedure for returning finished transcription to the person who dictated it. Transcribed materials are usually returned to the dictator in a folder with the most urgent messages on top ready for signing. An unused belt, disc, or tape, along with a new indicator slip, is placed in the folder with the completed dictation. Place the envelope for each letter face up with the flap over the top of the letter and any **accompanying** enclosures. If the folder is sent to the dictator by messenger or through the company mail system, it may be placed in a large envelope which is addressed to the recipient.

accompanying:
existing or going
along with

Transcribing Suggestions

Your rate of transcription can be increased and the number of time-consuming errors can be reduced if you follow the suggestions of experienced transcribers listed below.

1. Listen to the corrections and special instructions before transcribing any of the dictated material.
2. Use the indicator slip as a guide for the proper placement of material to be transcribed.
3. Be sure that you understand the meaning of the dictation before typing so that you will avoid
   (a) errors in grammar
   (b) errors in punctuation
   (c) errors in spelling
   (d) confusion of **homonyms**, such as *their* for *there*
4. Develop the ability to remember dictation in order to avoid backspacing so often.
5. Develop the skill of an expert — keep the typewriter moving as much as possible but stop the transcribing unit when necessary. Listen one phrase ahead of your typing.
6. Use the parts of the typewriter to advantage, especially the tabulator and the variable line spacer.

homonyms:
words pronounced
alike but different in
meaning and spelling

Improving Transcription

Transcribing ability is improved through correct practice and knowing about transcribing problems you will **encounter**. Some of the common transcribing problems and solutions are discussed below.

encounter:
come across; meet

Incorrect Information

Incorrect information such as a wrong price, date, or name may have been dictated. If the dictator did not know about the mistake, correct it if you are absolutely sure of the correct information. Always attach a note to the letter indicating what was changed and why.

If the dictator knows about the mistake, the error will be corrected at the time by recording over it (this is possible only on magnetic media dictating machines) so that you hear only the corrected version. On other machines the dictator may mark the indicator slip where the error occurs and dictate the correction where space is available on the recording. Before you start transcribing, listen to the error and then to the correction. Type only the corrected information.

Incomplete Information

Occasionally the dictator may not have information, such as a current address, readily available, and may ask that you find the information and insert it in the correct place in the transcription. In such a case, you may have to look in the files or in accompanying correspondence to find the information.

occasionally:
once in a while

Grammatical Errors

If you are certain there is a **grammatical** error in the dictation, it is proper for you to correct it. But if you are not certain, or if your correction would change the message in any way, you should check with the dictator before making the **revision**. Most grammatical errors are easily corrected by changing, adding, or deleting a word or two.

grammatical:
relating to the correct use of words

revision:
correction or improvement

Punctuation Errors

Dictators may make errors in punctuation, if they dictate punctuation. If you are not sure whether there is a punctuation error, check a reference manual. Most dictators do not give punctuation; therefore, it is the responsibility of the transcriber to supply correct punctuation marks.

Homonymns and Unfamiliar Words

Keep an eye out for homonymns. Normally you will be able to determine which word was intended (*mail* or *male*, *piece* or *peace*, etc.) from the way it is used in the sentence. If not, consult a dictionary, your supervisor, or the dictator.

You may not know the spelling or the meaning of some unfamiliar words. Sometimes these words will be spelled for you on the recording. If they are not, you should first check the accompanying correspondence, the files, or a dictionary. If you can't find the words ask your supervisor or the dictator.

Other Uses of Dictating Equipment

Dictation equipment can be used in many different ways to increase the efficiency of an executive by conserving time and energy. For example, many companies have form letters which have been prepared to answer routine correspondence. The busy executive does not want to take time to dictate a complete letter when a form letter is available. The executive need only supply extra information required to complete the form letter. Therefore, the executive dictates the needed information and requests that the transcriber type the letter and include the extra facts in their correct places.

Many executives also use portable dictating units to record messages or reminders to themselves or to their staffs. The messages are later transcribed and distributed as directed.

Some executives want transcripts of speeches they make, and these can be made with dictating equipment. Meetings can be recorded, and minutes can be typed from the recording. The efficiency of a business can be greatly increased by using dictating equipment.

REVIEWING IMPORTANT POINTS

1. What is the approximate cost of an average business letter?
2. What does the term *word processing* mean?
3. Under what circumstances would a portable dictating unit be considered a good purchase?
4. What is the purpose of an indicator slip?
5. Should the dictator keep the recording medium constantly in motion once dictation begins?
6. What does the "backspace" mechanism on a transcribing machine allow you to do?

7. What skill do you need to keep your typewriter moving smoothly as you type from a transcribing machine?
8. Is it a good practice for you to correct errors in grammar or punctuation made by the dictator?
9. What should you do if you come across a word that is very unusual, and you don't know how to spell it or what it means?
10. What are some of the other uses of dictating equipment in business today?

MAKING IMPORTANT DECISIONS

1. Whenever Miss Torkman dictates material on a dictating machine, she seldom remembers to prepare an indicator slip. How would you ask her to remember to prepare one for you?
2. Alice regularly finds that the final words of the dictator are inaudible on the tapes she must transcribe. What would you do about this problem?

LEARNING TO WORK WITH OTHERS

Miss Carrie Holman is a transcriber for Mr. R. P. Sherman. He dictates almost all his correspondence on a dictating machine, and Miss Holman transcribes it. Miss Holman has trouble understanding many of his sentences, because he dictates slowly in a very low voice and he mumbles. This has presented quite a problem for Miss Holman, because it takes her so long to transcribe the material. She has to listen to almost every sentence at least twice. Even then she is not always sure that she has transcribed the material correctly.

Should Miss Holman tell Mr. Sherman about this problem? How can Miss Holman encourage Mr. Sherman to speak plainly when dictating?

IMPROVING LANGUAGE SKILLS

Words that are pronounced alike but are different in meaning are known as homonyms. They can be very confusing when you are transcribing material from a dictating machine. On a separate sheet of paper type the word that correctly completes the following sentences:

1. Although she had (herd, heard) his voice many times, she did not recognize it on the dictation tape.
2. After Lionel had worked in an office, he found it was better not to (meddle, medal) in other people's business.
3. As Tom became more experienced in his new job, he was (allowed, aloud) to take over many more responsibilities.
4. Christi searched (threw, through) four files before she found the misplaced letter.

5. Enrolling in an office procedures (coarse, course), Lynn would learn how to operate a transcribing machine.
6. In a letter he transcribed, John misspelled Frankfort, the (capital, capitol) of Kentucky.
7. Linda did not like the (bare, bear) wall in the office; so she painted a landscape picture to put there.
8. (There, Their) jobs were carefully analyzed to determine which tasks they performed.
9. Use the indicator slip (to, too, two) guide you in properly placing a letter on the page.
10. There were (to, too, two) dictating units in the office — a standard unit and a combination unit.

IMPROVING ARITHMETIC SKILLS

Mr. Henderson, your employer, has decided to order two new transcribing machines for the office. He has asked you to go through some brochures and make suggestions concerning which transcribing machines you think would be best. You have narrowed the choice down to three different models which are basically the same. Your next step is to compute the price of each of the models to determine which would be least expensive. The Carter A-II Model sells for $175 per unit, and the company will allow $40 per unit if you trade in your two older transcribing machines. The Foxwell 204 Model sells for $160 per unit, and the company will allow $30 each if both of the older models are traded in. The Atom 800 Model sells for $145 per unit, and the company does not accept trade-ins. Which machine is the most economical purchase?

DEMONSTRATING OFFICE SKILLS

1. Write letters to several dictating machine dealers and ask for information on their latest standard and portable dictating units. Prepare a bulletin board display with the information you receive.
2. If dictating and transcribing machines are available, dictate the following letter on a machine and then transcribe it. This letter contains several errors which you should correct as you dictate and transcribe.

   If dictating and transcribing machines are not available, type the letter in rough draft form, make the corrections needed, and type the letter in block style with open punctuation.

   Use the letterhead from the *Supplies Inventory* or plain paper.

   This letter is to go to Mr. T. Y. Singer, Vice-President, T I W Hotel Associates, 1579 Avenue of the Americas, New York, NY 10032. I am surprised at the letters I'm receiving since that short presentation I made in Houston two weeks ago. I now realize that many companies are having problems in finding "quiet time" for executives. (¶) our plan is really as simple as I stated it was: We have an official quiet time from 7:30 to 10 every morning. No meetings are held, conversations are discouraged, and the paging system is silenced. Secretaries screen incoming telephone calls and only the most essential ones are put through. In checking, we find that no more than two calls get through to our staff of 200 executives! (¶) Yes, we feel that communications are at the center of our business, but we realized our managers didn't have time to plan their day, to think through the significance of what they had to do. So, when we instituted the four-day work week, we felt we could use the first two and a half hours of a nine-hour day for organization, planning, and thinking. (¶) We realized that to consider only quantity in relation to communications was to underestimate the powerful value of quality. Much communication was worthless, because it was initiated somewhat thoughtlessly. (¶) We plan to prepare a somewhat detailed story of our experience, and when this is available, we shall send you a copy. Sincerely yours, Richard T. King, Sales manager

IMPROVING OFFICE SKILLS (Optional)

Your instructor will dictate letters (or you will be able to listen to them from a recorded medium) that you are to transcribe on plain paper. Note the ease with which you are able to understand the corrections made by the dictator. Also, note the manner in which you made each correction. Proofread carefully.

Typewriting Reports and Legal Papers

Part 1

Preparing Reports

Shannon McGee has been working in the sales department of Hester's Industrial Equipment Company for almost three years. She realizes more and more how much of the information needed for the company to run smoothly is communicated by business reports. Shannon assists her employer in preparing reports which are used only by their office and reports which are distributed to other branch offices. She saves her employer valuable time by gathering and sorting information needed for the reports. She can type the reports quickly, because she knows the basic report format by memory. If her employer asks her to include special charts, illustrations, or a bibliography, Shannon knows exactly where the different sections will be located in the report. It is not unusual for Shannon to type several drafts of a report before she and her employer are satisfied. Shannon takes great pride in composing and typing all reports because she knows these reports represent her company to many people.

Importance of Business Reports

A business report may be only one or two pages and take the form of a memo or letter; or it may be a long, formal report of many pages. As businesses continue to grow and as the amount of information needed to operate a business increases, it is more and more difficult to communicate this **vast** amount of knowledge in person. Business reports make it possible for a busy executive to present information to others without talking to each person individually. Some reports are sent to personnel within the company while others are sent to interested people outside the company. Since so many people will be reading the report, it is extremely important that the information it contains be accurate.

When you work in an office, you will no doubt have an opportunity to help prepare reports. As you gain experience and **demonstrate** the ability to assume responsibility, you may even be asked to help gather information that is used in the reports.

vast:
great in size, amount, or degree

demonstrate:
show

Illus. 4-1

Gathering and checking information for a report may be one of your clerical responsibilities.

Photo courtesy of Manpower, Inc.

Parts of a Report

A long and detailed business report may contain many specific parts which are classified under three main headings: the introductory parts, the body of the report, and the supplementary parts. Before **binding** they are arranged in this order:

A. Introductory Parts
    1. Cover
    2. Title page
    3. Preface or letter of transmittal
    4. Table of contents
    5. List of tables, charts, and illustrations
    6. Summary

B. Body of the Report
    1. Introduction
    2. Main body or text
    3. Conclusions and recommendations

C. Supplementary Parts
    1. Appendix
    2. Bibliography
    3. Index

The body of the report must be developed first; so it is usually typed first. Then the supplementary parts and the introductory parts of the report are typed.

The Cover

The cover should contain this information: the title of the report, the name of the person submitting it, and the date it was submitted.

The Title Page

The items of information that usually appear on the title page are the title of the report, the name of the author, the date, and the place of preparation. Sometimes reports include the name of the person (with appropriate title) for whom the report was prepared. (See Illustration 4-10 on page 139).

Preface or Letter of Transmittal

The purpose of the preface or letter of transmittal, illustrated on page 140, is to interest the reader enough to read the entire report. The preface or letter of transmittal is written in a less formal, more personal style than the body of the report.

The preface or letter of transmittal usually contains the following information:

1. The name of the person or organization that asked that the report be prepared.
2. The main purpose of the report.
3. The scope, or extent of coverage, of the report.
4. An acknowledgement of assistance in the preparation of the report.

If a separate summary is not included in the report, it is usually included in the letter of transmittal.

Table of Contents

The table of contents, shown on page 140, gives an overview of the material covered in the report by listing the main topics or chapter titles with their page numbers.

Before you type the final copy of the Table of Contents, check the titles and page numbers to make sure they are correct, particularly if any last-minute changes were made.

List of Tables

A list of tables is actually a separate table of contents used in reports which contain several tables, charts, figures, or other illustrations. The List of Tables contains the title of each illustration and indicates the page on which it can be found. Usually the List of Tables is typed as a separate page, but it can be a part of the Table of Contents.

Summary

The summary of the report is written after the entire report is completed. It gives the reader a quick overview that saves time and makes it easier to understand the detailed statements contained in the body of the report.

Introduction

The purpose of the introduction is to tell the reader exactly what problem is going to be studied in the report. The reader is told how the problem developed and how the report will analyze and deal with the problem.

Main Body

The main body of the report presents the information which was collected and applies this information to the problem with the idea of presenting a solution to the problem. The main body, of course, is the bulk of the report. It is where the information is analyzed and compared and where relationships and trends are identified and evaluated.

solution:
answer to a problem

Conclusions and Recommendations

The conclusions are the results of what has been presented in the report. The recommendations contain the writer's suggestions about action that should be taken as a result of the conclusions.

Appendix

The text of a long report may be followed by an appendix; it is omitted in a short report. The appendix usually contains extra reference material not easily included in the text. It may also include tables containing complete original data, general reference tables, and other materials which will help to interpret and to add interest in the report.

interpret:
explain the meaning of

Bibliography

All documentary sources (written material) referred to in a business report — books, articles, and periodicals — should be included in the bibliography. It should also include all the references consulted which contained worthwhile information related to the report. The references listed in the bibliography should be arranged in alphabetical order by author, by editor, or by title if the authors' names are not available. Examples of references in a bibliography are illustrated on page 147.

Steps in Report Writing

There is no *one* standard way to write a report; there are many ways. In drafting and revising a business report, however, you and the preparer of the report, sometimes called the "originator," will usually take these steps:

1. The originator develops a broad idea of the problem to be covered in the report.
2. The originator prepares either a sketchy or a detailed outline of the contents.
3. The originator composes the first draft. The entire draft may be written in longhand or may be recorded on a dictating machine.

Illus. 4-2

An employer may record the first draft or the revision of a report on a dictating machine.

4. You type the first draft in rough draft form.
5. The originator reorganizes and edits the first draft for content, wording, and sentence structure (usually with your help).
6. You type a second draft of the report.
7. The originator edits the second draft to insure the best presentation of the contents.
8. You type the report in its final form.
9. You double-check each page for accuracy, particularly accuracy of numbers.
10. You **collate** pages of the report.

collate:
collect and arrange in order

Gathering Information

Your employer may not have all the information that is needed to complete either the footnotes or the bibliography. Only a little information may be given to you such as, "I think the title of the book is *Business Organization and Management* and the author is Tyler, but I'm not sure." Of course, your employer may not remember the author's first name or even how to spell the name. As for a newspaper article referred to, all your employer may remember is that it was in the *Times* last week. The rest is up to you.

Illus. 4-3

To compile information for a report many sources may be consulted.

There is even more to it than that. Very often in quoting material your employer may not correctly remember each word and may not have the exact statistics or the dates. Checking those quotations and figures in the proper sources is your responsibility too. After checking the original sources, you make the changes that are necessary, and inform your employer if the changes are major. You should not bother your employer with minor details however.

You may have to check reference books such as the *Reader's Guide to Periodical Literature*, *The New York Times Index*, and *The World Almanac*. In compiling reports or writing manuscripts, you will need to know what to look for, where to look, and how to get accurate information rapidly. Company purchased reference books, public libraries, trade journals, and business and local newspapers will be your best sources of information. Appendix H, page 712 contains a list of reference books which should also be of assistance to you.

compiling:
collecting; composing

Typing the Outline

Before writing the report itself, your employer will prepare an outline for you to type. An outline is necessary because it gives your employer a chance to organize thoughts and rearrange the contents of the report before it is actually written. It also permits the originator to see if everything is included in the report.

An outline may be written in sentence form or in topical form. *Topical form* uses words or phrases for headings. The *sentence form* uses complete sentences. Parallel construction should be used; that is, if the outline starts out in sentence form, all headings and subheadings should be sentences. This makes it easier for the reader to understand the outline. Topical and sentence headings should not be mixed in a single outline. No main heading or subheading should stand alone. For every Roman numeral "I," there should be a Roman numeral "II"; for every letter "A," a letter "B"; for every Arabic "1," an Arabic "2."

In the outline illustrated on page 129, each identifying number or letter is followed by a period and two spaces and begins just below the first word of the previous line.

REVIEWING IMPORTANT POINTS

1. Why are business reports important?
2. What are the three main parts of a business report?
3. What specific parts may be included in the introductory section of a report?

```
                        ANALYSIS OF OFFICE OPERATIONS

     I.  Introduction

         A.  Purpose of analysis

         B.  Summary

    II.  Proposed changes

         A.  Personnel
             1.  Designate an Administrative Manager
             2.  Standardize hiring procedure
             3.  Develop positive attitudes about office work
             4.  Improve morale
             5.  Provide inservice education for staff and partners
             6.  Evaluate and reward staff

         B.  Procedures
             1.  Standardize some office procedures
             2.  Delegate more office work to staff
             3.  Improve communication
             4.  Adopt an organizational chart
             5.  Adopt a work allocation chart
             6.  Develop a follow-up system
             7.  Improve reception and telephone services
             8.  Utilize automatic typewriters
             9.  Adopt an office manual

   III.  Prognosis for improvement

    IV.  Plan of action

     V.  Financial implications

    VI.  Conclusions and recommendations

   VII.  Appendices
```

Illus. 4-4   A topical outline of a report

4. What information should the cover of a report contain?
5. What is the purpose of a letter of transmittal?
6. Which part of a report gives an overview by listing the main topics or chapter titles?
7. When is the summary of a report written?
8. What is the purpose of the introduction?
9. What are conclusions and recommendations?
10. What is parallel construction in an outline for a report?

MAKING IMPORTANT DECISIONS

Before leaving town, your employer, Mr. Gilbert, hands you the final copy of an annual report and asks you to photocopy the report and mail it. The report must reach the national office the day after tomorrow. While photocopying the report, you notice that the page which should contain several charts is missing. You cannot locate the missing page, but you find one of the earlier drafts in Mr. Gilbert's desk. Most of the corrections seem to have been made on the draft in pencil. What would you do about the missing page?

LEARNING TO WORK WITH OTHERS

Saul Goldman, assistant to Mrs. Boyd, was asked to supervise the collating (assembling in correct order) and binding of a ten-page financial report. Since the operation would have to be done by hand, Saul asked Norma, a clerk/typist, to begin collating and stapling the report. Saul left Norma to work by herself for about an hour. When he returned to help, Saul observed that most of the reports had been stapled in a most haphazard fashion. He frowned at the thought of restapling all of the reports and wondered how he should approach the problem with Norma. What suggestions would you make to Saul in handling the matter? How could he have prevented this situation?

IMPROVING LANGUAGE SKILLS

The question mark has three usages:

A. After a direct question: "What time is it?"
B. In a series, if special emphasis is desired: "Where is my watch? my wallet? my keys?"
C. To indicate uncertainty: "She was graduated in 1969(?)."

(It is not necessary to use a question mark after a polite request: "Will you let us have the information quickly.")

On a separate sheet of paper type the following sentences and insert question marks and other punctuation where needed.

1. Please include these pages in the appendix.
2. Where are the figures for September he asked.
3. What happened to my first draft my carbon paper my notes.
4. What happened to the title page the table of contents the list of tables.
5. When do you expect to have the final draft completed.

6. She asked him to retype the letter of transmittal.
7. The amounts for the five-year period 1973–1978 were included.
8. The figures for 1974, 1975, 1976, 1977, and 1938 were given to the sales manager.
9. He asked her if she would complete the reports by Tuesday.
10. Can't this report be reduced to less than 45 pages the president asked.

IMPROVING ARITHMETIC SKILLS

Tom Wilkins works from 9 a.m. until 5 p.m. five days a week. He gets an hour for lunch. Today (Tuesday), as soon as he arrived at work, his employer handed him the final draft of a 52-page report to be typed and ready to take on a business trip. The employer must leave the office at 4 p.m. Wednesday to catch the plane. What is the least number of pages Tom can type an hour to meet the employer's deadline?

DEMONSTRATING OFFICE SKILLS

1. Using a letterhead from the Supplies Inventory, or plain paper, type the transmittal letter below in block style with open punctuation.

Mr. Nathan Lombard, President, Automated Industries, Inc., 7000 Broad Street, Lake Charles, LA 70632

Dear Mr. Lombard (¶1) Here is the report, ANALYSIS OF UTILIZA-TION OF OFFICE EQUIPMENT, covering our study of Automated Industries, Inc. (¶2) A summary of high priority implementation recommendations is given on Page 2 of the report. Primary and secondary courses of action are listed with suggestions for implementing and supervising. Additional equipment and personnel needs are discussed and justified in recommendations listed on Page 6. (¶3) Automated Industries has a reputation for being a front-runner in implementing modern office procedures and equipment. We believe that by following the recommendations in our analysis, your company will continue to be a front-runner. Furthermore, we believe that profits will be increased and the morale of your employees will be heightened considerably. (¶4) We would like to express our appreciation for the cooperation we received in compiling this report. We are ready to discuss the implementation of the report at your convenience. Sincerely Jonathon Swinson, Office Procedures and Equipment Analyst

2. Type the following in correct, topical outline form, making all necessary corrections in numbering, capitalization, or punctuation:

COST OF TRANSCRIBING MACHINES FOR HOME OFFICE

1. introduction:
   A. Purpose
      1. To recommend Improvements
      2. to increase profitability
   B. Need for Study
      1. To Examine effectiveness of present use of transcribing machines:
      2. To determine Future transcribing machine requirements.
      3. to Investigate costs of Various Models.
   B. Procedure —
      1. secure Information from company files
      2. Observe hours spent Using transcribing machines
      3. To gather information from Sales Representatives.
2. Analysis of Information:
   A. Strong Points
   B. Weak Points
III. Proposed Solution:
IV. Conclusions and recommendations.

Part 2

Typing Reports

Zachary was pleased to learn that his new position in the sales department of the Wilkerson Medical Supplies Corporation would involve compiling and typing several weekly and monthly reports. In high school, Zachary learned the basic rules for typing reports including procedures for setting margins, typing headings, numbering pages, and typing quoted material and footnotes. He looked forward to the opportunity to apply the rules he learned to different situations. Zachary knew that by presenting material in a logical, flawless form, his reports would be easy to read and understand. After Zachary studied the types of reports he would be responsible for, he quickly located the reference books which would be at his disposal. He also met the people who could assist him when he needed specific information. Zachary was now prepared to begin his new job, and he was anxious to demonstrate his skills and reliability.

One of the major responsibilities in preparing a report is typing the manuscript. Once you have a clear understanding of procedures, methods, and shortcuts in typing a report, you can type the copy with great confidence of success.

manuscript: copy; final draft

Setting the Margins

The margins for typed reports are determined by the binding. If the following table of margins for unbound, side-bound, and top-bound reports is carefully followed, the report will be attractive.

A light pencil mark about 1½" from the bottom edge of the page will tell you that you have only one line left to type at the bottom of the page. Be sure to erase this pencil mark when you are proofreading your final copy.

It may be helpful to use a guide sheet like the one in Illus. 4-6. On a plain sheet of paper, make rulings with very dark ink to show the left

MARGINS FOR TYPING BUSINESS REPORTS

Margins	Unbound	Side Bound	Top Bound
Top margin			
First page	2 inches	2 inches	2½ inches
All other pages	1 inch	1 inch	1½ inches
Side margins			
Left	1 inch	1½ inches	1 inch
Right	1 inch	1 inch	1 inch
Bottom margin	1 inch	1 inch	1 inch

Illus. 4-5

and right margins. Numbering the horizontal lines on the right edge of the page is useful in allowing space for footnotes. The guide sheet is

Illus. 4-6

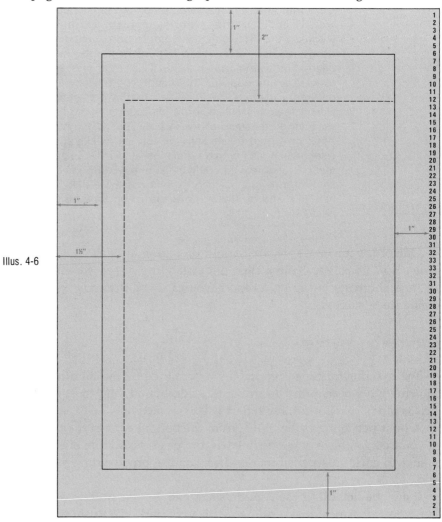

placed behind the original in the typewriter and followed for proper placement.

The Rough Draft

A rough draft is your employer's first attempt to get important thoughts down on paper where they can be edited and improved. The draft may be revised and retyped many times. The following ten suggestions should help you:

1. Use typing paper strong enough to withstand erasing. Do not use manifold paper or expensive letterhead paper.
2. Type double spacing so that the changes can be clearly marked and easily seen and followed.
3. Allow margins of 1½ inches at the top, bottom, and on both sides of each page to provide enough room for corrections.
4. X out typing errors and **deletions** in the first draft instead of taking time to erase them.

   deletions:
   items to be taken out
5. A carbon copy or photocopy should be made in case the original is lost. You may also wish to have an extra copy to cut up and paste when reorganizing the material.
6. Number each page in the draft in its proper sequence. Also assign a number to each succeeding revision of a draft and type the date on it.

Illus. 4-7

Sometimes cutting and pasting up a copy of a report is the easiest way to reorganize the material.

7. Type a long insertion on a separate sheet of paper and give it a corresponding page number and letter. For example, the first insertion to be included on page 8 should be numbered "8A" and you should clearly mark "Insert 8A" at the point where it is to be inserted.

8. Type quoted matter of four lines or more single spaced and indent it in the same form as it will appear in the final draft.

9. Type footnotes single spaced at the bottom of the page, on a separate sheet, or, preferably, insert them in this manner immediately after the reference in the text but separated from the text by solid lines.

---

[1]Mary Ellen Oliverio and William R. Pasewark, <u>Secretarial Office Procedures</u> (9th ed.; Cincinnati: South-Western Publishing Co., 1977), p. 152.

---

10. Keep all rough drafts in a file folder until the final draft has been approved. Your employer may decide to include words, phrases, and sentences deleted from previous drafts in the final draft of the report.

Need for Proofreading

All typewritten reports and manuscripts should be proofread carefully. The text can be checked most effectively, particularly if it contains statistics, by having one of your co-workers read the original copy aloud to you while you check the reading against the final copy.

statistics:
numerical data

You must also be absolutely sure that all numbers are accurate. An incorrect letter in a word is undesirable, but seldom does this kind of error cause the reader to misunderstand the entire report. An incorrect number, on the other hand, may mean the difference between a profit and a loss on a business transaction. You will find the following suggestions for reading and checking numbers helpful:

1. Read 2948 as *two nine four eight*.
2. Read 0 (the number) as *oh*.
3. Read decimal point as *point*.
4. Read .00032 as *point oh oh oh three two*.
5. Read down columns, not up or across.
6. Verify totals by addition. This is a double check on the original and on the copy.

verify:
check

The names of persons, places, and other proper nouns should be spelled by the reader, at least the first time that they appear in the copy, in order to avoid errors.

Use of Proofreaders' Marks

Proofreaders marks are used to indicate corrections and revisions in rough drafts of business reports because they are clearly understood and easily followed. Their use greatly reduces the chance of error in the re-typing of a draft. Standard proofreaders' marks, as they are indicated in a rough draft and corrected in the text, are shown below. You will need to know their meanings in order to type rough drafts of business documents efficiently.

PROOFREADERS' MARKS

Mark in Margin	Meaning of Mark	Correction or Change Marked in Text	Corrected or Changed Copy
⋀	caret; indicates insertion is to be made	If you are interested ⋀ we	If you are interested, we
⌣	close up	on the pay⌣roll	on the payroll
≡ or caps	capitalize	Mutual life of New York	Mutual Life of New York
¶	new paragraph	two or more lines. ¶ One caution	two or more lines. One caution
]	move to right	centered over the]columns and then typed	centered over the columns and then typed
[	move to left	cc: Joseph H. Morrow [Gerald A. Porter Allen A. Smith	cc: Joseph H. Morrow Gerald A. Porter Allen A. Smith
tr or ∼	transpose	monthly benefits	monthly benefits
ℒ	take out; delete	We wished you	We wish you
stet	leave it as it was originally	commencing starting next month	starting next month

Illus. 4-8 Proofreaders' marks

Typing the Report

The final draft of a business report should be typed on white bond paper (8½" × 11" in size) of good quality, preferably of 20-pound substance. The body of the report, except for footnotes and long quotations, should be double-spaced. The report should be typed so that it is attractive and easy to read. The typing line should be 6 to 6½ inches long: 60–65 pica spaces or 72–78 elite type spaces.

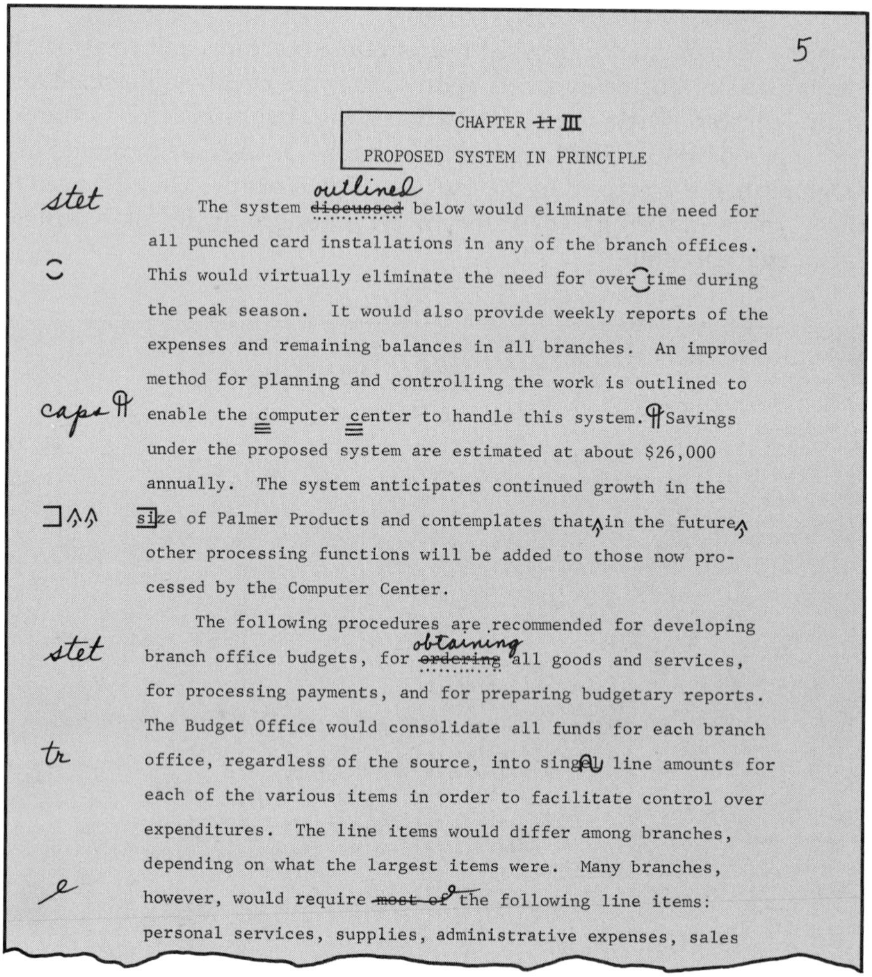

CHAPTER ~~II~~ III

PROPOSED SYSTEM IN PRINCIPLE

stet   The system ~~discussed~~ *outlined* below would eliminate the need for all punched card installations in any of the branch offices. This would virtually eliminate the need for over time during the peak season. It would also provide weekly reports of the expenses and remaining balances in all branches. An improved method for planning and controlling the work is outlined to enable the computer center to handle this system. Savings under the proposed system are estimated at about $26,000 annually. The system anticipates continued growth in the size of Palmer Products and contemplates that in the future, other processing functions will be added to those now processed by the Computer Center.

      The following procedures are recommended for developing branch office budgets, for ~~ordering~~ *obtaining* all goods and services, for processing payments, and for preparing budgetary reports. The Budget Office would consolidate all funds for each branch office, regardless of the source, into single line amounts for each of the various items in order to facilitate control over expenditures. The line items would differ among branches, depending on what the largest items were. Many branches, however, would require ~~most of~~ the following line items: personal services, supplies, administrative expenses, sales

Illus. 4-9

Rough draft report with proofreaders' marks

Title Page

The title page must be attractively typed with the information carefully spaced to give the page a balanced look. The information presented on the title page should be centered horizontally on the line of typing.

Letter of Transmittal

The letter of transmittal may be typed in any acceptable letter style. An illustration of an acceptable letter of transmittal appears on page 140.

```
ANALYSIS OF OFFICE OPERATIONS
ASSOCIATED INSURANCE CORPORATION




For
Richard L. Lindell, President
Associated Insurance Corporation




By
Charles R. Bruner
Office Management Consultants
2380 Peachtree Street
Atlanta, GA 48812
404-638-2291




July 2, 19--
```

Illus. 4-10

Title page of a report

Table of Contents

The heading, *Table of Contents*, should be centered two inches from the top of the page and typed entirely in capital letters. Double spacing is used before the titles of chapters or main topics, and single spacing in all other instances. All important words in the chapter or main topic title should be capitalized. Important words include the first word and all others except articles (a, an, the), conjunctions (and, but, for, neither, nor, or), and short prepositions (to, in, of, on, with). Each chapter title should be preceded by its number which is typed in capital Roman numerals and followed by a period and two spaces. The Roman numerals

TABLE OF CONTENTS

Illus. 4-12

Table of contents

OMC Office Management Consultants

2380 Peachtree Street   Atlanta, GA 44812   404-638-2291

July 3, 19--

Mr. Richard L. Lindell, President
Associated Insurance Corporation
2243 Sixteenth Street, N.W.
Washington DC 20134

ANALYSIS OF OFFICE OPERATIONS

Here is the report, ANALYSIS OF OFFICE OPERATIONS, covering our study of Associated Insurance Corporation.

On page 2 is a summary of priority items to implement for the Associated Insurance Corporation. The first course of action should be to designate an Administrative Manager who would be responsible for all of your office operations. A suggested procedure for hiring this person is described on page 3 of the report.

Associated Insurance already has an excellent foundation on which to develop efficient office systems. Your organization is success oriented, morale is high, and both partners and staff seem receptive to changes in your office. We believe the aims of the analysis, to increase profits and to make office work more pleasant, can be obtained by adopting the recommendations in the report.

Everyone we worked with at Associated Insurance was helpful to the study and I wish you would express appreciation to each of them. We are ready to discuss the implementation of the report after you have had a chance to review it.

Charles Bruner
Office Systems Analyst

bb

Illus. 4-11

Letter of transmittal

should be lined up with the periods directly beneath each other. Leaders (periods and spaces alternated) should extend across the page from each title to guide the reader in finding the page number at the right. The periods in the leaders should also be in vertical alignment (each in line above the other). This can be done easily by typing all periods at even (or odd) numbers on the typewriter line scale. Before the final copy is typed, the table of contents should be checked against the text for correctness of titles and accuracy of page numbers.

alternated: first one and then the other

List of Tables

The heading *List of Tables*, like all other main headings, is centered two inches from the top of the page and typed entirely in capital letters. The table numbers are typed in Arabic numerals followed by a period and two blank spaces. The first letter of every important word in the title of a table is typed with a capital letter. Leaders extend from the title to the Arabic page numbers at the right. Lists of charts and other illustrations are typed in the same form as the *List of Tables*.

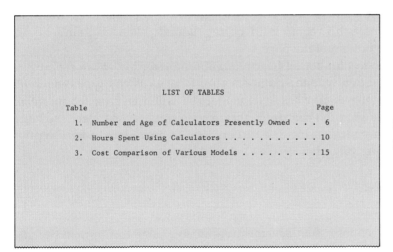

LIST OF TABLES

Table		Page
1.	Number and Age of Calculators Presently Owned . . .	6
2.	Hours Spent Using Calculators	10
3.	Cost Comparison of Various Models	15

Illus. 4-13
List of tables

Body of the Report

The division headings in the body of the report should be the same as the titles that appear in the table of contents. Each division should begin on a new page with the word *Chapter* or *Section* centered two inches from the top of the page. It should be typed entirely in capital letters and followed by a chapter or section number typed in large Roman numerals. The title of the chapter or section is centered one blank line below and also typed in capital letters. A very long title should be broken into two or more lines and divided at the point where the thought in the title changes. With a long title the inverted pyramid style may be used — the top line longer than the second, and the second line longer than the third. Two blank lines should be left between the title and the first paragraph of the report.

Numbering Pages

Small Roman numerals (ii, iii, iv, etc.) are used to number the pages of the introductory parts of the report. The title page is considered as page "i" but no number is typed on it. The numbers are centered and typed one-half inch from the bottom of the page, and they are not followed by periods or any other punctuation.

consecutively: one after the other in order

Arabic numerals, without punctuation, are used to number the pages in the rest of the report. They begin with "1" and run consecutively throughout the report. The number on the first page of each section is centered and typed one-half inch from the bottom of the page. The pages that follow are numbered one-half inch from the top and even with the right margin. If the report is to be top bound, all page numbers are placed at the bottom of the page.

It is wise to number all pages at one time after the entire report has been typed. If you type the numbers on the pages as you type the report and a rather long change has to be made, you will then have to renumber all pages following the change. Before page numbers are typed, they can be written in pencil on the first carbon copy to assist you in keeping the pages in numerical order.

Headings

You will choose from several types of headings to improve the appearance of the typed matter and to indicate the relationship of its parts. Headings make a report easier to read and understand. If the material is well organized, the headings and subheadings will serve as a basic outline for the report.

Main Headings. Main heading are usually centered on the page and typed in all capital letters. A main heading is normally followed by two blank lines.

Subheadings. There are two kinds of subheadings — side headings and paragraph headings.

CHAPTER II

PROPOSED CHANGES

A comprehensive analysis of Associated Insurance (AI) operations resulted in obvious changes to proposals that will increase office productivity. These changes are in the major categories of Personnel and Procedures.

Personnel

Some suggested changes in personnel are as follows:

Appoint an Administrative Manager. The most important priority for AI is to appoint an Administrative Manager who will be responsible for all office operations. Other possible names for this position could be Office Manager or Office Administrator.

The justifications for this new position are:

1. Partners would not have to spend so much time in the office and could devote more of their time and attention to outside selling that produces income.

2. The Administrative Manager will be responsible for the continuous improvement of present office procedures and the introduction of new procedures as AI grows.

3. Improved office procedures will permit us to serve our clients better which will improve our image and encourage additional business.

4. The present size of five partners and nine office staff and the complexity of AI's organization warrants an Administrative Manager.

5. The nature of the partner's major function of selling, requires them to be out of the office. Someone must be in the office at all times and be responsible for its operation.

6. Partners are well educated about selling insurance but none of the present personnel is educated to "back up the sales" in the office. Some of AI's selling strengths can be diluted by ineffective servicing of the policies we sell.

Illus. 4-14

A typed page of a report with headings and subheadings

Side Headings. Side headings are used to **indicate** major divisions of the main topic. They are typed even with the left margin with the main words starting with a capital letter. Side headings are followed by one blank line. They may also be underlined.

indicate: show; point to

Paragraph Headings. If the text needs to be divided further, paragraph headings may be used. Paragraph headings are indented and underlined. Usually the main words of the heading are capitalized, and the heading is followed by a period.

Quoted Material

Material from other sources is frequently quoted in business reports. All direct quotations should be typed exactly as they are written in the quoted source — in wording, spelling, punctuation, and paragraphing.

1. A brief quotation of fewer than four lines is typed in the text and enclosed with quotation marks.
2. A quotation of four lines or more is started on a new line and typed on shorter, single-spaced lines indented from both the left and right margins. No quotation marks are used.
3. A quotation of several paragraphs need not be indented, but a quotation mark should precede each paragraph and should follow the final word of the last quoted paragraph.
4. A quotation within a quotation (an inside quotation) is enclosed with single quotation marks. The apostrophe is used as a single quotation in typed material.
5. Omissions in a quotation are shown by typing an ellipsis — three spaced periods for an omission within a sentence or between sentences, four periods for an omission at the end of a sentence.

Permission should be obtained to quote copyrighted material if it is to be widely distributed in duplicated reports or printed manuscripts. Material may be quoted from government publications without obtaining permission.

Footnotes

Footnotes refer the reader to information outside the text of a report. They are inserted to **acknowledge** and identify the source of the quoted information, to support points made by the author, to provide additional material for the reader, or to **elaborate** on a statement within the text. The Arabic number of a footnote is typed in the text just after the statement to be documented but slightly above the line of writing. For raised numbers, the platen is turned toward the typist a half space before the number is typed. The footnote itself, if it is the first reference to a particular work, should identify the author and the title of the work referred to, give facts about the publication of the work and the copyright date, and **cite** a specific page reference.

Later references to the same source need not repeat all these details; only *ibid.*, the abbreviation for *ibidem* (meaning *in the same place*), and the page number are used when references to the same work follow each other. The author's name, *op. cit.*, the abbreviation for *opere citato* (meaning *in the work cited*), and the page number are used when a previous reference has been made to the same source but other references come between. The author's name and *loc. cit.*, the abbreviation for *loco citato* (meaning *in the same place*), are used to refer to the same passage in a reference previously cited.

acknowledge:
give credit to

elaborate:
to expand in detail

cite:
quote; refer to

The footnotes below show the use of *ibid., op. cit.,* and *loc. cit.*

----

¹H. Webster Johnson, <u>How to Use the Bus-</u><u>iness Library</u> (4th ed., Cincinnati: South-Western Publishing Co., 1972), p. 148.

²Paul S. Burtness and Robert R. Aurner, <u>Effective English for Colleges</u> (5th ed., Cincinnati: South-Western Publishing Co., 1975), pp. 217-243.

³<u>Ibid.</u>, p. 399.

⁴Johnson, <u>op. cit.</u>, pp. 142-146.

⁵Burtness and Aurner, <u>loc. cit.</u>

Footnotes should be typed according to the following guides:

1. They are separated from the text by a short, solid horizontal line of 15 pica or 18 elite spaces typed with the underscore key one line below the last line of the text.
2. The first line of the first footnote is typed one blank line below the short horizontal line. It is indented the same number of spaces as the paragraphs in the report. The succeeding lines of the footnote begin at the left margin.
3. The reference number, which corresponds with the footnote number in the text, is also typed slightly above the line of writing. It is typed without punctuation or a space between it and the first word of the footnote.
4. All footnotes are typed single-spaced. A blank line is left between footnotes.
5. Footnotes are usually numbered in sequence from the first to the last page of a report.

Appendix

The word *Appendix* can be centered horizontally and vertically on a separate sheet of paper and used as the first page of the Appendix; or you can treat the first page of the Appendix as a special page. Center the word *Appendix* two inches from the top of the page, and then continue with the material you want to include in the Appendix.

Bibliography

The bibliography is the list of publications which are referred to in the report. They are listed in alphabetical order by author.

Developing positive attitudes about office work is probably the most important challenge for Associated Insurance to increase office productivity. Office work is more difficult to measure and control than work on the farm and in the factory. AI must be sure to hire competent employees, then keep morale high so that all employees are working at their capacity. The result, hopefully, will be that while we cannot measure each employee's work accurately, we can, with reasonable assurance, expect that our office productivity is comparatively high.

Each partner must be convinced that while selling insurance policies is the first step toward a successful, profit-oriented business, servicing the customers' policies in the office is a necessary and important phase of the business. The time and effort of a partner to sell an insurance policy will be wasted if we lose the customer because the processing of the policy in the office was slow or inaccurate. The staff must be convinced of the importance of their work and the need to decrease the time, effort, and material to improve efficiency, reduce costs, and increase profits.[1] The partners and the office staff should be convinced of the vital role of the office at AI after they read the Conclusions and Recommendations, Chapter II, of this report.

---

[1]Charles J. Howard, _Controlling Office Costs_ (3d ed.; Detroit: National Publishing Co., 1977), p. 61.

Illus. 4-15   A typed page of a report

REVIEWING IMPORTANT POINTS

1. What determines the margins of a typed report?
2. What is a rough draft?
3. Why shouldn't you use expensive letterhead paper for a rough draft?
4. Why is a rough draft usually double-spaced?
5. Why might an incorrect figure in a report be a critical mistake?
6. What are the advantages of using proofreaders' marks to show corrections in reports and manuscripts?
7. How should the final draft of a business report be typed?

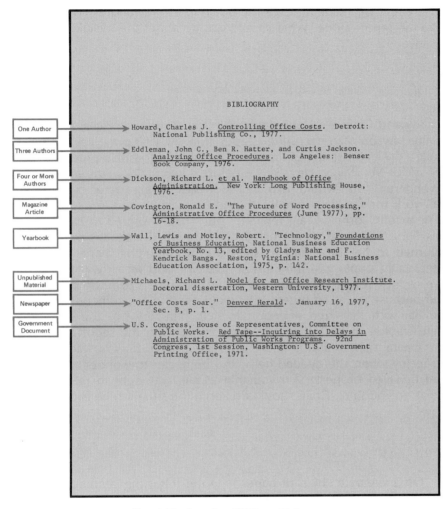

BIBLIOGRAPHY

One Author — Howard, Charles J. <u>Controlling Office Costs</u>. Detroit: National Publishing Co., 1977.

Three Authors — Eddleman, John C., Ben R. Hatter, and Curtis Jackson. <u>Analyzing Office Procedures</u>. Los Angeles: Benser Book Company, 1976.

Four or More Authors — Dickson, Richard L. <u>et al</u>. <u>Handbook of Office Administration</u>. New York: Long Publishing House, 1976.

Magazine Article — Covington, Ronald E. "The Future of Word Processing," <u>Administrative Office Procedures</u> (June 1977), pp. 16-18.

Yearbook — Wall, Lewis and Motley, Robert. "Technology," <u>Foundations of Business Education</u>, National Business Education Yearbook, No. 13, edited by Gladys Bahr and F. Kendrick Bangs. Reston, Virginia: National Business Education Association, 1975, p. 142.

Unpublished Material — Michaels, Richard L. <u>Model for an Office Research Institute</u>. Doctoral dissertation, Western University, 1977.

Newspaper — "Office Costs Soar." <u>Denver Herald</u>. January 16, 1977, Sec. B, p. 1.

Government Document — U.S. Congress, House of Representatives, Committee on Public Works. <u>Red Tape--Inquiring into Delays in Administration of Public Works Programs</u>. 92nd Congress, 1st Session, Washington: U.S. Government Printing Office, 1971.

Illus. 4-16   Examples of bibliographic forms

8. Why is it wise to number all pages of a report at one time after the entire report has been typed?
9. What three types of headings are used in business reports?
10. What information is contained in a footnote?

MAKING IMPORTANT DECISIONS

The day before a very important business meeting, your employer asks you to proofread for the final time a lengthy report which will be presented at the meeting. While proofreading, you find that the pages are numbered incorrectly because page number 15 was skipped. You are the one who numbered the pages, and you know it is your mistake. Your employer plans to leave the office in a few minutes and wants to take the report along. What should you do about the mistake you have discovered?

LEARNING TO WORK WITH OTHERS

Joy and Craig are stenographers in the security services department of the Lawson Manufacturing Corporation. At 1:00 p.m., Joy rushed to Craig's desk and said, "Craig, I'm in a real bind to finish proofreading a report for Mr. Bailey. He needs it before a two o'clock staff meeting, so I wondered if you would help me proofread?" Craig had all of his essential work for the day completed, and he was working on some filing. "I'm awfully sorry," Craig replied, "but I really wanted to catch up on this filing." Joy was somewhat disturbed with Craig's answer, but she returned to her desk and finished the proofreading alone. Two days later, Craig's boss gave him a report to type and said it was needed by five o'clock. Craig knew that he would need help to finish the report, and because it was so urgent, he would need to ask someone who was familiar with that kind of report to help him. Joy was the only other stenographer in the office who was familiar with the report, but Craig was hesitant about asking her. Craig remembered how he had responded to Joy when she needed help, and he began to wonder whether he had behaved properly. Do you think Craig was right in refusing Joy? What do you think Craig should do about the situation he is faced with now?

IMPROVING LANGUAGE SKILLS

On a separate sheet of paper type the following sentences and insert punctuation marks where needed. Change the dollar and decimal fractions to numbers.

1. It was two pm when she finished reading the report which left her little time to drive to the airport for her 345 pm flight
2. We are studying the use of the comma
3. The letter bore the initials CRF
4. Dr Williams received his PhD at Kent State University
5. The total account was eleven dollars and twelve cents
6. The report was written in our office in Wasington D C on Mar 13 1978
7. She read the summary (pp 120–25) before writing the letter
8. His grade average was eighty-seven point five
9. R M Stone left town today
10. John T Rhodes recently won an award

IMPROVING ARITHMETIC SKILLS

You have an elite typewriter (12 spaces to an inch). There are 6 vertical typewriter spaces to an inch. On a separate sheet of paper answer the questions below.

1. Where would you set your left and right margin stops for an unbound report?
2. Where would you set your left and right margin stops for a side-bound report?
3. How many lines from the top would you go down to type the page number?
4. What is the center point for a report that will be bound at the side?
5. If a report is to be bound at the side, at what point would you start typing each of the following lines on the title page:

COST OF TRANSCRIBING MACHINES FOR HOME OFFICE
By
Jan Murray
January 11, 19--
Minneapolis, Minnesota

DEMONSTRATING OFFICE SKILLS

1. Type the following five items of information in the form of a title page for a report:
   (a) Title: RESEARCH REPORT ON WORD PROCESSING
   (b) For: Nigel Westoner, President of the Westoner Development Company
   (c) By: Walter A. Starr, Director of Research and Development
   (d) At: Indianapolis, Indiana
   (e) On: November 30, 19--
2. Using plain paper type the following TABLE OF CONTENTS with appropriate margins on a single page:

	Page
Letter of Transmittal	ii
Table of Contents	iii
List of Tables	iv
List of Charts	v
Summary	vi
Chapter	
I. Introduction	1
Prices	2
Outlook	3
Earnings and Dividends	4
Employment	5

3. Type the following paragraphs in manuscript form with indented paragraph headings.

Incorporating an Established Business. Owners of sole proprietorships or persons doing business as a partnership may wish to incorporate the business and continue its operations as a corporation. In such a case, the same type of information is provided in the application for a charter as that provided when a corporation is formed to promote a new business. Each subscriber to the capital stock of the corporation indicates on the subscription list the number of shares of stock subscribed to and the method of paying the subscription when the charter has been granted. The owner or owners of the established business usually take stock in payment for their interest in the business.

Goodwill. Frequently the incorporators of a corporation being formed to continue the operations of an established business will agree to pay the owner of the established business more than the value of his proprietary interest in the assets of the business as shown by the balance sheet. This excess value is known as goodwill. The incorporators agree to pay more for the assets of the business than the owner's proprietary interest because the owner has an established trade, and the customers he has served will continue as customers of the corporation.

4. Type the following page from an annual report to the stockholders. The page is to be typed double space with margins set for binding at the side. The heading is *Research and Development*.

The Corporation's long-standing emphasis on research and development continues to be directed to new products, to improved products, and to more economical processes and equipment. These activities, located at Yorktown Heights, New York, are conducted to assure the future success of the Corporation. The organization is composed of separate groups with personnel well trained in scientific fields related to the Corporation's business, that is, in chemistry, in physics, in engineering, and in textile technology. Each group has adequate up-to-date facilities and equipment to do modern research in fields of expanding technology. (¶) The combination of the various technical talents at one location enables groups to conduct coordinated research on new fibers and packaging films — and basic or exploratory research directed toward the discovery of new products. Through research the competitive position of fiberglass tires has been improved by developing a method of processing fiberglass so that it is flexible and strong. As a result of this development, passenger car tires have been made even more durable under difficult road conditions.

Part 3

Typing Financial Reports

When Sylvia Marsh first applied for a typing position in the Shelton Electric Company, she told the personnel director that she enjoyed working with numbers. She was given a job in the accounting department where she typed statistical data. Sylvia proved to be a very accurate and efficient typist, so one morning Ms. Finch, the Accounting Manager, asked Sylvia if she would like to begin typing financial statements and reports. "Sylvia," Ms. finch explained, "these financial statements and reports are vital to our organization because they tell us exactly how healthy and profitable our company is. They also help to point out the areas in our organization which are causing problems. Since many managerial decisions will be based upon the information contained in these reports, it is important that they be 100% accurate! Do you think you can handle this job?" "I would certainly do my best," Sylvia replied. She knew this new position would require even more concentration and skill than her present one, but she was excited about the chance to advance and become more valuable to her company.

Understanding Financial Reports

A business, like a person, at times, needs a checkup. The family doctor provides a check on the physical condition of a person. After examining the patient thoroughly, the doctor analyzes the findings and locates the cause of any physical problem the patient may have. The doctor is then able to prescribe medication for the problem.

Those who manage a business can discover the financial health of a business by studying reports called *financial reports*. The two reports common to all types of businesses which furnish the information necessary for management to determine the financial health of a business are the *balance sheet* and the *income statement*.

Balance Sheet

A balance sheet, like a physical examination, reveals whether a business is healthy on a particular date. Analysis of the main parts shown in the balance sheet on page 156 enables management to tell whether, on a specific date, the business is healthy or sick. These parts are (1) *assets* (what the business owns), (2) *liabilities* (what the business owes), and (3) *capital* or — the owners' share of the business.

On every balance sheet, the total assets always equal the total liabilities plus capital ($A = L + C$). The form of the balance sheet should make this basic bookkeeping equation clear to the reader. Double lines typed beneath the figure representing *Total Assets* and beneath the figure representing *Total Liabilities and Capital* attract the reader's attention so it is obvious at a glance that the figures are equal.

equation: a mathematical statement that shows equality

obvious: easily seen

Income Statement

The income statement shows the financial progress of the business. It shows how successful or unsuccessful a business has been during the period stated in the heading of the report: for example, "For the Year Ended December 31, 19--." Success is measured in terms of net income, or net profit. A *net profit* results when the income is greater than the expenses. A *net loss* occurs when the opposite happens.

Below the heading, the income statement shows in convenient form the income of the business, the cost of merchandise or services sold, the expenses, and the net income or net loss that resulted from the operation of the business during the fiscal period. The *fiscal period* is the time covered by the financial statement.

convenient: suitable; handy

The double lines beneath the last dollar amounts listed on page 157 make the Net Income $470,133 immediately noticeable to the reader. Since this is the most important number on the income statement, the emphasis is justified. By studying the remaining numbers in the same column, the reader can understand why and how the net income occurred. For more detailed information, study the remaining columns on the report.

Producing Typewritten Financial Statements

You will have several major responsibilities in producing final copies of the financial statements. If the statements are to be correct and pleasing in appearance, careful study and planning are necessary before you begin to type.

Study Previous Reports

Before you type any financial statements for your employer, it is a good idea to examine earlier copies of income statements and balance sheets in the company files. Because executives compare new financial statements with previous ones, they usually prefer that the same general form be followed year after year.

Check Accuracy of Calculations

With a calculating machine, check to make sure that the addition and subtraction shown on the rough draft submitted for typing are correct. It is also wise to verify, by machine, the accuracy of the addition and subtraction of the figures typed on the final typewritten product.

Illus. 4-17

Double check all calculations by machine to be sure that every typed figure in the final report is correct.

Type the Financial Statements

A look at the financial reports of several companies would show many similarities and only minor differences in style. Points of similarity might include the following:

1. *Use of descriptive titles to introduce groups of similar accounts.* For example, in the balance sheet on page 156, assets which, during the normal course of business operations, will be converted to cash are listed under the title Current Assets. Notice that the first letter of the first word and important words in these introductory titles are capitalized.

2. *Identations from the left to indicate subdivisions of larger units of information.* In the income statement on page 157, the depth of the horizontal indentations before federal income taxes and State income taxes indicates that both types of expense are of equal importance, and that both are subdivisions of a larger grouping labeled Operating Taxes. The additional depth of indentation before Current Taxes shows that it is a subdivision of Federal income taxes.

3. *Use of commas in the amount columns to separate each three digits, beginning to the left of the decimal point.* For example, in the income statement on page 157, the Local service figure for 1978 is $1,351,364.

4. *Vertical alignment of the decimal point in a column of figures.* Also, when one or more of the items in the amount columns indicate cents, every entry in any column should contain a decimal. For example:

$2,550.42
350.00
1,670.90
80.00

5. *Single line extending the width of the longest item in the column, typed beneath the last figure, to indicate addition or subtraction.*

6. *Double lines typed beneath figures at the bottom of the column to identify the final figure in a column.*

7. *Use of leaders (a line of either spaced or unspaced periods) to guide the reader's eye from the explanation column to the first column of amounts.* Leaders are especially necessary when the items in the explanation column vary widely in the amount of horizontal space used or when, on single spaced copy, there is so much space between the explanation column and the first amount column that it may be difficult to read across the page. Leaders should be aligned vertically on either even or odd spaces on the typewriter scale and should end at the same horizontal point.

8. *Information given in the heading of the financial statement.* Answers to each of the questions, Who?, What?, When?, should be given on separate lines in that order. The balance sheet should answer the question, When?, with a specific date; the income statement will answer it with a phrase which identifies the fiscal period covered.

9. *Use of the dollar sign with the first figure listed vertically in each amount column.* In the balance sheet on page 156, notice that in the first column the In service figure ($8,456,037) includes a dollar sign. Be sure to use a dollar sign with every figure which has double lines typed directly beneath it.

CENTENNIAL UTILITIES
Balance Sheet
December 31, 1979

Assets

	December 31, 1979	December 31, 1978
Plant:		
In service...........................	$8,456,037	$7,774,099
Under construction...................	344,383	296,399
Other (held for future use).........	4,874	3,914
	8,805,294	8,074,412
Less: Accumulated depreciation...	1,770,614	1,673,448
	7,034,680	6,400,964
Current Assets:		
Cash.................................	32,234	34,237
Receivables.........................	399,870	355,382
Material and supplies...............	41,289	30,329
Prepaid expenses....................	38,840	37,497
	512,233	457,445
Deferred Charges......................	85,908	69,224
Total Assets..........................	$7,632,821	$6,927,633

Liabilities and Capital

	December 31, 1979	December 31, 1978
Equity:		
Common shares--par value $13 1/7 per share................................	$2,408,399	$2,408,399
Preferred shares--par value $100 per share, 7% cumulative..............	82,000	82,000
Capital in excess of par value......	336,566	336,566
Reinvested earnings.................	553,289	476,159
	3,380,254	3,303,124
Long and Intermediate Term Debt........	3,197,000	2,647,000
Interim Debt..........................	128,481	246,050
Other Current Liabilities:		
Accounts payable....................	248,410	214,385
Advanced billing and customers' deposits...........................	58,041	50,949
Dividends payable...................	51,806	51,806
Interest accrued....................	48,494	42,732
Taxes accrued.......................	32,766	38,148
	439,517	398,020
Deferred Credits:		
Accumulated deferred income taxes...	339,021	209,996
Unamortized investment tax credits..	139,184	114,691
Other...............................	9,364	8,752
	487,569	333,439
Total Liabilities and Capital.........	$7,632,821	$6,927,633

Illus. 4-18   A balance sheet

CENTENNIAL UTILITIES
Income Statement
For Year Ended December 31, 1979

	Year 1979	Year 1978
Operating Revenues:		
Local service......................	$1,351,364	$1,213,285
Foreign service....................	1,500,990	1,365,028
Advertising........................	138,147	128,773
Less: Provision for uncollectibles.	31,061	25,738
Total operating revenues.......	2,959,440	2,681,348
Operating Expenses:		
Maintenance........................	657,404	610,182
Depreciation.......................	417,452	386,628
Customer services..................	500,491	452,303
Pensions and other employee benefits	234,907	210,797
Services received under License		
Contract.......................	30,308	25,216
Other operating expenses...........	173,786	154,811
Total operating expenses......	2,014,348	1,839,937
Net operating revenues........	945,092	841,411
Operating Taxes:		
Federal income taxes:		
Current........................	70,916	77,647
Deferred.......................	116,832	84,412
Investments tax credits.........	24,493	22,513
State income taxes:		
Current........................	23,482	20,607
Deferred.......................	12,193	5,812
Property, social security, and		
other taxes....................	227,043	217,304
Total operating taxes.........	474,959	428,295
Net income..................	$ 470,133	$ 413,116

Illus. 4-19   An income statement

The important guideline to apply for minor points of style is to *be consistent.* Apply the test of consistency when making decisions related to the following points:

1. *Vertical spacing.* When deciding whether to single-space or double-space within a financial statement, consider:
   (a) Length of statement relative to the amount of vertical space available. The common practice is to avoid, if possible, two-page financial statements.
   (b) Ease of reading. Those who analyze financial statements are normally top-management people who have many demands on their time, attention, and efforts. Blank vertical lines scattered among single-space copy attract attention; therefore, use them for emphasizing especially important figures.
2. *Capitalization.*
   (a) In the heading. Some executives prefer that the entire heading of financial statements be typed in all capitals; others require all capitals for only the name of the business. The current trend seems to be away from the practice of using all capitals for every word in the heading of a financial statement.
   (b) In the explanation column. A common practice is to capitalize the first letter of the first word and each important word included in the explanation column. However, some executives prefer that only the first character of an account title be capitalized. (This practice is followed in both the income statement on page 157 and the balance sheet on page 156.)
3. *Colon.* A colon following a title is used to introduce like accounts (for example, on the income statement a colon following Operating Revenues). The colon indicates that a listing follows.
4. *Indentations.* The depth of the indentations depends on the amount of horizontal space available in relation to the number of horizontal spaces needed to type the necessary columns across the page. The important thing to remember is that categories of equal importance (such as Maintenance and Depreciation on the income statement on page 157) should be indented the same number of spaces.

Proofread the Final Product

Proofreading is easier, faster, and more accurate if the person reading the final typewritten product does not have to glance back and forth from the original to the copy being proofread. Either (1) ask another worker in the office to help — choose one who is particularly good at noticing details, or (2) dictate from the original copy onto a dictating machine and then check the final draft as you listen carefully to the recording.

The oral reader should be careful to indicate all capitalization, punctuation, use of dollar signs in figure columns, underscores, blank vertical spacing, and depth of indentations. Unless emphasized orally, these details are likely to be overlooked by the proofreader.

A common technique for proofreading columns of dollar amounts is to read down the columns, rather than across the columns.

File Carbon Copy of Final Draft

Before filing, on the copy write the name of the person responsible for the original preparation of the financial statement. Some executives require that the rough draft original submitted to a typist be filed along with the carbon copy of the final typewritten product.

REVIEWING IMPORTANT POINTS

1. What two financial reports help a business determine its financial situation?
2. Name three kinds of information contained in a balance sheet.
3. What basic bookkeeping equation should be obvious to one looking at a typed balance sheet?
4. What is the purpose of the income statement?
5. What is *net profit*?
6. Why do businesses ordinarily prefer that financial reports follow the same basic form, or design, year after year?
7. What major responsibilities might a typist have in producing final copies of the financial report?
8. What is the fastest and most accurate way for a typist to check the figures in a financial report?
9. What is the most important guideline to remember when making a decision on typing style?
10. How can a typist speed up the proofreading process?

MAKING IMPORTANT DECISIONS

1. Some people believe that the person who typed the final copy of the financial report should proofread while a second person reads out loud from the original. Others believe that the person who typed the final copy should be the oral reader and a second person, one unfamiliar with the copy, should do the proofreading on the final copy. Which is your choice and why?

2. Norm usually checks the accuracy of any calculations on financial reports with his calculator. However, today his machine is out of the office for repairs, and he has a financial report which needs to be proofread and sent out. Since he does not have a calculator, Norm decides to forget this part of the proofreading. The calculations on these financial reports are rarely wrong anyway. What do you think of Norm's decision?

LEARNING TO WORK WITH OTHERS

Because you are a fast and efficient proofreader, Mr. Sizemore often asks you to proofread the financial reports prepared by others in the office. While proofreading an annual report being compiled for the company's stockholders, you discover a wrong figure. You immediately report the error to Dan, the typist who typed the report. Dan listens to you, but doesn't really seem concerned about his mistake. What could you say to emphasize the importance of complete accuracy in preparing financial reports?

IMPROVING LANGUAGE SKILLS

Three important uses of the colon are:

A. To introduce a long or formal direct quotation.

   Example: The presiding officer began with these words: "It is on an occasion such as this that we must all remember that we are bound by ties of loyalty, tradition, and learning."

B. To introduce a number of examples or a formal list of any sort which contains a *summarizing* word.

   Example: The teacher introduced the following marks of punctuation: period, quotation mark, colon, and semicolon.

C. To introduce an independent sentence or clause when the second gives an illustration of a general statement in the first.

   Example: The purpose of a newspaper should be twofold: It should be the friend of all that is good and the foe of all that is evil.

Type the following sentences on a separate sheet of paper and insert colons where necessary according to the above rules.

1. Her original contention was justified that in time those who study, prepare their assignments, and apply themselves to their classes will receive good grades and be prepared to accept positions in business offices.

2. The Head of the Board began his address by saying it is with deep emotion that I must submit my resignation effective June 30, since the United States Government has requested that I direct an organization in South America dedicated to relieving poverty in Peru and bordering countries.
3. We learned that the following six terms are found on the balance sheet current assets, fixed assets, current liabilities, long-term liabilities, capital stock, and retained earnings.
4. Bring with you the income statement, the balance sheet, the December monthly report, and the sales and production figures for January to date.
5. Every detail indicated that Mary was interrupted at her work and intended to return to it the uncovered calculator, the unfinished income statement in her typewriter, the totaled columns of figures on her desk, the uncapped pen.

IMPROVING ARITHMETIC SKILLS

You are responsible for obtaining enough reams of paper from the stockroom to run off a report which will be sent to a variety of stockholders, company officials, and other interested persons. The report is 26 pages long, and you have determined that you will need 110 copies of the report. However, all of the reports will not include the entire 26 pages. Out of the 110 copies of the report, 55 will contain all 26 pages, 40 will contain only the first 20 pages, and 15 will contain only the first 10 pages. How many reams of paper will you need for this job? (A ream of paper contains 500 sheets.)

DEMONSTRATING OFFICE SKILLS

1. From the following data prepare a balance sheet for Fulton Enterprises as of December 31, 1979. Using plain paper, type the balance sheet in the same form as the illustration on page 156. Use a calculator to verify totals. (The first set of figures in each category represents 1979 figures; the second set, 1978.)

Assets:

```
Plant:  In service $6,574,099     $7,256,027
        Under construction $96,399     $44,383
        Other (held for future use) $13,914     $14,874
        (total):  $6,684,412     $7,315,284
        Less: Accumulated depreciation $673,448     $770,614
        (total):  $6,010,964     $6,544,670
```

Current Assets: Cash $16,237 $162,234
                 Receivables $455,382 $499,870
                 Material and supplies $20,329 $31,289
                 Prepaid expenses $27,497 $28,840
                 (total): $519,445 $722,233
Deferred Charges: $169,224 $185,908
Total Assets: $6,699,633 $7,452,811

Liabilities and Capital:

Equity: Common shares — par value $13¹/₇ per share
         $2,308,399 $2,308,399
         Preferred shares — par value $100 per share,
         7% cumulative $72,000 $72,000
         Capital in excess of par value $236,566 $236,566
         Reinvested earnings $576,159 $653,289
         (total): $3,193,124 $3,270,254
Long and Intermediate Term Debt: $1,840,331 $3,147,000
Interim Debt: $546,050 $428,481
Other Current Liabilities: Accounts payable $14,385 $48,410
                            Advanced billing and customers' de-
                            posits $60,949 $68,041
                            Dividends payable $41,806 $41,806
                            Interest accrued $32,732 $38,494
                            Taxes accrued $48,148 $42,766
                            (total): $198,020 $239,517
Deferred Credits: Accumulated deferred income taxes
                   $109,006 $239,011
                   Unamortized investment tax credits
                   $104,691 $109,184
                   Other $18,752 $19,364
                   (total): $233,439 $367,559
Total Liabilities and Capital: $6,010,964 $7,452,811

2. From the following data prepare an income statement for Fulton
Enterprises for the year ending December 31, 1979. Using plain
paper, type the income statement in the same form as the illustration on page 157. Use a calculator to verify totals. (The first set of
figures in each category represents 1979 figures; the second, 1978.)
Operating Revenues: Local service $1,451,364 $1,313,285
                     Foreign service $500,990 $365,028
                     Advertising $138,147 $128,773
                     Less: Provision for uncollectibles
                     $71,061 $65,738
                     Total operating revenues
                     $2,019,440 $1,741,348

Operating Expenses: Maintenance $607,404 $560,182
Depreciation $317,452 $186,628
Customer services $50,491 $52,303
Pensions and other employee benefits
    $434,907 $310,797
Services received under License Contract
    $50,308 $85,216
Other operating expenses $273,786 $254,811
    Total operating expenses
        $1,734,348 $1,449,937
    Net operating revenues
        $285,092 $291,411

Operating Taxes: Federal income taxes:
    Current $90,916 $97,647
    Deferred $16,832 $24,412
    Investments tax credits $24,493 $22,513
State income taxes:
    Current $3,482 $2,607
    Deferred $2,193 $2,812
Property, social security, and other taxes
    $27,043 $37,304
        Total operating taxes $164,959 $187,295
        Net income $120,133 $104,116

Part 4

Typing Legal Papers

Mr. Bert Kyle began working for Taylor, Holland, and Motley attorneys-at-law in a work-study program while he was in high school. After he graduated, Mr. Kyle continued working for the firm full time. He is learning a lot about the legal profession by transcribing a wide variety of legal documents from a transcribing machine. Mr. Kyle looks forward to typing the different contracts, wills, deeds, and leases that have been dictated by the attorneys. He realizes that he has a great responsibility to his employers to type error-free documents and also a great responsibility to the clients to keep all information confidential. Mr. Kyle finds his work very interesting and he enjoys the challenge of being a fast and accurate typist.

Legal Papers

legal:
relating to law

documents:
official papers

There are various kinds of **legal** papers, or **documents** — contracts, wills, deeds, leases, affidavits, powers of attorney. Some may be typewritten; others are printed and merely require filling in various blanks to complete them. Some require the services of a notary public; others require witnesses only. At some time or other you will probably be called upon to type or complete a legal document.

Typewritten Legal Papers

Legal documents may be typed on standard 8½" × 11" paper, however, most are typed on legal size paper which is 8½ inches wide and may vary from 13 to 15 inches in length. This paper may have printed left and right margin lines. The left margin rule is usually a double line; the right margin, a single line. In typing material on legal paper with printed margin rules, you should set the margin stops on your typewriter so that the margins of typewritten material will be at least two spaces within the printed margin lines. If paper without printed margin rules is used for typing a legal paper, you should allow a 1½-inch left margin and a ½-inch right margin. Minimum margins of 2 inches at the top and 1 inch at the bottom are usually allowed. You should prepare enough carbon copies of all legal papers so that each person interested in the paper will have a copy, including at least one copy for the lawyer and one for the court record. An example of a typewritten legal document is shown on page 169. Note particularly the space between the printed margin lines and the left and right margins of the typewritten material, the spacing (triple spacing between the title and the first line, double spacing thereafter), the use of all capitals for certain words in the contract, the punctuation, and the arrangement of the closing lines.

Spacing. Typewritten legal documents are usually double-spaced, but you may single-space some of them, including wills and *affidavits* (sworn statements in writing made under oath).

A type of legal paper may be purchased with consecutive numbers printed down the page at the left of the printed left margin line. The number "1" is approximately two inches from the top edge and indicates the postion of the typewritten title. The other numbers indicate the positions of the typewritten lines of material and make possible easy reference to any particular part of the legal paper when its contents are being discussed. If the legal paper used does not contain these printed numbers, and if your employer wants to have such numbers on the completed document, it will be a simple matter for you to type them as you type the document.

Erasures. Because a legal paper states the rights or privileges and duties or obligations of the parties who sign it, and later may be **submitted** in a

submitted:
presented; offered

Illus. 4-20

Some corrections will require retyping a legal document.

court of law as evidence, you should prepare each paper accurately and proofread it carefully. You may erase and correct some errors in typing legal papers; others may not be corrected. If the error and erasure affect only one or two letters in a relatively unimportant word, you may erase and make the correction. If, on the other hand, the error you make involves a word which might be important to the meaning of the part of the contract — substituting the word *may* for *must,* for example — or, if an error involves an amount of money, name, or date, the erasure should not be made but the complete paper should be retyped. In some cases, however, such corrections may be made if the corrected paper is initialed by all parties. If you are in doubt, you should ask your employer if it is necessary to retype the legal paper or if it is permissible to erase and correct the error.

Numbers, Dates, and Titles. Quantities in legal documents are usually written in both words and figures, as follows:

A scholarship of one thousand dollars ($1,000)
Under the terms of the will they will receive five thousand (5,000) dollars
A twenty (20) year mortgage
Fifty (50) shares of Exxon common stock
Five (5) percent interest

Dates are written in several forms. No one form, however, is more legal than another; therefore, there is no reason why you should not type a date in a legal form as you would type it in a letter. Variations are:

On this, the third day of November, 19—
This 16th day of June in the year 19—
This sixteenth day of June, in the year of our Lord, one thousand nine hundred and seventy-seven

Personal titles — Miss, Mr., Mrs. Ms. — are not used with names in legal documents. Professional titles — Dr., Prof. — are not ordinarily used either.

Printed Legal Forms

Legal documents may be prepared by typing the necessary information on a printed legal form. Standard forms for bills of sale, deeds, leases, mortgages, and wills may be purchased in stationery stores. However, important legal documents, even though they are on a printed form, should be checked by a lawyer.

When typing on printed legal forms, if the item of information that is filled in is important, such as a sum of money, the space that remains on either side of the item after it is typed should be filled in with hyphens. This eliminates the possibility of figures, letters, or words being added later to change the meaning of the typewritten insertion.

The same margins used for the printed matter should be used for the typewritten matter. When carbon copies are prepared, the position of the printed matter on each copy must be checked carefully so that the typewritten additions will appear in the proper places on all copies. Unless this check is made, the typewritten matter on a carbon copy may be written over some of the printed matter, and the copy may be illegible.

Notarized Legal Papers

Many legal documents are notarized. This means a signed statement is added by a *notary public* (a public official **authorized** by the state) to show that the paper has been signed in the notary's presence and that the signers have sworn that they are the same persons referred to in the document. The statement by the notary public usually is shown at the bottom of the same paper on which the legal document is typed. It may be shown on a separate page, however, if there is no room for it on the page that contains the legal material.

authorized:
given right or power

SINGLE ACKNOWLEDGEMENT

THE STATE OF TEXAS,
COUNTY OF ....*Bexar*.................... }   BEFORE ME, the undersigned authority,
in and for said County, Texas, on this day personally appeared ....*Don Knight and*............................
Nancy Knight..
....
known to me to be the person..*S*..whose name...*S*......subscribed to the foregoing instrument, and acknowledged to me
that *T*..he*y*.executed the same for the purposes and consideration therein expressed.
    GIVEN UNDER MY HAND AND SEAL OF OFFICE, This..*7th*....day of...*Friday*........................,A.D. 19.---.
    (L.S.)   *Vicky Raines*..
                    Notary Public............*Bexar*...........,County, Texas
                    My Commission Expires June 1, 19...---......

Illus. 4-21

Statement of a notary public

Do not be surprised if your employer wishes you to become a notary public. In large offices one of the employees usually acts in this **capacity**. In an office building containing a number of small offices, an employee in one of them may act as a notary public for all offices in the building.

capacity:
position to carry out a duty

The laws for becoming a notary public differ in the various states. In many states an application accompanied by statements that show that the applicant is a citizen and a resident of the state, of the required age, and of good character is submitted to the governor's office. If the application is granted, the notary public secures a notary's seal, which is a

embosses:
imprints by raising the surface of the paper

metal, hand-operated instrument that embosses on a legal paper the design of a seal containing the name of the notary. A notary's commission lasts for a limited period of time, usually for two years, but it may be renewed.

Typical Legal Documents

A discussion of a simple contract, a will, a deed, a lease, an affidavit, and a power of attorney — legal papers that are frequently prepared in a business office — will explain how to type legal papers.

Simple Contract. A *contract* is an agreement that can be enforced at law. It creates legal rights and responsibilities. It may be either oral or written; however, some contracts, such as those for the purchase of real estate, must be in writing. Before you type a contract, you should check to see that it includes the following essential information:

1. The date and the place of the agreement.
2. The names of the parties entering into the agreement.
3. The purpose of the contract.
4. The duties of each party.
5. The money, services, or goods given in consideration of the contract.
6. The time period.
7. The signatures of all the parties.

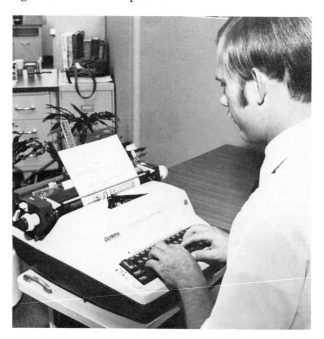

Illus. 4-22

Contracts are one type of legal document the clerical office worker may encounter.

```
                    AGENCY  CONTRACT

          This  agreement,  made  and  entered  into  on  this,  the  tenth
    day  of  May,  19--,  by  and  between  TRAMMEL  TRADE  COMPANY,  a  corporation
    of  Toledo,  Ohio,  the  party  of  the  first  part,  and  Marvin  Partain,
    of  Enid,  Oklahoma,  the  party  of  the  second  part,
          WITNESSETH:    That,  whereas,  the  party  of  the  first  part
    is  about  to  open  a  branch  office  to  be  located  in  Dallas,  Texas,
    for  the  sale  of  its  products,  the  said  party  of  the  first  part
    hereby  engages  the  services  of  Marvin  Partain,  the  party  of  the
    second  part,  as  manager  of  that  office.
          The  party  of  the  first  part  hereby  agrees  to  pay  the
```

Illus. 4-23

A simple contract
typed on legal paper

```
    first  part  from  time  to  time.
          IN  WITNESS  WHEREOF,  The  parties  have  hereunto  affixed
    their  hands  and  seals  on  the  day  and  in  the  year  first  above
    written.
                              TRAMMEL  TRADE  COMPANY
    Witnesses:

    Barbara Davis                    Julian Hooper  (Seal)
    ─────────────                    ─────────────
                                     President
                                Party  of  the  First  Part

    Paul Forest                      Marvin Partain  (Seal)
    ─────────────                    ─────────────
                                Party  of  the  Second  Part
```

The illustration above shows parts of a simple contract prepared on legal paper with printed margin lines.

Will. A *will* is a legal document which provides for the distribution of a person's property after death. The person who makes the will is the *testator* (man) or *testatrix* (woman). The testator or testatrix may designate an *executor* (man) or *executrix* (woman) to probate the will; that is, prove its

LAST WILL AND TESTAMENT OF CARL THOMAS RIEDEL

I, CARL THOMAS RIEDEL, of the County of Harris, State of Texas, being of sound and disposing mind and memory, and above the age of eighteen (18) years and lawfully married to THELMA JOYCE RIEDEL, do make, declare and publish this my Last Will and Testament revoking all Wills and Codicils previously made by me.

First: I direct that all of my just debts and funeral expenses

be paid out of my estate as soon as they can be conveniently done without the unnecessary sacrifice of any properties of my estate by my Executrix or Executor, as the case may be, hereinafter appointed.

Illus. 4-24

The format of a will

IN WITNESS WHEREOF I have hereunto set my hand at Houston, Texas, hereby declaring this to be my Last Will and Testament, on this the 13th day of September, A D., 19--.

Carl Thomas Riedel
Carl Thomas Riedel
Testator

The above instrument was now here published as his Last Will, and signed and subscribed by CARL THOMAS RIEDEL, the Testator, in our presence and we, at his request, in his presence, and the presence of each other, sign and subscribe our names thereto as attesting witnesses.

Paul F. Vetter
Witness

Nancy Klosterman
Witness

SUBSCRIBED and ACKNOWLEDGED before me by the said CARL THOMAS RIEDEL, Testator and subscribed and sworn to before me by the said witnesses, this the 13th day of September, A.D., 19--.

Margaret Neeld
Notary Public, Harris County,
Texas

validity:
legal force or
effectiveness

provisions:
requests; terms

real:
in law, fixed or
permanent

validity to the court for the purpose of carrying out its provisions. Making a will is a technical matter and should be entrusted only to a qualified attorney. Illustration 4–24 shows a properly prepared and correctly typed will.

Deed. A *deed* is a formal written instrument by which title to real property is transferred from one person to another. All of the details of the

This Lease Witnesseth:

THAT Bruce D. Damson and Denise L. Damson, husband and wife,

HEREBY LEASE TO Charles L. Burroughs

the premises situate in the City *of* Miami *in the County of*

Dade *and State of* Florida *described as follows:*

Building to be used as a restaurant located at 4531 Collins
Avenue, Pensacola, Florida

with the appurtenances thereto, for the term of ten (10) years *commencing*

June 1, *19 __ at a rental of* Seven hundred fifty (750)

dollars per month *, payable* monthly.

      SAID LESSEE AGREES *to pay said rent, unless said premises shall be destroyed or rendered untenantable by fire or other unavoidable accident; to not commit or suffer waste; to not use said premises for any unlawful purpose; to not assign this lease, or underlet said premises, or any part thereof, or permit the sale of* his *interest herein by legal process, without the written consent of said lessor* s*; to not use said premises or any part thereof in violation of any law relating to intoxicating liquors; and at the expiration of this lease, to surrender said premises in as good condition as they now are, or may be put by said lessor* s*, reasonable wear and unavoidable casualties, condemnation or appropriation excepted. Upon nonpayment of any of said rent for* thirty *days, after it shall become due, and without demand made therefor; or if said lessee or any assignee of this lease shall make an assignment for the benefit of his creditors; or if proceedings in bankruptcy shall be instituted by or against lessee or any assignee; or if a receiver or trustee be appointed for the property of the lessee or any assignee; or if this lease by operation of law pass to any person or persons; or if said lessee or any assignee shall fail to keep any of the other covenants of this lease, it shall be lawful for said lessor* s*,* their *heirs or assigns, into said premises to reenter, and the same to have again, repossess and enjoy, as in* their*first and former estate; and thereupon this lease and everything herein contained on the said lessor* s*'behalf to be done and performed, shall cease, determine, and be utterly void*

      SAID LESSORS AGREE *(said lessee having performed* his *obligations under this lease) that said lessee shall quietly hold and occupy said premises during said term without any hindrance or molestation by said lessor* s*,* their *heir or any person lawfully claiming under them.*

      Signed this first *day of* May *A. D. 19 __*

IN THE PRESENCE OF:

Mark Patterson	*Bruce D. Damson*
Richard Markay	*Denise L. Damson*
	Eugene R. Hooper

Illus. 4-25

Lease

transaction should be approved by a lawyer before the deed is registered with the proper government agency.

Lease. A *lease* is a contract by which one party gives to another the use of real or personal property for a fixed price. This relationship exists when one person, the *lessee*, under an express or implied agreement, is given possession and control of the property of another, the *lessor*. The amount given by the lessee is called *rent* (for real property) or *consideration* (for personal property).

The lease shown on page 171 illustrates the typing problems involved in completing a printed form for a legal document. Observe where typewritten material has been inserted, the method of indicating the amount in words and figures, and the completion of certain words by adding letters that keep the sentences containing those words consistently in plural form.

Affidavit. An *affidavit* is a written statement made under oath that the facts set forth are sworn to be true and correct. It must be sworn to before a proper official, such as a judge, justice of the peace, or a notary.

Power of Attorney. A *power of attorney* is a legal document authorizing one person to act as the attorney or agent of another person, called the grantor. The power of attorney may be given to a trusted employee by the employer. This power enables the employee to act for the employer. It may authorize the employee to sign checks and other legal documents for the employer. The power of attorney **specifies** the acts which the agent is authorized to perform for the **principal**. It may be granted for an indefinite period, for a specific period, or for a specific purpose only. It must be signed by the principal and should be notarized.

specifies:
names

principal:
person giving
instructions or having
authority

REVIEWING IMPORTANT POINTS

1. How does legal paper differ from other paper used in business?
2. What are the minimum margins usually allowed on typewritten legal paper?
3. How many carbon copies should be made of legal documents?
4. What is the advantage of using legal paper on which the lines are numbered?
5. What type of error may be erased and corrected in a legal paper?
6. How are quantities usually written in legal papers?
7. How can a typist eliminate the possibility of figures or words being added later which would change the meaning of a typewritten insertion in a legal form?
8. What is meant by the term *notarized*?
9. What information should a contract contain?
10. What is a deed?

MAKING IMPORTANT DECISIONS

Sherri has worked for Ms. Annell Petersen, corporate lawyer for Hamilton Industries, for five months. On Monday morning Ms. Petersen asked Sherri to prepare a contract that would be signed by executives from three corporations that afternoon. The contract included many provisions with dates and statistics and was quite lengthy. When Sherri got to the end of the second page, she realized that she had typed "July" rather than "June" in some instances. Sherri went back and corrected her errors. She observed that the only way one could tell there had been errors was by holding the paper up to the light. Sherri was proud of her corrections and submitted the contract to Ms. Petersen for signatures that afternoon. Do you believe Sherri made the right decision? Why?

LEARNING TO WORK WITH OTHERS

As a typist in the legal department of a firm, Ms. Stephens types contracts, wills, and other documents which contain a great deal of confidential information. She understands the importance of secrecy about such information and never discusses such matters with anyone else. While having lunch with Mr. Phillips, a new member of the firm's stenographic pool, Ms. Stephens is surprised when Mr. Phillips casually comments about the terms of a contract drawn up by the firm. What is Ms. Stephens' responsibility in this situation?

IMPROVING LANGUAGE SKILLS

There are four important usages for parentheses ( ):

A. To enclose figures or letters in a series of enumerated elements.

> **Example:** Miss Jefferson asked for three things: (1) the contract, (2) the reference book on contract law, and (3) the addresses of the persons who signed the contract.

B. To enclose figures verifying a number which is written in words.

> **Example:** The agreement specified that twenty thousand dollars ($20,000) would be paid yearly for the use of the building.

C. To enclose matter that is only indirectly related to the main thought of the sentence.

> **Example:** At 3:30 p.m. (the time agreed upon at the conference the evening before) the meeting began.

D. To enclose matter introduced as an explanation.

> **Example:** He told her to check the *Federal Reserve Bulletin* (March, 1971) page 103 for a review of the case.

Type the following sentences and insert parentheses where they are needed.

1. You may name an executor man or an executrix woman to probate your will.
2. Some typical legal documents are: a a will, b a deed, c a lease, and d a power of attorney.
3. The amount given by the lessee is called *rent* for real property or *consideration* for personal property.
4. The lease specified that for a term of eight 8 years rent was to be three hundred fifty 350 dollars a month payable monthly.
5. She left at 4:30 she had told them she would leave at 3:30, but she arrived at the airport in time to get on the plane.

IMPROVING ARITHMETIC SKILLS

Jim Jansen has worked in a law office a number of years. His employer has asked Jim to prepare a schedule of payments for a lease agreement. The lessee agrees to pay rent monthly for a leased building at the rate of $10 a day for one year, beginning January 1 of next year. Rent is due in advance on the first day of each month. On a separate sheet of paper prepare a schedule showing each month's payment.

DEMONSTRATING OFFICE SKILLS

1. Type the lease below on legal paper, making one carbon copy. Use the current date. If ruled legal paper is not available, rule in ink the necessary vertical lines on regular 8½ " × 11" paper. Use a one-inch top margin.

LEASE AGREEMENT

This agreement of lease, entered into this _____ day of _____, 19--, by and between George Cain hereinafter called Lessor, and Mr. and Mrs. Tom Irwin hereinafter called Lessee,

WITNESSETH:

Lessor does hereby rent and lease unto Lessee that certain furnished/unfurnished apartment designated as Apartment A, within an Apartment House known as Cedar Lake Apartments, located at 3920 Harmony in Randall County, Texas for the term of six months commencing December 8, 19--, and ending May 8, 19--, to be used by Lessee as a private residence and not otherwise, Lessee paying therefore the sum of eighteen hundred dollars ($1,800), payable three hundred dollars ($300) per month in advance on the first day of each month, as the same shall fall due to Lessor at 6739 Salem, Amarillo, Randall County, Texas.

The rental from the date of execution of this contract to the first day of the following month is three hundred dollars ($300) payable upon tenants taking possession. This includes all utilities.

At the end or other expiration of the terms, Lessee shall deliver up the demised premises in good order and condition, reasonable deterioration, damage by fire, tornado, or other casualty and the elements only excepted.

Lessee agrees to give access to Lessor or his agent within reasonable hours in order to show said premises for rent, sale, repair or inspection, as well as access to repairers for the purpose of maintaining said property. WITNESS, THE SIGNATURE OF THE PARTIES HERETO IN DUPICATE, THIS _____ DAY OF _____, 19--.

Lessee: _____   Lessor: _____

2. Type one original and one carbon copy of this will following the form on page 170. If ruled legal paper is not available, rule in ink the necessary vertical lines on regular 8½" × 11" paper.

LAST WILL AND TESTAMENT OF ROBERT LEWIS JONES

I, ROBERT LEWIS JONES, of Ada County, Idaho, do make, publish and declare this to be my Last Will and Testament, hereby revoking all Wills and Codicils previously made by me.

I hereby give, devise and bequeath my entire estate of every kind and character as follows: (a) To my wife, Linda Jones, my entire estate, if she survives. (b) If my wife shall not survive me, my entire estate shall be distributed, subject to the provisions of paragraph 2, to my then surviving issue, per stirpes. At the present time, my issue consists of my son, Ted R. Jones; my daughter, Lisa J. Jones; and my daughter, Jeanie A. Jones.

In the event that any share of my estate, or any share of a trust created under this Will shall otherwise be distributed at my death or upon the termination of such trust to a beneficiary who has not attained the age of twenty-three (23) years, such share shall be held by the Trustee as a separate and distinct trust for such person until such person attains the age of twenty-three (23) years, at which time that trust shall terminate and the trust estate shall be distributed outright to such person, but if such person shall die prior to attaining the age of twenty-three (23) years, upon such person's death such trust shall terminate and the trust estate shall be distributed to such person's issue, but if none of such person's issue is then living to such person's then surviving brothers and sisters in equal shares, if none, to my then surviving issue, per stirpes.

In any event, and anything to the contrary notwithstanding, any trust created herein shall terminate upon the expiration of twenty-one (21) years after the death of the last to die of my wife and such of my issue as are living at the date of my death. Upon such termination the trust estate shall be distributed, free and clear of trust, to the beneficiary who is entitled to such trust estate.

No Trustee shall be liable for decreases in value or other losses, save and except only those which occur by reason of the Trustee's intentional misconduct, fraud, or gross negligence.

No part of any trust estate, under any circumstances, shall ever be liable for or charged with any of the debts, liabilities or obligations of the beneficiary or subject to seizure by any claimant or creditor of the beneficiary. The beneficiary, under any circumstances, shall not have the power to assign, convey, pledge, charge or otherwise encumber or in any manner anticipate or dispose of his or her interest in any trust estate until the same shall have been actually transferred, conveyed or paid over to him or her, free and clear of such trust.

I direct that all my just debts, funeral expenses and expenses in connection with my estate be paid as soon as practicable after my death.

The revenues, receipts, proceeds, disbursements, expenses, deductions, accruals or losses of each trust shall be allocated or apportioned between corpus and income in the discretion of the Trustee, and the determination of the Trustee need not necessarily be in accordance with the provisions of the Idaho Trust Act, which shall control only if such discretion is not exercised by the Trustee.

The Trustee herein provided for shall have and is hereby granted the powers and authority vested in Trustees under the Idaho Trust Act as the same now exists, or as it shall hereinafter be amended. In addition thereto, but not by way of limitation, my Trustee shall hold, manage, control, use, invest and reinvest, sell, exchange, encumber and lease the trust estate in the sole discretion of the Trustee in all things and under all circumstances, and to the same extent as if the Trustee was the owner thereof in fee simple, and all rights and privileges and powers given the Trustee may be exercised without application to any Court.

I hereby appoint my wife, Linda Jones, Independent Executrix under this Will and of my estate. In the event my wife should fail or cease to act, for any reason, I hereby appoint my sister, Lynn Smiley, as Independent Executrix under this Will and of my estate, and Trustee of all trusts created herein. In the event Lynn Smiley shall fail or cease to act, for any reason, I hereby appoint my brother, Leonard Donald Jones, as Independent Executor under this Will and of my estate, and Trustee of all trusts created herein. In the event Leonard Donald Jones shall fail or cease to act, for any reason, I hereby appoint my cousin, Joyce Fields, as Independent Executrix under this Will and of my estate, and Trustee of all trusts created herein. In the event Joyce Fields shall fail or cease to act, for any reason, I hereby appoint NORTHWESTERN NATIONAL BANK of

Boise, Idaho, as Independent Executor under this Will and of my estate and Trustee of all trusts created herein, provided however, that any of the individuals appointed above, while acting as Trustee, may appoint another bank to act as successor Trustee in place of the NORTHWESTERN BANK of Boise, Idaho. No bond or other security shall be required of any Executor or Trustee and the Executor shall be independent of the supervision and direction of the Probate Court to the full extent permitted by law. I direct that no action shall be had in any court of probate jurisdiction in connection with this Will and the administration and settlement of my estate other than the probating and recording of this Will and the return of an inventory, appraisement and list of claims as provided by law. All references to Executor in this Will shall refer also to the Executrix then acting under the terms of this Will. In addition to having all the powers of an Independent Executor under the law of Idaho, the Executor shall have all the powers given the Trustee herein.

In the event my wife predeceases me or in the event of a common disaster, I hereby appoint my sister, Lynn Smiley, as guardian of the person of each of my surviving minor children. In the event that my sister fails or ceases to act, I appoint my brother, Leonard Donald Jones, as guardian of the person of each of my minor children. In the event that both my sister and brother fail or cease to act as guardian, I appoint my cousin, Joyce Fields, as guardian of the person of each of my minor children. I direct that no bond be required of any of the above named guardians.

I hereby bequeath and donate my body to the WESTERN UNIVERSITY SCHOOL OF MEDICINE for the advancement of medical science and /or any parts of my body as replacements to aid living persons.

IN TESTIMONY WHEREOF, I have signed my name to this my Last Will and Testament at Boise, Idaho, on this the _____ day of _____, 19--.

_____
Robert Lewis Jones

The above instrument was now here published as his Last Will, and signed and subscribed by ROBERT LEWIS JONES, the Testator, in our presence and we, at his request, in his presence, and the presence of each other, sign and subscribe our names thereto as attesting witnesses.

_____
Witness

_____
Witness

SUBSCRIBED and ACKNOWLEDGED before me by the said ROBERT LEWIS JONES, Testator and subscribed and sworn to before me by the said witnesses, this the _____ day of _____, 19––.

_____

Notary Public, Ada County, Idaho

IMPROVING OFFICE SKILLS (Optional)

Using plain paper, type the following report with footnotes as page 4 of side-bound report.

where to look for information.[1] Communicating information in a report is not an easy task because of the vast amount of information that is usually covered. An effective report has no unnecessary words or sentences. If you simplify your writing so that your reader will have a clear understanding of all the terms you use, your report will be much more meaningful. Choosing just the right words to express your thoughts is imperative in conveying a clear message.[2]

In composing reports, you should try to use everyday language. Visualize yourself talking face-to-face with your reader, and try to use the actual words you would employ in normal conversation. Use the simplest words you know which will convey the thought clearly.[3]

Give your reports personality by using words which are strong and vigorous. However, avoid using many adjectives and adverbs because they take the reader's attention away from the important nouns and verbs. Avoid words which are fuzzy and have vague meanings. Stick to concrete words, which are usually short, familiar words.[4]

Since verbs are the strongest parts of speech, make frequent use of active-voice verbs in your report writing. Use your words economically in composing sentences which are concise.

[1]Gilbert C. Stone, *Using Business Reference Books* (3rd ed., Seattle: Western Publishing Co., 1977), p. 15.
[2]Robert D. Maxwell and Arthur M. Woodward, *Report Writing* (4th ed., Seattle: Western Publishing Co., 1977), pp. 221–222.
[3]*Ibid.*, p. 238.
[4]Stone, *op. cit.*, pp. 42–45.

5

Meeting the Public

Part 1

Receiving Callers

Tiffany Lawton works as a receptionist/typist in a large, international advertising agency on Madison Avenue in New York City. She was hired for her job when she graduated from high school a few months ago. She finds her job very interesting. All the clients and visitors come by her desk; she knows how to take care of them promptly and graciously. She maintains a master calendar for the senior account executives who are very busy people. She likes the demands of her job and feels she is in a position where she can learn all about the company, which means she will have opportunities for advancement.

Person-to-Person Meetings

transacted:
performed; conducted

You are aware that much business is **transacted** in person. You have undoubtedly seen the receptionist who handles appointments in a dentist's or doctor's office or clinic, or you have been helped by a receptionist/clerk at a local delivery office. Office workers who greet the public are found in all kinds of organizations. They provide valuable assistance and are the link between the company and the public.

Special Skills and Abilities of Receptionists

Receptionists must have special skills and abilities to handle their jobs. Their constant communications with the public make their tasks different from many other jobs in the office. The skills and abilities possessed by successful receptionists are discussed in the following paragraphs.

Alertness and Attentiveness

Receptionists are people who enjoy being with others and being helpful. Therefore, they respond quickly and graciously to others. Callers are greeted immediately on arrival, for the receptionist is always aware of the entrance of a new person.

While talking with others, receptionists give their full attention so that they understand the purpose of the visit or inquiry.

Illus. 5-1

A friendly receptionist makes visitors to the office feel welcome.

Knowledge of Company Personnel and Policies

Receptionists must direct callers and answer questions about their organizations, so they must have a thorough understanding of their companies. The organization chart in some company manuals shows who currently holds each executive job. Sometimes such manuals provide information about job responsibilities. Receptionists review such manuals carefully so that they know the person to whom a caller should be referred. Also, the receptionists must clearly understand company policies so that they can answer questions accurately and intelligently.

> Cheryl works as a receptionist in a large printing company that does many small jobs for individuals and small businesses in the town. She is constantly receiving prospective customers who want to know about the type of jobs that can be handled by the firm and what the basic charges are. Cheryl maintains at her desk several brochures that contain the answers to the most frequently asked questions. Cheryl knows the contents of the brochures thoroughly and patiently discusses the contents with prospective customers.

Quickness in Using Reference Materials

Many receptionists provide information that they are not expected to know from memory. They are expected, however, to read and understand directories, atlases, maps, timetables, and other references. Receptionists learn how to use such references quickly by carefully reading the introductory material when a new reference is added to their collection. In their free moments receptionists become fully familiar with the contents of all the reference materials at their desks so that when a question is raised they can locate the desired information quickly.

Louise Valentine works as a receptionist at the Information Center at Hershey World. Thousands of visitors arrive daily to see this internationally known place. They ask millions of questions in the course of a year. Louise spends her day answering questions and giving maps and brochures to people from around the world. There are extended periods during the summer when the area around her counter is so crowded that she hardly pauses between answers to questions. She never grows impatient or indifferent; she likes being kind to those on vacation who have arrived for a good time. Seldom does a day go by that she doesn't have to refer to one of her many references to provide information for an unusual question.

Illus. 5-2

This worker at a large amusement center answers hundreds of questions from visitors each day.

Photo by Mark Payler
Kings Island

Techniques for Handling Receptionist Duties

techniques:
special methods

In addition to the special skills and abilities that a good receptionist must have, there are certain techniques that must be learned in order to become a valuable employee. Mastering these techniques makes a receptionist an asset to the company.

Scheduling Appointments

Appointments are a common way for people to meet in many organizations. In law offices, doctors' offices, dentists' offices, medical clinics, employment agencies, and insurance offices, appointments keep the waiting time to a minimum. A receptionist is often responsible for maintaining the schedule of appointments so that all persons are taken care of in a smooth and efficient manner.

Jayme Fenli is as a receptionist in a medical clinic for the golden-age citizens in a retirement center near Miami Beach, Florida. There are doctors in the clinic from 8 a.m. until 7 p.m. six days each week. Jayme works only 40 hours a week, however. There are 18 doctors who spend from four to nine hours a day at the clinic. Jayme maintains a comprehensive calendar for a six-month period in advance so that she can easily schedule appointments by telephone and in person. A page from her calendar is shown below.

comprehensive: very complete

JANUARY 14

	Dr. Altman	Dr. Cross	Dr. McNutt	Dr. Haynes	Dr. Froehlich
8:00	R. Grace 821-4211	M. Koenig 882-7277			M. Steible 281-1988
8:30	O. Baker 371-6864				
9:00		J. Minor 846-8534			W. Porsutti 591-4222
9:30	S. Page 562-9123	C. Fong 269-9925			
10:00					D. Moskowicz 591-3008
10:30	P. Delansandro 555-3723	L. Boechle 451-8696	N. Hernandez 844-3112		H. Parker 452-1707
11:00	G. Henderson 882-9568		V. Goldfarb 961-4454		
11:30					L. Steinberg 561-5976
12:00	T. Barnard 281-7954		E. O'Brien 269-2934		
12:30			A. Silvercloud 798-2677		
1:00		N. Klosterman 457-8496		B. Bartell 291-2091	
1:30				J. Markels 422-8072	
2:00	A. McDougle 831-3370	R. Polsky 291-5542	L. Fiedler 777-3434	J. Kincaid 271-4711	R. White 269-5679
2:30	S. Ervin 997-6842		W. Fogel 882-5437	B. Nicholson 561-1212	P. Staedler 422-9572
3:00	N. Cassano 821-3913				
3:30			I. O'Neil 555-4937	S. Rieschl 561-7559	A. Simpson 846-3987
4:00	J. Herrer 844-4719		G. Bemis 591-9995		
4:30			G. Trice 846-9239	M. Martienssen 271-7643	R. Armstrong 228-8544
5:00			C. Marvin 491-4731		
5:30					C. Stowell 791-3031
6:00					J. Schulz 422-8553
6:30					

Illus. 5-3

Appointment calendar page

Often appointments are made in person. In such instances, the receptionist might give the person requesting an appointment a card with the exact time of the appointment. Illustration 5-4 shows an appointment card used by the receptionist in a dental clinic.

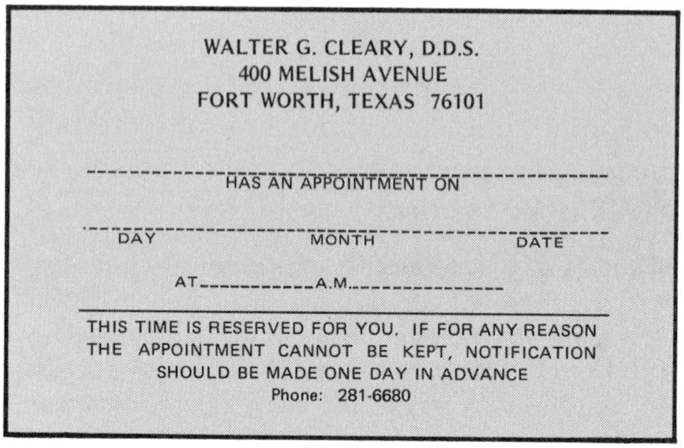

Illus. 5-4

Appointment card

```
WALTER G. CLEARY, D.D.S.
400 MELISH AVENUE
FORT WORTH, TEXAS  76101


----------------HAS AN APPOINTMENT ON-------------
----------------------------------------------------
    DAY              MONTH            DATE
AT_____A.M._____

THIS TIME IS RESERVED FOR YOU.  IF FOR ANY REASON
THE  APPOINTMENT  CANNOT  BE  KEPT,  NOTIFICATION
SHOULD BE MADE ONE DAY IN ADVANCE
Phone:  281-6680
```

Maintaining a File of Callers

Receptionists keep records on the people who call for information or receive help from their organization. A receptionist in a law firm, for example, maintains a file of all the clients of the firm. A receptionist in a large university department maintains a file of all students **currently** enrolled. Such records are often on a rotary file for easy reference. Each record contains the full name, complete address, and telephone number. Other details important for the particular office may be maintained. For example, the receptionist in a large accounting firm lists the partner responsible for each client; the receptionist in a large university economics department lists the departmental adviser for each student.

currently:
at present

Illus. 5-5

Rotary file card

```
Rollson, William R.
139 Peach Street
Atlanta, GA  30311




Telephone: 421-6922
```

The receptionist is responsible for getting full information from callers on their first visit so that a card can be typed and filed in the rotary file.

Greeting Callers

Friendliness is an important attitude in the office. As you talk with visitors you will want to convey a feeling of friendliness so that visitors feel at ease. Barbara Shaw, who is a receptionist in a large trade association office in Chicago, greeted a caller in this way:

Barbara (as the caller approaches her desk): "Good morning. May I help you?"

Caller: "Good morning. I have this manuscript for Ms. Redford. Is her office here?"

Barbara: "Yes, it is. I can take the manuscript for Ms. Redford."

Caller: "Would you sign this form for me?"

Barbara: "Yes. I'll see that this manuscript is placed on her desk immediately. Thank you for delivering it."

Caller: "Thank you. And have a good day."

On another occasion, Barbara was busy typewriting when a caller arrived at her desk. She handled the caller in this manner:

Barbara: "Good afternoon. May I help you?"

Caller: "Good afternoon. Yes, I am Tom Waters from Denver. I am in the city for some appointments and since I had a free hour, I thought I would come by here to see if I might talk briefly with Mrs. Elwood about some activities in our company. I'm with the Western Petroleum Corporation. Is Mrs. Elwood in?" (Barbara wrote down the caller's name and company quickly.)

Barbara: "Mrs. Elwood's office is on the third floor. Let me call her office to see if she is free to talk with you. Won't you have a seat while I call her secretary."

Caller: "Thank you." (Mr. Waters takes a seat on the couch.)

(Barbara telephones Mrs. Elwood's office.)

Barbara (on the telephone): "Terri, this is Barbara. Mr. Tom Waters of Western Petroleum Company from Denver is here. He would like to talk with Mrs. Elwood briefly, if Mrs. Elwood has a few minutes. He has appointments elsewhere in the city today." (There is a pause) "Thank you, Terri, I'll give Mr. Waters directions to your office; he'll be there in a few minutes."

Barbara (walks over to the couch where Mr. Waters is sitting): "Mr. Waters, Mrs. Elwood is free and will talk with you now. Her office is one flight up, in Room 324. Her secretary, Mrs. Terri Foster, is expecting you."

Mr. Waters: "Thank you very much."

Illus. 5-6

Even if busy momentarily, the receptionist acknowledges the visitor in a friendly manner.

Barbara used several good techniques that show how efficient and courteous she is.

1. She gave the caller her full attention immediately upon his arrival.
2. She wrote his name and company on a pad as he told her who he was so that there was no need to ask him to repeat that information prior to making her telephone call.
3. She asked him to be seated so that he would be out of range of the telephone conversation as she attempted to determine Mrs. Elwood's availability.
4. She knew whom to call and knew the secretary by name.
5. She walked over to Mr. Waters (she didn't shout from her desk) to give him the message.
6. She told Mr. Waters the location of Mrs. Elwood's office.

availability:
state of being free and of service

Announcing Callers

escorting:
accompanying

You will find that in some offices receptionist duties may involve escorting visitors to executive offices and announcing them. The following are courteous techniques for handling these situations:

An expected caller whom the receptionist knows:

Caller: "Good afternoon."
Receptionist: "Good afternoon, Mrs. Winston. Mr. West is expecting you. Let me check to see if he is free. Won't you have a

seat?" (The receptionist goes immediately into Mr. West's office and returns quickly.)

Receptionist: "Mrs. Winston, Mr. West is ready to see you." (The receptionist then returns to the front desk.)

An expected caller who has not been in the office before and does not know the person with whom he has an appointment:

Caller: "Good afternoon, I am Harvey Dickens."

Receptionist: "How nice to meet you, Mr. Dickens. Mr. West is expecting you. Let me see if he is free. Won't you have a seat?

Caller: "Thank you."

Receptionist: (Calls Mr. West's office) "Mr. West is free and can see you now." (The receptionist walks into the office with Mr. Dickens and introduces him to Mr. West.) "Mr. West, Mr. Dickens." (The receptionist then leaves the office quietly.)

Good techniques in announcing callers include:

1. Being aware of who is expected for appointments.
2. Asking the caller to have a seat.
3. Checking to be sure that the executive is free to see the caller.
4. Taking the caller into the office when he or she hasn't been there before.
5. Introducing the caller to the executive when necessary.

Talking with a Difficult Caller

From time to time you may encounter a difficult caller. The difficult caller may refuse to tell you who he or she is or what the purpose of the visit is. Such a caller may speak rudely or become angry. On such an occasion you must be firm in your replies and try to learn the caller's purpose. If the caller will not state the purpose of the visit, you will have to refuse the request. Here is a technique that is often successful:

(Caller approaches the desk with no comment.)

Receptionist: "May I help you?"

Caller: "I want to see the president."

Receptionist: "Please, may I have your name and the purpose of your visit?"

Caller: "It is none of your business. What are you, a screening device? I want to see the president."

Receptionist: "I am very sorry, but I am unable to grant your request without this information."

Caller: "Will you tell me where his office is; I'll go in myself?"

Receptionist: "I am sorry, but I cannot do this. I would suggest that you write the president a letter. If you would like to see him in addition to telling him of your business in the letter, indicate in your letter when you can come in for an appointment."

Caller: "That's not the way I want to handle my business, but I guess I have no choice." (The caller leaves the office.)

primarily:
mainly

The receptionist was successful in handling the difficult caller primarily by following these techniques:

1. Remaining calm but firm.
2. Not using the name of the president or saying where the president's office was.
3. Suggesting that the caller write a letter stating the problem and requesting an appointment.
4. Promising nothing. While telling the caller to request an appointment, the receptionist did not indicate the caller would get one.

Keeping a Record of Callers

Receptionists often receive callers for a number of executives. They must keep track of who is waiting, who is in what office, and other details. Some companies keep a record of callers. Illus. 5-7 shows a form that would be used to register callers. Notice that neat handwriting is important if this register is to be legible.

Illus. 5-7

Register of callers

JANUARY 14, 19--

Time of Arrival	Name	Affiliation	Person Seen	Time of Departure
8:50	H. Kuralt	Bibb-Kern, Inc.	A. Smith	9:30
9:00	T. Janes	Info-Systems Inc.	B. Holmes	9:15
10:10	M. Markoff	Huber Associates	S. Macy	10:35
10:12	L. Singleton	Broca Corporation	A. Smith	11:15
10:30	W. Perry	Nelson Security	L. Laman	11:30
10:45	B. Morris	Connant Corporation	W. Mayes	11:00

Handling Emergencies

As a receptionist, you should keep in a convenient place the telephone numbers of the organization's doctor, the nearest hospital, the police department, the fire department, the maintenance department, and any other sources that are likely to be of assistance in case of an emergency. You will find that the receptionist is frequently one of the first persons notified in an emergency, and you should remain calm and handle the tasks that must be done quickly and efficiently in such an event.

Covering the Receptionist's Desk

Reception desks should never be left unattended. If you are assigned to such a desk, you must be sure that you make arrangements for someone to **relieve** you when you are called away or go to lunch. You must also remember that the responsibility for handling receptionist duties does not allow you to spend time talking with friends either in person or by telephone. Adequate coverage requires attention to the business matters of your position at all times.

relieve:
give aid or help to;
take the place of

REVIEWING IMPORTANT POINTS

1. How does a receptionist assist in person-to-person meetings in business?
2. What kind of information should a receptionist have on hand about the company in which he or she is employed?
3. What are some reference books that might be found at a receptionist's desk in a large company?
4. Explain how a receptionist is efficient in maintaining a schedule of appointments for several executives.
5. How is an appointment card helpful?
6. What important information about a frequent caller is recorded on a permanent card by a receptionist?
7. Why should a receptionist record the name of an unfamiliar caller when the caller first gives his or her name?
8. Can a receptionist assume that all callers are acquainted with the executives with whom they have appointments? Explain.
9. How should the receptionist respond to callers who refuse to give names or purpose of visit?
10. What are some of the telephone numbers a receptionist should have listed for emergency purposes?

MAKING IMPORTANT DECISIONS

1. Nadia is a receptionist in a large broadcasting company. All visitors to the company come to her desk, including applicants for positions in the company. One afternoon an elderly woman came to her desk and asked: "Young lady, with whom do I talk about a position as a

typist? I would like to work for a fine company such as this one."
Nadia knows that everyone in the company must retire at 65 and
the lady seems to be in her late 70's.

What do you think Nadia should say?

2. Tina is a receptionist in a large printing office. The actual printing
center is a couple of blocks away from the office. Tina was given a
very brief orientation to her job. After about a week, she realized
that many callers were asking her for basic information about the
work of the company and she couldn't answer their questions. For
example callers would ask:

"Is it possible to get embossing done here?"

"Does your company print catalogues on newspaper print?"

"Is it possible to get stationery within a week of an order?"

Tina noticed that the persons who talked with potential customers
were very busy. In fact, there were always several persons waiting to
see each member of the staff. Often the callers were not able to
wait; they merely wanted a simple answer. Tina wondered what she
might do to be more helpful.

What suggestions do you have for Tina?

LEARNING TO WORK WITH OTHERS

Karita works as a receptionist in a large manufacturing company in
Seattle. She has several directories at her desk to which she must often
refer. During the time she is off for a coffee break or for lunch, Frank
serves as a relief receptionist. Frank is very pleasant, but he doesn't
seem to be concerned about keeping the directories at the desk. Apparently, when someone asks for an office number, Frank just gives the
person a directory and the person walks off with it. Constantly, Karita
must call the Central Supply Office to request additional directories.
She is often without a directory when a caller arrives and asks a question
about a staff member. She isn't able to do her job as she would like to
do it.

What do you think Karita can do about her problem with Frank?

IMPROVING LANGUAGE SKILLS

Some responses made by receptionists to callers are given below.
On a separate sheet of paper indicate for each whether the response is
appropriate or inappropriate. Rewrite those responses that you believe
are inappropriate.

1. Lana: "I can't find my directory. I think Mr. Jonstone's office
is on the fifth floor. Why don't you go up there and
just ask anyone you see where Mr. Jonstone's office
is."

2. Evelyn: "Good morning. May I help you? Do you have an appointment with someone here?"

3. Patrick: "If you are going to shout at me, I won't talk with you. You need to be polite in this office. You have no business talking to me that way."

4. Effie: "I guess you have a ten o'clock appointment with Mr. Stone. Well, be prepared to wait because he has someone in there who won't be finished with his business for at least another 30 minutes. Sorry!"

5. Celia: "Good morning, Ms. Rogers. Mrs. Weiler is expecting you. Won't you have a seat and I'll check to see if she can see you now."

6. Peggy: "I'll call Mr. Burns to see if he is free. Will you have a seat in the meantime?"

7. Richard: "Goodbye, Mrs. Reins. Have a pleasant day."

8. Winnie: "I'm very sorry that Miss Bryant is out of town. Would a time one day next week be convenient for you?"

9. Jill: "Mr. Collins is in, but he is very busy, and he doesn't want to see anyone this morning. Sorry!"

10. Vivian: "Mr. Bradford, Mr. Thomas Abelson of Electronics Equipment Company; Mr. Abelson, Mr. Theodore Bradford."

IMPROVING ARITHMETIC SKILLS

The receptionist in a small architectural firm in Boston, Massachusetts, was asked to figure out the length of each long-distance call made during the preceding week. These are the figures she recorded on her worksheet. On a separate sheet of paper determine the length of each call as well as the total time spent in long-distance conversations.

	Time Started	Time Ended		Time Started	Time Ended
11/15	9:15	– 9:20	11/17	2:15	– 2:19
	10:15	– 10:29		2:25	– 2:30
	11:45	– 11:50			
	1:15	– 1:21	11/18	10:00	– 10:15
	2:10	– 2:30		11:01	– 11:16
	3:15	– 3:19		11:45	– 11:51
				2:19	– 2:35
11/16	10:05	– 10:25			
	11:10	– 11:45	11/19	9:30	– 9:45
	12:58	– 1:10		9:50	– 10:20
	1:45	– 2:09		11:03	– 11:29
	2:10	– 2:20		2:15	– 2:45

DEMONSTRATING OFFICE SKILLS

1. Assume one of the following two roles:
   Receptionist in an Employment Office of the Federal Government.
   Mrs. Theresa Swann, an unemployed person who has never before visited an Employment Office.

   Situation: It is 9:30 in the morning. Mrs. Swann comes in to learn about job opportunities in ceramics factories. She would like very much to go back to work. The employment interviewer for factory jobs is temporarily out of his office, but he is due back in ten minutes. There are three people waiting to talk with him. Act out the conversation between Mrs. Swann, the unemployed factory worker, and the receptionist.

2. Assume one of the following two roles:
   Receptionist in a large brokerage house, where many persons come to tour the facilities as well as to talk with agents of the company.
   Mr. Arnold Inge, a teacher of an Office Procedures class.

   Situation: The teacher arrives at your desk with 15 students for a tour he says is scheduled for 2:30. Mr. Gordon, who conducts such tours, is not around. (It is now about a minute before 2:30.) On your tour schedule you find no listing of a tour with Mr. Gordon at 2:30. Act out the conversation between Mr. Inge, the teacher, and the receptionist.

3. Assume that you are the receptionist for a textile trade association in Atlanta, Georgia, where you schedule appointments for three executives. You have made the following appointments for Mr. McNally, Ms. Jones, and Ms. Beech for Thursday, December 7. Design and draw an appropriate calendar form and record the following appointments.

   Mr. McNally: 9:30 appointment with James Hanson from Washington, D.C. (202-567-8900 Ext. 45)
   Noon luncheon engagement with Wesley Horton (354-6789)
   3:00 appointment with Joan Waterman of Advertising (Ext. 467)
   4:00 appointment with Teresa Sallows (342-2345)

   Ms. Jones: 9:00 appointment with Ted Norris (451-4671)
   10:00 appointment with Richard Manley (567-3791)
   11:30 appointment with William Bates (465-8999)
   2:00 appointment with Barbara Colliers from Raleigh (919-567-4689)

   Ms. Beech: 9:30 appointment with George Wienberg (532-0975)
   10:30 appointment with Millie Elliott (680-3223)
   Noon meeting at the Towers Inn — Breakmore Room (out until 2:30)

Oral Communications in Business

Sherry Tobey realizes how important good speech is in her job as receptionist at an international company with offices in Boston. People from many countries around the world come to her desk. They all know English, but some have only a limited **facility** with the language. She is very careful to speak clearly, directly, and slowly so that what she says is understood. She knows that she must practice good speech habits if she is to do her job successfully. Persons from other countries are frequently grateful; many tell her: "Oh, how easy it is to understand what you are saying. A foreigner like me finds your speech a pleasure!"

facility:
ease in performance

Considerations for Good Business Communications

In business, the ways of talking are similar to those used in ordinary conversations with others. In general, though, the speech of the business office may be slightly more **formal** than that used with close friends and family members. Most business speech has a specific purpose, such as to communicate information, to convey instructions, or to transmit decisions. To achieve these purposes, it is important that oral communications be clear, precise, and complete.

formal:
according to set rules

Use of Standard Language

Standard language is that vocabulary which is acceptable in personal and business communications, both oral and written.

As you know, the language of a society is constantly changing. In fact, we talk of "living language" because we are always adding new words and dropping words that are no longer used. New developments, such as space exploration, have introduced new words into our daily vocabulary. Many dictionaries have a special section in which the new words that have been added to the language since the dictionary's last edition are defined. You may want to look through such a section to get an idea of the types of words that are being added to our language.

The language that you learned in your study of English as well as in your other courses is appropriate for the business office. A broad vocabulary will be a great asset in your business communications.

Clear Speech

You know how pleasant it is to listen to someone who speaks clearly. You hear each word that is spoken and can **respond** to the person accurately. Some common habits that prevent people from speaking clearly include:

respond:
reply in words

1. Speaking so rapidly that words run together.
2. Speaking in a very low voice.
3. Speaking in a very loud voice.
4. Speaking so that the ends of sentences are mumbled.
5. Speaking before you know exactly what you want to say so that phrases and sentences that are spoken are disconnected and jumbled.

If you will think of your listener as you talk, you will find that you can improve the **clarity** of your speech. If you speak as though you want to be heard, each word will be clearly **audible**.

clarity:
clearness

audible:
able to be heard

Illus. 5-8

When you speak clearly, others will be able to respond directly.

Unit 5 • Meeting the Public

Proper Pronunciation

Most words have standard pronunciations. This means that there is only one correct way of saying the word. There are some words, though, that have more than one acceptable pronunciation. For example, the usual pronunciation for *progress* is *präg res*, yet *pro gress* is also correct; the usual pronunciation for *tomato* is *ta mat o*, yet *ta mät o* is also correct.

You will also find that pronunciation differs from one part of the country to another. What is acceptable in Atlanta may sound strange in New York. However, if you work some place other than where you grew up, you will find people **tolerant** of speech differences. In fact, you should not try to imitate the pronunciation of the new community if it differs from your natural way of speaking. Such imitation is called *affected* speech and may be **offensive** to the listener.

tolerant: accepting

offensive: unpleasant; insulting

A good habit to follow is to check the preferred pronunciation of a word in a dictionary. Also you should be aware of careless speech habits that cause you to pronounce words improperly. Here are a few types of speech errors that you should avoid.

	FAULTY	CORRECT
Dropping the ending of a word:	*workin'*	working
	talkin'	talking
Dropping a syllable within a word:	*accracy*	accuracy
	sophmore	sophomore
Substituting one vowel for another:	*fur*	for
	fill	feel
	git	get
	fella	fellow
Substituting one syllable for another:	*libery*	library
	granite	granted
	purty	pretty

Proper Enunciation

When you speak each word precisely, you are enunciating properly. Care in enunciating words is important if you are to be understood by the person listening to you. Some words that are often confused because they are not enunciated carefully are the following:

accept	charted	metal	sense	than
except	chartered	mental	since	then
				work
affect	eminent	picture	statue	word
effect	imminent	pitcher	stature	worth

Avoidance of Colloquialisms and Slang

As you learned, our language is constantly changing and the value of certain words and expressions also changes. There are two classes of words that change rather quickly. These are colloquialisms and slang. *Colloquialisms* are words that are satisfactory for informal conversation and are often natural to a person's speech. However, such words should be avoided in written communications and in conversations where standard language is more likely to express your thoughts clearly. Below are a few frequently heard colloquialisms that are avoided by careful speakers.

COLLOQUIAL	PREFERRED
around for *about*	He should arrive *about* (not *around*) noon.
contact for *get in touch with* or *call* or *talk with*	Will you *talk with* (not *contact*) Miss Sanders this afternoon?
posted for *informed*	Mr. Keller kept us *informed* (not *posted*) while the negotiations were in progress.

Illus. 5-9

Giving directions is only one situation where precise communication is essential.

Although colloquialisms are sometimes acceptable, slang is out of place in a business office. Slang is made up of widely used current terms which have a forced meaning such as *to get with it* meaning *to cooperate* or *dig this* meaning *understand this*. Words or expressions of this type are contrary to good language usage.

The wide usage of certain slang words and phrases, such as *cut the mustard* or *to miss the boat*, has caused them to lose some of the undesirable quality that they had in the past; however, their usage in the business office should be extremely limited. A vocabulary made up of *gross, lousy, guy,* and other slang terms is an indication of a very weak English background. It is difficult to convey ideas precisely with such language.

Use of Correct Grammar

Both oral and written communications require that you give attention to correct grammar. It is very easy for grammatical errors to creep into your speech and to become so common that you are not aware that you are speaking incorrectly. Be aware of the errors you tend to make and then try to improve your grammar. Some common errors are listed below:

Using a subject of one number and a verb of another	Incorrect: *He don't* need that many sheets of paper. Correct: *He doesn't* need that many sheets of paper.
Using the wrong case for pronouns	Incorrect: Both *her* and *me* will go to the meeting tonight. Correct: Both *she* and *I* will go to the meeting tonight.
Using adjectives as adverbs	Incorrect: She did *good* in the contest. Correct: She did *well* in the contest.
Using the improper past tense for irregular verbs.	Incorrect: He *sat* it on the shelf. Correct: He *set* it on the shelf.

Elimination of Mannerisms

Mannerisms are gestures, facial expressions, or speech habits that detract from your ability to communicate clearly with others. It is possible to eliminate mannerisms by careful attention to them.

Nicholas is a conscientious young man, but he has a distracting habit of mumbling. It is seldom possible to understand what he is saying the first time he makes a comment. He works in the shipping room of a large paper company. His supervisor finds him a good worker but he often hears people ask: "What did you say, Nicholas?" One day he decided to talk to Nicholas about the problem. He told him that he felt he was a wonderful beginning worker, but that he needed to do something about his habit of mumbling. Nicholas was surprised. He didn't realize that he didn't speak clearly. His supervisor imitated his way of speaking for him; Nicholas realized that that was the way he spoke. He told the supervisor he would try to "speak up." He also said that he would be alert to how often someone asked him to repeat what he had just said.

Non-Verbal Influences

influence:
affect

interactions:
encounters;
exchanges

In addition to your use of language, there are some important considerations that influence your interactions with others. Among these is courtesy. Courtesy is reflected in the following ways:

1. By the full attention you give the person to whom you are talking.
2. By the patience you show as you talk with others.
3. By your willingness to respond to what you have been asked.

When an office supervisor was asked to describe a beginning worker who was courteous and one who was not, the following descriptions were provided:

When I think of the courteous beginning worker, I immediately think of Len. He is a gracious, pleasant young man. He is soft-spoken, but he speaks clearly so that there is no problem in understanding what he is saying. When he is talking with me, for example, he never looks away, no matter who is talking. If I pause to think before I say the next word, he stays attentive and never rushes to complete my thought or looks away in impatience. He is also an excellent listener. He *hears* exactly what I am asking and responds directly to any question I must ask him.

On the other hand, I immediately think of Arnie when I think of a young worker who has much to learn about courtesy. First, Arnie is constantly talking. In fact, I don't think he even knows what he is saying much of the time. He doesn't give the other person time to finish a full sentence. He interrupts, often with a comment that is unrelated to the discussion, he looks away, and his mind seems to wander. Arnie never listens to a question. He begins to respond before the question is completed, assuming he knows what is being asked. His response, therefore, is often unrelated to the question. I've tried to talk with him, but I've had trouble getting him to understand the problem. I think he would be a much more productive employee if he could change some of these habits.

REVIEWING IMPORTANT POINTS

1. What is the style of speaking most common in modern offices?
2. Where can you find a listing of new words that have been added to the language?

3. Describe what a person might do to improve the clarity of his or her speech.
4. There is only one right pronunciation for each word. Do you agree with this statement? Discuss.
5. Give two examples of faulty pronunciation that you have heard in recent conversations.
6. What habit should you develop if you want to be sure to distinguish between words like "accept" and "except" or "work" and "word" when you are speaking?
7. Why should slang expressions be avoided in the business office?
8. Explain why the sentence "There is several ways to get that job done" is incorrect gramatically.
9. How does one go about eliminating a mannerism?
10. Describe a person who is courteous when he or she is talking with another person.

MAKING IMPORTANT DECISIONS

1. Fran was born in Atlanta and lived there until she was eighteen. Then she moved to Boston, where she got a job as a receptionist. Fran was very self-conscious about her speech, which she felt was totally out of place in the North. She liked the style of speaking in Boston and decided to imitate it. She believed that no one would be able to detect the fact that she was not a native of Boston. What do you think of Fran's decision?
2. Mary Lou worked as a clerk in the stockroom of a large appliance store that carried all types of recording equipment. One day she and a co-worker were asked to check a tape recorder that a customer claimed was defective. Mary Lou and her co-worker recorded their conversation so that they could check the machine. Then they listened to the conversation. Mary Lou discovered that her friend's speech was clearer than her own. In fact, Mary Lou couldn't understand much of what she said. Some of her words ran together, some were mumbled, others were incomplete. What could Mary Lou do to improve her speech?

LEARNING TO WORK WITH OTHERS

Margret was recently hired as a clerk in the central filing department of a manufacturing company. Margret was born in Germany and lived there until three years ago when her family moved to New Orleans. She studied English earnestly when she came to the United States, but she continues to have difficulty in speaking English so that the listener will understand her easily. She knows her problem and after she was introduced to Beth, whose desk is next to hers, she said to Beth, "Will you help me with my English? When you hear me say something wrong, will you please tell me about it? I really want to improve my English."

What do you think Beth should say and do?

IMPROVING LANGUAGE SKILLS

Some words in the English language are pronounced alike but are different in meaning. Other words have pronunciations which are similar, but not exactly alike. Often people pronounce these words as though they are alike. Below are pairs of words, some of which are pronounced alike but have different meanings and others which are not pronounced the same. Use a dictionary to check the pronunciation of each word as well as the meaning of the word. On a separate sheet of paper write a sentence for each of the words. Underline those words that are pronounced the same.

1. absorb absurd	9. precede proceed
2. accept except	10. profit prophet
3. affect effect	11. relative relevant
4. bare bear	12. sew sow
5. beau bow	13. sight site
6. cents sense	14. then than
7. formally formerly	15. weather whether
8. pair pear	16. which witch

IMPROVING ARITHMETIC SKILLS

Mike is a receptionist in a management consulting firm. He has been given a number of duties including typing reports, but his primary responsibility is to greet callers and handle the telephone calls that come into the company. In an effort to learn how much work there is at his desk, Mike has been asked to keep a record of how many callers come to the office each day and how many telephone calls he receives and makes each day. Below are the tallies for one week. Compute the total number of calls for each day and prepare a report on plain paper showing how many callers were taken care of for the week of November 5.

MONDAY, November 5, 19--

Outgoing local calls: 卌 卌 卌 //
Outgoing long-distance calls: 卌 //
Incoming calls: 卌 卌 卌 卌 /
Office callers: 卌 卌 //

TUESDAY, November 6, 19--

Outgoing local calls: 卌 卌 卌 卌
Outgoing long-distance calls: 卌 卌 ///
Incoming calls: 卌 卌 卌 卌 /
Office callers: 卌 //

WEDNESDAY, November 7, 19--

Outgoing local calls: 卌 卌 卌 卌 ////
Outgoing long-distance calls: 卌 ///
Incoming calls: 卌 卌 卌 ///
Office callers: 卌 卌 卌 /

THURSDAY, November 8, 19--

Outgoing local calls: 卌 卌 卌 ///
Outgoing long-distance calls: 卌 ////
Incoming calls: 卌 卌 卌 //
Office callers: 卌 ////

FRIDAY, November 9, 19--

Outgoing local calls: 卌 卌 卌 ///
Outgoing long-distance calls: 卌 /
Incoming calls: 卌 卌 卌 /
Office callers: 卌 ///

DEMONSTRATING OFFICE SKILLS

1. Assume that you are a receptionist in a large company and that you are soon to go on vacation. Your supervisor has asked you to talk with Gail Winters, a clerk in the mailing department, who will substitute for you while you are away. Develop and type on plain paper an outline of the responsibilities of your job that you would plan to discuss with Gail when you talk with her. (You may imagine the situation in which you are working.)

2. As you consider your own speech habits and mannerisms, which ones do you think should be eliminated? Describe those you would like to eliminate. On plain paper, write a brief outline of what you believe you should do in the next six months in order to eliminate your poor habits and mannerisms.
3. On plain paper, make a list of slang words and expressions you hear daily that you believe would not be appropriate for business communications. For each slang word or expression, write the definition. Opposite the definition, write the word or words of standard English that you believe should be used to express the meaning intended by the slang word or phrase.

IMPROVING OFFICE SKILLS (Optional)

If a tape recorder is available, make a tape of the following:
a. A conversation with a fellow student in which you discuss the importance of good speech for the office worker.
b. Directions given by a receptionist (played by you) to a visitor from another country. (You may choose the directions: how to get to an office, a nearby drugstore, a coffee shop, etc.)
Then, listen to your recording and answer the following:
a. How friendly do you sound as you talk?
b. How clearly do you speak?
c. What are the words that you could pronounce more clearly?
d. What improvements do you think you should make in your speaking style and in your vocabulary?

UNIT

6

Using Communication Services

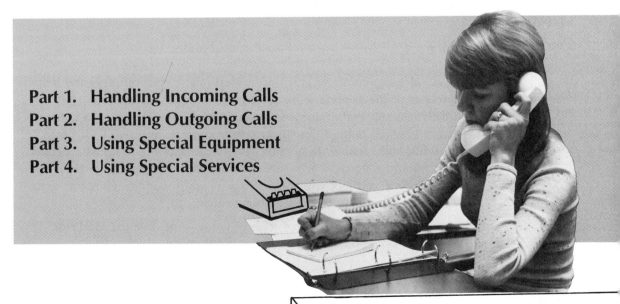

Part 1. Handling Incoming Calls
Part 2. Handling Outgoing Calls
Part 3. Using Special Equipment
Part 4. Using Special Services

Part 1

Handling Incoming Calls

Nora Thorne works as a clerk in a large architectural firm in downtown Atlanta. Her office is a busy place. There are three architects for whom Nora and two co-workers do many office tasks. Nora has primary responsibility for telephone calls. She takes each call in a relaxed, friendly manner. All three architects are available to respond to all calls when they are not in meetings. They are frequently away, however, so Nora often takes messages for them.

The telephone is one of the most important means of communication in today's office. Using the telephone is likely to be one of your daily tasks. You will probably answer the telephone and from time to time place calls. Learning the proper techniques as well as understanding the various telephone services available will be helpful in your work.

Telephone Manner

Your interest, your knowledge, and your concern for others are all conveyed when you talk with others on the telephone. People to whom you talk form impressions on the basis of your speech and your voice.

impressions:
effects or opinions
produced by
something

Voice

A voice can convey a spirit of interest, alertness, courtesy, and helpfulness over the telephone; or it can reflect an attitude of indifference, impatience, and inattention. A pleasant voice is much easier to listen to than one which is loud, harsh, or shrill. You can improve your voice if you think and speak with a smile. Try to think of the caller as a person —not merely a voice — who needs your help. You can have the *voice with a smile* if you talk with callers in a pleasant manner. Here are some suggestions to improve your telephone voice:

indifference:
lack of interest or
concern

1. *Speak clearly.* A normal tone of voice — neither too loud nor too soft — carries best over the telephone.

Illus. 6-1

The voice with a smile gives the caller a favorable impression.

American Telephone & Telegraph Corporation

2. *Use a low-pitched voice.* A low-pitched voice carries better over the telephone and is kinder to your listener's ear. A high-pitched voice tends to become irritating.

irritating: producing anger or impatience

3. *Use voice inflection.* The rise and fall of the pitch of your voice not only put your thoughts across but also add personality to your voice. A monotonous voice sounds indifferent, and makes it difficult for the listener to give close attention to what is being said.

monotonous: not varying; without change

Speech

Your speech habits are just as important as your voice: a pleasant voice makes you easy to listen to; good speech habits make you easy to understand. You should pronounce words clearly and correctly so that callers understand what you are saying. It is important that callers hear your message correctly.

Below are some suggestions for good telephone speech.

1. *Speak carefully.* Distinct speech is essential, since the listener can neither read your lips nor see your expression. Be careful to pronounce each word clearly; don't mumble or slur syllables.

distinct: clear; easily understood

2. *Talk at a proper pace.* A moderate rate of speech is easily understood, but the pace should be related to the ideas you are expressing. You should give some information more slowly, such as, technical information, lists, numbers, names, foreign or unusual words, and any information the listener is writing down.

moderate: reasonable; medium

3. *Use emphasis with words.* The stress or emphasis placed on words, or groups of words, may change the meaning of what you are saying.
4. *Consider the listener's comments and questions.* Allow the listener's ideas to be expressed.

Illus. 6-2

Good speech habits convey efficiency to the caller.

American Telephone & Telegraph Corporation

Vocabulary

Your ideas should be stated simply. Technical, awkward, and unnecessarily lengthy words may confuse the other person and may require an explanation or may even create a misunderstanding.

Be careful not to use language which will offend the listener or create a bad impression of the company you represent. Avoid trite words, phrases, and slang expressions. *Yes* sounds much better than *Yeah* or *OK*.

Courtesy

Courtesy is just as important in a telephone call as it is in a face-to-face conversation. Callers should not be interrupted or kept waiting without an explanation. Listen carefully to what the person is saying. Develop patience and concern for the party calling and you will find you are naturally courteous.

Incoming Calls

As part of your office duties, you will probably answer the telephone. You may also be expected to answer the telephone when your employer is away from his or her desk. The suggestions given below and on the following pages will aid you in performing this important function.

Answering Promptly

You should answer all incoming calls promptly and pleasantly, on the first ring whenever possible.

As you reach for the receiver, reach for your notebook. Be ready to take notes immediately. *You should hold the mouthpiece about an inch from your lips* and speak directly into the telephone in a normal conversational tone of voice.

Identifying Yourself

A telephone conversation cannot really begin until the caller knows that the right number has been reached. Therefore, you should identify yourself and your firm, office, or department immediately. Never answer by saying merely "Hello" or "Yes?" — these greetings add nothing to the identification.

If you answer an outside line, give your firm's name, followed by your name, as in Ramey Construction Company, Jane Foley." If your company has a switchboard, your operator has already identified the company; and you may answer your employer's telephone by saying, "Mr. Meade's office, Jane Foley." When answering an office extension in a department, identify the department and give your name: "Planning Department, Jane Foley."

Screening Calls

There is a practice in some offices of screening calls. Screening calls means determining who is calling and, at times, the purpose of the call before the person being called is informed of the call. In some offices, much time is saved through screening, for an office worker may be able to transfer the call immediately to the proper person. However, some companies feel that screening creates the impression that callers aren't welcome, and that the office worker is trying to determine what calls are *important* enough to transfer to the person being called.

You will find that practices differ among companies. You will need to learn the practices in the office where you are employed and **adhere** to them. If screening is a practice, calls would be handled as follows:

adhere:
follow closely

Office worker:	"Good afternoon. Mr. Wallace's office, Nevin Jones."
Caller:	"I'd like to talk with Mr. Wallace, please.'
Office worker:	"Yes. May I tell him who is calling?"
Caller:	"This is Dora Peck of Modern Electronics."
Office worker:	"Thank you, Ms. Peck. Just one moment and I'll ring for Mr. Wallace."

If the person requested is out of the office or in a meeting, the office worker can handle the situation in this manner.

Office worker:	"Good afternoon. Mr. Wallace's office. Nevin Jones."
Caller:	"I'd like to talk with Mr. Wallace, please."
Office worker:	"I'm sorry, Mr. Wallace is away from his desk. May I take a message?"
Caller:	"When will he back at his desk?"
Office worker:	"Mr. Wallace will be back by three. May I take a message?"
Caller:	"This is Dora Peck of Modern Electronics. I would like to talk with him briefly before I leave town this evening. Could he call me when he returns at three?"
Office worker:	"Yes, Ms. Peck, I'll leave a message for Mr. Wallace to call you. Where can he reach you shortly after three? How long will you be in your office this afternoon?"
Caller:	"I can be reached at 567-5432. I'll be in until about 4:30. Thank you so much for taking the message, and I'll expect to hear from Mr. Wallace."
Office Worker:	"Thank you for calling, Ms. Peck. Mr. Wallace will call you. Goodbye."
Caller:	"Goodbye."

Giving Information

You must be very careful when giving information if your employer is not available for telephone calls. For instance, a reply such as "Mr. Meade left for Denver this morning" may convey just enough information to let a competitor know, for example, that Mr. Meade is interested enough in a certain construction contract to make a personal trip to the construction site. Unless you are absolutely sure that your employer would want others to have the information, do not give details over the telephone to outside callers.

competitor:
a competing or rival
business

Say	Rather than
"He is out of the city. May I ask him to call you when he returns on Monday?"	"He was called to Denver to inspect a construction site."
"He is not at his desk. May I take a message?"	"He is discussing the merger with the comptroller."
"He will be in tomorrow morning. May I ask him to call you then?"	"He has taken off for the afternoon to see his dentist."

Getting Information

Some telephone callers do not care to give their names; others prefer not to say why they are calling. You will frequently have to find out *who* is calling and, if the name does not help you, *why* the person is calling. Try to obtain the information as tactfully as possible by using an appropriate response, such as:

> Mr. Meade has a visitor at the moment. If you will give me your name and telephone number, I will ask him to call you just as soon as he is free.
>
> or
>
> Mr. Meade is not at his desk just now. May I give him a message for you?
>
> or
>
> Mr. Meade is talking on another line. May I help you?

If you must ask a direct question to get the information, state it as a request rather than as a demand: "May I tell Mr. Meade who is calling?"

Taking Messages Accurately

A pad of forms for recording the details of incoming telephone calls should always be kept near the telephone to take messages when your employer is out or is busy. On returning, your employer can use the messages to return the calls, a practice which promotes better customer relations. It is very important, therefore, that you record all the details of every message accurately. It is a good practice to verify all names and telephone numbers.

The message, written clearly, should include

1. Name of the caller and company.
2. The telephone number, including extension and area code.
3. Message.
4. Initials of the person who wrote the message.
5. Exact time of call and the date.

Illus. 6-3 Memo of call

MEMO OF CALL

TO: _Mrs. Werner_

FROM: _Mr. Lang, Capital Savings Bank_

PHONE NO. _606-433-8331_

☑ Telephoned   ☑ Will Call Again
☐ Please Phone   ☐ Returned Your Call
☐ Came To See You   ☐ Wishes To See You

Message: _Wants you to refer to deposit on 3/15, deposit slip #1212 (slip is attached)_

Date: _5/17_   Time: _11:30_   Received By: _gf_

Illus. 6-4

Always be prepared to make a record of telephone messages.

Transferring Calls

Sometimes you will have to transfer a call to another extension or number. Calls are usually transferred when the caller has reached a wrong extension, when the caller wishes to speak with someone else, or when the caller's request can be handled better by someone else. Tell the caller why the transfer is necessary, and be sure that the call is being transferred to the proper person. You may say to the caller:

> Ms. Udall is no longer at this extension. I'll ask the operator to transfer you to extension 4521. Just one moment, please.

> or

> I am sorry. You have reached the wrong extension. You want to talk with someone in our Public Affairs Department. The extension is 4530. Just a moment; I'll ask the operator to transfer this call.

You will want to learn how to transfer a call in the office where you are employed. Telephone equipment differs from office to office. There is always a procedure for transferring calls, however, whether the office has automatic equipment or a manual system with an operator.

When a call is disconnected, the calling party should be the one to place the call again. If you were the party called, you should not use the telephone for awhile so that the calling party can get through to you quickly. If you placed a long-distance call that was disconnected, you should call the Operator (0) and explain that you were disconnected.

Automatic Answering and Recording Set

A telephone answering and recording set will automatically answer the telephone and record a message after business hours or during the regular business hours if there is nobody to answer the telephone. Here is how it works:

1. A message, such as the following, is dictated to the machine.
   "This is Hubert Quinn speaking. This is a recording. When you hear the signal, you may record a message which I shall listen to when I return to the office at 9 a.m. on Wednesday, December 6."
2. The dictator listens to the message to be certain it is clear and complete.
3. The machine is set to operate when the telephone rings.
4. The messages are reviewed as soon as the dictator returns to the office. At times, an office worker who returns shortly before the executive may record the messages on regular telephone message forms and give them to the executive.

Telephone Answering Service

With a telephone answering service you know that all your calls will be answered when you are unable to receive them personally. The telephone answering service operator takes your calls for you and relays the messages to you. The names of firms that supply telephone answering service are listed in the Yellow Pages.

Terminating Calls

Every telephone conversation should end in a friendly, unhurried manner. You should not hang up **abruptly**. To do so is to show disinterest and impatience. As the conversation ends, thank the caller with an appropriate comment, such as:

abruptly: suddenly

> Thank you very much for calling, Mrs. Feathers.

> or

> Thank you for calling back with the information, Mr. Rotherman.

> or

> Thank you. I'll see that Mrs. Elsman gets your message when she returns to her office this afternoon.

Following such a remark, a simple "good-bye" is a fitting ending. After the caller has hung up, replace the receiver *gently*. If you were the one to place the call, you should hang up first.

Personal Telephone Calls

governing:
controlling

urgency:
need for immediate
attention

The policy governing the use of a business telephone for personal calls differs from office to office. Some firms permit a limited number of personal calls; others discourage all personal calls. Brief, to-the-point personal calls that have some degree of urgency are generally allowed in most offices. There are times, of course, when changes in your schedule require that you make a personal call. One young office worker described the situation in his office in this way:

> We have a flexible policy, I'd say, about using the telephone for personal calls. None of us takes advantage of the freedom allowed us, though. Our supervisor knows that there are times when someone at home or a friend must get in touch with us during the day; such calls are very brief. For example, I was supposed to have dinner with a friend the other evening. However, he had to work about an hour beyond the time he ordinarily leaves the office. So, he called me to suggest that we change our dinner time. That kind of call requires less than a minute. No one minds an occasional call in our office.

REVIEWING IMPORTANT POINTS

1. On what basis does a telephone caller form an impression of you as you answer the telephone?
2. What kinds of attitudes can you convey with your voice?
3. How does a person speak "with a smile"?
4. Why is a low-pitched voice better than a high-pitched voice when talking on the telephone?
5. What is the meaning of "voice inflection"?
6. Why should you avoid speaking rapidly over the telephone?
7. Why should you identify your office and yourself when answering a business telephone?
8. What should you do if a call you placed is disconnected?
9. How should a telephone conversation be concluded?
10. What type of personal call is usually allowed in the office?

MAKING IMPORTANT DECISIONS

1. Carlos works in an office with three other clerks. Jessie is responsible for answering the telephone when she is at her desk. When she is not at her desk one of the other clerks is expected to answer the telephone. Carlos noticed that when Jessie is away, everyone in the office seems to assume that someone else is going to answer the telephone. The telephone rings and rings and rings. Then, after about the fifth ring all three rush to the desk. Sometimes the calling

party has hung up by the time a person reaches to answer the telephone. Carlos thinks there must be a better way to handle the telephone when Jessie is away. What would you suggest that Carlos say to his co-workers?

2. Every time Ms. Anslow tells the accountant in whose office she works that he has a telephone call, he asks: "Who is calling?" Ms. Anslow always says, "I don't know. The caller didn't say." The accountant never says anything further, but one afternoon Ms. Anslow realized that the accountant had asked her seven times who was calling. She felt she should change how she handles calls. What would you suggest to Ms. Anslow?

LEARNING TO WORK WITH OTHERS

Rose is a friendly, hard-working young woman. She often has a task that consists of simply checking one list of names against another list. When she is doing this job, she will often place a telephone call to a friend to chat. There is only one telephone in the small department where Rose works. There are several calls in and out each day, but calls aren't as frequent as they are in other offices. Rose feels that, since the telephone isn't used very much, she isn't keeping anyone from calling. The other two office workers are unhappy about Rose's practice. Even though Rose does her work accurately while chatting, the others feel that she isn't working as quickly as she could. Also, they have heard others in the company say that it is difficult to get through to them when other departments need information from their department.

What do you think Rose's two co-workers should do?

IMPROVING LANGUAGE SKILLS

Below are three simple rules to help you correctly add *ing* endings to verbs.

1. An *e* is usually dropped before the *ing*.
   Examples: advise   advising
                 come   coming

2. Before adding *ing*, *ie* is changed to *y*.
   Examples: lie   lying
                 tie   tying

3. When the final syllable contains a long vowel, the *ing* will be preceded by a single consonant.
   Example: reveal   revealing
   When the final syllable contains a short vowel, the *ing* will be preceded by a double consonant. (In recent years usage has

tended toward a single consonant. Check your dictionary for the preferred usage.)

Examples: program   progra*mm*ing or progra*m*ing

                cancel   cance*l*ing or cance*ll*ing

On a separate sheet of paper type the following words using the correct *ing* ending. Check the dictionary for the correct form if you are in doubt.

1. accompany
2. begin
3. charge
4. compel
5. claim
6. concern
7. consist
8. continue
9. deny
10. face

11. finance
12. forego
13. include
14. near
15. obtain
16. operate
17. proceed
18. qualify
19. travel
20. reaffirm

IMPROVING ARITHMETIC SKILLS

Mr. Sanders, for whom you work, asks you to do an analysis of all the long-distance calls made in his office last month. He asks you to indicate the number of calls made to each number, the length of each call, and the total time for all calls placed to the same number. He suggests the following form:

Number Called	Number of Calls	Time per Call						Total Time
		1	2	3	4	5	6	

The statement sent to you from the Central Telephone office is shown opposite:

```
CENTRAL TELEPHONE OFFICE                AREA CODE  513   271-5042 [EXT. 395]

                              DETAIL OF ITEMIZED CALLS   MARCH 19--


    DATE     TIME    MIN         CITY -- STATE                NUMBER
    304     859AM    06     LOUISVILLE  KY           606 734-5311     1.83
    304     922AM    03     COLUMBUS    OH           614 457-8496      .86
    308    1109AM    06     LOUISVILLE  KY           606 734-5411     1.83
    311     906AM    02     COLUMBUS    OH           614 457-8496      .73
    311     114PM    12     BOSTON      MA           617 831-3370     4.24
    315    1005AM    04     CLEVELAND   OH           216 271-8811     1.35
    316     906AM    08     SEATTLE     WA           206 885-7643     3.20
    317    1116PM    02     CLEVELAND   OH           216 271-8811      .75
    319     224PM    05     CLEVELAND   OH           216 271-8811     1.65
    319     230PM    03     COLUMBUS    OH           614 457-8496     1.05
    319     234PM    07     LANCASTER   OH           614 561-9623     2.25
    323    1014AM    03     AKRON       OH           216 846-8834     1.05
    323     155PM    04     AKRON       OH           216 846-8834     1.35
    324     943AM    13     COLUMBUS    OH           614 457-8496     2.97
    325     936AM    08     CLEVELAND   OH           216 271-8811     2.55
    325    1002AM    01     LANCASTER   OH           614 561-9623      .45
    329    1115AM    13     LANCASTER   OH           614 561-9623     4.05
    330     330PM    07     COLUMBUS    OH           614 457-8496     2.25

                                                           TOTAL    34.41
```

Type your report on plain paper to be submitted to Mr. Sanders.

DEMONSTRATING OFFICE SKILLS

1. Role play the following situations. If there is recording equipment available, you may want to record the conversations so that you can later listen to your own performance to note what you are doing well and what might be improved. While two students are acting out a situation, the other members of the class should make notes for evaluating the conversations. In evaluating telephone conversations, note especially the "message" conveyed by the voice and the words used.

   Situation 1: The telephone rings. You are answering the telephone for the Mail Room, where you are employed as a clerk. The person calling is Mr. Georgio Missoni who thinks he has gotten the office of the vice-president in charge of advertising, Mr. Howard Beeby. You and a fellow student, who plays the caller, Mr. Missoni, present your telephone conversation.

   Situation 2: You are an office worker in the office of Mrs. Geraldine Buchman, the director of cafeterias in your organization. Mrs. Buchman wants a sales representative for the

Bowdon Company to come by to see her because she needs new cooking utensils for one of the kitchens. Mrs. Buchman asks you to call the Bowdon Company to see if a representative can visit her at 3 on next Monday or at 10 on next Wednesday. You are able to dial direct to the Sales Office, where you talk with a receptionist. You and a fellow student, who assumes the role of the receptionist at the sales office of the Bowdon Company, present your telephone conversation.

2. The following telephone calls were received on December 2 while the persons called were not at their desks. Write messages for each call. Use message forms from the *Supplies Inventory* or prepare a form similar to the one shown in Illustration 6-4.

   a. Nancy Thomas called Roger T. Daniels at 9:15 regarding a conference plan that needs his approval. She would like Mr. Daniels to call her at his earliest convenience. She is at 578-9042.

   b. David Hirsch called Roger T. Daniels at 9:30. He is beginning a new project and needs some advice. He will call back this afternoon when he returns to his office.

   c. Midge Jones needs a quick answer to a problem. She called Frank G. Kercado at 9:35. He will call back at 2 this afternoon.

   d. Lannie McMahon received Frank C. Kercado's letter. He would like to talk with Mr. Kercado. Would he call at his convenience. Mr. McMahon can be reached at 543-5678 until 6:00 this evening.

Handling Outgoing Calls

Luis Carreno is a clerk in the delivery department of a large store in downtown Brooklyn. Often orders are delayed because of manufacturing problems. Therefore, calls must be made to customers. Luis often calls dozens of customers each day to give them up-to-date information about their orders. He enjoys his telephone work, and he is careful to be courteous while he talks with each customer. Often the customer is disappointed about the postponement of the order, but Luis strives to end each conversation pleasantly. He assures the customer that his department is sorry for the delay, but is doing what can be done to meet the new schedule.

Many business details are handled by telephone. You will find that often you will place a call in order to get information that you need or to get information for someone else in your office. To make each outgoing call **expeditiously**, it is important that you understand thoroughly the reason for your call and that you have at hand all the information related to the call.

expeditiously: quickly and efficiently

Telephone Directories

Telephone directories are valuable references. You should be able to reach them quickly and use them effectively. You may have a personal directory for frequently used telephone numbers, as well as a company directory, the alphabetical directory for your city (white pages), and the Yellow Pages in those large cities where this is a separate book. If you work in an office that makes calls to certain large cities frequently, it is likely that out-of-town directories will also be available.

You will always want to be sure that you have the right number before you place a call. You should **consult** the appropriate directory, and only if the number is not listed should you call Information. Your local telephone directory will give you details for dialing Information in your area, as well as for dialing beyond that area. In some areas a charge is made for calling Information.

consult: refer to

Personal Telephone Directory

An up-to-date list of frequently called local and out-of-town telephone numbers will save you and your employer a great deal of telephoning time. Booklets to be used as personal telephone directories can be obtained from most telephone companies. For the small firm or office, an "automatic finder" can be used. By moving the indicator on the finder to the correct letter of the alphabet, you can reach the desired page immediately. A large personal listing can be kept more easily on cards in a revolving visible file on your desk.

Alphabetical Directory

The names of subscribers are listed alphabetically in this directory. Individual names and firm names are easily located, unless the spelling of a name is unusual, and then it is cross-referenced as:

Brook — *See also* Brooke
Kaufmann — *See also* Kauffman, Kauffmann, Kaufman
McClelland — *See also* McClellan, McLellan

For the convenience of their customers or clients, business and professional people often list their home numbers directly below their business listings: for example,

Gaylord, James L advtg 70 East56...............................456-3219
    Res Rockeligh NJ...201 765-4332

It is often necessary to call government agencies to request information or answers to questions which are constantly arising about government regulations. Government agencies are listed under three categories:

categories:
classes; groups

Federal agencies under
United States Government .............U.S. Government
                                State Dept of
                                Treasury Dept

State agencies under
state government..........................Oklahoma State of
                                Motor Vehicles Dept of
                                Parks & Recreation

County and municipal agencies
under local governments................Louisville City of
                                Human Resources Administration
                                Landmarks Preservation
                                Mental Health

The first few pages of the alphabetical directory contain useful information including instructions for making emergency calls, local and long-distance calls, service calls (repair, assistance, etc.) and special calls (overseas, conference, collect, etc.). In addition, area codes for the United States and Canada, sample rates, and telephone company business office addresses and telephone numbers are listed.

Yellow Pages

The Yellow Pages are used when you wish to find out quickly where you may obtain a particular product or service. The names, addresses, and telephone numbers of business subscribers are listed alphabetically under the name of the product or service. Many business organizations use advertising space and artistic displays to tell their customers about the organization's operations, including brands carried, hours, and services. Nationally advertised or trademarked products may be listed with the names, addresses, and telephone numbers of most of the local dealers arranged alphabetically under a word or trademark design.

For instance, your employer may ask you to reorder master sets and copy paper for the A. B. Dick spirit duplicator. Under the heading, "Duplicating Machines & Supplies," the A.B. DICK trademark is displayed. Many local dealers are listed below "WHERE TO BUY THEM."

Illus. 6-5

In the Yellow Pages, you can locate a business by the product or service it offers.

At another time your employer may ask you to call a certified public accountant named Jones who has an office on North Fifth Street. Since there are so many Joneses listed in the alphabetical section, it will be much easier to refer to the heading in the Yellow Pages "Accountants —Certified Public" to find this particular Jones.

Placing Long-Distance Calls

At times you may have to place long-distance calls. The two major types of long-distance calls are *direct dialed calls* and *operator-assisted calls*.

Direct Dialed Calls

Direct distance dialing (DDD) is a method of placing all station-to-station calls by using the dial on your telephone. A *station-to-station call* is one made to a certain telephone number. This type of call is made if you are willing to talk with anyone who may answer the telephone or if you are fairly certain the person with whom your employer wishes to speak is within easy reach of the telephone. No assistance is needed from the operator in order to complete the call. The front pages of the telephone directory provide complete instructions for direct distance dialing.

Illus. 6-6

Dialing direct is economical and timesaving.

Gene Daniels — Black Star

Unit 6 • Using Communication Services

In order to dial direct in making a station-to-station call, you must generally first dial the number 1, which is a prefix code, to get a long-distance line. Then, you dial the area code and the seven digits of the particular telephone number you wish to reach. For example, suppose you were in Franconia, New Hampshire, and wished to call the Carter Supply House in Boston, Massachusetts. The telephone number for this Boston firm is (617) 453-6789. You would dial 1-617-453-6789.

1 is the prefix code to get a long-distance line
617 is the area code for Boston
453-6789 is the telephone number of the Carter Supply House

Station-to-station calls may also be made with the operator's assistance, but such calls generally cost more than calls dialed direct.

Operator-Assisted Calls

Operator-assisted calls are those which require some operator assistance. Person-to-person calls, credit card calls, and collect calls all require operator assistance.

Person-to-person calls. When you wish to speak with a particular person in a large company, you may need to place a person-to-person call. A *person-to-person call* is directed to a specific person, room number, extension number, or department. Make this type of call only if you must talk with a particular person and you are not sure whether the person will be available. This type of call costs more than a station-to-station call. In making such a call, you must generally dial the operator and ask that the call be placed for you. Give the information to the operator in this order: area code, telephone number, and the name of the person with whom you wish to speak. For example, you should say, "I'm making a person-to-person call to (412) 675-4320. I would like to speak with Dr. Helen O. Anderson."

In many cities, it is also possible to use direct distance dialing for person-to-person calls. You must first dial a special prefix code. This special prefix code signals the telephone company's computer that you wish to make a person-to-person call with DDD. You then dial the area code and the particular telephone number. The operator will come on the line and ask for the name of the person you are calling. When that person answers, the operator notes the start of the call. This is required for billing purposes.

You should remain at the telephone until your call is completed or until you receive a report from the operator that the person you want is not available. If the person isn't available, you may place the call later or ask the operator to call the party at a specified time.

Collect calls. You can call "collect" if the person or firm you are calling agrees to pay the charge. If you want to make a "collect" call, tell the operator when you place the call. Additional information about collect calls is given in Part 4.

Credit card calls. Customers who have telephone company credit cards may place calls and charge them to their credit card numbers. These calls require that the operator record the credit card number when the calls are placed. Additional information about credit card calls is given in Part 4.

Time Factor

It is important that you be aware of the time differences when placing long-distance calls. The continental United States is divided into four standard time zones: Eastern, Central, Mountain, and Pacific. Each zone is one hour earlier than the zone immediately to the east of it. When it is 3 p.m. Eastern Standard Time, it is 2 p.m. in the Central zone, 1 p.m. in the Mountain zone, and noon in the Pacific zone. This means that when it is 1 p.m. in New York, it is 10 a.m. in Los Angeles.

You must be aware of 17 different time zones when placing calls to other countries. When it is 9 a.m. in Chicago and Mexico City (both are

Illus. 6-7

Map of telephone area codes and time zones

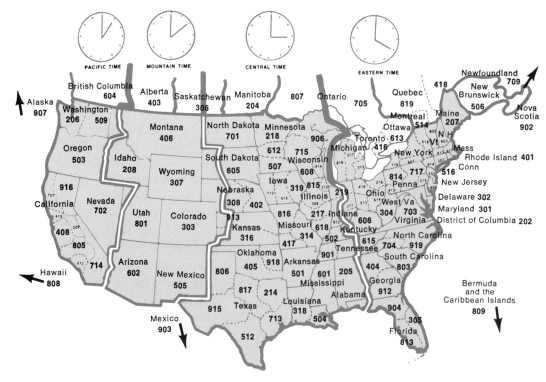

Unit 6 • Using Communication Services

in the same time zone), it is noon in Rio De Janeiro, 2 p.m. in London and Lisbon, 4 p.m. in Athens, and midnight in Tokyo.

The Cost of Telephone Service

The cost of telephone service is determined by the kinds of equipment the business has and the ways in which the equipment is used.

Cost for Local Calls

Businesses are charged in many different ways for their telephone service. In most communities the business is charged a basic rate for its telephone service, and it then can make as many local calls as it wishes. In a few large cities you are allowed a certain number of calls for a base rate and are charged for each extra call.

Costs for Long-Distance Calls

Charges are made for all out-of-town telephone calls or calls made beyond the local service area. Charges depend upon the distance, the type of call, the time of day or night that the call is made, and the length of the conversation. You should know when it is **advisable** to make each type of call and the relative costs of the calls.

advisable: recommended

The cost of a station-to-station call is less than the cost of a person-to-person call because a call can be made to a particular number in much less time than a call to a particular person. Long-distance calls you dial yourself are less expensive than calls for which you need the operator's assistance.

The rates for direct-dialed calls are based on an initial charge for one minute while the rates for operator-assisted calls are usually based on an initial charge for three minutes. Lower rates are in effect between 5 p.m. and 8 a.m. on weekdays and also apply all day on Saturdays, Sundays, and some holidays. You will find the rate schedule in the front pages of your current local telephone directory.

REVIEWING IMPORTANT POINTS

1. What types of phone directories are provided by your local telephone company?
2. What phone numbers are likely to be listed in a personal telephone directory?

3. How are names of subscribers listed in the Yellow Pages?
4. Under what letter of the alphabet would you look to find the Employment Office of the federal government?
5. Where would you find information about the procedure for making emergency calls?
6. When would you use the Yellow Pages?
7. How does a person-to-person call differ from a station-to-station call?
8. For what reason must you use the prefix "1" in some communities when you dial a long-distance number?
9. What information does an operator need when you ask for assistance in placing a person-to-person call?
10. Why should you be aware of time zones when making calls to various parts of the country?

MAKING IMPORTANT DECISIONS

1. When Ken Nathan answered the telephone in his office, the operator said: "This call is for Mr. Frank Hunter. Is Mr. Hunter there?" Ken knew that Mr. Hunter was in a meeting in a nearby conference room where there was a telephone. He was not sure what his response should be. What do you think Ken should say to the operator now?
2. Mr. William F. Solomon asked Mitch Randall, one of the office workers in the department, to place a call to George Weston in Springfield, Illinois. When Mitch placed the call, the operator reported that Mr. Weston wasn't in his office. He was expected back at 3:00. The operator wanted to know if a message should be left for Mr. Weston. Mitch didn't know what to say. What do you think Mitch's response should be?

LEARNING TO WORK WITH OTHERS

Eva Klein and Curtis Jeffrey work together in an adjustment department of a large department store. Often when Curtis is out for lunch or in the file room getting records, Eva takes messages from customers who have already talked with Curtis. Generally Eva records the name of the customer inaccurately. This means that Curtis has difficulty trying to determine who has called him. At times the telephone number is also wrong. These inaccurate messages are useless in many cases. Curtis is unhappy about the situation.

What do you think Curtis should do in this situation?

IMPROVING LANGUAGE SKILLS

The following words are spelled both correctly and incorrectly. On a sheet of paper type the correct spelling of each word. Then write a sentence using the word or a form of the word.

1.	additionally	addetionaly
2.	alphibitecal	alphabetical
3.	approximately	approximetly
4.	assistance	assistence
5.	carryed	carried
6.	comunities	communities
7.	conection	connection
8.	equipement	equipment
9.	extention	extension
10.	intial	initial
11.	operetor	operator
12.	repiar	repair
13.	reppresantive	representative
14.	residance	residence
15.	spetial	special
16.	techneques	techniques
17.	transfering	transferring
18.	terminating	terminateing
19.	unnecessary	unnecessery
20.	vocabulery	vocabulary

IMPROVING ARITHMETIC SKILLS

Determine the cost of each of the following Station-to-Station, DDD calls using the table on the next page.

Tuesday at 10:00 a.m., a 5-minute call from New York City to St. Louis, Missouri

Wednesday at 1:30 p.m., an 8-minute call from New York City to Denver, Colorado

Wednesday at 5:35 p.m., a 4-minute call from New York City to Los Angeles, California

Thursday at 6:50 p.m., a 2-minute call from New York City to Portland, Maine

Friday at 3:30 p.m., an 11-minute call from New York City to New Orleans, Louisiana

Saturday at 9:30 a.m., a 6-minute call from New York City to Philadelphia, Pennsylvania

What would each call cost if it were a person-to-person call?

Long distance rates to other states (excluding Alaska and Hawaii)

CALLS TO:	STATION-TO-STATION											PERSON-TO-PERSON				
	DIRECT DISTANCE DIALED (Paid by calling party)						OPERATOR-ASSISTED									
	FULL WEEKDAY RATE Mon.–Fri. 8 AM–5 PM		35% EVENING DISCOUNT Sun.–Fri. 5 AM–11 PM		60% NIGHT & WEEKEND DISCOUNT Every Night 11 AM–8 PM All Day and Night on Sat. to 5 PM Sun.		ALL DAYS & HOURS	OVERTIME			ALL DAYS & HOURS	OVERTIME				
								WEEKDAYS 8 AM–5 PM	35% EVENING DISCOUNT Sun.–Fri. 5 AM–11 PM	60% NIGHT & WEEKEND DISCOUNT Every Night 11 AM–8 PM All Day and Night on Sat. to 5 PM Sun.		WEEKDAYS 8 AM–5 PM	35% EVENING DISCOUNT Sun.–Fri. 5 AM–11 PM	60% NIGHT & WEEKEND DISCOUNT Every Night 11 AM–8 PM All Day and Night on Sat. to 5 PM Sun.
	Init. 1 Min.	Ea. Add. Min.	Init. 1 Min.	Ea. Add. Min.	Init. 1 Min.	Ea. Add. Min.	Init. 3 Mins.	Ea. Add. Min.	Ea. Add. Min.	Ea. Add. Min.	Init. 3 Mins.	Ea. Add. Min.	Ea. Add. Min.	Ea. Add. Min.
Atlanta, Ga.	.50	.35	.32	.22	.20	.14	1.80	.35	.22	.14	2.80	.35	.22	.14
Atlantic City, N. J.	.41	.26	.26	.16	.16	.10	1.35	.26	.16	.10	1.80	.26	.16	.10
Boston, Mass.	.44	.29	.28	.18	.17	.11	1.50	.29	.18	.11	2.10	.29	.18	.11
Chicago, Ill.	.50	.35	.32	.22	.20	.14	1.80	.35	.22	.14	2.80	.35	.22	.14
Cleveland, Ohio	.48	.33	.31	.21	.19	.13	1.70	.33	.21	.13	2.50	.33	.21	.13
Denver, Colo.	.54	.38	.35	.24	.21	.15	1.90	.38	.24	.15	3.10	.38	.24	.15
Detroit, Mich.	.49	.34	.31	.22	.19	.13	1.75	.34	.22	.13	2.65	.34	.22	.13
Hartford, Conn.	.41	.26	.26	.16	.16	.10	1.35	.26	.16	.10	1.80	.26	.16	.10
Houston, Tex.	.54	.38	.35	.24	.21	.15	1.90	.38	.24	.15	3.10	.38	.24	.15
Los Angeles, Cal.	.56	.40	.36	.26	.22	.16	1.95	.40	.26	.16	3.55	.40	.26	.16
Miami, Fla.	.52	.36	.33	.23	.20	.14	1.85	.36	.23	.14	2.95	.36	.23	.14
Milwaukee, Wisc.	.50	.35	.32	.22	.20	.14	1.80	.35	.22	.14	2.80	.35	.22	.14
New Orleans, La.	.52	.36	.33	.23	.20	.14	1.85	.36	.23	.14	2.95	.36	.23	.14
Phialdelphia, Pa.	.40	.25	.26	.16	.16	.10	1.25	.25	.16	.10	1.70	.25	.16	.10
Portland, Maine	.46	.31	.29	.20	.18	.12	1.60	.31	.20	.12	2.30	.31	.20	.12
St. Louis, Mo.	.50	.35	.32	.22	.20	.14	1.80	.35	.22	.14	2.80	.35	.22	.14
Seattle, Wash.	.56	.40	.36	.26	.22	.16	1.95	.40	.26	.16	3.55	.40	.26	.16
Washington, D.C.	.45	.30	.29	.19	.18	.12	1.55	.30	.19	.12	2.20	.30	.19	.15

Unit 6 • Using Communication Services

DEMONSTRATING OFFICE SKILLS

1. Role play the following situation:

   You are a clerk in a shipping department where one of your fellow workers has just slipped on a piece of a carton that was left accidentally on the floor in one of the storage rooms. It seems he has hurt his wrist. Although it isn't bleeding, it is quite painful. The supervisor asks you to call the local hospital to see if he can be taken care of immediately.

   One student should play the role of the receptionist at the hospital, another the role of the clerk calling about an immediate appointment.

2. On a separate sheet of paper type answers to the following questions. (Use your local alphabetical directory and Yellow Pages to find the answers):

   a. What number do you call to report a fire?
   b. What number do you call to get in touch with the local police department?
   c. What is the number of an automobile repair service?
   d. Under what heading would you look for the name of a lawyer?
   e. Under what heading would you look for the name of a doctor?
   f. Under what heading would you look to find a source for stencils and direct process masters?
   g. Under what heading would you look to find a place with banquet facilities?

Part 3

Using Special Equipment

Eloisa Prieto has just returned from a very interesting demonstration in one of the classrooms in the training department of the large insurance company where she works. The local telephone representative gave a very effective demonstration of the new equipment that is being installed. Eloisa now understands how to use the equipment and the reason the company is making the change. The new telephone equipment means that the work of the office can be done more efficiently than it was before.

Increasingly, companies are installing telephone systems that allow direct dialing from outside to particular offices as well as direct dialing within the company. Each telephone has a number which, when added to the company prefix, can be dialed from outside.

Example: G. T. Walters & Company   730-2300
             Personnel Office   730-2343

When the company number (730-2300) is dialed, the central switchboard responds. With direct dialing systems, the central switchboard staff is much smaller than that required in a non-direct dialing system. The operator in the central office can transfer calls that come in through the main number. It is also possible to dial the personnel office, for example, from outside by dialing 730-2343. A person calling that office from within the company needs to dial only 2-3-4-3. When someone from within the company wishes to dial a number outside the company, it is necessary to dial for an outside line first, generally 9, and then the full number of the party desired.

Switchboards

Many companies continue to use a private business exchange (PBX) system or switchboard to handle telephone calls. Such a system requires one or more operators who receive calls from outside, place all outgoing calls, and handle calls within offices of the company.

A PBX system has three main functions:

1. To receive incoming calls.
2. To place outgoing calls.
3. To make calls between offices within the business.

Usually companies have special switchboard operators. Sometimes, however, office workers are asked to fill in at the switchboard at the noon hour or at other times during the day.

Cord Switchboard

Cord switchboards are used in large businesses where many telephone lines are needed. The switchboard operator receives all incoming calls, makes the connection for interoffice calls, and either places outgoing calls or provides the outside line to dial the call.

Cordless Switchboard

There are many kinds of cordless switchboards. Usually companies that do not have a great volume of telephone calls will use a cordless board. A full-time operator is not needed since incoming calls usually can be made to any extension number and employees can place their own outgoing calls. The operator will normally answer only calls that are of a general nature.

Illus. 6-8

A cordless switchboard is used by companies that do not handle a great number of telephone calls.

Call Director

The Call Director is a small desk switchboard which permits you to answer many lines from one location. You can also transfer calls and make outside calls. An executive can both make and receive calls without assistance.

Illus. 6-9

In a busy office a Call Director is a time-saver for both office worker and executive.

Touch-Tone Telephone

depress:
push down

Touch-tone telephones have buttons instead of a rotary dial. Listen for the dial tone; then **depress** the numbered buttons for the telephone number. As each button is depressed you will hear a tone.

Touch-tone calling systems are being installed throughout the country and are available to both home and business users. The advantage of this calling system is the increased speed in dialing. More and more firms also use touch-tone buttons to send data to computers.

Key Telephone

Key telephones have almost completely replaced the two or three individual telephones that were formerly found on the busy executive's desk. A key telephone may have from one to six keys along its base, but the six-key variety is most common.

Arrangement of the Keys

The keys on a six-key telephone should be arranged and labeled in this order:

1. The *hold* key is the key on the left side of the telephone. When it is depressed you will be able to hold a call while you make or answer another call. The first caller is then unable to overhear your second conversation. The hold key does not remain depressed but returns to normal when you release it. However, if you do not use it before pressing another key to accept a second call, the first caller will be cut off.
2. The pick-up keys, Keys 2, 3, 4, 5, and 6, are used to make and receive outside calls. A line will be connected when you depress the correct key.

Illus. 6-10

With a six-key telephone more than one call can be handled on a single extension.

Key 1	Key 2	Key 3	Key 4	Key 5	Key 6
Hold	2368	2369	2370	2371	2372

Operating a Key Telephone

A number of calls can be handled on a key telephone at the same time. The steps involved in the receiving and handling of two incoming calls follow.

1. Depress the *pick-up* key connected with the ringing line before lifting the receiver. (Pick-up keys usually light up when in use.)
2. If a call comes in while you are talking on another line, excuse yourself, depress the *hold* key, then depress the pick-up key connected with the ringing line and answer it.
3. When the second call is completed, return to the first call by depressing the key for that line.

Custom-made arrangements, designed to meet the special needs of a particular office, are found in many offices. For instance, a *signal* key may be used as an internal buzzer that allows the executive to signal an assistant for help.

Speakerphone

You need not pick up the receiver at all when you use the Speakerphone. When a call comes in, you press a button and talk as you would to a visitor in your office. The caller's voice comes from a small loudspeaker on your desk. The **volume** of the loudspeaker can be adjusted to suit your desire. Your own voice is picked up by a microphone **sensitive** enough to hear your voice anywhere in your office or all the voices in an office conference. You can talk and listen with both hands free to take notes or to look up records. When you want to make a private call, you can pick up the receiver and your Speakerphone automatically becomes a regular telephone again.

volume:
loudness

sensitive:
receiving sounds
easily

Automatic Dialing Telephones

There are several automatic dialing telephones commonly used in business offices. Automatic dialing telephones save a great deal of telephoning time, and they eliminate the possibility of dialing a wrong number.

Card Dialer

The Card Dialer uses small plastic cards for numbers you call frequently. They should be coded and placed in the storage area in the unit. To place a call, you insert the proper card in the dial slot, lift the receiver, and when you hear the dial tone, press the start bar. There is no need to dial the number each time you want it.

Unit 6 • Using Communication Services

Illus. 6-11

The Card Dialer is useful for placing volume calls.

American Telephone & Telegraph Company

Touch-A-Matic

The Touch-A-Matic is a Touch-Tone automatic dialer. It is a combination of a six-key touch-tone telephone and a magnetic tape dialer with a storage for up to 500 telephone numbers.

Illus. 6-12

The Touch-A-Matic tape dialer is another telephone convenience feature.

American Telephone & Telegraph Company

Bellboy

The Bell System provides a personal signaling service called the Bellboy. The Bellboy is actually a pocket radio receiver with a 40-mile radius that, by means of a tone signal, alerts the carrier to call the office or home for a message.

> Mrs. Leslie works for Dr. Nagel, a very busy doctor who is often called to the three hospitals in the county. The doctor finds the Bellboy service invaluable. There are times when Mrs. Leslie receives a distressing call about a very ill patient. She is able to signal the physician, who immediately calls her for the message. Dr. Nagel's schedule can then be changed to enable her to go to the site of the emergency.

Mobile Telephone

A mobile telephone provides telephone service in a car or truck. It is possible to receive or place calls in the same way as in an office. This radio telephone service provides a listed number for the car or truck that is part of a nationwide dial network. Sales representatives, doctors, and municipal officials are among the common users of this special telephone service.

REVIEWING IMPORTANT POINTS

1. What do you believe is one of the major advantages of a direct dialing system when compared with a private business exchange system?
2. How are calls within a company handled in a direct dialing system?
3. Why is the Touch-Tone telephone considered an improvement to the rotary dial type of telephone?
4. What is the function of the hold key on a telephone?
5. How can you determine if someone is speaking on a line if there are 4 keys on the telephone?
6. What is the usefulness of a Card Dialer?
7. What is an advantage of a Speakerphone?
8. What is the key feature of the Touch-A-Matic?
9. What is the usefulness of the Bellboy?
10. What service does the mobile telephone provide?

MAKING IMPORTANT DECISIONS

1. Miss Ellis received a memorandum from Administrative Services inviting her to a presentation and demonstration of new telephone equipment that is to be installed in all the offices, including hers. She thinks: "A telephone is a telephone . . . so what could I learn at the demonstration?" What do you think of her decision not to attend the presentation?

2. Steve Herlitz has taken a new job as a clerk in a busy office. He notes that there is a small tray with plastic cards, each with a different number. He has no idea what these cards are for. He imagines they were used at one time in the office. Since they are taking up space on the desk, he decides that he will put them in a bottom drawer of a file cabinet where there seems to be some space. What do you think of Steve's decision?

LEARNING TO WORK WITH OTHERS

Kia Kwan works as a receptionist/typist in the central office of a large psychology department in a state university. When the telephones in the faculty offices are not answered on the third ring, the call is automatically transferred to Kia's telephone line, so she answers the telephone for the faculty member. In order to be helpful to callers, Kia needs to know the schedule of the professors, as well as basic information about courses, hours of classes, and office hours. Most employees of the professors are very helpful; however, the office assistant for Professor Hudnut is not. This office assistant never gives Kia a schedule, and never answers the telephone even when she is in her office. Then, after the call is transferred to the professor, the assistant calls Kia and asks, "Who was *that* who just called our office?"

Kia wishes the office assistant were more helpful. What do you think she might do about the situation?

IMPROVING LANGUAGE SKILLS

Adverbs, like adjectives, can be used in comparisons.

A. The *positive* degree is the simple form in which no comparison is indicated.
   Example: Bella said she would find the telephone number in the directory *quickly*.

B. The *comparative* degree is a form that makes a comparison between two possibilities.
   Example: Bella can find telephone numbers in the directory *quicker* than Gene can.

C. The *superlative* degree indicates the greatest degree of a quality among three or more possibilities.
   Example: Bella finds telephone numbers in the directory *quickest* of all of us clerks in the office.

On a separate sheet of paper, type the following sentences selecting the appropriate adverb in each instance.

1. Jan said that she can dial (fast, faster) on the Touch-Tone telephone than on the dial telephone.
2. The Card Dialer is (an accurate, a most accurate) means of getting a number you want.
3. Darrel learned how to use the telephone (more rapidly, most rapidly) of the four clerks.
4. The ring of this telephone is (soft, softer) than that of the telephone in my former office.
5. The third, and last, demonstration was the (clearer, clearest) one, I felt.
6. Mat types (fast, fastest).
7. Of all these boxes, I think this one is (better, best).
8. Bill arrived (sooner, soonest) than Ted and Sally.
9. John listened (carefully, most carefully) to the instructions for typing the report.
10. Our receptionist, Etta Hamilton, receives all callers (kindly, most kindly).

IMPROVING ARITHMETIC SKILLS

You have been asked to do some computing and then type up a report. One of the operators in the central telephone office of your company tallied the incoming calls on seven extensions for two time periods. When there are more than 15 calls per hour, it is generally advisable for an office to have a second extension. You are to add the number of calls for each extension for each of the hours. Then, you are to take an average of the two to determine if there were more than 15 calls per hour. After you have done the computations, type your report on plain paper so that it can be easily read by the supervisor.

Extensions: Calls between 9:30 and 10:30   Tuesday, October 21

4321 . . . . .
4322 . . . . .
4323 . . . . .
4324 . . . . .
4325 . . . . .
4326 . . . . .
4327 . . . . .

Extensions: Calls between 1:45 and 2:45   Thursday, November 7

4321 . . . . .
4322 . . . . .
4323 . . . . .
4324 . . . . .
4325 . . . . .
4326 . . . . .
4327 . . . . .

DEMONSTRATING OFFICE SKILLS

You are a clerk/typist in a small magazine publishing company. You have been asked to set up the telephone directory, which will be duplicated on heavy cardboard in a size appropriate for desk use. You are to type the directory on standard size plain paper in the form you believe will be most useful. Below is a list of the staff with their titles and telephone extensions. The first two listings will be:

Advertising Sales Director
    James W. Rutman...5637

Allen, Mortimer S.
    Production Editor...5645

Norman Krauss, Editor in Chief x5691
Patricia Weaver, Executive Editor x5679
William M. Graves, Managing Editor x5611
John P. Walsh, Art Director x5613
M. Jane Podell, Senior Editor x5651
Roy Flori, Senior Editor x5632
Giovanna Sparci, Senior Editor x5644
Ruth Landman, Senior Editor x5690
Gail Cassel, Associate Editor x5670
Robert S. Stephens, Associate Editor x5678
John M. Hill, Associate Editor x5643
Mortimer S. Allen, Production Editor x5645
Sally T. Fox, Associate Art Director x5622
Lawrence G. Zackman, Assistant Art Director x5688
Jean R. Leeper, Art Assistant x5689
Carol Cohen, Editorial Assistant x5603
William C. Hyde, Editorial Assistant x5647
Davis Roberts, President x5609
John T. Norris, Publisher x5612
Dee Bowman, Associate Publisher x5673
James W. Rutman, Advertising Sales Director x5637
Marilyn T. Podell, Special Projects Director x5633

Part 4

Using Special Services

Debbie Davidson works for an international public accounting firm. She is a clerk/typist and enjoys the variety of jobs she does each week. One of her primary jobs is sending messages around the world. She knows how to send messages via the company's teletypewriters, and by mailgram, telegram, and cablegram. Since much of the company's business is related to multinational firms, communications to other parts of the world are very important.

Special Long-Distance Calls

Commonly used long-distance services include:

1. Collect calls.
2. Credit card calls.
3. Conference calls.
4. Wide Area Telephone Service (WATS).
5. Overseas telephone calls.

The front pages of your local telephone directory contain the instructions for using each of these services. You should read that material carefully if you have responsibility for handling such calls.

Collect Calls

If you want the charges reversed, that is, if you want the station or the person you are calling to pay the charges, notify the operator when you place the call. This gives the station or person you are calling an opportunity to accept or refuse the call before the connection is made. The charges may be reversed on both station-to-station and person-to-person calls.

Credit Card Calls

Many business executives have credit cards from the telephone company that allow them to charge long-distance calls. Credit card telephone service is convenient for making long-distance calls when traveling.

If you are asked to place a credit call, you must be sure you have the credit card number. The card number, together with the area code and the telephone number, must be given to the operator who handles your call. The charge for the call will be billed to the executive's account.

Conference Calls

A conference call is a telephone call that enables several persons at different locations to talk to each other at the same time. As many as ten locations can be connected for a conference call. To arrange such a call you should give the operator the names, telephone numbers, and locations of the persons to be connected for the call. Be certain to give the exact time of the scheduled conference.

Wide Area Telephone Service (WATS)

Some of the telephone lines used by the company for which you work may be called "WATS" lines, and some phones may be called "WATS" phones. This means that the firm offers its customers, without charge, Wide Area Telephone Service. Customers and potential customers are able to call them without cost. Firms that use this service believe that, if they offer their customers this free service, they will get more business. Many hotel and motel chains use WATS service in order to make it easier for the customers to make room reservations.

potential: possible

The WATS phones or lines are used only for making and receiving station-to-station long-distance calls. To determine whether the company you wish to call offers this service, dial Area Code 800 and then 555-1212. The 800 is the standard area code for all WATS lines, and the 555-1212 is for operator assistance.

Overseas Telephone Calls

Underseas cables, satellites, and radio now make it possible to telephone cities and towns throughout the world. Each year more places can be reached through direct dialing. There are still many places, however, where you must seek the assistance of the operator. When placing a call to another country, you must be aware of the difference in time between the town where you are placing the call and the city or town you are calling. Recall the discussion in Part 1 of this Unit about the 17 time zones around the world.

Teletypewriter Service

A teletype is a typewriter-like machine which operates on the same principle as a telephone except that the typewritten, rather than the spoken, word is transmitted. Messages typed on the standard typewriter keyboard of a teletypewriter are transmitted and reproduced as they are typed. A message may be reproduced on a single machine or on many machines, depending on the kind of service the business wants.

Teletype equipment is often used for communication between offices of the same firm and between offices of different firms when speed is an important factor and when a written record of the message is desired. There are basically two types of teletype service: teletypewriter exchange service and teletypewriter private line service.

Illus 6-13

Teletype machines make possible the rapid transmission of written messages.

Western Union Data Services Company

Teletypewriter Exchange Service (TWX)

Teletypewriter exchange service (TWX) operates through a Western Union service. Each **subscriber** has a teletypewriter number and is furnished with a directory of all teletypewriter subscribers in the United States.

subscriber:
user of a service

Before sending a message, the teletype operator signals the TWX equipment being called and types the exchange and the number to be reached. After the connection has been made and the called unit is ready to receive, the teletype operator types the message. As the sending operator types the message, the receiving machine instantly copies it. The rates for teletyped messages are much lower than the rates for station-to-station telephone calls.

Teletypewriter Private Line Service (TWPL)

Teletypewriter private line service (TWPL) or leased wire service messages do not go through a central Western Union office. The machines are connected by direct wires. They are used for interoffice communications by firms with a number of branch offices and plants throughout the country.

Data-Phone Service

Data-phone service provides the means for computers to "talk" to computers. Payrolls, inventories, sales figures, and other business data can be transmitted rapidly from one location to another.

Illus. 6-14

Data-phones transmit large quantities of business data over regular telephone lines.

American Telephone & Telegraph Company

Data-phones can handle data prepared on punched cards, paper tape, or magnetic tape. Machine signals from the punched cards or tape are converted into tones that are sent over regular telephone lines. The Data-phone at the receiving offices changes the transmitted tones back into whatever is required: punched cards, paper tape, or magnetic tape.

Data-phone sets are capable of transmitting at speeds of up to 4,500 words per minute. The charge for this service is the same as it would be for a regular long-distance call.

Domestic Telegraph Services

A network of communications services is provided by Western Union for those persons who wish to send messages quickly from one place to another across the United States. Messages can be transmitted to a Western Union office in person or by telephone and from that office it is quickly forwarded to the recipient's town or city.

The Telegram

The telegram is a rapid means of written communication. It can be sent anywhere in the country and is often delivered within a few hours of the time of its transmission. A telegram sent a distance of 1,500 miles will be delivered in less than an hour, while the average business letter requires two to three days for delivery to such a distance.

Selecting the Service

The telegraph company provides two different types of telegrams. Messages are sent and delivered according to the type of telegram used. Some are sent and delivered immediately; others are sent during the night and delivered early during the following morning. The two types are the full-rate telegram and the overnight telegram.

Full-Rate Telegram. When there is great urgency about the message or when speed in having the message received is important, you will send the full-rate telegram. A full-rate telegram, usually referred to simply as a telegram, is the faster type of telegraph service. The message is sent immediately at any time during the day or night and, if it is received during business hours, it is telephoned or delivered to the addressee at once. Delivery is made within five hours of receipt of the message. Although it is a more expensive type of service, it is used most frequently by businesses because of the speed with which it is sent and delivered.

The basic charge is made for a message of 15 words or less; a small charge is made for each additional word in the message.

Overnight Telegram. An overnight telegram is more economical than a fast full-rate telegram but it is a slower type of telegraph service. It will be accepted by the telegraph office any time up to midnight for delivery the following morning. The basic charge is for a minimum of 100 words. Additional words are charged at the rate of approximately 3 cents a word. It is used mostly for messages of considerable length such as business proposals, progress reports, and detailed instructions.

Preparing a Telegram

You must prepare a telegram carefully if it is to be delivered without delay and if it is to be understood by the one who receives it. The secret of a well-worded telegram is to state your message as clearly and briefly as possible. The suggestions listed below should be kept in mind when preparing a telegram.

Since charges are based on the number of words beyond a minimum, you should secure from your local Western Union office the current basis for charges. You should acquaint yourself with the way in which numbers and special symbols are counted so that you can carefully write your messages to take advantage of the lowest cost available.

The following suggestions will aid you in preparing telegrams:

1. *Use Western Union telegram banks.* You can obtain pads of telegram blanks free of charge at any Western Union office. However, a telegram may be typed on plain paper.
2. *Type three copies of the telegram.* Ordinarily the original goes to the telegraph company, the second copy to the correspondence file, and the third to the addressee so that the message can be checked to see if it was transmitted correctly.
3. *Type the message with capital and lower case letters.* The message should be double spaced. Do not divide a word at the end of a line.
4. *Indicate whether the message is to be sent paid, collect, or charge.* If it is to be charged, indicate the account below the heading, CHARGE TO THE ACCOUNT OF.
5. *Indicate the type of service desired.* Type an "X" in the box before Over Night Telegram at the upper right of the blank if you want to send an overnight telegram. Unless the box is checked the message will be sent as a full-rate telegram.
6. *Type the date.*
7. *Type the full name of the addressee.*

8. *Type the complete address and telephone number of the addressee*. Whenever possible give the office number. Spell out such words as *North* and *South*. Do not use suffixes with street numbers (34 not 34th Street).
9. *Write the message clearly and include punctuation*. The use of punctuation marks makes the message clearer. There is no extra charge for them.
10. *Include your address and telephone number*. After the signature type the sender's telephone number, name, and address. This is important if hotel or travel reservations are requested.

Filing a Telegram

A message can be provided to the Western Union office for transmission in any one of the following ways:

1. *Over the Counter*. A prepared message can be taken to a Western Union office or a message can be written at the counter.
2. *Over the Telephone*. A telegram can be filed over the telephone. When a message is telephoned to a Western Union office, care must be taken to be sure that names and unusual words are transmitted **accurately**. Such words should be spelled out to the operator to avoid confusion.
3. *Tie Line Service*. Tie lines are used when the firm sends and receives a large number of telegrams. A tie line is a system of direct wires between the business and the telegraph company.
4. *Teleprinter Service*. A specially installed printing machine, the teleprinter, permits the operator to type a message that is **simultaneously** recorded on a tape or a message form in the telegraph office.

Paying for Service

Telegraph service may be paid for in any one of four ways:

1. *With cash at the time the message is sent*. Cash may be required of an infrequent telegraph user.
2. *Through business charge accounts*. Charge accounts are carried by the telegraph company, particularly for large firms that send many telegrams every business day. These accounts are billed on a monthly basis.
3. *Through telephone subscribers' accounts*. An individual may send a telegram from a telephone or from a Western Union office and have it charged to the individual's telephone bill.
4. *By the person receiving the message*. A message may be sent collect. This means that the receiver of the telegram pays for it upon delivery. To send a telegram collect, type the word *Collect* beneath the heading PD OR COLL. at the top of the blank.

accurately:
without error

simultaneously:
at the same time

Sending Money

One of the quickest and safest ways for you to send money is to send a telegraphic money order. The amount to be sent is given to the telegraph office together with the name and address of the recipient and any accompanying message. There is a charge for sending the money order and a slight additional charge for any accompanying message. You will be given a receipt for the amount of money sent.

The recipient is notified when the money order arrives. To receive the money, the recipient will have to provide proof of identity, such as a passport.

Delivery Telegrams

A telegraphic message may be delivered in any one of the following ways:

1. *By messenger.* The message may be delivered in a sealed envelope by a Western Union messenger.
2. *By telephone.* The telephone is often used instead of the messenger for speed and convenience, especially when the addressee is located at a distance from the telegraph office. The Western Union operator will mail a copy of a telephoned message to the addressee upon request at no extra charge.
3. *By teleprinter.* This machine, described under "Filing a Telegram" on page 244, automatically receives and prints the messages.

When the telegraph company fails to deliver a message or makes an error in the transmission of the message, it is **liable** for damages. The limits of liability are stated on the back of each telegram blank.

liable: responsible

Using Special Telegram Services

When messages are of a legal nature or of serious concern to both sender and recipient, two additional services are available.

Repeat Back. At the time the message is filed with the telegraph company, you may decide that the message is important enough to need special attention. For example, the message may contain figures, names to be published, or dates. For an additional charge, a message may be repeated back from its **destination** to the sending office to be checked for possible errors. If errors are discovered, the corrected message is then sent at no additional charge. *Repeat Back* must be typed at the top of the telegraph blank if this additional service is desired.

destination: place to which something is sent

Report Delivery. Occasionally written evidence of the time of delivery and the address of the person or firm to whom the telegram was delivered is considered necessary. To get this additional information, you must pay the cost of a return telegram and type *Report Delivery* or *Report Delivery and Address* at the top of the telegraph blank. These words of instruction are counted and charged for.

Differences in Time Zones

A branch office in Portland wishes to contact your office in Atlanta. It is 5 p.m. in Portland. The message is long and will be reported at a branch meeting on the following afternoon. The office worker in Portland wisely sends it as an overnight telegram. You will receive it when you arrive at work the next day. If a telegram is to be sent any great distance east or west, the office worker must be aware of the difference in time between the sending office and the receiving office to decide upon the correct service.

The Mailgram

The Mailgram combines features of a letter and a telegram. This means of communication is available through Western Union, which uses the facilities of the U.S. Postal service for final delivery.

It is possible to send a mailgram by calling the local Western Union office number, which is a toll-free number, or by Telex or TWX. Each message is routed by wire to the post office nearest the addressee and printed out individually. The Mailgram receives **preferential** treatment and may be delivered the day it is received if the regular mail of that day is not yet delivered. Delivery is guaranteed for the following day in the 48 **contiguous** states.

The Mailgram is less expensive than the telegram, yet it provides for speedier delivery than an ordinary letter. It is placed in a **distinctive** blue and white envelope and is credited with gaining the attention of the recipient more readily than does an ordinary letter. There are special rates for sending the same message to a number of persons.

Mailgrams, just like telegrams, may be sent at any time, day or night, seven days a week.

International Telegraph Service

Many businesses have transactions with foreign companies. International communications are very common. Cablegrams may be sent to foreign countries by means of cables under the seas and by radio.

preferential:
priority

contiguous:
joined; touching

distinctive:
eye-catching; standing out

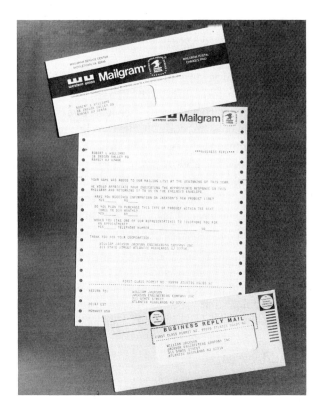

Illus. 6-15

Mailgram

Kinds of Service

International telegraph service and domestic telegraph service are similar. There are three types of international telegraph service: *Full-Rate* (FR) messages, *Cable Letters* (LT), and *Ship Radiograms*.

Full-Rate Messages (FR). A full-rate message is the fastest and most expensive type of overseas service. It is transmitted and delivered as quickly as possible. It may be written in any language that can be expressed in letters of ordinary type, or it can be written in code. A minimum charge is made for a message of seven words or less.

Cable Letters (LT). A cable letter, or letter telegram, is transmitted during the night and delivered at its destination the following morning. The message must be written in plain language, not code. A minimum charge is made for a message of 22 words or less. The cost is only one half that charged for full-rate messages.

Ship Radiograms. Plain language or code may be used in sending radiograms to and from ships at sea. A minimum charge is made for a message of seven words or less.

Code Messages

domestic:
within the country

Cablegrams and radiograms are more expensive than **domestic** telegrams. Not only are the rates higher but many more words are counted and changed for. In order to reduce the cost of overseas messages, many firms send their messages in code. One five-letter code word may be used in place of a common phrase that would normally take four or five words. For example, the code word *ODFUD* may be used in place of the statement, "Please cable at once," and only one word would be charged for instead of four.

You count chargeable words for international messages in about the same way that you do for domestic telegrams. The major differences are:

1. Each word in the address is counted and charged for.
2. Code words are counted as five letters to the word.
3. Each punctuation mark is counted as one word.
4. Special symbols, such as ¢, $, and #, must be spelled out because they cannot be transmitted.

Cable Code Addresses

Because each word in the address is counted as a chargeable word, firms that have a great many international messages often use a single code word as the business's cable address. Below are the regular address and the cable code address of Jones Lang Properties in London.

Regular Address	*Cable Code Address*
Jones Lang Properties	Jolpr
43 St. James Street	
London, England U.K.	

There is a small annual charge for registering the cable address with the telegraph company.

Differences in Time

Time differences will determine, in part, the service you choose. If you work in an office that has a heavy volume of overseas communications, be sure you have a chart of the time zones around the world.

REVIEWING IMPORTANT POINTS

1. How does a collect call differ from a credit card call?
2. Describe a situation where a conference call would be useful.

3. Why do companies use WATS?
4. Describe the nature of teletypewriter services.
5. What does Data-phone service provide?
6. How might you file a telegram?
7. What is the nature of "repeat back" service?
8. How does a Mailgram differ from a letter?
9. What are the basic types of international telegraph service?
10. Why do companies often use a single code as their business cable address?

MAKING IMPORTANT DECISIONS

1. Nancy Ann Howard was asked by her supervisor to find out if there were six rooms available at the Seaside Hotel in Miami, Florida, where a training seminar is to be held next month. Nancy is in Fremont, Nebraska. She doesn't have the number of the hotel. What would you suggest that she do?
2. Dave Robinson must send a message to about a dozen persons in different locations. The message should reach the persons within 24 hours if possible, but it is not of the greatest urgency. Should he use telegrams or mailgrams? Why?

LEARNING TO WORK WITH OTHERS

Eric has the task of checking the statements for toll calls in his large department. One afternoon while checking the statements for the various executives in the department, he noted several calls to New Orleans during a one-week period when Mr. Yates' family was visiting relatives there. He left the statement on Mr. Yates' desk with a note asking him to check the calls that were personal and thus would be paid by him. He returned the statement with a note: "All these calls were business calls."

What do you think Eric should do at this point?

IMPROVING LANGUAGE SKILLS

The pairs of words listed below are frequently misused. In each of the sentences, select the correct word. Type each sentence using the correct word on a separate sheet of paper.

1. *All ready* and *already*
   (a) Betsy had (all ready, already) arrived when we reached the main office.
   (b) They were (all ready, already) to depart by 7 this morning.

2. *Among* and *between*
   (a) Must I choose (among, between) these two attractive pictures?
   (b) There were no major differences (among, between) the several candidates for the presidency of the association.
3. *Beside* and *besides*
   (a) (Beside, Besides) these four awards, we will present three smaller ones.
   (b) Would you ask Mrs. Lang to sit (beside, besides) Mr. Wilson at the head table?
4. *Can* and *may*
   (a) (Can, May) this applicant type at the required rate of 60 words per minute?
   (b) (Can, May) Gail come to my office about 3:00 this afternoon?
5. *Doesn't* and *don't*
   (a) They (doesn't, don't) think his office is too noisy.
   (b) It (doesn't, don't) take long to complete a final draft once I have a corrected first draft.
6. *Farther* and *further*
   (a) I don't have complete instructions; therefore, I can't go any (farther, further) with this job.
   (b) Will there be (farther, further) instructions for this job?
7. *In* and *into*
   (a) She hurried (in, into) Ms. Halley's office.
   (b) He was (in, into) his car when the telephone rang.
8. *Set* and *sit*
   (a) The transcribed letters have been (setting, sitting) on her desk all day.
   (b) Would you please (set, sit) the plant near a window where the sun shines in each morning?
9. *Affect* and *effect*
   (a) What was the (affect, effect) of the announcement?
   (b) The drop in the stock market may have a telling (affect, effect) on employment opportunities.
10. *Raise* and *rise*
   (a) Let me (rise, raise) the window for you.
   (b) Price (raises, rises) were announced by every major automobile manufacturer.

IMPROVING ARITHMETIC SKILLS

Below is a reproduction of a portion of a Western Union Telegraph Company statement covering a company's charges for the months of March and April. What is this company's current balance?

AMOUNT ENCLOSED_____

PLEASE DETACH

BATCH	DATE	DESTINATION		TYPE		WD. CNT.	CHARGES	CREDITS	BALANCE
							PREVIOUS BALANCE		58.16
								58.16	
	4/21/--	PAYMENT							
35376	3/20/--	WASHINGTON	DC	PD	D	18	5.61		
35377	3/21/--	NEWROCHELL	NY	NL			1.70		
35378	3/22/--	CHICAGO	IL	PD	D	16	5.37		
35378	3/22/--	BALTIMORE	MD	PD	D	21	5.97		
35378	3/22/--	AMHERST	MA	PD	D	12	5.25		
35384	3/27/--	DAYTON	OH	NL			1.30		
35398	4/03/--	BATONROUGE	LA	NL	D		3.20		
35412	4/13/--	STPETERSBU	FL	NL	D		3.20		
35416	4/17/--	CHARLESTON	SC	NL	D		3.20		
35417	4/17/--	HONOLULU	01	FR		45	9.45		
		FIXED EQUIP					8.00		

DEMONSTRATING OFFICE SKILLS

1. Type the dialogue that would take place between you and the operator in the following situations:
   a. Your employer has asked you to place a conference call with John T. Smithers at 202-561-3456 (Washington, D.C.) and Ted Kreidel at 212-786-5432 (New York City) for 3 o'clock on the following afternoon. You work for Miss Adele Isman at 617-422-9727 (Boston).
   b. You are asked to place a credit card call for an executive working temporarily in your office. His name is G. R. Toothman and his card number is 567-71891. He wants to call Mr. G. H. Barnes at 412-561-5301 (Pittsburgh)
   c. You are asked to place a collect call for a caller who wants to talk with her home office. She is Ms. F. T. Gordon and she is calling 513-567-5432 (Cincinnati, Ohio) to talk with Ms. H. J. Lawson.
2. Your employer, Mr. E. S. Carson, asks you to send a telegram to Mrs. Anna W. Elsworth telling Mrs. Elsworth that he will not be able to see her at 3:00 p.m. on Friday afternoon because his plans have been changed and he won't be getting to Rochester until the following Monday. If Mrs. Elsworth is free on Monday afternoon, she should leave a message at the Royal Hotel, indicating the time after 3:00 p.m. when she might meet Mr. Carson. Prepare the message as clearly and concisely as you can on the blanks provided in the *Supplies Inventory* or on plain paper. Make one carbon copy on a form and one on plain paper.

IMPROVING OFFICE SKILLS (Optional)

1. Visit a local telephone office for a demonstration of the newest equipment available for local business. Note the improvements of such equipment over previous models. After your visit, write a brief report in which you describe the advantages to a company that are to be realized with the use of such equipment.

2. Your employer is concerned that a supply of special letterheads for a forthcoming national conference has not yet been received. He asked you to send a telegram to the firm inquiring about the order. According to your files, your order number was P-4561, and the order was placed six weeks prior to today's date. Delivery was assured for a week ago. On plain paper, prepare the message for the telegram as concisely as possible.

7

Filing Records in the Office

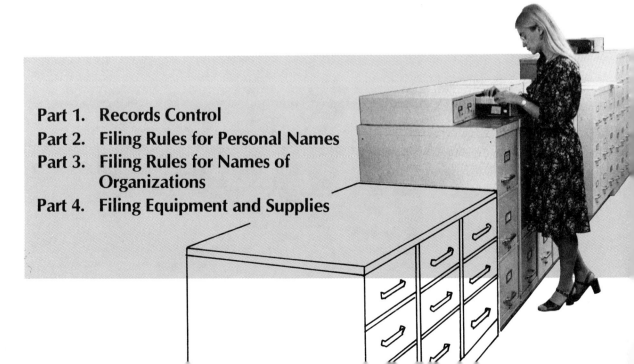

Part 1

Records Control

As Mr. Ellis and Ms. Chandler were having lunch, Ms. Chandler related an embarrassing incident that took place that morning in which a client had called about a loan. After asking the file clerk to locate the client's file, Ms. Chandler resumed the telephone conversation. When the clerk did not return with the file, she asked what was wrong. It seems that the file could not be found! Ms. Chandler apologetically explained the situation and asked to return the client's call. Thirty minutes later the file was found. Mr. Ellis understood Ms. Chandler's problem and said, "No one thinks that filing is important until you can't find something. Then it's too late."

Because of one filing error, both the executive and the office worker may suffer embarrassment and the possible loss of a client. Most file clerks maintain efficient and orderly filing systems. They know that by following filing rules, they can locate information quickly.

Illus. 7-1

Your employer doesn't expect to have to wait for urgently needed materials that have been filed

Even in our high-speed "computer age," paper work must accompany every business action. A telephone call may require papers to place an order, report on a shipment, or make a payment. The information contained in these papers forms the basis for a variety of decisions and moves the business forward.

All the records which you will file will be important to the continued successful operation of your firm. The records become part of the *memory* of the organization. Not only do the records provide a history of the business, but they also provide a basis for future decisions. In today's business offices, important decisions are based upon available up-to-date information. The risks are too great for an executive's decisions to be based upon guesses or hunches.

The proper care of records is also important to every family. Everyone has records to keep — insurance policies, appliance guarantees, bills, receipts. When personal records are not kept in order, insurance policies soon lapse because the premiums have not been paid; service cannot be obtained when an appliance breaks down because the guarantee cannot be found; bills become overdue; or an item is charged for twice because the receipt from the first payment cannot be found.

lapse: cease

premium: amount paid for insurance

Records Control

Every important record, whether it belongs to the nation's largest business or to its smallest, must be stored where it can be found when needed. The way in which a business keeps track of its records and correspondence is called *records control*. Since business information is created and spread about in so many different ways, a records control program plays an important role in providing the "business intelligence" of any firm for which you may work.

Four main areas with which records control is concerned are:

1. *Files Management* — Developing effective information (or filing) systems, deciding upon the particular type of equipment and supplies needed for each of the systems, and controlling and improving the different systems.
2. *Information Retrieval* — Developing effective and rapid methods of retrieving filed information.
3. *Records Protection* — Deciding what the vital records of a firm are and developing a program for protecting them. (*Vital* records are the important papers of a business that are needed to continue operating after a fire or some other disaster.)
4. *Records* **Retention** *and* **Disposition** — Determining which records should be kept, where, and for how long; deciding when and how outdated records should be destroyed.

retention: keeping

disposition: throwing out

Files Kept by the Office Worker

As an office worker, you will be responsible for keeping your employer's business records in an orderly condition. You may be expected to decide which material should be filed, where it should be filed, and how it should be filed. A great deal of mail that is addressed to your employer (advertisements, announcements, and other third-class mail) need not be filed at all. When you are first employed, a brief discussion of the files with your employer should prove helpful in deciding which material should be discarded and how the material to be filed should be classified. Most large firms have a records retention schedule which helps classify materials according to their importance. In addition to the regular business files of your office, you may be asked to keep a separate file of your employer's semi-personal correspondence which may include records of civic and professional activities.

Central Files

Many firms find it economical to maintain a central file of all materials that may be needed by different departments or by the entire organization. It is also possible that a large department within an organization, such as the purchasing department, may centralize its own files.

Because the file clerks in a central file department are well-trained specialists and are properly supervised, faster and better filing service is possible. A central file department eliminates the keeping of duplicate copies of material and makes for more efficient use of filing equipment and filing floor space. The central file department should also serve as an active information file — not just as a place for filing old and unneeded records. As an office worker, you will work with the central file department. You will have to decide which material must be filed in central files and which material should be kept in your own office. You will also have to know how to call for information kept in the central files.

Filing

Filing is a system of arranging and storing business papers in an orderly and efficient manner so that they can be located easily and quickly when they are wanted.

Filing is one of the most important, yet one of the most neglected, duties performed by most office workers. Errors in filing may appear to be funny in cartoons, but they are costly and embarrassing in a business office. Your employer doesn't expect to have to wait for filed copies of correspondence of other business papers.

To *find* material efficiently, you must *file* material efficiently. You must follow standard rules and procedures of filing. Not only must you know the rules of filing and apply them but you must also keep your files up to date by setting aside some part of every day to filing. Otherwise you may get so far behind that you will have to search through the files and then rummage through the unfiled material on your desk to produce requested information.

Filing Systems

The most important reason for having a filing system is to locate information quickly. Filing systems should be developed according to the way records are called for, or the way they are used.

Alphabetic Name Files

Since most business records are referred to by the name of a firm, these names determine the type of filing system that will be used. This system of filing, known as an *alphabetic name file*, is the most widely used in business. When you look for a firm name in a telephone directory, you are using this system.

Alphabetic Subject Files

Another filing system found in most business offices is an *alphabetic subject file*. The Yellow Pages of a telephone directory are arranged in alphabetic subject file order. Under the letter *E* in the Yellow Pages you will find such subject headings as Employment Agencies, Employment Contractors, Employment Counselors, and Employment Service. Most offices have both an alphabetic name file and also an alphabetic subject file. Sometimes these two systems are combined into one file.

Geographic Files

To find the names of customers and prospective customers in the parts of the country in which they are located some offices maintain geographic files. A geographic file may be set up alphabetically according to the name of a state and then be further subdivided by the sales territories within the state, or by cities, towns, or counties. Many sales offices and magazine publishers use geographic filing systems.

Numeric Files

Since some business papers are identified by number rather than by name, numeric files are frequently used. Life insurance companies file their policies by the policy number. In addition to the main numeric file, an alphabetic file by the names of all policyholders (listing policy numbers as well) is kept on cards or computer tape for fast retrieval.

Chronological Files

Another basic filing system is the chronological file, a file maintained in the order of time according to the year, month, and day. For example, an automobile insurance company would keep a chronological file showing the exact day of the year on which each automobile owner's insurance policy expires. This helps the company prepare and mail new policies to owners before their current automobile insurance expires.

expires:
runs out

Since it is almost impossible to remember everything that must be done on a given business day, a chronological file should be developed and checked daily so that proper action may be taken at the right time. A desk calendar is one form of chronological filing. Other chronological files of unfinished, pending, or follow-up work may be kept in a *tickler file*, a file arranged according to the days of the month.

pending:
not yet decided

The Care of Records

For business purposes, records are classified in four general groups: vital, important, useful, and nonessential. All records considered critical to the operation and growth of an organization, such as the financial statements, legal papers, and tax records, are classified as *vital records*. Many business firms that lose their vital records in a fire, flood, or tornado are forced to go out of business. These records should be protected by microfilming them (photographing on a narrow film) and storing the microfilm in a fireproof cabinet, or by photocopying them and filing the copies in another location.

critical:
extremely important

Important records are those which could be replaced, such as personnel records, but only at great expense. These records should also receive protection because of their confidential nature. *Useful records*, such as the records of accounts payable, are those which can be replaced — but with some delay and inconvenience. They should be kept in regular file cabinets.

confidential:
secret

Illus. 7-2

These records survived a scorching fire because they were stored in fireproof cabinets.

The Shaw-Walker Company

Non-essential records, such as press releases, are those which soon outlive their usefulness — perhaps some of them should never have been filed in the first place. They should be destroyed to save valuable file space and floor space. Records management experts estimate that approximately 85 percent of all files are never referred to again.

Records Control in the Office

Much of your time will be spent on records control. When you type a letter or sales order, you are preparing a record (the carbon copy) for the files. When you read and decide what to do with incoming mail, you are preparing materials for filing. The result of almost all your office duties will be placed in the files. To be effective in any office, you must thoroughly understand business filing and records control procedures.

REVIEWING IMPORTANT POINTS

1. Why do business firms keep records?
2. Name and describe each of the four main areas of records control and management.
3. What is the purpose of a central filing department?
4. Define the term *filing*.

5. Name five systems of filing.
6. Give an example of each of the following terms: vital record, important record, and useful record.

MAKING IMPORTANT DECISIONS

Mr. Carson is an office worker for the service manager of an air conditioning company. To avoid filing each document one at a time, he places them in a tray on his desk. There are very few days when he finds the time to file, so the documents accumulate in the tray day after day. Most of the time, Mr. Carson can remember what is in the tray so he really doesn't worry about filing daily. What do you think of Mr. Carson's daily filing practices?

LEARNING TO WORK WITH OTHERS

Ms. Charlene Kelly, a recent high school graduate, accepted her first full-time position as a stenographer in the purchasing department of a very large company. During her first two weeks of work, Mrs. Williams, supervisor of the department, acquainted her with the department's operations. The supervisor also explained the tasks and duties for which Ms. Kelly alone would be responsible.

After introducing Ms. Kelly to her co-workers and giving her an overview of the purchasing department and what it does, Mrs. Williams explained to Ms. Kelly the filing system used in the department. Ms. Kelly was then given several correspondence files to read and prepare for filing. While having lunch with several of the employees in the department, Ms. Kelly commented that she didn't know if she would stay on this job or not. "After all," she said, "I accepted this position to be a stenographer, not a file clerk."

Is Ms. Kelly correct in having doubts about her new position? Could the supervisor have chosen another way of teaching her the basics of her job? How can reading correspondence and preparing it for filing help a new employee?

IMPROVING LANGUAGE SKILLS

On a sheet of paper list the words in Column 1. Then write the number of the correct definition for each word from Column 2. The first one is done for you in the example below.

Example: (a) retrieval   (3) act or process of recovering or finding

Column 1	Column 2
(a) retrieval	(1) a person who engages the professional services of another
(b) manually	(2) arranged by date or by order of occurrence
(c) retention	(3) act or process of recovering or finding
(d) confidential	(4) a maximum measure of content or output
(e) chronological	(5) an orderly collection of papers
(f) file	(6) relating to or involving the hands
(g) document	(7) an official paper that conveys information
(h) capacity	(8) of a secret nature
(i) client	(9) to set down in writing as evidence
(j) record	(10) act of keeping in possession or use

IMPROVING ARITHMETIC SKILLS

1. Your present files for individual folders have tabs in three different positions which make folders difficult to find. You and your employer decide that much time would be saved if tabs for individual folders were only in the third position. You can type 10 labels in one minute. There are 20 filing drawers with approximately 90 folders in each drawer. If you typed without stopping, how long should it take you to revise all of the folder labels?

2. Other employees in the office agreed to help you type the labels in their spare time. Each employee kept a record of how much time was spent typing labels. By using the following data, how much time did it actually take to revise all of the folder labels?

Sherry:	1 hour, 25 minutes
Jim:	1 hour, 10 minutes
Linda:	40 minutes
Terry:	30 minutes

DEMONSTRATING OFFICE SKILLS

You have been employed recently by State Bank and Trust, 906 South Main Street, Albany, New York 12210. Because of the many records that must be kept, the bank is quickly running out of filing space, and the current filing system needs updating. Your employer has asked you to be responsible for locating a filing equipment company to obtain information about microfilming equipment and filing efficiency.

Consult the Yellow Pages of your local telephone directory under Filing Equipment, Systems & Supplies, and then compose and type letters to be sent to at least two companies explaining your problem, requesting information, literature, and the assistance of one of their representatives. Use the letterheads in your *Supplies Inventory*, if available, or use plain paper.

Part 2

Filing Rules
for Personal Names

During a unit on filing, Mrs. Gibson, Vocational Office Education teacher, told the students that in the average company about 1 in 100 documents is misfiled; and each misfile costs about 68 cents. She explained that many factors must be considered when figuring this cost, such as the time to locate the missing file and the inconvenience to others.

The students were surprised by this information and realized the importance of knowing and applying their filing rules properly. Because the students used filing in some way in their afternoon jobs, one student suggested that they each compile a notebook of the rules of filing learned in class. The notebook would be used as a reference while on the job. The class agreed that this would be a very helpful and worthwhile assignment.

A filing system is costly to set up and maintain. Therefore, if the system you use is to be worth this high cost, the information in it must be available when it is needed. This means that business correspondence and other filed materials must be arranged in an exact and established order.

Filing Rules

Every filing method makes use of filing rules. Only if you know the standard rules for filing, and apply them the same way every time, can you find the filed materials quickly when they are needed.

The most widely used method of filing is based on the alphabet; however, because of difficulties involved in deciding how some materials are to be filed, or because of the great volume of materials filed, other filing methods have been developed. These are numeric, geographic, and subject filing.

By following one set of filing rules and recognizing the importance of records control, you will be of great assistance to your employer and play an important role in the successful operation of your office. Since every business, regardless of its size, uses one or more of the alphabetic filing methods, it is important that you learn the rules for alphabetic filing. In certain cases, where more specialized filing procedures are used, you will need on-the-job training to fully understand these methods.

Alphabetic Indexing for Individuals

The first step in filing procedures is *indexing*. When you arrange names for filing purposes, you are indexing. The rules for alphabetic indexing follow.

1. Order of Indexing Units

When you consider the name Walter B. Anderson, each word and each initial or abbreviation is a separate *indexing unit*. Thus, you have three indexing units. The units of an individual's name are considered in this order: (a) last name (surname); (b) first name, initial, or abbreviation; (c) middle name, initial, or abbreviation. Therefore *Anderson* is the first indexing unit, *Walter* is the second, and *B.* is the third. (In the examples below, the names are in alphabetic order.)

Names	INDEX ORDER OF UNITS		
	Unit 1	Unit 2	Unit 3
Walter B. Anderson	Anderson	Walter	B.
Harriet Boughman Brown	Brown	Harriet	Boughman
Edward J. Cox	Cox	Edward	J.
A. B. Davis	Davis	A.	B.

2. Last Names (Surnames)

When the last names of individuals are different, the alphabetic order is determined by the last names alone. *The letter that determines the order of any two names is the first letter that is different in the two names.* In the following lists the underlined letter in each last name determines the alphabetic order of that name when compared with the preceding name. Note that when one last name (Johns) is the same as the first part of a longer last name (Johnston), the shorter name goes before the longer. This is often called the *nothing before something* rule of filing order.

Last Names	Last Names	Last Names
Hall	Hoffman	Johns
Hill	Hoffmann	Johnston
Hull	Hofmann	Johnstone

3. Last Names Containing Particles or Articles

A last name containing a foreign particle or article (also called prefixes) is considered as one indexing unit. The common prefixes include *D', De, Del, du, Fitz, La, Mac, Mc, O', Van, Von*, and *Von der*. Spacing between the prefix and the rest of the last name, or capitalization of the prefix, makes no difference when indexing.

Names	INDEX ORDER OF UNITS		
	Unit 1	Unit 2	Unit 3
Frances C. D'Arcy	D'Arcy	Frances	C.
Mario L. Del Favero	Del Favero	Mario	L.
Robert J. du Pont	du Pont	Robert	J.
Malcolm Paul MacDonald	MacDonald	Malcolm	Paul
Mabel J. Manning	Manning	Mabel	J.
Helen C. McConnell	McConnell	Helen	C.
Charles H. Mead	Mead	Charles	H.
Mary M. O'Shea	O'Shea	Mary	M.
Henry T. Van Allen	Van Allan	Henry	T.
Carol A. Van Derbeck	Van Derbeck	Carol	A.
Elsie D. von Koch	von Koch	Elsie	D.

4. Compound Last Names

Compound last names such as *Fuller-Smith* and *San Martin* are indexed as two separate units. When the compound name is hyphenated, the hyphen is ignored. In a compound last name such as *St. Claire*, *St.* is considered to be the first unit (in spelled-out form as *Saint*) and *Claire* the second unit. *St.* is not considered a prefix as in Rule 3 because it is an abbreviation for the word *Saint*. None of the prefixes under Rule 3 are abbreviations.

INDEX ORDER OF UNITS			
Names	Unit 1	Unit 2	Unit 3
Michael Ross-Harris	Ross(-)	Harris	Michael
Ruby J. Ross	Ross	Ruby	J.
Allen Ross-Sanders	Ross(-)	Sanders	Allen
Ethel J. Rosse	Rosse	Ethel	J.
Edwin St. Claire	Saint	Claire	Edwin
Gerald St. John	Saint	John	Gerald
John San Martin	San	Martin	John
Marie T. Satone	Satone	Marie	T.
Minnie Twigg-Porter	Twigg(-)	Porter	Minnie

5. First Names (Given Names)

When the last names are alike, you consider the first names in determining the alphabetic order. When the last names and the first names are both alike, the middle names determine the alphabetic order, as illustrated below.

INDEX ORDER OF UNITS			
Names	Unit 1	Unit 2	Unit 3
Willa A. Smith	Smith	Willa	A.
Winifred C. Smith	Smith	Winifred	C.
Gladys Clark Thompson	Thompson	Gladys	Clark
Gladys Crane Thompson	Thompson	Gladys	Crane

6. Initials and Abbreviated First or Middle Names

A first initial is considered an indexing unit and goes before all other names that begin with the same letter. An abbreviated first or middle name (*Wm.* for *William*), is usually treated as if it were spelled in full. Nicknames — *Bob* for *Robert*, *Larry* for *Lawrence*, etc., are indexed as written.

	INDEX ORDER OF UNITS		
Names	Unit 1	Unit 2	Unit 3
R. Robert Brogan	Brogan	R.	Robert
Robt. R. Brogan	Brogan	Robert	R.
Robert Richard Brogan	Brogan	Robert	Richard
Sam F. Brogan	Brogan	Sam	F.
Sam'l George Brogan	Brogan	Samuel	George

7. Unusual Names

When you can't decide which part of a name is the last name, (as in a foreign name) the last part of the name as written should be considered the last name. (This type of name is often cross-referenced as explained on page 287.)

	INDEX ORDER OF UNITS		
Names	Unit 1	Unit 2	Unit 3
Juan Maria Mallendez	Mallendez	Juan	Maria
Boyd Nelson	Nelson	Boyd	
Arthur Patrick	Patrick	Arthur	
Lee Kuan Yew	Yew	Lee	Kuan
Geza Zsak	Zsak	Geza	

8. Identical Personal Names

When the full names of two or more individuals are exactly the same, the parts of the addresses are used to determine the filing order. The parts of the address are not considered indexing units but *identifying elements*. Identifying elements are another means of determining the alphabetical order when the names are identical.

The order in which the parts of the address are used for determining the alphabetical order is as follows:

(a) Town or City Name
(b) State Name
(c) Street Name
(d) House Number (in numeric order)

Names	INDEX ORDER OF UNITS			IDENTIFYING ELEMENTS			
	Unit 1	Unit 2	Unit 3	City	State	Street	House Number
Carla G. Grant 145 Beach Street Kingston, IL 60145	Grant	Carla	G.	Kingston	Illinois	Beach	145
Carla G. Grant 204 Pearl Street Kingston, NY 12401	Grant	Carla	G.	Kingston	New York	Pearl	204
Carla G. Grant 177 State Street Kingston, NY 12401	Grant	Carla	G.	Kingston	New York	State	177
Carla G. Grant 350 State Street Kingston, NY 12401	Grant	Carla	G.	Kingston	New York	State	350

9. Seniority in Identical Names

Terms indicating **seniority**, such as *Senior* or *Junior*, or *II (Second)* or *III (Third)*, is not considered an indexing unit. The terms are used as identifying element in determining the alphabetic order for filing purposes. The titles "Junior" (Jr.) and "Senior" (Sr.) are arranged in alphabetical order. The titles "I," "II," and "III" are arranged in numeric order.

Names	INDEX ORDER OF UNITS		IDENTIFYING ELEMENTS
	Unit 1	Unit 2	Seniority Titles
John Young	Young	John	
John Young, Jr.	Young	John	(Junior)
John Young, Sr.	Young	John	(Senior)
George Zack II	Zack	George	II
George Zack III	Zack	George	III

10. Titles and Degrees

Below are the rules for indexing a personal or professional title (Mayor, Dr., Senator) or a degree (Ph.D., M.D., D.D.).

(a) A personal or professional title (Mayor, Dr.) or degree (Ph.D.) is usually not considered in filing, but it is put in parentheses at the end of the name.

(b) When a religious title (Father) or foreign title (King) is followed by a first name only, it is indexed as written.

	INDEX ORDER OF UNITS		
Names	Unit 1	Unit 2	Unit 3
(a) Mayor Alfred G. Brown	Brown	Alfred	G. (Mayor)
Arlene E. Brown, Ph.D	Brown	Arlene	E. (Ph.D)
Raymond C. Ellis, M.D.	Ellis	Raymond	C. (M.D.)
Mme. Jeannine Patou	Patou	Jeannine (Mme.)	
Dr. John J. Ryan	Ryan	John	J. (Dr.)
Lieut. Mary T. Stewart	Stewart	Mary	T. (Lieutenant)
Senator Bella Williams	Williams	Bella (Senator)	
(b) Brother Andrew	Brother	Andrew	
Father Henry	Father	Henry	
King George	King	George	
Lady Anabel	Lady	Anabel	
Prince Philip	Prince	Philip	
Princess Margaret	Princess	Margaret	
Sister Mary Martha	Sister	Mary	Martha

11. Names of Married Women

If it is known, the legal name of a married woman should be used rather than her husband's name for filing purposes. When a woman marries, the only part of her husband's name that she legally may assume is his last name. Her legal name then includes either (a) her first name, her maiden last name, and her husband's last name, or (b) her first name, her middle name, and her husband's last name. In other words, a married woman's legal name could be *Mrs. Jane Foster Burke* or *Mrs. Jane Melinda Burke* but not *Mrs. Marvin J. Burke*.

The title *Mrs.* is put in parentheses after the name but *it is not considered in filing*. A woman's husband's name is given in parentheses below her legal name and is often cross-referenced, as explained on page 287.

	INDEX ORDER OF UNITS		
Names	Unit 1	Unit 2	Unit 3
Mrs. Mary Parker Smith (Mrs. Thomas Smith)	Smith	Mary	Parker (Mrs.)
Mrs. Herta Marie Zeller Mrs. Theodore Zeller)	Zeller	Herta	Marie (Mrs.)

REVIEWING IMPORTANT POINTS

1. Using your own name, illustrate indexing units.
2. What is meant by the *nothing before something* rule?
3. Explain the difference in the filing rules applied to St. John and Von Schmidt.
4. How is an abbreviated name like *Benj.* treated for filing?
5. If two people have the same names (first, middle, and last), what determines the order in which they are filed?
6. Explain identifying elements.
7. How are terms indicating seniority used in determining the order for filing purposes?
8. How is the *Dr.* in *Dr. James B. Moulton* treated in filing?
9. How are religious and foreign titles treated in indexing?
10. Which is the correct legal name: Mrs. Peter G. Bryce or Mrs. Janet Cox Bryce?

MAKING IMPORTANT DECISIONS

Miss Diaz, a file clerk at a small realty firm, was far behind in her filing. She knew that her employer, Ms. Grier, would be unhappy if she didn't have all of the filing done by Friday. At 4:15 on Friday, Miss Diaz realized that she would not be able to finish the filing by herself. In desperation, she called Mr. Carmichael, a stenographer, to help her. Miss Diaz didn't take time to explain the filing procedure to Mr. Carmichael. She assumed that everybody knew the alphabet. On Monday morning, Mr. Grier called for the file on Harold De Forrest. Miss Diaz could not find the file so she asked Mr. Carmichael if he knew where it was. Mr. Carmichael cheerfully replied that he knew exactly where it was. "Look under 'F' for Forrest," he said. Miss Diaz was relieved that she found the file under "F," but was worried about how many more folders were improperly filed. What do you think of Miss Diaz's decision to have Mr. Carmichael help her. Why?

LEARNING TO WORK WITH OTHERS

Miss Susan Randle is an office worker in a small office. Since the office is small, she handles all the filing. Her files contain such records as personnel information, contracts, and other confidential files. She is often called from her desk to handle other matters. Rather than wait for her return, many of the salespeople in the office get the information they need from her files without her knowledge.

Should her files be open to all employees? If not, how can she correct this situation?

IMPROVING LANGUAGE SKILLS

A good practice is not to use a capital unless a rule exists for its use. Four basic rules of capitalization are:

A. Capitalize the first word of a sentence.
   Example: He asked if we were ready to go.
B. Capitalize the first word of a direct quotation.
   Example: She asked, "Are you ready to go?"
C. Capitalize proper nouns and adjectives.
   Example: Beaumont High School   Mexican music
D. Capitalize the important words of titles
   Example: *A Short History of the English People*

Type the following sentences on a separate sheet of paper using capitalization wherever necessary.

1. a condensed version of his new novel will appear in the march issue of the reader's digest.
2. the new york firm had all its vital records on microfilm stored underground at a secret location in altoona, pennsylvania.
3. she asked, "is the albany contract being considered?"
4. when she opened the drawer marked contracts and agreements, she was surprised at the number of files it contained.
5. dean lindsey told his secretary to file the volume entitled an inquiry into the nature of certain nineteenth century pamphlets in the school library.

IMPROVING ARITHMETIC SKILLS

1. Emma's supervisor asked her what materials she had ready for the files. When Emma checked her desk, she found four stacks of documents for the files. One contained 15 contracts; the second contained 11 letters; the third consisted of 20 case histories; and the

fourth was a miscellaneous stack of 7 different items. How many documents did Emma have to file before she would be ready for another assignment?

2. There are 40 file folders with Barrett as the first indexing unit, 15 with Baxter as the first unit, and 20 with Benson as the first unit. There are 200 folders under the letter "B." Barrett, Baxter, and Benson together make up what percentage of all the "B" folders?

DEMONSTRATING OFFICE SKILLS

In completing the following filing exercise, you will need one hundred 5" x 3" filing cards, or plain paper cut to about that size. (When the dimensions of a card are mentioned, the first number indicates the width of the bottom edge, and the second number indicates the depth. With a 5" by 3" card, the 5" means that the bottom edge is 5 inches wide, and the 3" means that the card is 3 inches in depth. Normally, however, these cards are referred to as 3" by 5" cards.)

(a) Type each of the following names in index form at the upper left side of a card.

(b) Type the number of each name in the upper right corner of the card. (These numbers will aid in checking the answers.)

(c) After the names have been properly indexed and typed, arrange the cards in alphabetic order.

1. Dr. Hermione G. Hofmann
2. Salvatore L'Abbate
3. Joan Neuhaus
4. Shirley M. Schecter
5. Mrs. Adele C. Welsh
6. Mrs. Minnie B. Ballau
7. Ernestine Sanford Black
8. Lloyd C. Carpenter
9. Marian F. Corey
10. Ruth Forbes-Watkins
11. Harry D. Van Tassell
12. Stanley Schechter
13. Laura Neuhaus
14. Hedda M. Kaufmann
15. George A. Heinemann
16. Vicki Forbes
17. Maryalice Corey
18. Mrs. Evelyn M. Cannon
19. Sidney J. Bernstein
20. Susan Theron Baldwin
21. Hartzell P. Angell
22. Mrs. Bessie Berkowitz
23. Joseph A. Colombo
24. Mrs. Agnes F. Burns
25. John A. Farrell
26. Arnold H. Hansen-Sturm
27. Mae Jacobs
28. Robert L. Michalson
29. Viggo Rambusch
30. W. Anthony Ullman
31. E. Cooper Taylor
32. Nichola Rambone
33. Vera D. McLean
34. C. Albert Jacob, Jr.
35. Rev. Herbert W. Hansen
36. Jean Farrell
37. Paul G. Clarke, Jr.
38. Gina Borsesi
39. Thomas L. D. Berg
40. Bette P. Albert, M.D.
41. Robert S. Hackett
42. Olga Ellison

43. Mrs. Evelyn E. Clarke
44. Charles W. Borman
45. Thomas L. Beckett, Ph.D.
46. Norma J. Abrams, D.D.S.
47. Mrs. Sharon Ennis
48. Edwin C. McDonald, Jr.
49. Alfred H. Phillips
50. Anthony Y. Szu-Tu
51. Julia B. Fee
52. N. R. Heinneman
53. Julia Ann Kaufman
54. Kazan Michel
55. William St. John
56. Cynthia C. Ullmann
57. Patrick Colombo
58. George L. Cady
59. Norma T. Bernstein
60. Mrs. Lillian M. Backer
61. David B. Bandler, Jr.
62. Malcolm Carpenter, M.D.
63. Mrs. J. Black
64. D. Howard Daniels
65. Maxine Friedman
66. Richard D. Hoffman
67. Annette C. LaBelle
68. Arabelle J. O'Brien, M.D.
69. Madelyn Russell Segal
70. Harold A. Welch
71. Richard D. Zirker

72. Mrs. Gladys Smythe
73. James F. O'Neill
74. R. O. Ennis
75. James A. Gilmartin
76. Lorraine M. Ellis
77. Samuel H. Clark
78. Roberta D. Block
79. Edward J. Barrett
80. Albertina V. Marcus
81. Joseph Lloyd Barnett
82. Samuel Clark
83. A. Marvin Gillman, M.D.
84. Leo J. Madden, D.D.S.
85. William M. Smith
86. Gloria Younger
87. Dr. William Bloch
88. A. V. Danielson
89. Hariet A. Humphries
90. Carol Philipps
91. Barbara Ann Barken
92. Denise R. Young
93. Joseph E. Black
94. Irving T. Siegel
95. James E. Clark, Jr.
96. William J. O'Neil
97. Malcolm MacDonald
98. Vivian S. Humphreys
99. Louis M. Friedmann
100. Henry L. Daniels

Part 3

Filing Rules for Names of Organizations

Because Miss Dolores Rivera was leaving her job at PYCO, Inc., Mr. Singleton hired Mr. Larry Anderson to replace her. One of Miss Rivera's last duties was to train Mr. Anderson for the responsibilities of the job. Miss Rivera set aside two afternoons to explain the efficient filing system that she had established at the beginning of her job with PYCO. Mr. Anderson was very impressed with the complete and up-to-date system. He began to realize how many companies depended on PYCO for their products. He knew that maintaining this filing system would be a key responsibility and a very satisfying one.

Alphabetic Indexing for Business Firms and Other Organizations

The alphabetic indexing rules presented in Part 2 are also used in filing for business firms and other organizations. Business names, however, can sometimes present special indexing problems. A mastery of the following rules should give you the confidence you need to file materials for business names other than names of individuals.

12. Business or Firm Names

The following rules determine the indexing of a business or firm name:

(a) As a general rule, the units in a firm name are indexed in the order in which they are written. The word *and* is not considered an indexing unit.

(b) When a firm name includes the full name of a person, the person's last name is considered as the first indexing unit, the first name or initial as the second unit, the middle name or initial as the third; and then the rest of the firm name is considered.

274   *Unit 7 • Filing Records in the Office*

(c) Occasionally a business name contains the name of a person (for example, *Arthur Murray* or *Fanny Farmer*) who is so well known that it would confuse most people if the name were to be transposed. In such cases, the name is indexed as it is popularly known and cross-referenced. (See page 287.)

(d) The name of a hotel or motel is usually indexed in the order in which it is written. However, if the word *Hotel* or *Motel* appears first, it is **transposed** to allow the most clearly identifying word to become the first indexing unit (for example, *Hotel McKitrick* is indexed as *McKitrick Hotel*).

transposed: reversed

(e) The names of banks are indexed first by the name of the city in which they are located. (For example, *First National Bank, Cincinnati*, is indexed as *Cincinnati First National Bank*.)

	INDEX ORDER OF UNITS			
Names	**Unit 1**	**Unit 2**	**Unit 3**	**Unit 4**
Ames Art Shop	Ames	Art	Shop	
Hotel Ames	Ames	Hotel		
Brown and Son Realty Co.	Brown (and)	Son	Realty	Company
Campbell Soup Company, Inc.	Campbell	Soup	Company	Incorporated
Canton National Bank	Canton	National	Bank	
John Hancock Mutual Life Insurance Co.	John	Hancock	Mutual	Life
John H. Kramer Shoe Repair Shop	Kramer	John	H.	Shoe
Trust Bank, Minneapolis	Minneapolis	Trust	Bank	
Modern Tile Store	Modern	Tile	Store	
Montgomery Ward and Company	Montgomery	Ward (and)	Company	
Motel Morris Gift Shoppe	Morris	Motel	Gift	Shoppe
L. Morrison Moss Supply Co.	Moss	L.	Morrison	Supply
Singer Wallpaper and Paint Company	Singer	Wallpaper (and)	Paint	Company

13. Alphabetic Order

The first units of firm names determine the alphabetic order when those units are different. The second units determine alphabetic order when the first units are alike. The third units determine alphabetic order when the first and second units are alike.

	INDEX ORDER OF UNITS			
Names	Unit 1	Unit 2	Unit 3	Unit 4
Gunn Printing Company	Gunn	Printing	Company	
Gunn Radio Shop	Gunn	Radio	Shop	
Hess Beauty Shoppe	Hess	Beauty	Shoppe	
Mary Hess Beauty Salon	Hess	Mary	Beauty	Salon
Hess Specialty Shop	Hess	Specialty	Shop	
Irwin Shoe Distributors	Irwin	Shoe	Distributors	
Irwin Shoe Mart	Irwin	Shoe	Mart	

14. Articles, Prepositions, and Conjunctions

The articles (*a, an, the*); prepositions (*of, on, for, by*, etc.); and conjunctions (*and, &, or*) are *not* considered as indexing units and should be put in parentheses. However, when a preposition is the first word in a business name (as in *At Home Bakery* or *In Town Motel*), the preposition is treated as the first indexing unit.

	INDEX ORDER OF UNITS			
Names	Unit 1	Unit 2	Unit 3	Unit 4
L. S. Andrews & Co.	Andrews	L.	S. (&)	Company
A Bit of Scotland	Bit (of)	Scotland (A)		
By the Sea Inn	By (the)	Sea	Inn	
First National Bank of Cincinnati	Cincinnati	First	National	Bank (of)
The House of Design	House (of)	Design (The)		
In Between Book Store	In	Between	Book	Store

Illus. 7-3

Carefully managed files are essential to the smooth operation of every busines.

Photo furnished courtesy
Browne-Morse Co.
Muskegon, MI

15. Abbreviations

An abbreviation in a firm name is indexed as if it were spelled in full. Single-letter abbreviations are also indexed as though spelled in full.

Names	INDEX ORDER OF UNITS			
	Unit 1	Unit 2	Unit 3	Unit 4
Amer. Paper Co.	American	Paper	Company	
Ft. Lee Stores, Inc.	Fort	Lee	Stores	Incorporated
Penn Central R.R.	Penn	Central	Railroad	
St. Vincent's Hosp.	Saint	Vincent's	Hospital	
U.S. Rubber Co.	United	States	Rubber	Company
YWCA	Young	Women's	Christian	Association

16. Single Letters

When a firm's name is made up of single letters, each letter is considered as a separate indexing unit. The spacing between the single letters is not considered in indexing. Firm names made up of single letters are filed before words beginning with the same letter because of the *nothing before something* rule.

	INDEX ORDER OF UNITS			
Names	**Unit 1**	**Unit 2**	**Unit 3**	**Unit 4**
A & A Auto Parts	A (&)	A	Auto	Parts
ABC Printers	A	B	C	Printers
A C Cleaners	A	C	Cleaners	
A–Z Dry Cleaners	A (–)	Z	Dry	Cleaners
Acme Rug Co.	Acme	Rug	Company	
WNBC	W	N	B	C
X-Cel Advertising Service	X (-)	Cel	Advertising	Service

17. Hyphenated Names and Words

(a) Hyphenated firm names are indexed as if they were separate words; thus, they are separate indexing units (for example, *Allis-Chalmers*).

(b) Each part of a hyphenated **coined** word (such as *The Do-It-Yourself Shop*) is considered to be a separate indexing unit.

(c) A single word written with a hyphen (a word containing a prefix, such as *anti-, co-, inter-, mid-, pan-, trans-, tri-*) is filed as one indexing unit.

	INDEX ORDER OF UNITS			
Names	**Unit 1**	**Unit 2**	**Unit 3**	**Unit 4**
(a) McGraw-Edison Company	McGraw(-)	Edison	Company	
Shaw-Walker	Shaw(-)	Walker		
Stokens-Van Buren, Inc.	Stokens(-)	Van Buren	Incorporated	
(b) Bar-B-Q Drive-Inn	Bar(-)	B(-)	Q	Drive(-)
C-Thru Window Company	C(-)	Thru	Window	Company
Econ-O-Me Cleaners	Econ(-)	O(-)	Me	Cleaners
(c) Inter-State Truckers Assoc.	Inter-State	Truckers	Association	
Mid-City Garage	Mid-City	Garage		
Pan-American Insurance Co.	Pan-American	Insurance	Company	

18. Two Words Considered as One

If separate words in a firm's name are often considered or written as one word, these words as a group should be treated as one indexing unit. The use of a hyphen or spacing is of no indexing significance. This rule does away with the separating of similar names in the files. Examples of such words include *airlines, carload, crossroads, downtown, eastside, goodwill, halfway, mainland, railroad, seaboard*, and points of the compass words, such as *northeast, northwest, southeast*, and *southwestern*.

Names	INDEX ORDER OF UNITS	
	Unit 1	Unit 2
Down Town Garage	Down Town	Garage
Good Will Agency	Good Will	Agency
The Half-Way Restaurant	Half-Way	Restaurant (The)
Northeastern Airlines	Northeastern	Airlines

19. Titles in Business Names

(a) A title in a *business name* is treated as a separate unit and is indexed in the order in which it is written.

(b) The titles *Mr.* and *Mrs.* are indexed as written *rather than* spelled in full.

Names	INDEX ORDER OF UNITS			
	Unit 1	Unit 2	Unit 3	Unit 4
Dr. Posner Shoe Co., Inc.	Doctor	Posner	Shoe	Company
Madame Adrienne French Cleaners	Madame	Adrienne	French	Cleaners
Mr. Foster's Shops	Mr.	Foster's	Shops	
Sir Michael, Ltd.	Sir	Michael	Limited	

20. Compound Geographic Names

Compound geographic names containing two English words (such as *New York*) are treated as two separate indexing units, but compound names written as one word (such as *Lakewood*) are considered as one indexing unit.

INDEX ORDER OF UNITS				
Names	Unit 1	Unit 2	Unit 3	Unit 4
Ft. Wayne Finance Co.	Fort	Wayne	Finance	Company
New Jersey Thruway Res't	New	Jersey	Thruway	Restaurant
Newport Knitting Co.	Newport	Knitting	Company	
St. Louis Post Dispatch	Saint	Louis	Post	Dispatch

21. Numbers

A number in a business name is treated as though written in full and is considered one indexing unit (regardless of the length or number of digits). In order to use a smaller number of letters to **indicate** a number, four-digit numbers are written in hundreds and five-digit numbers are written in thousands. For example, the four-digit number *1,250* would be written *twelve hundred fifty* instead of *one thousand two hundred fifty*. The five-digit number *10,010* would be written *ten thousand ten*.

indicate:
show; point out

INDEX ORDER OF UNITS				
Names	Unit 1	Unit 2	Unit 3	Unit 4
A-1 Envelope Co.	A(-)	One	Envelope	Company
40 Winks Motel	Forty	Winks	Motel	
42nd Street Playhouse	Forty-second	Street	Playhouse	
40,000 Investment Association	Forty Thousand	Investment	Association	
The 400 Cake Shop	Four Hundred	Cake	Shop (The)	
4th Federal Loan Co.	Fourth	Federal	Loan	Company

22. Foreign Names

(a) Each separately written word in a compound foreign name is considered as a separate indexing unit. The words *San* and *Santa* mean *Saint* and are, therefore, indexed separately.
(b) A foreign prefix is combined with the word that follows it and is indexed as one filing unit (as explained in Rule 3, Part 2, page 265).
(c) Unusual foreign names are indexed as written.

Unit 7 • Filing Records in the Office

Names	INDEX ORDER OF UNITS			
	Unit 1	Unit 2	Unit 3	Unit 4
(a) Mesa Verde Distributors	Mesa	Verde	Distributors	
Puerto Rico Travel Bureau	Puerto	Rico	Travel	Bureau
San Francisco Chronicle	San	Francisco	Chronicle	
Terre Haute City Service	Terre	Haute	City	Service
(b) Du Bois Fence & Garden Co.	Du Bois	Fence (&)	Garden	Company
LaBelle Formal Wear Shops	LaBelle	Formal	Wear	Shops
Las Vegas Convention Bureau	Las Vegas	Convention	Bureau	
Los Angeles Wholesale Institute	Los Angeles	Wholesale	Institute	
(c) Ambulancias Hispano Mexicana	Ambulancias	Hispano	Mexicana	
Iino Kauin Kaisha Imports	Iino	Kauin	Kaisha	Imports
Mohamed Esber, Cia	Mohamed	Esber	Cia	

23. Possessives

The *apostrophe s* (*'s*), the singular possessive, is *not* considered in filing. An *s apostrophe* (*s'*), the plural possessive, *is* considered as part of the word. Very simply, consider all letters in the indexing unit up to the apostrophe; drop those after it.

Names	INDEX ORDER OF UNITS			
	Unit 1	Unit 2	Unit 3	Unit 4
Brook's Jewelry Store	Brook('s)	Jewelry	Store	
Brooks' Brothers Clothing	Brooks'	Brothers	Clothing	
Paul's Limousine Service	Paul('s)	Limousine	Service	
Pauls' Real Estate Agency	Pauls'	Real	Estate	Agency

24. Identical Business Names

(a) Identical names of two or more businesses are arranged in alphabetical order according to the names of the cities in the addresses. The name of the state is disregarded unless the towns have the same name.

(b) If several branches of one business are located in the same city, the names of those branches are arranged alphabetically or numerically by streets. If more than one branch is located on the same street in the same city, the names are arranged according to the numeric order of the building numbers. Names of buildings are not considered unless street names are not given.

Names	INDEX ORDER OF UNITS			IDENTIFYING ELEMENTS			
	Unit 1	Unit 2	Unit 3	City	State	Street	House Number
(a) Office Supplies Company Akron, Ohio	Office	Supplies	Company	Akron	Ohio		
Office Supplies Company Canton, Ohio	Office	Supplies	Company	Canton	Ohio		
Office Supplies Company Lansing, Michigan	Office	Supplies	Company	Lansing	Michigan		
(b) National Food Market 225 Main Street Columbus, Ohio	National	Food	Market	Columbus	Ohio	Main	225
National Food Market 187 Prospect Street Columbus, Ohio	National	Food	Market	Columbus	Ohio	Prospect	187
National Food Market United Building 341 Stone Drive Columbus, Ohio	National	Food	Market	Columbus	Ohio	Stone	341
National Food Market 722 Stone Drive Columbus, Ohio	National	Food	Market	Columbus	Ohio	Stone	722
National Food Market Young Building Columbus, Ohio	National	Food	Market	Columbus	Ohio	Young	

25. Churches, Synagogues, and Other Organizations

(a) The name of a church or synagogue is indexed in the order in which it is written unless some other word in the name more clearly identifies the organization.

Names	INDEX ORDER OF UNITS		
	Unit 1	Unit 2	Unit 3
First Baptist Church	Baptist	Church	First
The Chapel at Brown & Vine	Chapel (at)	Brown (&)	Vine (The)
Congregation of Moses	Congregation (of)	Moses	
Trinity Lutheran Church	Lutheran	Church	Trinity
St. Paul's Church	Saint	Paul's	Church

(b) The name of a club or any other organization is indexed according to the most clearly identifying unit in its name. For example, the most clearly identifying unit in *The Ancient Order of Mariners* is *Mariners*.

Names	INDEX ORDER OF UNITS		
	Unit 1	Unit 2	Unit 3
Fraternal Order of Eagles	Eagles	Fraternal	Order (of)
Loyal Order of Moose	Moose	Loyal	Order (of)
Retail Store Employees Union	Retail	Store	Employees
Rotary Club	Rotary	Club	

26. Schools

(a) The names of elementary and secondary schools are indexed first according to the name of the city in which the schools are located, and then by the most distinctive word in the name.

Names	INDEX ORDER OF UNITS			
	Unit 1	Unit 2	Unit 3	Unit 4
Indian Prairie School, Kalamazoo, Michigan	Kalamazoo	Indian	Prairie	School
Oakwood Elementary School, Kalamazoo, Michigan	Kalamazoo	Oakwood	Elementary	School
Oakwood Junior High, Kalamazoo, Michigan	Kalamazoo	Oakwood	Junior	High
Pershing School Portage, Michigan	Portage	Pershing	School	

(b) The names of colleges or universities are indexed according to the most clearly identifying word in the name.

Names	INDEX ORDER OF UNITS		
	Unit 1	Unit 2	Unit 3
Albany Business Col.	Albany	Business	College
Indiana Business School	Indiana	Business	School
Iowa State University	Iowa	State	University
University of Iowa	Iowa	University (of)	
Northwestern University	Northwestern	University	
Slippery Rock State College	Slippery	Rock	State

27. Newspapers and Magazines

(a) The name of a newspaper is indexed in the order in which it is written unless the city of publication does not appear in its name. In that case, the name of the city is inserted before the name of the newspaper.

Names	INDEX ORDER OF UNITS			
	Unit 1	Unit 2	Unit 3	Unit 4
The Canton Herald	Canton	Herald (The)		
The Journal Gazette Ft. Wayne, Indiana	Fort	Wayne	Journal	Gazette (The)
The New York Times	New	York	Times (The)	
The Wall Street Journal, New York, NY	New	York	Wall	Street

(b) The name of a magazine is indexed in the order in which the name is written. (A cross-reference may be made listing the publisher, as described on page 287.)

Names	INDEX ORDER OF UNITS		
	Unit 1	Unit 2	Unit 3
Administrative Management	Administrative	Management	
Harvard Business Review	Harvard	Business	Review
The Office	Office (The)		
Reader's Digest	Reader's	Digest	

28. Federal Government Offices

The names of all federal government agencies and offices are indexed under United States Government. They are indexed according to the order given below.

(a) United States Government
  (three indexing units)
(b) Name of the department
(c) Name of the bureau
(d) Name of the division or subdivision
(e) Location of the office
(f) Title of official, if given

District Director
Internal Revenue Service
Indianapolis, Indiana 46204

would be indexed

United States Government
  Treasury (Department of)
  Internal Revenue Service
  Indianapolis
  District Director

GOVERNMENT OFFICE	WOULD BE INDEXED

District Director
Agricultural Research Service
Federal Building
Tallahassee, Florida 33602
	United States Government
	  Agriculture (Department of)
	  Agricultural Research Service
	  Tallahassee
	  District Director

Bureau of International Commerce
U.S. Department of Commerce
Philadelphia, Pennsylvania 19108
	United States Government
	  Commerce (Department of)
	  International Commerce (Bureau of)
	  Philadelphia

Division of Employment Statistics
Bureau of Labor Statistics
U.S. Department of Labor
Cleveland, Ohio 44199
	United States Government
	  Labor (Department of)
	  Labor Statistics (Bureau of)
	  Employment Statistics (Division of)
	  Cleveland

Customs Service
U.S. Department of the Treasury
San Francisco, California 94102
	United States Government
	  Treasury (Department of the)
	  Customs Service
	  San Francisco

Data Processing Center
Veterans Administration
St. Paul, Minnesota 55511
	United States Government
	  Veterans Administration
	  Data Processing Center
	  St. Paul

(Note: Rule 28 also applies to foreign government offices.)

29. Other Political Subdivisions

The names of other political subdivisions — state, county, city, or town government — are indexed according to:

(a) Geographic name of the subdivision, such as *New Jersey, State (of); Westchester, County (of);* or *Philadelphia, City (of)*
(b) Name of department, board, or office
(c) Location of the office
(d) Title of the official, if given

Names	INDEX ORDER OF UNITS			
	Unit 1	Unit 2	Unit 3	Unit 4
Police Department Alliance, Ohio	Alliance	City (of)	Police	Department
Clinton Co. Park Commission Dubuque, Iowa	Clinton	County (of)	Park	Commission
Municipal Public Works Div. Lancaster, Pa.	Lancaster	City (of)	Public	Works
State Health Department Columbus, Ohio	Ohio	State (of)	Health	Department

30. Subjects

Sometimes it is better to file materials according to subject rather than under the name of the person or business. This is done because the subject may be more important than the name of the person or business. Applications for employment are examples of this type of indexing. The applications are of major importance; the names of the applicants are of secondary importance.

secondary: lesser

Names	INDEX ORDER OF UNITS			
	Unit 1	Unit 2	Unit 3	Unit 4
C. J. Browning (Advertiser)	Advertisers:	Browning	C.	J.
R. M. Smith (Advertiser)	Advertisers:	Smith	R.	M.
H. L. Kramer (Application)	Applications:	Kramer	H.	L.
Jack Myer (Application)	Applications:	Myer	Jack	
J. Fran Smith (Application)	Applications:	Smith	J.	Fran

Cross-Referencing

What will you do when a letter or other material to be filed could be asked for by more than one name? Examples are firm names that consist of two or more surnames, the names of married women, and the names of magazines. You may look for the name according to an indexing order that is not shown on the piece of correspondence or on the file card. For example, you may remember only the name *Goodman* in the firm name *Bergdorf Goodman*; you may not remember a married woman's legal name — you may remember only that her husband's name is *Thomas Devine*; or you may remember the name of a magazine, *Business Week*, but not the name of the publisher, *McGraw-Hill, Inc.*

consist: are made up

In such instances, a cross-reference sheet or card should be filled out and filed under the other title. It should indicate where the material is actually filed. If a photocopying machine is available, it is more efficient to make a photocopy than to fill out a cross-reference sheet. The photocopy should then be filed under the other title.

Although cross-referencing is important for locating filed information quickly, care should be taken in deciding which records really need to be cross-referenced. Too much cross-referencing takes excessive time and a lot of space. Too little cross-referencing will cause needless and costly delays in getting important information. A more detailed discussion of cross-referencing is given on pages 314–315.

Cross-Reference for a Company Known by More than One Name

If the name of a firm is *Rogers-Turner Food Mart*, the original piece of correspondence should be indexed as it is written. You should, however, make a cross-reference card or sheet for the second name in the title. Consequently, if you remember only the second name, *Turner*, you will find on the cross-reference for *Turner* "See Rogers-Turner Food Mart."

Cross-Reference for the Name of a Married Woman

You will file the original piece of correspondence for a married woman under her legal name, that is, her given first name, her maiden last name, and her husband's last name, if she has assumed it. Her husband's given name might be cross-referenced to find the filed piece of correspondence faster. If the legal name of a married women is *Mrs. Martha Lee Laidly*, this name should be indexed on the original piece of correspondence; and a cross-reference card or sheet based on her husband's name should be prepared.

```
┌─────────────────────────────────┐   ┌─────────────────────────────────┐
│ Laidly, Martha Lee (Mrs.)       │   │ Laidly, Thomas Q. (Mrs.)        │
│─────────────────────────────────│   │                                 │
│ Mrs. Thomas Q. Laidly           │   │ See Laidly, Martha Lee (Mrs.)   │
│ 1700 Maple Street               │   │                                 │
│ Shaker Heights, OH  44120       │   │                                 │
│                                 │   │                                 │
│                                 │   │                                 │
│                                 │   │                                 │
│                                 │   │                                 │
└─────────────────────────────────┘   └─────────────────────────────────┘
           Illus. 7-4                            Illus. 7-5
```

REVIEWING IMPORTANT POINTS

1. In what order are the units of a business name considered for filing purposes.
2. What is done when units of an individual name are included in a firm name?
3. How are the words *and*, *of*, and *for* treated in indexing?
4. What rule is used when filing firm names made up of single letters?
5. In a firm name what differences are there in indexing between two words combined with a hyphen and a single word containing a hyphen — for example, Walker-Gordon Mills, Inc., and Mid-Hudson Electric Co.?
6. State simply the rule for indexing possessive words.
7. How would the following be indexed: Federal Reserve Bank, Branch Office, Dallas, Texas?
8. Give examples of subject titles that would be used in preference to the names of the persons or businesses that are concerned.
9. What is a cross-reference card?
10. Give two examples of types of names that are frequently cross-referenced.

MAKING IMPORTANT DECISIONS

Miss Bradford has been the file clerk for a trucking firm for five years and has become familiar with the names of the regular customers. Wednesday, however, Miss Bradford was at home sick. Mr. Grimshaw, her employer, decided to look for a certain file for some customer research he was doing. He remembered a particular pottery company that had shipped with them once last year, but had not done so again. Since it had been so long ago, he could not remember the exact name of the pottery company. He was sure the name had a "Hartley" in it somewhere, but when he looked under Hartley in the files, there was no record of a pottery company. Miss Bradford had not been using a cross-reference sheet for any of her files, so Mr. Grimshaw had to wait until Miss Bradford returned to find the file. What do you think of Miss Bradford's decision not to maintain a cross-reference sheet? Why?

LEARNING TO WORK WITH OTHERS

Mr. Neil has been with the ABC Printing Company for fifteen years. He developed the filing system for the firm and is now supervisor of the central files. His filing procedures are used in all the executive offices so that materials sent to the central files can be filed and found quickly.

He has his own ideas about filing rules; for instance, the customer's names beginning with Mac and Mc are placed ahead of all the other names in the M section of the alphabetic filing at the ABC Printing Company.

New employees are confused because the system is so different from the rules of filing they have been taught. They waste much time and energy filing and finding correspondence.

If you were employed as a file clerk at the ABC Printing Company, how would you attempt to reconcile the differences between company practice and the filing rules learned in school? Since his system has been in use for 15 years, should you expect Mr. Neil to change his filing procedures to fit those taught in school? How would you plan to get along with him?

IMPROVING LANGUAGE SKILLS

On a separate sheet of paper write the plural form of each of the following business words. After you have written the plural forms, check your answers in a dictionary.

1. prefix	6. business	11. studio
2. attorney	7. series	12. company
3. salesperson	8. chief clerk	13. trade-in
4. belief	9. statistic	14. delivery
5. secretary	10. city	15. youth

IMPROVING ARITHMETIC SKILLS

1. Ten years ago your company had 8 separate files on the Morgan Corporation. Today you have 24 files. The number of files increased by what percentage?
2. The price of a desk lamp is reduced 30 percent from the original price of $11.95. How much will you pay for the desk lamp at the reduced price?

DEMONSTRATING OFFICE SKILLS

1. On a separate sheet of paper type each of the following. Underline the first indexing unit and circle the second indexing unit.

   (a) R. Harold Dana
   (b) The Holden Paper Co.
   (c) Hubert Smith-Johnson, Jr.
   (d) Woodward & Lothrop Dept. Store
   (e) Lois J. McDowell
   (f) A to Z Cleaning Service
   (g) National Association of Life Underwriters
   (h) Trans-Canada Air Lines
   (i) Father Francis
   (j) North West Wholesale Furriers
   (k) Provident Bank & Trust Company of Cleveland
   (l) Tommy Tucker's Toys
   (m) Mrs. Sally (John) Hanson
   (n) Johnson-Hardin Produce Co.
   (o) President Walter C. Schott
   (p) San Bruno Public Warehouse
   (q) Disabled American Veterans
   (r) A-1 Window Washers
   (s) Attorney Edward K. Wilcox
   (t) St. Louis Pharmaceuticals, Inc.
   (u) University of Cincinnati
   (v) Holy Angels Nursery School

2. Is the order of the names in each of the following pairs correct? Type the pairs of names on a separate sheet of paper. Make any corrections in indexing order that are necessary.

   (a) H. M. Jones
       Henry M. Jonas
   (b) Carl O'Bannon
       J. B. Obannon
   (c) Mrs. Rena Lawson Carter
       Harold Lawson-Carter
   (d) Professor Leslie Hampton
       Leslie Hampton
   (e) George Carpenter, II
       George Carpenter, III

(f) Sister Julia
Julia Sisson
(g) Ernest V. Mellon, Sr.
Ernest V. Mellon, Jr.
(h) Dr. Beverly Tarkington
Beverly D. Tarkington
(i) Francine the Florist
Francis J. Flanagan
(j) Charlie's Place
Charlie Porter, Plumbing

3. On a separate sheet of paper, type the order in which the parts of the following titles are considered in indexing.

(a) Board of Education
Hamilton County, Oregon
(b) Pennsylvania State Department of Highways
(c) Central Trust Company of Delaware
(d) Department of Public Welfare
City of Minneapolis, Minnesota
(e) Phillips & Woods (Real Estate)
(f) Division of Unemployment Compensation
Ohio State Employment Service
(g) Oakwood First National Bank
(h) M. Meredith Weatherby (Application for Employment)
(i) The Gerald Gerrard Gun Shop
(j) The War College
U.S. Department of Defense

4. On a separate sheet of paper, type the following names in correct alphabetic order in each group.

Group 1

(a) H. Duncan McCampbell
(b) Mack Campbell
(c) The Campbell Soup Company
(d) J. C. MacCampbell

Group 2

(a) Martin and Ulberg
(b) Martin C. Ulberg
(c) Martin-Ulberg, Inc.
(d) K. Martin Ulberg, M.D.

Group 3

(a) Rosewood Delicatessen
(b) Olde Rosewood Tea Shoppe
(c) Rose Wood (Mrs.)
(d) Roselawn Public Library

Group 4

(a) Five Corners Car Wash
(b) Five-Corners Creamery
(c) Five O'Clock Shop
(d) 15th Avenue Apartments

Group 5

(a) Williams Ave. Brake Service
(b) William's Coiffures
(c) Williams' Associates (Brokers)
(d) Williamson Heating Company

Group 6

(a) La Maisonette
(b) Lamson & Towers Advertising
(c) Lamps & Lighting, Inc.
(d) Laap Family Furniture

Group 7

(a) 2 in 1 Cleaning Service
(b) 22d Street Theater
(c) Twenty-One (Restaurant)
(d) Twosome Dance Club

Group 8

(a) Ms. J. C. (Barbara) Sands
(b) Santa Barbara Police Dept.
(c) St. Barnaby's Episcopal Church
(d) Barbara St. John

Group 9

(a) Eagle's Nest (Restaurant)
(b) Anne Eagles
(c) Fraternal Order of Eagles
(d) Save the Eagle Committee

Group 10

(a) J. & L. Fruit Market

(b) Jones & Laughlin Steel

(c) J. L. Jones, Jr.

(d) J. L. Jones, Sr.

Group 11

(a) Southern Railway

(b) South Boston Beanery

(c) South Western Printing Company

(d) Rachel W. Souther

Group 12

(a) Black's

(b) Blacks'

(c) Blacks' Super Market

(d) S. Black & Co.

Group 13

(a) K-P Kitchenware

(b) Kennedy-Porter Fencing

(c) Arthur P. Kennedy

(d) P. Kennedy Arthur

Group 14

(a) St. Joseph's Orphanage

(b) St. Joseph (Missouri) Railroad Depot

(c) San Jose Growers' Assn.

(d) Sanjor Coffee House

5. In completing this exercise you will need 50 5″ x 3″ file cards or plain paper cut to about that size.

(a) Type each of the following names in index form at the top of a card. Type the number of each name in the upper right corner of the card. (These numbers will aid in checking the answers.) Type the name and address below the indexed name. (See Illus. 7-4 on page 288.)

(b) After the names, numbers, and addresses have been typed, arrange the cards alphabetically.

(c) Save these cards for use in assignments in Unit 8, Parts 1 and 4.

(1) Janitrol Heating Service, 6602 No. Clark St., Chicago, IL 60626.

(2) Kitty's Korner Kitchen, Cooper Bldg., Marietta, OH 45750

(3) Mlle. Jeanette Cecil Sagan, 3 Rue de la Pais, Paris, France

(4) Janitor Supplies & Equipment Co., 9 W. 7th St., Akron, OH 44314

(5) Robert P. Van der Meer, 221 Watervliet St., Detroit, MI 48217

(6) Jeanette Labelson, Apt. 3B, 60 Sutton Place, South, New York, NY 10022

(7) Williams & Williams, Tax Consultants, Suite 12, Statler Hotel, Cleveland, OH 44141

(8) Jasper J. Seaman, Chalfonte Hall, Campus Station, Durham, NC 27707

(9) Meyer Lufkin & Son, Commercial Bldg., 9th & Walnut, Omaha, NE 68108

(10) Julia Meyer Employment Agency, 210 N. State St., Albany, NY 12210

(11) Youman & Garties Mfg. Company, 316 Spring St., N.W., Atlanta, GA 30308

(12) The World-Telegram News, Dallas, TX 78421

(13) Rachel J. Vandermeer, 3920 Alamo Drive, Houston, TX 77007

(14) Mid Way Service Station, Junction State Routes 7 & 9, Osburn, ID 83849

(15) Ringling Bros.-Barnum & Bailey Circus, Winter Headquarters, Sarasota, FL 33580

(16) Greenstone Zion Reform Temple, Cor. Reading & Vine Sts., Greenstone, PA 17227

(17) William's U-Fix-It Shop, 4920 Carthage Rd., Richmond, VA 23223

(18) Seamen's Rest, 60 Front St., New Orleans, LA 70130

(19) Wati Rajhma, Room 2100, United Nations Secretariat, New York, NY 10017

(20) Oberhelman Bros. Flooring, Inc., 420 Vine St., Seattle, WA 98121

(21) P. M. Diners' Clubhouse, 22 Regent St., Louisville, KY 40218

(22) Society for the Sightless, 1404 K St., N.W., Washington, D.C. 20005

(23) J. & K. Seaman Hauling Line, 160 N. First St., Ottumwa, IA 52501

(24) 29th Street Mission, 13 - 29th St., San Francisco, CA 94110

(25) La Belle Dresses, 18 Circle Drive, Rogers, CT 06263

(26) Rosenswig's Dept. Store, 6920 Appletree Rd., Wilmington, DE 19810

(27) R. & L. Benjamin & Company, 14 West Decatur St., Ft. Smith, AR 72901

(28) Mayor Ella O'Berne, City Hall, Baltimore, MD 21202

(29) Midway Seafood House, 3109 Collins Ave., Miami Beach, FL 33839

(30) The Hobby Shop, 1010 Pacific Blvd., Portland, OR 97220

(31) Automatic Food Dispenser Co., 112 High St., Colorado Springs, CO 80904

(32) Automatic Food Dispenser Co., 19th & Ewald Sts., Camden, NJ 08105

(33) Automatic Food Dispenser Co., Camden, OH 45311

(34) Hobby Haven, 730 Pine St., St. Joseph, MO 64504

(35) Lufkin Central Savings Society, 9 So. Main St., Lufkin, TX 75901

(36) Rosen's Fresh Fruit Market, 1403 La Cienega St., Los Angeles, CA 90035

(37) Kitty-Kat Products, Ashport, TN 38003

(38) Long Island Railroad, 69–75 Rockefeller Plaza, New York, NY 10020

(39) Adolph G. Meier Lumber Co., First St. at B. & O. R.R., Columbus, OH 43201

(40) Dr. Mary W. Barnhart, 22 Medical Arts Bldg., Oak Park, IL 60403

(41) Mary Barnhart, 635 Capitol Ave., Springfield, IL 62701

(42) Drury Hill Farms, Inc., Box 10, Route 4, Drury, PA 18222

(43) Carthage Mills, Inc., Springvale, GA 31788

(44) Police Department, Drury, PA 18222

(45) P. M. Dinersman Company, 1614 Meridian St., Indianapolis, IN 42625

(46) Branford & Branford Co., Artesia, MS 39736

(47) Branford, Branford and Branford, Attorneys, Union Life Bldg., St. Louis, MO 63155

(48) Olde Seaport Inn, Front and Plum Sts., Alexandria, VA 22313

(49) Mary Lee Barnhart, 2226 Washington Avenue, Fargo, ND 58102

(50) Ninety and Ninth Apartments, 90th St. at 9th Ave., New York, NY 10024

Part 4

Filing Equipment and Supplies

As Mr. Boyle was searching the files for some information, he noticed how crowded the drawer was. He asked his receptionist, "Mr. Crume, must these file drawers be so packed? It's difficult to find anything!"

"I know what you mean, Mr. Boyle, but this is our only filing cabinet. We could certainly use another one."

"Why don't you call some office supply stores, Mr. Crume, and ask their advice on the type of filing equipment best suited for our office. We have sufficient space to add more files. Anything you can do will be appreciated."

Knowing the indexing rules for filing is absolutely necessary. But, unless you have the proper filing equipment and the correct supplies, you will not have an efficient filing system.

Filing Equipment

Good tools are necessary to make your filing system work for you. In large offices filing equipment is usually ordered through the purchasing department, and filing supplies are available from the supply room. However, in a small office you may make **recommendations** and assist your employer in purchasing equipment and supplies. This will require careful study to make correct decisions. Whether you work in a large office or a small office, you will be more efficient if you are familiar with the kinds of equipment and supplies that you will be using on your job.

recommendations: suggestions

Proper storage of records is necessary in all businesses. The *size* of the material to be filed is the first factor to be considered; the *number of items* to be filed each day is second.

Standard filing cabinets are available for storing the two most common sizes of business records: letter size (8½" x 11") and the legal size (8½" x 13" or 8½" x 14"). Other cabinets are designed to **house** card files, visible records, punched cards, computer print-outs, blueprints, and other materials.

house: contain

Vertical Files

The typical pull-out drawer file cabinet — the **vertical** file — is used in most business offices. Vertical file cabinets are manufactured in two-, three-, four-, and five-drawer units. Two-drawer vertical file cabinets are used beside the desk and contain only the most active records. Three-drawer vertical file cabinets are often referred to as counter-height cabinets. Five-drawer vertical file cabinets are replacing four-drawer units since they occupy the same amount of floor space, but contain an additional drawer.

Office space in the business districts of many large cities is very expensive, so a saving in floor space for filing cabinets can greatly reduce the cost of housing records.

Every business office has correspondence files. Some typical contents of correspondence files include letters, telegrams, teletype messages, purchase orders, invoices, memorandums, reports, and interoffice messages. Reading the correspondence files of any company is the easiest way to learn the nature of its business and the history of its transactions. Active correspondence files are sometimes kept in desk-side, two-drawer files; while files on completed transactions are kept in three-, four-, or five-drawer files in other areas of the office.

vertical: upright

Illus. 7-6

Vertical file cabinets, of various heights, are the most common type of office file.

Lateral and Shelf Files

lateral:
from the side

Because of the increasing number of records that must be kept in expensive office space, many organizations are now using lateral and shelf files. The lateral cabinets look like a chest of drawers and are frequently used as area dividers or low partitions. Often the secretary and the executive will have lateral cabinets behind their desks to house the records they refer to constantly such as current correspondence, sales reports, price lists, production reports, trade handbooks, and periodicals of the industry.

Illus. 7-7

Lateral file cabinets

In shelf filing, papers are held in folders placed on shelves in an upright position. Some shelf files are built with open shelves (like the shelving for library books); others are equipped with sliding doors to protect the records. Still others have sliding shelves which draw out sidewise, similar in operation to the pull-out drawer in a typical file cabinet.

maximum:
greatest

Units that are seven or eight shelves high provide the maximum amount of filing area for the floor space while keeping the records within reach. While much floor space can be saved by using shelf files, many records management consultants believe that individual records cannot be filed or found as quickly as in vertical files, particularly when sliding doors are used to protect the shelf files. They believe shelf filing is most effective for storing records that are not frequently used.

In addition to the standard filing equipment mentioned here, there is a great deal of specialized filing equipment that is used in microfilming and in the data processing field which is described and illustrated in Part 4 of Unit 8. You will usually be most concerned with vertical files and lateral files since your files should contain only materials that are needed frequently. Shelf files and special files are usually found in the central filing department where less frequently called for materials are stored.

Illus. 7-8

These shelf files, with open shelves, save much floor space.

Filing Supplies

Since your filing duties will be concerned mostly with alphabetic name and subject files, which are often combined in one system, you should know how to use the tools within a file drawer to their greatest advantage.

Each drawer in a correspondence file contains two different kinds of filing supplies — guides and file folders. The *guides* in an alphabetic correspondence file divide the drawer into alphabetic sections and serve as signposts for quick reference. They also provide support for the folders and their contents.

File folders hold the papers in an upright position in the file drawer. They are made of heavy paper stock and serve as a container to keep papers together.

Guides

Guides are heavy cardboard sheets which are the same size as the folders. Extending over the top of each guide is a tab upon which is marked or printed a notation or title called a *caption*. The caption indicates the alphabetic range of the material filed in folders behind the guide. For example, a guide may carry the caption *A* which would tell you that only material starting with the letter *A* would be found between that guide and the next guide. This tab may be part of the guide itself, or it may be an attached metal or plastic tab. Sets of guides may be purchased with printed letters or combinations of letters and numbers that may be used with any standard filing system. Other guide tabs are blank, and the specific captions are made in the user's office.

eyelet:
ringed hole

Guides may be obtained with a small projection that extends below the body of the guide. The projection contains a metal **eyelet** through which a file drawer rod may be run, thus holding the guides in place and preventing the folders from slipping down in the drawer.

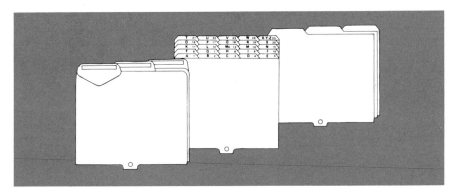

Illus. 7-9

File guides with metal eyelets for projection rods.

Kinds of Guides. Guides are classified as primary or secondary. The *primary guides* indicate the major divisions — alphabetic, numeric, subject, geographic, or chronological — into which the filing system is divided. *Secondary guides* (also called auxiliary or special name guides) are subdivisions of the primary guides and are used to highlight certain types of information, for example, to indicate the placement of special folders (such as those for *Advertising* or *Applications*). They are also used to indicate a section of the file in which many folders with the same first indexing unit are placed. For example, if a file contains many individual folders for the name *Brown* behind the primary guide with the caption *B*, a secondary guide with the caption *Brown* might be placed in the file drawer to aid in finding one of the *Brown* folders.

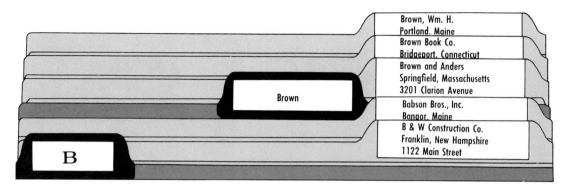

Primary Guide	Secondary Guide	Individual Folders

Illus. 7-10

Number of Guides. If individual folders are to be located quickly, not more than ten should be filed behind any one guide. The number of guides, however, will depend on the actual use of the file and the amount of material in each folder. Anywhere from 15 to 25 guides in each file drawer will help in finding and filing in most filing systems.

Folders. A folder is made of a sheet of heavy paper that has been folded once so that the back is about one-half inch higher than the front. Folders are larger than the papers they contain so that they protect them. Two standard folder sizes are *letter size* for papers that are 8½″ x 11″ and *legal size* for papers that are 8½″ x 13″ or 8½″ x 14″.

Folder Cuts. Folders are cut across the top so that the back has a tab that projects above the top of the folder. Such tabs bear captions that identify the contents of each folder. Tabs vary in width and position. The tabs of a set of folders that are *one-half cut* are half the width of the folder and have only two positions. *One-third cut* folders have three positions, each tab occupying a third of the width of the folder. Another standard tab is *one-fifth cut* which has five positions. Other folders "hang" from a metal frame placed inside the file drawer.

projects:
sticks out

captions:
explanatory headings

Miscellaneous Folders. A miscellaneous folder is kept for every alphabetic primary guide. It is called a *miscellaneous* folder because it contains filed material from more than one person or firm. When there are fewer than six pieces of filed material to, from, or about the same person or firm, these documents are placed in a folder bearing the same caption as the primary guide it serves. For example, if the caption on the primary guide is *B*, the caption on the miscellaneous folders will also be *B*.

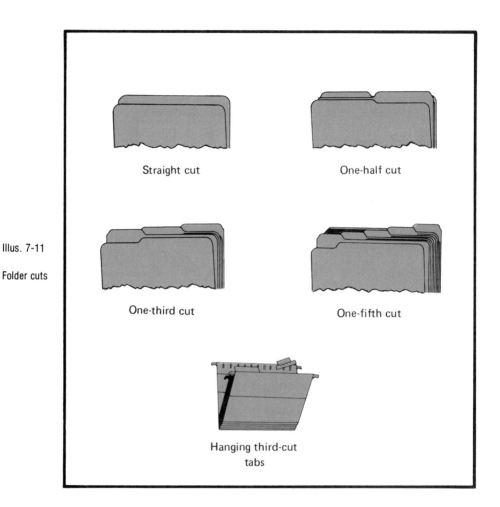

Illus. 7-11

Folder cuts

Straight cut

One-half cut

One-third cut

One-fifth cut

Hanging third-cut
tabs

Individual Folders. When a certain number of pieces of filed material (generally about six) to, from, or about one person or subject have accumulated in the miscellaneous folder, an individual folder for this material is prepared. The caption on the tab of an individual folder identifies the correspondent. Obviously materials will be found faster if they are filed in an individual folder rather than in a miscellaneous folder.

accumulated:
collected; piled up

Special Folders. When an organization files a large amount of material that relates to one subject (such as applications for employment), all this related material is placed in a special folder. The caption identifies the subject or the name of the material. A special folder may be prepared to file all identical last names, thus removing them from the miscellaneous folder. For example, all the *Smiths* may be removed from the miscellaneous folder and placed in a special folder, thus permitting material filed under *Smith* to be found faster.

Capacity of Folders. Folders should never become overcrowded. Each separate folder should contain not more than one inch of filed material. Most file folders have *score lines* at the bottom that are used to widen each folder and thereby increase its capacity. When the folder begins to fill up, the first score line is creased; as more pieces of filed material are inserted, the remaining scores are creased.

When a folder can hold no more material it should be subdivided into two or more folders. Subdivisions may be made according to date or by subject:

Jones Company   Jones Company
January-March   Orders
Jones Company   Jones Company
April-June   Receipts

A subdivided folder should be properly identified. *Folder 1* or *Folder 2* does not indicate what is in the folder. Miscellaneous folders should be examined often so that individual and special folders may be prepared to expand the filing system logically.

Labels

There are two principal kinds of labels for filing — folder labels and file drawer labels.

Folder Labels. Folder labels come in a variety of colors. Each company has its own system of identifying file folders by the use of color. The use of color coding in filing is a great help in locating particular files in a matter of seconds and thus helps in keeping costs under control.

The captions on folder labels should be typewritten. It is better if they are typewritten because they can be read more easily.

Consistency in typing captions on labels is important. The captions should always be typed in exact indexing order (*Brown John A* — not *John A. Brown*). Punctuation other than a hyphen or dash is usually omitted. In order to insure uniformity in the files you should type the first letter in the caption at the same point on each label, usually two spaces from the left edge. Type the name on the label so that after the labels have been attached to the folders, the names will appear at the top edge of each tab. For ease in reading, upper and lower case letters should be used. In a subject file, however, the caption of the main subject is sometimes typed in all capital letters to make it stand out. The subdivision file labels are then typed in upper and lower case.

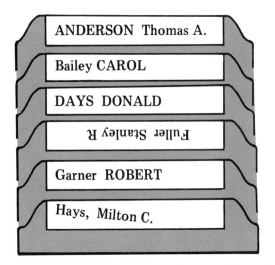 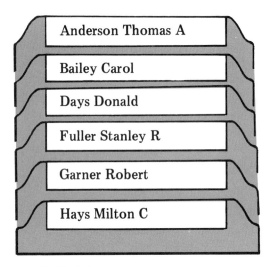

Illus. 7-12   The captions at the left are inconsistent in their
punctuation, capitalization, and placement. Captions may be
typed in all capital letters or as shown at the right.

Labels must be kept in good condition and should be replaced when
they become torn or difficult to read. Hard-to-read or torn labels tend to
delay the filing and finding of materials.

Drawer Labels. Drawer labels are used to identify the contents of each file
drawer. To locate filed material quickly, the labels must be specific, easily
read, and up to date. The information should appear on the drawer as
illustrated below.

Illus. 7-13

```
GENERAL  CORRESPONDENCE

AA-BZ

197-

SALES  DEPARTMENT
```

Line 1 — Description
    2 — Index
    3 — Year
    4 — Unit or department

When the contents of a cabinet are changed in any way, the drawer label
must be corrected immediately.

Positions of Guides and Folders

Since the tabs on guides and folders take up only part of the horizontal edge from which they extend, they may appear in several positions.

In any filing system, the tabs in each position should be of the same width. Specific positions should be reserved for each type of guide and folder. When guide positions are made with regard to the position of the folders, the filing system becomes well organized. An example of this is an alphabetic system in which four filing positions are used.

1. First position: Reserved for primary guides indicating the major divisions of the system.

2. Second position: Reserved for miscellaneous folders. Miscellaneous folders carry the same caption as the primary guides and are placed at the end of each category, *immediately in front of the next primary guide.*

3. Third position: Reserved for individual folders filed directly behind the primary guides.

4. Fourth position: Reserved for secondary guides or out guides. (An out guide is put in the file to indicate that a folder has been borrowed.)

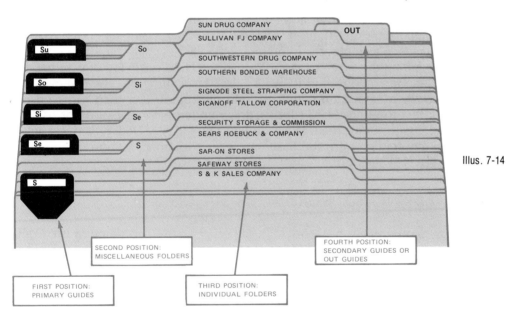

Illus. 7-14

Filing Accessories

In addition to filing cabinets, guides, and folders, there are many accessories that will make your filing job easier. Some of these are a table or desk to be used when arranging material for the files, file boxes or baskets into which material is placed, and a sorter, illustrated on page 315 for arranging papers before they are filed.

accessories: extra but not essential items

REVIEWING IMPORTANT POINTS

1. Why would a five-drawer vertical file be preferred to a four-drawer file?
2. What is a miscellaneous folder, and where is it placed in relation to the primary guide and the other folders?
3. When should an individual folder be prepared?
4. What information should a drawer label contain?
5. What is the purpose of an out guide?

MAKING IMPORTANT DECISIONS

Mr. Dodson prides himself on his efficiency. Tuesday he noticed some empty file folders in a box in the basement of the plant. Mr. Dodson was delighted to see them because now he would not have to order more file folders. By using the folders in the basement, he would save money by not having to order more folders and would save time by not having to wait for the order to come in. He brought the folders from the basement upstairs to his office, but noticed that the folders from the basement were thinner and shorter than the folders now in his cabinet. Mr. Dodson didn't think it mattered that much. Thursday, Miss Mayes, Mr Dodson's employer, asked him to find a file while she was on "hold" with a long distance call. Mr. Dodson searched every file drawer for the folder. He couldn't find it! After Miss Mayes hung up, she came out to see why Mr. Dodson could not find the folder. Just then Mr. Dodson saw that the folder had slipped down underneath several other folders and could not be seen. What do you think of Mr. Dodson's decision to use the folders from the basement even though they were thinner and shorter? Why?

LEARNING TO WORK WITH OTHERS

Scott Thomas has worked in the office of the Top Name Music Company for three months. The company has six employees.

When Scott was hired, Mrs. King, the owner of the company, asked him to "be generally in charge of the files." Mrs. King explained that while everyone will need to use the files, she is asking Scott to be responsible for such things as "keeping the files neat and making sure that all of the papers are in the proper order." Mrs. King said that "all of the employees will help you in this job."

That sounded all right when Mrs. King explained the responsibility to Scott, but it's not working out that way. For example, some employees remove folders from the file cabinets and do not return them for several weeks. When employees cannot find a folder in the files, they ask Scott where it is. Also, since the employees know that Scott is responsible for keeping the files neat, some of them will open the file drawer and simply place a folder on top of the other folders instead of inserting it back in its proper place between the other folders.

Scott knows that the files are not neat, and he is sure that Mrs. King also knows this, but just doesn't say anything to Scott. Scott hasn't tried to get the other employees to improve their filing habits, because they are all older than Scott.

This situation is beginning to bother Scott. He knows he is expected to do a good job, but, yet, he doesn't seem to be able to do what is expected of him. What should he do?

IMPROVING LANGUAGE SKILLS

Ten of the following words are misspelled. Type the entire list giving the correct spelling of each.

1. accessories
2. appostrophie
3. asist
4. chronalogical
5. consistency
6. correspondance
7. efficiency
8. equitment
9. facilitate
10. foreign
11. guarentees
12. initial
13. miscellaneous
14. partition
15. possessive
16. reciepts
17. refered
18. retrieval
19. similiar
20. sirname

IMPROVING ARITHMETIC SKILLS

1. You have been asked to order additional filing folders for a new department that is being set up. You will need approximately 750 folders. If the folders come in boxes of 60 each, how many boxes should you order?

2. If you earn $130 a week, how much will you make each month (four weeks to a month)? If you save $10 a week, how much will you save in a year (before annual interest is added)? If your rent is $120 a month, how much will housing cost you for a year? If your insurance policy premium is $40.36 annually, how much do you pay semiannually? On a separate sheet of paper show your answers as well as how you computed them.

DEMONSTRATING OFFICE SKILLS

List five or more places where your name is on file indicating in each instance just how it is filed. For example, list how your name is filed for

Social Security purposes, for school records, for life insurance, for a charge account, for a driver's license, for a public library card, in a telephone directory.

IMPROVING OFFICE SKILLS (Optional)

You work for a national insurance company. Records of policyholders are placed in an alphabetic file and also in a chronological file set up according to the dates the policies are accepted. The names, addresses, and policy dates listed below are for policyholders whose records must be added to each filing system. Type the information on a 5" × 3" card in index form at the upper left corner of the card. Type the number of each in the upper right corner to aid in checking the answers.

For the alphabetical file, type the last name first with the address and policy date underneath. Arrange the cards alphabetically. For the chronological file, type the policy acceptance on the first line with the name and address underneath. Arrange these cards chronologically.

(1) Ms. Adrienne Thurman
5414 Highland Road
Denver, CO 80214
Policy: 11/21/77

(2) Mr. Tom Freeman
253 Garver Heights
Stockton, CA 95201
Policy: 1/26/77

(3) Ms. Cathy Green
34 Melrose Drive
Denver, CO 80202
Policy: 1/29/78

(4) Mr. Glen Caldwell
8254 South Willow Road
Syracuse, NY 13271
Policy: 8/14/77

(5) Mr. John Buckner
6333 Hudson Avenue
Seattle, WA 98112
Policy: 6/12/77

(6) Ms. Mallory Young
8731 First Street
Memphis, TN 38122
Policy: 2/10/78

(7) Mr. Fred Sellers
3212 53rd Street
Little Rock, AR 72214
Policy: 5/18/77

(8) Mr. Curtis Banks
5445 Linden Avenue
Pittsburgh, PA 15221
Policy: 10/2/77

(9) Ms. Linda Meyers
334 Madison Road
Santa Fe, NM 87501
Policy: 9/4/77

Records Management in the Office

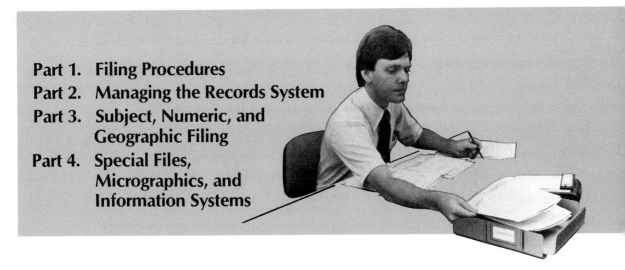

Part 1. Filing Procedures
Part 2. Managing the Records System
Part 3. Subject, Numeric, and Geographic Filing
Part 4. Special Files, Micrographics, and Information Systems

Part 1

Filing Procedures

Miss Melba Morgan began her job as file clerk five years ago under the supervision of Mr. Wilbur Simms. Mr. Simms emphasized the importance of proper collection, inspection, and cross-referencing of materials to be filed. He also stressed the fact that a good file clerk never falls behind in filing papers.

Miss Morgan followed these tips in filing and formed good work habits. After several promotions, she has become assistant to Mr. John Ramsey, vice-president of sales. Among her fine qualifications is her experience in filing. Mr. Ramsey has been very impressed by her simple and efficient filing system.

Effective filing procedures begin long before any material is actually placed in the files. If they are properly applied, systematic filing procedures will in the long run save you time which you can use to perform other office duties. Even more important, well-organized and carefully followed filing practices insure the prompt retrieval of filed records.

Collecting Papers for the Files

The basic reason for having a filing system is so that you or your employer can find desired information when it is needed. Unless materials are filed promptly and accurately, this is not possible.

Correspondence and other business papers that are to be filed should be collected in an orderly manner. Materials to be filed should be kept in a special basket or tray which is usually marked *File*.

Several times a day you should gather the materials to be filed from both your desk and your employer's. Occasionally it may be necessary to go through the papers on your employer's desk (with permission, of course) to gather materials that should be filed.

Illus. 8-1

Materials to be filed should be placed in a special tray.

Inspecting

The next step in the filing process is **inspecting** each document that is to be filed. During inspection you should separate those current materials that will go into your own or your employer's files from those that will go to the central filing department. In large offices several times a day a messenger collects the papers to be filed in the central files.

During the inspection process you look for a *release mark*, which is your **authority** to file each letter. This mark indicates that action has been taken on the letter, and it is released for filing. The release mark usually is indicated by your initials or those of your employer. These initials are placed in the upper left corner of the letter.

Since it is assumed that carbon copies are ready to file, they do not bear release marks. Many firms prepare carbon copies on paper with the words F I L E C O P Y printed in large outline letters across the face of the sheet. Frequently colored paper is used for the file copy.

In addition to checking for the release mark, you should examine records for completeness. All correspondence that is clipped together is examined and stapled (if it belongs together) in the upper left corner. The reply is stapled on top of the incoming letter. Paper clips, rubber bands, or straight pins are never placed in the file drawer. Torn papers should be mended at this time.

inspecting: examining

authority: right to proceed

Indexing

significant:
important

Although every step in the filing process is important, the indexing step is particularly **significant**. *Indexing* is the process of determining how a document is to be filed. An incorrect decision at this time may mean a lost letter. At the very least, it means extra time to locate the letter. It is necessary, therefore, to scan or read each letter carefully to determine the *key name* or *title* (first indexing unit) that best identifies the material.

The way materials are requested usually determines the way they should be indexed. An incoming letter could be filed under the name appearing on the letterhead, the name of the person signing the letter, the name of a person or business mentioned in the body of the letter, or the subject of the letter. For example, a letter announcing a new fire-resistant file cabinet would probably be filed under the heading "Office Equipment" in a folder labeled "Filing Cabinets" rather than under the name of the distributor appearing on the letterhead.

Copies of outgoing letters could be filed under the name of the addressee, the name of a person or business mentioned in the letter, or the subject of the letter. If a letter is of a personal nature, it is filed under the name of the person to or by whom it is written, even though the letter may have been written on a company letterhead. If there is any doubt about how a document should be indexed, the person who has released the record for filing should be consulted.

Coding

coded:
labeled with symbols

After the exact indexing order has been chosen, the document is marked or **coded**. A document may be coded in several different ways. The indexing units may be underlined:

Alamo Dry Cleaning Corporation

R. Robert Wilson

or the units may be numbered:

    1   2   3   4
Alamo Dry Cleaning Corporation

  2   3   1
R. Robert Wilson

If the name or subject does not appear in the letter, it must be written in, preferably in the upper right corner of the paper. All coding is

CROSS REFERENCE RECORD

Name or Subject ___Gary P. Lord___ File No. ___L371___

Date ___October 1, 19--___

Remarks ___Procedure to collect bad accounts___

SEE ___Kipley's Collection Agency___ File No. ___K442___
___253 Ludlow Avenue___
___Austin, TX 78714___

Authorized by ___Marilyn Garcia___ Date ___Oct. 1, 19--___

File Cross-Reference Record under name or subject listed at top of this sheet, and in proper date order. The document referred to should be filed under Name or Subject listed under "SEE".

Illus. 8-3   Cross-reference for a letter

PHONE: 512-321-4122

Kipley's Collection Agency
253 LUDLOW AVENUE
AUSTIN, TX 78714

ALG

19- OCT 1 AM 9:30

October 1, 19--

Mrs. Alice L. Freeman, President
Arden Manufacturing Company
5328 Belview Road
Austin, TX 78702

Dear Mrs. Freeman

Every company has to deal with difficult-to-collect accounts receivables. They are costly in both time and money.

Kipley's has developed a procedure for collecting bad accounts that has helped our clients increase their profits. A brochure and sample copies of letters to collect your accounts are enclosed. Just give us your accounts that are uncollectible and we do the rest!

To reduce the costs of bad accounts and to increase your profits, please call me collect at 512-231-4122 for more information.

Sincerely

Gary P. Lord X

Gary P. Lord
Representative

Enclosures

ag

Illus. 8-2   Letter properly released and coded

done with a colored pencil. Coding aids in filing the record each time it is removed from the file as it does not need to be reread.

Cross-Referencing

relatively:
measured in
comparison

Although selecting the indexing caption is relatively simple in most cases, there are always some records that might be requested in more than one way. For example, your firm might receive a letter from a good customer recommending an applicant for a position. Obviously this letter of recommendation should be filed with other records referring to the applicant and would be filed in the applicant's folder in the "Applications" section. It may be wise, however, to keep a record of the letter in the customer's folder. The name of the applicant, therefore, is underlined on the letter as the primary indexing unit. The customer's name (of secondary importance in this instance) is also underlined and an X placed at the end of the line in the margin to show that a cross-reference should be made.

cross-reference:
alternate indexing
caption for a
document

A cross-reference sheet (usually of a distinctive color) is prepared with the name and address of the customer, the date of the letter, a brief description of the letter, and where the letter is filed following the "SEE." This cross-reference is then placed in the customer's folder, in its proper

sequence:
order

sequence by date with the other papers, as a record of the letter.

Rather than prepare regular cross-reference sheets, many companies prefer using a photocopy of the original. This speeds retrieval since a complete copy of the record is available at each file point. Do not forget, however, to underline the primary indexing unit and put an X on each copy, so that you will know in which folder each is to be filed.

Many hard-to-index documents should be cross-referenced in several places; it is up to you to think of the number of ways in which materials may be requested. Too much cross-referencing requires considerable time as well as filing space; however, too little cross-referencing may hold up retrieval.

manila:
a durable,
buff-colored paper of
smooth finish

If a permanent cross-reference is desired, a cross-reference guide is prepared. This is a manila card the same size as a file folder, having a tab in the same position as those used for individual folders. A situation requiring a permanent cross-reference guide might be as follows: The name of a company with which you do a great deal of business is changed. Another folder is prepared for the new name and all material is placed in this folder. The old folder is now replaced with a permanent cross-reference guide with the necessary retrieval information on its tab:

Adams and Smith Manufacturing Co.
See Adams and Jones Manufacturing Co.

If the special cross-reference guide form is not available, use the back half of the folder as a cross-reference guide by cutting off the front flap of the folder at the score line. The cross-reference guide remains in the file as long as the name or subject is still active. (See page 287 for additional information on cross-referencing.)

Sorting

After the records have been coded and the necessary cross-reference sheets prepared, the material is ready to be sorted. *Sorting* is the process of arranging the records in indexing order before placing them in the folders.

Sorting serves two important purposes. First, it saves actual filing time. Since the records are in exact indexing order, you are able to move quickly from drawer to drawer, thus saving time and energy for other important tasks. Second, if documents are requested before they are filed, they can be found quickly.

If the volume of filing is high, special sorting trays or compartments should be used. Sorting trays are equipped with alphabetic, numeric, or geographic guides, depending upon the classification system you are using. When you sort materials alphabetically, for example, records

Illus. 8-4

A sorting tray helps to reduce daily filing time.

beginning with the letter *A* are placed behind an *A* guide; those beginning with *B*, behind a *B* guide, and so on through the alphabet. After the materials have been rough sorted, they are removed from the sorting tray and placed in exact alphabetic order (fine sorting). If the volume of material is low, this same procedure may be followed on your desk top.

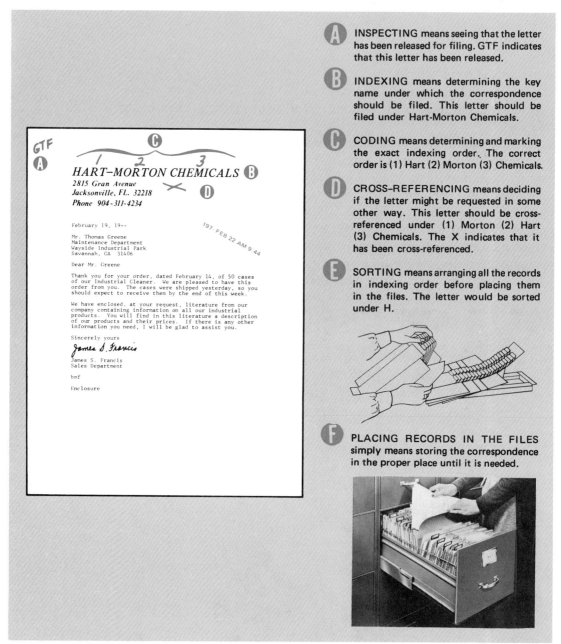

A INSPECTING means seeing that the letter has been released for filing. GTF indicates that this letter has been released.

B INDEXING means determining the key name under which the correspondence should be filed. This letter should be filed under Hart-Morton Chemicals.

C CODING means determining and marking the exact indexing order. The correct order is (1) Hart (2) Morton (3) Chemicals.

D CROSS-REFERENCING means deciding if the letter might be requested in some other way. This letter should be cross-referenced under (1) Morton (2) Hart (3) Chemicals. The X indicates that it has been cross-referenced.

E SORTING means arranging all the records in indexing order before placing them in the files. The letter would be sorted under H.

F PLACING RECORDS IN THE FILES simply means storing the correspondence in the proper place until it is needed.

Illus. 8-5   Basic filing procedure

Unit 8 • Records Management in the Office

Placing Records in the File

After the records have been fine sorted they are placed in the files. A systematic routine should always be followed:

1. Locate the proper file drawer by examining drawer labels.
2. Scan the primary guides in the drawer to locate the major alphabetic section desired.
3. Check to see if an individual or special folder has been prepared for this material. If so, file the record here.
4. If no individual or special folder is available for this particular record, file the letter in the miscellaneous folder for the section.

scan:
look over quickly

Arranging Materials in Folders

Letters should always be placed in folders with the front of the letter facing the front of the folder and the top of the letter at the left side.

In *individual* folders, letters are arranged according to date, with the *most recent* record in front. In *miscellaneous* folders, the documents are arranged alphabetically by name; if there are two or more records for the same individual or company, they are arranged according to date, with the most recent record first. In a *special* folder, the records are arranged alphabetically by name and then by date in each group of names.

Filing Efficiency

Twenty filing suggestions made by experienced filing supervisors are given on the following pages.

1. Follow systematic procedures. Well-organized, carefully administered files encourage accurate filing and rapid retrieval. What's more, you'll enjoy filing!
2. Don't economize needlessly on file supplies. Good quality supplies hold up through continued hard use; poor quality supplies soon wear out and hinder the efficiency of the system. Choose the right supplies for the right records with a particular system in mind.
3. Set aside a definite time each day for filing. Remember: records belong in the file — not in or on desks.
4. Keep your system simple. If others must use materials from your files, be certain they understand how the system works, but insist that you do all the filing and refiling. Provide a handy place for them to place the materials they have removed from the files. They will be glad to cooperate — and it will guarantee file accuracy.

hinder:
prevent; hold back

Illus. 8-6

Bulging, messy folders encourage filing errors. Materials in an organized file are found without delay.

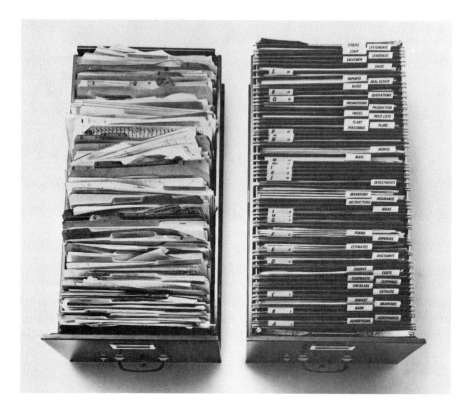

Oxford Pentaflex Corporation

jog:
shake slightly

5. Before refiling any folder that has been removed from the files, quickly examine its contents. You may find a lost document by performing this simple procedure. Always jog the contents of a folder before returning it to the file.

6. Constantly analyze your filing system and recommend ways in which it can be improved. Your employer will appreciate any suggestions that will improve the information system. Seek the advice of your office supplies dealer. Constantly review the various business publications. They'll keep you informed on the latest products and new developments in the field of records management.

7. Protect the tabs on guides and folders. Always lift a folder or guide by the side — never by the tab. Replace folder labels as soon as they are difficult to read.

8. File the most active records in the most easily reached parts of the file cabinets. Active records belong in the top drawers, less active documents in bottom drawers.

9. Use your filing cabinets only for filing, not for storing office supplies and other items. File only vital records in the special

Unit 8 • Records Management in the Office

fire-resistant equipment that has been purchased for their protection.

10. To avoid accidents, close a file drawer immediately after using it; and open only one drawer at a time.

11. Don't allow folders to bulge. Bulging folders encourage filing errors. When necessary, subdivide individual folders into monthly folders. Expand your system by preparing special and individual folders whenever necessary.

expand: enlarge

12. Don't fill a file drawer to capacity. Leave at least six inches of working space in each file drawer. It speeds up your work and prevents papers from being torn.

13. Mend all torn documents before placing them in a file folder.

14. If smaller than normal-sized documents are placed in file folders, glue or tape them to standard size paper. They will be easier to find.

15. If a particular document was difficult to find, cross-reference it when it is finally retrieved. This will save time when it is requested again.

16. Let color help. Use different color labels for different file years or periods. A well-planned color scheme will aid in prompt filing and retrieving.

17. Separate records that must be maintained in the files for long periods of time from those of temporary value.

18. Use the proper filing tools. A rubber finger helps separate documents; a file shelf makes you more efficient at the file; sitting on a file stool conserves your energy.

19. Follow a regular program of removing inactive records from the active files.

20. Be certain to follow, without variation, the office procedures that have been established to protect vital records.

REVIEWING IMPORTANT POINTS

1. How are letters and other papers gathered together for filing and by whom?
2. What does a release mark mean and how is it recognized?
3. Why is indexing so important?
4. What are the various captions under which incoming letters could be filed?
5. Under what captions may copies of outgoing letters be filed?
6. Under what caption is a personal letter filed?
7. Illustrate two ways of coding.
8. What is cross-referencing?
9. What are two important purposes of sorting?

10. How are letters arranged in *individual* folders? In *miscellaneous* folders? In *special* folders?

MAKING IMPORTANT DECISIONS

1. You notice that in another department the files are neat and orderly, similar to those on the right-hand side of page 318. Your files look like those on the left. What should you do to improve the appearance of your files?
2. It is said that cross-referencing can be overdone. Under what circumstances might this be true?

LEARNING TO WORK WITH OTHERS

In the office of the Kruger Packing Company, Mr. W. E. Hedges has received a letter asking for an answer to an earlier letter written by the Brooks Grocery Store. The unanswered letter was found in the *special* folder of the Brooks Grocery Store. The letter bears the initials *WEH* as a release-for-filing mark, but Mr. Hedges says he does not remember initialing the letter. The initials were actually placed there by mistake by Mr. Hedges' secretary. What should the secretary do in this situation?

IMPROVING LANGUAGE SKILLS

The twenty words listed below are used in filing. After you have studied the example, type the key word and the word or phrase you believe is *nearest in meaning* to the key word.

Example: facilitate — (a) appreciate (b) depreciate (c) *make easier* (d) negotiate

1. *adhere* — (a) expect (b) hold closely (c) part (d) loosen
2. *appropriate* — (a) approximate (b) apt (c) fitting (d) unsuitable
3. *caption* — (a) finishing stone (b) heading or title (c) rank of captain (d) seizure
4. *comprehensive* — (a) compelling (b) complex (c) extensive (d) limited
5. *consistent* — (a) consonant (b) incompatible (c) incongruous (d) tribunal
6. *conventional* — (a) contrary (b) customary (c) jovial (d) well informed
7. *distinctive* — (a) distasteful (b) sound harsh (c) intemperate (d) individual

8. *document* — (a) a particular principle (b) an established opinion (c) any written item (d) ownership of land
9. *effective* — (a) exhausted of vigor (b) flowing out (c) producing intended results (d) show enthusiasm
10. *identical* — (a) idealistic (b) matching (c) unlike (d) visionary
11. *initial* — (a) beginning (b) concluding (c) inheriting (d) suggesting
12. *legible* — (a) branch of military science (b) multitude (c) valid (d) capable of being read
13. *primary* — (a) humble (b) last (c) main (d) proud
14. *procedure* — (a) disposition (b) course of action (c) to defer action (d) to progress
15. *propel* — (a) foretell (b) multiply (c) project (d) prove
16. *retention* — (a) silence (b) rejoinder (c) remedy (d) memory
17. *retrieval* — (a) recovery (b) retraction (c) retrenchment (d) retribution
18. *sequence* — (a) separation (b) series (c) seriousness (d) sermon
19. *variation* — (a) deviation (b) sameness (c) truthfulness (d) word for word
20. *vital* — (a) unimportant (b) expendable (c) resounding (d) essential

IMPROVING ARITHMETIC SKILLS

1. By using the following data, determine how many items you will need to file.

        14 incoming letters
        36 carbon copies of outgoing letters
         7 sales representatives' reports
         3 company contracts

2. Of the 75 folders in one filing drawer, 11 need to be divided in half because they are too bulky. How many folders will be in the filing drawer when you divide the folders?
3. Your company estimates that the time it takes you to file each day using color-coded file labels is 15 minutes shorter than the time it takes to file without color-coded file labels. How much time does this save a week, a month (4 weeks), a year?

DEMONSTRATING OFFICE SKILLS

1. The following letters pertaining to the application of Irene Newberry are filed in the "Applications" folder of the firm where you work. Indicate the order, from front to back, in which the letters should be placed in this folder.

(a) Henry & Currier Company's March 8 letter of recommendation
(b) Irene Newberry's March 12 letter concerning her call on March 15
(c) Your firm's March 3 letter to Ms. Newberry asking her to come in for an interview
(d) Irene Newberry's March 18 letter accepting the position
(e) Your firm's March 5 letter to the Henry & Currier Company asking for information about Irene Newberry
(f) Your firm's March 11 letter to Ms. Newberry asking her to come in for a second interview
(g) Your firm's March 17 letter offering Ms. Newberry a position in the cost accounting department
(h) Irene Newberry's March 1 letter of application
(i) Your firm's March 9 letter to Henry & Currier Company thanking them for their cooperation

2. The following letters are filed in the Harvey O. Jackson individual folder. Indicate the order, from front to back, in which the letters should be placed in this folder.
(a) Harvey O. Jackson's order of April 1
(b) Your firm's letter of April 8 enclosing the April 6 invoice
(c) Harvey O. Jackson's letter of April 30 enclosing a check
(d) A cross-reference sheet dated April 10
(e) Your firm's letter of May 3 acknowledging the check of April 30
(f) Your firm's invoice of April 6 for the April 1 order

3. The letters listed below are filed in the "To-Tw" miscellaneous folder. Indicate the order, from front to back in which the letters should be placed in this folder.
(a) Your firm's letter of September 30 to Arthur Towne, Jr.
(b) The receipted invoice sent to you on September 21 by Amy Town
(c) Towne and Lovitt's order of September 2
(d) Your firm's letter of September 28 to Richard G. Twitchell
(e) Your firm's invoice of September 6 covering the September 2 order from Towne and Lovitt
(f) An advertising circular and letter dated September 14 sent to your employer by H. J. Tweed

4. This is a continuation of the alphabetic indexing exercise begun in Unit 7, Part 3.
(a) Type the following names in index form on 25 file cards. Type the number in the upper right corner and the name and address below the indexed name as you did in Unit 7, Part 3.
(b) Combine these 25 cards in proper filing order with the 50 cards prepared in Unit 7, Part 3.
(c) Save the cards for the Performing Secretarial Tasks assignment in Unit 8, Part 4.

(51) X-Cel Paints & Varnishes, 532 Mill St., Pittsburgh, PA 15221

(52) Theodore C. Haller, 59 E. 10th St., Charleston, WV 25303

(53) Henry R. Elston, II, 660 N. Michigan Ave., Chicago, IL 60611

(54) XYZ Electrical Repair Service, 2d and Main Sts., Lexington, KY 40507

(55) Countess Flora's Dance Academy, Chase Hotel, St. Louis, MO 63166

(56) Mrs. K. D. Ingles (Hazel Parks), 40 Sheridan Dr., Providence, RI 02909

(57) Quick Brothers Florists, 6720 Turkey Run Rd., Nashville, TN 37202

(58) Charlene T. Hallam, 4600 Pueblo St., Phoenix, AZ 85041

(59) Hall-Kramer Printing Co., Inc., 7700 S. Wells St., Chicago, IL 60621

(60) R. Nelson Forrester, 377 Desert Drive, Reno, NV 89504

(61) Robert N. Forrest, 781 University Ave., Minneapolis, MN 55413

(62) Sister Julietta, Sacred Heart Academy, Racine, WI 53401

(63) William A. Graves, 239 N. Vineyard Drive, Kenosha, WI 53140

(64) Mrs. Arthur P. Matthews (Helen), 5229 Crest Drive, Cleveland, OH 44121

(65) Town & Country Furniture Co., Town & Country Shop-In, Centerville, IN 47330

(66) U.S. Electrotype Corp., 2101 - 19th St., Long Island City, NY 11105

(67) Prince George Hotel, St. Thomas, Virgin Islands 00801

(68) Les Trois Chats Inn, 48 Henri St., Quebec, Province of Quebec, Canada

(69) 29 Palms Motel, U.S. 60 First St., Twenty-Nine Palms, CA 92277

(70) Venice Yacht Club, 29 Oceanside Drive, Venice, CA 90291

(71) Mr. Morris Book Store, 6th & Pike Sts., Mt. Morris, IL 61054

(72) State Auditor, Columbus, OH 43216

(73) Hire-the-Handicapped Committee, 30 Le Veque Tower, Denver, CO 80201

(74) Hamilton County SPCA, Colerain & Blue Rock Sts., Cincinnati, OH 45223

(75) Port-au-Prince Imports, Inc., 21 Main St., Gulfport, MS 39501

5. The following letter has just come to your office. Properly date, code, and if necessary, cross-reference the letter. (Use the letter provided in the *Supplies Inventory* or type the letter shown below. If cross-referencing is necessary, use the form from the *Supplies Inventory*, if available or type one similar to that on page 313.)

CRM

2
1 3
William Carter co.

815 Lakeland Dr. Kansas City, MO 64151 Area Code 816 891-1129

June 14, 197-

Allis-Bowen Products, Inc.
9621 East Tracy Street
Los Angeles, CA 90028

19-- DEC 12 AM 11:00

Attention Mr. B. P. Warren

Ladies and Gentlemen

Thank you for your letter of June 12 in which you in-
quired about the possibility of our printing for you
a booklet giving a short description of your company
and an illustrated description of the products that
you manufacture.

Before we are able to quote prices on a publication of
this kind we need the following information:

    1. An estimate of the length of the booklet

    2. The approximate number and dimensions of
       illustrations

    3. The size of the page desired

    4. The kind and quality of paper and cover
       stock.

We shall be glad to give you an exact quotation on cost
of the booklet as soon as we receive this information.

At the present time we are in a position to give you
prompt as well as efficient service. We can assure you
of an attractive booklet with suitable type, clear illustrations, and strong binding.

              Very truly yours

              Earl E. Whitmore

              Earl E. Whitmore

ecb

Part 2

Managing the Records System

Ms. Diane Malone has been with Spinner Corporation for many years as supervisor of the central files. When she first started her job, the filing system was very small and easily managed. Through the years it has grown into a very large, complex system. Ms. Malone has put into effect many aids for controlling the files. One of them is the use of the charge-out system, which provides a record of who has each folder that has been removed from the files. This saves time when it comes to locating the folder. When workers at Spinner need a certain file, they can be sure that Ms. Malone has it or knows where it can be found.

Records are kept because they contain useful information; filing systems are developed in order to retrieve this information promptly and efficiently. Yet if records are often removed from the files without *charging* them to the borrower, the system will soon become useless. It will certainly not be worth the time, effort, and money that have gone into its development and maintenance.

Since the people who borrow records from the files are busy, they may neglect to return these documents to the files. Although every worker should feel responsible for maintaining an effective office information system, it is your responsibility to protect the records placed under your control. Therefore, some type of charge-out and follow-up system must be developed to insure the return of borrowed documents to the files.

Charge-Out

There are times when other executives or employees will need materials that are stored in your files. When materials are borrowed from your files, you should prepare a form that identifies the records removed. This form (usually 5" × 3" or 6" × 4") is known as a *requisition* card and has spaces for a full description of the material borrowed, the name and the department of the borrower, the date the material was removed from the file, and the date it is to be returned. The requisition cards may later be used to analyze the activity of the files. A tabulation of the cards will determine how often the files are used and which records are most active.

Charge-Out Forms

In addition to the requisition card, four kinds of forms are commonly used when material is taken from the files. They are *out guides, out folders, carrier folders,* and *substitution cards.*

Out Guides. An out guide is a pressboard guide with the word *OUT* printed on its tab. It is placed in the files when an entire folder is borrowed. There are two forms of out guides. One type is ruled on both sides, and the charge information is written directly on the guide. When the folder is returned, the out guide is removed and the charge information crossed out. The guide is then ready for further use.

The other kind of out guide has a pocket into which a requisition card is placed. This form is preferred since it is faster to use and the charge information is usually more legible.

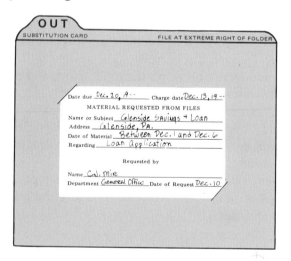

Illus. 8-7   Ruled out guide   Illus. 8-8   Out guide with inset

Out Folders. Some firms prefer using out folders when an entire folder is requested from the files. If additional material reaches the files before the regular folder is returned, it is temporarily filed in the out folder. This material is then filed in the regular folder when it is returned.

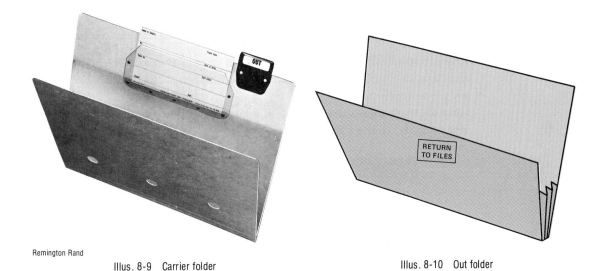

Remington Rand

Illus. 8-9   Carrier folder   Illus. 8-10   Out folder

Carrier Folder. A carrier folder is useful in reminding the borrower to return records to the files. It is a different color from the regular folders and has the words *RETURN TO FILES* printed on it. The requested material is removed from the regular folder and sent to the borrower in a carrier folder. An out card or guide is placed in the regular folder containing the charge-out information. The regular folder remains in the file to hold any material placed in the file before the carrier folder is returned. A carrier folder saves the regular folder from the wear and tear it would receive when removed from the files.

Substitution Cards. A substitution card is a tabbed card, usually salmon-colored, that is placed in a folder when single documents are borrowed. The word *OUT* is printed on the tab. The charge-out information may be recorded on the card itself or on a requisition form inserted in a pocket of the substitution card. A substitution card is basically the same as an out guide.

Photocopies

To avoid removing important papers from the files, some firms prepare photocopies of a requested record. When this method is used, the document is removed from the files and copied on a copying machine. The original document is then refiled and the photocopy sent to the borrower with instructions to destroy it after use. This method is generally used when single documents are requested rather than an entire folder.

Length of Charge Time

Borrowed materials are used by the borrower immediately and should be returned to the files as soon as possible. The longer records are away from the files, the more difficult it is to get them back; furthermore, they are likely to be lost or discarded. Most firms charge out records for only one week (with weekly extensions, if found necessary). It is best to have short charge-out periods and prompt follow-up of materials that are not returned to the files.

Illus. 8-11

File requests may be made in person, by phone, or through interoffice mail.

White Power Files, Inc.

Follow-Up

How will you remember the many matters that will require attention in the future? Since you cannot rely on your memory, you will find it necessary to devise a system that will call your attention to these matters at the exact date when action must be taken. A file that is designed for this purpose is called a *follow-up file* and is arranged in chronological order. Two common follow-up files are the card tickler file and the dated follow-up folder file.

chronological: arranged by date or time

Card Tickler Files

A card tickler file consists of a set of 12 monthly primary guides and 31 daily secondary guides. Important matters to be followed up are recorded on cards and placed behind the appropriate month and day guides in the file. A card tickler file may be used to follow up records that have been borrowed from the files or to follow up other matters that require attention.

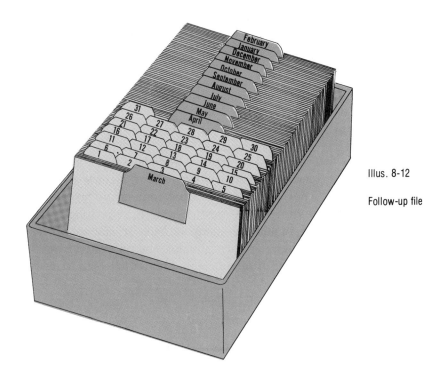

Illus. 8-12

Follow-up file

Dated Follow-Up Folders

This file resembles the card tickler file except that a folder is allowed for each day of the month. Items that require follow-up are placed in the correct day folder, and the folder is then placed behind the appropriate monthly guide. For example, a folder may contain a photocopy of an incoming letter or an extra carbon of an outgoing letter that requests an answer by a certain day. On that particular day you should check to see if an answer to the letter has been received. If not, follow-up action is taken. By using photocopies and extra carbons for follow-up, the correspondence can be filed in its proper place and the official folder is always complete. This procedure saves a great deal of time.

Transfer

inactive:
not often used

retain:
keep; store

Office files should contain only those records that are needed to operate efficiently. If inactive or outdated records are never removed from the files, needed information becomes more and more difficult to retain and retrieve. Every organization should adopt a plan of removing inactive documents from the active files by *transferring* these records to a records center.

Removing inactive records from the office files serves three important purposes:

1. Active records can be filed and retrieved quickly.
2. Expensive office space and file equipment are kept at a minimum.
3. Costs are reduced since transferred records are housed in inexpensive file equipment, usually cardboard transfer cases.

Transferring File Folders

Records that must be kept for long periods of time should be separated from those of temporary value when placing records in transfer cases. Miscellaneous, special, and individual folders are usually transferred from the active to the inactive files when they are no longer needed. Each transferred folder should be stamped *Transfer File* to prevent it from being returned to the active files should it be requested from the records center. Many firms use different colored folder labels to identify different file periods.

The Records Center

A records center is an important part of any transfer program. This center houses documents no longer needed for daily reference. Records may be stored at the center indefinitely or for a temporary period only. Inactive records are inexpensively maintained in the center, since all the floor space can be utilized (floor to ceiling filing) and inexpensive equipment can be used to house the records.

Documents maintained in the center must be accurately indexed and controlled so that they will be available if requested. Without adequate indexing, protection, and control of these inactive records, all the time and effort spent in the transfer program have been wasted.

Retention

Every organization is faced with the problem of how long to retain its records. Because of the growing volume of paper work, many firms

have established *record retention schedules*. Such a schedule identifies the retention value for every type of record created or received by an organization and determines which records must be retained and for how long. Useless records occupy expensive floor space and costly equipment; they hinder the rapid retrieval of needed information.

While certain documents must be retained permanently, most records created and received in the average business organization have a limited period of usefulness. The National Records Management Council estimates that 95 percent of all corporate paper work over a year old is rarely, if ever, referred to again. Record authorities estimate that 40 percent of all stored records can be legally destroyed.

Even though every organization must develop its own retention schedule, factors that affect the retention value of business records include:

1. Legal requirements (federal, state, and local)
2. Office use (those records needed to operate on a daily basis)
3. Historical documents
4. Vital records

A retention schedule can be adopted only after the record requirements of a particular organization have been thoroughly studied. Legal counsel should always be sought. Once a schedule is adopted, it must be continually revised to meet changing conditions and needs.

REVIEWING IMPORTANT POINTS

1. Why should all materials taken from files be *charged out* to the person taking them.
2. What information is included on a requisition card?
3. What are the two types of out guides? Which is better?
4. What is the difference between an out guide and a substitution card?
5. How is the out folder used?
6. Why are carrier folders used?
7. Describe a card tickler file and tell how it is used.
8. What is the difference between a card tickler file and a dated folder file?
9. Why is it less expensive to store inactive records in a records center?
10. What four factors affect the retention schedule of business records?

MAKING IMPORTANT DECISIONS

Miss Kittle, the receptionist of a large law office, is also supervisor of the legal library. Because of her varied duties, she cannot devote her full time to the library. Files are often misplaced because someone failed to fill out a charge card or a file is several weeks overdue. What suggestions can you make for improving this system?

LEARNING TO WORK WITH OTHERS

An important folder is missing from the files. Your employer asks you if you have it or know where it is. After looking around your work station, you say "No." The next day as you are looking through a stack of materials on the table behind your desk, you find the missing folder. What should you do?

IMPROVING LANGUAGE SKILLS

Type the following sentences and insert the correct capitalization and punctuation.

1. Yes she said Ill take the folder with me
2. What are these Xs for
3. The management of jefferson and company considered the workers grievances three of which were justified but the other problems needed further negotiation
4. Smiths folder was removed early Tuesday morning it should have been returned by Thursday afternoon
5. Mr. green requested that you bring the harden jonas and mitchell folders to the board of directors meeting

IMPROVING ARITHMETIC SKILLS

On a separate sheet of paper solve the following problems:

1. If Mary could file 80 files in a half hour, how many could she file in two hours?
2. In your office about 25% of the files are used during the month. If there are 1,600 files in the office, how many are used during the month?
3. If a file cabinet costs $185 and your employer will receive a 20 percent discount, how much will the file cabinet cost?

DEMONSTRATING OFFICE SKILLS

1. Type captions on folder labels for each of the following authors, who contributed articles to a recent issue of *The Office*, a magazine of management, equipment, and automation. (If folder labels are not available, type the names on blank sheets of paper approximately 3½" × 1½".) Type the name without punctuation on the lower half of the folder label about two spaces from the left edge, as illustrated.

Lucy H. Harmon	Jan E. Torrence
Aretha L. Ratz	Charlene A. Agemian
Fritz H. Jordan, Jr.	Denise S. Greensmith
J. A. Mosher	Hollis K. Cobb
Wesley S. Bagby	T. M. Galloway
Eva G. Morris	E. Philip Kron
Richard I. Tanaka	Patrick R. Gaffney
Fran Plasha	Lee Ann Golgart
Fay B. Blackstone	John H. Dunham
Jane Goldstein	Roberta E. Bennis
G. Peter Ignasiak	Eleanor H. Morse
Clarissa E. Franke	K. R. Atkins, Jr.
James D. Parker, Jr.	Glenna F. Evans
William W. Newell	Mary M. Carlson

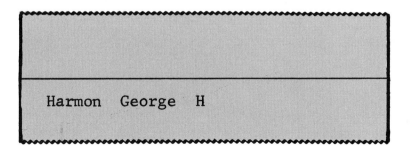

2. After the names in Problem 1 are indexed in alphabetical order type the list on a single sheet of paper. Center the heading, AUTHORS OF THE JANUARY ISSUE, and then type the list in two double-spaced columns.

Part 3

Subject, Numeric, and Geographic Filing

New office workers hired by Marsh Clothing Distributors, Inc. always spend one week in the filing department. The management feels this experience acquaints each worker with the different filing systems used within the company. In addition to the alphabetic system, Marsh uses a numeric system for orders and stock numbers, a subject system for the different types of clothing, and a geographic system for the sales territories.

As an office worker, you will probably be more concerned with alphabetic correspondence filing methods than with subject, numeric, or geographic. To assist your executive properly, however, you may need to understand other filing systems and how they operate. You may be required to request records from a filing department that uses one of the other systems. You may also be required to code correspondence for storage in the central files.

Records must be filed according to how they will be requested — by name, by subject, by number, or by geographic area. When you have correspondence with a customer, you know that it will be filed alphabetically by the company name. All the forecasts of anticipated expenditures for your department for the coming year will be filed by the subject caption *Budgets*, not under *Controller Jamison*. If your executive asks that copies of the sales reports be sent to the managers of each territory, you will make use of a geographic file. In a purchasing department, you will keep a numeric file by the purchase order number.

forecasts:
predictions of the future

Subject Filing

Every organization has materials which are important because of their content rather than because of the person to whom or by whom they are written. For these materials a *subject* filing system is necessary. Your duties may not bring you into direct contact with this system of filing. However, in case you are needed to assist with this kind of filing, it is good to have a knowledge of it. Subjects are arranged in alphabetical order, and related subjects may be grouped together. A folder labeled "Applications" with the subheading "Sales Representatives" is an example. The names of all sales applicants are not easily remembered; therefore, the names are of secondary importance in filing, and letters should be placed in a special subject folder labeled "Applications — Sales Representatives." As long as there are only a few subject folders, they are filed in a regular alphabetic or numeric system along with all the other folders.

The following list shows some typical subject filing captions:

Advertising	Finance	Payroll
Applications		Personnel
Associations	Government — Federal	Price Lists
Audit Reports	Government — Municipal	Production
	Government — State	Public Relations
Balance Sheets		
Budgets	Insurance	Real Estate
		Reports
Conferences and	Legal Matters	Research
Conventions		
Contracts	Maps	Sales
Credits and Collections	Methods and Procedures	Speaking Invitations
	Minutes	Statistical Data
Directors' Meetings	Mortgages	
		Taxes — Federal
Employee Benefits	Operating Overhead	Taxes — Municipal
Equipment & Supplies	Operating Policies	Taxes — State

Guides and Folders Used in Subject Filing

In a subject file you will make use of several different types of guides and folders. The main subject titles are used as captions for primary guides. These serve the same purpose as primary guides in an alphabetic file. Secondary guides are used for the subordinate titles that are related to the main subjects on the primary guides behind which they are placed.

subordinate:
of less importance

There is a miscellaneous folder for each main subject in which all papers relating to that topic are filed. Individual folders are made for subdivisions of the main subject when sufficient papers (usually six or seven) accumulate for the subtopic. Subdivisions may be made by subject, name, or date.

Subject: *Name:*

Safety   Associations

      Accident Prevention   American Bankers Assocation

      Accident Reports   American Manufacturers Association

Date Periods:

Production Reports

      January–June, 19––

      July–December, 19––

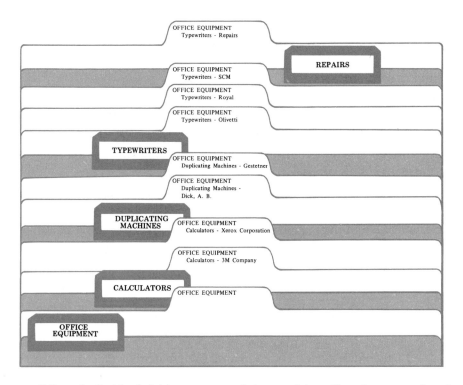

When individual folders are used in a subject file, they are placed behind the primary or secondary guides that classify the subject matter of the correspondence in those folders. In this way correspondence is doubly identified — by subject, as shown by the guide captions; and by titles, as shown on the folder captions. Main subject and subdivision captions must be shown on each folder tab.

Subject Filing Procedures

When filing by subject, there are six basic steps which you should follow.

Inspecting. Each letter should be checked to see that it has been released for filing.

Indexing. The letter must be read carefully to determine under which subject it should be filed. Thorough familiarity with the outline of subjects and their subdivisions is necessary.

Coding. When the subject of a letter has been determined, the caption is written on the letter in the upper right corner or it is underlined if it appears in the letter.

Cross-Referencing. If more than one subject is involved in a letter — a very frequent occurrence — a cross-reference caption is underlined and an X is placed at the end of the line in the margin. An extra carbon copy, a photocopy of the letter, a cross-reference sheet, or a 5" × 3" index card should also be prepared.

Some companies distribute copies of the main subjects of the filing system (and possibly a definition of each) to each department for its use in dictating letters or when requesting materials from the files.

Sorting. Material is sorted first according to the main subjects and second by the main subdivisions.

Placing Material in Folders. Material that is placed in an individual folder is filed with the latest date in front. If there is no individual folder, the material is filed in the miscellaneous folder for the main subject in alphabetic order according to subdivisions or in date order, most recent date in front.

Combination Subject and Name Files

In many offices there may not be enough files to have separate subject and name files, so subject and name folders may be filed in the same drawer as shown below.

Numeric Filing

repetitive:
occuring over and
over

With the widespread use of data processing systems for repetitive and statistical operations in many organizations, numbers have become important in identifying many records in today's businesses. In general, only large systems use numeric filing. Records that are frequently identified by number and filed in a numeric sequence are insurance policies, purchase orders, sales orders, contracts, licenses, customers' charge accounts, bank accounts, and credit card accounts. Many large government agencies such as the Social Security Administration, the Veterans

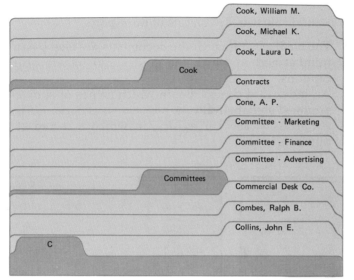

Illus. 8-15

A combined subject and name file

Administration, and state motor vehicle bureaus file their records in numerical order.

Since it would be impossible to remember the file number of every business paper, an alphabetic card index of the numerically filed material is maintained by name or by subject as a cross-reference. Numeric filing systems are *indirect* in filing and finding because, in many instances, reference must be made to the alphabetic card index before a document is found or coded.

Illus. 8-16

Business and government agencies with large volumes of records typically use numeric files.

A numeric file usually consists of three parts:

1. The file itself, in which the documents are filed by an assigned number and in which the guides and folders bear numeric captions.
2. An index card control file, in which names or subject titles are arranged alphabetically.
3. An *accession book* or *register*, in which a record of assigned numbers is kept.

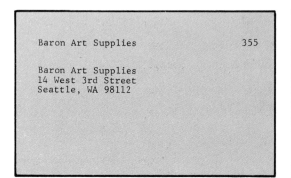

Illus. 8-17   Alphabetic and subject index control cards for a numeric file

Numeric Arrangements

There are several arrangements of numbers that may be used in numeric filing:

1. The numbers may be in consecutive order (consecutive number filing).
2. Certain portions of a long number may be used as the first indexing unit (terminal-digit and/or middle-digit filing).
3. The number may be combined with letters of the alphabet (alpha-numeric filing).

terminal:
last or ending

Consecutive Number Filing

In this arrangement documents are filed in strict numeric sequence. The number is written in the upper right corner of the paper, and an alphabetic card is typed as a cross-reference to the assigned number. The papers are filed in numerical sequence in folders, and the card is filed alphabetically in the index. Additional papers related to the same subject are checked against the card index and coded with the same number.

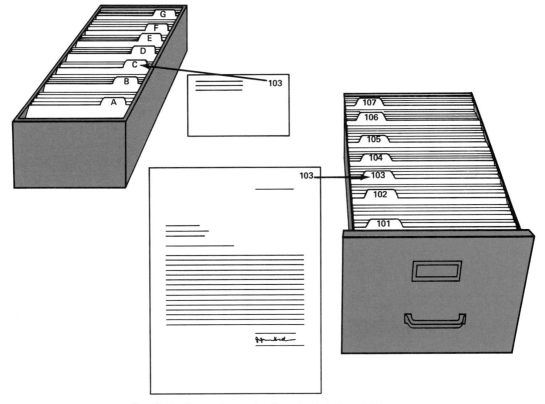

Illus. 8-18   Consecutive number file and alphabetic card index

Legal Files. In legal firms a number (for example, 607) is assigned to a client and as additional matters are handled for the same client, they are given a secondary number (607-1 — Will) to separate the new material. An alphabetic cross-reference card is made for each client as well as for each item the legal firm is taking care of for the client. Individual folders are prepared for each and are filed numerically:

client: customer

607   John W. Rodgers
607-1   Will
607-2   Real Estate Holdings
607-3   Income Tax Records
607-4   Insurance

Project and Job Files. Consecutive numeric filing is used for these two types of records primarily because there are related drawings, blueprints, and artwork connected with the correspondence and such material is controlled more easily through a numbering system. Almost always it is necessary to subdivide the correspondence by subject. Drawings will have secondary numbers for parts of the project or job, and dates for revisions of drawings become an important identifying factor. Numbers are obtained from the accession book. The alphabetical card index is an essential key for locating material by name or subject.

Numeric Correspondence Files. Because it is a slow and indirect method, ordinary correspondence today is seldom filed numerically. The need to keep papers confidential is the primary reason for using this system. Numbers are assigned in consecutive order from the accession book, and individual folders are made for each correspondent. All papers for this correspondent are placed in this folder, with the most recent material in the front. An alphabetic index card is made. Neither the accession book nor the card index is available to unauthorized personnel.

Illus. 8-19

A confidential correspondence file in which numbers and names have been combined.

Shaw-Walker

Terminal-Digit Filing

Terminal-digit filing is a method of numeric filing based on reading numbers from *right to left*. It is ideal for any large numeric file with five or more digits. In terminal-digit filing, the numbers are assigned in the same manner as for consecutive number filing, but the numbers are read in small groups (00–99) beginning with the terminal (or final) group. It is widely used by banks for depositors' savings accounts, mortgages, and loans; by hospitals for medical case records; and by insurance companies for policyholders' applications.

In the terminal-digit system, the primary division of the files is based on the last two digits of a number, the secondary division upon the next two digits, and the final division upon the first digits. For example, if you were to look up life insurance policy number 225101, you would read the numbers from right to left in pairs of digits instead of from left to right as whole numbers.

22	51	01
Final	Secondary	Primary

You would first locate the drawer containing those materials or records whose numbers end with 01. Then you would search down the guides in that drawer for the number 51. Lastly, you would file or find the material in proper order behind the number 22. Numbers of fewer than six digits are brought up to that figure by adding zeros to the left of the number.

When even larger numbers are common, they may be broken down for filing in groups of three digits, 000 to 999.

Illus. 8-20

Terminal-digit filing is useful in numeric files with five or more digits.

Shaw-Walker

Alpha-Numeric Filing

Banks now identify the checking accounts of their depositors by numbers. In some banks an individual account number is assigned to each depositor according to an *alpha-numeric plan*. This is a method of assigning numbers to accounts in such a way that even with additions and deletions, accounts filed in numeric sequence will also be in alphabetic sequence. Originally the accounts are arranged in exact alphabetic sequence and assigned account numbers with uniform gaps between numbers to allow for additional accounts. This number is printed with a special magnetic ink on a set of blank checks before the checks are given to the depositor. After a check has been drawn, cashed, and returned to the bank, a machine automatically "reads" the number and charges the account of the depositor. The canceled checks are filed daily in front of check size guides, which usually contain the signature card of the depositor, and are accumulated until the time of the month when the statement and canceled checks for the period are returned to the depositor.

There are other alphabetic-numeric filing systems which are highly specialized and are used in large filing departments with special problems that these systems are designed to solve. Your office duties may indirectly bring you into contact with these various filing systems. Filing personnel who work with alphabetic-numeric systems are given on-the-job training before being assigned to the operation of such systems. On-the-job training is normally necessary because of the differences in the systems.

Guides and Folders Used in Numeric Filing

The type and quantity of supplies used in numeric filing will depend on the arrangement that is used. Individual folders can be made for each number, with the number on the tab, or with the number and name typed on a label affixed to the tab. Guides are normally inserted for every ten folders.

Geographic Filing

If you are using a geographic filing system, geographic location is the prime indexing factor. In the United States, for instance, materials would be arranged alphabetically first by states, then by cities or towns within the states, and finally alphabetically by the names of the correspondents in the cities or towns. A geographic file may also be based upon sales territories, upon cities in a single state, or upon districts or streets for local correspondence.

Typical users of geographic filing systems are publishing houses, mail-order houses, radio and television advertisers, real estate firms, and organizations dealing with a large number of small businesses scattered over a wide area. The personnel in many of these small businesses change frequently; therefore, the name of the individual owner or manager is often less important than the location of the business.

Geographic filing is an indirect method of locating folders for individual correspondents. It is slower to operate since papers must be sorted as many as three times, depending on the geographic arrangement that is selected.

Arrangement of a Geographic File

The primary guides in a geographic filing system bear the names of the largest geographic divisions. The specific arrangement will depend on the needs of the company and the volume of records. For example, a geographic filing system based on states would have each guide tab printed with the name of a state; and all correspondence with people in that state would be filed behind that guide. These state guides are usually arranged alphabetically; thus, Alabama is first, followed by Alaska and the other states in alphabetic order. They would also be arranged by a division of the country into areas, such as "West Coast"; and behind these guides the secondary guides or folders for the states of California, Oregon, and Washington would be filed.

The secondary guides bear the names of the geographic subdivisions. For example, behind each primary state guide there are secondary guides with captions that provide for the alphabetic arrangement of cities and towns within that state.

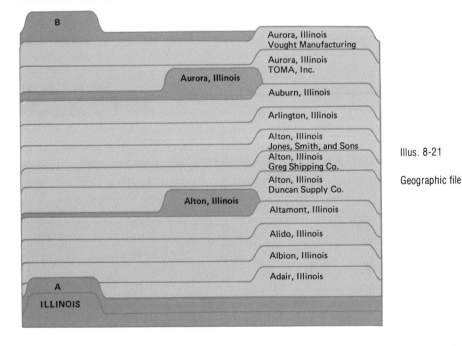

Illus. 8-21

Geographic file

A geographic file may include several different kinds of folders, such as individual folders, city folders, and state folders. Individual folders in a geographic file are used in the same manner as in an alphabetic file. They differ, however, in their captions, because in a geographic file, the caption on an individual folder includes the name of the city and state, as well as the name of the correspondent. The geographic identification should appear on the top line, the correspondent on the second. This arrangement of the captions aids in the correct placement of the folders behind the appropriate state and city guides.

If there is no individual folder for a correspondent, communication from that correspondent is filed in a city folder. If there is not enough correspondence to warrant the use of a separate city folder, the communication is placed in a miscellaneous state folder at the back of the appropriate state section of the file.

For larger cities, several city folders are sometimes necessary. These are assigned alphabetic captions and placed behind a secondary city guide. For example, five Chicago folders might be used, the first for those Chicago correspondents whose names fall into the alphabetic range of A–C; the second, D–H; the third, I–M; the four, N–R; and the fifth, S–Z.

Cross-Reference for Geographic Filing

As in alphabetic filing, there are times when cross-references must be prepared on a letter. The geographic location, the correspondent's name, and other information about the letter are recorded on the form.

Card Index

In geographic filing you must know the name of the city and state in which a person or business firm is located to find a letter referring to that correspondent. Because this information is not always known, it is advantageous to keep a card index with a geographic correspondence file. This is usually a 5" × 3" card file, which includes a card for each correspondent giving the name and address of the correspondent. The card index is arranged alphabetically by the names of the correspondents.

Geographic Filing Procedure

The filing procedure for a geographic file is similar to that for alphabetic filing, except that the state and city are of primary importance in

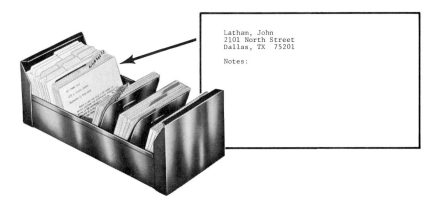

Illus. 8-22

Card index and individual
correspondent card

Shaw-Walker

coding and filing. In coding it is desirable to mark on each letter the city and state as well as the name of the correspondent. The location may be circled and the name of the correspondent underlined.

Materials are sorted by geographic units, starting with the key unit for the first sorting and continuing until all the units involved in the filing system have been used. For example, the first sorting might be on the basis of states, the second sorting on the basis of cities or towns, and the final sorting on the basis of correspondents.

Letters are arranged in the different types of folders as follows: (1) in an individual folder by date, (2) in a city folder by the names of the correspondents and then by date, (3) in an alphabetic state folder by the names of cities or towns and then by the names of correspondents according to date. In each case, of course, the most recent letter is placed in front.

Summary of Filing Methods

Each filing method has its advantages and disadvantages. On page 348 is a summary of the outstanding features of the four methods.

There are many types of commercial filing systems. All make generous use of color to code classifications of primary and secondary guides, include individual and miscellaneous folders, and are designed for efficiency and ease of operation.

"Office-Made" Filing System

In many small businesses and separate offices in large businesses, it is not economical to purchase commercial filing systems. You may be asked to devise or reorganize a file system in such circumstances.

METHOD	ADVANTAGES	DISADVANTAGES
Alphabetic	1. Direct filing and reference. 2. No index required. 3. Records may be grouped by individual or by company name. 4. Simple arrangement by guides, folders, and colors. 5. Easy to locate miscellaneous records.	1. Possibility of error in filing common names. 2. Related records may be filed in more than one place. 3. Too little or too much cross-referencing.
Subject	1. Records grouped by subject in technical or statistical files. 2. Unlimited expansion.	1. Extensive cross-referencing necessary. 2. Difficulty in classifying records for filing. 3. Difficulty in filing miscellaneous folders. 4. Index necessary to determine subject heading or subdivision.
Numeric	1. Most accurate of all methods. 2. Unlimited expansion. 3. Definite numbers to identify name or subject when requesting files. 4. Uniform system of numbers used in departments of company. 5. Cross-referencing permanent and extensive. 6. Complete index of correspondents and subjects.	1. Specialized training required. 2. High labor cost. 3. Indirect filing and reference. 4. Miscellaneous records require separate files. 5. Cumbersome index.
Geographic	1. Direct filing and reference for geographic area (indirect for individual correspondence). 2. Provision for miscellaneous records. 3. Records grouped by location.	1. Location as well as name required. 2. Triple sorting necessary — by state, by city, by alphabet. 3. Increased labor cost. 4. Increased possibility of error. 5. Reference to card index necessary to find correspondent. 6. Detailed typed descriptions on folder labels. 7. Confusion in miscellaneous files.

A practical, inexpensive system using one-third cut folders would include:

1. First position: primary guide that is also a miscellaneous folder for that letter in the alphabet. The letter of the alphabet is printed on the label.
2. Second position: special guide that is also a miscellaneous folder for that section of the file.
3. Third position: individual folders.

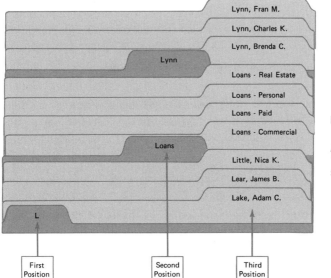

Illus. 8-23

A basic, three position "office-made" filing system

First Position | Second Position | Third Position

REVIEWING IMPORTANT POINTS

1. Why must an office worker be acquainted with all the basic types of filing systems?
2. When is a subject filing system preferable to other systems
3. How is a letter coded in a subject file?
4. Name the three parts of a numeric filing system. What is the purpose of each?
5. How is terminal-digit filing read?
6. What is the disadvantage of geographic filing?
7. What kinds of guides and folders are used with a geographic filing system?
8. What is of primary importance in coding and filing in a geographic filing system?
9. With a geographic system, how are materials arranged in an individual folder? in a city folder? in an alphabetic state folder?
10. An "office-made" file system is likely to be used in what type of business?

MAKING IMPORTANT DECISIONS

Warren has just started working for a newly established insurance company. He has been asked by his employer, Mr. Stevens, to help set up a filing system for each sales representative's accounts. Warren decides to set up a geographic file based upon the territories of the sales representatives. He also suggests using color coded folders for each of the sales representatives. What do you think of Warren's decision about color coding?

LEARNING TO WORK WITH OTHERS

An office worker filing under a subject system must read letters and papers carefully since they may contain references to more than one subject. Leonard Nelson, with whom you work, fails to read the material to be filed, and, as a result, there is much misfiling and improper cross-referencing. Whenever the chief file clerk corrects him, Leonard becomes impatient and tells the chief clerk the system is stupid and does not make sense.

How would you help Leonard to improve his work habits and to understand the importance of proper operation of the filing system?

IMPROVING LANGUAGE SKILLS

The relative pronouns *who* and *whom* are frequently misused. When a relative pronoun is the subject of a subordinate clause, *who* is used. When a relative pronoun is the object of a verb or a preposition, *whom* is used. Type each of the sentences below inserting the correct pronoun.

Examples: Samuel Todd is the player *who* can score the touchdown.
Gretel is the person *whom* we chose for the job.

 1. Sally is the one _____ knows the system better than anyone.
 2. Don't you know _____ called me?
 3. _____ do you want to do the job?
 4. For _____ are you waiting?
 5. To _____ did you wish to speak?
 6. The matter of _____ shall pay for the delay is still to be decided.
 7. Do you know _____ is going to get the promotion?
 8. Was it _____ I thought it was?
 9. He is the one _____ should be fired.
10. Have you noticed _____ is always late?

IMPROVING ARITHMETIC SKILLS

1. The sales reports are filed according to geographic divisions of Eastern, Central, Mountain, and Pacific. Reports were received from the following cities:

Seattle, Washington   Denver, Colorado
Des Moines, Iowa   New York, New York
Philadelphia, Pennsylvania   San Francisco, California
Los Angeles, California

How many reports will be filed in each geographic division?

2. The claims in your office are filed according to claim number. Place the following claim numbers in correct order.

6654	5746	8767
6655	5766	6632
7632	5776	6691
0965	5976	5461
7877	5970	5413
6666	6759	7676

3. On a separate sheet of paper state the value of N in the following equations.

Example: $13 + 14 = N$ Answer: 27

$$N - 8 = 42 \qquad N = 14 - 12$$
$$16 - N = 7 \qquad 5 + 9 = N$$
$$3 \times N = 24 \qquad 15 \div N = 3$$
$$4 \times N = 36 \qquad 14 + N = 40$$
$$N \div 2 = 15 \qquad N = 9 \times 7$$

DEMONSTRATING OFFICE SKILLS

Type the following twenty business firm names, addresses, and account numbers on 5″ × 3″ cards. Arrange them three ways as for filing: (1) alphabetically, (2) geographically, and (3) numerically.

5001 Cobin & Co., Washington, D.C. 20013

5004 Connel Manufacturing Co., Seattle, Washington 98111

5009 The Cole Manufacturing Co., San Francisco, California 94101

5006 Crawford, Crawford and Croll, Cincinnati, Ohio 45201

5003 Cone, Lambert and Ulysses, Chicago, Illinois 60690

5002 Corn and Frederick, Dallas, Texas 75221

5005 Max Collier & Sons, Tallahassee, Florida 32302

5007 Conwit Tailors, Gainesville, Florida 32601

5008 Cone, Arnold & Co., New York, New York 10001

5010 Cobbs Corporation, Boston, Massachusetts 01432

5019 Conklin Company, Erie, Pennsylvania 16512

5015 Conner Corporation, Cleveland, Ohio 44101

5016 The Samuel Collins Company, St. Louis, Missouri 63177

5013 Colton Company, Boise, Idaho 83707

5012 Conrad & Matthew, Reno, Nevada 89504

5011 Coyne Corporation, Los Angeles, California 90053

5014 Craig & Stanton Corporation, San Luis Obispo, California 93401

5017 Cole & Monford Co., Nashville, Tennessee 73202

5018 Conners Metal Manufacturing, Inc., Cicero, Illinois 60650

5020 Conover & Sterling, Baton Rouge, Louisiana 70821

Part 4

Special Files, Micrographics, and Information Systems

"Mr. Houghton, will you call Ms. Peterson, with Peterson, Vickers, and Sanford law firm, please?"

"Yes, Mr. Rice."

Although Mr. Houghton does not know Ms. Peterson's number, he can easily and quickly find it by using his rotary file. Mr. Rice can always depend on him to either have the requested information or know where it can be found.

In a matter of minutes, Mr. Houghton is able to say, "Ms. Peterson is on the telephone, Mr. Rice."

Card Files

From small to large, practically all offices make use of card files. You may keep a small card file on your desk that contains the names, address, and telephone numbers of people whom you call or write to frequently. Receptionists for doctors and dentists usually have card files containing information about patients; teachers often have a card file for each of their classes; libraries, of course, have card catalogs covering all the books in the library. A card file is needed as a cross-reference in subject, numeric, and geographic filing. Card files are used in almost every department in a business firm; shipping, receiving, purchasing, inventory control, personnel records, payroll, and stock records may be maintained on cards.

Cards used in filing are usually 5" × 3", 6" × 4", or 8" × 5". The size selected usually depends upon the amount of information that will be written on the card. The 5" × 3 " is the most widely used card size.

When typing information on the cards for the files, follow this simple procedure:

1. Type the name in exact indexing order.
2. If the card is not ruled, begin typing on the third line from the top of the card. If the index card is ruled, begin typing above the first printed line.

3. Indent two spaces from the left edge of the card file and set a margin.
4. Use upper and lower case letters. They are easier to read.
5. Abbreviations may be used since space is limited.
6. Be consistent in spacing, capitalization, punctuation and style.

Vertical Card Files

These are the types of files in which the card stands on edge, usually the width of the card. Thus, a 5″ × 3″ card rests on the 5-inch edge; the 6″ × 4″ card rests on the 6-inch edge; the 8″ × 5″ card rests on the 8-inch edge. There are, however, exceptions to this; some cards are filed according to the depth of the card. The cards may or may not be ruled, depending upon whether they will be typed or handwritten.

Illus. 8-24

A numeric vertical card file

Ohio National Life Insurance Company

Just as guides are needed to divide the file drawer to keep the folders in order, it is also necessary to divide the cards in an alphabetic card file into convenient alphabetic sections with a set of *card guides*. These card guides indicate on projecting tabs the various alphabetic sections into which the file drawer is divided. In some cases special primary and secondary guides are used, and cards will often be color coded.

The notations on the tabs of the guides consist in most cases of letters, such as *Alf, Alli, Alm, Alt, Am, An*; but they may consist of common surnames such as *Allen, Anderson, Andrews,* as you will notice in the illustration below. They indicate the alphabetic range of the cards filed in each section. The file cards are placed in alphabetic order behind the appropriate guide just as the folders are placed behind the guides in the file drawer.

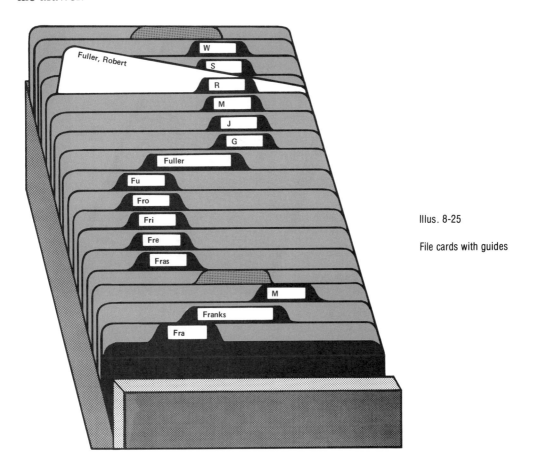

Illus. 8-25

File cards with guides

Visible Card Files

These are files in which a portion of the card is visible at all times, that portion generally showing the name, department, or product to which the card record refers. These cards are generally placed in pockets on horizontal trays, or on vertical sheets, or in files that appear in book form. The total card becomes visible as the overlapping cards are raised to provide a view of the whole card.

Illus. 8-26

Visible record card book

Signals on Visible Records. In addition to cards that are especially printed for use with visible files, small metal or plastic signals are available. These may be placed in various positions on the cards to indicate something important about the record. For example, if a visible file is used for collection records, the signal may indicate that the account is in good standing, or that it is overdue. Some signals may be used to indicate that it is very much overdue or that the firm with the account is no longer to be given credit because of poor standing. These signals are sometimes placed in special positions on the card and frequently are in different colors. For example, blue may indicate a good credit standing, yellow may mean mildly overdue, orange may mean very much overdue, and red may tell you that no further credit is to be extended.

Reference Visible Systems. These files usually carry only a strip instead of a whole card, the strip containing perhaps a name, address, and telephone number of persons who are called fairly often. The strips are usually referred to as visible panels and are generally limited to one or two lines.

356

TAG NO.	DESCRIPTION	MONTHLY INSPECTION CONTROL
385	Bench Grinder	JAN FEB MAR APR MAY JUN JUL AUG SEP OCT NOV DEC
386	Rivetting Machine	JAN FEB MAR APR MAY JUN JUL AUG SEP OCT NOV DEC
387	Knob Machine	JAN FEB MAR APR MAY JUN JUL AUG SEP OCT NOV DEC

Illus. 8-27

Signals on visible records

ITEM	PART NO.	WEEKS SUPPLY ON HAND
Cam Shaft Gear	398	1 2 3 4 5 6 (7) 8 9 10 11 12
Crank Shaft Gear	225	1 2 3 4 5 (6) 7 8 9 10 11 12
Driving Shaft	187	1 (2) 3 4 5 6 7 8 9 10 11 12
Feeder Arm Right	339	1 2 3 4 5 6 (7) 8 9 10 11 12
Feeder Cam	358	1 2 (3) 4 5 6 7 8 9 10 11 12
Feeder Pump Cover	186	1 2 (3) 4 5 6 7 8 9 10 11 12
Impression Cylinder	116	(1) 2 3 4 5 6 7 8 9 10 11 12

Rotary Files

A rotary file is used where quick reference to a large number of cards is needed. Cards used with this type of equipment are punched or cut at the bottom or at the side depending upon the style of wheel. There are small rotary files for desk-top use and also large rotary motorized equipment that is used when a great deal of information must be available for fingertip retrieval.

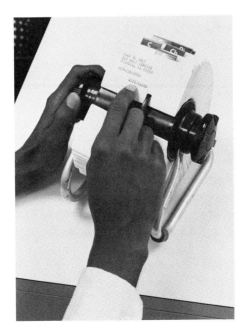

Illus. 8-28

Rotary file

Random Files

In this kind of system, the cards not only have typed or printed information on them, but are also equipped with strips of metal teeth which are attached to the bottom edge of the card. These teeth are cut in relation to magnetic rods that run under the cards. These files are operated by a keyboard, and the depression of certain keys causes one or more cards to be pushed up, thus locating them and making them available quickly. This system has the advantage of allowing one card to be identified under one of several possible captions. It is often found in banks, savings and loan associations, and finance companies where fast reference to a customer's file assures prompt service and goodwill.

Illus. 8-29

At the touch of the keys this file automatically selects the right card.

Acme Visible Records

Elevator Files

This type of file is power driven and is in a sense a multiple card file with trays arranged on shelves which may be brought to the level of the operator by the use of an elevator or power-driven system. The shelves in this kind of a file operate on the same principle as a ferris wheel at an amusement park. The shelves may be wide enough to take four, five, or more trays of 5" × 3" cards; and any single machine may include a large number of shelves. The operator pushes a button to move any particular shelf into position. At that point the operator may work directly on some cards, or may remove a complete tray of cards and turn them over to someone else to work on.

Illus. 8-30

Elevator file

Sperry Univac

Micrographics

Micrographics refers to the various processes of photographically reducing information on paper onto some type of film. The word "micrographics" is comparatively new and is sometimes used interchangeably with the more familiar word "microfilm." An 8½ × 11 inch sheet of paper can be reduced to 1/24 of its original size in one second.

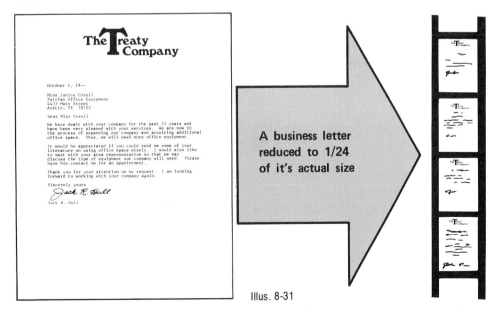

A business letter reduced to 1/24 of it's actual size

Illus. 8-31

There are several types of micrographics: microfilm, microfiche, aperture card, and computer output microfilm (COM).

Microfilm

The original documents are photographed on a roll of film, similar to motion picture film, which is placed in a 4 × 4 inch cartridge.

cartridge:
protective case

The Process. (See Illustration 8-32) A roll of microfilm in a **cartridge** is snapped into the camera (1). The original document (2), for example, a letter, is fed into the machine and photographed instantly. The camera reads out the location of the document on the film (3) and this location is indexed on the outside of the cartridge for future retrieval.

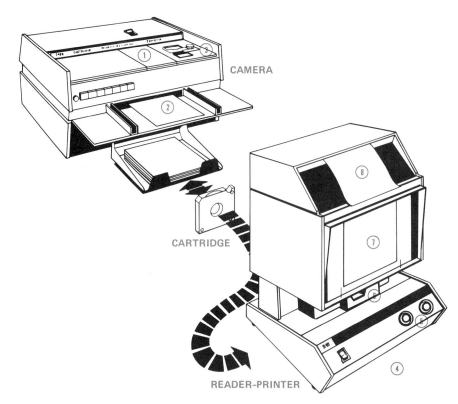

CAMERA

CARTRIDGE

READER-PRINTER

Illus. 8-32

A microfilm filing system.

3M Company

When a specific document is to be retrieved, the cartridge is placed on a reader-printer (4). Turning the dial (5) on the front of the machine permits the operator to scan the film. When the reading on the printer (6) matches the location of the document on the index of the cartridge, the document appears on the screen of the reader (7). If hard copy (paper copy similar to the copy from a copying machine) is desired, the print button is pressed and the reader-printer produces an exact copy (8) of the picture on the screen.

Advantages. Microfilming has the following advantages:

1. *Space saving.* About 3,000 letter-size documents can be placed on a 100-foot role of microfilm.
2. *Accurate filing.* All of the documents in the cartridge are always in the same sequence and cannot be misfiled.
3. *Efficient retrieval.* A letter on a microfilm can be located in a few seconds while the operator is seated at the reader-printer.
4. *Security.* An extra copy of the microfilm can easily be made which can then be stored in a different, protected location.
5. *Duplication.* Documents can be duplicated **inexpensively**. The copies are as good as the originals even though hundreds of copies are made.

inexpensively: at very little cost

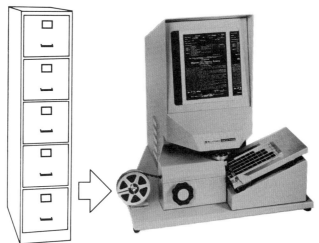

Illus. 8-33

A single role of microfilm contains the same number of documents as a five drawer file cabinet.

Microfiche

Microfiche (pronounced *micro feesh*) is a 4" × 6" sheet of microfilm that can contain 98 business documents (8½ × 11 inch) reduced to ¹/₂₄ of their original size. Typed information is recorded on the top of the microfiche so that it can be filed and retrieved. Duplicate copies of 4" × 6" film can be made inexpensively. Six microfiche can be mailed in an envelope as first-class mail.

Aperture card

Aperture cards are punched cards that contain a piece of microfilm. The holes in the card make it possible to file and retrieve the cards on a sorter as described in Unit 10, Part 3, page 440.

Illus. 8-34

Aperture card

Courtesy of Eastman Kodak Company

Computer Output Microfilm

Computer output microfilm (sometimes abbreviated COM) makes it possible to place information stored in a computer directly onto microfilm. Information can be recorded at the rate of 20,000 typewritten lines a minute. This is approximately 20 times faster than the computer can print the same information onto paper.

Electronic Data Processing

Electronic data processing equipment can store more information and retrieve it faster than any other system. Specially trained people handle the equipment for both input and retrieval of data. If you work in a data processing department, you would be very much concerned with the equipment and how it is used. If you work in any other department, you should be familiar with how the data processing equipment can aid your employer and you. In almost all cases, however, you would need the assistance of the people in the data processing department in order to store or retrieve information.

Tabulating (Punched) Cards

extensive:
broad

With the tremendous increase in the use of electronic data processing equipment, most companies have **extensive** tabulating card files. The tabulating or punched cards are often stored in vertical files. In the drawers of the filing cabinets, the cards are stored in removable trays. Alphabetic, numeric, and alpha-numeric indexing systems are used.

Computer Tapes and Disks

Magnetic tapes and disks can hold more information in less space than can punched cards. The tapes and disks are usually stored in fire- and heat-resistant cabinets or safes.

Some electronic data processing equipment uses punched paper tape to store information. The punched paper tapes themselves are usually placed in specially designed folders that contain pockets for the tape.

Retrieval

Retrieval of information stored in a computer is quite rapid. When you request information from a computer, it may print out the information on a continuous sheet of paper or on specially prepared business forms. It is possible that you may work in a business that has visual display units for retrieving information. With visual display units, the information you request is shown on a television-like screen.

Illus. 8-35

Visual display unit for retrieving information

Inforex, Inc.

Which Filing System?

considerable:
much

If a filing system is to operate effectively, considerable time must be given to its development. A good filing system cannot be designed casually. The solution to many records management problems is neither simple nor easy. The development of an effective filing — and finding — system must be based on careful analysis and extensive experience.

Here are some factors that should be considered when developing a filing system:

1. *The record requirements of the office.* What kinds of records are retained? How are these records created or received? What is the total volume of records retained each week, month, or year? What about future expansion of the system?
2. *Using the system.* How are the records requested and used? How active are the records? How long must the records be retained in the file?
3. *Storing the records.* What type of classification system should be used? Will a centralized or decentralized file plan be most effective? Where will the inactive records be stored?
4. *Equipment and supplies.* What specific types of equipment and supplies — out of the vast array available — would be most appropriate for this system in this office?

array:
variety of items

Since every office has different records requirements, a system used in one office is not always suitable for another. Remember that you are storing important information that must be retrieved quickly — you are not merely keeping pieces of paper.

Every filing system should be as simple as possible to use. In addition, the system should be efficient and reliable in providing needed information and should be economical to operate and maintain.

When an office decides to install a new filing system or to change an old one, three methods may be considered. A qualified person in the office may analyze the particular information requirements and develop an "office-made" system, a system may be purchased from a filing equipment and supplies manufacturer, or a records consultant may be engaged to design a tailor-made filing system to meet the company's particular needs.

REVIEWING IMPORTANT POINTS

1. Why are card files needed?
2. What procedure should be followed for typing information on cards for filing?

3. Why are metal or plastic signals used with visible card records?
4. When are cards filed on rotary files?
5. Give one of the advantages of a random file.
6. Give one of the advantages of an elevator file.
7. List the major types of "micrographics."
8. What are the five advantages of microfilming?
9. Why are magnetic tapes and disks preferred to punched cards in electronic data processing systems?
10. What are four of the factors to be considered in developing a filing system?

MAKING IMPORTANT DECISIONS

Miss Estelle Weeks began working for Cliffside Advertising Agency as a file clerk during their busiest period of the year. She soon discovered that many of the materials were misfiled, that proper procedures were not being followed for charging out materials, and that the firm also was in need of some new and more appropriate filing equipment. Miss Weeks decided to do her best under the current circumstances and to talk with her employer as soon as possible about some changes that should be made after the company's business slowed down. Do you think Miss Weeks' decision not to try to make changes at this particular time was a wise one? Why or why not?

LEARNING TO WORK WITH OTHERS

When Kenneth was promoted, he was asked to train Howard as his replacement. Kenneth spent a considerable amount of time teaching Howard the different filing systems used by the department. For several weeks Kenneth has been available to answer Howard's questions. During the last week, however, Howard has been repeating the same questions. Kenneth feels that Howard is depending too heavily on him for answers and not thinking through situations on his own. How can he encourage Howard to become more independent?

IMPROVING LANGUAGE SKILLS

Type each of the following sentences using the correct form of the word in parentheses.

1. My sister and (I, me) went to the movies last night.
2. The folders fell (off, off of) the table.
3. She types (better, more better) every day.
4. Dan (can hardly, can't hardly) work because his telephone rings so often.
5. The invitation included my friend (too, also).
6. We don't have (no, any) more carbon paper.
7. Please (bring, take) that letter here, and I'll photocopy it.
8. Where do the typists place (there, their) initials on the letters?
9. Resort reservations are not (so, as) expensive this summer as they were last summer.
10. Mary (sure, surely) knew her filing rules.
11. (Try to, Try and) picture a more perfect setting.
12. They work (well, good) together.
13. (Leave, Let) me answer the phone, please.
14. (It don't, It doesn't) matter if you are a bit late.
15. Everyone in our class (has, have) seen the filing movie, *It Must Be Somewhere.*
16. You were (very, real) thoughtful to call.
17. They (should of, should have) mailed it sooner.
18. We (differ with, differ from) you in our opinion of such elaborate planning.
19. Act (as if, like) you were interested in the suggestion.
20. Please (lay, lie) down to rest at the end of the day.

IMPROVING ARITHMETIC SKILLS

1. You are starting to transfer documents onto microfilm. Each cartridge holds approximately 320 letters. If you had 35 cartridges, how many letters could you transfer onto microfilm?
2. The computer presently prints the 15,000 address labels needed to mail the company's annual report. Each address label has four lines. Your employer would like a permanent record of this mailing list on microfilm. If the COM can record 20,000 lines of typewritten information in one minute, how long will it take to record all of the address labels?

   (a) Since a COM prints 20 times faster than a computer does, how long will it take the computer to print out the labels?
   (b) If you didn't have a computer, obviously someone would have to type all of the address labels. If you type 8 address labels in a minute, how long would it take you to type all of the address labels?

DEMONSTRATING OFFICE SKILLS

This is the conclusion of the alphabetic indexing exercise begun in Unit 7, Part 3, and continued in Part 1 of this unit.

Prepare your last 25 index cards from the names listed below and integrate them with the 75 cards you now have compiled from the earlier assignments.

(76) Henry R. Elston, IV, 2728 Germantown Rd., Germantown, PA 19144

(77) Chamber of Commerce, 12th & Olive Sts., Joliet, IL 60433

(78) Chief Engineer, Safety Division, Arkansas State Highway Dept., Ft. Smith, AR 72901

(79) Horace Mann Junior High School, 2500 Euclid Ave., Erie, PA 16511

(80) St. Mark's Episcopal Church, Oakwood, MO 63401

(81) University of New Mexico, Albuquerque, NM 87103

(82) Wm. A. Graves, 1620 N. Vernon Place, Winnetka, IL 60093

(83) Second National Bank, 8th & Race Sts., Spokane, WA 99202

(84) Garden Gate Antiques, 49 W. Elm St., Independence, KS 67301

(85) Security Savings Society, 74 Ohio Ave., Watertown, NY 13601

(86) Vera's Beauty Salon, 29 W. Adams St., Bennington, VT 05201

(87) Jack the Tailor, 536 S. 29th St., Oklahoma City, OK 73129

(88) Downtown Merchants Assn., 1200 Transportation Bldg., Wheeling, WV 26003

(89) Countess Mara Cosmetics, 128 W. 63rd St., New York, NY 10023

(90) Citizens Bank & Trust Co., Manchester, NH 03105

(91) Hartford Water Department, Hartford, CT 06101

(92) U.S. Marshal, Justice Dept., Federal Bldg., Boise, ID 83707

(93) Arnold A. Townley-Jones, 5021 Eastman Blvd., Chicago, IL 60622

(94) Chief Inspector, Food & Drug Administration, Health & Welfare Dept., Post Office Bldg., Butte, MT 59701

(95) United Fine Arts Fund, Terminal Bldg., Dallas, TX 75222

(96) Baldwin-Wallace College, Berea, OH 44017

(97) Harold McArthur & Sons, 4587 Roland Ave., Glendale, CA 91209

(98) MacArthur Sportswear, 688 Jefferson St., Kalamazoo, MI 49007

(99) Bernice L. McAdoo, 3 Alpine Terrace, Trenton, NJ 08610

(100) Perkins-Reynolds Insurance Agency, 200 Nicollet Ave., Minneapolis, MN 55401

IMPROVING OFFICE SKILLS (Optional)

Arrange the following items into an "office-made" filing system. Type them in the proper order on a separate sheet of paper. Indent to show first, second, and third position folders.

1. Sporting Goods Department
2. Dodson, Jane R.
3. Derrick, Lance
4. Departments
5. Music Department
6. Furniture Department
7. Dearing Office Supplies
8. Appliance Department
9. Derryman, Samuel
10. Dodson, Rosemary

Using Mail and Shipping Services

Part 1. Handling Incoming Mail
Part 2. Handling Outgoing Mail
Part 3. Volume Mail
Part 4. Air and Surface Shipping

Handling Incoming Mail

Miss Fulton has the responsibility of keeping a record of packages other companies have said they have mailed to her company. Since many departments depend on her records, she makes sure they are kept up to date. When Mr. Casey from the marketing department asked Miss Fulton if his package from Lenning, Inc., had arrived yet, she was able to give him the information quickly. "It was sent five days ago, but it hasn't arrived yet." Based on that information, Mr. Casey decided to notify Lenning that he had not received the package. Mr. Casey has confidence that Miss Fulton's records are accurate, and he is grateful that he can depend on her for current information. Miss Fulton knows that keeping accurate records makes her job easier and also helps other departments to be efficient.

The United States Postal Service presently handles about 90 billion pieces of mail every year. One of your regular duties may be to help process the daily mail.

The procedure for handling incoming mail will depend upon the size and type of business in which you are employed. In a large office the incoming mail is opened, sorted, and distributed by the mail department. In a small office, handling the incoming mail may be just one of several tasks handled by an office worker.

Opening the Mail

When the volume of incoming mail is very large, letters are opened in the mail department with an electric mail opener. This machine trims a narrow strip off one edge of each envelope. The amount taken off is so small that there is little risk that the contents of the envelope will be damaged. To reduce the chances of cutting the contents, the envelopes may be jogged on the table before they are placed in the opener so that the contents will fall away from the edge that is to be trimmed.

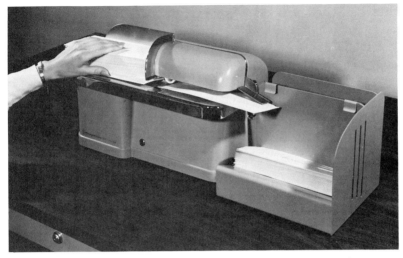

Illus. 9-1

Electrically operated
letter opener

After you have opened the envelopes, remove the letters and other enclosures carefully. Look at each letter and its enclosures as soon as they are removed and attach the enclosures to the letter. If an enclosure is missing, you should note the omission in the margin of the letter.

Illus. 9-2

Opening letters by
hand

Keep the envelopes until you have examined each letter for the signature and the address. If either is missing on the letter, attach the envelope to the letter. Sometimes a check is received with no other means of identification except the envelope in which it was mailed. If the date of the letter is different from the postmark, keep the envelope. Sometimes the envelope of an important document is stapled to the document

identification:
a means of telling to
whom something
belongs

because the date of mailing may prove to be of some importance. If, after you have thrown away the envelope, you notice that the return address is not printed or typed on a letter, you may be able to find the address in a telephone directory, a city directory, or in the correspondence files.

If by error you open a letter marked "personal" or "confidential," immediately place the letter back in the envelope and write on the outside "Sorry — opened by mistake," and add your initials. Do not read the contents of a personal letter. Examine each letter carefully before you open it so you don't make this error often.

Dating the Mail

After you have checked the incoming mail for enclosures, return addresses, and signatures, mark it with the date and time. You can do this with a pen or pencil, a rubber stamp, or a time stamp machine.

The date and time on the incoming mail may be important in correspondence about contracts, insurance, and some financial agreements. The receiving date also reminds the recipient of when the correspondence was received and may encourage a prompt reply.

Illus. 9-3

A time stamp machine records time, date, and identifying mark on letters, telegrams, and other documents.

Cincinnati Time Recorder Company

Sorting and Routing Mail

If you work in a small office, you may have many responsibilities related to the mail. After you have opened the mail, you check it carefully for addresses, signatures, and enclosures. Next, you will date and time stamp the mail. Then you will *route* the mail, which means sorting it according to addressee or department.

In the mail room of a large company, the mail is sorted by department. Sorting bins or trays, with a separate compartment for each department, are used for this purpose. After the mail has been sorted, it is delivered by a mail clerk or a messenger. Usually the mail is delivered several times a day, the first mail of the day being the heaviest.

When sorting and routing the mail in a large company, usually all orders are directed to the order department. Correspondence regarding credit is sent to the credit department. Inquiries concerning products are sent to the sales department. Checks and correspondence related to the payment of bills are sent to the accounting department. Personal and confidential mail is delivered *unopened* to the addressee. Correspondence addressed to individuals in the company is routed directly to them.

Illus. 9-4

Mail sorting bins, postage meters and scales in a small mail department.

Kwik-File

Special delivery letters and registered mail are usually not delivered with the regular mail. They should be handled promptly upon receipt and brought to the addressee's attention quickly.

Your incoming mail may sometimes contain correspondence or important articles from magazines or newspapers that need to be routed to more than one executive or department. Many firms have rubber stamps or a duplicated routing slip that has all of the names of the executives or departments in the company on it. The mail is either rubber stamped or attached to a routing slip. If a particular executive or department is not to be included in the route, that executive or department is crossed off the list. This leaves only the executives or departments that are supposed to receive the mail. This mail is then routed and delivered with the regular mail.

Illus. 9-5

Routing slip

```
                Albert Martin, Director
                Public Relations Department

                                         Date 3/25/--

                   ROUTING SLIP
                                            Date
                                          Forwarded
            _____ Everyone            _____
            _____ Babb, B.            _____
             ✓    Gryder, H.            3/25
            _____ Igo, J.             _____
            _____ Mundt, K.           _____
             ✓    Primrose, N.          3/25
             ✓    Roehr, P.             3/28
            _____ Slaughter, G.        _____
             ✓    Tucker, C.            3/28
            _____ Wingfield, M.        _____
             ✓    Brown, M.             3/28


            Will you please:

            _____ Read and keep
            _____ Read and pass on
            _____ Read and return
             ✓    Read, pass on, and return
```

Keeping Mail Records

As you read certain letters, you will notice promises of materials that are being sent under separate cover, meaning in another envelope or package. To be sure that you receive them, you should keep a record of mail expected in another package. Check at least twice a week to see which items have not been received so that you can remind your supervisor or the addressees of delayed mail. When the delayed mail is received, send it to the department or the person to whom the original letter was routed. One type of record for separate cover mail is illustrated below.

Illus. 9-6

Register of mail expected under separate cover. Note that the last item has not arrived yet.

DATE OF ENTRY	ARTICLE	FROM WHOM	DATE SENT	DEPARTMENT	INDIVIDUAL	DATE RECEIVED
9-5	Book	Welch Bros.	9-3		A. Ward	9-6
9-12	Folders	Hill Supply	9-10	Filing		9-14
9-23	Report	Lehman & Cole	9-21	Research		9-25
10-1	Catalog	Tate Mfg. Co.	9-30	Purchasing		10-4
10-3	Tickets	Jack Wylie	10-1		H. Lewis	

Because of its special importance, you may find it necessary to keep a record of the mail received that is insured, special delivery, or registered. Use a form similar to the one illustrated below.

RECEIVED		FROM WHOM		FOR	KIND OF MAIL RECEIVED
DATE	TIME	NAME	ADDRESS	DEPARTMENT OR INDIVIDUAL	
4-5	3:20pm	J.J. McIntosh	St. Louis, Mo.	Purchasing	Insured
4-6	9:15am	Grove Mfg.	Memphis, TN	Sales	Special Delivery
4-9	10:45am	Mo. P. Williams	Des Moines, Il	M. Jones	Registered

Illus. 9-7

Register of insured, special delivery, and registered mail

Photocopying Mail

When reading the mail for sorting and routing, you may notice that the subject matter is important to more than one person or department. For instance, a letter addressed to the order department might contain an order and also an inquiry about a new product. To speed delivery to both the order department and the sales department, you will photocopy the letter. Make a notation on the original that is being sent to the order department that you have sent a copy to the sales department.

Illus. 9-8

It may be necessary to photocopy some correspondence for fast delivery to several departments.

Distributing the Mail

Depending on the size of the company you may or may not be responsible for distributing the mail. If you are, you will have the necessary supplies to carry out this task. Your equipment may be a cart, a lightweight mail basket, or something as simple as an alphabetized expanding folder.

REVIEWING IMPORTANT POINTS

1. When opening incoming mail with an electrically operated letter opener, how do you avoid cutting the contents of the envelopes?
2. What should you do if you open an envelope that is missing an enclosure mentioned in the letter?
3. When is it desirable to attach the envelope to the contents of a piece of mail?
4. How should personal mail be handled and what should be done if you open a personal letter by mistake?
5. Why are letters time-stamped upon receipt?
6. What does it mean to "route" the mail?
7. The regular mail is delivered at 3 p.m. A special delivery package has just arrived. When should you deliver this package?
8. What is a method of routing one piece of correspondence to several executives or departments?
9. How will you know if a package that was sent under separate cover is overdue?
10. You have made a photocopy of an incoming letter. What should you do before you deliver the original?

MAKING IMPORTANT DECISIONS

Your employer, the office manager in a medium-sized company, has learned that there are many problems in handling incoming mail. You have been asked to study the situation and report your findings to the office manager. You have found the following practices used throughout the company:

a. The mail is opened by hand by the receptionist who also handles the switchboard. When the mail is too heavy for the receptionist to take care of it alone, one of the stenographers in the office who happens not to be busy helps out.
b. Enclosures that are referred to in letters frequently do not accompany the letters that are distributed to the various executives. The executives are therefore uncertain whether the enclosures have been received or whether they have been received and have become separated from the letters.

c. Often a letter is not answered until long after it is received, but the executives do not know whether the delay is in their own offices or whether the letter has not been delivered to them promptly.

d. Before an order is filled, it is handled by a the credit department, the sales department, and the order department. In some cases, it goes first to one department and in other cases, first to another department, depending on where the mail clerk is going first.

e. Sometimes in a letter, reference is made to a package being sent under separate cover. The executive, however, usually never sees the package or knows if it arrived.

After studying your report the office manager asks you for suggestions for eliminating these problems. What methods for solving these problems would you suggest?

LEARNING TO WORK WITH OTHERS

A special delivery letter came to your employer, Mr. Randy Vega, while he was away at lunch. During his absence you began working on a long and involved project; consequently, you forgot to give him the letter. The next morning as Mr. Vega was walking by your desk, he noticed the letter.

How should you handle your mistake? Should you just ignore the situation and hope he says nothing to you?

IMPROVING LANGUAGE SKILLS

Semicolons are used to punctuate complex elements in a sentence. Below are three uses of the semicolon:

A. Between independent clauses not joined by a conjunction.
   Example: Letters marked "personal" are for the person addressed only; they should not be opened by the mail clerk.

B. Before a conjunction joining two independent clauses when one clause (or both) has internal punctuation.
   Example: By dating incoming mail, the receiver is reminded of when it arrived; and responsibility for delay can be established.

C. After each independent clause in a series when one (or more) has internal punctuation.
   Example: The mail clerk removed the letter from the envelope; he checked the enclosures against the list at the bottom of the letter; and then he clipped together the letter, the price list, the booklet, and the sample.

Punctuate the following sentences based on the three semicolon rules you have reviewed above.

1. Some pieces of correspondence may be attached to a routing slip other pieces of correspondence may need to be photocopied.
2. After reading the letter Mr. Lacey decided that Mr. Strickland should handle the request but as it turned out Mr. Strickland was out of town until Friday.
3. Advertising materials should be kept on the left orders should be kept on the right correspondence should be kept in the center unopened personal and confidential mail should be delivered unopened checks and other enclosures should be attached to letters.
4. In most offices correspondence is stamped orders are stamped invoices are stamped including both copies if they are sent in duplicate advertising materials as a rule are not stamped.

IMPROVING ARITHMETIC SKILLS

1. All employees are asked to record the number of photocopies they make on a tablet near the copier. You have 3 pieces of mail that need to be sent to the following individuals or departments:

Mail	Individual or Department
Two-page magazine article	President
	Vice President of Marketing
	Sales Department
Three-page report	Claims Director
	Vice President of Traffic and Safety
One-page letter	Vice President of Finance
	Internal Auditor

How many photocopies will you record on the tablet by the copier?

2. If the first letter on Tuesday was stamped at 8:40 a.m. and the last letter on the same day was stamped at 4:35 p.m., how much time was there between the first letter and the last letter?

DEMONSTRATING OFFICE SKILLS

1. The mail listed below is expected under separate cover. Record the information on the form in your *Supplies Inventory*, if available, or draw a form like that on page 374.

May 1 A letter from Boyd C. Waggoner refers to a mailing list that was sent under separate cover on April 28, to the Advertising Department.

May 1 In a letter dated April 29, David Hard stated that he was returning a parcel post package to the Shipping Department.

May 2 In his letter of April 30, Margo B. Jennings said that she was shipping a catalog to the Purchasing Department.

May 3 In a letter dated May 1, Jack D. Clary stated that he is returning a desk calculator to the Service Department.

May 4 In his letter of May 1, Carrie J. Michaels stated that she sent her analysis of our operations systems to Keith McIntire.

May 4 Margaret Russell, in her letter of May 1, said that she shipped 16 reams of 8½ × 11, S-20, green duplicating paper to the Duplicating Department.

May 5 In a letter of May 2, Lee Alberts stated that she returned a rental typewriter to the Rental Department.

May 6 Francis Brooks, in his letter of May 2, stated that he sent a book to the Accounting Department.

May 6 In a letter of May 3, Gary T. Campbell stated that he sent pamphlets to the Sales Department.

May 6 A letter from Cynthia McLarty refers to a package of folders sent on May 3 to the Research Department.

May 7 A letter from Mallory P. Boucher refers to an art booklet that was sent under separate cover May 4 to the Advertising Department.

2. The insured, special-delivery, and registered mail listed below has been received by your company. Record the information on the form in your *Supplies Inventory*, if available, or draw a form similar to that on page 375.

May 15 At 9:30 a.m. a registered letter was received from Ms. Aeja F. Davidson, Phoenix, Arizona. It was referred to the Sales Department.

May 15 At 11:25 a.m. an insured package was received from Ms. Katherine Whitely, Augusta, Maine, addressed to the Advertising Department.

May 16 At 2:15 p.m. a registered letter was received from Mr. Jesse R. Pennington, Memphis, Tennessee, for the Accounting Department.

May 17 At 10:40 a.m. a special-delivery letter was received from Ms. Beverly Anne Hayes, Chicago, Illinois, for the Purchasing Department.

May 17 At 3:15 p.m. a registered letter was received from Mr. Douglas J. Fullerton, Mobile, Alabama, addressed to the Sales Department.

May 18 At 4:00 p.m. a special delivery letter was received from Mr. Kevin E. Sealy, Flint, Michigan, for Larry Fannon.

May 19 At 11:05 a.m. an insured package was received from Mr. Walter D. Kemp, New York, New York, for the Maintenance Department.

May 19 At 1:30 p.m. a registered letter was received from Miss Ada B. Conwell, Seattle, Washington, for the Sales Department.

Part 2

Handling Outgoing Mail

"Mr. Chun, I have several packages that need to be wrapped and mailed as soon as possible. Please take care of them." Mrs. Crim knows that Mr. Chun is well informed about postal requirements, rates, and services. He knows how to wrap each package; and according to the contents, he can decide how each package should be sent.

Outgoing mail may mean one letter sent to thousands of persons. It may mean first to fourth class and even mixed mail; or it may mean domestic, foreign, and special service mail. Your knowledge and understanding of postal services and mail handling procedures can save your employer time and money and can increase the overall efficiency of the business.

You should be able to select the proper mailing service for all the different types of outgoing mail. A complete list of postal services with the details for their use can be found in the Postal Service Manual of the United States. Postal services and rates are changed from time to time; therefore, it is important that you have an up-to-date copy of the Postal Service Manual in your office. It may be purchased from the Superintendent of Documents, United States Government Printing Office, Washington, D.C. 20402.

You can speed the mail delivery and reduce the cost of mailing if you use the right mailing service at the right time. A United States Postal Service official states that millions of dollars are wasted each year because of the general lack of knowledge of the various postal services. The official estimates that extravagance adds at least 10 percent to the annual cost of all mailing in the United States. You can always get up-to-date postal information free of charge at the Information window of your local post office, or you can call the local postmaster or the customer service representative for the latest information.

extravagance: spending much more than necessary

Handling Outgoing Mail

The system of handling outgoing mail, like the system of handling incoming mail, depends upon the size and type of business in which you are employed. In a small office a mail clerk is usually responsible for all the details connected with outgoing mail. In a large office the mail is collected from each department several times throughout the day by a messenger or a mail clerk and taken to the mailing department where it is sealed and stacked near the *postage meter*, a machine that automatically prints the amount of postage, the postmark, and the mailing date on the envelope.

Folding and Inserting Letters

Folding a business letter properly is not a difficult task. Care should be taken so that the creases are straight and are made without detracting from the neatness of the letter. A letter should be inserted in an envelope in such a way that it will be in reading position when it is removed from the envelope and unfolded. Paper, 8½″ × 11″, to be inserted in a small envelope (No. 6, 6½″ × 3⅝″) is folded and inserted as follows:

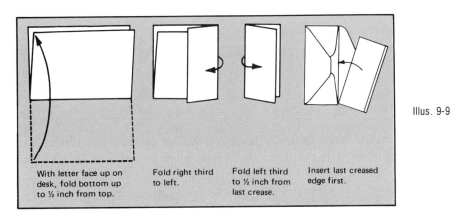

With letter face up on desk, fold bottom up to ½ inch from top.

Fold right third to left.

Fold left third to ½ inch from last crease.

Insert last creased edge first.

Illus. 9-9

Only two folds are necessary if the letter is to be placed in a large envelope (No. 10, 9½″ × 4⅛″):

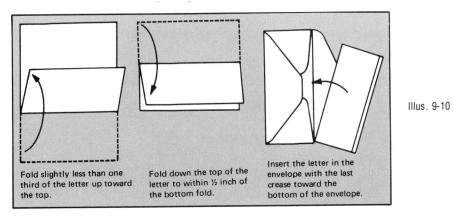

Fold slightly less than one third of the letter up toward the top.

Fold down the top of the letter to within ½ inch of the bottom fold.

Insert the letter in the envelope with the last crease toward the bottom of the envelope.

Illus. 9-10

The enclosures that accompany the letter should be folded with the letter or inserted so that they will come out of the envelope at the same time the letter is removed.

For a large No. 10 window envelope, 8½″ × 11″ letter sheets are folded as shown below:

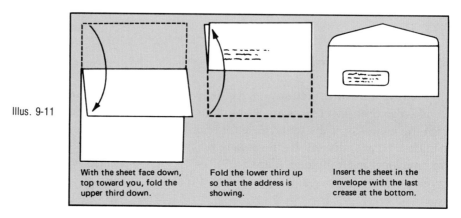

Illus. 9-11

| With the sheet face down, top toward you, fold the upper third down. | Fold the lower third up so that the address is showing. | Insert the sheet in the envelope with the last crease at the bottom. |

Small No. 6 window envelopes are also available; they are used mostly for bills or statements that are designed to fit with only a single fold.

Sealing Envelopes

If you should have to seal a large number of envelopes without the use of a sealing machine, spread about ten envelopes on a table, address

Illus. 9-12

Sealing envelopes by hand

down, flap open, one on top of the other with gummed edges showing. Brush over the gummed edges with a moist sponge or a moistener to soften the glue so that the flaps can be closed quickly and sealed. When sealing, start with the top envelope, the one nearest you, and work down to the first one placed on the table.

Stamps

You may also put postage stamps on rapidly by arranging six to eight envelopes on top of each other, showing just the upper right part of each one. Moisten the strip of stamps with a damp sponge and put on one stamp after the other. You can save time and increase your **efficiency** this way.

efficiency: productivity without waste

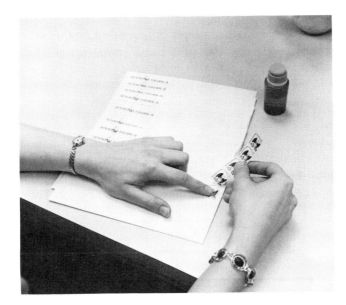

Illus. 9-13

Applying stamps by hand

Postage stamps may be purchased in sheet, booklet, or coil form. The bound booklets of stamps are preferred for personal and home use; business firms find it better to work with the 100-stamp sheets or the coiled stamps. Coiled stamps are often used in business because they can be placed on envelopes and packages quickly and because they are less likely to be lost or damaged than are individual stamps.

Precanceled Stamps and Envelopes

For an advertising campaign your employer may wish to use precanceled stamps or precanceled stamped envelopes. Their use reduces the time and cost of handling mail. Precanceled stamps and envelopes are purchased from the post office with the cancellation lines already stamped on them. When the sorted mail is returned to the post office, it is not necessary for the letters to go through the canceling machine again. Therefore, the mail is dispatched more quickly. Precanceled stamps and envelopes cannot be used for first-class mail.

dispatched:
sent out

Stamped Envelopes and Cards

denominations:
kinds or classes

Another means of saving time when handling mail is through the use of stamped envelopes of different denominations which may be purchased in various sizes — singly or in quantity lots. The return address will be printed on them by the post office for a small fee if the envelopes are purchased in quantity lots.

First-class postal cards may be purchased in single or double form. The double form is used when a reply is requested on the attached card.

Spoiled stamped envelopes and cards (if uncanceled) may be exchanged for new stamps, stamped envelopes, or postal cards. You may also obtain an exchange on stamps if you buy the wrong denomination.

Metered Mail

The most efficient device you can use to put postage on any class of mail is the postage meter machine. This machine prints the postmark and the proper amount of postage on each piece of mail. The imprint of

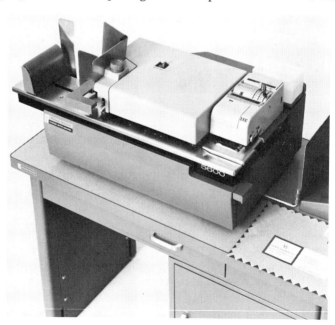

Illus. 9-14

In a small office a desk-top postage meter is used for stamping and stacking outgoing mail.

Pitney Bowes Corporate Communications

Unit 9 • Using Mail and Shipping Services

a fully automatic metering machine may also carry a slogan or a line or two of advertising, such as IT'S SMART TO BE THRIFTY, next to the postmark. Metered mail does not have to be canceled or postmarked at the post office; therefore, it is processed and dispatched quickly.

The meter of the postage machine is set at the post office for the amount paid at the time. The meter registers the amount of postage used on each piece of mail, the amount of postage remaining in the meter, and the number of pieces that have passed through the machine. The meter locks when the amount paid for has been used; it is then necessary to take it to the post office again to pay for more postage. Additional postage should be bought before the meter locks. You will find the postage meter very easy to operate, and it will save you a great deal of time.

ZIP Codes

To assure prompt delivery of your mail always use ZIP Codes. Their use increases the speed, accuracy, and quality of *all* mail service. The ZIP Code is a five-digit number that identifies the destination of a piece of mail. For instance:

9	45	77
Area	Sectional Center	Local Zone
	or Large City	

The 9 identifies one of ten large areas made up of three or more states into which the entire country has been divided. The next two figures, 45, represent the sectional center or large city within that area. And, finally, the 77 represents the local delivery zone within that city or sectional center.

The code should appear on the last line of *both* the envelope address and the return address following the city and state. One space should be left between the last letter of the state and the first digit of the code. The address should be typed in block form:

> Fisk Division
> The Radcliff Company
> 2350 Washington Avenue
> San Leandro, CA 94577

All Zip Codes can be found in the *National Zip Code Directory.*

Optical Character Reader (OCR)

The post office has installed Optical Character Readers, electronic equipment which speeds up the processing of mail. This equipment can read printed or typewritten addresses and can sort letters rapidly and accurately.

Whether or not your post office has OCR equipment, the following rules will help to speed the processing of your outgoing mail.

1. *Basic Format.* The address should be single-spaced in block form.
2. *Street Address, P.O. Box,* or *Rural Route.* These should be shown on the line immediately above the City, State, and ZIP Code.
3. *Unit Number.* Mail addressed to occupants of a multi-unit building should include the number of the apartment, room, suite, or other unit. The unit number should appear immediately after the street address on the same line — never above, below, or in front of the street address.
4. *City, State,* and *ZIP Code.* They should appear in that order on the bottom line of the address.

occupants: those living in a particular place

Illus. 9-15

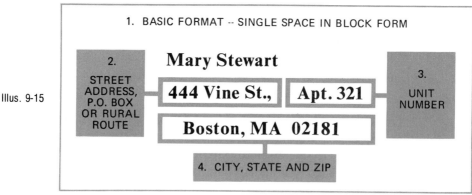

Items to Check Before Mailing Letters

Before mailing your outgoing correspondence, check each letter first to be sure that:

1. Any enclosures noted at the bottom of the letter are actually enclosed in the envelope.
2. Numbers, such as order numbers, referred to in the correspondence are correct.
3. Carbon copies for others are prepared for mailing.
4. Your initials appear below your employer's signature on any letter you have signed for your employer.

Then check each envelope to be sure that:

1. The address on the envelope agrees with the inside address of the letter.

2. The ZIP Code is typed on the last line of *both* the envelope address and the return address.
3. Any special notations, such as Registered or Special Delivery, have been noted on the envelope.
4. The typed address on a label for a package to be sent separately agrees with the address on the envelope.

Finally, to skip one sorting operation at the post office, separate and identify the *Local* and the *Out-of-Town* mail. Free self-sticking, wrap-around labels are available from most post offices.

Domestic Mail Service

Domestic mail is mail sent within the United States, its territories and possessions, Army-Air Force (APO) and Navy (FPO) post offices, and also mail for delivery to the United Nations, New York City.

Classes of Domestic Mail

Your employer will expect you to know the different kinds of domestic mail most widely used by business firms. The five kinds of domestic mail listed below will be considered separately.

1. First-class mail — letters, postal cards, and postcards
2. Second-class mail — newspapers and periodicals
3. Third-class mail — circulars and other miscellaneous printed matter
4. Fourth-class mail — parcel post
5. Mixed classes of mail

First-Class Mail

First-class mail usually takes the form of sealed letters; however, the following mail must also be sent first-class:

1. All matter sealed against postal inspection.
2. Postal cards (cards sold by the post office with stamps imprinted on them) and postcards (privately purchased mailing cards which require stamps).
3. Business reply cards and envelopes.
4. Matter, partly in written form, such as statements of account, checks, punched cards, and filled-in forms.
5. Other matter in written form, such as typewritten reports and documents.

Second-Class Mail

bulk:
great mass or quantity

Certain newspapers and magazines are sent at second-class rates of postage which are lower than third- and fourth-class mail. Authorization to publishers and news agents to mail at **bulk** second-class rates must be obtained from the Postal Service.

Third-Class Mail

Almost every day you receive in your own home circulars and advertisements that have been sent through the mail at third-class rates. This rate is used for materials not otherwise classified as first- or second-class mail that weigh less than 16 ounces. The same material in parcels weighing 16 ounces and over is considered fourth-class mail. The following may be sent by third-class mail service:

1. Circulars, books, catalogs, and other printed matter
2. Merchandise samples

Envelopes may be sealed if marked *Third Class* on the address side of the envelope. In the absence of such a marking, sealed envelopes will be subject to first-class mail rates.

Fourth-Class Mail (Parcel Post)

Fourth-class mail is also known as parcel post. It includes merchandise, printed matter, and all other mailable matter not included in first-, second-, or third-class mail that weighs 16 ounces or more. Parcel post rates are determined according to (1) the weight of the parcel and (2) the distance the parcel is being sent. There are limitations on the weight and size of parcel post packages.

Parcel post packages may be sent sealed or unsealed. Unless it is clearly marked *First Class* a sealed package is usually treated as parcel post by the postal sorters regardless of the amount of postage paid.

Mixed Classes of Mail

Sometimes it is better to send two pieces of mail of different classes together as a single mailing to be sure that they both arrive at the same time. A first-class letter may be attached to the outside of a large envelope or parcel of a different class of mail, or it may be enclosed in a large envelope or parcel. When a first-class letter is *attached*, the postage is **affixed** to each part separately. When a first-class letter is *enclosed*, its

affixed:
fastened; attached in
any way

postage is added to the parcel postage and affixed on the outside of the package. The words *First Class Mail Enclosed* must be written, typed, or stamped below the postage and above the address. A piece of mixed mail is handled and transported by the post office as the class into which the bulky portion falls — not as first-class mail.

Mailing Suggestions for Fast Delivery

There are many ways to help the United States Postal Service send your mail rapidly. Here are four suggestions to speed the processing and delivery of your outgoing mail:

1. *Mail early and often.* To avoid getting mail caught in the five o'clock rush, mail early in the day and as often as possible. Most post offices receive about three quarters of the day's mail in the late afternoon or early evening.
2. *Check collection times.* If you ordinarily mail from a building lobby or street mail box, check the "Hours of Collection" listing on the box. Collections are made only once a day at some street mail boxes. If you should miss the last daily collection and want your mail to move fast, take it directly to the nearest post office.
3. *Keep Local Mail separate from Out-of-Town Mail.* Use separate labels for *Local Mail* and *Out-of-Town Mail* to make certain that your mail skips one sorting operation at the post office.
4. *Use ZIP Codes in both the mailing address and in the return address.* To assure speedy delivery of your mail, *always use ZIP Codes.* Make sure your addressing is clear, complete, and correct. Check to be sure that you have written the *correct street number* in the mailing address. Remember that all envelopes should carry your return address with your ZIP Code so that undeliverable mail can be returned to you.

International Mail

Mail is now sent to all parts of the world, either by air or surface transportation, in ever-increasing volume. International mail is divided into two general categories — postal union mail and parcel post. Postal union mail is further divided into two groups — *LC* mail and *AO* mail. LC mail (letters and cards) consists of letters, letter packages, and postal cards. AO mail (articles, other) includes printed matter, samples of merchandise, matter for the blind, and small packets.

The postage for letters and postal cards mailed to Canada and Mexico is the same as that for the United States. To all other countries the rates

international: between or among different nations

are higher and the weights are limited. Overseas parcel post packages must be packed even more carefully than those for delivery within the continental United States. A *customs declaration* form must be attached to each parcel with an accurate and complete description of its contents.

Special Postal Services

The United States Postal Service also provides many special services, such as:

1. Special Delivery
2. Special Handling
3. Registered Mail
4. Certified Mail

5. Insured Mail
6. COD Service
7. Tracing Mail
8. Recalling Mail

Special Delivery

Special delivery provides the fastest handling and delivery service for any kind of mail. Special delivery mail is handled at the post office of destination with the same promptness given to first-class mail and, in addition, is given immediate delivery (within prescribed hours and distances). The fees charged are in addition to the regular postage. They vary according to the weight of the letter or parcel. The mail must be stamped or marked *Special Delivery*.

Special Handling

On payment of a fee in addition to the regular postage, a parcel labeled *Special Handling* will be given the same prompt handling and delivery service as is given to first-class mail. Special handling parcels are delivered the same way that parcel post is ordinarily delivered — on regularly scheduled trips, not special delivery. The fees are lower than special delivery fees. Special handling services may be used only with parcels sent as third- or fourth-class mail.

Registered Mail

Mail is registered to give protection to valuable and important contents. Money, checks, jewelry, stock certificates, and bonds are included in the valuable items frequently sent by registered mail. Important items include contracts, bills of sale, leases, mortgages, deeds, wills, and vital business records. Registration provides insurance, a receipt for the sender, and proof of delivery. Mail may be registered for insurance up to

$10,000 if no other insurance is carried. If other insurance is carried, postal insurance liability is limited to a maximum of $1,000. All classes of mail may be registered provided the first-class rate is paid.

You will be given a receipt showing that the post office has accepted the registered mail for transmittal and delivery. For an additional fee you may obtain a *return receipt* to prove that the mail has been delivered.

Certified Mail

If your mail has no value of its own (such as a letter, a bill, or an important notice) and yet you want proof of mailing and delivery, send it as *Certified Mail*. It provides a receipt for the sender and a record of delivery. No insurance coverage is provided for certified mail.

Insured Mail

Third- or fourth-class mail may be insured for up to $200 against loss or damage. A receipt is issued for insured mail. It should be kept on file until the insured mail has arrived in satisfactory condition. If an insured parcel is lost or damaged, the post office will **reimburse** you for the value of the merchandise or the amount for which it was insured, whichever is the smaller.

reimburse:
pay back

COD Service

Merchandise may be sent to a purchaser COD, that is, *collect on delivery*, if the shipment is based on an order by the buyer or on an agreement between sender and addressee. The seller may obtain COD service by paying a fee in addition to the regular postage. The maximum amount collectible on one package is $300. The total fee varies with the amount to be collected, the weight of the package, and the distance it is to travel.

Tracing Mail

If mail has not been delivered within the expected time, you may make a written request to have it traced. The post office will supply you with a form for tracing a piece of mail. Although the post office will cooperate in every possible way, it is almost impossible to trace unregistered, uninsured, or uncertified mail, especially if it does not carry a return address. Consequently, all mail should carry a complete return address and valuable or important mail should be registered, certified, or insured.

Recalling Mail

Occasionally it may be necessary to recall a piece of mail you have already mailed. This will require prompt action on your part. Go to the post office in your mailing zone to recall a letter mailed to a local address or to the central post office to recall a letter mailed out of town. Fill in Form 1509 (*Sender's Application for Withdrawal of Mail*) and the post office will have the piece of mail returned to you.

REVIEWING IMPORTANT POINTS

1. If you are uncertain as to how to mail a package, who can you call for assistance?
2. What is a postage meter?
3. Why are ZIP Codes now used with all classes of mail?
4. What are the four rules of addressing mail?
5. What are some of the items to be checked in a letter and so on an envelope before they are released as outgoing mail?
6. What kind of mail must be sent at the first-class rate?
7. What are some suggestions to speed up delivery of the mail?
8. How do *Special Delivery* and *Special Handling* differ?
9. What are the differences between *Registered Mail* and *Certified Mail*?
10. Once you have mailed a letter, can you ever get it back again, If so, how?

MAKING IMPORTANT DECISIONS

Linda Nichols works in the mail room of a large manufacturing firm. One of her responsibilities is to keep the postage machine adequately filled. On Wednesday Linda sent a large number of items through the postage machine. On Thursday she had a big packaging and mailing job to handle. When she was finished with that task, she was tired and didn't bother to fill the postage machine even though she knew it was getting low. On Friday at 4:45 p.m. the postage machine locked in the middle of a very important batch of letters announcing an unscheduled stockholders' meeting for Tuesday morning. It would take Linda 20 minutes to go to the post office which closes at 5 p.m. How well do you think Linda handled her responsibility of keeping the postage machine adequately filled? Explain. How would you have handled the responsibility differently?

LEARNING TO WORK WITH OTHERS

In the office where Charlie works, the mail goes out four times a day — 8:30, 11:30, 3:30, and 5:15. Early on Monday morning Charlie received a telephone call from an executive in the branch office. She urgently needed a shipment of typewriter ribbons to fill a customer's order. Charlie assured the executive that he would get the shipment into the 11:30 mail. After getting the ribbons, Charlie told the mail clerk that the package had to go out in the 11:30 mail. Several hours later he checked to see if the package had been mailed. It was still in the mail room and had missed the 3:30 mailing. Should Charlie approach the mail clerk for an explanation and hope that the package would be put in the 5:15 mail, or should he leave the office to mail the package himself?

IMPROVING LANGUAGE SKILLS

1. The following terms were taken from Unit 9, Parts 1 and 2. Write the meaning of each term. Consult the text or a standard dictionary if you are not sure of the definition.

   a. metered mail
   b. LC and AO international mail
   c. mixed mail
   d. OCR

   e. precanceled stamps
   f. return receipt
   g. parcel post
   h. domestic mail

2. Type the correct spelling of each of the following words used in mailing:

a. denominations	denomunations
b. catagories	categories
c. cataloges	catalogs
d. certified	certefied
e. circulars	circulers
f. exceding	exceeding
g. optical	opticle
h. receipt	reciept
i. transmited	transmitted
j. confidential	confedential

IMPROVING ARITHMETIC SKILLS

Monday morning the post office put $200 worth of postage into the company postage machine. There was $3 already in the machine before the new postage was added. By Friday you had mailed the following items:

4 manuscripts	$.19 ea
500 form letters	$.13 ea
1,800 advertising circulars	$.05 ea (bulk rate)

The next Monday you have the following pieces of mail that need to be sent:

350 statements	$ .13 ea
3 reports	$ .21 ea
1 manuscript	$ .17 ea
2 books	$1.79 ea
7 letters	$ .13 ea

1. How much postage was used the first week?
2. How much postage was left in the machine after the first week?
3. How much postage is needed for next Monday?
4. How much more postage does the machine need before all of Monday's mail can be sent?
5. The pieces of correspondence are of equal importance. If you wanted to mail as many items as possible without adding postage, which item(s) would you NOT mail on next Monday?

DEMONSTRATING OFFICE SKILLS

1. Using an 8½" × 11" sheet of paper and an ordinary No. 6 envelope, fold the paper as you would a letter and insert it in the envelope.
2. Using three sheets of 8½" × 11" paper and a large No. 10 envelope, fold the three sheets together and insert them in the envelope.
3. Using an 8½" × 11" sheet of paper and a large No. 10 window envelope, fold the sheet and insert it in the envelope. (If you do not have a window envelope, fold the sheet as if it were to be inserted in a window envelope.)
4. Ask one of the employees at your local post office how much it would cost to mail from your town the following:
   a. Parcel post package weighing two pounds — destination is Tampa, Florida.
   b. Registered envelope weighing less than one ounce containing a check for $1,000, return receipt requested — destination is Milwaukee, Wisconsin.
   c. First-class package containing typed reports weighing 10 ounces — destination is Ponca City, Oklahoma.
   d. First-class letter less than one half ounce — destination is Paris, France.

Part 3

Volume Mail

Willie Ramirez had found a summer job between his junior and senior year in high school as an assistant to Ms. Hansen, the director of public relations for a large bank. At three o'clock on the third day of his new job, Mr. Ramirez was asked to address and mail the monthly newsletter by four o'clock. There were over 1,000 names on the mailing list. Mr. Ramirez panicked! Mr. Ramirez had to tell Ms. Hansen that he would not be able to finish that afternoon. Startled, Ms. Hansen asked him why not. Mr. Ramirez said, "There are 1,000 names on this list! I can't type that fast." Ms. Hansen laughed at the expression on Mr. Ramirez's face and said, "Obviously I didn't tell you about our addressograph." Mr. Ramirez was very relieved to find out he didn't have to type 1,000 addresses by four that afternoon.

Aids for Volume Mailing

There are several mailing aids to business firms for use in advertising campaigns and for announcements of new products and services.

Mailing Lists

Many firms keep lists of their customers, prospective customers, subscribers, clients, or others to whom they address mail repeatedly. A firm may use a number of mailing lists for different purposes — for instance, to advertise a new product, to announce a new service, or to initiate a new policy. Special mailing lists of all kinds of prospective buyers, both nationwide and regional, can be purchased. One of your duties may be to develop the mailing list and keep it up to date.

repeatedly:
over and over

initiate:
begin

Mailing Lists on File Cards

Names and addresses for a mailing list are frequently kept on 5″ × 3″ cards that are filed in alphabetic order. These cards may be grouped

stationers:
sellers of office
supplies

under various classifications, such as doctors, druggists, jewelers, and stationers. The different groupings may be indicated by colored tabs, or the cards for each group may be filed in separate drawers or compartments in the card file.

The cards may also be filed by subject — the subject that the prospective customer has been interested in or may be interested in later.

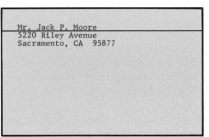
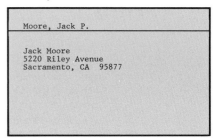

Illus. 9-16

File cards in address style and index style for a mailing list

Up-to-Date Mailing Lists

Unless mailing lists are kept up to date, they soon lose their usefulness. The names on all mailing lists are constantly changing as newcomers move into the sales area and others move out. Additions, deletions, and corrections of names and addresses should be made whenever new information is received. You learn of many of the necessary changes in addresses when mail is returned because of nondelivery.

The post office will assist you in maintaining an up-to-date mailing list. It will make corrections on a mailing list or correct individual addresses if requested to do so. For a small fee it will also supply the ZIP Codes for an entire mailing list.

Chain Feeding of Envelopes for a Mailing List

If a mailing list is used infrequently, the names and addresses on the list are usually typed individually on the envelopes. A chain feeding method of inserting and addressing the envelopes will save a great deal of time when typing from the list. The basic steps in the widely used *front-feed* method follow:

1. Stack the envelopes *face down*, with the flaps toward you, at the side of the typewriter.
2. Address the first envelope; then roll it back (toward you) until a half inch shows above the alignment scale.
3. Insert the next envelope from the front, placing it between the first envelope and the cylinder.

4. Turn the cylinder back to remove the first envelope and to position the second one. Continue the "chain" by feeding all envelopes from the front of the cylinder.
5. The envelopes will stack up in order at the back of the cylinder. Remove them after about every sixth envelope is typed.

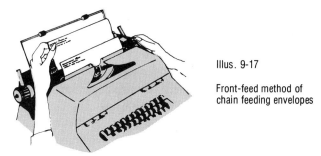

Illus. 9-17

Front-feed method of chain feeding envelopes

The steps in the *back-feed* method are:

1. Stack the envelopes *face up* at the left side of the typewriter.
2. Insert the first envelope to typing position; place a second envelope behind the cylinder in the "feed" position.
3. Address the first envelope. As you twirl the first envelope out of the machine with the right hand, feed another envelope in the "feed" position with the left hand.
4. As the first envelope is removed, the second envelope will be moved into typing position. Continue the "chain" by placing a new envelope in the "feed" position each time the addressed envelope is removed.

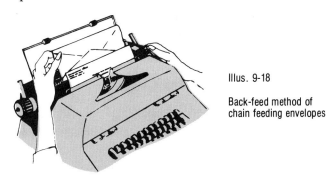

Illus. 9-18

Back-feed method of chain feeding envelopes

Addressing Machines and Addressing Services

You may use an addressing service or, if your office has it, an addressing machine for addressing a large number of envelopes. Because mailing lists are used over and over again, the names and addresses are often stenciled or embossed so that the envelopes can be automatically addressed on an addressing machine. Addressing machines print from metal plates or stencil plates. Some businesses use their computers for addressing large numbers of envelopes.

Metal Plates. Metal plates are often used for addressing envelopes and cards for permanent mailing lists. They may also be used to print the inside addresses on letters or to print names, addresses, numbers, and other identifying information on bank statements, monthly bills, time cards, paychecks, dividend checks, and other business forms. The plates can be coded so that an automatic selecting device can be used as the letters are addressed. Classification tabs can be attached to the address plates of a particular mailing list, and the automatic selector will then select and print only these plates without changing the order of any of the plates in the file.

Illus. 9-19

The metal plate addresser-printer has many uses in volume mailing.

Stencil Plates. Stencil plates can be prepared on a typewriter. When a small attachment is used, the small stencil plates are typed in much the same manner as ordinary stencils. The stencil addressing equipment is not often used to print inside addresses on letters or other material that should give the appearance of having been typed. The plates are useful, however, for mailing lists with frequently changing addresses.

Computer Addressing. Some large firms use their computers for addressing envelopes and cards. The computer can print the addresses directly on the cards and envelopes, or it can print address labels which have an adhesive backing. When adhesive-backed labels are printed, they are then attached to the front of the envelopes.

Presorting Volume Mail

You will get faster delivery of a large volume of important mail if you presort and separate it by the five-digit ZIP Code areas. For ease in handling, mail should be presorted three times:

1. From 0 to 9 according to the first digit of the ZIP Code to route each piece of mail into one of the ten large geographic areas of the country.
2. According to the second and third digits to route the mail into a large post office or designated sectional center within the geographic area.
3. According to the fourth and fifth digits which represent the delivery area or the post office of delivery.

For example, a letter with the ZIP Code 60635 following the mailing address would be routed into the Midwest by 6, the first digit in the ZIP Code; into Chicago by 06, the second and third digits; and into a local

Illus. 9-20

This postage meter machine for heavy volume mail feeds, seals, meter stamps, counts, and stacks 200 envelopes a minute.

Pitney Bowes Corporate Communications

post office in Chicago for delivery by *35*, the fourth and fifth digits in the ZIP Code.

Mail separated by five-digit ZIP Code areas bypasses all state and sectional center sorting operations, and arrives at the delivery area or post office of delivery ready for sorting into the carriers' mail routes.

Traying Volume Mail

You can speed the processing of a large volume of first-class mail through the postal system by switching to trays, modern mail containers recommended by the Postal Service. The trays will be provided by the Postal Service and picked up at your place of business at no cost. However, your mail must be placed in the trays with the addresses and postage faced in one direction. Traying saves valuable processing time and permits the Postal Service to dispatch your mail sooner.

For assistance with presorting or traying volume mail you can call your local post office and ask for either the postmaster or the customer service representative.

REVIEWING IMPORTANT POINTS

1. What steps can you take to be sure your mailing lists are current and correct?
2. List the steps in the front-feed method of addressing envelopes.
3. How should you presort the mail three times?
4. What is the advantage of presorting volume mail by five-digit ZIP Code areas?
5. What is meant by traying volume mail?

MAKING IMPORTANT DECISIONS

Miss Seward is a receptionist for three doctors in a medical building. Any time a patient changes his or her address, Miss Seward makes a note in the margin of the appointment book to save time. During a free moment she transfers the changes of address to the permanent files. After the monthly statements were mailed in June, two were returned to the office stamped "Return to Sender, Address Unknown." Miss Seward was surprised to see the statements because she thought she had transferred all the changes of address to the permanent file. A quick check in the appointment book showed that she had missed two address changes. How would you improve Miss Seward's procedure for keeping the mailing list up to date?

LEARNING TO WORK WITH OTHERS

You have been hired to help with traying volume mail for a large manufacturing company. The mail room supervisor, Ms. Carter, has stressed to you the importance of placing the mail so that the addresses and postage face in one direction in the trays. Kevin Gunn, who has worked in the mail room for over a year, has been assigned to tray with you. Mr. Gunn feels he has been demoted and he tries to finish traying as fast as possible. On Tuesday you find some letters that are turned upside down in the trays. You think that you or Mr. Gunn has made a simple mistake so you position the letters correctly. After a week, you find that you spend much of your time re-traying mispositioned letters. Ms. Carter has started to get complaints from the post office about the envelopes not facing the same direction. You think Ms. Carter holds you responsible for traying incorrectly, but she hasn't mentioned it to you yet.

What should you do?

IMPROVING LANGUAGE SKILLS

1. A few of the more important comma usages are:

   A. To set off a nonrestrictive phrase or subordinate clause. (A phrase or clause is nonrestrictive if the main clause in the sentence expresses a complete thought when the nonrestrictive phrase or clause is omitted.)
   B. To set off phrases or expressions at the beginning of a sentence when they are loosely connected with the rest of the sentence.
   C. To set off parenthetical words, clauses, or phrases.
   D. To set off words and phrases used in apposition.
   E. To separate two or more adjectives if they both precede or follow the noun they modify, provided each adjective modifies the noun alone.

   On a separate sheet of paper type the following sentences and insert commas where needed.

   1. Mr. Reed a sales representative from the West Coast joined us for lunch.
   2. You know of course that our deadline is next week.
   3. The dusty worn-out typewriter was in the attic.
   4. Since she left early she missed the announcement.
   5. For example look at the warehouse.

2. Type the correct spelling of each of the following words used in mailing:

a.	envalopes	envelopes
b.	adressed	addressed
c.	lable	label
d.	dividend	divadend
e.	accurate	acurate
f.	applicable	applicible
g.	bulky	bulkey
h.	mailible	mailable
i.	prescribed	perscribed
j.	underlinning	underlining

IMPROVING ARITHMETIC SKILLS

1. You have received a statement from your local post office for $16.10 for placing ZIP Codes on a volume mailing list. If the post office charges $1.15 per thousand names for this service, how many thousand ZIP Codes were furnished?
2. An envelope has been prepared for each address on the mailing list of 15,000 names. If the postage machine can feed, seal, meter stamps, count, and stack 200 envelopes per minute, how long will it take to finish this set of envelopes?
3. Of the envelopes being sent in Problem 2, 25% are to Vermont, 15% to New Hampshire, 10% to Maine, and the rest to Massachusetts. How many letters were sent to each state?
4. You have been assigned to prepare 600,000 labels for a special sales promotion program. The machine you will use to prepare this mailing will print 1,000 labels a minute. How many hours will it take to complete this job?

DEMONSTRATING OFFICE SKILLS

Using a chain feeding method, address No. 6 or No. 10 envelopes for the following names and address. If envelopes are not available, type the addresses on slips of paper of envelope size. These names and addresses were taken from the classified directory of St. Louis, Missouri.

A-1 Copy-Printing, 36 N. Central Avenue, 63105

Broadway Office Interiors, 2115 Locust Avenue, 63103

Burroughs Business Forms, 8630 Delmar Blvd., 63124

Business Forms and Supply Company, 76 Grasso Plaza, 63123

Business Guidance Corporation, 11960 Westline Industrial Road, 63141

Business Service By Professionals, 9322 Manchester Road, 63119

Clayton Business Service, 1670 South Brentwood Blvd., 63144

Leewood Business Supply Center, 2374 Grissom Drive, 63141

Missouri Envelope Company, 10655 Gateway Blvd., 63132

Moore Business Forms, 1015 Locust Avenue, 63101

Officeplus, 7777 Bonhomme Avenue, 63105

Quality Office Outfitters, 8574 St. Charles Rock Road, 63114

Quill and Ink Office Supplies, 3230 Olive Avenue, 63101

Shaw-Walker Office Furniture, 520 Olive Avenue, 63101

Steelcase Office Furniture, 11902 Lackland Road, 63141

Supreme Filing Systems, 705 Olive Avenue, 63101

Tomkins Printing Company, 922 Pine Avenue, 63101

Typographic Studio, 608 North Skinker Blvd., 63130

When you have finished typing, place the envelopes or slips in ZIP Code order.

Part 4

Air and Surface Shipping

John Larson was recently employed for the summer in the mail department of Northwood Electronics. When he applied for the job, he was told that he would deliver company mail, file literature requests, handle outgoing volume mail, and operate mailing equipment.

The job has become a challenge. John has learned to perform all his duties well. He had never realized how much mail was involved in a company or how important it was to use systematic procedures when handling mail.

"What's the best way to send the package?" your employer may ask. It may be just a small parcel urgently needed by a customer, or it may be a large package of advertising materials. Your employer may consider the speed of delivery to be of much more importance than the cost. Whatever the case may be, you must be familiar with all the available types of ground and air shipping services.

commodities: goods bought and sold

Every business firm uses a number of different shipping services to deliver parcels and to distribute large commodities. As an alert and intelligent office worker, you should be familiar with the advantages of each type of service. You may be required to decide how small parcels should be sent, or you may be called upon to prepare the necessary forms for express and freight shipments by train, plane, truck, or bus. Occasionally you may be asked to prepare the forms for tracing a shipment or for filing a claim for goods damaged in transit.

transit: movement from one place to another

Recent Developments in Shipping

With a great increase in volume, the shipping of goods in the United States and Canada has undergone many rapid changes in the past few years. Trucks have replaced trains for a great deal of shipping across the nation, and shipping by air is becoming widespread.

Improved packaging has also aided the shipping process. Lightweight, theft-proof containers are used in place of heavy wooden crates.

In addition, shipping terminals and airports are equipped with automatic equipment that uses high speed conveyor belts to move packages of all sizes. Railroad terminal yards are equipped with automatic switching equipment and closed-circuit TV to save time and shipping costs.

Methods of Shipping

Goods may be shipped to various points by railway, truck, bus, planes, or by a combination of two or more of these services. Each of these services has its own advantages: some offer faster delivery; some offer a higher degree of safety; some are less expensive; and some are much more convenient for the shipper, for the receiver, or for both. The values of each of these services should be known to the shipper so that the most suitable shipping service can be selected.

Shipping Guides

Where can you look for the information you and your employer need about shipping? There are several guides which are widely used in business offices and which you will find very helpful in selecting the method that is best for each shipment.

The United States Postal Service Manual gives complete information about all classes of mail.

The Express and Parcel Post Comparative Rate Guide gives a complete list of all express stations and the comparative charges between express and parcel post shipments.

Leonard's Guide gives rates and routings for freight, express, and parcel post.

Parcel Post

Also called fourth-class mail, parcel post is a method of transporting goods that is used most often when small items are to be shipped to widely scattered places. Some details of parcel post service are discussed in connection with the classes of mail in Unit 7, Part 2. Parcel post shipments are handled by the United States Postal Service. The cost of sending a package parcel post depends on the weight of the package and the distance it is to travel.

Priority Mail

When speed is important in the delivery of a package, you will probably send the parcel by priority mail. By using this postal service, the delivery time can be greatly reduced. The rates are higher than for ordinary parcel post. Increasingly, priority mail is being used to send merchandise to distant and isolated places. This is especially true for Hawaii and Alaska and other areas when delivery by surface travel would require longer time.

isolated:
alone; far from other places

Express Mail

Designed to meet the demand of business and industry for fast and reliable delivery, express mail is based upon a network of metropolitan areas in the United States and some foreign countries. Anything up to 50 pounds can be sent by express mail. The shipment is insured at no extra charge and is guaranteed delivery within 24 hours. This service receives top priority on the airplane, which means express mail is first to be loaded on the plane. There are five options for pick up and delivery; the options are flexible to meet the sender's schedules.

metropolitan:
relating to a large, important city

Air Express

Air express is the swiftest method of commercial transportation. This service includes shipping by air to all parts of the United States and to most foreign countries. Air express shipments receive special pick-up and delivery service. Almost all types of goods, including machine parts, perishable foods, printed materials, and flowers, are moved by air express. Small packages or shipments may be placed on regular passenger planes. Large or bulky shipments are usually sent by special air freight cargo planes.

perishable:
liable to spoil or decay

Bus Express

Most bus lines throughout the country offer package express service. This is a particularly useful service when destination points are located where there is no airport and when speed of delivery is important. Many points receive same day delivery — many within a few hours — which may be even faster than air service. Frequent and direct bus trips between the cities and the fact that terminals are usually located in business districts account for the speed of handling and delivery.

United Parcel Service

United Parcel Service is a specialized carrier of small packages that weigh no more than 50 pounds. Its rates are competitive with parcel post. The service is provided in all 48 contiguous states plus the island of Oahu in Hawaii.

competitive:
compare with favorably

Illus. 9-21

Businesses depend on the services of specialized carriers of some packages.

United Parcel Service

Truck Transportation

Another shipping service which your employer may use is truck transportation. The truck is the best type of local transportation available. Arrangements can easily be made with a trucking company to make regular calls at your place of business to pick up and deliver goods. Truck transportation is available for long-distance hauls as well. Some long-distance trucking firms offer overnight service to insure prompt delivery.

Railway Freight Service

For shipping bulky articles and goods for which the speed of delivery is less important, railway freight service is often used. Shipping by rail is generally less expensive than shipping by truck or any other method.

Illus. 9-22

Railway freight service, while slower than other methods of shipping, is generally less costly.

Union Pacific Railroad Photo

Packaging

Goods for shipment must be packaged properly if they are to be delivered without damage. It is the responsibility of the shipper to properly package the item for shipment. The item to be shipped, the method of transportation to be used, and the distance to be traveled will determine the type of packaging. The decision on a damage claim is often decided on the basis of how well the goods have been packaged.

Marking Goods for Shipment

Whether goods are shipped by freight, express, parcel post, or some other way, it is important to the prompt movement and proper delivery of shipments that the goods be marked correctly. The rules of the carriers require that the shipper mark each package plainly, legibly, and durably. In marking shipments, the following rules should be observed:

1. The addressee's name, address, and ZIP Code must be shown.
2. The word *From* should precede the name and address of the shipper. This explanation is of great assistance to both the shipper and the carrier if the shipment gets lost, is unclaimed, or is refused by the addressee.
3. Packages containing articles easily broken should be marked *Fragile* or *Handle with Care*. Packages containing merchandise that is perishable, such as fruit, should be marked *Perishable*.

Illus. 9-23

Packaging goods durably and marking them plainly insures prompt delivery.

Unit 9 • Using Mail and Shipping Services

4. Marking should be done with a brush, stencil, crayon, or rubber stamp. If lettered by hand, a bold, clear style of lettering should be used. Labels should be prepared on a typewriter and fastened securely to the packages.

Tracing

It may be necessary to trace a shipment if the goods are not delivered within a reasonable time. All carriers in all **modes** of transportation provide tracing services. Information required to trace a shipment includes:

modes: styles, kinds, or methods

1. Shipper's name and address.
2. Name and address of the person to whom the goods were shipped.
3. Shipping date.
4. Quantity of packages involved.
5. Shipping receipt.
6. Routing used.

Claim for Loss

A claim to the transportation company should be submitted for a total or partial loss if the shipment is not delivered, if it is totally or partially destroyed, or if it is delivered in a damaged condition. Claims for loss are presented by either the shipper or the addressee, depending upon who owns the goods.

REVIEWING IMPORTANT POINTS

1. Name some of the more recent developments in shipping services.
2. What are four methods of shipping?
3. What shipping guides are commonly used in business offices?
4. What factors determine the cost of parcel post?
5. What are the advantages of express mail?
6. What are the advantages of air express?
7. When might bus express be useful?
8. What are some advantages of shipping by truck?
9. What are some of the rules you should follow in marking goods for shipment?
10. What information is needed to trace a shipment?

MAKING IMPORTANT DECISIONS

You received a package containing fragile items. When you opened the box, about half of the contents were broken. Whom should you talk with about replacing the broken items? Who should handle the claim if the package was insured?

LEARNING TO WORK WITH OTHERS

Ms. Fay Little, an executive of a large brokerage firm in New York City, asked her new office assistant, Miss Barbara Weaver, to photocopy the entire folder of a client with a large account. The client had moved to Hawaii, so Miss Weaver was asked to wrap the photocopies and mail them by priority mail to the manager of the firm's branch in Honolulu.

Two weeks later Ms. Little received a telephone call from the manager of the Honolulu branch. She said that the records had not been received. Much to her embarrassment, the client had already called but she could not suggest investments because she had no record of the customer's holdings.

Ms. Little then learned that Miss Weaver had delayed mailing the photocopies because she said that she did not have the time to wrap them. Furthermore, she felt that it was not her job to wrap and mail packages because that was the responsibility of the mail department. When she finally had them ready, she mailed them by ordinary parcel post.

What do you think of Miss Weaver's attitude with regard to the wrapping and mailing of packages? What was wrong with shipping the records by ordinary parcel post? What would you have done?

IMPROVING LANGUAGE SKILLS

Adjectives are used to indicate an increasing or decreasing degree of quality, quantity, or manner. The three degrees of comparison are positive, comparative, and superlative.

Example: *Positive*	*Comparative*	*Superlative*
light	lighter	lightest
useful	more (less) useful	most (least) useful

On a separate sheet of paper list the adjectives in the sentences below and indicate which degree of comparison is used.

1. The typist's work gets better every day.
2. Of all the merchants on Fifth Avenue, Mr. Clay had the prettiest window display.
3. Jane received a fine compliment from her employer because her work in the department was the most efficient.
4. The package was wrapped with less paper than it should have been.
5. The typewriter, the books, the stove, and the produce had to be crated before shipment to either a near or a far destination.
6. He put it in the largest box available.
7. The driver was calm now even though the anger showed on his face.
8. Mr. Nance is the most organized executive in that section.
9. The book that I ordered is on the Best Seller list.
10. The building offered much ventilation, more light than, and the most space of any of the warehouses they examined.

IMPROVING ARITHMETIC SKILLS

1. It takes a shipment 3½ hours to travel from Seattle, Washington, to Boston, Massachusetts, by air. If the shipment left Seattle at 11:15 (Pacific time) what time did it arrive in Boston (Eastern time)?
2. A firm ships 450,000 packages a year as follows:
   25 percent by air express.
   40 percent by truck.
   15 percent by railway freight.
   2 percent by bus.
   The remainder are shipped by parcel post.
   How many packages are shipped by each method? On a separate sheet of paper compute your answers.

DEMONSTRATING OFFICE SKILLS

1. Make a study of the following shipping services available in your community and be prepared to report your findings orally to the class and in writing to your teacher.
   a. Express Mail
   b. Bus Express
   c. United Parcel Service
   d. Truck Service
   e. Railway Freight Service
2. What transportation service would you suggest for shipping the following items from your community:
   a. Two swivel office chairs to a branch office 400 miles away.
   b. The 24 volumes of the *Encyclopaedia Britannica* to a relative 230 miles away.
   c. An overhead projector with a case of transparencies to a rural school 70 miles away.
   d. A portable electric typewriter to a field office 100 miles away.
   e. A 500-pound refrigerator to the company's recreation center 45 miles out of town.
3. Mrs. Koehler, the office manager at Crane, Inc., has become concerned because mailing expenses have increased about 4% in each of the first five months of this year. If costs keep increasing at this rate, mailing expenses would be up 48% by the end of the year. In discussing the problem with you, Mrs. Koehler told you:
   a. Employees send packages by air express to Philadelphia which is only 300 miles away, on Thursdays and Fridays. The packages do not arrive until Monday morning. Parcel post mail, at a less expensive rate, will also arrive on Monday morning.
   b. The company is doing more business than last year. There is no way to avoid the additional expense because of this.
   To identify and correct the problem, she asked you to list the possible reasons for the increase and some ways to keep the costs down. For ideas, check your textbook, your Post Office Customer Services

representative, or office workers you know. Mrs. Koehler suggests
that you and she discuss your findings at lunch tomorrow.

IMPROVING OFFICE SKILLS (Optional)

You work in the main office of a large plastics corporation. Every day
you are responsible for seeing that certain correspondence is mailed out
in time to reach branch offices across the state on certain dates. You
have updated the following outgoing mail schedule and are ready to
type it in final form. Type the schedule in an attractive form on plain
white paper.

OUTGOING MAIL SCHEDULE

Depart Post Office	Destination	Via Flight	Arrive
6:10 AM	Fresno	BL-174	9:50 AM
	Anaheim	~~BL-273~~ CA-132	7:55 AM
	Stockton	"	7:45 AM
	Pasadena	"	9:30 ~~9:25~~ AM
	~~San Francisco~~	~~CA-273~~	~~10:25 AM~~
	Santa Rosa	"	11:05 AM
9:10 AM	Pasadena	~~ST-389~~ BL-180	10:50 AM
	Santa Rosa	CA-283	11:15 ~~11:10~~ AM
	~~San Francisco~~	~~ST-392~~	~~11:55 AM~~
	Fresno	"	11:55 PM
12:55 PM	Stockton	BL-197	2:00 PM
2:30 PM	Fresno	~~CA-234~~ BL-349 2:55	~~3:35~~ PM
	Anaheim	ST-454	4:40 PM
	Pasadena	"	4:55 PM
	San Francisco	~~"~~ CA-127 5:30	~~5:00~~ PM
	Stockton	"	5:05 PM
5:15 PM	San Francisco	CA-384	6:40 PM
	Santa Rosa	ST-234	9:05 PM
	Pasadena	~~BL-233~~ CA-128 10:25	~~10:10~~ PM
	Anaheim	~~BL-224~~ "	11:15 ~~11:21~~ PM
7:30 PM	Anaheim	BL-214	8:40 ~~8:35~~ PM
	Fresno	"	11:30 PM
	Santa Rosa	"	12:00 AM
	Pasadena	CA-441	4:25 ~~4:00~~ AM
8:25 PM	Fresno	~~BL-220~~ ST-211	5:00 AM
	Pasadena	"	6:14 AM
	Stockton	CA-311	7:19 AM

Unit 9 • Using Mail and Shipping Services

UNIT 10

The Office Worker and Data Processing

Part 1. **Processing Data**

Part 2. **The Data Processing Cycle**

Part 3. **Machines for Processing Data**

Part 4. **Electronic Data Processing**

Part 1

Processing Data

Mr. Jim Herrera has been working for a large manufacturing firm for several months. He has been successful in this job because of his desire to learn all he can about the different departments in the firm. At lunch one day he told a friend that he had difficulty understanding data processing and would like to know more about that department. His friend suggested that he attend a course offered by American Data Processing Systems. The course is designed to help office workers understand the principles of data processing. Immediately after lunch Jim called American Data Processing Systems to inquire about the course.

The Office Worker Processes Data

The increasing use of electronic data processing (often abbreviated EDP) equipment in the modern office has changed office procedures and office work. Some of the **routine** tasks usually performed by an office worker are now performed by machines. For example, many companies maintain inventories, make out payrolls, and prepare monthly statements through the use of electronic data processing equipment. This frees the office worker to perform other duties.

As an office worker today, you must be familiar with the **vocabulary** of data processing. You may be directly involved with the data processing department and you should be familiar with the most common words used by the people who work in the data processing department.

You probably will not actually operate electronic data processing computers, although you may operate small electronic calculators. Your job may involve gathering the data to be processed and using the information after it has been processed. This means you must know the many uses of the records and reports that are provided by the data processing department.

routine:
regular and often repetitious

vocabulary:
collection of words and phrases

Illus. 10-1

Data processing plays
an important role in
decision making by
providing useful
information about
business transactions.

What is Business Data Processing?

Data is generally defined as detailed or factual material of any kind. Included in data are facts, figures, letters, words, charts, maps, tables, and other basic elements of information. Data and *information* are used more or less interchangeably. If a distinction is made, data is generally considered to be original figures and facts which may or not have meaning in themselves. Information is the knowledge that grows out of data when it has been processed and analyzed. The goal of *data processing*, then, is to turn raw data into useful information. *Business data processing* means arranging words, numbers, and symbols about business transactions to provide useful information.

Whether you realize it or not, you are constantly processing data mentally. Consider the following situation:

Nan asked Roberta to go to the movie. Before she could decide, Roberta had to consider the following data:

1. The cost of the movie.
2. The length of the movie.
3. The distance from home to the theater.
4. The subject of the movie.
5. What she might do instead of going to the movie.

After analyzing each of the factors, Roberta decided she would go with Nan.

In deciding whether she would or would not go, Roberta was processing data. Although business decisions usually involve other types of matters, the procedures used are similar.

Data by itself is often meaningless. For example, if twenty sales invoices arrived in your office, it would be difficult to know the total dollar amount of sales by simply looking at the twenty separate invoices. The data must be added together to arrive at a total. This adding of numbers is processing data. The report which results from processing the data can be useful to your employer in making decisions about the business.

Data about business transactions is collected, processed, and then reported to provide information. The data needed by a business depends upon many factors, such as the size and type of business. The information needed by the owner of a small service station would not be the same as that needed by an executive in a large steel corporation. The more complex the operation of a firm the more different types of information it needs. The method for processing data will depend on such factors as the amount and kind of data and the time and money available for processing the data.

Some people think that data processing is a recent development. The term *data processing* is new, but the activity is not. The processing of numbers, words, and symbols has progressed from manual methods through stages to sophisticated electronic computer methods.

The Need for Processed Data

derived:
based on; obtained
from

Data is needed for internal use (within the company) and for external use (outside the company). Information **derived** from data is used internally to perform the daily activities of the business and to plan the future of the business.

External information is provided to stockholders (owners of the business), government agencies, unions, customers, suppliers, and creditors. Some data serves several purposes. Payroll records, for example, give internal information for payment of salaries and also external information for financial reports to the government and unions.

Methods of Processing Data

similarities:
likenesses

Data may be processed by manual, mechanical, electronic unit record, or electronic computer means. There are **similarities** among these methods as well as differences.

Processing Data Manually

The human mind was the earliest tool for processing data. When a person hears or sees something, it becomes data stored in the brain. The brain is the processor which performs operations upon the data. The information that results can take the form of the written or spoken word, or both.

Let's say you are asked to process an order. With the manual method of processing data, you would write a sales slip giving data, such as the date, customer's name, customer's address, terms, quantity, and other vital information. Other records such as the invoice, journal entry, ledger, and customer's statement would be copied in handwriting.

It is easy to make errors in routine work, such as copying data from one form to another. The speed and accuracy with which the data is manually processed are comparatively low; and, for large volumes of work, the cost to process each document is relatively high.

comparatively: estimated or judged

Illus. 10-2

Manual means of processing data

Processing Data Mechanically

When the intelligence of the office worker is combined with the speed and accuracy of machines, an efficient system has been created. Office machines, such as calculating machines, typewriters, and bookkeeping machines (see Part 2 of this Unit), are combined to perform operations more quickly than they could be performed manually.

If you were processing a sale by using mechanical means of processing data, you would probably write out the sales slip but you would

The adding machine is one means of processing data mechanically.

perform the calculations with an adding machine. By using a bookkeeping machine, the journal and ledger entries could be posted and the customer's statement prepared. Thus, you would combine your intelligence with the speed and accuracy of machines to form a mechanical data processing system.

Processing Data Electronically

In recent years many mechanical data processing machines have been replaced by electronic machines which cost hardly any more to

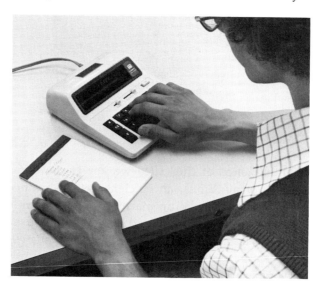

Illus. 10-4

Electronic calculators are more efficient than mechanical machines.

purchase and are more efficient than mechanical machines. For example, electronic calculators multiply and divide automatically, compute rapidly, and many calculator models can store data in memory registers.

Processing Data by Unit Record

In the *unit record* system each individual or unit of record is kept on one punched card. Sometimes it is called a *punched card* system. Sometimes it is called a *tabulating system* because one of the important machines in the system is a tabulator.

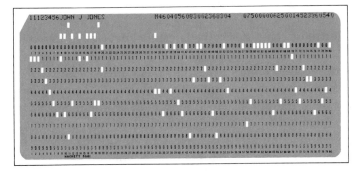

Illus. 10-5

Punched card

Compared with manual and mechanical systems of data processing, unit record equipment handles large volumes of data with greater speed and accuracy at a relatively lower cost. The system consists of the *card punch, verifier, sorter, collator, interpreter, reproducer,* and *tabulator.* Some of these machines are illustrated in Part 3 of this Unit.

Illus. 10-6

Tabulating means of processing data

Ohio National Life Insurance Company

If you processed a sale by this method, you would handwrite or typewrite the sales slip. It would provide the information needed to process the data by the unit record method. The sales slip data would be punched into a punch card and *verified*, or checked, for accuracy. The punched holes convey the information in the form of a code that can be accepted by the card punch machines. The punched cards would be processed by machine to produce the journal entries, ledger entries, and the statement.

Processing Data by Electronic Computer

The electronic computer is the latest tool developed to aid in processing data. For business or government agencies dealing with great numbers of records, none of the previously mentioned data processing methods is fast enough. It is almost impossible to describe a computer's many uses. The computer helped land men on the moon. It is used for arranging class schedules, sorting and routing mail, assisting doctors in **diagnosing** and controlling diseases, printing this book, navigating ships, verifying income tax returns, and keeping airline reservations in order. Part 4 of this Unit will take you through the basic steps of electronic computer processing.

diagnosing: identifying the cause of a condition or problem

Let's say that you are asked to supply a sales slip for the processing of a sale using electronic data processing equipment. You may either

Illus. 10-7

Electronic means of processing data

Unit 10 • The Office Worker and Data Processing

handwrite or type this sales slip. Information from the sales slip is then recorded on media such as punch cards that are processed by the computer. The processing, or arranging, of the data is performed by a list of instructions for the computer called a *program*. Computer programs are sometimes referred to as *software*. The computer consists of several units which will be discussed in Part 4 of this Unit. The computer can prepare the invoice, journal entry, ledger entry, and statement for the customer. It can also store the information for future reference.

REVIEWING IMPORTANT POINTS

1. Define business data processing.
2. What factors determine the method of data processing to be used?
3. Distinguish between internal and external uses of information.
4. Identify the five methods of processing data and briefly explain each.
5. What are the disadvantages of processing data manually?
6. Why is a punched card system in data processing also called a unit record system?
7. What are the advantages of electronic calculators over mechanical machines?
8. Name the five machines that make up the unit record system.
9. What is the latest method of processing data?
10. List five ways in which electronic data processing is used.

MAKING IMPORTANT DECISIONS

1. Paula said, "I don't need to know anything about data processing. I'm a clerk-typist." Do you agree that Paula has no need to know about data processing? Explain.
2. Do you think all businesses should use electronic data processing? Explain why or why not.

LEARNING TO WORK WITH OTHERS

Max and Chris have been friends since Max came to the company three years ago. Both are competent keypunch operators. Chris has been with the company for eight years; however, Max was recently offered a promotion because of his ability to learn quickly. Chris resents Max because he felt that his longer service with the company should qualify him for the promotion. Max would like to accept the promotion, but he does not want to end their friendship. How should Max handle the situation?

IMPROVING LANGUAGE SKILLS

Quotation marks are used:

A. To mark the beginning and end of a direct quotation.
   Example: The speaker said, "People entering business must understand how data is processed."

B. To set off quotations that are a grammatical part of a sentence.
   Example: His letter stated that there are "several languages used in data processing" and that he "intends to master all of them."

C. To set off a specific part of a complete work. (The title of the complete work is put in italics.)
   Example: "Estimating Answers" is a section in the instruction book *Electronic and Mechanical Printing Calculator Course*.

Type the sentences below on a separate sheet of paper and correctly insert the quotation marks.

1. Earlier in the chapter the author states that copies made on an offset duplicator are of a much finer quality than those made on a stencil or fluid duplicator.
2. Since ball point pens have no carbon in their ink, said the salesperson, images made by them cannot be reproduced by the thermal process.
3. Constant Division is the title of a section in the *Electronic Display Calculator Course* book.
4. The teacher told the students that they should always clear the machine before starting the solution to a problem.
5. Under the section Types of Copiers it states the flatbed copier permits you to copy the pages inside of a bound book by placing the page of the book face down on the glass.

IMPROVING ARITHMETIC SKILLS

You are an office employee for Simpson's Wholesale Distributors. Simpson's is a small company and does not have a mechanical or electronic data processing system. All data must be manually processed. As one of your duties you must determine the amount of inventory from data sheets which are prepared by your co-workers.

Figure the total value of the goods in the following partial inventory. Then type the list on a separate sheet of paper, filling in the Amount column.

Item	Quantity	Price	Amount
J12	6 doz.	$2.38 doz.	
K96	19	5.97 ea.	
Z54	7¼ doz.	4.60 ea.	
Q29	56	1.29 ea.	
S31	18 doz.	7.69 doz.	
R63	24	8.44 ea.	
T17	79	2.99 ea.	
B49	11	6.10 ea.	

DEMONSTRATING OFFICE SKILLS

1. Visit a local company that uses electronic data processing and write a report on your visit. Include in your report the advantages and disadvantages of electronic data processing for the firm and your reaction to the employees' acceptance of the system.
2. The following letter was received from a customer complaining about an error made by a computer on the customer's monthly statement.

Ladies and Gentlemen:

Again, I am returning this statement to you because it is incorrect. As I wrote you last month, I did not purchase the clock-radio charged to me August 5; yet it has not been subtracted from my account.

Will you please straighten out your computer? I will pay my bill as soon as this correction is made.

Sincerely yours,

Herman Jackson

Herman Jackson

You check the records and discover that an error was made by the sales clerk when writing the account number on the sales slip so the computer charged the clock-radio to the wrong account. Using a letterhead from the *Supplies Inventory* or plain paper, write a letter explaining the situation to Mr. Jackson at 1011 Hudson Avenue, Cheyenne, WY 82001. Then answers these questions:
a. Was the error the computer's fault?
b. How does an error like this affect customer relations?
c. What can be done to prevent errors like this from happening again?

Part 2

The Data Processing Cycle

Sylvia Stercz decided that she needed a part-time job for extra spending money while she attended college. She saw an ad on the school's help-wanted bulletin board for a part-time keypunch operator, no experience necessary. Sylvia was hesitant to apply for the job because she knew very little about data processing. However, when she went to the interview she was pleasantly surprised. The department manager told Sylvia that data processing is basically a series of steps to be followed. The manager outlined these steps for her. She explained that as a keypunch operator Sylvia would be arranging data for input into the computer system. Sylvia soon learned all about operating a keypunch machine and how her work fit into the data processing cycle.

The Data Processing Cycle

Before a final report is prepared, the data to be used in the report must follow a series of steps called the data processing cycle. Regardless of the method used, the steps in the data processing cycle are: (1) origin, (2) input, (3) processing, and (4) output.

Step 1 — Origin of Data

Origin means the beginning or start of something. In business the information to be processed originates in a variety of business papers. The business papers used to record data for the first time are called *source documents*. For example, when you go to a store to buy a stereo on a charge account, the sales clerk fills out a sales slip with your name and address, telephone number, description of the item you bought, and the price. This information written on the sales slip is the origin of data about your purchase of the stereo. The sales slip is the source document. Other source documents may include invoices, time cards, or checks.

Step 2 — Input of Data

The data recorded for processing is called *input*. The input of the data from the source document is recorded in such a form that it can be easily manipulated, or processed. If the information is to be processed man ually, this step may involve putting the information about the sale in a sales journal so that the store can get a total sales figure for the month. If the information is to be processed by electronic equipment, this step will involve recording the data from the source document onto cards or tapes so that it can be processed on electronic equipment.

Step 3 — Processing of Data

The next step is to actually process the data. This may involve classifying, calculating, or summarizing the data. When you purchased your stereo, the facts and figures concerning the sale were written on a sales slip. The data on the sales slip is processed (added, subtracted, multiplied, divided, or summarized) to provide a monthly bill for you and to provide reports, such as the Monthly Sales Report, that are needed to run the business efficiently. The different machines used to process the data, known as *hardware*, will be discussed in Part 4 of this Unit.

Step 4 — Output of Data

The final step in the data processing cycle provides the output of data. In this step the data that has been processed is organized and arranged in a usable form. The output document may take a variety of

Illus. 10-8

Utility bill in the form of a punched card

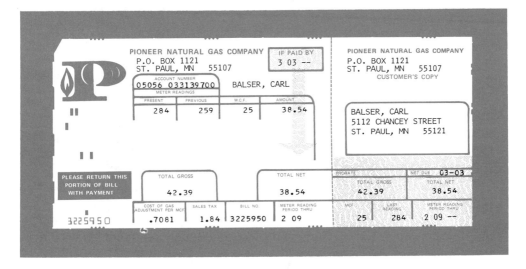

forms. Quite often it is a statement, an invoice, or a report. The output from your purchase of a stereo may include a monthly bill to you and a sales report for the store. When data is processed electronically, the output is often another punched card rather than a written report. You are familiar with the monthly utility bill you receive at your home; it is usually in the form of a punched card. This punched card can be processed automatically when it is returned to the company with payment.

Flowchart Symbols

The steps in the data processing cycle can be shown using a *flowchart*, which is a diagram showing step-by-step how something moves or flows in a business. Flowcharts are used in business because symbols make it easier to **visualize** the processes than words do. Also, flowchart symbols can save time because fewer words have to be used.

visualize:
form a mental image
or picture

Some of the symbols and their meanings are shown below.

Illus. 10-9

Flowchart
symbols

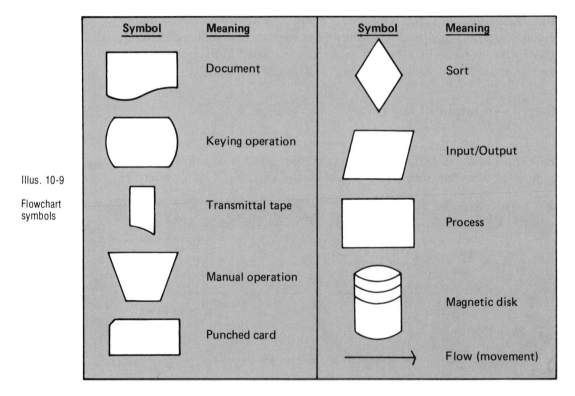

Symbol	Meaning	Symbol	Meaning
	Document		Sort
	Keying operation		Input/Output
	Transmittal tape		Process
	Manual operation		Magnetic disk
	Punched card		Flow (movement)

The record of a sale of a tape deck using a combination of manual, mechanical, unit record, and electronic computer methods would be charted as shown on page 427.

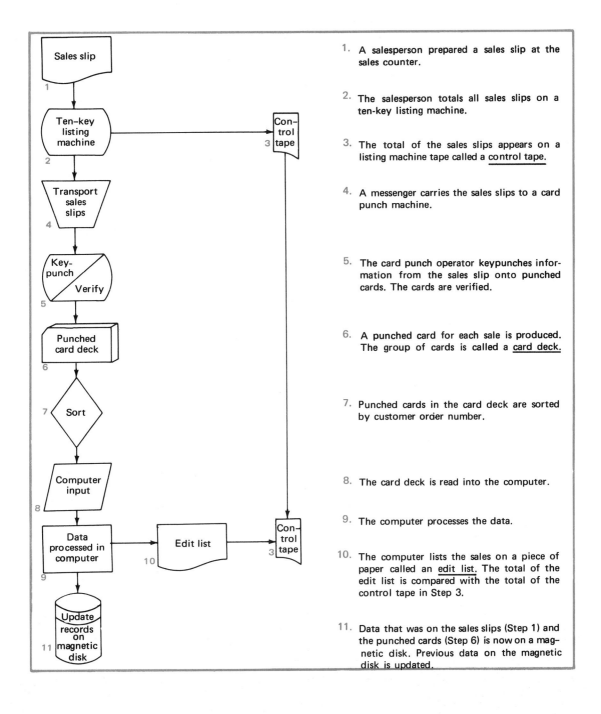

1. A salesperson prepared a sales slip at the sales counter.

2. The salesperson totals all sales slips on a ten-key listing machine.

3. The total of the sales slips appears on a listing machine tape called a control tape.

4. A messenger carries the sales slips to a card punch machine.

5. The card punch operator keypunches information from the sales slip onto punched cards. The cards are verified.

6. A punched card for each sale is produced. The group of cards is called a card deck.

7. Punched cards in the card deck are sorted by customer order number.

8. The card deck is read into the computer.

9. The computer processes the data.

10. The computer lists the sales on a piece of paper called an edit list. The total of the edit list is compared with the total of the control tape in Step 3.

11. Data that was on the sales slips (Step 1) and the punched cards (Step 6) is now on a magnetic disk. Previous data on the magnetic disk is updated.

Illus. 10-10   Record of a sale through various data processing steps

Common Machine Language

unites:
joins together

Data recorded by one machine can be transmitted to and processed by other machines. This process that **unites** the work of data processing machines is sometimes called *integrated data processing* or *IDP*. The processing of data by machines with a minimum of human involvement is called *automation*.

So that one machine can process data from another machine, data must be recorded in a form that can be understood by both machines; this is called *common machine language*. Common machine language takes the form of holes punched in paper or magnetic impulses (invisible electrical signals) on plastic tape similar to the plastic tape on a tape deck. The holes in the paper and the magnetic impulses on the plastic tape represent letters, numbers, or symbols that can be understood and therefore processed by machines.

Machines That Can Read Print

Data represented by holes in punched cards and magnetic impulses on tape can be read by machines, but it cannot be read very well by people. Printed data can be read by people, but until recently it could not be read by machines. This meant that printed data on paper had to be converted to holes in paper or to electrical impulses on plastic tape before it could be understood by machines.

There are machines now, however, that make it unnecessary to convert printed data on paper into another form for the machines to read. *Magnetic ink character recognition (MICR)* and *optical scanning* machines can read printed characters (data). In the MICR method, characters are printed on documents with special magnetic ink that machines can read.

Illus. 10-11

Check with magnetic ink numbers

RACHEL HARTHOUSE
2219 BLANCHARD CIRCLE
BILOXI, MISSISSIPPI • 39530

101

19_____   88-0
          1120

PAY
TO THE
ORDER OF _____ $_____

_____ DOLLARS

FIRST NATIONAL Bank and Trust
GULFPORT, MISSISSIPPI

⑈1120⑈0000⑈   12 345 6⑈

KORB PC

In the optical scanning method, numbers are printed with ordinary ink; but each character has a special shape which can be read by a light beam. The light beam is then converted into electrical impulses on magnetic tape or in printed form on other documents. Some optical scanning machines can even read handwritten numbers.

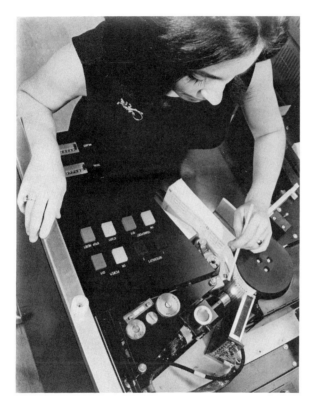

Illus. 10-12

Optical scanning machine

REVIEWING IMPORTANT POINTS

1. What are the four basic steps in the data processing cycle?
2. Define and give an example of a *source document*.
3. What does input consist of?
4. What does manipulating the data mean?
5. Processing data may involve three steps. List them.
6. What is the final step of the data processing cycle?
7. Name three forms that an output document can take.
8. What is a flowchart?
9. Why are flowchart symbols used in business?
10. What do magnetic ink character recognition and optical scanning machines do?

MAKING IMPORTANT DECISIONS

You often hear the statement, "People are being replaced by machines." Do you think electronic data processing will ever completely take the place of people in the business world? Explain why or why not.

LEARNING TO WORK WITH OTHERS

You are a clerk in the collection department of the Masterson Company, which employs about 250 people. To better understand job requirements for hiring new workers, the Personnel Office has asked for one volunteer from each department to flowchart the work activities of the various jobs performed in that department. A co-worker volunteers you for the task in your department without asking you first. How should you handle this situation? Should you confront your co-worker or just go ahead and do the work and hope that it won't happen again? State reasons to support your decision.

IMPROVING LANGUAGE SKILLS

A preposition connects a noun or a pronoun with some other element of the sentence and shows the relationship between them. Some often misused prepositions are *in, into, between,* and *among.* Study how each of these words should be used and then type the correct preposition for each of the phrases below on a separate sheet of paper.

> *in* — used after a verb expressing the idea of rest or, in some cases, motion within a certain place.
>
> *into* — used after a verb that indicates the motion of a person or a thing from one place to another.
>
> *between* — used only in reference to two persons or objects
>
> *among* — used only in reference to three or more persons or objects

1. to distinguish _____ the two steps (between, among)
2. to walk _____ a dark room (in, into)
3. to divide the bonus _____ us three (between, among)
4. to keep money _____ the vault (in, into)
5. to work _____ the data processing department (in, into)
6. a discussion _____ the group of managers (between, among)
7. to go _____ the computer rental business (in, into)
8. a talk _____ father and daughter (between, among)
9. to choose _____ the four of them (between, among)
10. to cross from one country _____ another (in, into)

IMPROVING ARITHMETIC SKILLS

You work for Johnson's Hardware. Mr. Johnson always takes advantage of any discount for prompt payment offered by his suppliers. Mr. Johnson has asked you to figure the amount he must pay on the invoices he received today. The steps in determining this amount can be flowcharted as follows:

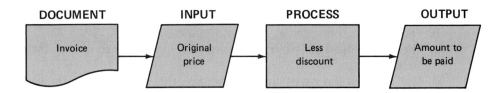

DOCUMENT	INPUT	PROCESS	OUTPUT
Invoice	Original price	Less discount	Amount to be paid

How much would Mr. Johnson pay on these invoices?

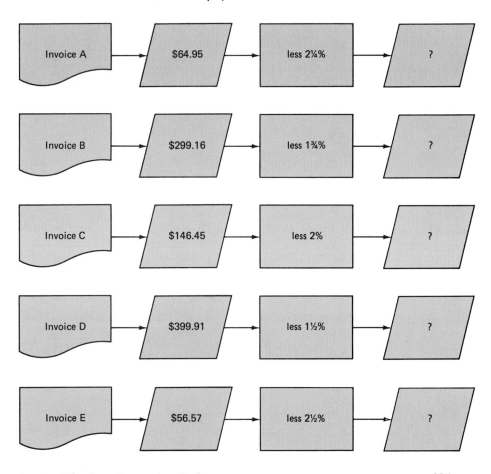

Invoice A	$64.95	less 2¼%	?
Invoice B	$299.16	less 1¾%	?
Invoice C	$146.45	less 2%	?
Invoice D	$399.91	less 1½%	?
Invoice E	$56.57	less 2½%	?

DEMONSTRATING OFFICE SKILLS

1. Your employer would like to learn more about MICR and optical scanning equipment. On plain paper prepare a report which briefly covers the following points:
   a. How each works.
   b. For what purposes the machines are used.
   c. What businesses use such equipment.
2. Make a flowchart showing the cash sale of a record player. Show the following steps:
   a. The salesperson prepares a sales slip at the sales counter.
   b. The salesperson receives cash from the customer.
   c. The salesperson determines the amount of change to give to the customer.
   d. The salesperson gives the change and the merchandise to the customer.
   e. All sales slips for the day are added on a ten-key listing machine to get the total sales for the day.
   f. The total of the sales slips appears on a listing machine tape called a control tape.

Part 3

Machines for Processing Data

While Bob Willard was working in the payroll department, two of the latest data processing machines available were installed. The machines came with manuals to help each person learn to operate them correctly. The sales representative, however, suggested that one person in the department be taught everything about the machines. Bob was chosen to receive instructions. After three days he had learned proper operation and care of the data processing machines. He was also given some valuable time-saving hints for efficient use of the machines.

In the course of your work, you may have to check columns of figures, discounts, or percentages for a report or a letter. It may also be your responsibility, in a small office, to handle payrolls for several departments, sales analyses, financial statements, and expense reports. These business records contain many calculations that can be easily and accurately produced with the aid of an office machine. Computing and recording machines have been installed in modern business offices to handle the ever-increasing volume of paper work. You will frequently work with processed records when you are employed as an office worker, and you should have a clear understanding of how to operate common data processing machines.

Calculating Machines

The amount of work you do on a calculator will depend on the business in which you are working. Some of the duties you may perform using a calculator are checking amounts and figures for payroll, budget, and expense reports.

There are several kinds of calculating machines. Since there are many manufacturers of these machines, there are many different models of each type. Don't let this confuse you. If you know the basic features of each machine and how to operate one model of each type, you will be able to operate other models with a little additional practice. As a comparison, if you know how to drive one model of automobile, with very little practice you can drive another model automobile.

Electronic Calculators

The electronic calculator is the most modern of all the calculators and is replacing many other types of calculating machines. Models are available that will perform every kind of computation that is needed in a business office.

Electronic calculators compute very rapidly because numbers are entered on a keyboard with a touch system, and calculations are made electronically. They multiply and divide automatically; and, because of their computing speed, they are very efficient for multiplication and division problems. Some models can store amounts in separate memory registers until needed later in the calculations.

There are two types of electronic calculators — printing and display. Computations are done electronically on these calculators, but on most machines the printing is mechanical; that is, a wheel or bars strike the paper tape to print answers. Computations of electronic printing calculators are shown on a paper tape so that they can be checked for accuracy against the original document.

Computations for electronic display calculators are shown by lighted figures in a window directly above the keyboard. They are used when a printed record of the calculations on a tape is not needed. Display calculators have no moving parts and are completely silent. Portable, battery-operated models that can be held in one hand are available.

Illus. 10-13   Electronic printing calculator

Illus. 10-14   Electronic display calculator

Illus. 10-15   Portable electronic calculator

Ten-Key Listing Machines

As the name implies, a ten-key machine has only ten figure keys on the keyboard. Ten-key listing machines are used for addition and subtraction. Amounts are entered on the keyboard and printed on the paper tape in the order in which they are read. Each figure key, including the 0, or cipher key, is struck separately. For example, to list $50.60 you would strike the 5, 0, 6, and 0 keys and then strike the motor bar.

Because the machine has only ten figure keys, all within easy reach, you will be able to enter amounts on the keyboard without looking at the keys after a few hours of practice. Touch operation will increase your production rate and greatly reduce your chances of omitting amounts or transposing figures in an amount.

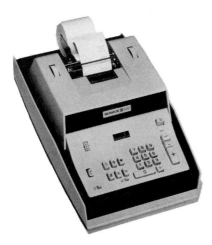

Illus. 10-16

Ten-key listing machine

Mechanical Printing Calculators

Mechanical printing calculators are still found in some offices, but in time they will be replaced with electronic printing calculators. Mechanical printing calculators have ten-figure keyboards and like the other ten-key machines can be operated by touch.

Calculations printed on the tapes can be checked against source documents from which the computations are made. They are all-purpose machines with automatic multiplication and division. Some models have memory storage.

Full-Keyboard Listing Machine

A full-keyboard listing machine (also known as a *full-bank adding machine* has from five to twenty columns of keys ranging in **ascending** order from 1 to 9. There are no 0 keys on the keyboard; zeros are printed automatically. The full-keyboard listing machine is used primarily for addition and subtraction.

Some listing machines have movable carriages which hold statements and ledger cards. If you work in a small company, you will be able to do your billing work on the listing machine itself.

Cash Registers

The cash register is widely used in business to process data. It can be used to record a transaction and also to give a receipt to the customer.

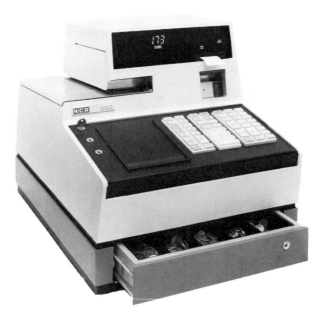

Illus. 10-17

Electronic cash register with audit tape

NCR Corporation

Special cash registers are available that also show the correct change due a customer.

The cash register records all cash sales, charge sales, receipts on account, or paid-out items on an audit tape. At the end of each day, the audit tape is used to determine whether the amount of cash in the cash register drawer agrees with the cash amount on the tape.

audit tape: paper tape on which transactions are recorded

Bookkeeping Machines

Bookkeeping machines are also known as *billing* machines. The main advantages of bookkeeping machines are their ability to tabulate from one position to another and to print at high speeds. Records such as statements, invoices, and checks can be prepared on a bookkeeping machine much more rapidly and accurately than they can be handwritten. Bookkeeping machines can perform addition; subtraction; and, with a special attachment, multiplication and division. They are particularly valuable in preparing repetitious data related to customer billing.

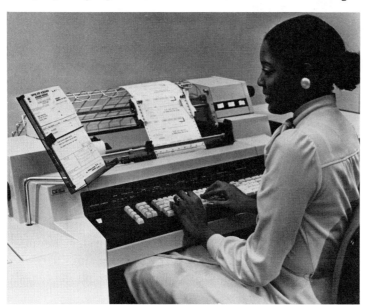

Illus. 10-18

Bookkeeping machine

NCR Corporation

Accounting Machines

These machines work faster and more automatically than bookkeeping machines. They are not, however, as efficient as computers. This machine has a *central processing unit* (sometimes called a *CPU*) that programs the work for the machine to do. The program is stored on paper tape in cabinets beside the machine. The operator sends data into the system using a keyboard similar to a typewriter but having additional keys.

Illus. 10-19

Accounting machine

Unit Record System

As was mentioned in Part 1 of this Unit, the unit record method of processing data is also called the punched card system because data is recorded by punching holes in a card. The five machines used in the unit record system are illustrated here, and a brief description of how they are operated is given.

Card Punch Machine

The purpose of the card punch machine is to transfer data into a card by means of a punched code. The card punch operator reads the source document and strikes keys that punch the appropriate holes in the cards. The holes represent numbers, letters, and symbols. The machine automatically feeds, positions, and ejects each card. The operator must strike the proper keys in the correct sequence.

Illus. 10-20

Card punch machine

Courtesy of International
Business Machines

Verifier

Since accuracy is so essential, card verifying is necessary to check original card punching. A different operator usually verifies the original punching by striking the keys of a verifier while reading from the same source of information used to punch the cards. The verifying machine compares the key struck with the hole already punched in the column on the card. A difference between the two causes the machine to stop.

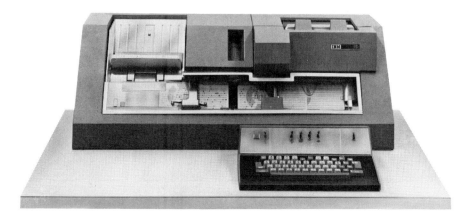

Illus. 10-21

Card Verifer

Courtesy of International
Business Machines

Sorter

Imagine sorting from 800 to 1,000 cards a minute with complete accuracy! This is one of the outstanding advantages of the punched card system. After the punched cards have been verified, they are sorted into numeric or alphabetic order according to the information that has been punched in them. Payroll cards, for example, may be sorted alphabetically according to the last and first names of the employees or numerically according to their time card numbers.

Illus. 10-22

Sorter

Tabulator

After the cards have been sorted, they are fed through a tabulator to transcribe and print automatically the information punched in the cards. The tabulator will print names and other descriptive information from a group of cards, add or subtract punched amounts, and print totals and grand totals only, without listing either the descriptive information or the separate amounts punched into the individual cards. Tabulating machines operate at speeds ranging from 100 to 150 cards a minute depending upon the type of machine used.

Illus. 10-23

Tabulator

Collator

merged:
combined; united;
blended

Sometimes information is required from two or more card files. The cards from the files must be brought together and merged or matched before further processing is possible. A collator is used for this purpose.

A collator can: (1) merge two decks of punched cards in numeric sequence, (2) match the cards from two files having the same numeric data punched in them in a particular field, (3) select from a deck of cards only those cards having a certain number or a series of numbers in a specified field, or (4) check a file of cards to make sure that they are in sequential order.

Illus. 10-24

Collator

REVIEWING IMPORTANT POINTS

1. Under what circumstances might you use calculating machines?
2. Name the two types of electronic calculators.
3. Why is an electronic printing calculator more efficient than a ten-key listing machine or other mechanical calculators?
4. Where do the computations of a display calculator appear?
5. What is one of the chief advantages of a ten-key listing machine?
6. Why use the touch method when entering amounts on the ten-key listing machine?
7. How is the audit tape used to check accuracy in business?
8. What are the main advantages of bookkeeping machines?
9. What do the punched holes in a data card represent?
10. What purpose does the verifer serve?

MAKING IMPORTANT DECISIONS

1. James must find the total for this column of numbers:

$$14.71$$
$$88.33$$
$$6.17$$
$$245.04$$
$$37.53$$
$$\underline{183.78}$$

He should list the numbers and check his answers on a paper tape. Close to his desk are a full-keyboard listing machine and an electronic printing calculator. Which machine should he use? Why?

2. Mr. Thaxton has been an efficient clerk with the Bankacharge Credit Card Company for six years. At 4:45 p.m., Mr. Matthews, his employer, asked him to record a small amount of data on punched cards by closing time at 5 p.m. Mr. Thaxton was positive of his accuracy and by not using the verifier machine he was able to punch the cards for Mr. Mathews by 5 p.m. Mr. Thaxton was proud that he finished the task on time. What do you think about his decision not to use the verifier?

LEARNING TO WORK WITH OTHERS

You have recently been hired as a bookkeeper by the National Building Suppliers. There are four other bookkeepers in the office. Elaine, who has the most seniority, has been asked to assist you in learning how to operate an electronic calculator. Elaine resents having to spend her time teaching you and, as a result, often speaks sharply to you. What can you do to help decrease the tension in this situation? Is a willingness to help others a necessary trait for a good office worker?

IMPROVING LANGUAGE SKILLS

Using the suffixes *able* or *ible*, convert the following words into adjectives. Type both the root word and the adjective.

Examples: *Root Word*   *Adjective*
predict   predictable
defense   defensible

1. accept	6. present
2. conceive	7. knowledge
3. force	8. convert
4. manage	9. verify
5. recognize	10. consider

IMPROVING ARITHMETIC SKILLS

You work in the credit department of Millhouse Fashions. Some of the customer accounts are shown below. The amounts on the left side of the accounts are debits (amounts customers owe). The amounts on the right are credits (amounts customers have paid).

What is the balance (debits less credits) for each account?

Which calculating machine in the office would you use to get the answers? Explain your choice.

a.   M. Caruso   d.   P. Quincy

$425.50	$350.00
75.88	
126.97	

$ 73.50	$ 65.00
81.80	

b.   L. Havenhill   e.   H. Holder

$ 44.35	$ 50.00
91.20	

$ 49.99	$ 49.99
161.17	100.00
34.40	

c.   G. Brombeck   f.   D. Arden

$ 31.29	$ 18.25
57.66	
18.25	

$ 23.00	$ 93.75
54.00	
16.75	

DEMONSTRATING OFFICE SKILLS

1. Write to one or more manufacturers of adding and calculating machines asking for literature on their machines. Use this material for a bulletin board display.
2. If calculating machines are available to you, use one of the machines to do the following problem. If calculating machines are not available, do the problem manually.

   You purchase the following items from the Hobart Office Supply Company:

		Total Due
15 boxes	Fluid Masters @ $3.51	$52.65
7 reams	Duplicating Paper @ $3.19	22.37
3 boxes	Carbon Paper @ $2.72	8.16
4 boxes	Envelopes @ $2.38	9.52
25	Pens @ $.25	6.50
6	Typewriter Ribbons @ $2.20	13.01
		$92.21

a. Carefully check each item to make sure all extensions and totals are correct. On a separate sheet of paper indicate any corrections and the correct total.
b. Hobart Office Supply Company gives you a 2 percent discount if you pay your bill within ten days. What would be the total amount you should pay Hobart Office Supply Company if you paid the bill within the ten days?

Part 4

Electronic Data Processing

Ms. Rennie White had worked as an office assistant at an airline computer center for two years. During this time Ms. White worked with everyone in the department at one time or another. She enjoyed her job and worked hard to learn all about the tasks performed in the center as well as how the computer operated. When a job of assistant night shift operator opened up, Ms. Hoopes, the director of the center, asked Ms. White if she would be interested in training for the job. Ms. Hoopes said that Ms. White's active interest and eagerness to learn about the computer center had prompted the job offer. Ms. White made a good trainee and soon mastered the basics of her new job.

Features of Electronic Computers

The computer plays a vital role in our lives today. The business world needs faster and more accurate information for decision-making. The computer can supply this information because of three main features — speed, accuracy, and storage.

Speed

If you were asked to multiply two 10-digit numbers, say 3,575,212,134 by 2,456,754,137, it would be a difficult task with a pencil and paper. This would be an impossible task if you tried to perform the calculations mentally and to remember the original numbers along with the answer for future reference. Most electronic computers, however, could do this calculation and store the results in a few *nanoseconds* (a nanosecond is equal to one billionth of a second).

Accuracy

Accuracy is very important in all businesses. When large numbers of items are processed, errors are frequently made. When using computers, however, errors can be reduced because the information is verified before it is put into the computer. The computer then follows the same instructions each time without getting tired or bored. Often, human beings become tired and inattentive when doing repetitious work and, as a result, make errors.

Storage

Many different types of data can be stored in a computer until they are needed. Usually the data to be processed and the instructions for processing the data are stored in the computer on magnetic drums, tapes or disks. The computer is able to find this data very quickly when it is needed.

Illus. 10-25

The electronic computer is a highly sophisticated means of processing data.

Courtesy of International Business Machines Corporation

How a Computer Works

unreliable:
not dependable or trustworthy

The human mind is an adaptable but very **unreliable** processor of information. Human beings, however, are needed to handle situations where judgment is required. EDP combines the talents of people who are slow, inaccurate, and intelligent with computers which are fast, accurate, and not intelligent. Combining the advantages of the human mind and the electronic computer gives business an efficient system of providing information for decision making and service to customers.

Computers are associated with the term *electronic data processing* — the processing of records electronically. A typical electronic data processing system uses three groups of linked devices or machines to perform steps in an operation.

Input

Computers are fed data to be processed along with a program that tells the computer how to process the data. The program and data are recorded on different media. The major media are punched paper cards, magnetic plastic tape, and magnetic disks.

Punched Paper Cards. Information can be put into a computer with the same punched cards used in the unit record system described on page 419.

Magnetic Plastic Tape. Just as you cannot see your voice recorded on the plastic tape of a tape deck, you cannot see the magnetic impulses or spots on the plastic tape used for processing data. When you play back a tape recorder, music is produced. When you play back the data processing tape, information in the form of words, numbers, and symbols is printed on paper.

Magnetic Disks. A magnetic disk can be compared with a home phonograph record as a magnetic tape can be compared with a reel of tape on a tape deck. Magnetic disks have an advantage over magnetic tape because the computer can go directly to an item of information and retrieve it without examining all the data on the disk. To retrieve information that is stored on magnetic tape, you must start at the beginning and play the tape through until you locate the desired information. This technique of locating information on magnetic disks is called *random access*.

Data on the media is sent into the computer by input devices and machines that may be located in the same room as the computer. It is also possible to enter data into the computer via machines that are far away from the computer but connected to the computer with electrical wires.

via:
by way of; through

Business is constantly searching for ways to automatically collect accurate data at its source and record it in a common language that can be processed later. This makes it possible to process data accurately and rapidly with the least amount of human effort. For example, to decrease the number of times the same data about a sale must be rewritten, some modern cash registers send sales data, such as the customer's name, the date, the articles purchased, and the price, directly to a computer to which they are connected.

Illus. 10-26

Magnetic tape is one kind of input in electronic computer data processing.

NCR Corporation

Central Processing Unit

The central processing unit (CPU) includes:

1. The *storage section* which stores data, instructions, final results, historical data, master records, and any other information that can be **advantageously** stored within the computer.

advantageously: favorably

2. The *process section* which manipulates the data. Computing — addition, subtraction, multiplication, and division — is performed here.

3. The *control section* which could be called the nerve center of the data processing system. It receives each instruction of the program and analyzes it to determine the operation to be performed. The movement of data into or out of storage is supervised by the control section. It controls the actual execution of the operation. It **monitors** and supervises the flow of data within the system and notifies the operator when attention is required.

monitors: checks; regulates

Output

The output devices are used to take the results of the processing out of the system. Output information can be on a continuous form, called a

Illus 10-27

A central processing unit

Courtesy of International Business Machines Corporation

print-out; on up-dated magnetic tapes or disks, punched paper tape or cards; or displayed on a television-like screen at a terminal unit.

Visual display units are connected directly to a computer close by or many miles away. For example, a branch office in Tucson may not keep a complete set of records on its customers. The sales representative may want to know the type of merchandise that a certain customer ordered

Illus. 10-28

Visual display terminal

Mohawk Data Sciences Corporation

Part 4 • Electronic Data Processing

during the last three months, and this information is stored in the home office computer in Denver.

The operator types into the terminal unit a request for information from the computer. In a few seconds the computer responds by producing the information on the screen of the terminal unit.

By having a knowledge of the ways data can be processed, you are better prepared to perform your job in a modern office whether you work with computer software or printed documents such as payrolls, ledgers, and statements.

REVIEWING IMPORTANT POINTS

1. List three features of an electronic computer system and comment briefly on each.
2. How does the electronic computer provide businesses with a more efficient system?
3. What are the three linked steps in a typical electronic data processing system?
4. What is the function of an input device?
5. List three types of media used to record data.
6. What is the advantage of magnetic disks over magnetic tape?
7. What are the three sections in a CPU?
8. Why is the control section called the nerve center of the data processing system?
9. Output devices are used for what purpose?
10. How can a visual display unit be used?

MAKING IMPORTANT DECISIONS

You have been employed by Henderson Savings & Loan for seven years. You have always been considered a valuable employee. Your employer asks your opinion on whether your company should purchase a computer which uses punched cards for inputs or one which uses magnetic tape. How will you reply? State the reasons for your decision.

LEARNING TO WORK WITH OTHERS

Sam is employed by a machines supply house. One afternoon as he is leaving work he sees Mary carrying a box of office paper to her car. She looks embarrassed when she notices Sam watching her. Then she says, "Oh well, taking home a little paper couldn't hurt a big company like this. Besides, everybody else does it."

How should Sam react? Should he tell the supervisor about the incident? What would you do?

IMPROVING LANGUAGE SKILLS

Numbers can be written as figures or as words. Two very frequent uses of numbers in business are to write amounts of money and dates. Amounts of money, except in legal documents, should be written in figures. Amounts less than one dollar are written in figures with the word *cents* following. In writing even sums of money, the decimal and ciphers are omitted.

Except in formal or legal writing, the day of the month and the year are usually written in figures. You use an *st, d,* or *th* only when the day is written before or is separated from the month.

> We enclose our check for $21.75
> The meeting was held on the 5th and 6th of July.

On a separate sheet of paper rewrite any of the following sentences in which numbers are expressed incorrectly.

1. The cash register showed the total of the purchase was $128.43.
2. The purchase price of the electronic calculator was three hundred twenty dollars and fifty-eight cents.
3. Mr. Hanna had used his ten-key listing machine since the 12 of August, 1973.
4. A roll of paper tape for the ten-key listing machine costs $.89.
5. Although Mrs. Harrison knew the bookkeeping machine was very good, she did not want to pay over $150 for a used machine.
6. Ms. Turner's full-keyboard listing machine had a trade-in value of about $60.00.
7. The business machines dealer said the new calculators would be delivered on the 3 of January.
8. On April seven, 1977, Mr. White purchased a printing calculator for the Accounting Department.
9. Ms. Morris estimated that the electronic display calculator and the ten-key listing machine would cost about $350.00.
10. The Business Machines Conference will be held on the 10th and 11th of October.

IMPROVING ARITHMETIC SKILLS

Your company uses time clocks which operate on the 24-hour system. That is, midnight would be designated 0000, 6 a.m. as 0600, 12 noon as 1200, 3 p.m. as 1500, and 9 p.m. as 2100.

As one of your duties, you are to use the time cards to add and record the exact hours and minutes that each person in your department has worked for the week.

Below are several time cards for you to figure. There are blanks for regular hours and overtime hours. Any time over 40 hours for the week is considered overtime. Figure the hours and minutes on a separate sheet of paper. Show your work.

Employee #1		
	IN	OUT
M	0759	1617
T	0800	1700
W	0830	1749
TH	0731	1650
F	0750	1715
Regular _____		
Overtime _____		

Employee #2		
	IN	OUT
M	1645	0113
T	1753	0301
W	1807	0200
TH	1900	0251
F	1833	0227
Regular _____		
Overtime _____		

Employee #3		
	IN	OUT
M	0000	0800
T	2330	0815
W	2345	0830
TH	0017	0901
F	0022	0930
Regular _____		
Overtime _____		

DEMONSTRATING OFFICE SKILLS

Writing effective letters is an important office skill. Using the letterheads from the *Supplies Inventory* or plain paper, compose and type letters to cover the following situations. Use block form with regular punctuation.

a. You are an assistant to Ralph Sutton, personnel manager at Cline, Inc. He asks you to write a letter for him informing Mr. H. G. Cornell, 3315 East Ada Street, Camden, NJ 48304, that there are no openings in data processing at Cline, Inc., at this time. His name will be kept for consideration for future openings.

b. You are to write a letter to be signed by your employer, Mrs. Helen Bruce. Write to Mr. James Robertson, 504 Southern Place, Carrollton, Georgia 33214, confirming his appointment with Mrs. Bruce on Friday, April 15, at 9 a.m. Ask him to send his notes on the Brown case right away so that Mrs. Bruce can review them before the meeting.

IMPROVING OFFICE SKILLS (Optional)

Visit one or more offices in your community and do the following:

a. Find out what adding and calculating machines are being used.

b. Determine what particular kinds of jobs are being done on the various machines.

c. Request some of the business forms that are used in connection with these jobs.

Prepare a typed report on your visit and attach the forms collected.

11

The Office Worker and Reprographics

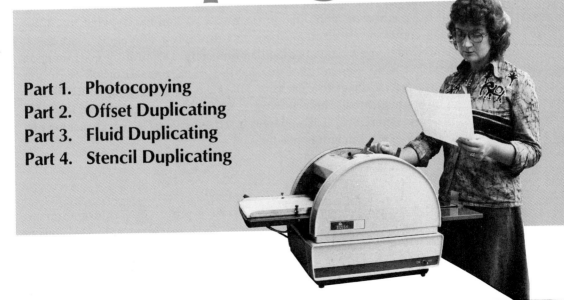

Part 1

Photocopying

Last summer Ron Stewart worked in the Patient Services Department of a hospital. He passed by a room that was called "Reprographic Services." In this large room there were many different kinds of complicated looking machines. These machines were used to duplicate and copy work for all departments of the hospital. Ron never had the time to find out exactly what the machines were and how they were used.

Yesterday Ron's Office Procedures class started the unit on copying and duplicating machines. The teacher had put up illustrations on the bulletin board similar to the machines that Ron saw in the hospital. Ron is pleased to know that he will now learn all about the machines he saw on his job last summer.

Manufacturers are introducing many new types of duplicating and copying machines. Sometimes these machines are combined with each other for greater efficiency. Because of these developments, the word "reprographics" is being used more often to describe duplicating and copying processes.

Both copying and duplicating machines reproduce printed material, but the method of reproduction for each is different. Copying machines make copies of an original document through a photographic process. Hence, this type of copy is called a photocopy. Duplicating machines, on the other hand, depend on a surface-to-surface transfer of ink or carbon from a master sheet to each copy. Because photocopying equipment is more sophisticated, photocopying tends to be more expensive than duplicating. Therefore, it is generally used when just a few copies or just one copy of a document is needed.

Photocopiers

The demand for machines that can rapidly copy information on paper has been growing in recent years. Such machines are called *copiers* or *photocopiers*. In business the machines are also called by the trade names of the companies that manufacture the machines, such as *Xerox* or *Thermo-Fax*. They are now standard equipment in most offices, and you may work in an office that has more than one copier. There may be a floor model which is used when many copies are needed, in addition to a small model on a desk or table near you which you can use to make a few copies quickly.

Features of Photocopiers

Photocopiers have the following features:

1. They can produce exact copies of an original. This can be important when the item to be reproduced is a complicated drawing or illustration.

   complicated:
   complex; having many parts

2. They reproduce small quantities rapidly. It is not necessary to prepare a stencil or a master from the original.
3. They can be used when one or many copies are needed, although combined copier-duplicator equipment will reproduce an unlimited number of copies.
4. They are inexpensive when only a few copies are made from the original.
5. Photocopiers are easy to operate. You simply set the dial for the number of copies desired and insert the original into the machine. The original is scanned by the camera and copied. The copy of the original then passes out of the machine.
6. Some models prepare transparencies that can be projected on a screen. These may be used by your employer to illustrate important points in a business meeting.
7. Some models prepare offset mats, fluid masters, and stencils which are placed on duplicating machines. Many copies can then be reproduced rapidly.
8. Most copiers reproduce only in black. Some copiers will reproduce color but the cost per copy is considerably higher.

Types of Photocopiers

Photocopiers may be the pass-through type or the flatbed type. With the pass-through copier you insert the original in an opening of the copier and rollers pass the original through the copier, ejecting both the original and the copy. With the flat-bed copier, you place the original on a sheet of glass at the top of the copier where it is copied. The flat-bed copier permits you to copy the pages inside a bound book by placing the pages of the book face down on the glass.

ejecting:
throwing out or off from inside

Copying machines prepare copies through different processes, but you will probably use the electrostatic and infrared copiers most frequently in the office.

Electrostatic. There are more electrostatic copiers in offices than any other type of copier. Electrostatic copiers produce dark black copy that can look very much like the original. Corrections, if you make them properly on the original, are not **visible** on the copy.

The electrostatic copier is simple to operate. After turning on the machine, you insert the original in the machine and the copy is automatically ejected within a few seconds. Most models have a feature that permits you to set a control for the number of copies needed. On some models the original must be reinserted for each copy.

You can make copies at the rate of one a second on some machines. You can also make enlargements or reductions on some models during the copying process. This process is frequently called *Xerox*, after the brand name of one of the companies that makes this type of copier.

visible:
able to be seen

Illus. 11-1

Electrostatic copier

Courtesy of International
Business Machines
Corporation

Infrared. An infrared copier requires a special paper. The *image* (material to be copied) must contain carbon, for example, lead pencil and print such as in this book. Since ball point pens have no carbon in their ink, images made by them will not reproduce by this process. The infrared copier will not copy all colors, particularly red, blue, and green. You can prepare offset mats and fluid masters on the infrared copier. An infrared copier can make copies in as little as five seconds. Sometimes this process is called *Thermofax*, after the brand name of a company that first manufactured this type of copier.

To operate this copier, start the machine to warm it up. Place a sheet of special copy paper on top of the original and feed both into the machine. The copy is produced in a few seconds.

Illus 11-2

Infrared copier

Special Uses of Photocopiers

Your employer may sometimes use copiers for answering letters, as shown on page 459. Handwritten notations are made on the original letter and it is then copied. The letter is mailed back to the sender, and the copy is placed in the office files. This saves your employer's time since an answer does not have to be dictated. It also saves your time since a reply letter does not have to be typed. Both the letter and the reply are on one sheet of paper, so filing space is saved as well.

Since this method of answering letters is somewhat informal, it is used when corresponding with persons who know your employer quite well or when the subject of the letter requires an immediate or brief reply.

Photocopiers may be used to make copies of complicated drawings or illustrations that would be difficult to reproduce on a stencil or master. Special kinds of copiers can send and receive printed information

Illus. 11-3

This photocopy equipment can transmit printed information long distances by telephone.

3M Company

through telephones. A telephone receiver is placed in the copier. The original is placed in the sending copier and a light beam scans the dark printed matter on the white paper. The dark print is converted into sound that is sent through telephone wires. At the receiving end, the procedure is reversed and a copy is reproduced.

Photocopiers are frequently used to make copies of letters for cross-referencing.

Collators

Any time you have a duplication job of two pages or more, you must collate it — that is, the pages must be assembled in proper order and fastened into sets. The simplest method of collating is to place the copies of each page in individual stacks on a table, then lift the top page from each stack until a complete set is assembled. This method, however, is both tiring and time-consuming.

Mechanical collating machines are often used in offices where there is a great deal of duplicating and collating. The pages of a duplicated job are stacked in separate compartments of the collator. A rubber-tipped metal rod rests on each stack and pushes a page out of each compartment as the foot control is depressed. The pages are gathered in sets and criss-crossed for stapling or binding after each depression of the foot control.

Richardson
ART SUPPLY 1643 DURRETT AVENUE OMAHA, NE 68109

April 20, 19--

Mr. Robert P. Nelson
Hauser Art Center
15 North Park Blvd.
Bismarck, ND 58501

Your Invoice 79822

Dear Bob

Our Receiving Department just informed me that on March 15 we ordered 25 cases of quarter inch paint brushes on our Purchase Order 472566. On March 21 we received your invoice showing that the paint brushes were shipped on March 18.

Sorry Adam, our error; 10 cases placed on back order

We received 15 cases of the paint brushes on March 29. As yet we have not received the other 10 cases. Will you please let me know immediately if the additional paint brushes were placed on back order or if they were shipped separately?

Also, we need about 250 additional advertising sheets on the pastel chalks for distribution to our customers. Bob, will you please let me know by return mail when we can expect this shipment.

Shipping today by separate package

Thanks.

Sincerely

Adam

Adam Tabler
Manager

gh

Illus. 11-4   Copy of letter with notations

For a great deal of collating, an automatic collator may be used. This machine will automatically collate and staple sets of papers. These collators may be attached to certain models of copiers.

Part 1 • Photocopying   **459**

Illus. 11-5

Collator combined with electrostatic copier.

Xerox Corporation

REVIEWING IMPORTANT POINTS

1. What is reprographics?
2. What are four features of photocopiers?
3. Briefly describe the two types of photocopiers.
4. Which photocopiers are most frequently used in offices?
5. What is one disadvantage of infrared photocopiers?
6. How may photocopiers be used for answering letters?
7. What must you consider before using a copier in answering a letter?
8. What are some special uses of copiers?
9. Define collating.
10. Explain how a mechanical collating machine operates.

MAKING IMPORTANT DECISIONS

Your employer has never told you when to make a carbon copy of correspondence and when to type an original and make a copy of it on the photocopying machine. How do you determine when to use each procedure?

LEARNING TO WORK WITH OTHERS

During the last year, Mr. Randolph, President of Randolph Corporation, was concerned about the huge increase in the number of copies made and the expense of the copying machine. He asked the Administrative Manager, Ms. Mitchell, to find a solution to the problem.

Ms. Mitchell found that employees made more copies than they actually needed, used the copying machine when a duplicator would have been more efficient, and made copies of personal papers.

To overcome the problem, it was decided that everyone, including Mr. Randolph, would bring all work to be copied to you. You would record the date, number of copies, and the person for whom copies were made on a Copy Record sheet. All of the employees, except Mrs. Simpson, the vice-president, follow this procedure very well. Mrs. Simpson strides past your desk directly to the copying machine and makes her own copies. You notice that sometimes she records the information on the Copy Record sheet and sometimes she does not.

At the end of the month you know that the number of copies on the counter of the machine will not be the same as the number of copies on the Copy Record sheet. What should you do?

IMPROVING LANGUAGE SKILLS

The word *get* is one of the most overworked terms in the English language. In the sentences below, substitute a word that will improve the sentence by eliminating the *get* construction. (Do not rewrite or rephrase the sentence.)

1. *Get* a contract form for me, please.
2. *Get* a reservation for me at the Hilton Hotel in Los Angeles for the night of April 13, late arrival.
3. We ought to *get* a new file cabinet to replace the one in Mrs. Anderson's office.
4. The Atlanta office *got* the order we sent.
5. The shipment *got* broken when the clerk dropped it on the floor.
6. He *got* control of the company through purchase of the stock.
7. We must *get* to the meeting immediately.
8. He was surprised to learn he had *gotten* the promotion.
9. The Minneapolis office *got* the award for selling the most policies.
10. She *got* the information, but with great difficulty.

IMPROVING ARITHMETIC SKILLS

Your employer, who is active in a civic organization, has asked you to typewrite a 14-page report and then use the office copier to prepare 9 copies for a meeting. Since this is a report for the civic club, he has asked that you figure the cost of the copy paper so that the club can reimburse your company. The copy paper is priced at $4.80 for a hundred sheets. What will be the cost to the civic club for the paper?

DEMONSTRATING OFFICE SKILLS

1. Assume that the following material is to be reproduced on an office copier. Type the copy in an attractive style on plain paper. Arrange items in descending order with the largest number of shareholders at the top of the list.

PROFILE OF SHAREHOLDERS

This list shows the types of shareholders who own Investment Fund shares and the amount of their holdings as of June 30, 19––.

Men, 3,972, $39,000,000; Women, 9,672, $114,200,000; Joint Accounts, 9,815, $72,500,000; Custodians for Minors, 2,379, $5,400,000; Individual Fiduciaries, 2,123, $24,300,000; Bank Fiduciaries, 205, $5,600,000; Corporate Retirement Accounts, 430, $7,760,000; Self-Employed Retirement Accounts, 1,152, $7,140,000; Union Welfare Funds, 19, $2,190,000; Municipal and State Welfare Funds, 10, $1,250,000; Charities Including Hospitals and Religious Organizations, 190, $5,300,000; Educational Institutions, 121, $2,200,000; Other, 320, $5,100,000.

2. Type a guide copy of the following report to the stockholders of the Wakefield Gypsum Company. Use your best judgment in planning the layout of the guide copy. Correct all errors and make the layout as attractive as possible. The report is to be photocopied.

To the stockholders —

Profits for the first nine months and the third quarter of this year, compared with corresponding periods of last year, were as follows —

	this year		last year	
	Amount	Per share	Amount	Per share
9 months				
Consolidated Companies;				
Profit before income taxes ...	$13,894,371	$4.86	$12,474,298	$4.36
Less United States and Foreign Taxes on Income	7,030,558	2.46	6,405,100	2.24
Profit after income taxes	6,863,813	$2.40	6,069,198	$2.12
Dividends from *Subsidiaries* NOT CONSOLIDATED	$84,725	.03	188,140	.07

3rd Quarter
Consolidated Companies;

Profit before Income Taxes	4,808,157	$1.68	$4,407,167	$1.54
Less United states and foreign Taxes on Income	2,469,175	.86	2,253,296	.79
PROFIT AFTER INCOME TAXES	$2,338,982	$.82	$2,153,871	$.75
Dividends from SUBSIDIARIES NOT CONSOLIDATED	22,887.00	.01	71,199.00	.03
NET Income.........................	$2,361,869	$.83	$2,225,070	.78

Part 2

Offset Duplicating

Phyllis Gregory started her first job the week after she graduated from Central High School. She was confident that her high school training in courses like typing, accounting, office machines, and office procedures had prepared her to be a valuable office employee. When she was asked to prepare the master for a special announcement that was to be duplicated on the offset machine and sent to all the stockholders in the company, she was excited about the assignment. She remembered what she had studied in class about this method of duplication and applied her knowledge to the task.

Phyllis was proud to present an attractive, well-planned offset master to her supervisor for approval. When the copies were returned from the duplicating center, Phyllis showed them to her employer, who complimented her on the quality of her work.

Features of Offset Duplication

Copies made on an offset duplicator are of a much finer quality than those made on a stencil or fluid duplicator. The offset duplicator has the following features:

1. Copies of excellent quality are produced. The copy looks like the type on the page of this book.
2. Thousands of copies can be produced from a master.
3. Cost is moderate for short runs and inexpensive for long runs.
4. Masters are easily prepared, but machine operation is fairly difficult.
5. Copies can be produced in many colors.
6. Many copies can be produced quickly.
7. Copies can be printed on a variety of weights, sizes, colors, and qualities of paper.
8. Illustrations can be reproduced.

Types of Offset Duplicators

One of your office tasks will probably be to prepare offset masters to be used on one of the three major types of offset duplication models.

Table Model. New table model offset duplicators are easy to operate. The operation has been simplified, and secretaries and other office workers can operate the machine.

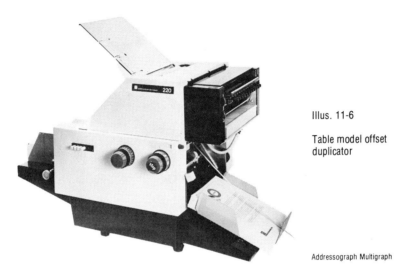

Illus. 11-6

Table model offset duplicator

Addressograph Multigraph

Floor Model. These machines are usually in a central duplicating department and are run by skilled operators.

Illus. 11-7

Floor model offset duplicator

A. B. Dick Company

Continous Copy Model. With this model, originals are fed into a copier which produces an offset master. The master moves on a belt to a machine that processes the master without being touched by the operator. The master is then automatically attached to the cylinder of the offset duplicator, and many copies can be duplicated very rapidly.

Illus. 11-8

Continuous copy model

Addressograph Multigraph
Corporation, Multigraphics
Division

Principles of Offset Duplication

There are three basic methods of preparing masters for use in the offset process.

In the first method, images (typewritten, handwritten, or drawn) are placed directly on the paper master (or "mat") by a special typewriter ribbon, carbon typewriter ribbon, pencil, crayon, or ink. Because of this direct application, the method is called "direct image."

In the second method, an original or layout is prepared on a plain sheet of paper and photographed. The resulting negative is then placed over a **sensitized** master (or "plate") and the plate is "exposed."

sensitized:
made sensitive

substituting:
replacing

In the third method, a master is made by **substituting** special offset sensitized master paper for the regular copy paper in some models of copying machines. The original or layout is processed as a regular original would be copied.

The offset process operates on the principle that "grease and water will not mix." The master is placed on the cylinder and comes in contact with rollers that have ink and water on them. Ink adheres to grease on the master. Water keeps ink from adhering to other parts of the master.

deposited:
put down

A reverse-image results when the ink on the master is **deposited** on a large drum of thick rubber called a "blanket." The ink is then transferred from the blanket to the copy paper being fed through the machine when the impression roller presses the copy paper against the rubber blanket.

Unit 11 • The Office Worker and Reprographics

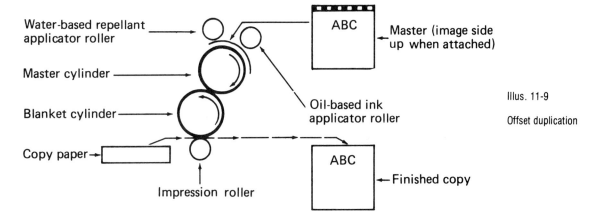

Water-based repellant applicator roller

Master (image side up when attached)

ABC

Master cylinder

Oil-based ink applicator roller

Blanket cylinder

Copy paper

ABC

Finished copy

Impression roller

Illus. 11-9

Offset duplication

Preparing an Offset Master

Preparing a paper master with the use of a typewriter or special writing tools is a simple process. It is outlined in the following paragraphs.

Collect the Supplies

The only supplies needed for typing an offset master are the duplicating master and a soft, nongreasy eraser.

The Offset Master. There are two types of offset duplicating masters — paper masters and metal masters (sometimes referred to as aluminum plates). Short-run, medium-run, and long-run masters may be purchased. Up to 5,000 copies can be obtained from a single long-run paper master, but 25,000 or more copies can be run from an aluminum plate. The short-run paper masters are the least expensive; the aluminum plates are the most expensive.

Since special techniques and supplies are necessary to prepare an aluminum plate, you will probably not work with a metal plate master. The paper master is more common. It is made of a specially treated paper and contains guide marks to help you achieve neatly positioned copies.

Eraser. You will need a very soft, nongreasy eraser to get best results when making corrections on the offset master. You can purchase a special offset eraser or use a soft typing eraser.

Plan the Placement of Materials on the Master

Typing a paper master is very much like typing on regular paper because you don't have to work with carbon (as you do in the fluid process), and you don't have additional sheets that require special care (as you do in the stencil process). Nevertheless, planning how you are going to put the material on the page is very important because you do not want to waste masters. You should try to get the placement right the first time you type it. A special pencil can be purchased that will enable you to write directly on the master as you are planning the layout of the material. The pencil marks will not reproduce when the master is run.

Prepare the Typewriter

When typing an offset master, the typefaces should be clean and the paper bail rollers and platen free of ink smudges. You must use typewriter ribbons of carbon plastic, carbon paper, or special grease fabric because they are **receptive** to the special offset ink.

receptive:
able to accept

Move the paper bail rollers outside the left and right boundary markings on the master to prevent the rollers from smearing the type.

Type the Offset Master

Insert the offset master in the typewriter so that the markings on it face you. Use the markings on the master to guide you as you type. Set the pressure control on an electric typewriter to the lowest position where all characters will print. You should type with a firm, even touch to get an evenly dark image; a touch that is too heavy creates embossing on the **reverse** side of the master and appears as hollow-looking letters on the duplicated copy.

reverse:
opposite; back

Correct Errors

Use a soft, nongreasy eraser or a special offset eraser to make corrections on a paper master. Erase the image very lightly with a *lifting* motion, being careful not to damage the slick finish on the master. It is necessary only to remove the greasy deposit. It is not necessary to remove the ghost image left as this image will not reproduce. Keep the eraser clean by frequently rubbing it on a piece of clean paper.

Proofread

Offset masters are easy to proofread since the copy is clear. Carefully proofread in order to catch every error before removing the master from the typewriter.

Operating an Offset Duplicator

As mentioned earlier, it is relatively easy to type a master to be run on the offset duplicator, but it is difficult to actually run the duplicator. In fact, a skilled operator is needed to run these machines. Your job will probably be to prepare the offset master, and a central duplicating department will do the actual duplicating. However, should your duties involve operating an offset duplicator, you will receive special training on the particular machine you are to run.

Illus. 11-10

Offset duplicating requires the skill of a well-trained operator.

Addressograph-
Multigraph Corporation,
Multigraphics Division

Storing the Offset Master

Storing an offset master is very important because the master can be used many times. Storing it correctly will insure good copies no matter how many times you run it.

Before storing the master, carefully wipe the surface with a ball of cotton containing a special fluid which will remove any ink or grease smudges. Cover the master with a thin coat of gum solution to preserve the typed images. Allow it to dry. Place the master in a file folder and store it in a file cabinet. If several paper masters are stored in one file folder, slip a piece of clean paper between them to prevent small amounts of oil and ink from being transferred from one master to another. If this is not done, when the master is rerun, smudges will appear where the ink and oil were deposited.

Machine Preparation of Masters and Stencils

Placing information on an offset master, fluid master, or stencil is called *imaging*. When you typewrite, write, draw, or rule information on the master or stencil as explained in this unit it is called *direct imaging*.

There are many ways of preparing masters and stencils. As mentioned on page 455, you can insert special masters and stencils instead of copy paper into regular copiers and complete the imaging process.

Image makers, also called *master makers*, that are similar to copiers will prepare masters, stencils, and transparencies. Some machines will make all these items; others will prepare only one or two of them.

Illus. 11-11

A master maker will serve a variety of needs in a busy office.

American Type Founders

An electronic scanner will prepare stencils. The original is wrapped around one half of the cylinder, and the stencil is wrapped around the other half of the cylinder. When the machine is started the original is exactly reproduced on the stencil.

Machine preparation of masters and stencils is faster than direct processing. Also, it completely eliminates the need for proofreading the master or stencil because an exact copy is produced, whether it is an engineer's drawing, a complicated tabulation, a detailed business form, or an interoffice communication.

tandem:
one behind another

For fast production of much duplicated work, the image maker can be connected in **tandem** to an offset duplicator. The originals are fed into the image maker from one side and an offset master is prepared. The master moves on a belt to a machine at the right of the offset duplicator that processes the master without being touched by the operator. The master is then automatically attached to the cylinder of the offset machine where many copies are duplicated very rapidly. The process is sometimes called a continuous total copy system.

REVIEWING IMPORTANT POINTS

1. What are four features of offset duplication?
2. Name the three types of offset duplicators.
3. Describe briefly the three methods of preparing offset masters.
4. The offset process operates on what principle?
5. What are the two types of offset masters?
6. What causes embossing? How does it appear on the duplicated copy?
7. How do you correct errors on an offset master?
8. How do you store an offset master? Why would you store it?
9. Define the term *imaging*.
10. What are two advantages of a machine stencil maker?

MAKING IMPORTANT DECISIONS

The Mansfield Advertising Agency is a small, newly established company. You are employed by the firm as a general office worker. Your employer knows that you have had experience with office machines in your Office Procedures class in high school. Your employer has decided to purchase an offset duplicator for the agency's use and asks for your opinion. Which model would be best for Mansfield Advertising?

LEARNING TO WORK WITH OTHERS

Due to the large amount of duplicating which must be done daily, your company has decided to establish a central duplicating center. You and one of your co-workers have both applied for the job of supervisor of the new center, a position of responsibility which would merit an increase in your salary. You have heard that your co-worker has spread false rumors around the office in an attempt to discredit you and cause you to lose your chance at this job. What action should you take?

IMPROVING LANGUAGE SKILLS

On a sheet of paper, write the plural form for each of these words.

1. copy	6. speech
2. process	7. company
3. desk	8. invoice
4. attorney-at-law	9. ratio
5. opportunity	10. typist

IMPROVING ARITHMETIC SKILLS

On a sheet of paper, complete the following problems.

1. 721
    $\times \; 63$

2. $7{,}678$
    $- \;\; 513$

3. 412
    23
    7
    1029
    18
    712
    $+ \;\;\; 4$

4. $26 \overline{)6942}$

5. $7 \; 2/9 \times 5 \; 4/5$

DEMONSTRATING OFFICE SKILLS

Prepare a guide copy of the following letter and certificate. The material will be duplicated on an offset duplicator. The material should be arranged in such a way that the customer can tear the certificate from the letter to mail in with the order.

Best Products Co., Inc.
4722 South Wayland Road
Indianapolis, Indiana 46227

Dear Customer:

This may be the last catalog we can send you. We have been happy to send you catalogs since you requested your first one. But, in order to keep our prices low, we must keep our costs down. And to do this we have to send catalogs only to those people who buy from us.

We know that you have enjoyed our catalogs and have been pleased with our money-saving prices. Just one order from you will keep you on our mailing list. Because we want to keep you as a customer, we have attached a special certificate that entitles you to a five percent discount on anything you order.

Your first order will show you how easy and economical it is to order from us. Just attach the certificate to your order and claim your discount. It's that simple.

Sincerely yours,

Sales Manager

Special Discount Certificate

This certificate is worth five percent discount on anything in our catalog. Attach this certificate to your order to claim your discount. Please use this certificate within 30 days of its date.

Date:

Part 3

Fluid Duplicating

Miss Marsha Hunt is a typist in the Personnel Department of the main office of Clovis Toy Manufacturing Company. She is frequently asked to prepare materials for duplication. Today, Miss Hunt's employer, Ms. Greenwell, asked Marsha to prepare a colorful, illustrated poster announcing the company bowling tournament. About 25 copies are needed to be placed at various locations in the building. Marsha quickly decided that the fluid duplicator would be best for this job since several colors of carbon can be used to produce the master, and drawing and shading on fluid masters is easy and reproduces well.

Features of Fluid Duplication

You will probably find that the fluid duplicating process is the easiest to learn. When many copies are needed but the quality of the copies is not of great importance, you should probably use a fluid duplicator. Fluid duplication has the following features:

1. It is used when up to 200 copies are needed; although, with a well-typed master and careful operation of the duplicator, as many as 300 copies can be made from a long-run master.
2. Fluid duplication is probably the least expensive duplicating process for about 10 to 30 copies.
3. A master is easy to prepare and the duplicator is easy to operate.
4. Copies are not as attractive as those produced by most other duplicating methods.
5. Several colors can be duplicated.
6. Smooth-finished, glossy paper of any color prints the best.
7. The masters can be saved to be used again.
8. The purple dye from the master soils your hands very easily.
9. Handwriting and artwork can be reproduced easily and quickly.

10. It is used mostly for interoffice communications such as notices of meetings, informal reports, safety rules, and company activities.

Preparing a Fluid Master

The five elements necessary for fluid duplication are a master sheet, carbon sheet, copy paper, fluid, and the fluid duplicator.

A master sheet is attached over the carbon side of a carbon sheet. Pressure on the face of the master with a typewriter or writing instrument deposits a carbon image on the back of the master sheet in reverse image.

The master sheet is placed on the cylinder of the fluid duplicator. As the cylinder rotates, the master comes in contact with a sheet of copy paper which has been moistened with an alcohol-like fluid as the paper enters the duplicator. The fluid causes a very light coating of carbon to transfer from the master sheet to the copy paper.

Illus. 11-12

Fluid duplication

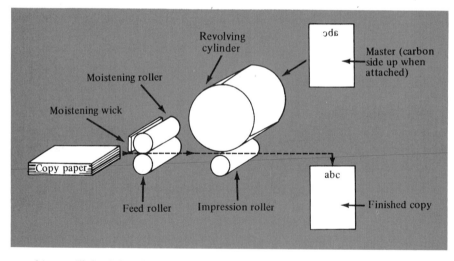

A. B. Dick Company

achieve:
attain; reach

You will find fluid masters easy to prepare, and you will **achieve** the best results by following these steps:

Collect Needed Supplies

The materials you will need to prepare a fluid master are the master itself and a razor blade or knife.

The Master Set. The master set is composed of a sheet of master paper and a sheet of carbon which are fastened together at one end. The master set has a tissue sheet between the master and carbon sheet, which you should remove before you insert the set in your typewriter. Save the tissue sheet to use to protect the master sheet after it has been typed.

Razor Blade. You need a razor blade or knife when correcting errors. When you are typing a fluid master, your typing puts carbon deposits on the back of the master sheet. When you make an error, you have carbon where you do not want it. Use the razor blade to carefully scrape off the unwanted carbon.

Plan the Placement of the Copy of the Master

You will seldom find it necessary to type a guide copy; however, you will have to plan the placement of the material on the master before you begin typing. When planning the placement, you must remember to leave at least one-half inch blank space at the top or bottom of the fluid master. This allows space for the master to be clamped onto the cylinder. (Either end of the master can be attached to the cylinder.)

Prepare the Typewriter

To insure good copies when using the fluid duplication process, you must carefully clean the type faces on the typewriter. Give extra attention to type faces where ink is likely to accumulate, such as *e, a, w, g,* and *o.*

Type the Fluid Master

Remove the tissue sheet from between the master sheet and the carbon sheet before inserting the fluid master in the typewriter. As mentioned before, the carbon sheet and master are fastened together on one end. To aid in correcting any errors you may make, insert the open end of the master set in the typewriter first, with the carbon sheet next to the platen. In this way you can make corrections on the back of the master sheet without first separating the master sheet from the carbon sheet.

If your typewriter does not have a smooth, medium hard platen, place a sheet of heavy paper or thin, **pliant** plastic behind the carbon sheet to serve as a backing sheet.

pliant: flexible

An electric typewriter automatically gives the even pressure needed for typing a master. If you are using a manual typewriter, you will probably obtain better results if you type a little slower than your usual rate. Type with firm, even strokes.

Illus. 11-13

Fluid master in the typewriter

Correct Errors

Because of the position of the materials in the typewriter, typing results in a positive ribbon image on the front of the master sheet which can be proofread. A reverse reading carbon image is formed on the back of the master sheet.

To correct an error on a fluid master, follow these steps:

1. Separate the master sheet from the carbon sheet. Corrections are made on the reverse side of the master sheet. Since you inserted the open end of the master set into the typewriter first, you can simply pull the master sheet toward you; and the reverse side of ihe master sheet, on which you will make your corrections, is exposed.

    The section of the master sheet where you will be making the correction should rest on the flat part of the typewriter or on a flat surface, such as a typewriter shield, that you have placed on top of the typewriter.

2. Lightly scrape off the unwanted carbon with a razor blade or knife, being careful not to make a hole in the master sheet.

3. Fluid carbon paper can be used only once; and at that point where you typed an error, you have already used the carbon. Therefore, you must provide some new carbon before you can type in the correction. You can cut fresh carbon from the unused portion of that carbon sheet, or you can cut a small piece from another carbon sheet that you are using for that purpose. Insert this fresh carbon behind the error with the carbon side

facing the master sheet. Type the correction. Remove the extra carbon slip before resuming your typing.

resuming:
beginning again

Although the method described above is used most often, there are several other ways to correct errors on a fluid master. If you have several lines to delete, you can simply cut them out with a razor blade; or you can cover them with cellophane tape. You can also buy a special adhesive correction tape which has the same surface as the master sheet. To correct an error, place this special tape over it and type the correction. This eliminates the need to scrape off the unwanted carbon.

Proofread

Always proofread and make corrections before removing the fluid master from the typewriter. Even though you have been proofreading as you are typing, reread the entire page.

Remove the Fluid Master from the Typewriter

Disengage the paper release and remove the master, being careful not to wrinkle the master sheet. Cover the carbon side of the master sheet with the tissue sheet to protect it until it is attached to the machine for duplicating.

Prepare Illustrations

You may use a pencil, a ball point pen, or a stylus for drawing illustrations on a fluid master. You will usually save time and get a better copy if you first draw the illustration on bond paper because you can make corrections easily and quickly. Place the drawing on top of the fluid master set and trace the outlines, using an even pressure. A machine master maker (see page 470) is sometimes used to produce the masters, especially when detailed drawings must be copied.

stylus:
a sharply pointed instrument used to write or draw on a stencil

Operating a Fluid Duplicator

In a large office with a separate duplicating department, you would be expected to run off copies only in an emergency. In a small office, however, preparing masters and turning out copies on a fluid duplicator may be one of your duties. Instructions for operating the various makes of fluid duplicators vary slightly, but the following general instructions apply to all makes.

1. *Attach the master.* Clamp the master copy to the cylinder, carbon side up. Take care to insert the master copy across the width of the drum in the slot evenly. This will avoid wrinkling the master. Wrinkle marks will reproduce and ruin the copies. Then hold lightly to the unattached end while you turn the drum one complete revolution.

Illus. 11-14

Turn the drum one complete revolution to test for fluid control, pressure, and margin alignment.

2. *Adjust the fluid control.* This mechanism determines how much the paper being fed into the machine is moistened. The wetter the paper when it comes into contact with the master copy the more carbon is transferred from the master copy to the paper. Therefore, when this mechanism is set on *high*, each individual copy produced will be very dark; but, you will get fewer copies than with a low setting.
3. *Position the copy paper in the feed tray.* Align the sides of the copy paper on the feed tray with the sides of the master copy on the drum. This permits the duplicated copies to have the same margins as the master copy.
4. *Set the pressure control.* This mechanism controls the force with which the moistened paper is pressed against the carbon side of the master copy. When a low setting is used, each moistened sheet will be pressed only *lightly* against the master, resulting in relatively light copies. More copies, even though light in color, can be produced in this manner.
5. *Run the copies.* Both electrically and manually operated machines are available. The speed of the manual machines may be adjusted. The greater the speed the weaker the color

strength of the copies produced and the greater the number of copies possible. Slower speeds give shorter runs with greater color strength.

Storing the Fluid Master

Although the total number of copies a fluid master can produce is limited, fluid masters can be stored and used again. Copies will not be as good, however, if the fluid master is very old and dried out. You should protect the carbon side of the fluid master sheet with the tissue paper that comes with the fluid master set before you store it.

Fluid masters can be placed in a regular file folder and stored in a file cabinet, or they can be laid flat and stored in the fluid master box. They should be protected from the sun and extreme heat to prevent them from drying out.

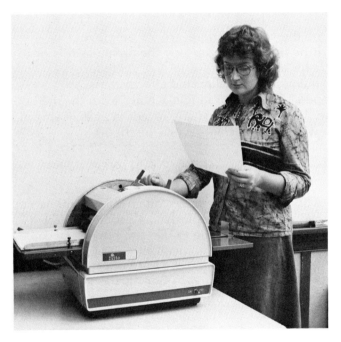

Illus. 11-15

Inspect the first copy and make any adjustments before proceeding to run remaining sheets.

REVIEWING IMPORTANT POINTS

1. What are some of the advantages of fluid duplication?
2. Why is this machine called a "fluid" duplicator?
3. What are the three parts of a master set?
4. When planning placement of material on the master, why should you leave one-half inch blank space at either the top or bottom of the page?

5. What procedures should you follow for preparing the typewriter and typing the master?
6. Describe the method of correction most frequently used on a fluid master.
7. What may happen if the master is not attached properly to the cylinder? What will this do to the copies?
8. Why should you turn the drum one complete revolution before running all the necessary copies?
9. What two machine controls can be adjusted to determine color strength of copies and length of run? Explain.
10. Explain how you would store a fluid master.

MAKING IMPORTANT DECISIONS

1. Your employer found a magazine article that she would like to have reproduced so that each employee can have a copy. The article is two pages and has a colorful diagram explaining the important points of the report. There are 25 employees in the company. Would it be better to photocopy the article as it is or to prepare a fluid master and duplicate it by that method? Make your decision based on time, cost, quality, and effectiveness.
2. Many operators of duplicating machines learn the methods of operation on the job. What then are the advantages, if any, of becoming familiar with these machines while in school?

LEARNING TO WORK WITH OTHERS

Dennis works in an office where much duplication is done. Executives who need a master and copies place a rough draft in a basket with instructions as to which machine to use and how many copies to make. Any worker not busy at the moment gets duplication work from the basket and processes it.

Most of the workers complain about this duty. They claim that the duplication is too messy; consequently, Dennis does more than his share of the duplication work. How should he handle the situation?

IMPROVING LANGUAGE SKILLS

Type the correct spelling of each of the following words:

1. accommodate	acommodate	accomodate
2. accumulate	acumulate	acummulate
3. recievable	recievible	receivable
4. receed	recede	resede
5. annoyance	annoyence	annoiance

6. cecede	seceed	secede
7. exceed	excede	exsede
8. procede	proceed	prosede
9. responsable	responsible	responseble
10. comitte	comittee	committee

IMPROVING ARITHMETIC SKILLS

On a separate sheet of paper show your computations and answers for the following problems:

1. 563 is _____% of 212,739.
2. 45 is 12% of _____.
3. 29% of $951 is _____.
4. .051 = _____%.
5. .31 = _____%.

DEMONSTRATING OFFICE SKILLS

The schedule below is to be prepared on a fluid duplicator for distribution to all company sales representatives. Use the calendar for next month. Set the schedule up on a fluid master and insert the following information under the correct dates. (If fluid masters are not available, use plain paper.)

First Saturday, 7:30 p.m.: Company awards banquet
First and third Monday, 9:30 a.m.: Sales meeting
Second weekend, Friday through Sunday: Chicago sales convention
Each Tuesday: Weekly sales reports are due by 5:00 p.m.
Third Thursday, 10:30 a.m.: Meeting for all sales representatives with the company president
Fourth Wednesday: Deadline for submitting material for monthly newsletter
Last day of the month: Monthly report due by 5:00 p.m.

Part 4

Stencil Duplicating

Mr. Goodwin, director of purchasing for Plains Manufacturing Company, has decided to develop new requisition forms for the company employees. He consulted his assistant, Miss Margie Smithson, and together they planned a concise, adaptable, and simple form to be used in all departments. Since many requisitions are made each week, a large number of duplicated forms must be on hand at all times. Miss Smithson suggested that the forms be prepared by stencil duplication. This method will allow several hundred copies to be run off at a time and the stencil can be stored for future use when the supply runs low.

Features of Stencil Duplication

versatile:
having many uses

Many offices today use stencil duplicating, also called mimeograph duplicating. The stencil duplicator is a very dependable and **versatile** machine. You should know how to prepare stencils and how to operate the duplicator.

Stencil duplication has the following features:

1. Up to 10,000 copies can be produced.
2. Copies are inexpensive for long runs and comparatively expensive for short runs.
3. Compared with fluid duplication, copies are of better quality; compared with offset duplication, copies are poorer quality.
4. Cutting stencils and operating the duplicator are not difficult.
5. Illustrations can be traced onto the stencil or manufactured insets may be purchased and used.
6. Color can be reproduced.
7. Stencils can be stored and used again when more copies of an item are needed. For example, 200 to 300 copies of an inventory form may be run off and the stencil stored until the supply must be **replenished**.

replenished:
filled again; restocked

8. **Absorbent**, rough finished paper of any color makes the best copies.

absorbent:
taking in; spongelike

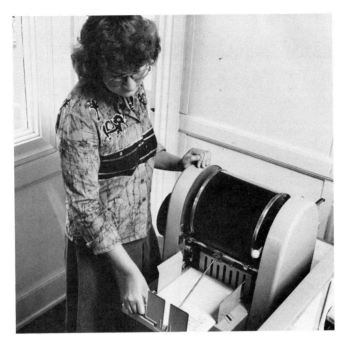

A stencil duplicator is used when many copies are needed.

Preparing a Stencil

A stencil is prepared by pushing aside the wax coating on the stencil sheet with a typewriter key or stylus. (Preparing a stencil with a machine stencil maker is discussed on page 470.) This is called *cutting a stencil* or *stencilization*. When the stencil is placed on the mimeograph machine, ink flows through the openings made by the typewriter keys and forms an impression on the copy paper. To get good copies on a stencil duplicator requires careful planning. The steps for preparing a stencil correctly are discussed on the following pages.

Collect Needed Supplies

The supplies you will need to prepare a stencil are the stencil itself, a burnisher, and stencil correction fluid.

The Stencil. Most stencils have guidelines to aid you in properly placing the material to be duplicated on the page. If you carefully follow the guidelines and numerals on a stencil as illustrated on page 484, your copies will be attractively positioned.

A Burnisher. A *burnisher* is any smooth, rounded object that you can use to lightly rub an error before stencil correction fluid is applied. Special

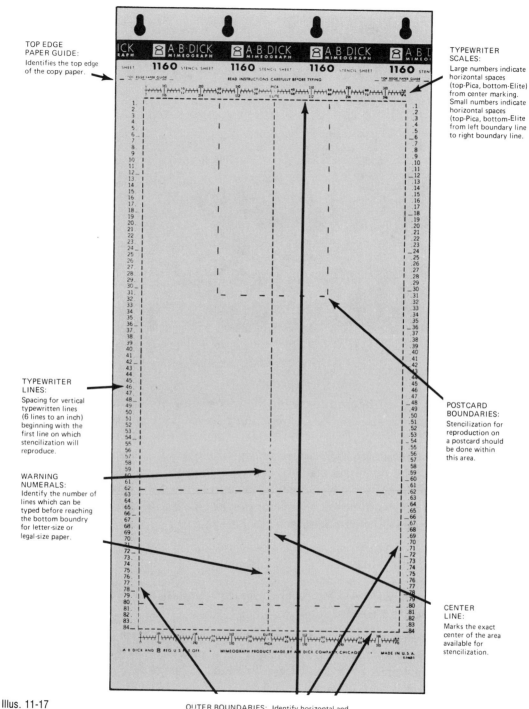

TOP EDGE PAPER GUIDE: Identifies the top edge of the copy paper.

TYPEWRITER SCALES: Large numbers indicate horizontal spaces (top-Pica, bottom-Elite) from center marking. Small numbers indicate horizontal spaces (top-Pica, bottom-Elite from left boundary line to right boundary line.

TYPEWRITER LINES: Spacing for vertical typewritten lines (6 lines to an inch) beginning with the first line on which stencilization will reproduce.

POSTCARD BOUNDARIES: Stencilization for reproduction on a postcard should be done within this area.

WARNING NUMERALS: Identify the number of lines which can be typed before reaching the bottom boundry for letter-size or legal-size paper.

CENTER LINE: Marks the exact center of the area available for stencilization.

OUTER BOUNDARIES: Identify horizontal and vertical area available for stencilization. Nothing typewritten or drawn outside these boundaries will reproduce.

Illus. 11-17

Stencil sheet markings

A. B. Dick Company

burnishers can be purchased; however, the rounded end of a paper clip can be used quite effectively.

Burnishing helps correct the error by smoothing a small amount of the surrounding stencil coating over the error. To insure an unnoticeable correction, you must very carefully burnish each error before applying correction fluid.

Stencil Correction Fluid. To complete the correction process, stencil correction fluid must be applied. Stencil correction fluid is a chemical compound much the same as the stencil coating itself. For a complete discussion on correcting errors on stencils, see pages 487–489.

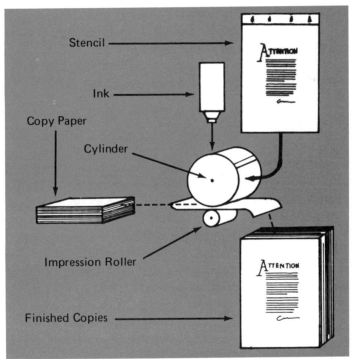

Illus. 11-18

Stencil duplication

A. B. Dick Company

Prepare the Guide Copy

To assure proper positioning on the stencil and on duplicated copies, you should type the material for the stencil on ordinary typing paper first. (Be sure to use the same size paper that will be used to run off the duplicated copies.) Since you will be using the guide copy when you begin typing the stencil, it is very important that you carefully place each item on the page. Stencils are expensive; be sure to get the material placed correctly on the stencil the first time. You will have some leeway because the mimeograph machine can be adjusted to raise or lower the copy on the page, but it will save time if the placement is correct on the stencil itself. As you gain experience in preparing a stencil, usually it will not be necessary to prepare a guide copy unless the job is very difficult.

Prepare the Typewriter

To prepare the typewriter to type a stencil, you should shift the ribbon control to the *stencil* position. This **disengages** the ribbon and allows the typeface to strike the stencil directly.

To get a good *cut* on the stencil, you should always clean the typefaces on the typewriter before beginning to type. A typeface covered with ink deposits from the ribbon will not give a good clear image.

Finally, you should move the paper bail rolls so that they are just outside the markings on the stencil sheet.

Prepare the Stencil

Before inserting the stencil in the typewriter, remove the protective sheet that is usually over the stencil and place the guide copy that you have prepared directly beneath the stencil sheet. Be sure that the top edge of the guide copy is aligned with the paper guide markings on the stencil. Since you can see through the stencil sheet, it is easy to check the position of the guide copy beneath. On the stencil, mark the position of important parts (such as paragraphs and illustrations) of the guide copy with dots of correction fluid so that you will have no trouble in positioning the material when you begin typing. After you have marked the stencil, remove the guide copy and type the stencil from it.

If the stencil assembly you are using has a protective sheet, discard it. This sheet protects the stencil sheet until it is ready for use.

Insert a cushion sheet between the backing sheet and the stencil sheet. If you are using a waxed cushion sheet, insert the cushion sheet with the waxed side up. A tissue cushion sheet may be inserted with either side up since it is the same on both sides. A tissue cushion sheet helps to produce fine-line copy. A waxed cushion sheet helps to produce medium- to bold-line copy.

If the stencil set has a cellophane film, place it on top of the stencil sheet, aligning the bottom edges. Smooth the cellophane film over the stencil sheet. You are now ready to insert the entire stencil set in the typewriter.

Type the Stencil

With the backing sheet next to the platen, carefully roll the stencil set into the typewriter, taking care to avoid wrinkling the stencil. To straighten the stencil, disengage the paper release, match top and bottom right corners and top and bottom left corners of the stencil set, and engage the paper release.

An electric typewriter automatically gives the even pressure needed for typing a stencil. If you use a manual typewriter, however, you will probably obtain better results if you type a little slower than your usual rate. Strike with greater force those letters and special characters that have a large printing surface, such as *M, W, E, A, $, #, &,* and *@,* so that the entire typeface area will cut through the stencil. Strike with less force letters and punctuation marks having small sharp printing surfaces, such as *c* and *o,* the comma, and the period, Notice the difference between a poorly cut stencil and a correctly cut stencil.

```
Dear Vacationers:

    It is about time to start planning for
to work  Yes  the summer recess must end s
letter is to notify you  f the preopening

    We have all of you ha e had g   d vacat
you will share your experiences wi h us  O
seems from the cards we have received that
```

Illus. 11-19

A poorly cut stencil.

```
Dear Vacationers:

    It is about time to start planning for t
to work.  Yes, the summer recess must end so
letter is to notify you of the preopening n

    We hope all of you have had good vacatio
you will share your experiences with us.  On
seems from the cards we have received that
```

Illus. 11-20

A correctly cut stencil

A. B. Dick Company

Correct Errors

Errors should be corrected immediately after they are made to prevent your overlooking them later. To correct an error you should:

1. Lift the paper bail and turn the stencil up several lines so that you can work at the point where the typing error occurred.

2. If you have a cellophane film over the stencil, pull it loose from the top of the stencil set and lay it over the front of the type-writer. The correction must be made on the stencil sheet itself.

3. Lightly rub a rounded object such as a paper clip or a special glass rod burnisher in a circular motion over the error. Burnishing smoothes a small amount of the surrounding stencil coating over the error.

Illus. 11-21

Burnishing to correct an error

4. Apply a thin coat of stencil correction fluid with a single, up-ward stroke for each incorrect character. Stencil correction fluid, after drying, is similar to the stencil coating itself. You are actually covering up the error so that you can recut the correct letter or letters. Replace the brush in the bottle and cap the bottle as quickly as possible to prevent the fluid from becoming dry and thick. Allow 30 to 60 seconds for the fluid to dry.

Illus. 11-22

Replacing stencil coating with correction fluid

5. Roll the stencil back to the typing position and type the correction, using a stroke slightly heavier than normal.

Proofread

Although you have been proofreading as you have been typing, you still must reread the entire page and make any additional corrections before removing the stencil from the typewriter. It is much more difficult to correct an error after the stencil has been removed from the typewriter because you must **realign** the stencil in the typewriter in the same position as it was originally.

realign:
line up again

Before removing the stencil from the typewriter, check to make sure that you have not left out a paragraph. Also be sure you have enough space remaining for any illustrations.

Prepare Illustrations

Drawings and illustrations can be placed on a stencil by using a lighted drawing board and one of several styluses. You can purchase a stylus to draw straight or curved lines, dotted lines, shaded lines, or shaded areas. Several stencil manufacturers also provide booklets or leaflets with cartoons and drawings which you can trace onto a stencil. These drawings are easy to use and make very attractive copies. A machine stencil maker, described on page 470, is sometimes used to prepare stencils, especially when detailed drawings must be copied.

Operating a Stencil Duplicator

Detailed instructions for operation may be obtained from the manufacturer of your machine. Some machines have step-by-step directions mounted on the duplicator. Since these instructions are designed for a particular machine, it is wise to study them carefully before attempting to duplicate copies.

The following is an outline of the general steps involved in duplicating on a stencil machine, regardless of the brand of machine that may be used.

1. *Prepare the stencil.* After the stencil has been cut and proofread, remove the cushion sheet and the cellophane film if one was used.
2. *Attach the stencil.* With the backing sheet up, attach the stencil face down. Tear the backing sheet from the stencil sheet along the perforation. Stretch the stencil sheet carefully around the cylinder.

Illus. 11-23

With the backing
sheet up, attach the
stencil carefully, face
down, around the
cylinder.

3. *Load the copy paper.* Place a supply of copy paper on the feed table. Adjust the left and right paper guides so that the paper fits snugly into the area appropriate to the size paper you are using.

4. *Preparing the receiving tray.* The completed copies drop neatly into the receiving tray. This is particularly important when duplication is necessary on both sides of the paper. Like the feed table, the receiving tray can be adjusted to accommodate various lengths and widths of paper.

5. *Review and follow carefully instructions for inking and counting copies.* Duplicate a trial copy; inspect it to see if the margins are correct. Copy may be raised or lowered by adjusting controls on the machine. Side margins can easily be adjusted by moving the left and right paper guides on the feed tray.

If the copies are too light the duplicator may not be receiving enough ink. If necessary, add ink according to instructions on the machine. Run off a few more copies. If copies are dark enough and evenly inked, run off the entire number needed.

All machines have some mechanism by which copies may be automatically counted as they are run through the machine.

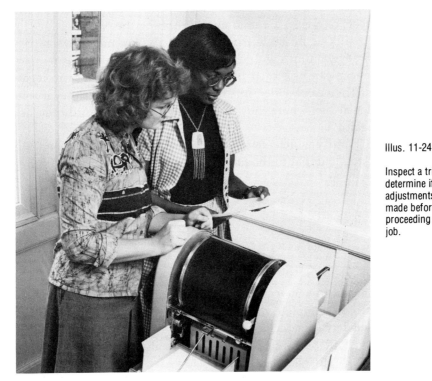

Illus. 11-24

Inspect a trial copy to determine if any adjustments must be made before proceeding with the job.

Some machines register one on the counting device each time a sheet of paper is fed through. When the machine begins to produce the quality desired, the operator sets the counter register at zero and operates the machine until the counter shows that the desired number has been reproduced.

On the other models, it is possible to preset the counting device to the number of copies desired. When that number has been fed through the machine, a bell will sound and the feeding mechanism will automatically stop the flow of paper into the machine.

6. *Remove the stencil.* If the stencil is not to be reused, discard it by placing it inside an old newspaper and depositing it in the wastebasket.

Storing the Stencil

Since up to 10,000 copies can be made from a single stencil and since it is difficult to store large amounts of duplicated copies, a small number of a particular item may be duplicated and the stencil can be saved for reuse when the supply must be replenished.

To prepare a stencil for filing, clean the stencil by placing it between two sheets of newspaper and gently rubbing the entire surface to remove as much ink as possible from the stencil. You may have to repeat this process several times with clean newspaper until all ink is removed.

Stencils can be stored in special stencil wrappers or in legal size file folders. They can be filed in a legal size file cabinet, or they can be placed in a stencil box where they are kept dry and clear until they need to be used again.

To identify which stencil is in a particular folder, attach a copy of the duplicated material to the file folder or write a description of the item on the file folder.

Selecting a Reprographics Process

Many offices have a variety of duplicating and copying machines that are used to complete different types of reprographic work. Sometimes you will have to decide which process to use. Most of the time your decision will be guided by your general knowledge of the process as outlined in the following chart:

USING THE PROPER COPYING AND DUPLICATING PROCESS

Process	Used Primarily For
Electrostatic copier	Quick copies; excellent quality; few copies
Infrared copier	Quick copies; few copies; quality not important
Offset duplicator	Many copies; excellent quality
Electrostatic copier/ offset duplicator	Many or few copies; excellent quality
Stencil	Many copies; good quality; moderate cost
Fluid	Low cost

Sometimes it will take more specific information about the reprographic processes to make a decision. You will then analyze the work to be done more precisely and consider the features of each process described on this chart:

FEATURES OF DUPLICATING AND COPYING PROCESSES

Process	Optimum number of copies in relation to cost	Quality of copies	Comparative labor cost to prepare and run	Comparative cost of equipment	Ease of preparing original/ master/ stencil	Ease of operating machine
Electrostatic	1–10 per original	Excellent	Inexpensive	Expensive	Very easy to moderate	Very easy
Infrared	1–10 per original	Fair	Inexpensive	Moderate	Very easy to moderate	Very easy
Electrostatic Copier/Offset Duplicator	10–many thousands	Excellent	Inexpensive	Very expensive	Very easy	Complicated
Offset	10–many thousands	Excellent	Expensive	Expensive	Moderate	Complicated
Fluid	50–300	Fair to poor	Moderate	Inexpensive	Moderate	Easy
Stencil	50–3,000	Good	Moderate	Moderate	Difficult	Moderate

REVIEWING IMPORTANT POINTS

1. What is another term for a stencil duplicating machine?
2. What are some of the features of stencil duplication?
3. Why is the stencilization process called "cutting a stencil"?
4. What is a burnisher?
5. Give reasons why you should prepare a guide copy when first learning to make a stencil.
6. How do you prepare the typewriter to cut a stencil?
7. Describe how to make a correction on a stencil.
8. What are the main steps in operating a stencil duplicator?
9. What is a stylus used for?
10. Describe the method for storing a stencil.

MAKING IMPORTANT DECISIONS

1. If you had prepared and run off a stencil and the copies were not sharp and clear, how would you decide what could be done to correct the situation?
2. Which typewriter do you think would prepare better stencils — one with pica type or one with elite type? If you think there is a difference, how do you account for it?

LEARNING TO WORK WITH OTHERS

Amy Cook has just been hired by Grant Placement Center. You have been instructed to show Amy around and help her get started on her new job. Amy's duties are typing and filing. After several days, you notice that Amy wastes a large amount of supplies, particularly typing paper, stencils, and masters. She starts over several times on each assignment. What could you do to help both Amy and the firm?

IMPROVING LANGUAGE SKILLS

Semicolons are used to punctuate complex elements in a sentence. Below are two important uses of the semicolon:

A. Between independent clauses in place of a conjunction
   Example: She prepared the stencil; it was then run off on the mimeograph machine.

B. Before a conjunction joining two independent clauses when one clause (or both) has internal punctuation
   Example: She had three stencils to type, four letters to file, and a report to complete; but she completed the work, with time to spare, before her employer left on his trip.

On a separate sheet of paper type the sentences below punctuating them based on the two rules you have reviewed above.

1. The office manager told the new employee that the company used several kinds of duplicating machines depending on the size of the job but he should consult Maxine Smith the supervisor or Joe Camp the assistant supervisor if he was not sure which method to use.
2. There were four stencils that had to be prepared three of which had to be run off that day however Susan had to delay the work because the data processing department did not have the information completed in time.
3. Wayne did all the typing on the stencils however Ed was in charge of the illustrations duplication and lettering.
4. Because of the flood water in the duplicating room it was impossible to do any work there so the company had to send the work out and the employees in the duplicating department helped out in the mail room and shipping department temporarily.
5. We hope to finish duplicating the manuals by five o'clock otherwise we will have to work late to meet the deadline.

IMPROVING ARITHMETIC SKILLS

Figure the total cost for the following supplies you are ordering for your office from the National Office Supply Company.

24 ballpoint pens at 25¢ each
2 pkgs. carbon paper at $6.50 per pkg.
5 boxes paper clips at 40¢ each
2 reams bond paper at $7.50 per ream
2 reams manifold paper at $3.40 per ream
4 bottles correction fluid at $1.00 each

DEMONSTRATING OFFICE SKILLS

1. Prepare a stencil for an Employee Information Roster form to be kept by each department. Include the following information in whatever style and order that you think best: name, address, position, date of employment, date of birth, telephone number, and additional information. If stencils are not available, use plain typing paper.

2. The material shown below is to be reproduced on a stencil duplicator. Type the material in tabular form on a stencil. Rule the form. If stencils are not available, use plain paper.

Comparison of Estimated and Actual Expenses

Last year:

Sales Salaries: Estimated, $7,000.00; Actual, $7,118.00
Office Salaries: Estimated, $7,500.00; Actual, $7,556.00
Delivery Expense: Estimated, $1,600.00; Actual, $1,591.05
Advertising: Estimated, $300.00; Actual, $312.95
Rent: Estimated, $1,500.00; Actual, $1,500.00
Supplies: Estimated, $300.00; Actual, $287.60
Insurance; Estimated, $2,100.00; Actual, $2,100.00
Depreciation: Estimated, $500.00; Actual, $521.16
Miscellaneous: Estimated, $350.00; Actual, $357.35

This year:

Sales Salaries: Estimated, $7,500.00; Actual, $7,439.00
Office Salaries; Estimated, $7,800.00; Actual $7,780.00
Delivery Expense: Estimated, $1,650.00; Actual, $1,612.45
Advertising: Estimated, $350.00; Actual, $365.75
Rent: Estimated, $1,500.00; Actual, $1,500.00
Supplies: Estimated, $350.00; Actual, $342.75

Insurance: Estimated, $2,250.00; Actual, $2,250.00
Depreciation: Estimated, $550.00; Actual, $565.32
Miscellaneous: Estimated, $400.00; Actual, $392.40

IMPROVING OFFICE SKILLS (Optional)

Your company is considering purchasing a copying machine. Your employer has asked you to prepare a one-page report discussing the advantages of having a copying machine and listing any points that should be considered before making such a purchase. Type the report on plain white paper.

UNIT
12

Working with Purchasing and Receiving

Part 1. The Purchasing Function
Part 2. Office Procedures for
Purchasing and Receiving

Part 1

The Purchasing Function

Stan Whaler works as a purchasing clerk in a large electrical products manufacturing firm in suburban Philadelphia. During the year, the purchasing agent and the staff purchase more than $25 million worth of raw materials, equipment, and services. Mr. Whaler's job is varied, but all tasks are related to efficient, prompt ordering of needed materials and follow-up on all orders. Mr. Whaler uses the typewriter for filling in forms and preparing tables. He also aids in maintaining departmental files and in using those files frequently each day. He likes his job very much; he has seen that what he does is an important link in the chain of tasks for which the purchasing agent has responsibility.

crucial:
extremely important

Crucial decisions of a company are made in the purchasing department. In many large companies the persons with responsibility for purchasing also help plan future development of their organizations.

Organization of the Purchasing Function

The purchasing function differs from company to company. The nature of the products or services provided by the organization will influence the manner in which the purchasing function is organized. In a large oil refinery, for example, the purchasing department is primarily concerned with locating large supplies of crude oil for a steady supply. This means that staff are actually located in those parts of the world where there are likely to be sources of oil. On the other hand, a large department store in the center of a city has specialized buyers for the many products they sell. The buyers for the department store attend shows, visit manufacturers in the United States and abroad, and study to improve their buying skills.

The general structure of the organization also affects the nature of the purchasing function. In some companies, the purchasing function is *centralized*, which means all purchasing for the organization is handled from one office. In other organizations, the purchasing function is *decentralized* so that each department makes its own decisions about purchasing. In still other companies, there is a combination of centralized/decentralized purchasing. A vice-president responsible for purchasing made the following comment:

> We find that a combination of centralized/decentralized purchasing works best for us. Some purchases must be made at the branch office where they are needed. Yet, some purchases can be made at the home office. I am responsible for all items that are considered to be of a "corporate nature"; this means that I buy those items that are used by all branches of our company. For example, all office furniture and equipment are purchased through my office. On the other hand, the lumber needed for manufacturing furniture in our North Carolina plant is purchased by a purchasing agent in that plant.

It is important to plan and carry out the purchasing function so that there will always be sufficient materials on hand to meet changing demands. In this way, the operations of a company are not stopped. This requires certain business procedures to be carefully followed.

Purchasing Tasks

A modern purchasing agent and staff, including clerks, typists, and secretaries, are acquainted with procedures that **simplify** their work. If you think about how you purchase an item in your own home town, you know that you must first decide where to look for it. Then you need to compare the various brands of the same item that may be available. The market place for many organizations is the world, so efficient ways of purchasing are extremely important.

simplify: make easier; streamline

Materials Acquisition

Selecting and securing materials that are to be used by a company for manufacturing goods or for selling to the public is an important task. This task is referred to as *materials acquisition*. For example, a candy manufacturer might need supplies of cocoa, sugar, and nuts; a glass manufacturer would look for sand, potash, lime, and cullet (waste glass); a sporting goods store might seek tennis rackets, golf clubs, and baseballs. Office workers help the purchasing agent by preparing purchase orders and letters of inquiry about new sources. Office workers also help by maintaining sources of information about suppliers of materials in catalogs and trade directories.

Catalogs. Catalogs with price lists are available to all business firms interested in purchasing a particular line of products. In addition to stock numbers and descriptions of the products, catalogs usually provide the prices for single and quantity purchases of the specific items.

Trade Directories. Nationally and internationally known products and services are listed in trade directories. These directories list the names, addresses, and telephone numbers of most of the manufacturers and wholesalers of a particular product or service. One widely used type of trade directory is the Yellow Pages of the telephone directory. It lists dealers in alphabetic order under subject headings.

Vendor Evaluation

Persons or sources from whom goods and services are purchased are known as *vendors*. Vendors must be responsible, dependable persons if an organization's work is to proceed on schedule. When companies need new sources of materials, purchasing agents spend a part of their time seeking reliable vendors. Office workers handle the forms, correspondence, and telephone messages that are often required to establish the rating of a prospective vendor.

Illus. 12-1

This purchasing agent examines fabric samples presented by a sales representative for an office furniture company.

Cost Estimation

To buy the best quality at the lowest price is one of the key goals of any purchasing department. Therefore, considerable effort is made to determine the relative costs of materials and services. The purchasing department staff must understand a great deal about each item desired to determine whether the price offered is a fair one. One purchasing agent described a situation in her own office:

> One of our young assistants was offered a quantity of wiping cloths at a price one third lower than what we had been paying. The assistant thought it was a good buy, so he changed suppliers. He later realized that the new supplier charged for replacement wipers. The cost of replacements was high — something he didn't realize when he made the decision to change — and three hours of a clerk's time was required each week to count the wipers, another cost that he had not considered. As a result of the change in suppliers, the year's supply of wipers cost 40 percent more; yet, the decision had been made on the basis of an estimate that was one third *less* than the price we had been paying to our earlier supplier.

Office workers handle figures and prepare reports. Those reports help purchasing agents and their assistants learn exactly how much goods and services will cost the firm.

Receipt of Goods and Services

The purchasing department maintains detailed records of all orders and delivery dates. Often it is necessary to follow up on orders to be sure that the promised delivery schedule is met. Office workers frequently assume responsibility for checking on orders and notifying managers when a particular order needs attention. Each organization has a set of procedures for accepting and checking goods.

Payment for Materials and Services

Before an order for materials or services is submitted, there must be a clear understanding between buyer and vendor of the prices and terms of payment. Purchasing agents have varying arrangements with suppliers depending on the quantity ordered, frequency of orders, and services provided. In some instances contracts are drawn up that give the details of price and shipment dates along with payment requirements. Some standard deductions are common in the purchase of goods and services for business use. These include:

1. *Cash discount.* The seller encourages prompt payment by offering a discount to the purchaser who pays within a short time after receiving the invoice. The discount usually applies up to ten days from the date of the sales invoice, which is usually the date the goods are shipped. The buyer who pays after day 10 (up to day 30) pays the full, or net, amount of the sale. Thus the terms of 2% discount would be expressed as 2/10, net 30. If an invoice of $9,000, dated March 14, with terms of 2/10, net 30, is paid on or before March 24, there would be a discount of $180. If the invoice is not paid within ten days, the full amount of $9,000 would have to be paid within 30 days — on or before April 13.

2. *Quantity Discount.* A buyer often gets a better price for buying in large quantities. For example, file folders may be listed in a catalog at $1.19 per dozen or $12.00 per gross. This means that each folder costs $.0992 if purchased in units of one dozen, or $.0833 if purchased in units of a gross.

gross:
12 dozen or
144 items

	Cost	Cost per Folder
Dozen folders (12)	$ 1.19	$.0992
Gross folders (144)	12.00	.0833

3. *Trade Discount.* Buyers are encouraged to stock a particular manufacturer's line of goods by the offer of trade discounts. Trade discounts are based on the suggested list price, the price printed in the manufacturer's catalog. Sometimes there is a single trade discount; at other times there are two or more discounts, referred to as a *chain discount*. For example, in one catalog the following items were listed:

Fantastic Cleaner No. 1 $11.50 per 100 lbs., less 20%
Detergent Special No. 11 $19.69 per 100 lbs., less 25%
                                       and 10%

$11.50 — Suggested list price
−2.30 — Trade discount ($11.50 × 20% = $2.30)

$ 9.20 — Retailer's cost price

$19.69 — Suggested list price
−4.92 — First discount of 25% ($19.69 × 25% = $4.92)

$14.77
−1.48 — Second discount of 10% ($14.77 × 10% = $1.48)

$13.29 — Retailer's cost price

In those instances where trade discounts are common, list prices generally remain the same for long periods of time; however, trade discounts may change from time to time.

Illus. 12-2

These office workers check bill payments against customer statements using automated equipment.

Service to the Company

In many companies, as noted earlier, some of the purchasing tasks are handled in a decentralized manner. In such instances, the central purchasing department aids in the purchasing tasks throughout the company. The central office may maintain information on sources, including catalogs and directories that are sent out on loan to other offices. The central office may also have up-to-date information on prices and new sources that are not yet included in standard directories. Information about exhibitions and trade shows of particular goods and services is also generally available to others in the firm who seek it.

REVIEWING IMPORTANT POINTS

1. What is the basic responsibility of a purchasing department?
2. How does centralized purchasing differ from decentralized purchasing?
3. What is meant by *materials acquisition*?
4. What tasks do office workers do as part of materials acquisition?
5. Why is vendor evaluation an important activity in many companies?
6. What is meant by *cost estimation*?
7. For what reason is a cash discount allowed?
8. What is a quantity discount?
9. How does a trade discount differ from a quantity discount?
10. What kind of information does a purchasing department provide other departments in an organization?

MAKING IMPORTANT DECISIONS

Frances Sills is a clerk in the purchasing department of a large university. One day a sales representative for classroom furniture comes to the office. Frances is alone in the office as all the others are out either taking a coffee break or attending a staff meeting. The sales representative told Frances that he would like to see the manager about a new line of furniture that he thinks would be appropriate for the new classrooms under construction. Frances is not responsible for making appointments, but everyone in the office knows the manager's schedule, which is on the secretary's desk. What should Frances do?

LEARNING TO WORK WITH OTHERS

Tom Gales works as a receptionist/clerk in the purchasing department of a large manufacturing company. There are many persons coming in and out of the office. Often clerks and secretaries from other offices in the corporation come to borrow catalogs. Although purchases are made through the central purchasing department, the various departments prepare their own requisitions from catalogs that Tom keeps. Tom maintains a record of catalogs taken out of the office so that he knows where they are at all times. One afternoon, Bette Stiles comes in to borrow a catalog. Tom realizes that Bette has borrowed about ten catalogs in the last month and has returned none of them. What do you think Tom should do at this moment?

IMPROVING LANGUAGE SKILLS

The dash indicates a sudden change in the thought or the structure of a sentence. Dashes should not be overused because such overuse tends to be distracting and may fail to communicate clearly the thoughts of the writer. The dash is used:

A. To show a sudden break in thought
   Example: If the stamp machine is empty — by the way, that one belongs to Purchasing — I don't think we can get a refill today.

B. Before a statement, or even a single word, which summarizes a series
   Example: Cash discounts, trade discounts, quantity discounts — all these are common in modern business.

C. In place of commas to show emphasis
   Example: This is the time — without doubt — to do something about the bottleneck in this office.

D. To give special emphasis to an appositive

Example: I want to see Miss Winters — our hard-working, cooperative mailroom supervisor.

Type the following sentences on a separate sheet of paper, inserting dashes where needed.

1. The vice-president for materials acquisition, the purchasing agent, the purchasing clerk these three were all carefully reading the contract when the receptionist came in the office.
2. Can we expect delivery immediately on the day of receipt of order for every part of this long order?
3. This reference book how fortunate we are to have three copies is possibly your best source for the appropriate titles for government officials.
4. Checks, money orders, bank drafts all provide means of making payments safely.
5. The Personal Banking Department made by far the largest contribution to the corporation's overall profits some 12 million dollars underscoring the importance of continued growth in our business.

IMPROVING ARITHMETIC SKILLS

On a separate sheet of paper, show your solutions to the following problems:

1. Determine the net cost for 108 file folders that are listed as $4.15 per dozen, less trade discounts of 30% and 10%.
2. Determine the amount to be paid to a company that has sold your firm a total of $4,500 worth of office furniture. There are trade discounts of 20% and 5% plus a cash discount of 2% for payment within 10 days. Assume that payment is being made within ten days.
3. Determine the cost per unit for an item which has the following quantity discounts.

	Cost per Dozen	Cost per Unit
Purchases in units of 12 dozen	$8.90	_____
Purchases in units of 144 dozen	7.50	_____
Purchases in units of 288 dozen	6.00	_____

DEMONSTRATING OFFICE SKILLS

You are a typist in the purchasing department of a large company. Mr. Chounard, the purchasing agent, is a member of a research committee for a national professional organization. He has prepared in longhand the following table, which he would like you to type up in good form.

Participation in General Management Functions
Compared to Prior Periods
(Questions 4, 6, 8)

Amount of Responsibility	Type of General Management Function	
	New Product Development	Long Range Planning
More	32%	46%
Less	4	4
Same	63	57
No Reply	1	3

Part 2

Office Procedures for Purchasing and Receiving

Miss Lilly Dasko began working as a clerk/typist in Golden Card Corporation's purchasing department when she graduated from high school six months ago. Her work is varied and so it allows her to learn much about the business in which she works. She determines prices for items, types orders, files, and deals with vendors. She knows that every detail must be accurate, so she gives full attention to her work each day.

As you become acquainted with some of the standard procedures in business, you will find that procedures tend to simplify office work so that it can be done with speed and accuracy. Office workers in departments other than purchasing often need to know about purchasing procedures, because they prepare purchase requisitions from time to time.

Purchasing Procedures

Procedures are organized so that one step follows another step in a logical order. Purchasing usually follows this procedure:

1. Requesting the goods, supplies, or services needed.
2. Obtaining price quotations and shipping information.
3. Handling orders.
4. Following-up on orders.

Requesting the Goods, Supplies, or Services Needed

Heads of the various departments in a company have the authority to request the purchase of goods and services that are necessary for their departments. To request a purchase, it is necessary to complete a *purchase requisition* form.

A *purchase requisition* provides space for the information needed by the purchasing department to order the desired goods or services. The information includes the name of the item or service, its catalog number, size, color, and quantity desired.

Generally two copies of a purchase requisiton are prepared. The original is sent to the purchasing department; the duplicate is maintained in the files of the department placing the order. Before the purchase requisition is sent to the purchasing department, it must be approved by the person in the department who has authority to make purchases, generally the head. There are times when a third copy of the purchase requisition is needed for the accounting department.

Illus. 12-3

Purchase requisition

Office Wholesale Distributors

400 Commerce Avenue   Des Moines, IA 50302   Area Code 515 376-9872

		Deliver To.:	Display Room	
Requisition No.:	21101	Location:	1 Floor	
Date Issued:	August 28, 19--	Job No.:	432-17	
Date Required:	September 30, 19--	Approved By:	B.E.L.	

Quantity	Description	Unit Price	Amount
100	Plastic interlocking letter trays #8658	2.39	239.00
24	Desk lamps, flourescent light #332C	35.95	862.50
6	Office desks #114D	124.60	747.60
18	Horizontal metal files, 4 slots #527Y	12.20	219.60
			2,069.00

J. W. Hopkins

Obtaining Price Quotations and Shipping Information

When a purchase requisition reaches the purchasing department, the quotation file is checked for prices. Purchasing departments maintain a quotation file of the latest prices for the products that they buy, together with the names and addresses of the suppliers that furnish them. The quotation file is usually made up of 6" × 4" cards on which information about the products and their prices is recorded. The product will probably be ordered immediately if the latest prices are on file. If the latest prices are not available in the quotation file, it is customary to send a *request for quotation* to the business firms that sell the product. The purchasing agent decides which companies are most likely to furnish the product by referring to a catalog file, to the *Thomas Register of American Manufacturers*, or to a similar general purchasing directory.

The request for quotation contains the name of the firm making the request, the current date, a description of the product, the quantity needed, and desired delivery date. To avoid any confusion on the part of the seller, the form is sometimes marked THIS IS NOT AN ORDER! in all capital letters.

Handling Orders

There are several ways of handling orders based on purchase requisitions: by filling in a purchase order, by filling out and mailing an order blank, by placing an order with a sales representative, by writing an order letter, by telephoning, and by sending a telegram. Business firms generally use purchase orders which they mail to the vendors. If the products are needed immediately, they are often ordered by telephone or telegraph; then a purchase order covering the transaction is prepared and mailed to the vendor or seller to serve as written confirmation of the order.

PURCHASE ORDER

Office Wholesale Distributors
400 Commerce Avenue   Des Moines, IA 50302   Area Code 515 376-9872

To: McMillan Manufacturing, Inc.
       305 East Hampton Road
       Ladue, IA 52251

Date: August 29, 19--

Order No.:   06138

Ship By: Truck

Terms: 2/10 net 30

Quantity	Descriptions	Cat. No.	Unit Price	Amount
100	Plastic interlocking letter trays	865S	2.39	239.00
24	Desk lamps, fluorescent light	332C	35.95	862.80
6	Office desks	114D	124.60	747.60
18	Horizontal metal files, 4 slots	527Y	12.20	219.60
				2,069.00

By *S. L. Brooks*

Illus. 12-4

Purchase order

The purchase orders bears the name, address, and telephone number of the firm issuing the order, the date the product is needed or the delivery schedule, the name and address of the vendor, the purchase order number, the quantity, the description of the items with their catalog numbers, the size of the items, the color, the price, the total amount of the purchase order, and the shipping instructions. Normally several copies of every purchase order are needed. Purchase order forms are made with carbon sheets between them so that all copies are made with one typing. After the copies have been signed by the purchasing agent, they are usually distributed in this manner:

Copy	Is Routed to:
Original	The vendor
Copy 1	The purchasing department to serve as a follow-up on the purchase order
Copy 2	The department from which the requisition came
Copy 3	The accounting department
Copy 4	The receiving clerk

Following-up Orders

confirmation: acknowledgement

Companies have established procedures for handling orders which include an immediate confirmation when an order is received. The confirmation generally states when the goods or services will be delivered. Often the purchaser has indicated when receipt is desired. The vendor, in the confirmation, states if that date can be honored.

Purchasing departments maintain a well-organized follow-up file of copies of purchase orders, usually according to the date of their expected delivery. This file is checked periodically and action is taken if any orders are late in arrival. A follow-up may be a personally dictated letter or a form letter depending on how urgently the shipment is needed. Sometimes a telegram is sent by the purchasing department to indicate the urgent need for a particular shipment. At other times a telephone call or a teletypewriter message to the supplier is used to find out why the shipment has not been made and when it may be expected.

Receiving Procedures

All purchases should be handled in a series of orderly steps when they arrive. These steps include the receiving, checking, recording, identifying, and storing of the goods.

Receiving

A complete and accurate record should be made of all incoming shipments as soon as they are received. When goods arrive at the receiving point, the receiving clerk should examine the unopened cartons, packages, boxes, or barrels very carefully. The receiving clerk should count the packages, inspect the condition of each, and see that the number and condition of the packages are recorded in the delivery receipt book. After the delivery receipt has been signed, a copy should be kept in case a claim for loss or damage should arise.

Checking

The receiving clerk next checks the goods received against a copy of the purchase order. If the check of the goods actually received does not agree with the quantities listed on the purchase order, the differences are brought to the attention of the purchasing agent. The receiving clerk also notes any items received in damaged condition. The purchasing agent will then inform the supplier of any differences in quantity or of any damaged goods.

When the merchandise has been shipped, the vendor usually mails an invoice to the purchasing department on the same day. The invoice is known to the vendor as a *sales invoice* and to the purchaser as a *purchase invoice*. An invoice usually includes the current date, the name and address of the vendor, the name and address of the purchaser, the invoice number, the buyer's purchase order number, the terms of payment, and

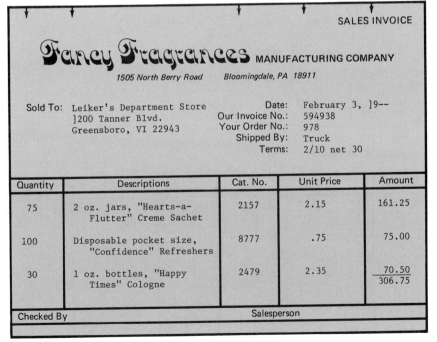

SALES INVOICE

Fancy Fragrances MANUFACTURING COMPANY

1505 North Berry Road   Bloomingdale, PA 18911

Sold To: Leiker's Department Store
]200 Tanner Blvd.
Greensboro, VI 22943

Date: February 3,]9--
Our Invoice No.: 594938
Your Order No.: 978
Shipped By: Truck
Terms: 2/10 net 30

Illus. 12-5

Purchase (sales) invoice

Quantity	Descriptions	Cat. No.	Unit Price	Amount
75	2 oz. jars, "Hearts-a-Flutter" Creme Sachet	2157	2.15	161.25
100	Disposable pocket size, "Confidence" Refreshers	8777	.75	75.00
30	1 oz. bottles, "Happy Times" Cologne	2479	2.35	70.50
				306.75

Checked By	Salesperson

the method of shipment. In addition, for each item it lists the quantity shipped and a brief description of the item with its price and amount. The total amount of the invoice, with the shipping charges included, is usually shown at the bottom of the last column. The invoice may also show trade discounts and other deductions.

If you become a clerk in a purchasing department, it may be your responsibility to check the purchase invoice against the terms and conditions of the purchase order to be sure that they agree in quantity and price. If they agree, the date, amount, and invoice number are entered on the reverse side of the purchasing department's copy of the purchase order. When the invoice is approved by the purchasing department, it is stamped *APPROVED*, initialed by the proper authority, and then sent to the accounting department for payment.

Sometimes goods have to be returned to a supplier for one reason or another. The merchandise may have been delivered too late to be of value; it may be the wrong kind, style, or color; or it may have arrived in a damaged condition. In cases such as these, the goods are returned to the supplier with a letter requesting credit. The supplier then issues a *credit memorandum* to your firm. The credit memorandum lists the items that were returned and the amount by which your firm's account has been reduced.

Illus. 12-6

Credit memorandum

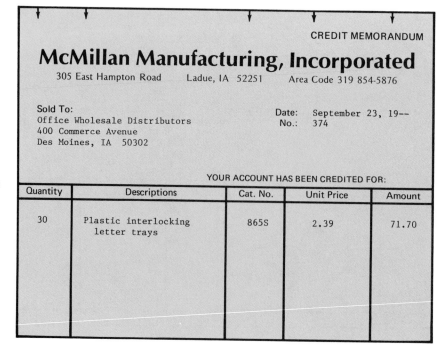

Recording

As the goods are checked, the receiving clerk fills in a *receiving record*. This is a record of the number of items received, the date, the vendor's name, the method of shipment, the transportation charges, and other facts about the receipt of the goods. The receiving record is very important because it is the first record of an incoming shipment. It is useful in determining whether goods have been received and whether they were in perfect condition.

```
                    RECEIVING RECORD
      Date  July 23          197-____      No. 05232
From  Byron Jackson & Co., Chicago, IL 60614
VIA  Truck                    Express Charges  $24.93
Memo _____

|      Quantity       |      Description of Article      |
|---------------------|---------------------------------|
|        35           | 622 spring assembly             |
|        200          | 230 bearings                    |
|        70           | 272 heavy duty relay 50v        |
|        490          | 478 screw sets                  |

                          Received by _____
```

Illus. 12-7

Receiving record

The receiving record is completed accurately and carefully and often is distributed in this way:

Copy	Is Routed to:
Original	The purchasing department
Copy 1	The accounting department
Copy 2	The receiving department to be filed
Copy 3	The stockroom

Identifying

As soon as the shipment has been completely entered in the receiving record, it must be identified. This means that the receiving clerk must assign a receiving number to the entire shipment and must then mark each package in the shipment with that number. The clerk writes on each carton with a crayon or marking pencil the receiving number assigned to the shipment, the department for which the goods are intended, and the number of packages in the entire shipment. For example, the first carton in an eight-carton shipment for the Filing Department, with the assigned receiving number 33, would be marked #33, *Filing Dept., 1 of 8.*

Storing

Often goods received will not be used or needed immediately; so they must be stored properly. Items should be stored as close as possible to the location where they will be used and in such a way that the identifying marks can be read easily.

Ethics

ethics:
standards of right and wrong

The generally accepted business **ethics** of fairness and honesty apply to the actions of all persons in purchasing departments. Large sums of money are often involved in the transactions between purchasing departments and vendors. Vendors are eager to sell, and purchasing agents want to get the "best buy." Professional workers in purchasing departments always consider the interests of their company first and try to carry out its established purchasing policies. To discourage showing favoritism to any vendor and to help insure getting the best buy, many companies prohibit accepting gifts from suppliers.

REVIEWING IMPORTANT POINTS

1. What are the main steps in the standard purchasing procedure?
2. Where do purchase requisitions originate?
3. What is a request for quotation?
4. How may an order be placed?
5. What information is important on a purchase order?
6. To whom are copies of purchase orders generally sent?
7. What are the key steps in the receiving procedure?
8. When is a credit memorandum necessary?

9. What is the purpose of a receiving record?
10. What ethical behavior is expected in the purchasing department?

MAKING IMPORTANT DECISIONS

Ken Howard, who is responsible for purchase requisitions from the various departments of the large construction firm for which he works, received a requisition for a type of flooring not maintained in the regular inventory. There was no price indicated, so he checked the files for the last order of this material. The previous order was received approximately 14 months earlier. Ken noted the price paid at that time and used that price for preparing a purchase order. What do you think of Ken's action?

LEARNING TO WORK WITH OTHERS

Janet Walsh works as a clerk/typist in the advertising department of a large office machines company. She is very busy most of the time and finds that she can save time when filling in purchase requisitions if she merely describes what she needs. She feels that the clerks in the purchasing department have more time than she has. Therefore, they can look up the numbers and sizes of the items needed in the department where she works. She has found that she doesn't always get the ordered items as quickly as she should. She feels the purchasing department staff is not being cooperative, so she has decided that in the future she will not be cooperative with them.

Do you think Janet is acting wisely? Why or why not?

IMPROVING LANGUAGE SKILLS

The following paragraph has several misspelled words. Type the paragraph with the misspelled words typed correctly.

We are sory to tell you that the specefications you indicated in your letter are not standerd and, therefore, the price you sighted is not correct. For special orders, it is necessary to charge ten percent abouve the reguler price.

You can be sure that we appraciate your order. We garauntee all our work. We have inclueed a card for your comvenience in letting us know if we should procede with the order at the higher price.

IMPROVING ARITHMETIC SKILLS

Use the prices below to complete the problems which follow.

JOB WORK ORDER FORMS

Duplicate form 211-2		Triplicate Form 211-3	
4,000 sets	$129.50	4,000 sets	$175.00
2,000 sets	74.50	2,000 sets	95.00
1,000 sets	46.50	1,000 sets	59.50
500 sets	26.95	500 sets	34.95
250 sets	17.50	250 sets	23.95

SALES AND SERVICE FORMS

Duplicate Form 307-2		Triplicate Form 307-3	
4,000 sets	$99.50	4,000 sets	$138.00
2,000 sets	59.95	2,000 sets	82.50
1,000 sets	35.95	1,000 sets	49.50
500 sets	21.50	500 sets	29.95
250 sets	14.95	250 sets	19.50

1. What would be the total cost of purchasing the following items:

2,000 sets	211-2	_____
1,000 sets	211-3	_____
4,000 sets	307-2	_____
2,000 sets	307-3	_____
	Total	_____

2. What is the cost *per set* of duplicate form 211-2 if purchased in sets of 4,000? if purchased in sets of 250? How much more expensive is each set if purchased in sets of 250 rather than sets of 4,000?

3. If you were to purchase 2,000 sets of Triplicate Form 307-3 instead of 500 sets, how much would you save per set? What is the percentage of saving?

DEMONSTRATING OFFICE SKILLS

If blank forms from the *Supplies Inventory* are not available for the following assignments, use plain paper and prepare forms that are similar to those shown in the Unit.

1. Type a purchase requisition in duplicate for Howell & Associates, Glenville, WI 54013.

Requisition No. 308 from the Purchasing Department for the Travel Department, 3d floor; Date issued: May 6, 19--; Date required: May 26, 19--; Approved by Frank Williams.

  1 Executive Desk, 78" × 38", Style 47765, Custom Finish. Price: $250.40

  1 Executive Chair, Style T-9931, Top Grain Leather. Price: $185.95.

2. Type a purchase order in duplicate from the following information taken from a purchase requisition sent to Natorp Garden Supplies, 1505 North Berry Road, Bloomingdale, PA 18911, on February 2, 19--. Items will be shipped by truck, terms: 2/10 net 30. The quantities and unit prices are given; you are to make all extensions and calculate the totals.

Rockwood Gardens, 51 Fairview Road, Salisbury, MD 21801:

  1,000 feet Privet Hedge, #351, at $3.98 per 50 feet

  1,000 plants Heather Ground Cover, #154, at $1.10 per 10 plants

  144 rose bushes (Western), #799, at $1.95 per plant

3. Type a credit memorandum from the following information for goods returned to Terrell Corporation, 868 Bethel Road, Canton, DE 19935, on October 1, 19--.

Memorandum No. 279 to Mason Manufacturing, 198 James Avenue, New York, NY 10003:

  2 Portable Display Calculators, Model St-099, #463, at $188.95 each

  2 Calculating Machine Desks, 60" × 30", Style 4832-H, #973, Olive Green, at $213.65 each

IMPROVING OFFICE SKILLS (Optional)

The director of the company cafeteria has forwarded a note to the purchasing department seeking some assistance in finding a source for plastic placements. The manager of your department has located the following three addresses. She asks you to write a brief letter to each of the three companies below asking the price for a standard reusable plastic placemat in quantities of 1,000 and 5,000. Colors desired are blue and yellow. You also need to find out how quickly an order could be shipped. Use plain paper for all of the letters.

  1. American Plastics Corporation
     11 Park Avenue
     New York, NY 10013

2. Chencel Corporation
   290 Davis Road
   Somerset, NJ 08775

3. Elrene Manufacturing Company
   11 Clinton Road
   Newark, NJ 07102

Working with Inventories

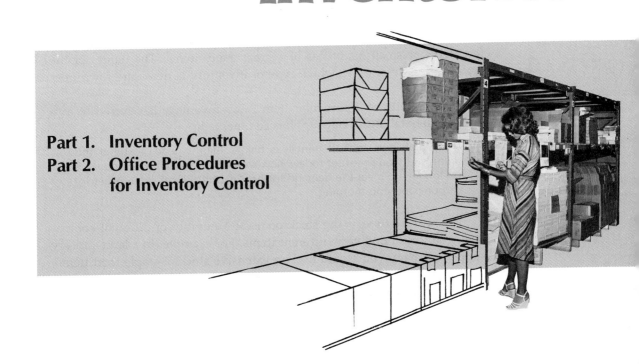

Part 1. Inventory Control
Part 2. Office Procedures
       for Inventory Control

Part 1

Inventory Control

Ms. Gail Wilson works as an inventory clerk at Seaside Cameras, a large camera store in downtown San Diego. For many years she has had an interest in cameras. She believes she was fortunate to secure a position with Seaside upon her graduation from high school about six months ago. She maintains the inventories for the more than 300 cameras the company sells. She finds it very interesting to maintain the records and to keep the stock of cameras in good order. She oversees the delivery of cameras to the stockroom. She is also responsible for filling orders from the selling departments when they need additional stock on the selling floors.

Varied Inventories in Modern Business

depleted:
used up

An *inventory* is a supply of items kept on hand by a business so that it can operate efficiently. If the supply of a necessary product is depleted, a serious delay can result. Inventories may contain large quantities of a few items or small quantities of a great many items. The nature of the organization determines which type of inventory is necessary for proper operation.

The quantity of a particular item in an inventory is referred to as a *stock*. A clerk talking about supplies commented:

> I think our stock of pencils is higher than it needs to be at this point, so I won't reorder today; however, our stock of carbon paper is far too low to meet the demand for next month. I'll call in an order for carbon paper this morning.

If you were to visit the stockrooms of a number of different companies, you would find very different items. For example, in a large grocery supply company you would find an extensive stock of staple food items, such as flour, sugar, vegetable oil, canned vegetables, and fruits. In a glass manufacturing company, you would find supplies of raw materials such as lime, potash, and sand. Bookstores' inventories include best sellers as well as classics. Department stores maintain thousands of items in their inventories, from buttons to beds.

Systems for Keeping Inventories

Companies have developed systems for keeping records of their inventories so that they know exactly how much of each item is on hand. They also know how many items are needed at particular times during the year. Computers have aided businesses tremendously in keeping accurate inventories.

Illus. 13-1

Office worker checking the accuracy of inventory records in the form of a computer printout.

The profits that companies earn depend, to some extent, on how carefully they purchase the materials and products needed to carry on their businesses. If they have too little stock, the work of the firm is interrupted. If they have too much stock, they are spending money needlessly. Therefore, knowing the best size for inventories is important to a firm.

Workers Needed

Many office workers are needed in all types of businesses to properly maintain inventories. Office tasks related to inventories and their control are interesting and very important. These tasks require alertness, accuracy, and orderliness.

Maintaining Inventory

Having the right materials and supplies on hand at the time they are needed means there must be inventory control. Many office workers are needed to maintain inventories properly. Generally a manager oversees inventory activities and is responsible for recordkeeping procedures. Working with the manager are assistants and inventory clerks who monitor the stock on hand, reorder items, receive items, keep an orderly arrangement in the stockroom, fill requisitions, and check the adequacy of inventories.

Records for Inventories

Managers of stockrooms decide on the right amounts of each item to be kept on hand. They have an important job. They know that if they keep stocks larger than are needed for normal operations they are tying up too much of the firm's money. Therefore, they must carefully review the past demand for each item and consider forecasts of the firm's activities. Office assistants see that the stocks are maintained at the levels established. There are basically two systems for keeping inventories, *periodic and perpetual*.

Periodic Inventory System. In some companies, the items in inventory are counted at established intervals. There are a number of variations of this basic system. One manager in a large home appliance company commented:

intervals:
spaces of time

variations:
different methods or ways

> We use the Unit Buying Count method, which means that every two weeks there is an actual counting of all the appliances that are in the stockroom as well as all that are on the selling floor. At this point, the quantity of stock available, which is listed on the tag of each item on the selling floor, is updated. In this way the salespersons know exactly how much stock is left for sale.

In firms where there is no need for an immediate knowledge of stock levels, the periodic inventory system is adequate. In small organizations, a skilled manager can scan the inventories regularly and replenish low stocks as needed.

Perpetual Inventory System. This system provides a continuous means of knowing the current status of each item in an inventory. Either manually or through the use of a computer, a record is made each time an item in an inventory leaves the stockroom or the sales floor. This system is considered essential in firms that need constant information about their inventories. The manager in a large, high-volume toy store commented:

status:
condition or state

Illus. 13-2

Inventory clerk taking periodic inventory

We have recently installed an important new network of cash registers in our store that are linked to a computer. The computer instantly tells which toys are moving rapidly on the selling floor. We monitor our stock daily in order to meet the demands of our customers. We don't want to have to say that something is "out of stock."

In many stockrooms, a stock record card is kept for each item. Every time a request is filled, the stock record card is updated. Then merely a glance at the card tells you what the stock is of that item.

Illus. 13-3

Attached to this cash register is a special tape recorder which stores information for inventory use later.

NCR Corporation

Reordering Goods

Well-organized stockrooms have a reordering procedure that goes into effect whenever an item reaches the minimum stock level. The minimum level is the point at which there is just enough stock to take care of normal demand until the new stock is delivered. Stockroom managers establish the minimum levels for all items. Generally some procedure is used for noting when the minimum level has been reached. When that minimum level has been reached, the reordering process begins. A clerk in a large automotive store commented:

> We have thousands of parts in our inventory, from spark plugs to carburetors. There are constant calls from the repair shops for parts, and they count on us to have all parts on hand. Customers are very unhappy if their automobiles can't be ready on the day they leave them for tune-up or repair because a part is "out of stock." As a warning, we have a large card stapled to the box that represents the beginning of our minimum stock. As soon as one of us sees that large card, we reorder.

Keeping an Orderly Stockroom

Goods must be located quickly if they are to be available to the people who need them. Therefore, there must be some system to the arrangement of all items in the stockroom. The system must be understood

Illus. 13-4

A well-organized
stockroom

Unit 13 • Working with Inventories

by everyone who works in the stockroom, and everyone must cooperate in maintaining the system. A manager of a large stockroom in a dress manufacturing company commented:

> We operate this stockroom very much like a systematic library. Clerks here automatically follow the same procedure each time they handle an item. When they work with incoming goods, they know that the goods are to be placed in their regular locations immediately. When a new item is ordered, arrangements are made for its placement on the shelves or in the bins immediately so that, when the goods arrive, the master layout shows the location of the new item. We have buttons, hooks, belts, buckles, trim, thread — in many styles — plus fabrics for dresses, for linings, and for interfacings. You can walk through our stockroom at any time and find it a clean, organized place. We don't like to work in chaos.

chaos:
state of confusion

Illus. 13-5

An office worker signs a requisition form in the presence of the stockroom clerk.

Requisitioning Goods

There must be an accounting for the total quantity of each item that is placed in stock. Therefore, you will find that every stockroom has a procedure for taking items out of stock. Persons from many departments in the company are likely to need goods from the stockroom. They must be informed of the procedures which are usually written down in some form. As an employee of the stockroom, you may have to explain the procedures to those who fail to read them. One clerk in a supplies stockroom commented:

We supply all the materials that secretaries and other office workers need to do their work. We receive requisitions by interoffice mail and in person. In case of emergencies, we do accept requests by telephone. All the office workers have the requisition forms in their offices, but we also carry a supply for those who arrive at the window without one. We are instructed not to issue any item without a requisition form that clearly identifies the budget to which the item is to be charged. Furthermore, every requisition must be signed by the person who is to receive the goods.

Variations in Inventories

Different kinds of businesses have different kinds of inventories. The inventories of stores are organized differently from the inventories of manufacturers which, in turn, are different from inventories of service organizations, such as hotels, car rentals, and plumbing companies.

Inventories in Distributive Firms

Firms that buy goods for the purpose of resale are called *distributive firms*. Department stores, drugstores, bookstores, supermarkets, wholesale fruit companies, and shoe stores are examples of distributive firms. Inventories are very important to such businesses. A customer who finds a shirt that he likes and then learns from the salesclerk that it is out of stock in his size is less likely to be a steady shopper in that store. Customer dissatisfaction often results from such poor inventory control.

Illus. 13-6

Retail stores must maintain large inventories of stock.

       Unit 13 • Working with Inventories

Inventories in distributive firms are organized by types of goods. You are likely to find many different stockrooms in a large firm. While some stockrooms, such as a shoe stockroom for a large department store, may house only one type of good, other stockrooms house several types of goods. In a store with a small linens department, you may find that linens are in the same stockroom with towels, fabrics, bedspreads, and draperies. Each distributive firm determines an appropriate division of its total merchandise lines for the purpose of inventory maintenance.

Inventories in Manufacturing Firms

A *manufacturing firm* processes raw materials in order to make a product. A shoe company is an example of a manufacturing firm. It uses raw materials to produce shoes which can be sold.

Important inventories for a manufacturing firm are these:

1. *Raw materials inventory.* Materials needed in the production process, such as leather, fabric, and thread.
2. *Components inventory.* Finished items that are needed for the final product but which are purchased from another company. An example would be shoe laces.
3. *Goods in process inventory.* Products which represent the output of a manufacturing firm at each step prior to the *final* step in the manufacturing process. For example, shoes are not made in a single step. There are several steps, and at each one

Illus. 13-7

Finished goods inventory of a furniture manufacturing company there is a partially finished shoe. The goods in process inventory is a means of keeping account of how many items are at each stage of production. This inventory provides a means of determining if there are sufficient items at each step to maintain production at the scheduled rate.

4. *Finished goods inventory.* Final output of a manufacturing company, such as shoes from a shoe manufacturing company. Finished goods are ready for sale and shipment.

Inventories in Service Businesses

Service businesses provide some useful work rather than products to their customers. Appliance repair companies, beauty salons, cleaners, hotels, and motels are service businesses. Lawyers, doctors, and accountants render professional services. In all instances, equipment and supplies are required to do the work involved.

render:
give; furnish

Service firms have the following inventories:

1. *Supplies and equipment needed to operate the business.* For example, a motel or hotel needs a wide variety of items to keep its facilities clean. Mops, dust cloths, brooms, paper towels, and many other items must be kept in stock.

2. *Supplies and equipment for direct customer services.* For example, a motel or hotel needs stationery, soap, furniture, water glasses, linens, and many other items in the rooms for guests.

Maintaining Security

The goods kept in stockrooms are valuable. Easy access to them may lead to a loss of goods. Persons who deal with inventories must be honest. Sometimes stockroom personnel who handle valuable goods are bonded. This protects the employer in case an employee is dishonest.

bonded:
insured against loss
by theft or dishonesty

REVIEWING IMPORTANT POINTS

1. Why are inventories maintained in modern businesses?
2. In what ways do inventories differ among companies?
3. Why does a firm not wish to keep a large surplus of goods in an inventory?
4. Describe the typical procedures involved in inventory control.

Unit 13 • Working with Inventories

5. How does a *periodic* inventory system differ from a *perpetual* inventory system?
6. Why is it a good idea to have some means of recognizing when the stock of an item is at a minimum level?
7. What is meant by the phrase "requisitioning goods"?
8. How do inventories in department stores differ from inventories in manufacturing firms.

MAKING IMPORTANT DECISIONS

1. Harold is a clerk in the stockroom of a large bookstore. Late one afternoon one of the salesclerks called to tell him six copies of a best seller were needed and requested that he bring them up right away. Harold found the books and took them up to the clerk. Since it was so near the end of his working day, he didn't make any record of this delivery; he knew that he could fill in the delivery form the next morning. What do you think of Harold's decision?
2. Anne is a clerk in the stockroom of a large office supplies store. By accident one day an excess supply of reams of typing paper was delivered to the selling floor. Since there was not enough space on the floor for all the paper, about 150 reams were returned to the stockroom. Anne realized that these reams would be needed in the near future, so she had them stacked up near the checkout window. She put a note on the top box, "Use from this stack when requests are received." What do you think of Anne's procedure?

LEARNING TO WORK WITH OTHERS

Dwight is a clerk in a large stockroom of office supplies for a large corporation. Secretaries and administrative assistants generally submit requisitons for supplies through interoffice memos. Dwight regularly receives from three secretaries requisitions that are incomplete as well as extremely difficult to read. Generally Dwight must call each of them to verify what is being requested. They don't refer to the catalog which was sent to each of them. Dwight feels that they are uncooperative. What do you think Dwight should do at this point?

IMPROVING LANGUAGE SKILLS

On page 530 is a list of frequently misused words and expressions. On a separate sheet of paper write a sentence using a more accurate word or phrase as a substitute for the misused word.

Example: would of

If I had known your plans, I *would have* met you at the theatre.

1. less people
2. different than
3. between us three
4. hisself
5. lots of
6. show up
7. real good
8. final end
9. enthuse
10. further on
11. seldom ever
12. these type
13. for free
14. hopeful optimism
15. but however
16. irregardless
17. join together
18. outside of

IMPROVING ARITHMETIC SKILLS

Assume that the figures given below are the beginning number of yards of material on bolts of upholstery material and the number of yards removed from each bolt. What is the present quantity on each of the bolts?

	Beginning Quantity	Quantity Removed	Present Quantity
a.	57½	4	_____
b.	97¾	2½	_____
c.	29⅞	3¼	_____
d.	67	4⅜	_____
e.	56½	5⅞	_____
f.	58½	5	_____
g.	19¼	3½	_____
h.	15	3¼	_____
i.	71⅛	10½	_____
j.	59¼	3½	_____
k.	41⅓	7¾	_____
l.	78½	16½	_____

DEMONSTRATING OFFICE SKILLS

1. You are employed in the stockroom of a large insurance company. The manager is preparing a new catalog to distribute to all the offices. You have been given this *rough draft* of one page to type perfectly on a sheet of plain paper so that your typed copy can be

photographed for reproduction. Arrange the items in order by stock number, from lowest to highest.

ITEM #	DESCRIPTION	250	500
8733	Reply Message 8½ × 7, 3 parts, cbnless	—	27.25
8793	Reply Message 8½ × 7, 3 parts	—	19.85
49300	#10 Window Envelope ~~(Imprinted)~~	—	18.75
81193	Reply Message 8½ × 11, 3 parts	—	29.50
91855	Tray for 8½ × 11 Forms $18.10 ea.	—	—
82194	Purchase Order 8½ × 11, 4 parts	*39.50* ~~38.70~~	~~44.00~~ *46.00*
82195	Purchase Order 8½ × 11, 5 parts	50.40	63.35
87193	Purchase Order 8½ × 7, 3 parts	15.85	21.05
87194	Purchase Order 8½ × 7, 4 parts	18.10	28.95
87195	Purchase Order 8½ × 7, 5 parts	28.05	37.40
81153	P.O. Follow-up 8½ × 11, ~~4 parts~~ *3 parts*	29.30	35.20
85013	Requisition 5⅔ × 7, 3 parts	*23.00* ~~21.20~~	~~25.30~~ *26.20*
81104	Request for Quotation 8½ × 11, 4 parts	30.10	40.10
81114	Quotation 8½ × 7, 4 parts, cbnless	42.15	50.60
81194	Quotation 8½ × 11, 4 parts, cbnless	51.00	60.30
82104	Invoice 8½ × 11, 4 parts	36.75	51.70
82105	Invoice 8½ × 11, 5 parts	44.95	54.45
87108	Invoice 8½ × 7, 3 parts	14.80	21.10
87104	Invoice 8½ × 7, 4 parts	*26.25* ~~24.50~~	~~29.85~~ *31.10*
87105	Invoice 8½ × 7, 5 parts	32.85	39.40
87204	Invoice w/Blockout 8½ × 7, ~~3 parts~~ *4 parts*	28.45	34.10
87205	Invoice w/Blockout 8½ × 7, 5 parts	33.45	40.15
49300	#10 Window Envelope (Imprinted)	17.30	18.75
83004	Monydu-Gram 8½ × 7, 4 parts	38.45	52.25
6712	Statement 5¾ × 7, 2 parts	—	12.65
6822	Statement 5¾ × 9½, 2 parts	—	19.45
6941	Continuous Statement 8 × 7, 1 part	—	16.90
6942	Continuous Statement 8 × 7, 2 parts	—	30.35
49104	#6¾ Window Envelope ~~(Imprinted)~~	—	19.40
49300	#10 Window Envelope ~~(Imprinted)~~	17.30	18.75
85453	Proposal Agreement 8½ × 11, 3 parts, cbnless	—	39.45
87114	Credit Memo 8½ × 7, 4 parts	30.75	36.30
87214	Debit-Credit Memo 8½ × 7, 4 parts	25.70	30.80
~~49550~~	~~Confidential Window Envelopes (Imprinted)~~	~~17.05~~	~~23.85~~
88113	Voucher checks — Blue	—	44.40
88123	Voucher Checks — Green	—	44.40

2. The manager of the stockroom, Ms. DiSalvo, has asked you to prepare an interoffice memo to send to all departments telling them that the central supply office will have new hours beginning the first of next month. The new hours are: Monday, Wednesday, and Friday, 9:30 to 11:00 a.m.; Tuesday and Thursday, 1:30 to 3:00 p.m. Use a memo form from the *Supplies Inventory* or plain paper.

Part 2

Office Procedures for Inventory Control

Mr. Don Reilly works as a clerk in the stockroom of a large household gifts and linen shop on fashionable Newberry Street in Boston. The goods that are maintained in inventory range from those that are modestly priced to those that are very expensive, and so must be handled very carefully. Mr. Reilly is responsible for checking merchandise as it is received and for filling requests that come from the selling floors. Handmade tableclothes, napkins, and placemats from over 15 different countries are in the store's stockroom. He finds the merchandise very interesting, and the job challenging.

Stockroom Recordkeeping

In order to maintain inventories, accurate recordkeeping is necessary. From the time a copy of a purchase order reaches the stockroom until the time goods are reordered, certain procedures must be followed to keep supplies of stock on hand for use as needed.

Receiving Goods

The stockroom keeps on file a copy of the purchase order (see Illus. 12-4, page 509) for goods to be received. When goods arrive, you will have to check what is received against what was ordered. The usual procedure for handling this task is:

1. Look for your company's order number on the invoice that accompanies the goods received.
2. Take from your files the copy of the purchase order and check it against the invoice you received to be sure you have the right order.
3. Compare the items listed on the invoice accompanying the goods against the items listed on the file copy of the purchase order. If there are any differences between these two, you

should note the difference on the invoice received as well as on the copy of the purchase order.

4. Open the goods and count them against the file copy of the purchase order. Every company has an established procedure for doing this. You will generally have assistance in opening cartons and placing the contents on a table or stand so that counting can be done easily. Counting should be done carefully, so it is important that you check the total contents of each carton.

5. Check the quality and condition of the goods received. For example, if you are checking letterheads, one ream should be opened to determine if the printing is clear and in the style and color requested.

Recording the Receipt of New Stock

For each item received in the shipment, you will find a control sheet or card. You will have to note the receipt of the order on this sheet or card. Notice in the illustration below that there is a record of the date the letterheads were ordered, plus the quantity ordered. If the quantity received is the same as the quantity ordered, then a checkmark is all that is needed. If there is any difference, then the actual quantity received is recorded.

Illus. 13-8

Supply control card

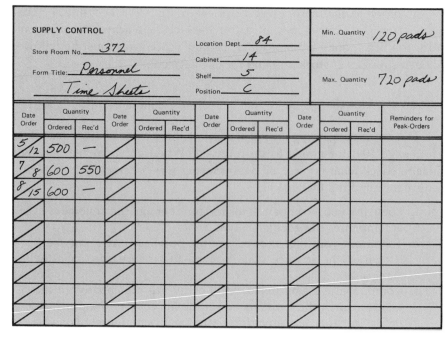

SUPPLY CONTROL										
Store Room No. *372*		Location Dept. *84*		Cabinet *14*		Shelf *5*		Position *C*	Min. Quantity *120 pads*	
Form Title: *Personnel Time Sheets*									Max. Quantity *720 pads*	

Date Order	Quantity Ordered	Rec'd	Date Order	Quantity Ordered	Rec'd	Date Order	Quantity Ordered	Rec'd	Date Order	Quantity Ordered	Rec'd	Date Order	Quantity Ordered	Rec'd	Reminders for Peak-Orders
5/12	500	—													
7/8	600	550													
8/15	600	—													

Unit 13 • Working with Inventories

Arranging Stock

Because many businesses must house a wide variety of items in their stockrooms, stockrooms must be orderly places. After goods have been checked, they should immediately be placed in their correct locations. You will find that the stockroom is carefully organized and often there is a directory for locating a particular item.

The stock should be arranged neatly at its correct location. It is standard practice to place old stock in the front so that it will be used first. This means that you will move the old stock to the side, while you place the new stock to the rear of the location.

Illus. 13-9

The labels and tag sheets on these shelves make goods in this stockroom easy to locate.

Counting Stock

As you learned in Part 1, the two most common systems for keeping a count of the inventory are the perpetual inventory system and the periodic inventory system. Each system has its own control card.

The Perpetual Inventory Card. The card used in a perpetual inventory system usually includes the following items.

A. The stock number of the item — which is the key identification for the item. Notice on Illus. 13-10 that the bottom line contains the same information as the top line. This is done so that the card can be arranged in a visible file for easy access.

B. The description of the item, including its size, finish, color. This card is used for appliances in a major retailing establishment with stores in many parts of the world.

C. Source of the item as well as shipping point. In this instance, the source may be either a store within the company or an outside vendor.

D. The ordering date for additional stock, that is, the length of time that it takes from the time goods are reordered until they arrive.

E. The current price at which the item is sold at retail.

F. Current sales which, you will notice, are recorded daily.

Illus. 13-10

Perpetual inventory control card

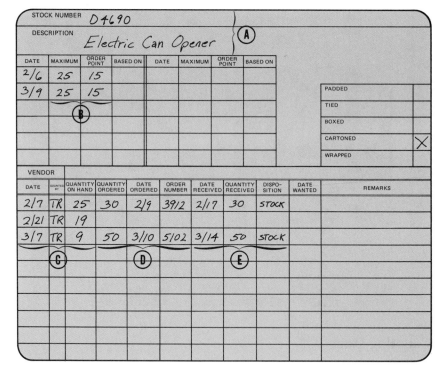

The Record for Periodic Counting. This form is used in a stockroom where a quick physical count is made once every two weeks. The count usually is taken at the beginning of the first working day of the week. The periodic count record form provides an up-to-date record of the actual

Unit 13 • *Working with Inventories*

amount of stock on hand and indicates those items that have reached minimum levels.

The following items are usually included on the form:

A. Stock number and description of the item.
B. Maximum and reorder quantities maintained.
C. Date of physical count and quantity on hand.
D. Quantity ordered, date ordered, order number.
E. Date received, quantity received, and disposition.

	STOCK No.	ITEM RATING	M.L. Page	DESCRIPTION		SIZE		FINISH	COLOR	Wt.
(A)	L-291	B	210	Coldright Side by Side	–	23 cu. ft.		—	white	298 lbs.

(B) LINE DESCRIPTION _Refrigerator – freezer on side_
Use Order Form No. _B-269_ Billing Price _310.10_
Enter in space below the exact availability which applies to your store.
Dist. No. ___
C.S. _12_ RTL. _4_ Card No. _14-21_
Dept. _12_ DIV. _4_
_12_ Wk. Count   YEAR 19 _--_

	Source Number	SOURCE (or Control Store)	ADDRESS	Source Zone	SHIPPING POINT	Par. Rec. Price	Latest Price
(C)	412	Coldright Manufacturing	Kalamazoo, MI	291	Kalamazoo, MI	429.	329.

	PERIOD	1	2	3	4	5	6
(D)	Ordering Date	3/14	6/14	7/30			
(E)	Current Selling Price	329.	329.	329.			
	On Hand	20 / 14	14 / 2	5 / 3			
	REGULAR ORDER	15	25	25			
	SPOT ORDER						
	Purchase Order No.	1212	3921	4983			
(F)	CURRENT SALES Enter Sales Daily Stroke Method	₩ ₩ / ₩ ₩	₩ ₩ / ///	₩ ₩ / ₩ ₩			
	Last Year Sales	29	31	42	34	49	61

	STOCK No.	ITEM RATING	M.L. Page	DESCRIPTION		SIZE		FINISH	COLOR	Wt.
(A)	L-291	B	210	Coldright Side by Side	–	23 cu. ft.		—	white	298 lbs.

Illus. 13-11

Periodic count record

The Annual Count. Most businesses find it necessary to take a thorough count of all items in inventory at least once a year. This inventory-taking activity often requires closing the stockroom for a day or longer. This process is necessary to get an accurate financial picture of the entire year's activities.

Before doing the actual counting, you will have to take care of some housekeeping chores in the stockroom. Even the best-managed stockroom is likely to have a few items that are not in their proper locations. Therefore, you and co-workers will be involved in straightening all the shelves, rearranging any items that are out of place, and putting on the shelves any unpacked items.

Generally you will work in teams of two for this job. The counting is generally checked by others; so it is important that the same procedures are used by everyone.

Requesting Stock

Each company has organized procedures that are used by all persons who need items from the stockroom. In most instances, a written request is required. However, many stockrooms do accept requests, especially emergency ones, by telephone. A written form is then prepared by the stockroom and the form is signed by the receiving office at the time of delivery.

Illus. 13-12

Signed requisition form

A requisition form is filled in by a clerk in the stockroom and is signed by the person who receives the stock. Notice in the illustration below that the quantity, code number, and a brief description of each item are listed.

183700031	05 14 7-	2 1		1	0843											CHECK DATA PRINTED WITH DELIVERED ITEMS	
BUDGET NO.	DATE			QTY.1 CODE		QTY.2 CODE		QTY.3 CODE		QTY.4 CODE		QTY.5 CODE					

BUDGET NO.		DATE		DEPARTMENT-PROJECT-OFFICE	FOR STORES USE ONLY
18-3700-031		5 24 --		Advertising	
REQUESTED BY		DELIVER TO		RECEIVED BY	
Toni Blair		RM 351 Macy Bldg.		Toni Blair	

	QUANTITY	CODE	DESCRIPTION	B.O.*
1	1	367	Casette Tape C 121	
2				
3				
4				
5				

B.O.*QUANTITY IN THIS COLUMN INDICATES OUT OF STOCK OR PARTIALLY DELIVERED. PLEASE REORDER UNDELIVERED ITEMS.

DELIVERY COPY

Delivering Stock

Persons who go to the stockroom for items frequently take the stock they need with them. Many times, however, a stockroom clerk puts together all the items requested by one person, or one office, and later delivers them by cart to the proper location. If you are given the responsibility for delivering goods, you will find it useful to always check on the following:

1. The items listed on the requisition should match the items you have packed.
2. The information about the location to which the items are to be delivered should be accurate.
3. Someone at the receiving office should sign a copy of the requisition so that you have proof that you have delivered the supplies.

REVIEWING IMPORTANT POINTS

1. What is the value of an invoice enclosed with a shipment received by a company?
2. How is a supply control card useful?
3. What information is likely to be included on a perpetual inventory control card?
4. What is the purpose of a physical count in a stockroom?
5. Why is an annual count of all items in a stockroom necessary?
6. How are items generally requested from a stockroom?
7. Who signs a requisition for stock from a stockroom?
8. What are the key housekeeping chores in a stockroom?
9. Of what value is the requisition form to the clerk who is to deliver the items requested?
10. What is the evidence that a supply order from a stockroom has been delivered?

MAKING IMPORTANT DECISIONS

1. Wade is a new clerk in the stockroom of a stationery store. He notes that incoming stock is in boxes that are clearly marked with the contents. He decides that he can easily check the contents by merely comparing the purchase order with the notations on the packing boxes. There is no reason, he believes, to open the packing box to determine if there are, in fact, 25 boxes of pencils. What do you think of Wade's idea?

2. Lynn works as a clerk in the stockroom of a large record and tape store. All the records and tapes are arranged first according to the name of the recording company and then by title. When additional copies are needed on the selling floor, the request is generally made by telephone, and the sales clerk generally gives the title only. Sometimes much time is spent in determining where that title is located. What do you think might be done in the stockroom to make it easier to fill requests?

LEARNING TO WORK WITH OTHERS

Bert is a clerk in a large stockroom of an insurance company. Requisitions are received through local mail, in person, and by telephone. Bert is hardworking and is very courteous to everyone who requests supplies. There is a new assistant to one of the vice-presidents who always seems to need supplies. She never anticipates her needs, and regularly makes emergency calls to the stockroom requesting that small items be delivered immediately. She generally says, "Please deliver the supplies *right now.*" Bert doesn't want to be discourteous toward her, but he feels that she is unreasonable in her constant requests. What would you suggest that Bert do?

IMPROVING LANGUAGE SKILLS

Write or type each of the following sentences on a separate sheet of paper, correcting the misspelled words.

1. The nineth page of your report is not fully leggible.
2. We won't know for several days weather the job can be done in his labartory.
3. The principle point of his argument was not clear from the ilustration he presented.
4. The meeting was planed carefuly but we don't think the president apreciated it.
5. On what type of containar should the lettering be enlarged?
6. Hans is an extremly conscientous clerk.
7. A perpetuel invantory is mainteined in this company.
8. Does she excell at typewriting?
9. Faith accepted the complement with a smile.
10. There will be severel atheletic activities during the all-day excursion next week.

IMPROVING ARITHMETIC SKILLS

A clerk made a physical count of the stock of linens at one counter on the selling floor. Listed below are the items found. Determine the total cost of the merchandise on hand at this counter.

Item	Unit Cost	Extension
4 dozen linen napkins	1.79 each	_____
10 sets of placemats/napkins	25.95 per set	_____
6 tablecloths (52″ by 52″)	19.95 each	_____
8 tablecloths (52″ by 60″)	29.95 each	_____
7 tablecloths (52″ by 90″)	35.95 each	_____
5 tablecloths (60″ by 90″)	45.95 each	_____
3 tablecloths (60″ round)	39.50 each	_____
2 tablecloths (90″ round)	49.50 each	_____
2 tablecloths (52″ by 90″)	79.95 each	_____
1 tablecloth (60″ by 110″)	115.50 each	_____

Total Cost _____

DEMONSTRATING OFFICE SKILLS

Use the purchase order form from the *Supplies Inventory* or draw up an order form like that illustrated on page 509. Use it for ordering the following from: A. G. C. Supply House, 39 Atlantic Avenue, Albany, NY 12204.

> 12 gross Pencils No. 456 @ 37 cents a dozen
> 15 doz. 3M Scotch Tape ½ × 1296 in. @ 69 cents a roll
> 12 doz. Yellow Pads 8½ by 11 No. 134 @ $3.69 a dozen

IMPROVING OFFICE SKILLS (Optional)

Assume that you are working in the office supplies center for a large corporation. From time to time, all users of office supplies are asked to make suggestions about the office supplies furnished by the center. The suggestions are then reviewed by the manager and several of the staff in the center, who use the information to make decisions about supplies to be purchased in the future. You have been asked to write an inter-office memo to be sent to all offices for suggestions. In your memo you should indicate:

1. The information about each item that you will need — type of forms, size, color, and use.
2. That you would like to know the experience the user has had with the item discussed.
3. That all suggestions should be sent to the center within two weeks.

14

Working with Sales

Part 1. The Selling Function
Part 2. Office Procedures
          for Selling

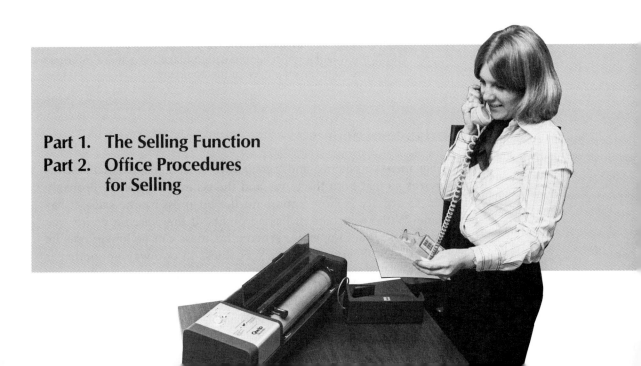

The Selling Function

After Jill Edwards graduated from high school, she decided that she would like to work in a large company. She wasn't quite sure what type of position she wanted, however. When Jill was hired for a job with the Bowman Hill Company, she told the personnel director that she had taken a wide variety of business courses in school, but she wasn't sure what office position she would enjoy the most. So that Jill would be able to view all the different activities of the company and decide upon a specific job, the personnel director put Jill on a rotating job schedule where she would spend several weeks each in the Sales, Warehouse, Traffic, Accounting, and Personnel Departments.

Jill's first assignment was in the Sales Department where she typed sales invoices from purchase orders which came in through the mail. Whenever she received a purchase order, Jill checked the company's catalog to make sure that the company sold the items requested. After completing the sales invoice, Jill sent one copy to the Warehouse Department. Jill began to realize how many people were involved in selling merchandise to the public. She looked forward to becoming familiar with the other departments. Jill knew that the rotating job schedule would make her a more informed and valuable employee of the company.

Importance of Selling

Selling means assisting and persuading customers to obtain goods and services so that both the buyer and the seller are satisfied. Probably no business activity is more important. If a business has no sales, it has no income. Without income, it has no profits. If there are no profits, the firm cannot continue to operate. When a business can no longer operate there are no jobs. Every job in every business in one way or another is **dependent** upon successful selling.

dependent:
relying upon

What Businesses Sell

All businesses sell something. They may sell *goods*, such as clothing, portable radios, soft drinks, or cameras. They may sell *services*, such as movie theater admissions, dry cleaning of clothing, or investment advice. Many businesses sell both goods and services. For instance, a store may sell television sets and service them; an automobile agency sells and services cars.

No matter what a business sells, customers must be satisfied if the company is to be successful. Its purpose is to provide those goods and services that the customers want. In addition, the firm must sell its goods and services in such a way that customers will come back.

Employees As Sales Representatives

Every employee of a business can be considered a sales representative of the firm. Each employee a customer meets helps to form the customer's opinion of the firm. If customers have favorable opinions, there is a good chance that they will continue to **patronize** the firm. It is, therefore, very important that all customers be treated fairly and courteously.

patronize: buy from

Sales Personnel. Those who have the most frequent and direct contact with customers are the sales personnel. These are the employees who directly assist the customer in buying those goods and services which will provide the most satisfaction. Like all other employees in a business, sales personnel are specially trained in assisting customers.

Nonselling Personnel. Although office workers are occasionally asked to perform direct selling functions, usually this is not the case. Rather, as a office worker, you may assist the salesperson and the customer in other ways. For example you may answer telephone inquiries or complaints from customers, you may type invoices for sales, or you may handle routine correspondence related to sales.

Even though it is unlikely that you will be involved in direct selling, you will affect the way in which customers view your business. If you treat customers in the office with courtesy and respect, a good impression of your company will be formed. On the other hand, if you are indifferent — or worse, rude — to customers or if you make an error in typing their monthly statements, a poor impression will be formed.

Every employee of the firm makes an impression on the customers. If that impression is not good, the customers and their future purchases may be lost.

Methods of Selling

How your business goes about selling its goods or services is very
important to you because the income from sales pays your salary. There
are two main methods of selling — personal selling and nonpersonal
selling.

Personal Selling

In personal selling a sales person speaks directly with a potential customer. This meeting may take place on the sales floor, in the customer's
home, or over the telephone. Although as an office worker you probably
won't be dealing with customers on the sales floor or in their homes, it is
possible that you may do some telephone selling. In that case you will
have to study the product, and learn how to deal with customer questions. You may also have to prepare reports on your telephone contacts.

Nonpersonal Selling

Nonpersonal selling takes place when an attempt is made to influence customers to buy without meeting them or talking with them. Three
common methods of nonpersonal selling are advertising, sales letters,
and catalog selling.

Advertising. Everyone is exposed to hundreds of advertisements daily in
newspapers and magazines, on billboards, on buses, and on radio and

television. Advertisements inform potential customers about goods and services for sale by businesses. Preparing advertising materials requires special training. A knowledge of advertising methods and techniques is very helpful to an office worker in an advertising agency or in a store that prepares most of its own advertisements.

Sales Letters. Most businesses use sales letters to inform customers of special goods and services that they have to offer. Sales letters are often

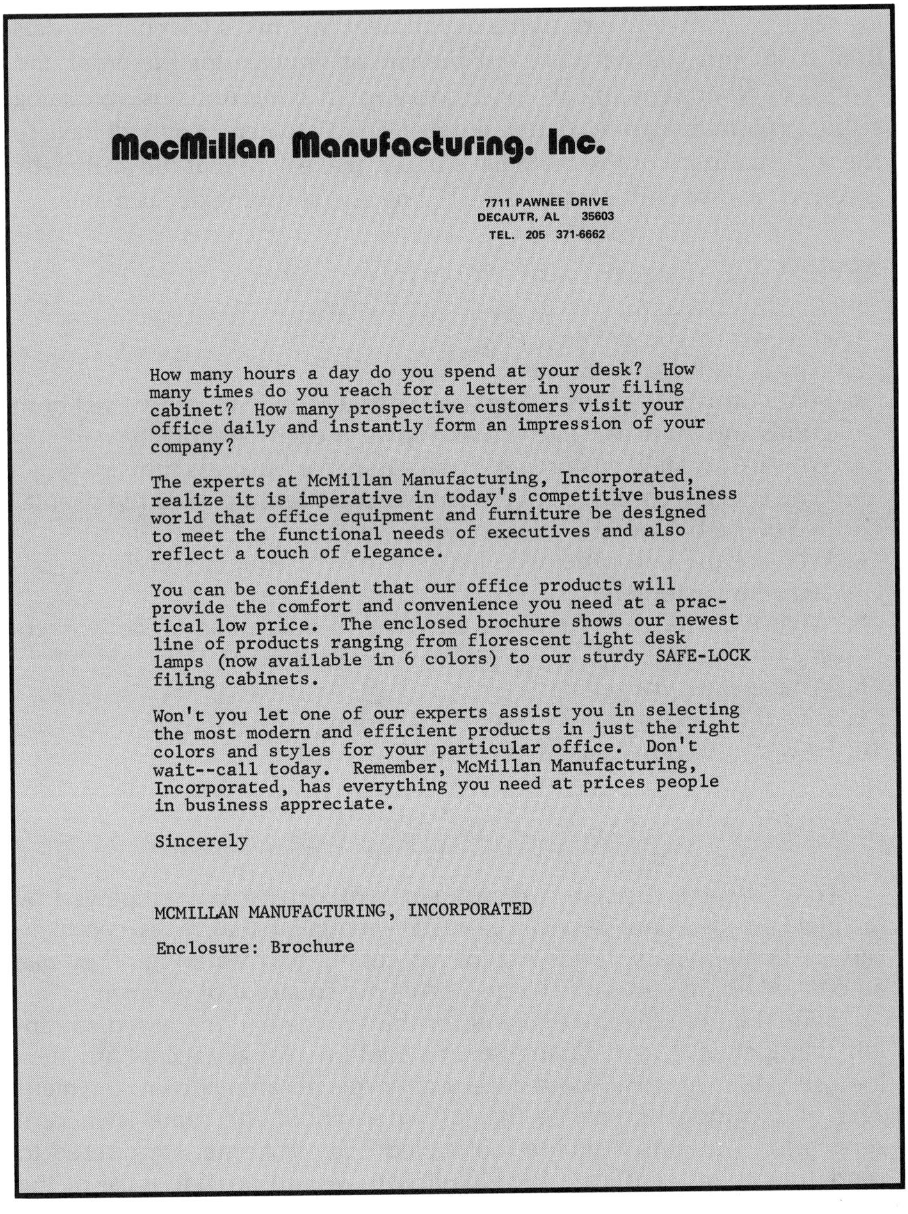

MacMillan Manufacturing, Inc.

7711 PAWNEE DRIVE
DECAUTR, AL 35603
TEL. 205 371-6662

How many hours a day do you spend at your desk? How many times do you reach for a letter in your filing cabinet? How many prospective customers visit your office daily and instantly form an impression of your company?

The experts at McMillan Manufacturing, Incorporated, realize it is imperative in today's competitive business world that office equipment and furniture be designed to meet the functional needs of executives and also reflect a touch of elegance.

You can be confident that our office products will provide the comfort and convenience you need at a practical low price. The enclosed brochure shows our newest line of products ranging from florescent light desk lamps (now available in 6 colors) to our sturdy SAFE-LOCK filing cabinets.

Won't you let one of our experts assist you in selecting the most modern and efficient products in just the right colors and styles for your particular office. Don't wait--call today. Remember, McMillan Manufacturing, Incorporated, has everything you need at prices people in business appreciate.

Sincerely

MCMILLAN MANUFACTURING, INCORPORATED

Enclosure: Brochure

Illus. 14-2

Sales letter

used to announce preseason sales, anniversary sales, and clearance sales to regular customers. These letters must be so carefully written that some firms employ specialists to write them. Even though you probably won't be writing sales letters, you may be responsible for typing them. If a large volume of sales letters is being sent to prospective buyers, you may have to use an automatic typewriter to prepare them as described in Unit 10.

Catalog Selling. Many office workers are employed in mail-order or catalog selling. You may work in the department that takes telephone orders from customers. In that case you prepare an invoice for the order and send it to other departments for processing. In other firms using catalog selling, you may receive written orders from customers. You will have to check the accuracy of the customer's order, make sure that the arithmetic is correct, and send the order to the billing and shipping departments.

REVIEWING IMPORTANT POINTS

1. How would you define *selling*?
2. Why is selling so important?
3. Some firms sell goods, others sell services, and still others sell both goods and services. Give two examples in each category.
4. Why are satisfied customers so necessary for business firms?
5. Why is every employee of a business considered a sales representative of the business?
6. Who are the personnel who have the most frequent and direct contact with customers?
7. What types of duties may be assigned to nonselling office workers in a business?
8. What is personal selling?
9. Give three examples of nonpersonal selling.
10. How do businesses use sales letters?

MAKING IMPORTANT DECISIONS

Toby Green's first job was in a small office. He was employed by Richfield Landscaping Service, a service company that takes complete care of homeowners' lawns except for cutting and watering. They use automated equipment and charge 5 cents per square foot of lawn.

By middle of May the demand for the service had increased so rapidly that Richfield Landscaping Service could no longer accept any new lawn service contracts. About a week after this became known, the manager of a competing service that provided about the same lawn care service for 5½ cents a square foot called Toby at home. He offered to send Toby a gift certificate for $100 if Toby would provide a list of the homeowners whose lawns Richfield Landscaping Service was unable to care for. Should Toby accept or reject this offer? Give reasons for your answer.

LEARNING TO WORK WITH OTHERS

Vicki Sterling has just been assigned to assist Louise Robinson in the Sales Department of Erickson, Lee, and Company. Her main responsibilities include typing and stuffing envelopes, preparing sales invoices, and answering telephone inquiries. One afternoon Louise overhears Vicki answering a telephone inquiry concerning a sale which will start the following day. The person calling apparently wants to know what items will be featured in the sale. Vicki, rather brusquely, informs the caller that the sale items are listed in the evening newspaper and suggests that the caller read the advertisement for the information she wants. After she finishes the call, Vicki rushes back to her desk which is piled high with work to be done. Louise realizes that Vicki was very busy when the call came in, but she also knows that her company might have just lost a customer because of the way Vicki handled the inquiry.

How might Louise approach Vicki concerning the importance of dealing tactfully with customers?

IMPROVING LANGUAGE SKILLS

The apostrophe has three principal uses:

A. To form the possessive of nouns and indefinite pronouns.
   Example: Hazel's desk should be repaired.

B. To denote the omission of letters or figures.
   Example: He hasn't been here today.

C. To form the plural of figures, letters, signs, and words (in some cases of current usage, it is not incorrect to omit the apostrophe — the 1960s).
   Example: When *and's* and *the's* are used in titles, they should not be capitalized, unless they are the first word.

On a separate sheet of paper type the following sentences, inserting apostrophes where necessary.

1. Where is todays paper?
2. Mr. Howard isnt ready to read Harriets report.
3. Its hard to read Janets writing because her es and ls look alike.
4. Wheres the final draft of this report?
5. Carls typewriter is broken and wont be ready this afternoon.
6. He wasnt clear about how he wanted the sales figures handled.

7. Why did she type the *2s* and *8s* so lightly?
8. Mens shoes, childrens shoes, and womens shoes were on sale all week.
9. He used +s and −s to indicate if sales for the month were ahead or behind.
10. The class of 70 had its reunion here.

IMPROVING ARITHMETIC SKILLS

1. Leslie Billings, a high school student, sells greeting cards in her spare time. She is paid a straight commission of 20 cents on each box of cards that she sells. During the month of June she sold 120 boxes of cards. What was the amount of her commission?
2. Jess Bailey, a sales representative, is paid a straight commission of 9% on the amount of his sales. During March his sales amounted to $10,700. What was the amount of his commission?
3. The cashier at a local movie theatre had $65 in change in the cash box of the ticket-selling window at the start of the day. During the day she sold 153 matinee tickets at $2.25 each and 534 evening tickets at $3.00 each. How much money should have been in the cash box when she proved the cash at the close of the day?

DEMONSTRATING OFFICE SKILLS

Prepare a Quarterly Sales Summary for Capital Industries, Inc.

1. Type a rough draft of the quarterly sales summary.
2. Complete the following calculations on the rough draft:
    (a) Subtract the listed amount of the Sales Returns and Allowances for each sales representative from Gross Sales to find Net Sales for the first quarter of the year. For example, the Net Quarterly Sales for the first sales representative, Sue Abrams, are $62,036 ($65,555 − $3,519 = $62,036).
    (b) Compare the amount of each sales representatives net first quarterly sales with his or her net quarterly sales for the first quarter of last year. Record the amount of the increase or decrease in the proper column. For example, Sue Abrams' net quarterly sales have increased by $2,248 ($62,036 − $59,788 = $2,248).
    (c) Add the columns and record their totals at the bottom of the Quarterly Sales Summary.
3. Type the final draft of the Quarterly Sales Summary on plain paper with two carbon copies.

CAPITAL INDUSTRIES, INC.
Quarterly Sales Summary
PERIOD ENDING March 31, 19--

Salesperson	Gross Sales for the First Quarter	Sales Returns and Allowances First Quarter	Net Sales for the First Quarter	Net Sales First Quarter (Last Year)	Comparison	
					Amount of Increase	Amount of Decrease
Abrams, Sue	$65,555	$3,519		$59,788		
Becker, Harry	68,706	4,221		64,823		
Carr, Frances	97,376	5,720		90,231		
Davis, Rhoda	72,064	4,472		70,947		
Ehrlich, Tom	57,649	2,170		54,923		
Fulton, Ross	62,630	3,702		57,005		
Goldberg, Celia	70,480	6,042		66,122		
Hansen, George	88,290	5,170		79,162		
Iorizzo, Manuel	90,592	5,517		80,216		
Johnston, Dale	72,575	3,433		67,980		
Kraft, Drew	62,195	2,155		59,944		
Lang, Eileen	66,444	3,414		65,082		
Mazer, Ruth	70,188	4,560		61,201		
Neale, Ronald	50,780	2,158		57,160		
O'Brien, Anita	98,490	7,269		85,396		
Parker, Patrick	56,333	3,908		55,013		
Quinn, Peter D.	72,403	5,501		65,161		
Roberts, Ginny	61,512	4,094		50,057		
Tsuyuki, Robert	73,488	3,408		66,567		
Van Tassel, Charlene	55,304	2,129		59,041		
TOTALS	$	$	$	$	$	$

Part 2

Office Procedures for Selling

Tom Bledsoe was a very fast and accurate typist in high school. His skill in typing helped him to get a job with the Weiss and Taylor Company. For six months, Tom worked in a typing pool. Because his work was always neat and accurate, Tom was assigned a new responsibility. Tom is now responsible for answering letters from customers. He has a notebook at his desk which contains over 100 form letters which his company frequently uses. Tom knows which letter to send to answer a customer's questions. His automatic typewriter does much of the work for him, but Tom must type in special information on each letter. He is valuable to his company because he does his job very well and with little supervision.

Sales Office Responsibilities

As was mentioned in Part 1, as an office worker you probably will not be responsible for selling directly to customers. However, it is quite likely that you will perform clerical functions that will aid your sales personnel and your customers in successfully completing sales. You may be responsible for handling telephone or mail orders from customers. A large amount of your time may be spent typing and filing the business papers related to selling. No matter what your responsibilities are, you must remember that every action you take may affect a customer's **attitude** toward your company.

attitude:
mental position, feeling

Routine Correspondence

Much of the correspondence that comes into a business contains routine requests for catalogs, information about products or services, and information about company policies. Office workers are often responsible for answering these requests. Since many customers ask similar questions, *form letters* are often used to answer their requests. All you have to do is find the form letter that will answer the customer's question. You may have to type in special details not covered in the basic form letter. Space is provided on the form letters for this information.

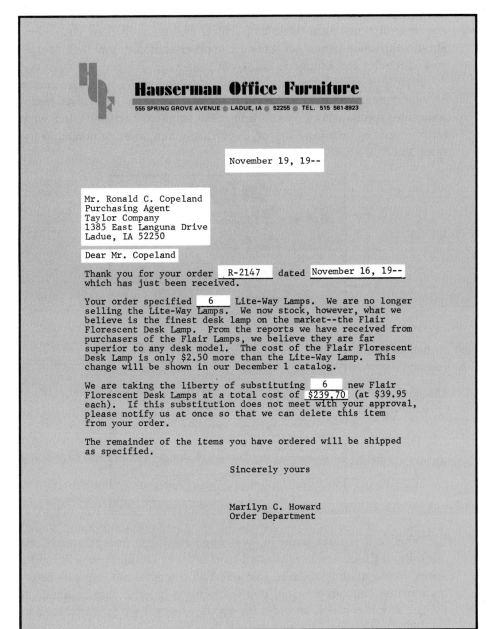

Illus. 14-3

Filled in form letter

Sales Personnel Records

If you work for a firm that has sales personnel who call on customers at their places of business, you may have the responsibility of assisting these representatives in serving their customers. The sales personnel may either work out of your office, or they may work in another city or state. If the sales personnel work out of your office, they will talk with you several times each week concerning the needs of their customers. Should the sales personnel work in another territory, you will receive mailed reports and telephone calls from them.

Each time sales representatives call on customers, they make a record of their conversations on *call reports*. On the call reports the sales representatives record who they call upon, the subjects discussed, and what action needs to be taken. The call reports are then taken or mailed to the sales office.

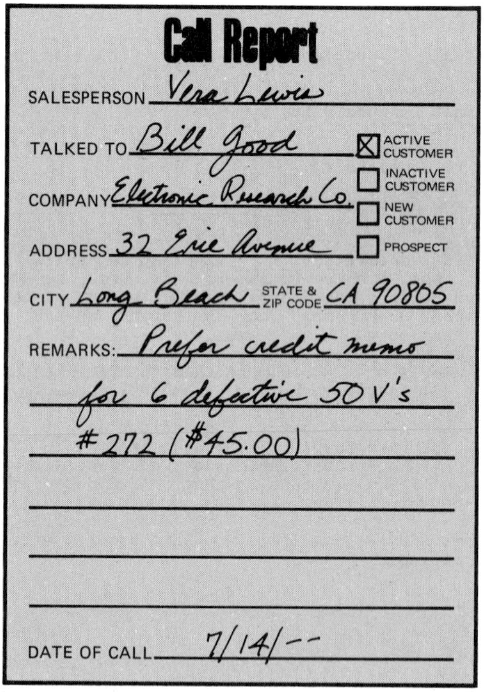

Illus. 14-4

Daily call report

Call Report

SALESPERSON *Vera Lewis*

TALKED TO *Bill Good*   ☒ ACTIVE CUSTOMER

COMPANY *Electronic Research Co.*   ☐ INACTIVE CUSTOMER

                                       ☐ NEW CUSTOMER

ADDRESS *32 Erie Avenue*   ☐ PROSPECT

CITY *Long Beach* STATE & ZIP CODE *CA 90805*

REMARKS: *Prefer credit memo*
for 6 defective 50 V's
#272 ($45.00)

DATE OF CALL *7/14/--*

When call reports come in, you must read and interpret each one carefully. If the customer requested a price list or catalog, you will send a notice to the mailing room to that effect. If the customer requests information that you can provide, you will write a letter to that customer. If the call report contains an order for goods, you will type the invoice and send it to the appropriate departments.

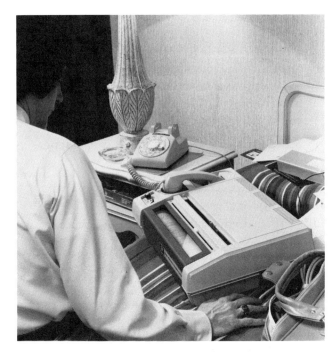

Illus. 14-5

A traveling sales representative transmits a rush order to the office using a portable telecopier.

After the proper action has been taken, the call report should be filed in the customer's file folder. Any letters or invoices that relate to the customer should also be placed in that file. In this way the file becomes a complete history of the customer's dealings with your company.

Illus. 14-6

An order department clerk receives a copy of the order from the sales representative.

Mail Requests

Mail-order houses are not the only businesses that receive mail orders. Most businesses get letters every day ordering goods. Some businesses include mail-in coupons in their advertisements to make it easier for customers to place orders.

Special procedures are usually necessary for handling mail orders.

1. If you are responsible for opening the envelopes, take care that you don't damage the contents.
2. Don't throw the envelope away until you are sure that the customer's name and address are included in the contents of the letter or order.
3. Handle with extreme care any checks or money orders received. Usually you will note on the letter or order that a check was received and indicate its amount. Checks are then normally sent to the cashier or the accounting department.
4. Check the order to be sure that it is complete and that the arithmetic is correct. Consult your supervisor if any important details are missing or incorrect. If the customer lives in your town, you may be told to call and get the information needed. If the customer lives in another town, you may have to send a written request for missing information (often form letters are available for this purpose).
5. Usually you will type an invoice for the order received. A copy of the invoice will go to the credit department for approval before charge sales are shipped.

Illus. 14-7

Mail orders must be checked carefully to see that they are complete and that the arithmetic is correct.

Photograph Courtesy of the Standard Register Co.

Telephone Requests

Every day business firms receive thousands of telephone requests for information about products and services. By using the telephone, customers show that they want action in a hurry. You must perform your duties in such a way that the customers are not disappointed.

Many businesses include their telephone numbers in their advertisements so that customers can call to order goods and services. If your duties include taking telephone orders, you should have copies of the latest advertisements handy for reference. This will aid you in answering questions and in knowing which goods the customer is ordering.

When a customer calls, you should have *sales order forms* and pencils and pens ready. You must listen very carefully to be sure that you know exactly what the customer wants. If anything is said that you do not completely understand, politely ask the customer to repeat the information. When writing the information on the order form, make sure that you write legibly. Be sure to get the customer's name (spelled correctly), address, telephone number, and charge account number, if it is a charge sale. Carefully record the items desired, the prices, and how the goods are to be shipped. To be sure that you have recorded the information correctly, read the order back to the customer.

After you have **concluded** your conversation with the customer, you should recheck the order for completeness and accuracy. Then you or a

Illus. 14-8

When a customer calls, order form and pencil should be at hand. Listen carefully to what the customer says.

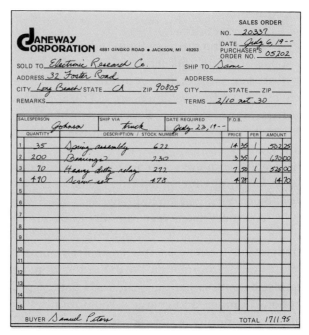

Illus. 14-9

Sales order filled in by hand

co-worker will usually type an invoice from the order form. Copies of the invoice are sent to the appropriate departments, including shipping and accounting.

Processing Orders

An order for goods or services may come to your business in many ways. It could come as a purchase order; it could come as a letter or telephone call; it could come in person from a visiting customer; or it could come as a result of a sales representative's call. No matter how the order is received, you must process it accurately and rapidly. Every action you take should be aimed at providing customer satisfaction.

Checking the order

When an order is received, you must check it to be certain that all needed information is provided and that what is given is correct. You should also check to see that the goods ordered are in stock. If the ordered goods are not in stock, your supervisor will decide whether to contact the customer or to send goods that are very similar to the ones ordered.

You must also check the accuracy of the prices shown on the order. Use a calculator to check all the arithmetic.

Approving Credit

When an order is received without an accompanying payment, it usually must be approved by the credit department before the merchandise is shipped. Most orders are from established customers who have proved their reliability. Those orders are given rapid credit approval.

If the order is from a new customer without an established credit rating or from a firm with an unsatisfactory record of past payments, the credit department may recommend that the goods be shipped *COD*, which stands for *cash on delivery*. This means that goods must be paid for as soon as they are delivered to the buyer. When a COD shipment is necessary, the seller often writes to the buyer to ask whether the goods should be shipped under these terms.

Illus. 14-10

A customer's credit rating is checked before an order is shipped.

Courtesy of Bankers Box/records, storage systems, Itasca, Illinois

Preparing the Sales Invoice

The sales invoice (illustrated on page 511) gives all the details of the sale. You must take great care in typing invoices to be sure that all the information is correct. The sales invoice shows a complete listing of the goods shipped, including the following information about each item: the quantity, description, catalog number, unit price, and the *extension* (the product of the unit price times the quantity of an item shipped). For example, a line on an invoice for office products might be:

```
6 DZ TYPEWRITER ERASERS   873   2.40 DZ   14.40
```

The sales invoice also carries the firm's name, the customer's name and address, the method of shipping, the customer's order number, the sales invoice number, the terms of payment, and the total amount of the invoice.

The copies of the sales invoices are usually distributed as follows:

Copy	Is Sent to
Original	Customer
First copy	Accounting Department for accounts receivable
Second copy	Filing Department for placement in the customer's file
Third copy	Shipping Department
Fourth copy	Sales Department or salesperson

Every well-organized business firm has an established procedure for preparing sales invoices. This procedure will differ with the number and the difficulty of the invoices prepared by each firm. If they require very little mathematical work, a small number of invoices can be prepared on a typewriter. Invoices with more complicated arithmetic will require the use of a desk calculator as well as a typewriter. If a large number of invoices is prepared every day, it may be more economical and efficient to use either special billing machines or data processing equipment. Most sales invoices prepared on billing machines or data processing equipment are written on continuous invoice forms with carbon paper between the copies.

Illus. 14-11

This office worker double-checks the extensions on a stack of invoices.

Billing the Customer

When the order is shipped by your firm, the bill or invoice is mailed to the customer. This important office operation is known as *billing*.

Statements. In addition to sending out invoices to customers when an order is shipped, most businesses send out monthly billing statements for each customer's account. The statement shows the amount the customer owed at the beginning of the month, the charges and payments made during the month, and the balance the customer owes at the end of the month.

Statements are usually prepared on bookkeeping machines, punched card tabulating machines, or other electronic data processing equipment, depending upon the number of statements sent out each month. The

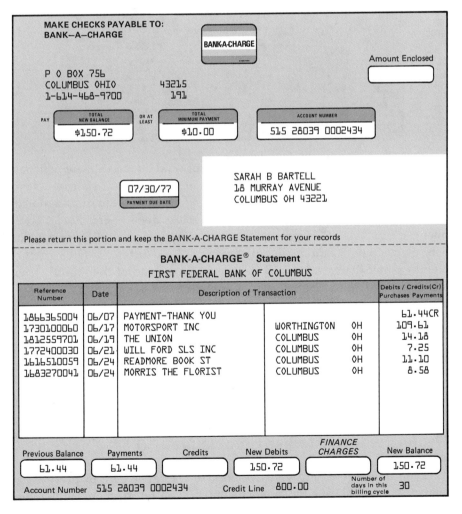

Illus. 14-12

A monthly billing statement

preparation of the statements is the responsibility of the accounting department in all but very small business firms, but it is sometimes necessary for the office workers in other departments to help in preparing statements, especially during rush periods.

Illus. 14-13

These volume sales invoices, prepared on continuous forms, are fed through a forms burster for separation.

Photograph Courtesy of the Standard Register Co.

Cycle Billing. The firm you work for may not send out all its statements at the end of the month. Some companies mail some of their statements on the first of the month; others on the fifth; still others on the ninth; and so on. This procedure is called *cycle billing*. Most department stores, telephone companies, and gas and electric companies have divided their lists of customers and mail out statements on different dates in the month, rather than mail out all statements at the end of the month. This makes it possible for the billing department to work steadily throughout the month, to avoid peak loads and overtime at the end of every month, and to send out statements as they are completed. Some companies divide their customer lists alphabetically; for example, statements may be mailed to customers whose last names are in the middle of the alphabet, beginning with either M or N, on the fifteenth of the month. Other companies divide their customer lists by districts, geographic locations, or sales territories.

Dealing with Customer Complaints

Even though you and your co-workers take great care in processing sales, there will always be some customers who return merchandise for one reason or another. The merchandise may have been delivered too late to be of value; the merchandise may have been the wrong kind, style, or color; or the merchandise may have been received in a damaged condition. Then, of course, there are also instances when customers return goods because what they ordered simply will not fit their needs. Usually after customers tell the seller that they are not satisfied with the shipment, they will be asked to return the shipment. In some cases, however, it may be more advantageous to the seller to grant a special allowance to customers to cover their losses if they decide to keep the merchandise.

Every time a customer has a complaint there is an opportunity to build goodwill for your firm. The more attention and courtesy the customer receives, the higher that person's opinion of your business.

Credit Memorandums

When merchandise is returned to the seller or when an allowance is granted to the customer, a credit memorandum (Illus. 12-6, page 512) is issued. This credit memorandum is very much like a sales invoice and has about the same information that appears on an invoice. At least three copies are made — the original for the customer, the second copy for the accounting department to be used in crediting the customer's account, and the third copy for the customer's file. Frequently additional copies are prepared — one copy for the receiving department to indicate the goods to be returned, and one copy for the sales department as a record of sales returns and allowances. All businesses try to keep sales returns and allowances to a minimum.

Adjustment Letters

Some customer complaints involve problems that cannot be solved by simply sending a credit memorandum. An adjustment letter may be necessary to more fully explain what caused the problem and what action will be taken. Beginning office workers are seldom asked to write adjustment letters; however, as you gain experience this may become one of your responsibilities. Adjustment letters usually contain the following information:

1. An acknowledgment of the customer's complaint and an expression of regret.
2. An explanation of the problem.
3. A suggestion for the adjustment of the complaint.

You should present the facts in a forthright manner, without anger or trying to fix the blame. Suggest the adjustment in a tone and manner that will reassure the customer. An example of an adjustment letter is shown in Illus. 14-14.

DAVIS BUSINESS INTERIORS

3449 York Road
Sioux City, IA 50317
Tel. 712 885-7643

May 14, 19--

Mrs. Eve Coffman
Curry Company
43 Lawndale Drive
Sioux City, IA 50317

Dear Mrs. Coffman

Thank you very much for your letter of May 10 regarding the eight defective swivel desk chairs, No. 44S. We are immediately issuing a credit memorandum for $889.28 to your account.

Arrangements have been made for the Ace Trucking Company to pick up these chairs on May 17 and return them to us. Every effort will be made to determine the cause of the defect. Please accept our apologies for the inconvenience this has caused your firm.

Thank you for your cooperation in this matter. We look forward to serving your needs in the future and to continuing the fine business relationship we have always had with your company.

Sincerely yours

Michael T. Millican

Michael T. Millican
Adjustment Supervisor

ks

Enclosure: Credit Memo 384 for $889.28

Illus. 14-14

Adjustment
letter

REVIEWING IMPORTANT POINTS

1. What is the purpose of a form letter?
2. What is a call report and why should a call report be carefully read and interpreted?
3. Why is it a good idea not to throw away the envelope as soon as you open a letter?
4. How should you handle checks and money orders enclosed in letters ordering goods?
5. What is the purpose of a sales order form?
6. What decision must be made if a customer orders goods which are not in stock?
7. Under what circumstances would a credit department recommend that goods be shipped COD?
8. What types of information are included on a sales invoice?
9. What information is shown on a customer's statement?
10. What is the main advantage of using a cycle billing system?

MAKING IMPORTANT DECISIONS

Jim Goodner, one of the sales representatives of the company, has just left several call reports on your desk to be processed. One of the reports is a rush item. You read the call report, but you are not sure about whether the quantity of merchandise ordered is seven or two boxes. However, you are almost positive the number is seven. You know Jim will not be back in the office until tomorrow. Should you process the order sending seven boxes instead of two, wait until you talk with him tomorrow, or contact the firm which placed the order?

LEARNING TO WORK WITH OTHERS

A new sales representative bursts into the sales department and happily displays her first large order — an order for over $1,000 from Haynes Developers. You suddenly remember that the credit department has been trying to collect $1,200 from Haynes Developers for over a year for a previous order.

Should you: (a) type the sales invoice for Haynes Developers and let the sales representative get the bad news from the credit department in a few days, or (b) tell the sales representative that you do not think the order will be approved because Haynes Developers still owes the company $1,200 for a previous order? Do you think she will hold it against you if you tell her now?

IMPROVING LANGUAGE SKILLS

The hyphen is used for dividing words at the end of a line when you don't have sufficient space to complete the full word. Rules to follow in dividing words are:

A. Words should be divided between syllables only.
   Wrong: regr-etable   **Right:** regret-able

B. Single Syllable words are not to be divided.
   Wrong: pa-int   **Right:** paint

C. Hyphenated words should be divided at the hyphen only.
   Wrong: self-rel-iance   **Right:** self-reliance

D. A one-letter syllable should not be typed at the end of a line or at the beginning of the next line.
   Wrong: a-ward   **Right:** award
              are-a   area

E. A two-letter last syllable should not be carried to the next line.
   Wrong: bodi-ly   **Right:** bodily

F. A single-letter syllable should be typed with the beginning portion of a divided word rather than with the end of the word.
   Wrong: ded-ication   **Right:** dedi-cation

On a separate sheet of paper type each of the following words indicating all the places where the word should be hyphenated if it appeared near the end of a line of typewriting.

1. allocate
2. applicant
3. balance
4. consolidate
5. illustration
6. license
7. manager
8. ounce
9. patriot
10. ratio
11. salutation
12. source
13. tentative
14. thousand
15. undergo
16. valuable
17. valid
18. warranty
19. yielding
20. zero

IMPROVING ARITHMETIC SKILLS

On a separate sheet of paper show the calculations and the answers to the problems below.

1. How much does the customer pay for a suitcase marked $45.50 if a retail discount of 12% is allowed?
2. Sleeveless blouses formerly priced at $13.50 were marked down 20%. What was the markdown price?
3. During a special sale, the price of a dining table is marked down 30% from $309.95. What is the special sale price?
4. The price of a desk is reduced 40% from the original price of $415.95. How much will the desk cost the purchaser at the reduced price?

5. For a sale $25 curtains were marked down 15%. What was the sale price of curtains?

DEMONSTRATING OFFICE SKILLS

1. If blank business forms from the *Supplies Inventory* are not available for this and the following problems, use plain paper and create the forms on your typewriter. Type the information that is ordinarily printed on such forms as shown in the illustrations in this part and in Unit 12, Part 2.

    Fill out by hand sales order forms for the following orders taken by phone for the Ames Furniture Company, 1600 Washington Avenue, Cincinnati, OH 45320, on December 3, 19––, terms 2/10, net 30 days. The quantities and unit prices are given; you are to make all extensions and calculate the totals.

    a. The Rockdale Publishing Company, 784 Catherine Street, Unionville, CT 06085. Ship by ABC Trucking Company. Our invoice NF 325 C. Customer Order K 725. Salesperson Canter. Department 16.

      7 Open Storage Bookcases (2 shelves), 48"H × 36"W × 12"D, Walnut veneer finish, No. SW47-1130. Price $86.50 each.
      6 Single Pedestal Desks, 60" × 30", Walnut veneer finish, No. SW48-976. Price $127 each.
      24 Desk Trays, Letter size, Walnut veneer finish, No. SW45-1360. Price $66 a dozen.
      3 Side Chairs with Walnut Arm Rests, Seat 18½" × 18"W × 3"D, No. SW44-204. Price $62.75 each.

    b. The Adams Distributing Company, 66 Canterbury Drive, Springfield, MO 65802. Ship by Beckel Transfer Company. Our Invoice NF 329 C. Customer Order DD 3184. Salesperson Waldorf, Department 16.

      3 Fluorescent Desk Lamps, 18" high, Translucent shade and wood grain walnut base, No. SD77-108. Price $32.95 each.
      36 Desk Pads with Walnut Panels, 20" × 34", No. SD78-3960. Price $92.25 a dozen.
      6 Reception Room Chairs, Seat 18½" × 20"W × 3"D, color: Spice brown, No. SW43-241. Price $41.50 each.
      3 Walnut Oblong Waste Baskets, 16" × 9", 14" high, No. SD75-356. Price $12.75 each.

2. Type credit memorandums in duplicate for the following credits allowed customers on January 14 by the Mod Furniture Company, Coral Gables, FL 33926.

a. Mr. J. B. Olds, 1462 Alhambra Circle, San Antonio, TX 78284:

      1 Captain's Chair $68.00
      1 Night Table....................$43.50

b. Mrs. Ellen Brock, 3714 Ponce de Leon Boulevard, Marcellus, NY 13108.

      3 Arm Chairs ....$99.50 each
      1 End Table $35.00

IMPROVING OFFICE SKILLS (Optional)

As an office worker in Barkley's Department store, you are asked to compose a first-draft sales letter that will:

a. Announce a Spring Sale on April 2 and 3.
b. Inform customers of the sales values given by the 20% discount on children's sportclothes, 10% discount on women's casual wear, and 15% discount on men's sportswear.
c. Persuade customers to attend the sale.

Type your draft on a plain white sheet of paper. Even though this is only a draft, it should be neat and easy to read.

The Office Worker and Financial Duties

Part 1

Banking Activities

Peggy Colson works in a small law office with two other office workers. The two lawyers for whom the three work provide all of the legal services in their small town. Because the office staff is small, Peggy and her two fellow workers help each other with all the tasks that must be done. However, because Peggy enjoys recordkeeping, she handles most of the financial tasks, including taking care of the banking activities for the office.

Banking activities in a large firm are handled by a specialized department within the firm. If you are employed by the department that handles banking activities, you will have specific tasks to complete according to established procedures. This is necessary to maintain a smooth, orderly relationship with the bank or banks with which the company does business. On the other hand, if you are employed in a small office, you may find that you will have some tasks that include some banking activities. Because every business must deal with banks, you will find it valuable to understand the basic services they provide.

premises:
property; buildings
and grounds

obligations:
financial duties

Business firms of all sizes use the services of commercial banks rather than maintain large sums of money on their own premises. Money deposited in checking accounts is then available for the payment of all types of obligations through writing checks. Cash, if used at all, is used for only the smallest transactions.

Checks facilitate the handling of financial transactions. Checks can be sent through the mail safely, and a canceled check can be used as a receipt for payment. Furthermore, checks can be transferred from one person to another by merely indorsing them properly. Of course, checks can be deposited in a commercial account either in person or by mail.

indorsing:
writing one's name on
the back of a check

reconciling:
bringing into balance

Office workers often handle bank accounts and therefore have the responsibility for making deposits, writing checks, keeping the checkbook, and reconciling bank statements. Occasionally office workers are authorized to sign checks and indorse those received for deposit. Financial matters must be handled in a confidential manner. Accuracy is also extremely important.

Opening a Bank Account

While banks have varying procedures for opening accounts, many do require some references in order to know that they will be dealing with a responsible group of people. Generally a new company is able to provide references with no difficulty.

All persons in the organization who will be authorized to sign checks must fill out signature cards. The signatures should be written exactly the way they will appear on all checks that are signed by these persons. Generally only a few individuals are authorized to sign checks for an organization.

Authorized Signatures of	Brooks, Alison R.	ACCOUNT NUMBER
FOR THE PEOPLE'S SAVINGS BANK, PORTLAND, MAINE		511-400-24

Below are duly authorized signatures, which you will recognize in the payment of funds or in the transaction of other business on my account. In making this deposit and at all times in doing business with this bank, I specifically agree to all of the terms and conditions printed on the reverse side hereof.

Date *May 26, 19--*

Signature *Alison R. Brooks*

Signature   Telephone No. *799-0624*

Signature   { *Alison R. Brooks*   Account

Signature   { *by William R. Nelson*   Accepted by *M.C.*

Address   200 Columbia Street

Business   Singers Department Store

Introduced by   Ralph M. Kennedy

Please honor the above signature on checks against my account or as endorsement on checks or drafts in my favor.

Illus. 15-1

Signature card

Making Deposits

Checks and cash received by an organization are generally deposited in the bank as soon after receipt as possible. In offices where the volume of funds received is great, there may be daily or twice-daily deposits in the bank. In other offices, deposits may be made only once or twice a week. Plan a schedule for depositing money so that large amounts of money — in either checks or cash — are not held in the office overnight.

A deposit slip must be prepared for every deposit. This form is supplied by your bank, and you should keep a stock of the forms in your office so that you can prepare the deposit slip before you go to the bank.

The information needed on a deposit slip includes:

1. Name and address of depositor.
2. Date.
3. Account number.
4. Items to be deposited.

Generally checks should be identified on the deposit slip in one of the following ways:

1. By transit number, which appears in fraction form in the upper right corner of the check and is assigned to each bank by the American Bankers Association. An illustration of a check is on page 573.
2. By name, if the bank is a local one.
3. By the city and state of out-of-town banks.

If, however, you have a large number of checks, you may show the total only on the deposit slip and attach an adding machine tape showing the individual items, as well as the total.

Illus. 15-2

Deposit slip

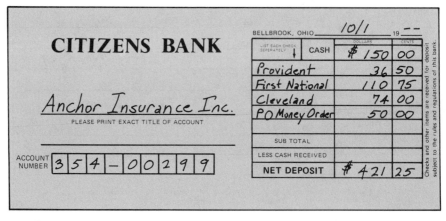

If you must regularly deposit large sums of coins and bills, you should get a supply of wrappers which the bank will provide. Coins and bills should be packaged in designated quantities. It is a general practice to write or stamp the name of the depositing firm on each roll of coins and each package of bills so that if one should be misplaced, it will be credited to the proper account.

Deposits consisting of checks only may be made by mail or in person. If by mail, a deposit will be acknowledged by the bank by a prompt return of a receipt. Deposits that include cash are made in person at a

Unit 15 • The Office Worker and Financial Duties

teller's window at the bank where the account is maintained. A teller receives your deposit, checks the items, and immediately issues you a receipt. This receipt should be filed when you return to your office.

Writing Checks

A *check* is a written order directing a bank to pay out the money of a depositor; therefore, it should be written with extreme care. The following procedures are generally acceptable.

1. Type checks or write them in ink — never in pencil.
2. Number each check if numbers are not printed on them. Be sure that the number of the check corresponds with that on the check stub.
3. Date the check on the exact date that it is written.
4. Write the name of the payee, the person who is to receive the money, in full. If you are not sure of the correct spelling, try to verify it in the telephone directory or from previous correspondence. Omit titles such as Mr., Ms., Mrs., Miss, Dr., or Prof.
5. Write the amount of the check in large, bold figures close enough to the printed dollar sign to prevent the insertion of other figures. In spelling out the amount, start at the extreme left, capitalize the first letter only, and express cents as fractions of one hundred:
   Two hundred fifty-two no/100 -Dollars
   Three thousand two hundred forty 75/100 - - - - - - - - - -Dollars
   If you should write a check for less than a dollar, precede the spelled-out amount with the word *Only* and cross out the printed word *Dollars* as:
   Only forty-nine cents -Dollars
6. Fill in all blank space before and after the name of the payee and after the written amount with hyphens, periods, or a line to prevent the insertion of other names or amounts.

Illus. 15-3

Check with stub

7. Write the purpose of the check, such as *In Payment of Invoice 1691*, at the bottom of the check. Some checks have a special blank line for this purpose.
8. Do not erase on a check. If you should make an error in writing a check, write the word *Void* across the face of both the check and the check stub. Save the voided check and file it in numerical order with the canceled checks when they are returned by the bank.
9. Do not sign blank checks. Anyone could fill them out and cash them.
10. Do not write a check payable to "Cash" unless you are in the bank and plan to present it for bills and coins immediately.
11. Write legibly. An illegible signature creates difficulties at the bank and is no protection against **forgery**.

forgery:
illegally writing
another's name

alterations:
changes

Frequently, a firm has a checkwriter, a machine that perforates and inks in the amount into the check paper to prevent **alterations**.

Maintaining a Record

The form of checks used in an office varies, but there is always some means of maintaining a record of checks written. Some checkbooks contain a stub for each check. Fill in the stub first, recording on it the exact information that will be included on the check itself. The stub has a place for the balance brought forward as well as the balance after the amount of the check being written is subtracted.

Indorsing Checks

Indorsements are necessary to make checks *negotiable*, that is, transferable from one person to another. There are several types of indorsements, each of which serves a different purpose and carries a different degree of protection. The most common types of business indorsements are *restrictive, full* or *special,* and *blank* indorsements. A knowledge of indorsements will help you safeguard checks.

A *restrictive indorsement* allows you to send an indorsed check safely through the mail. It transfers the ownership for a specific, stated purpose. For example, the following words may be written above the signature of the indorser: *For Deposit Only*. If you indorse a check in this way it can only be deposited in the account for which you have responsibility. Since the check cannot be cashed by anyone else, there is little danger if the check is misplaced, lost, or stolen.

Indorsements are usually written in ink, but restrictive indorsements made with rubber stamps are often used for depositing checks. This type

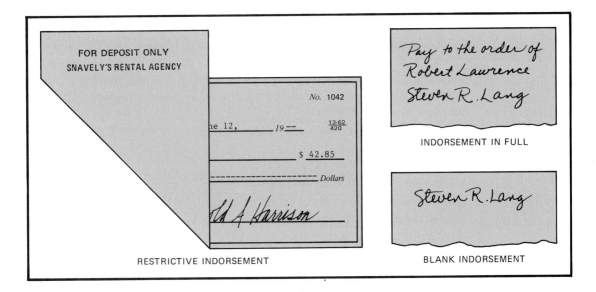

FOR DEPOSIT ONLY
SNAVELY'S RENTAL AGENCY

Pay to the order of
Robert Lawrence
Steven R. Lang

INDORSEMENT IN FULL

No. 1042

he 12,   19--   13-62
                              420

$ 42.85

----------------------- *Dollars*

Ed A. Harrison

Steven R. Lang

RESTRICTIVE INDORSEMENT

BLANK INDORSEMENT

of indorsement is satisfactory because it makes the checks payable only to the account of the depositor and would not benefit anyone who might obtain a rubber stamp and attempt to use it improperly.

An *indorsement in full,* or a *special* indorsement as it is sometimes called, shows the name of the person to whom the check is being transferred. For example, the words *Pay to the order of William T. Rosen* may be written before the indorser's signature. A check indorsed in this way cannot be cashed by anyone without William T. Rosen's signature. Therefore, you may send a check indorsed in this manner through the mail without danger if it is lost.

A *blank indorsement* consists only of a signature across the back of the check. It makes the check payable to anyone who may possess it. You should use this type of indorsement only when you plan to cash or deposit a check immediately. It is not the correct indorsement for a check that is being sent through the mail or for a check that could be lost or misplaced because the check can be cashed by anyone who holds it — even if that person has no right to it.

Stopping Payment on Checks

There are times when it is necessary to stop payment on a check. To "stop payment" means to inform the bank that it is not to pay a check when it arrives at the bank.

Payment on a check may be stopped for a number of reasons. Among them are: if a check is lost or stolen, if a check was written incorrectly, or if the check was written for goods or services that have been canceled.

Illus. 15-4

Generally it is a good practice to telephone the bank telling them of the check for which payment is to be stopped. The bank will need the following information: the name of the drawer (the one who signed the check), the date of the check, the amount of the check, and the name of the payee. It is also a good practice to follow up the telephone conversation with a letter or form confirming the information that was provided by telephone.

Overdraft

When a depositor writes a check on an account in which there are not sufficient funds to cover payment of the check, there is an *overdraft*. Inaccurate or incomplete recordkeeping on the part of the depositor or the bank may have caused the overdraft. Overdrafts occur infrequently in a well-organized office. One office worker related this experience:

> When I was called by the local bank about an overdraft, I was extremely surprised. My employer was a new lawyer in town, and we had carefully deposited sufficient funds to take care of our monthly bills. I told the banker that there had possibly been an error. I asked if the bank had recorded our deposit of May 30. They checked, and they had not. When the bank called back an hour later, they told me that the deposit had been credited to J. Noble by mistake. My employer's name is J. Nobel.

When a checking account is overdrawn, a bank is likely to return the checks marked *Insufficient Funds*. There are occasions, however, when someone at the bank will first telephone the depositor. A charge is generally made by the bank for handling a check written with insufficient funds to cover it.

Reconciliation of the Bank Statement

A bank statement and the canceled checks that the bank paid out of your firm's account are sent to you periodically, usually once a month.

As shown below, the Statement of Account will list the Statement Period — A; the Beginning Balance — B; Total Deposits — C; Total Checks — D; the Service Charge — E — for handling the account; and the Ending Balance — F — of the period.

This banking service permits you to check the accuracy of your checkbook against the bank records and to file the canceled checks as proof of the firm's payments.

You should compare the final balance on the bank statement with the checkbook balance and account for the difference. This process of accounting for the difference is called *reconciling the bank statement*. For the

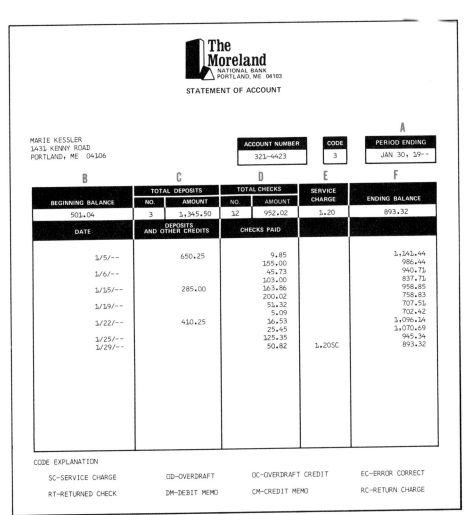

Illus. 15-5

Statement of
Account

The Moreland
NATIONAL BANK
PORTLAND, ME 04103

STATEMENT OF ACCOUNT

MARIE KESSLER
1431 KENNY ROAD
PORTLAND, ME 04106

ACCOUNT NUMBER	CODE	A PERIOD ENDING
321-4423	3	JAN 30, 19--

B	C TOTAL DEPOSITS		D TOTAL CHECKS		E SERVICE CHARGE	F
BEGINNING BALANCE	NO.	AMOUNT	NO.	AMOUNT		ENDING BALANCE
501.04	3	1,345.50	12	952.02	1.20	893.32

DATE	DEPOSITS AND OTHER CREDITS	CHECKS PAID		ENDING BALANCE
1/5/--	650.25	9.85		1,141.44
		155.00		986.44
1/6/--		45.73		940.71
		103.00		837.71
1/15/--	285.00	163.86		958.85
		200.02		758.83
1/19/--		51.32		707.51
		5.09		702.42
1/22/--	410.25	16.53		1,096.14
		25.45		1,070.69
1/25/--		125.35		945.34
1/29/--		50.82	1.20SC	893.32

CODE EXPLANATION

SC–SERVICE CHARGE	OD–OVERDRAFT	OC–OVERDRAFT CREDIT	EC–ERROR CORRECT
RT–RETURNED CHECK	DM–DEBIT MEMO	CM–CREDIT MEMO	RC–RETURN CHARGE

convenience of their depositors, many banks print a reconciliation form on the back of the monthly statement. The following steps should be taken to reconcile an account:

1. Compare the amount of each canceled check with the amount listed on the bank statement. This step will show any error made by the bank or the depositor in recording a check. Place a check mark beside each verified amount.
2. Arrange the canceled checks in numerical order.
3. Compare the returned checks with the stubs in the checkbook. Place a check mark on the stub of each check that has been returned.
4. Make a list of the outstanding checks — those that have not been paid and returned. Include on the list the number of each outstanding check and the amount.

5. Add the amounts of the outstanding checks and deduct the total from the balance shown on the bank statement.
6. Subtract the amount of the service charges listed on the bank statement from the checkbook balance.
7. After the service charge has been deducted from the checkbook balance, the remaining amount should agree with the balance shown on the bank statement after the total of the outstanding checks has been deducted.

Illus. 15-6

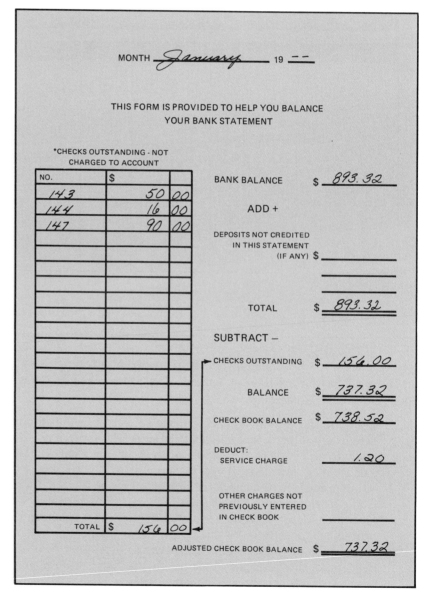

MONTH _January_ 19 _--_

THIS FORM IS PROVIDED TO HELP YOU BALANCE
YOUR BANK STATEMENT

*CHECKS OUTSTANDING - NOT
CHARGED TO ACCOUNT

NO.	$	
143	50	00
144	16	00
147	90	00
TOTAL	$ 156	00

BANK BALANCE $ 893.32

ADD +

DEPOSITS NOT CREDITED
IN THIS STATEMENT
(IF ANY) $ _____

TOTAL $ 893.32

SUBTRACT −

CHECKS OUTSTANDING $ 156.00

BALANCE $ 737.32

CHECK BOOK BALANCE $ 738.52

DEDUCT:
SERVICE CHARGE 1.20

OTHER CHARGES NOT
PREVIOUSLY ENTERED
IN CHECK BOOK _____

ADJUSTED CHECK BOOK BALANCE $ 737.32

Unit 15 • The Office Worker and Financial Duties

You will generally prepare a rough draft of a bank reconciliation in
pencil and, if necessary, type a final copy for your records. Bank recon-
cilations are maintained for at least a year. The form provided on the
back of the bank statement is generally a sufficient record, so it may not
be necessary to type another copy.

Following is an example of a typed reconciliation.

RECONCILIATION OF BANK ACCOUNT

January 30, 19--

```
Balance as shown on bank statement .......................... $893.32
Less checks outstanding:

                    143............... $50.00
                    144............... 16.00
                    147............... 90.00                     156.00
Adjusted Bank Balance ....................................... $737.32

Balance as shown by check book ............................ $738.52
Less January service charge ................................   1.20
Adjusted checkbook balance .................................. $737.32
```

REVIEWING IMPORTANT POINTS

1. What are the advantages of using the services of commercial banks?
2. What are common banking activities that office workers sometimes handle?
3. If you were authorized to sign checks for a company, what records at the bank would you have to sign? Why?
4. What is the purpose of a deposit slip?
5. When may a check be written to "Cash"?
6. Why must checks be indorsed?
7. Why is a checkwriter used?
8. When might payment be stopped on a check?
9. Why is a bank reconciliation prepared?

MAKING IMPORTANT DECISIONS

1. Roberta Townsend is responsible for preparing deposits for the bank. One day, she had a large number of checks to prepare for deposit. There were more checks than she could list on the last deposit slip that she had at her desk. She decided that a deposit listing wasn't really that important and merely took the stack of checks to the bank, along with the tape from her adding machine that indicated the total of the deposit. What do you think of Roberta's decision?
2. Phil was asked to prepare checks for several invoices. He was very busy so he neglected to prepare the checks on the day they were given to him by the supervisor. When he got around to the task, he found that in all three instances the discount period had ended three days ago. He wondered what he should do because he knew that his firm liked to take advantage of the discount. As he thought about the matter he realized that his supervisor hadn't cautioned him to do this job immediately. Therefore, he decided it wasn't his fault that they had lost the discount. Then he wondered what would happen if he merely dated the checks for the final day of the discount period. This seemed like a good idea to him. What do you think of Phil's decision to postdate the checks?

LEARNING TO WORK WITH OTHERS

Martin McClusky takes care of banking activities in a small office. From time to time the owner of the business writes a check but doesn't take time to fill in the details so that Martin knows the purpose of the check. Martin is responsible for maintaining all the banking records and he finds it difficult to do when the owner fails to keep records. Martin is relatively new in his position; the owner is hard-working and competent. Martin wonders what he should do about this problem.

What suggestions do you have for Martin?

IMPROVING LANGUAGE SKILLS

Type the following paragraph, capitalizing all words that should be capitalized.

during the year we arranged to purchase an idle flat glass plant on approximately 50 acres in henryetta, oklahoma. title closing was completed in december. we are converting this property to a glass container factory by utilizing many existing facilities and installing modern production equipment. henryetta is located 50 miles south of tulsa and 90 miles east of oklahoma city and has excellent highway and rail facilities to most of the population in the southwest. from this plant, we will be able to economically serve arkansas, kansas, louisiana, missouri, oklahoma, texas and other states. in line with our planned expansion program, the henryetta plant will enable us to expand sales to our present customers who operate in these areas.

IMPROVING ARITHMETIC SKILLS

You must prepare checks for payment of several invoices. Information necessary for determining the amount of each check is given below. Determine the amount for each check. Today's date is May 12.

1. Invoice date: May 2
   Terms: 2/10, n/30
   Amount of invoice: $498.71
2. Invoice date: April 27
   Terms: 2/15, n/30
   Amount of invoice: $1,190.45
3. Invoice date: May 2
   Terms: 2/10, n/30
   Amount of invoice: $390.56
4. Invoice date: April 15
   Terms: 2/10, n/30
   Amount of invoice: $1,456.54
5. Invoice date: May 3
   Terms: 3/10, n/30
   Amount of invoice: $986.54
6. Invoice date: May 3
   Terms: 2/15, n/30
   Amount of invoice: $198.54

DEMONSTRATING OFFICE SKILLS

1. The checking account balance for the Village Stationery Store on the first of April was $1,121.50. During the month there were deposits totaling $1,500.50. During the same period checks totaling $950.43 were written. On the last day of the month checks amounting to $321.25 had not yet been cashed. What is the checkbook balance on April 30? What is the bank balance on the same date?
2. Assume that you are responsible for handling banking tasks for your employer, who is a medical doctor. Among your tasks is the reconciliation of the bank statement each month. Assume that the following checks were written during the month of April:

No. 843	$ 50.45	853	$ 31.49
844	15.25	854	29.45
845	425.00	855	75.60
846	125.34	856	105.43
847	156.75	857	45.00
848	89.90	858	19.50
849	111.20	859	23.45
850	24.50	860	154.19
851	149.00	861	45.67
852	345.30	862	15.32

The checkbook balance after reconciliation on April 1 was $3,210.34. The deposits for the month were: $350.00, $1,325.50, $869.00, $1,140.40 and $890.40.

The bank statement for the month of April showed a balance of $5,936.86. The checks missing were: 858 for 19.50, 860 for 154.19 and 862 for 15.32.

Using the form provided in the *Supplies Inventory* or plain paper, prepare the reconciliation of the bank statement.

Part 2

Making Payments

Pamela Blair works as a clerk in the office of a small downtown bookstore. Among her responsibilities is taking care of all the payments that must be made. She has developed a procedure that allows her to write all checks for monthly expenditures at one time, so she doesn't have to return to this task often. She keeps all her records up to date because the owner of the business, Ms. Carla Haddad, must refer to them frequently.

Paying Monthly Bills

Your office will undoubtedly have a system for checking the accuracy of each bill received for payment. You will want to verify each statement before preparing the check necessary for payment. For example, if a payment reaches its destination later than expected, the statement for the following month may include an amount in arrears. You should determine, in such an instance, whether the preceding month's bill had been paid. When you find that a check has been written for the preceding month, you subtract the amount shown in arrears and write a check for the difference, representing the expense for the last month only.

arrears:
due but not yet paid

Your records will also indicate when payment must be made and in what form since there are some firms that do not accept ordinary checks.

Forms for Payments

Some of the various forms that are used in making payments include:

1. Ordinary check.
2. Voucher check.
3. Certified check.
4. Bank draft.
5. Cashier's check.
6. Postal and American Express money orders.

Ordinary Checks

You learned in the preceding Part how checks are written. For many payments, it is sufficient to write ordinary checks and send them by mail in time for arrival at their destination on the due dates.

Voucher Checks

Voucher checks are checks with vouchers attached which are perforated for easy detaching. The voucher provides details of the check's purpose. As shown in Illus. 15-8, the invoice number, a description of the goods purchased, the amount, the discount allowed, and the net amount are all included on the voucher. The voucher is detached before the check is deposited. The voucher is verified against the records of the receiving company, and if it agrees with that record, the voucher may be discarded or filed.

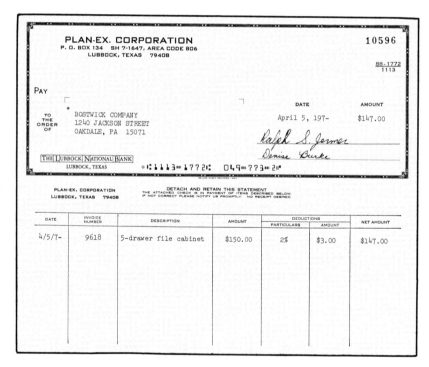

Illus. 15-8

Voucher check

Certified Checks

Certified checks are checks that the bank has confirmed will be paid when presented. You obtain a certified check by presenting an ordinary check to the bank and asking a bank official, usually a cashier, to certify it for you. The official will look at the account on which the check is drawn to see if there are sufficient funds to cover the check. If there are sufficient funds, the official will stamp CERTIFIED on the face of the check you prepared and add his or her signature. Immediately, the account is charged for the amount of the check. From this point on, the bank becomes responsible for payment of the amount indicated on the check. Because the bank now guarantees payment, the check is received by the payee without hesitation, even if the payee doesn't know the drawer. Such a check is deposited the same as an ordinary check.

Certified checks are generally requested when the payee does not know the business reputation of a person or company providing goods or services.

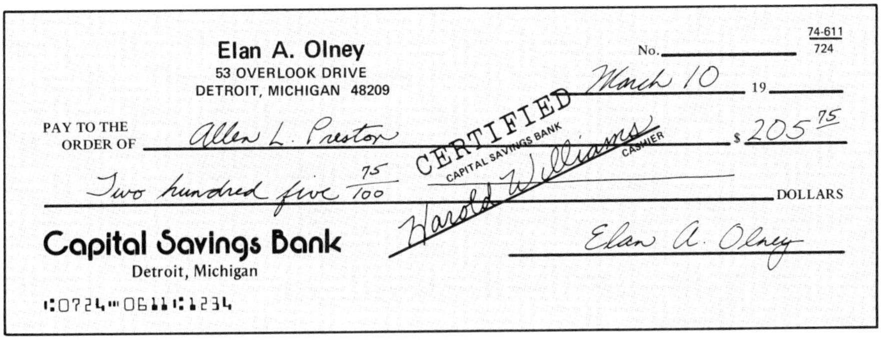
Elan A. Olney
53 OVERLOOK DRIVE
DETROIT, MICHIGAN 48209
No. ______ 74-611/724
March 10 19___
PAY TO THE ORDER OF Allen L. Preston $ 205 75/100
Two hundred five 75/100 DOLLARS
CERTIFIED
CAPITAL SAVINGS BANK
Harold Williams
CASHIER
Capital Savings Bank
Detroit, Michigan
Elan A. Olney
⑆0724⑈0611⑆1234

Illus. 15-9

Certified check

Bank Draft

A *bank draft* is an order drawn by one bank on its deposits in another bank to pay a third party. Since this type of draft, like a certified check, has the bank's assurance of payment, it is accepted more freely than an ordinary check. In the illustration, the Southern Trust Bank is the drawer; the First National Bank of Denver, Colorado, the drawee, is the bank that must pay the draft; and the payee is K and S Construction Co. The cashier of the Southern Trust Bank, Barbara J. Jones, merely signs for the drawer.

You may purchase a bank draft by presenting cash or your employer's check to a bank. The cashier will make out the draft. Ordinarily banks make a small charge for bank drafts.

A bank draft is usually used to **remit** to an individual or firm in a distant city who might not care to accept an ordinary check from a person or firm unknown to them. Although bank drafts and certified checks should be passed with equal confidence, business firms prefer bank drafts.

remit: send

Cashier's Check

Another type of cash payment you or your employer might use is the cashier's check. A *cashier's check* is written by a bank on its own funds. It serves somewhat the same purpose as a bank draft. It differs in that it is drawn by the cashier on funds in the cashier's own bank, whereas a bank draft is drawn upon deposits in another bank. When you wish to pay a person who may be unaware of your credit standing or to cash a check in a distant city, where you are not known and your personal check might be questioned, you could use a cashier's check.

You need not be a depositor in a bank to purchase a cashier's check. You may give the cashier your employer's check or cash to cover the amount of the cashier's check. The cashier will then write a check for the specific amount, payable to the person whom you designate. A small charge is usually made by the bank for issuing a cashier's check.

Illus. 15-10

Cashier's check

No. 5111	**SOUTHERN TRUST BANK**	23-322 / 1020

September 15 19 --

PAY TO THE ORDER OF *K and S Construction Co.* $ *1247 55*

The sum of $1247 and 55 cts _____ DOLLARS

THE FIRST NATIONAL BANK
Denver, Colorado

Barbara G. Jones

CASHIER

⑈⑆020⑈⑆0322⑈1234

Postal and American Express Money Orders

Postal money orders or *American Express money orders* are documents that are exchangeable for the sums indicated on them when they are presented at the proper offices. When payment must be made by a person who does not have a checking account, the postal or American Express money order provides a safe, secure way of sending money.

Domestic postal money orders may be purchased at all post offices, branches, and stations in the United States and its possessions; international postal money orders may be purchased at many of these same places. Express money orders may be purchased at any American Express Company or at many banks.

If you are sending an international money order, you must fill out a printed application form. None is required for a domestic money order or an American Express money order. When you purchase a domestic money order, you are required to enter on the appropriate lines the name of the payee, your own name, and your address.

Postal money orders are limited to $300, but two or more may be purchased to make up any desired amount.

To cash a postal money order, take it to a money order office within thirty days after issue; after that time, the orders will be paid only at the office designated on the order.

You may cash American Express money orders either at American Express offices or at banks. They are good indefinitely.

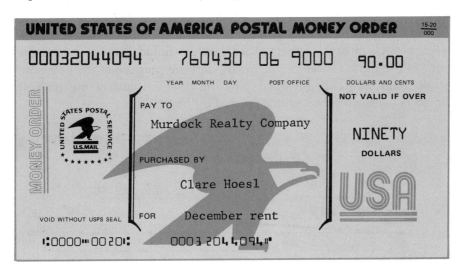

Illus. 15-11

Domestic postal money order

Petty Cash Fund

While most payments are made in the manner described in the preceding pages of this Part, there are small payments that are generally handled through what is known as a *petty cash fund*. This fund is used to pay for such items as special mail services, window washing, refreshments for a special coffee hour, and unusual, but inexpensive, office supplies.

Usually one person has responsibility for handling the petty cash fund. The person with the responsibility receives all requests for payments, sees that a proper record is made, and makes the payments in cash. The fund is usually maintained in a metal cashbox in the desk of the person responsible during the day and is placed in a safe at night.

Establishing the Fund

To establish a petty cash fund:

1. A check is written payable to Petty Cash for the amount to be placed in the fund.
2. The check is signed by an authorized person and cashed at the firm's bank.
3. The money is placed in the petty cash box.

Recording Payments from the Fund

Each time a payment is made from the petty cash fund, a receipt signed by the person receiving payment is placed in the petty cash box. In many offices, the receipts are numbered consecutively as a way of keeping track of each of them. Each receipt should show the date, the name of the person receiving payment, and the purpose of the payment. At all times, the cash on hand plus the total amount of the receipts should equal the original amount placed in the fund.

Illus. 15-12

Petty cash receipt

Jones Drug Company	
PETTY CASH RECEIPT	

No. *422* Date *April 30* 19--

Received of Jones Drug Company $ *1.05*

One and 05/100 Dollars

For *Postage due*

Account Charged: *miscellaneous* Signed *H. R. Burke*

Replenishing the Fund

Additional cash is placed in the fund whenever the amount of cash is judged to be insufficient to pay for expected expenses. To replenish the fund, follow this procedure:

1. Add all receipts to gain a total of payments made from the last date of replenishment of the fund.
2. Count the cash on hand.
3. Add the total of receipts to the amount of cash on hand. The sum should equal the amount originally placed in the fund.

This step is called "proving the petty cash fund." An illustration of a proof follows:

Total of receipts for payments	$72.09
Cash on hand	2.91
Total..	$75.00

(The original sum in the fund was $75.00.)

4. Prepare a report of petty cash expenditures. The receipts should be attached to the report.

SUMMARY REPORT OF PETTY CASH FUND
May 2 to June 16, 19--

Balance on hand, May 2	$75.00

Expenditures:

Office Supplies	$ 9.90
Cleaning Supplies	8.44
Taxis and Buses	14.75
Messenger Services.......................................	10.50
Window Washing Service...........................	12.50
Photographs	16.00
Total expenditures	72.09
Balance on hand, June 16..	$2.91

5. Write a check payable to "Petty Cash" for the amount of the expenditures made from the petty cash fund. (In the above illustration, the check would be written for $72.09.)
6. Submit the report with receipts attached and the check payable to "Petty Cash" to the person responsible for the establishment and replenishment of the fund.
7. Cash the check, after it is returned to you with the signature of the person responsible for the fund, and place the money in the petty cash fund.

In some organizations, a record of petty cash payments is maintained in a Petty Cash Book, a page of which is illustrated on page 590. You will note that the amount on the first line is the balance of petty cash on May 1. Each expenditure is recorded on the day of the payment and the explanation column identifies the nature of the payment. Several additional columns are provided in a Petty Cash Book to show the distribution of the payments. There are special columns for frequent expenses, such as "Office Supplies," "Messenger Service," "Taxis and Buses," and

"Window-Washing Service." All items that do not fit into one of the special columns are listed in the "Miscellaneous" column.

PETTY CASH BOOK

Date	Explanation	Receipts	Payments	Distribution of Payments				
				Office Supplies	Postal	Transportation	Messenger	Miscellaneous
May 5	Balance	100 00						
6	Cleaning supplies		5 90					5 90
7	Window washer		12 50					12 50
8	Delivery of contract		4 50				4 50	
18	Taxi		2 20			2 20		
19	Develop photographs		16 00					16 00
20	Immediate delivery of sale		5 00				5 00	
20	Taxi		5 30			5 30		
21	Postage stamps		13 00		13 00			
22	Miscellaneous office supplies		6 50	6 50				
23	Taxi		4 60			4 60		
25	Miscellaneous art supplies		12 45					12 45
31	Totals	100 00	87 95	6 50	13 00	12 10	9 50	46 85
31	Balance		12 05					
		100 00	100 00					
31	Balance	12 05						
31	Check No. 456	87 95						

Illus. 15-13

Petty cash book

REVIEWING IMPORTANT POINTS

1. What must you do to verify statements for payment?
2. What are some of the forms that are used in making payments?
3. How does an ordinary check differ from a voucher check?
4. How does a bank draft differ from a cashier's check?
5. Where can money orders be obtained?
6. What is a petty cash fund?
7. How many persons should be responsible for making payments from a petty cash fund?
8. What are the procedures for establishing a petty cash fund?
9. Who signs the receipt for a payment made from a petty cash fund?
10. When is a petty cash fund replenished?

MAKING IMPORTANT DECISIONS

1. Reggie Felty works as a clerk in the business office of a medium-sized manufacturing company. One day his supervisor asked him to

prepare checks for payments that were due. The supervisor explained how each statement was to be checked. However, when Reggie began preparing checks he felt that the statements *had* to be accurate and that it was a waste of time to do the checking. He found that he could prepare another check in the time required to check a statement. What do you think of Reggie's modification of the procedure?

2. Carrie Matthews was asked to prepare some voucher checks by her supervisor. She wasn't sure what a voucher check was and, as she looked at the forms, she couldn't understand why so much information needed to be sent to the person receiving the check. She believed that anyone who received a check would understand what it was in payment of. She decided she could save time by leaving the voucher blank. However, she typed in the information on the check very carefully. What do you think of Carrie's decision?

LEARNING TO WORK WITH OTHERS

Don Mori is responsible for the petty cash fund in his office. One day two of his fellow workers stopped by his desk to ask if they could borrow $20 from the fund. There was going to be a luncheon the next day for one of the clerks who was moving to the West Coast and they wanted to buy a small gift during the lunch hour on this day. They said that they would return the money on Friday afternoon when the received their paychecks. They were good friends with Don, and they were confident that he would cooperate.

What do you think Don should do?

IMPROVING LANGUAGE SKILLS

You may want to review *Plural Forms of Nouns* in Appendix C before doing this assignment.

Write or type the plurals of each of the following words. Be prepared to explain in class the reason for the plural form you chose.

1. analysis	11. itinerary
2. appendix	12. library
3. belief	13. memorandum
4. brother-in-law	14. money
5. crisis	15. parenthesis
6. curriculum	16. path
7. editor in chief	17. president
8. four-year-old	18. proof
9. gentleman	19. shelf
10. index	20. strength

IMPROVING ARITHMETIC SKILLS

You must prepare checks for payment of several invoices. Information necessary for determining the amount of each check is given below. Determine the amount for each check. Today's date is May 31.

1. Invoice date: May 21
   Terms: 2/10; n/30
   Amount of invoice: $987.59

2. Invoice date: May 21
   Terms: 1/10; n/30
   Amount of invoice: $1,178.90

3. Invoice date: May 22
   Terms: 2/10; n/30
   Amount of invoice: $1,350.00

4. Invoice date: May 1
   Terms: 1/10; n/30
   Amount of invoice: $2,500.39

5. Invoice date: May 22
   Terms: 2/10; n/30
   Amount of invoice: $356.89

6. Invoice date: May 21
   Terms: 2/10; n/30
   Amount of invoice: $145.69

DEMONSTRATING OFFICE SKILLS

You are given the following information about the Petty Cash fund transactions for the month of April:

April 1 Balance in the Fund is $1.39.
    1 Check No. 456 for $73.61 was cashed to replenish the fund.
    5 Paid Bright Windows Cleaning Service $12.50 to clean windows.
    6 Paid Airline Stationery Company $4.60 for special writing supplies.
    9 Paid $1.49 to a messenger from Fleet Messenger Service for delivery of a C.O.D. package.
    14 Paid $13.45 to Magic Kitchen Bakery for cakes for conference coffee hour.
    17 Paid $2.69 to send a letter by special delivery.
    19 Paid $24.50 to T. Jones for minor repair job on office files.
    25 Paid $3.50 for taxi to take report to T. W. Wells at his legal firm.
    30 Wrote check to replenish fund.

Prepare a summary report of petty cash expenditures for the month. Write a receipt for each of the payments made during the month. Use the forms provided in the *Supplies Inventory* or make up a form like the one on page 588.

Part 3

Payroll Recordkeeping

Jerry Mead is a payroll clerk in a medium-sized department store. He has been in his position since he graduated from high school about six months ago. He had a general idea of the work of the payroll department when he started but he has learned much about procedures since he began his job. Just recently Jerry was informed that the payroll would be handled by the computer, and he is taking an in-service course on the use of the computer for payroll accounting so that he will have complete understanding of his new duties.

Maintaining the records for the payroll is one of the most important financial tasks in any business. Every organization wants to pay its employees on the scheduled date; it wants the check or payment in cash given to each employee to be absolutely accurate. Furthermore, every organization wants a system that assures accurate recordkeeping for all payroll taxes and all contributions that the organization and the employees may make directly from wages and salaries.

Overview of the Payroll Function

Internal control refers to a system of maintaining records and preparing payments that reduces the possibility of fraud. To maintain good internal control, each part of the payroll system is likely to be handled by a different person, or, in a large firm, by a different department.

fraud: cheating; dishonesty

Internal control enters into the following:

1. *Hiring the employee.* When an employee is hired, a record is created that includes the rate of pay, deductions to be made from the payroll, and general terms of employment.
2. *Keeping the employee's time.* If employees are paid on an hourly basis, there may be a record maintained on a time clock. For those paid by the week or by the month, some type of record

is maintained in the department where employed, and this record is sent to the payroll department at times.

3. *Computing the wages or salary to be paid for each pay period.* In a large organization, there will be a payroll department that handles the timekeeping records and processes the information necessary for the preparation of the payroll.

4. *Paying wages or salaries.* In a large organization, the person who signs the checks or prepares the cash for distribution to employees is in a department other than the one that prepared the payroll. In a very small organization, a payroll clerk may have full responsibility for preparing checks, which are signed by the owner or manager of the business.

In this Part, you will have an opportunity to learn about those activities that are generally handled within the payroll department in a large business or by the payroll clerk in a small business.

Illus. 15-14

A payroll check in a sealed envelope is passed out to each individual in this department.

Wages and Salaries

interchangeably:
in place of each other

Although the terms "wages" and "salaries" are sometimes used **interchangeably**, *wages* refers to payment made for work on an hourly basis. *Salary* describes payment for work for a particular period of time.

Gross earnings refer to the amount earned before deductions. *Net pay* or *take-home pay* refers to the amount actually received by the employee after deductions. The supervisor of the payroll department in a large manufacturing company made this comment:

> We are careful to distinguish between wages and salaries. All the employees in our factories are paid on an hourly basis; when any of them work overtime, they are paid at the rate of 1½ times their basic rate. On the other hand, all of our office employees and the executives are paid a specified sum either for a week or a month; their pay is called a salary. In some instances, persons on salaries are paid for additional work after regular hours. Executives, however, are not paid for overtime work.

deductions: amounts taken out of the paycheck

Computing Wages and Salaries

There are various methods of computing wages and salaries depending on the type of organization, kind of work done by the employee, and regulations covering the employment situation.

Hourly Rate Method. Some employees are paid by the hour. The information you will receive for each hourly employee will include the number of hours each employee worked during the preceding pay period including overtime hours. Your own records would show the hourly rate of each employee. To compute gross wages, you would multiply the number of hours of regular time worked by the rate per hour. Then, if there are overtime hours you would multiply the number of overtime hours by the overtime rate. By adding the two products, you would have the gross wages.

> Harold Wingate worked a total of 45 hours during the week ending June 5. Forty hours were at the regular rate; 5 hours were at the overtime rate. Harold earns $4.50 per hour; 1½ times his base rate is his overtime rate.

$$40 \times 4.50 = \$180.00$$
$$+ \ 5 \times 6.75 = \underline{\quad 33.75}$$

Total (gross) wages earned for week ending June 5........... $213.75

Salary Method. An employee who is paid a salary receives a stated amount for each pay period. Thus, the stated salary is the same as gross pay for the period. For example, if Diane Ellman is earning a salary of $185 per week, her gross pay is $185 per week.

When a salary is stated on a weekly basis, it is possible to determine the yearly salary by multiplying the weekly rate by 52, the number of weeks in a year. Diane earns $9,620 per year ($185 × 52). Her monthly salary can be determined by dividing the yearly salary by 12.

Piece-Rate Method. In some jobs, the employees are paid a certain rate for each item produced. This method is often used in factories where workers produce varying numbers of items or pieces. The more skillful workers under such a plan produce more items in a given amount of time and, thus, earn more wages than persons who are less skillful. In some typewriting service centers typists are paid on the basis of the number of pages of usable copy they are able to produce.

> Jill Kallen works part-time for a typing service near a large university. Jill is a skillful typist and can produce up to 8 pages of manuscript copy per hour. She is paid at the rate of 95 cents per page of regular copy and at the rate of $1.36 per page of copy with quotations and/or footnotes. Recently she received a check for $129.20 for typing a manuscript of 136 pages.

Commission Method. In some positions, employees are paid on a commission basis. Often the sales representatives for an organization are paid on this basis. The commission basis means that an employee is paid a certain percentage of the dollar value of what is sold.

> Bertha Corr is a sales representative for a large optical goods manufacturer. She visits shops throughout the state of Iowa. She is paid monthly; her wages are seven percent of the total sales she has made. Last month she earned $1,456 based on sales of $20,800.

Determining Deductions

There are two kinds of payroll deductions: those required by law and those not required by law, called voluntary deductions.

Required Deductions. The payroll deductions required by law include:

1. Federal income tax.
2. FICA tax (generally identified as social security tax).
3. State income tax (where applicable).
4. City income tax (where applicable).

The amount of federal income tax that is deducted from wages or salaries each pay period depends on the number of exemptions claimed and the amount of income. Exemptions are allowed for those dependents that can legally be claimed by the employee. At the time of employment, each employee fills in an Employee's Withholding Exemption Certificate, referred to as the W-4 Form. If there are changes in the exemptions, the employee is responsible for notifying the payroll office. A copy of the W-4 form is shown in Illus. 15-15.

Form W-4
(Rev. May 1977)

Department of the Treasury
Internal Revenue Service

Employee's Withholding Allowance Certificate
(Use for Wages Paid After May 31, 1977)

This certificate is for income tax withholding purposes only. It will remain in effect until you change it. If you claim exemption from withholding, you will have to file a new certificate on or before April 30 of next year.

Type or print your full name	Your social security number
John Quist	202-54-7747

Home address (number and street or rural route)
1899 Blind Brook Drive

City or town, State, and ZIP code
Houston, Texas 77079

Marital Status

[X] Single ☐ Married
☐ Married, but withhold at higher Single rate

Note: *If married, but legally separated, or spouse is a nonresident alien, check the single block.*

1 Total number of allowances you are claiming 1
2 Additional amount, if any, you want deducted from each pay (if your employer agrees) . . . . $
3 I claim exemption from withholding (see instructions). Enter "Exempt" . . . .

Under the penalties of perjury, I certify that the number of withholding exemptions and allowances claimed on this certificate does not exceed the number to which I am entitled. If claiming exemption from withholding, I certify that I incurred no liability for Federal income tax for last year and that I anticipate that I will incur no liability for Federal income tax for this year.

Signature ► *John Quist*   Date ► March 15   , 19 --

Detach along this line

If you will look at the sample federal income tax table shown in Illus. 15-16, you will see that as the weekly wage increases, so does the federal income tax withheld. Also note that as the number of exemptions increases, given the same weekly wage, the federal income tax withheld decreases.

The amount of social security tax (FICA) deducted each payroll period is a percentage of gross pay up to a maximum amount. The employee's contribution to social security is matched by the employer. Each year the rates are reviewed and can be changed by Congress. The rate for 1978 was 6.05 percent; the maximum on which the rate applied was $17,700. You can secure the current rate by checking with the nearest Social Security Office.

Illus. 15-16

WEEKLY Payroll Period—Employee NOT MARRIED

And the wages are-		And the number of withholding allowances claimed is—									
At least	But less than	0	1	2	3	4	5	6	7	8	9	10 or more
		The amount of income tax to be withheld shall be—										
$110	$115	$13.50	$10.90	$ 8.30	$ 5.80	$ 3.50	$ 1.20	$0	$ 0	$0	$0	$0
115	120	14.40	11.80	9.20	6.60	4.30	2.00	0	0	0	0	0
120	125	15.30	12.70	10.10	7.50	5.10	2.80	.50	0	0	0	0
125	130	16.20	13.60	11.00	8.40	5.90	3.60	1.30	0	0	0	0
130	135	17.10	14.50	11.90	9.30	6.70	4.40	2.10	0	0	0	0
135	140	18.00	15.40	12.80	10.20	7.60	5.20	2.90	.60	0	0	0
140	145	18.90	16.30	13.70	11.10	8.50	6.00	3.70	1.40	0	0	0
145	150	20.00	17.20	14.60	12.00	9.40	6.80	4.50	2.20	0	0	0
150	160	21.60	18.60	16.00	13.40	10.80	8.20	5.70	3.40	1.10	0	0
160	170	23.80	20.60	17.80	15.20	12.60	10.00	7.40	5.00	2.70	.40	0
170	180	26.00	22.80	19.70	17.00	14.40	11.80	9.20	6.60	4.30	2.00	0
180	190	28.30	25.00	21.90	18.80	16.20	13.60	11.00	8.40	5.90	3.60	1.30
190	200	30.70	27.20	24.10	20.90	18.00	15.40	12.80	10.20	7.60	5.20	2.90
200	210	33.10	29.60	26.30	23.10	19.90	17.20	14.60	12.00	9.40	6.80	4.50
210	220	35.50	32.00	28.60	25.30	22.10	19.00	16.40	13.80	11.20	8.60	6.10

If the state and local community have income taxes, these too are deducted from gross pay in the payroll department of the employing firm.

Voluntary Deductions. In some organizations there may be voluntary deductions for a company-sponsored insurance program, a savings program, or a retirement plan.

Records Maintained for Payroll Accounting

After you have computed the employee's gross pay and deductions, you are ready to record the earnings of each employee. This information must be recorded so that it can be sent to state and federal agencies which require it. Payroll information is usually recorded on two records — the payroll register and the employee's earnings record.

Payroll Register

Time cards for hourly employees provide the information that is recorded in a *payroll register*. In Illus. 15-18 is a time card for a company using a time clock. Illus. 15-17 shows how the information from the time card is transferred and the deductions are made for each employee.

The Payroll Register lists all employees at work for the particular payroll period. The names of the employees are listed in alphabetical order.

Illus. 15-17

Payroll register

THE WAKEFIELD PUBLISHING COMPANY

PAYROLL REGISTER   DATE November 5, 19--

No.	Name	Allow.	Marital Status	Gross Earnings	Federal With. Tax	F.I.C.A.	Group Insurance	Hosp.	Bonds	Total Deductions	Net Earnings
9	BROCK, PERRI	1	S	78 00	6 30	4 56	1 60	1 75		14 21	63 79
13	FRANKS, CHRISTINE	1	S	90 00	8 60	5 27	1 60	1 75		17 22	72 78
35	GANGL, ALAN R.	4	M	162 92	10 40	9 53	4 10	2 25	5 50	31 78	131 14
11	GATES, STEPHAN M.	1	S	90 00	8 60	5 27	1 60	1 75		17 22	72 78
32	HEIDT, CAROL A.	2	M	150 39	14 20	8 80	2 85	2 25		28 10	122 29
26	JUNG, MAY	3	M	104 00	1 90	6 08	2 85	2 25	3 00	16 08	87 92
24	WERNER, CHARLES	2	M	101 00	4 30	5 91	2 85	1 75		14 81	86 19

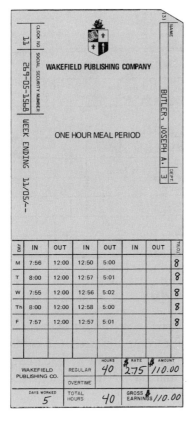

Illus. 15-18

Punched time card

Employee's Earnings Record

An individual *employee's earnings record* is kept for each employee. The earnings records are usually kept in alphabetic order on cards in a file or on loose-leaf sheets in a binder.

The employee's earnings record provides space for information for 13 weeks or a quarter of a year. The information to be recorded on the employee's earnings record is taken from the payroll register. The date for the pay period is entered in the first column. Gross earnings are recorded under the Earnings column and individual deductions for each pay period are recorded under Deductions. The amount actually paid each employee is recorded in the Net Pay column. Another column is added to the employee's earnings record. This is the Taxable Earnings Accumulated. This tells at a glance the total gross earnings of the employee. When an employee's earnings reach a certain amount, some taxes, such as social security, no longer apply. By using this column, you can make sure all deductions are accurately figured.

EMPLOYEE'S EARNINGS RECORD

Gates	Stephen	M.	289-54-3802
LAST NAME	FIRST	MIDDLE	SOC. SEC. NO.

Week	Period Ending	Earnings	Deductions						Net Pay	Taxable Earnings Accumulated
			Fed. With. Tax	F.I.C.A.	Group Ins.	Hosp.	Other	Total	Amount	
Total First Three Quarters		3537 60	340 80	206 95	62 40	68 25		678 40	2859 20	3537 60
1	10/8	90 00	11 00	5 27	1 60	1 75		19 62	70 38	3627 60
2	10/15	90 00	11 00	5 27	1 60	1 75		19 62	70 38	3717 60
3	10/22	83 50	9 50	4 88	1 60	1 75		17 73	65 77	3801 10
4	10/29	90 00	11 00	5 27	1 60	1 75		19 62	70 38	3891 10
5	11/5	90 00	11 00	5 27	1 60	1 75		19 62	70 38	3981 10
6										

Illus. 15-19

Employee's earnings record

Computerlinked Records

In many organizations, a computer system is used for payroll processes. The input for the computer are time cards, time sheets, and job tickets which indicate the time spent by each employee on the job. The output are the individual payroll checks and the earnings statements. Records are maintained on cards, disks, or magnetic tapes. While such records may seem very different physically from the ones described in the preceding paragraphs, remember that the basic records provide the same types of data. If you understand the nature of records maintained by a payroll clerk in a manual system of recordkeeping, you can understand a computer system for payroll with only a little explanation.

Paying Employees

After the payroll has been prepared, the next step is to pay each employee. In many firms payment is by check; in other firms, in cash; in still others, certain employees are paid in cash, and others are paid by check.

Paying by Check

Payroll checks, after being prepared by a clerk, must be signed by the person designated by the firm to do this. As a rule, however, if there are many checks, a check-signing machine is used.

Deductions are often shown on payroll checks in such a way that the employee will know the amount of each deduction. This information is usually printed on an attached check stub, or voucher, that the employee removes before cashing the check.

Checks for office employees are usually enclosed in envelopes for privacy and presented in packets to department heads, who **distribute** them to the individuals in their departments. In some organizations, checks are mailed to the employee's home or bank. Checks for salaried factory workers are sometimes enclosed in envelopes so that they will not become soiled from handling. They are distributed to the department heads or foremen, who pass them on to the employees. Checks for salaried store employees are usually given to department heads for distribution. While methods of payment vary with different businesses, the information provided on the check will always be the same as that developed in the payroll register; therefore, the check should be prepared using the payroll register as a source of information.

distribute: give out

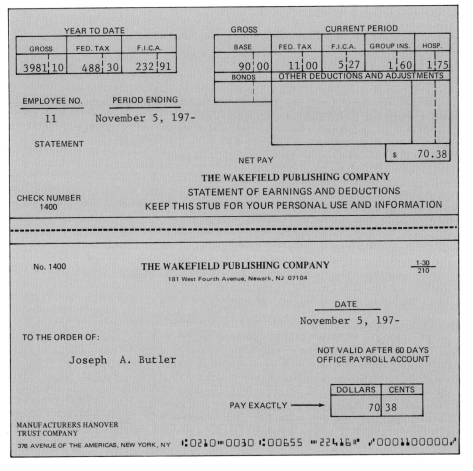

Illus. 15-20

Paycheck and stub

Paying in Cash

As a general rule, employees need their money immediately on pay-day. Therefore, some firms, as a service to their employees, pay by cash rather than by check.

When it is the policy to pay all or some of the employees in cash, a check is drawn for the net amount of the payroll, that is, the amount of the payroll less all deductions. The check is cashed and the money, along with a slip of paper showing gross pay, deductions, and net earnings, is placed in pay envelopes, which are distributed. Before someone is sent to the bank for the payroll money, it is customary to prepare two forms — a payroll change sheet and a payroll cash slip.

Payroll Change Sheet. A payroll change sheet or money tally shows the name of each employee and the amount of money earned. In the columns to the right of each employee's name are indicated how many bills and coins of each denomination will be needed to pay the worker. For example, if Robert T. Rowan makes a net amount of $169.55, he will be given

Illus. 15-21

Payroll change sheet

PAYROLL CHANGE SHEET											
DATE November 12, 19--											
EMPLOYEE	AMOUNT PAID	$20	$10	$5	$1	50¢	25¢	10¢	5¢	1¢	
Rowan, Robert T.	$ 70.38	3	1				1	1		3	
Cavallo, Rose M.	118.59	5	1	1	3	1			1	4	
Kirkland, Murray	70.38	3	1				1	1		3	
Rustagi, Pramode	80.99	4				1	1	2		4	
Dyer, Lena B.	126.64	6		1	1	1		1		4	
Grossman, Isidore	82.62	4			2	1		1		2	
Fairbanks, Joan	61.29	3			1			1		4	
TOTAL	$ 610.89	28	3	2	7	4	4	6	1	24	

eight \$20 bills, one \$5 bill, four \$1 bills, one 50¢ piece, and one nickel. After the salary amounts have been broken down into the various denominations and all columns have been totaled, the totals are transferred to a payroll cash slip so that the bank will know how many of each of the denominations are needed.

You will also notice that the payroll clerk handles the least number of pieces of currency and coins in the lists shown on the payroll change sheet. For Robert T. Rowan, the clerk handles fifteen pieces of currency and coins for a total of \$169.55. The fewer pieces of money handled the fewer the mistakes that might occur.

Payroll Cash Slip. Using the payroll change sheet as a source of information, the clerk prepares a payroll cash slip (illustrated below). This form shows the number of \$100, \$50, \$20, \$10, \$5, and \$1 bills and the number of half-dollars, quarters, dimes, nickels, and pennies that are needed. Because people find it difficult to change large bills, most firms use nothing larger than \$20 bills.

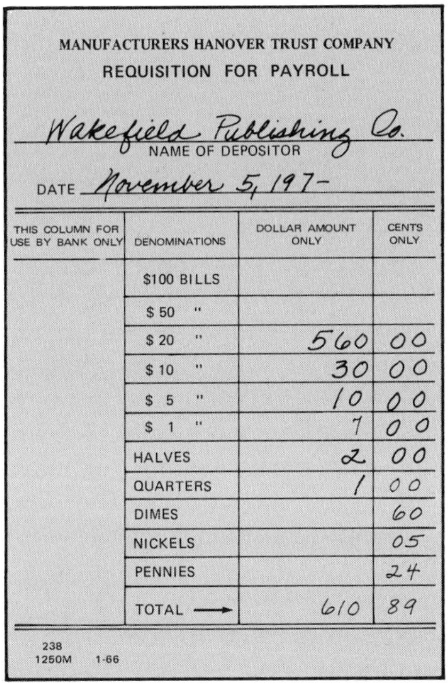

MANUFACTURERS HANOVER TRUST COMPANY

REQUISITION FOR PAYROLL

Wakefield Publishing Co.
NAME OF DEPOSITOR

DATE November 5, 197-

THIS COLUMN FOR USE BY BANK ONLY	DENOMINATIONS	DOLLAR AMOUNT ONLY	CENTS ONLY
	\$100 BILLS		
	\$ 50 "		
	\$ 20 "	560	00
	\$ 10 "	30	00
	\$ 5 "	10	00
	\$ 1 "	7	00
	HALVES	2	00
	QUARTERS	1	00
	DIMES		60
	NICKELS		05
	PENNIES		24
	TOTAL →	610	89

238
1250M 1-66

Illus. 15-22

Payroll cash slip

Distribution of Payroll Money. After the money has been received from the bank, it is usually counted and separated into various denominations and inserted in pay envelopes which have been prepared in advance. After the money and the slip **itemizing** deductions have been inserted, the pay envelopes are ready for distribution. If there are only a few employees in an organization, the pay envelopes are usually distributed to

itemizing: listing singly

them by an executive, the cashier, or the bookkeeper. In a large organization, where it might be unsafe and inconvenient to carry all the pay envelopes around to them, the employees are asked to call at a certain place for their pay. The employees are often asked to sign a receipt when the receive their pay.

REVIEWING IMPORTANT POINTS

1. What are two key characteristics of a good payroll system?
2. How is internal control maintained?
3. What are the key aspects of the payroll function?
4. Is the term *wages* the same as *salaries*? Discuss.
5. How does the hourly rate method differ from the salary method of payment for work performed?
6. Describe the piece-rate method of payment.
7. Why would a firm use the commission method for the payment of employees?
8. Is a person's pay check equal to gross pay? Explain.
9. What is the purpose of a payroll register?
10. What key information is provided in the employee's earnings record?

MAKING IMPORTANT DECISIONS

1. John Garner returned the Employee's Withholding Allowance Certificate (W-4 form) to the payroll department as instructed. When Claire, who works in the payroll department, looked at it, she noticed that he had failed to sign the form. Otherwise, he had provided all the other information. What do you think she should do?
2. Rob works in the payroll department of a medium-sized firm. Recently, he and his co-workers were called together for a meeting at which they learned that a new system for maintaining the payroll would be installed within six months. The new system would involve the use of a computer. The basic tasks would be the same, but they would be done in a different manner. Rob liked his work and the way he did it now. As he listened to the discussion of the new system, it appeared complicated to him. The next day he went to the personnel director to ask if he could be transferred to a department that would not be using a computer. What do you think of Rob's decision?

LEARNING TO WORK WITH OTHERS

Suzanne maintained the payroll records for all employees. She has knowledge of the wages and salaries earned by everyone in the firm.

Shortly after she had been given her present responsibilities, she had lunch with some of her former co-workers. They knew what her new job was. During lunch one said: "Suzanne, now you know all the salaries of the department heads and the top executives. Won't you tell us who gets the highest salary? Are the top salaries really high?"

Suzanne is a friendly, cooperative young woman. She likes her former co-workers very much. What do you think she should say to the questions?

IMPROVING LANGUAGE SKILLS

The following ten terms are among the 1,500 most frequently used words in the business world. You will use each word often when you begin your working career. On a separate sheet of paper write a sentence relating to something that you have learned in this course and use the word correctly. If you do not recall the meaning, you may check it in the dictionary before composing the sentence.

1. analysis   (noun)
2. capacity   (noun)
3. conference   (noun)
4. initial   (verb)
5. maintain   (verb)
6. maximum   (adjective)
7. participate   (verb)
8. procedure(s)   (noun)
9. range   (noun or verb)
10. specific   (adjective)

IMPROVING ARITHMETIC SKILLS

Determine the amount of FICA (social security) tax that must be paid on each of the following gross wages. The rate of tax is 6.05 percent.

	Gross Wages	FICA Tax
1.	$156.89	_____
2.	245.65	_____
3.	79.50	_____
4.	134.50	_____
5.	156.70	_____
6.	125.00	_____
7.	198.60	_____
8.	156.75	_____
9.	139.40	_____
10.	153.25	_____

DEMONSTRATING OFFICE SKILLS

1. On a separate sheet of paper prepare forms like those shown in this Part to complete the three parts of this problem or use the forms provided in the Supplies Inventory.

   a. Prepare a payroll register similar to the one illustrated on page 598. Use the following information to do the payroll register.

Employee				Deductions			
No.	Name	Exemptions	Gross Earnings	Fed. With. Tax	Group Ins.	Hosp.	Bonds
11	Better, John	1	68.00	7.00	1.00	1.25	
32	Carter, Rita	2	121.88	12.70	1.25	1.50	2.00
13	Dupont, Edna	1	66.75	6.60	1.00	1.25	
24	Frazer, Marvin	2	80.00	6.10	1.00	1.25	
35	Gross, Cheryl	4	155.75	13.30	1.50	1.50	2.00
26	Diaz, George M.	3	80.00	3.80	1.25	1.25	1.00
17	Kyoto, Fusai	2	100.00	9.50	1.25	1.50	1.00
28	Maloney, Michael J.	1	75.00	8.00	1.00	1.25	
19	Nielsen, Inger	1	89.05	10.60	1.00	1.50	
10	Presley, Thelma M.	2	63.75	3.30	1.00	1.25	
21	Reid, Ruth P.	2	88.43	7.40	1.25	1.25	
12	Sanchez, Julio P.	1	60.00	5.50	1.00	1.25	
23	Tenney, Mabel A.	3	111.25	8.80	1.25	1.50	1.00
34	Upton, Charlotte	1	80.62	9.10	1.00	1.25	
25	Walker, Arlene N.	2	64.75	3.60	1.00	1.25	

   Compute the FICA (Federal Insurance Contribution Act) tax at the rate of 6.05 percent of the total earnings of each employee.

   After the various deductions have been filled in, add them across to get the total deductions. Deduct the total deductions from gross earnings in order to determine the net earnings — the amount that should appear in the final column. Prove your work by adding all columns vertically. Add the totals of all deductions horizontally. This should equal the grand total of deductions. This amount, subtracted from the total gross earnings, should equal the total net earnings.

   b. Complete the payroll change sheet.
   c. Complete the payroll cash slip.

2. You are to complete the employee's earnings record of William P. Rudy, social security number 463-86-0526, for the last quarter of the year.

(a) Prepare an employee's earnings record by entering the following information on it.

Deductions

Week	Period Ending	Earnings	Federal With. Tax	FICA*	Group Ins.	Hosp.	Other
Total First Three Quarters		4,200.50	565.50	254.13	78.00	87.75	45.00
1	10/8	125.00	18.70	7.56	2.00	2.25	5.00
2	10/15	125.00	18.70	7.56	2.00	2.25	
3	10/22	142.85	21.80	8.64	2.00	2.25	
4	10/29	100.00	13.40	6.05	2.00	2.25	
5	11/5	135.71	20.80	8.21	2.00	2.25	5.00
6	11/12	75.00	8.00	4.54	2.00	2.25	
7	11/19	149.99	22.90	9.07	2.00	2.25	
8	11/26	125.00	18.70	7.56	2.00	2.25	
9	12/3	125.00	18.70	7.56	2.00	2.25	5.00
10	12/10	159.68	24.50	9.67	2.00	2.25	
11	12/17	130.00	19.70	7.86	2.00	2.25	
12	12/24	130.00	19.70	7.86	2.00	2.25	
13	12/31	152.26	24.50	9.21	2.00	2.25	

*FICA Tax Computed at 6.05%

(b) Complete the employee's earnings record by (1) adding each line horizontally to find the total deductions, (2) subtracting the total deductions from the total earnings to find the net pay, (3) extending the total earnings for the first three quarters to the Taxable Earnings Accumulated column and adding the successive total earnings for each week to the accumulated total to find the taxable earnings accumulated, and (4) adding vertically all columns except the Taxable Earnings Accumulated column to find the totals for the quarter and for the year. After the totals have been recorded, check the accuracy of your work by subtracting the deductions total from the earnings total; the remainder should equal the total of the Net Pay column. The last entry in the Taxable Earnings Accumulated column should be equal to the earnings total. *Note:* The items in the Other column represent payments made by Mr. Rudy for goods purchased from the company store.

IMPROVING OFFICE SKILLS (Optional)

Determine the net pay for each of the following employees. Employees are paid biweekly. This is the payroll for March 31.

Name	Gross Earnings	Federal Withholding	FICA	Group Insurance	Net
1. Andre, Roger T.	$660.00	106.30	?	2.50	?
2. Barclay, Lucile	697.50	118.50	?	2.50	?
3. Bargello, Shirley	450.00	75.40	?	2.50	?
4. Brizell, Victor	300.00	51.00	?	2.25	?
5. Chan Hung	540.50	98.50	?	2.50	?
6. Goldman, Lisa	320.00	55.60	?	2.25	?
7. Goretsky, Carl	420.50	51.60	?	2.50	?
8. Hanson, Carolyn	320.00	32.30	?	2.25	?
9. Harewood, Irving	490.00	56.90	?	2.50	?
10. Harragan, Winnie	520.00	58.80	?	2.50	?

You as an Office Worker

Part 1

Learning of Job Opportunities

Maria, Pamela, Michael, and José are seniors in a large high school in San Antonio, Texas, where they are studying clerical procedures. One afternoon after two hours in their laboratory session, the four began to talk about their future. They realized that they had learned a great deal about the modern office; they knew that they had good basic skills; they were confident they understood office procedures and could apply them in various situations. They were sure that they would find jobs that would be very interesting to them.

The Job Market

With your clerical business skills you will find that there are many opportunities for employment. Clerical workers are needed in all types of businesses and organizations. Traditionally, both large and small companies have sought high school graduates for beginning workers. These companies look for beginning workers with good basic skills and positive attitudes toward work.

traditionally: usually; as a cultural pattern

Beginners are hired for positions as typists, accounting clerks, file clerks, clerk/typists, word processing typists, receptionists, and office machine operators.

Types of Organizations

Organizations are classified in a number of ways. A classification based on the nature of activity carried on by the organization is given on page 611. What kind of organization would you find interesting?

Betsy grew up on a farm and loved everything about farming. Over the years she learned a great deal about farming equipment and found it extremely interesting. Near the end of her senior year, as she considered job possibilities, she decided to accept a job with a large distributor of farm equipment. She was hired as a clerk/typist in the maintenance department.

610

Warren worked as a volunteer librarian in his high school. He thoroughly enjoyed helping students select books and talking with them about books. He decided that he would like his first job to be with a large bookstore. He applied for a position with a large bookstore in the downtown section of his hometown. He was hired as a clerk/typist in the order department.

Office workers are needed everywhere. If you have some special interest in a particular field of work, you may want to consider the kinds of positions that are available in that area.

Organization	Activity
Manufacturing	Producers of household appliances, glass products, pianos, carpeting, textiles, electronics, automobiles
Mining	Coal, copper, silver
Construction	Housing, mobile homes, offices, hospitals and bridges
Transportation and Public Utilities	Trucking, airlines, railroads, bus lines, electricity, gas, telephone
Trade	Wholesale, central retailing chain, department store, grocery store, specialty store
Finance, Insurance, and Real Estate	Commercial banks, savings banks, security dealers and brokers, insurance companies, real estate brokers
Health Services	Hospitals, clinics, doctor's office, dentist's office
Community Agencies	YMCA, YWCA, Red Cross, 4-H, Boy Scouts, Girl Scouts
Religious	Church mission services of coordinated groups of churches
Communications	Periodicals, newspaper, book publishing, radio, television, films
Government	City government, state government, federal government
Education	Preschool centers, elementary schools, secondary schools, community colleges, colleges, universities, research centers
Professional	Law offices, counseling service, consultant services, architects' offices, theatre services

Sizes of Organizations

Organizations range from giant corporations with thousands of employees in offices and factories around the world to small, one-office businesses. As you enter the work world, you may want to consider whether you would prefer to work in a large, medium, or small organization or business.

Large organizations generally have specialized departments, including a separate personnel department. The policies and regulations are clearly specified, usually through written bulletins and reports. There is generally an established pattern for reviewing employees for promotion and salary increases. As you realize, a large firm must be well organized because so many people are participating in the activities needed to keep the firm running smoothly.

On the other hand, small organizations, and many medium-sized organizations, often have a more informal style of operation. Since the person with overall responsibility may have first-hand knowledge of the performance of every employee in a small organization, the need for written rules and policies is lessened. This doesn't mean that small organizations don't establish rules and policies. It merely means that such rules and policies are communicated through personal contact and not through formal bulletins and reports.

Illus. 16-1

In large organizations job tasks and promotional opportunities are well-defined.

Dora attends a small high school in western Kansas. Every time she goes to Kansas City, she is sure she wants to work in a large company in a major American city. She thinks it would be exciting to be a part of a major organization. She is planning to consider jobs in large companies when she graduates from high school.

Sean lives in a small town in eastern Ohio. During the past two years he has been working part-time in a local hardware store office. He likes his work and he is considering accepting a full-time job in the hardware store, which is owned by two local families. He likes working in a business that is small enough for him to know personally everyone who works there. He also knows practically everyone who comes there on business.

Illus. 16-2

In smaller organizations the working environment is frequently more informal and job duties often more diverse.

Location

Where do you want to work? Your choice is wide! There are jobs in downtown centers of large metropolitan areas, in suburban communities, in small villages. Jobs are available in places as different as Portland, Maine, and Miami Beach, Florida, or London, England, and Lima, Peru. Some beginning office workers expect to commute from their homes when they are working; others plan to relocate so that they may live near the place of their work.

commute: travel back and forth regularly

relocate: move to a new place

> Rodney loved his hometown, which he realized was smaller than many other towns in the region, and he had no desire to find a job elsewhere when he graduated from high school. He liked to be with people whom he knew; and bustling, large cities were no lure for him. Therefore, he applied at the public utilities office in his hometown when his high school graduation approached. He was hired as a mailroom clerk and messenger. His knowledge of the town made him a valuable employee immediately.
>
> Lynn had always dreamed of the time when she would have the skills to earn her own living and would be able to go to Washington, D.C., to work. She knew that Washington would be very different from the small suburb of 11,000 in Indiana where she had lived all her life. She passed the Civil Service Examination for typist. Soon after her high school graduation she left for Washington where she began working for the Department of Commerce.

Learning of Job Opportunities

There are many ways you can learn about the job opportunities in the community where you want to work. Take advantage of all of them as you search for the job that is best for you.

The Guidance Office in Your School

Most high schools provide counseling services which include job counseling. You should become familiar with the services provided by your guidance office. In many communities, businesses and other organizations that employ high school graduates inform the school's guidance office of job vacancies, both part-time and full-time. You should inquire about notices of job opportunities that have been received in your school's guidance office.

punctual:
on time

Guidance counselors will be able to advise you as you consider your first job after graduation. Sometimes counselors arrange interviews with employers seeking beginning workers. You should be punctual for such interviews and you should keep the counselor informed of your experiences at these interviews. From time to time, you may want to discuss your career plans, as well as current job opportunities, with a counselor.

Employment Agencies

In many communities there are both private and public employment agencies that will assist you in your efforts to find a position. Private employment agencies are sometimes specialized; so you will want to be sure that you are inquiring at one that does place office personnel. Private employment agencies earn their income from fees which are paid either by the individual who secures a position through the agency or by the company that hires the new employee. The fee is generally a percentage of the annual salary.

Public employment agencies provide a service without fee. Such agencies are supported through public funds. You may register at a public employment agency for aid in seeking a position. In large cities public agencies are specialized; so you will want to be sure that you visit the department that handles clerical positions.

Classified Advertisements

Many companies as well as employment agencies use the classified section of newspapers to announce vacancies. While many of the advertisements identify the company or agency seeking personnel for positions, some are listed as blind advertisements. A *blind advertisement* is

one that lists only a post office box number so that the identity of the company seeking an employee is not revealed. Blind advertisements are

FIGURE CLERKS

Career Opportunities
In Our Fashion
Buying Office.

Interesting entry level positions
at WARD.
You'll like our concern
for people.
Bring us typing skills (50
wpm) and good figure work
ability. Enjoy diversified
duties in a friendly atmosphere.
Lots of room for advancement.
Please visit our third floor Personnel
Department, Tuesday thru Friday only.
10AM to 4PM

MONTGOMERY

WARD

393 7th Ave.
(31st-32nd Sts)
RIGHT OPPOSITE PENN STATION
Equal Opportunity Employer

**Advertisement
by Employment
Agencies**

**Identified
Company**

**Blind
Advertisement**

RECEPTIONIST. Exciting opportunity for an ambitious individual to become involved in a customer oriented service industry. If you possess good judgment and a patient phone personality this may be the spot you have been looking for. Salary is commensurate with experience. This is an immediate opening. If you are interested come and see us at FRONT DESK PERSONNEL AGENCY. Our address is 15 E. 19th St. Our positions are fee paid and there are no contracts to sign.

RECEPTIONIST   FEE PAID

Travel Calif.

RECORDING CORP.
Must be able to travel twice a
year to the Coast & back. Work for
artist & repertoire director. Take
over responsibility. Good typing.
FEE PAID $165
BRENT agency, 505 5 Av(42 St)Rm 502

CLERICAL-FULL TIME

Genl asst for busy non-profit film library rental service. Typing 50 wpm. Attention to detail a must; send resume to X6513 TIMES.

screening:
selecting through
evaluation

used so that some preliminary screening can be done on the basis of written letters and data sheets submitted by interested applicants.

Direct Inquiry to Organization

Some people learn about office positions through relatives and friends who are employed in companies that are seeking new employees. If you are informed of an opening through such a source, your relative or friend may make the initial inquiry to the personnel department and arrange an interview for you. You will be expected to visit the company and indicate to the personnel officer who informed you of the opening.

If there is a company in which you have a special interest, it is perfectly proper to write a letter of inquiry and to describe the type of position you are seeking, along with your qualifications for such a position. If you are writing to a company that often hires beginning workers, your chances of being granted an interview are very good.

Civil Service Announcements

Many positions in government require that candidates take examinations and, therefore, there are general public announcements about the dates of such examinations. If you are interested in employment in government, you will want to note the announcements that are posted in public buildings and that appear in newspapers. Announcements for federal positions are often displayed in post offices and in regional civil service offices throughout the country. You can also write directly to the United States Civil Service Commission, Washington, DC 20415, for information on forthcoming examinations. Announcements of city civil service examinations are usually posted in the City Hall; announcements of county and state examinations, in the County Courthouse or principal county building. Also, you can consult your local telephone directory to find the Civil Service Commission office in your city and request information directly from that office.

REVIEWING IMPORTANT POINTS

1. Where in the job market can high school graduates with clerical skills look for positions?
2. What are some of the major categories of companies in the United States?
3. What are some businesses that would be classifed under "Trade"?

4. Why is a small organization not likely to have a specialized personnel department?
5. Is it necessary to go to a very large city to find a position as a clerical worker?
6. Why do private employment agencies charge a fee?
7. How do public employment agencies differ from private employment agencies?
8. In what section of the newspaper would you find notices of job openings?
9. What information is missing in a blind advertisement?
10. How can you learn about examinations for civil service positions in the federal government?

MAKING IMPORTANT DECISIONS

1. Jill and Bob were talking together one afternoon after school. Both had been studying office procedures for the year, and both were planning to begin full-time work shortly after high school graduation. Jill commented to Bob, "I'd love to work in a big city, but I'm afraid to apply to a giant company. Here in our small high school, we know practically everyone. I think I would find it interesting, but it would be very strange to work in a large place. Maybe I'd better settle for a job right here in our small downtown area." What do you think Bob might say in response to Jill's "thinking out loud"?

2. You are interviewed for a position in a small law office in your own hometown. There are two office workers in the office now, and you will be the only new person to be employed. Two lawyers share the practice. As you walk home after the interview, which ended with the lawyers offering you a position at an acceptable salary, what kinds of questions will you ask yourself to determine if this is the job you want?

LEARNING TO WORK WITH OTHERS

Denise and Trudy were very close friends. They had similar plans to enter the business world when they graduated from high school. Early in the spring of their senior year, they decided they would take the U.S. Civil Service Commission tests for the position of typist. Later, they applied to take the test. Two days before the Saturday scheduled for the tests, however, Denise called Trudy and said, "Trudy, I'm scared to death. I can't face that test on Saturday. Please, let's not go. We can get jobs right here at home without taking a test. Isn't that better? Don't you think it is silly for us to try the test?"

What do you think Trudy might say at this point to Denise?

IMPROVING LANGUAGE SKILLS

Some of the words listed below are written as one word, others are hyphenated, and others are written as two words. On a separate sheet of paper type the words according to proper usage.

1. airservice
2. altogether
3. background
4. bestseller
5. bimonthly
6. bondholder
7. byline
8. cityeditor
9. clearcut
10. coexist
11. coordinate
12. copartner
13. counterclaim
14. doorman
15. earphone
16. extraordinary
17. rosecolored
18. selfaddressed
19. shortchanged
20. vicepresident

IMPROVING ARITHMETIC SKILLS

Below are listed weekly salaries for several office employess. The table on page 597 shows the withholding tax deducted from a single person's salary. Also the employer deducts 6.05 percent of the gross salary for social security benefits levied under the Federal Insurance Contributions Act. On a separate sheet of paper indicate in the form of a table the net salary for each of these single employees, assuming that each claims one exemption.

Employee	Gross Pay	Federal Withholding Tax	FICA Tax	Net Salary
Alson, Robert T.	$140.00			
Arrigo, Barbara	144.00			
Baumann, James	153.00			
Borg, Etta	131.00			
Bufano, Fred T.	148.00			
Clune, Norman	150.00			
Conte, Frank	139.00			
Cruz, Marie	136.00			

Unit 16 • *You as an Office Worker*

DEMONSTRATING OFFICE SKILLS

1. Make a list of the sources of placement information that are available in your community to you and your classmates. For each source, write a brief statement about the nature of the service available and the hours during which you may seek assistance.
2. From your local paper, or from a paper in a nearby large city, clip several advertisements that announce jobs in which you think you might have some interest. For each advertisement, write a brief statement explaining why you are interested in the job. Be prepared to discuss your statement in class.

Part 2

Applying for a Job in Person

Marc Levere talked with his high school placement counselor and learned that there were openings in a local furniture manufacturing firm for clerks in several departments, including purchasing and inventory control. Marc enjoyed woodworking as a hobby and thought it would be interesting to work in a furniture manufacturing firm. The high school counselor called the personnel officer at the company and arranged for Marc to visit the company at 3:30 on a Thursday afternoon, several weeks before his graduation from high school.

prior:
earlier in time or order

While Marc had an appointment for an interview, it is common for many companies to accept applicants without **prior** scheduling. Whether you have an appointment scheduled or go directly to the company to talk with the person responsible for hiring beginning workers, you will want to prepare carefully for your meeting.

Personnel Department Hours

Many companies have personnel departments that interview applicants during certain hours, such as 9 to 4, Monday through Friday. The information you receive about job openings will generally indicate when you should apply. For example, a newspaper advertisement may state *Apply in person between 10 and 2, Monday through Friday*. Announcements that your school placement office receives will often specify *Apply in person*. In some cases, you may be asked to call for an appointment. When an appointment is scheduled, you should be sure to arrive promptly at the hour stated.

When you know where and when you are to apply for a job, you should think about what clothes you will wear, what information you should have with you, and how you can prepare yourself for a favorable interview.

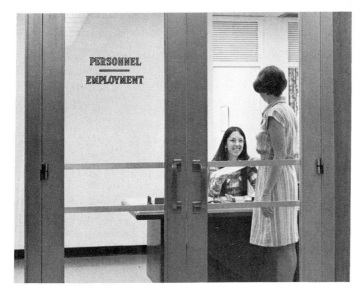

Illus. 16-5

A company forms its first impression of you in its personnel office.

Ohio National Life Insurance Company

Your Appearance

Business offices vary in what they consider appropriate dress for work. Clothing that is acceptable in your community and does not call attention to yourself is preferred in business offices. Fads in fashions that may be acceptable for parties or informal occasions generally are not appropriate for the business office. Plan carefully just what you will wear for your interview. Wear clothing that is basically standard for meeting people in your community. Your clothing should not be the casual, comfortable kind that you wear for leisure hours; neither should it be the formal clothing that you wear for special parties. Your appearance should give the impression that you are a well-groomed, neat, confident person. Your choice of clothes should show that you are aware of what is appropriate and what is becoming to you.

Arrival at the Office

In most organizations there is someone near the arrival area who will direct you to the right office. Often employment offices are located near the main entrance.

When you arrive at the right office, you should walk quietly and directly to the receptionist. If the receptionist is busy on the telephone or talking to another person, you will want to stand back far enough so that you are not likely to overhear the conversation. When the receptionist is free, you should state briefly why you are there. Then you should listen to what the receptionist says to you. Here is a portion of a conversation between an applicant and a receptionist in a large insurance company:

Receptionist: "Good morning. May I help you?"

Applicant: "Good morning. I am Scott Novello. The placement counselor at Central High School, Ms. Laura Snyder, suggested that I come here because you are looking for clerk/typists."

Receptionist: "I'm happy to meet you Mr. Novello. Yes, we are hiring clerk/typists. Let me give you an application form." (The receptionist takes an application from the desk, gets up, and walks with Scott to one of the tables at the far end of the large room.) "Please fill in all the questions on this application form. When you are finished, let me know. Then you may talk with Ms. Weston about job opportunities in our company."

Illus. 16-6

The receptionist in the arrival area is the first person you should speak to when you visit a company to apply for a job.

The Application Form

Most companies require that job applicants complete an application form. Although application forms vary from company to company, most of them request the same basic information.

To help you in filling in all the spaces on the application form accurately and completely, you may want to take with you information that you may not quickly recall when you are writing details on a form.

Among the facts that you may want to have on a small card or slip of paper are the following:

1. Your Social Security number.
2. Your weight and height.
3. A list of your activities while in high school.
4. The names and addresses of summer or part-time employers.
5. The periods of time during which you held jobs, the kind of work you did, and the weekly salary received.
6. The full names, addresses, and telephone numbers of at least three persons who would be willing to give references for you. Ask these persons for their permission to list their names. Former employers, your teachers, and your minister are references for your abilities, interests, and character. You should tell these persons that you are applying for a job and that they may be hearing from prospective employers.

Application forms should be filled in carefully and legibly. Since office workers must be careful in their work, interviewers look at the application form as an example of the kind of attention you will give to your work. Print the information where printing is requested. Print all the information if your printing is more legible than your writing.

If the question does not apply to you, write the notation NA (not applicable) or a dash(—) so that the interviewer will know that you did not overlook the item.

Illus. 16-7

Proofread your application before returning it to the personnel officer.

APPLICATION FOR EMPLOYMENT

WITH

Booth, Marcus, and Murdock Associates

(Applicants should complete in their own handwriting using pencil or pen)

GENERAL INFORMATION

Name *Nicholson, Mary Lee*	Date *August 1, 19--*
Street Address *3466 Kemper Lane*	Phone Number *621-1046*

City *Cambridge*	Zone *02138*	State *MA*	Social Security Number *368-05-6133*

In Case of an Emergency Notify *Mrs. Edna Nicholson*	Address *3466 Kemper Lane*	Phone Number *621-1046*

Date of Birth *May 12, 19--*	Type work desired *Clerk-typist*

Any defects in sight, hearing, or speech? *No*	How much time have you lost through illness in the past two years? *2 days*	Nature of illness *Cold*

Give names of any members in our organization with whom you are acquainted *Betty Morris*

Are you related to any of these people? *No*	If so, to whom? *—*

Who referred you to us for employment? *Campbell Business School*

Have you ever served in the United States Armed Forces? *No*	Rank and branch of service *—*

Are you now employed? *Yes*	If so, where? *William Paulson Advertising Company*

EDUCATION

High School attended *Jefferson High School*	City & State *Cambridge, MA*	Year Graduated *19--*
Business School attended *Campbell Business School*	City & State *Cambridge, MA*	Number of months attended *One year*
College or University attended	City & State	Year Graduated *—*	Degree

Business subjects studied while in school	HIGH SCHOOL *Typing, Office Procedures, Gen. Business, Accounting*
	BUSINESS COLLEGE *Typing, Business Law, Office Procedures*
	COLLEGE

Are you studying now? *Yes*	If so what? *Economics*	Where? *Boston University*

Other special training *None*	System of shorthand studied *Century 21*

In the space to the right indicate your present speed in shorthand and typing, if you have these skills. Place an (X) after the office machines you can operate.	Shorthand		Typing *60 words a min.*		Transcribing Machine	X
	Billing Machine		Bookkeeping Machine	X	Duplicating Machine	X
	Addressograph		Calculator	X	PBX Board	X
	Adding Machine		Key Punch		Other	
	Posting Machine		IBM Tabulator			

Illus. 16-8

Application blank — Page 1

EXPERIENCE AND REFERENCES

Business Experience & References (Show last position first)

	From	To	Period Yrs.	Period Mos.	Name of Company	City & State	Person to whom you reported
1	7/70	Now	2		Wm. Paulson Adv. Co.	Cambridge, MA	Thomas Adams
2							
3							
4							

Business Experience and References (Continued)

	GIVE TITLE AND NATURE OF YOUR WORK	Monthly Earnings	Why did you leave?
1	General Clerical Duties	$525	To seek work with more responsibility and higher potential earnings
2			
3			
4			

Character References: Do not refer to previous employers or relatives.

NAME	ADDRESS	OCCUPATION
Mrs. C. C. Clark	3470 Craigie St., Cambridge	Purchasing Agent
Mr. Donald Calhoun	South High School, Cambridge	Teacher – business subjects
Miss Mary Wagner	1312 Pearl St., Cambridge	Owner of clothing store

By signing this application I affirm that all statements made herein are true to the best of my knowledge. If employed by the company, I agree to consider my salary a confidential matter and to refrain from discussing it with other employees.

Mary Lee Nicholson
Signature of Applicant

APPLICANTS SHOULD NOT WRITE BELOW THIS LINE

Interviewed by:	Date of interview	Date applicant available for work	E G F P

Remarks:

Date Employed	Clock Number	Department	Classification
Enrolled in Group Insurance		Enrolled in Pension Plan	Blue Cross – Blue Shield Coverage ☐ Ind. ☐ Fam. ☐ Surg.
Date Employment Terminated	Reason		Consider for Re-employment

Illus. 16-9

Application blank — Page 2

Employment Tests

Many companies will ask you to take typewriting and clerical tests. You will find that these tests are similar to those you took in high school. The same general rules for taking tests apply in both situations. You should feel relaxed about the tests. Personnel interviewers try to make the situation as comfortable as possible and you should not be overly anxious about your performance.

Clerical Tests

Clerical tests which some companies require determine the applicant's general knowledge of clerical procedures. Listen carefully to all instructions as they are given to you. If permitted, take notes of the instructions. Read written instructions carefully so that you know exactly what you should do. Be sure to find out whether you are to be timed or are to proceed at your own pace and, if you are, let the person **administering** the test know when you have finished it. Below are some typical written instructions:

administering: giving

> INSTRUCTIONS: Read the following sentences carefully. Determine whether the practice is one that you would follow as an office worker. If it is a practice that you would follow, place a check mark in the "Yes" column. If it is a practice that you would not follow, mark the "No" column. Answer all the questions. You will have ten minutes to complete this part.
>
> Example: An office worker arrives at his or her desk no later than 30 minutes after the beginning of the work day.

Yes	No
	√

From these instructions, you learned that one of two responses is possible and how you are to mark each response. You also learned how much time you will have for this section of the test and that you should attempt to answer all of the items.

If you finish a timed test before time is called, use the extra time to reread the items and to check your answers. Careful attention to comprehending each item can help you avoid errors.

Performance Tests

The most common performance test given to applicants for office jobs is a typewriting test. It may be a timed typing test from straight copy, or

Illus. 16-10

Applicants for the clerk/typist position are usually asked to take a typewriting performance test.

it may be an office assignment, such as typing a letter from a rough draft. Listen carefully to the instructions so that you will know what you are to do and how long you will have for the completion of each test.

Generally you will have a chance to get used to the typewriter you are to use. Even though you may find that you will be typing on a machine that you have never used, you will quickly adjust to it during the practice period. Remember that typewriters are alike in basic operation. In just a few minutes you can learn how margins and tabulator stops are cleared and set. Then you can do a little straight typing to get the feel of the stroking action of the machine.

The interviewer is interested in learning about your general typewriting skill. You will have had sufficient practice in school so that the performance test should be relatively easy for you.

The Interview

In some companies, you will fill in an application form, take tests, and see an interviewer during the same visit. In other companies, the interview may come after you have filled in the application form, and you will be asked to return for the tests if the interview was considered satisfactory. In still other companies, you are asked to fill in an application form and take tests, which are evaluated before you are asked to come in for an interview. In some firms, you will be hired on the basis of

evaluated: rated

your application form and the interview. Some companies use the information about your skill development in school as the basis for assessing your abilities and, hence, give no tests.

Purpose of the Interview

Your application form and the results of your tests are in the hands of the interviewer. The interviewer is talking with you in order to tell you about the company and the job and to get additional information that may be helpful in deciding whether you are the best person for the job.

Illus. 16-11

The interview is your opportunity to evaluate the company for which you may be working.

You will be made to feel at ease so that you will be relaxed in answering questions and in talking with the interviewer. The interviewer will tell you about the following:

1. The nature of the company's business and what its general policies are.
2. What the specific job for which you are being interviewed requires and in what department it is located.
3. What the hours of work are, the salary, the benefits, including coffee breaks, health insurance, the pension plan, vacations, holidays, and tuition reimbursement, if provided.

You should not hesitate to ask questions about any of the topics that the interviewer discusses with you. The interview has three purposes:

1. To permit an official of the company to become acquainted with you.

2. To permit you to become acquainted with the company.
3. To provide you with information about the work you will be doing if you are chosen for a position.

Answering Questions

In addition to giving you information, the interviewer will ask you questions to get an idea of your interests and attitudes, as well as to learn how well you respond to questions. Listen carefully to the questions asked; respond directly to them. Make your answers brief, but not so brief that you give an incomplete answer or seem curt. Here is a portion of an interview between an applicant and an interviewer:

Interviewer: "What tasks did you learn to do in your clerical procedures class, Miss Rollins?"

Applicant: "Oh, we learned about all the tasks that are important in an office today. I think I can do anything that needs to be done."

This applicant, Miss Rollins, isn't telling the interviewer very much. The following response would have been more informative:

Applicant: "We learned about a variety of tasks in the clerical procedures course, including how to handle mail, how to an-
swer the telephone, how to type letters of various styles, how to type reports and legal documents, and how to use calculating machines to compute answers to many business transactions."

The Interviewer's Evaluation of You

The interviewer, by talking with you, forms an opinion of you as a worker. The interviewer will note particularly the following:

1. Your alertness in answering questions.
2. Your use of the English language.
3. Your voice.
4. Your appearance and your poise.
5. Your interest in the job to be filled.

If the interviewer receives a favorable overall impression based on these qualities, you will probably be considered a good candidate for the position.

Conclusion of the Interview

When the interview is over, the interviewer will tell you what the next step will be. In some companies, you may be offered a position immediately if you have made a favorable impression and if your skills are satisfactory. In other companies, the interviewer may tell you that you will be told the company's decision within a few days.

If a position is offered to you, you will be given some time to think over the offer. You should not respond at the time of the interview unless you are sure that this is the job you want.

Regardless of what the interviewer says in ending the interview, you should thank her or him for talking with you. Indicate that you will either call or write within the time given for a reply or you will await a call. You should then leave without delay.

Follow-up of the Interview

If you are offered a job at the end of the interview, you should call or write your decision within the time allowed you. Illus. 16-12 is a sample written response.

Illus. 16-12

Letter of acceptance

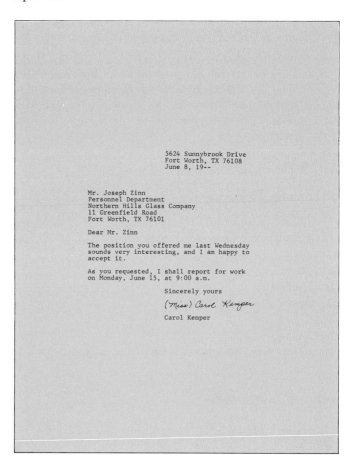

```
                                          5624 Sunnybrook Drive
                                          Fort Worth, TX 76108
                                          June 8, 19--

          Mr. Joseph Zinn
          Personnel Department
          Northern Hills Glass Company
          11 Greenfield Road
          Fort Worth, TX 76101

          Dear Mr. Zinn

          The position you offered me last Wednesday
          sounds very interesting, and I am happy to
          accept it.

          As you requested, I shall report for work
          on Monday, June 15, at 9:00 a.m.

                                  Sincerely yours

                                  (Miss) Carol Kemper

                                  Carol Kemper
```

If the interviewer promised to call or write to you, you should respond as soon as you hear from the company. If the interviewer calls you, it is appropriate to respond by telephone. However, a letter in reply to an offer is considered satisfactory.

REVIEWING IMPORTANT POINTS

1. Is it always necessary to have an appointment in order to apply for a job? Explain.
2. How would you decide what to wear to a company where you were seeking a job?
3. How does a receptionist aid the person inquiring about a job in a company?
4. What information should you take with you that will aid you in filling in an application form?
5. If a question on an application blank doesn't apply to you, what do you write in the space for an answer?
6. What kind of tests may an applicant for a clerical job be expected to take?
7. Why should an applicant listen to and read instruction for tests carefully?
8. What is the purpose of an interview between a company interviewer and an applicant?
9. How should an applicant respond to questions asked in an interview?
10. What does an interviewer observe about applicants in order to decide who will be most suited to the company and the job?

MAKING IMPORTANT DECISIONS

1. Ron was interested in working for a large textile company in his hometown. He called the personnel office to find out the hours when an applicant could be interviewed. The person with whom he spoke told him that applicants were interviewed between 10:00 and 4:00, Monday through Thursday, and that he should come at his convenience. He decided that he would skip school the next day in order to be there at 10 o'clock. He felt being prompt would impress the interviewer. What do you think of Ron's decision?
2. While Matt was filling in an application form in the personnel office of a large company, he came to the question: "What are your most enjoyable leisure time activities?" As Matt thought about that question he couldn't see its relationship to a job, so he just left the space for the answer blank and went on to the next question. What do you think of Matt's decision?

LEARNING TO WORK WITH OTHERS

When Sherri was being interviewed for a position as a typist in a local utilities office, the interviewer told her that she would have to take a typewriting test. Sherri, at this point, said to the interviewer: "I don't understand why I must take a typewriting test. I have with me a certificate of proficiency from my typewriting teacher. This certificate indicates that I can type 65 words a minute with no more than 3 errors during a five-minute test. Isn't this certificate a substitute for the test you administer?"

What do you think of Sherri's response to the interviewer?

IMPROVING LANGUAGE SKILLS

The exclamation point (!) is used to represent a full stop after an enthusiastic or strong comment.

Examples: Wait! You don't have the report.
The job is done!

The exclamation point is typed inside the quotation marks if the exclamation applies only to the quoted matter. It is placed outside the quotation mark if it applies to the entire sentence.

Examples: The crowd shouted "Bravo!" as we entered the campaign headquarters.
This package must be marked "Fragile"!

On a separate sheet of paper write or type each of the following sentences with correct punctuation.

1. Sally called from the bus stop Hurry you are going to miss this bus
2. We'll meet our quota shouted the sales representatives at the announcement of the challenge proposed
3. This is indeed a surprise
4. How many of you want to attend Friday's seminar
5. Good heavens this job can't be done in an hour

IMPROVING ARITHMETIC SKILLS

Clerks in many offices must compare numbers to see if they agree. Clerical tests administered to job applicants often include checking numbers for agreement. Opposite are two columns of numbers. On a separate sheet write these lists of numbers. Then place a check beside the second number if it is the same as the first number.

Example:	4,567	4,568
	34,223	34,223$\checkmark$

1.	467,987	467,987
2.	321,302	321,203
3.	56,789	56,798
4.	41,321	42,231
5.	56,675	65,675
6.	35,432	35,332
7.	781,098	718,098
8.	964,323	945,323
9.	13,134	13,143
10.	14,541	14,541
11.	43,516	43,516
12.	345,579	345,759
13.	345,324	354,324
14.	1,457	1,547
15.	68,432	86,432
16.	42,369	42,396
17.	57,890	57,890
18.	43,253	43,352
19.	98,654	98,654
20.	167,542	167,543
21.	453,208	435,208
22.	47,819	47,918
23.	5,471	5,471
24.	19,430	19,340
25.	71,012	71,012

DEMONSTRATING OFFICE SKILLS

1. Assume that you are preparing for an interview in a local company and you want to take with you information that would help you in filling in the standard application form. Make a list of the items you would include in this information and then type in the facts related to each item of information.
2. Assume that you have been asked to complete an application form for a clerical position. If the application form from the *Supplies Inventory* is available, complete it carefully in ink. If a form is not available, type a copy of the illustration on pages 624 and 625 and fill in the information in ink.

Part 3

Writing a Letter for a Job

Tess Stanley's family is moving to Hartford, Connecticut, shortly after she graduates from high school. She plans to go with them and wants to begin working in Hartford soon after her family moves there. She is now living in Hillside, New Jersey. Her placement counselor gave her the name of a large insurance company in Hartford that hires many high school graduates. Tess is preparing a letter to send to the personnel director at the company.

You may apply for a job by letter. In that case your letter and your personal data sheet should represent you in the best possible way.

The Personal Data Sheet

Before you apply for a job, you will want to prepare a personal data sheet. The personal data sheet tells a potential employer who you are and what you are trained to do.

Its Purpose

A prospective employer needs to become acquainted with you in very little time. A personal data sheet is helpful in achieving this purpose. A personal data sheet outlines in clear form the important facts about your background that will be of value in determining whether you are a good candidate for a position.

Its Content

Generally personal data sheets are divided into the following parts:

Personal information
Education
Extracurricular activities
Experience
References

Personal Information. The personal information asked for may vary from one company to another, but generally includes your name, home address, telephone number, your date of birth, and your physical condition (a general statement is sufficient).

Education. Under education you will give the complete name of your high school, plus the curriculum that you studied or the major courses taken, and the office skills that you have developed. You will want to add any scholastic awards that you received while in high school.

Extracurricular Activities. Extracurricular activities are of interest to prospective employers; so you will want to list all your organizational activities while you were a student and those activities in the community in which you continue to be active. Any offices that you held in a class or club should also be listed. This section of your personal data sheet reflects your special interests, your ability to work with other people, and your leadership qualities.

Experience. Experience at work, even though limited, should be listed. Begin with your most recent experience and list the jobs you have held for more than a few weeks. Give the job title first, then the name of the firm or organization, and the dates of your employment. If you have had little or no work experience for which you were paid, you will want to list all volunteer jobs that you have held in the community.

References. In evaluating candidates, prospective employers review references. You will want to list as references persons who know you well enough to judge you on the **traits** and attitudes that employers are concerned about. Generally it is a good idea to give at least one name for each of the following:

traits: qualities

1. Scholarship — The recommendation of a former teacher who can write about your achievements in school and your potential for handling the requirements of a job is valuable.
2. Character — The recommendation of a person who has known you for several years and can comment on your **integrity**, loyalty, and dependability is useful. Clergy, business, and professional people are appropriate references. You should not use relatives or neighbors for references.
3. Experience — If you have had even a part-time or temporary summer job, it would be appropriate to ask your supervisor for a recommendation. If you have not held a job for which you were paid, but you do have some volunteer work experience, you should consider asking the person who supervised your volunteer work to write a reference for you.

integrity: moral soundness; honesty

You should telephone or write notes to all persons whom you plan to list as references asking them if they are willing to allow you to list their names.

Its Appearance

Your personal data sheet should be organized logically and typewritten carefully. Be sure to proofread it so that it contains no uncorrected errors. Send the original to the prospective employer, and keep a copy for yourself.

If it is likely that you will need several data sheets, it is permissible to have the copies duplicated. You will want to be sure that the duplicated copies are attractive. Some photocopying machines are satisfactory for producing good copies of your original, typed copy.

Letter of Application

A short letter indicating your interest in a position should accompany your personal data sheet. A letter of application is a direct, concise letter in which you state clearly the position or type of work in which you are interested. If you are not certain if the company to which you are applying has a vacancy for the type of job in which you are interested, then your letter of application is also a letter of inquiry. Letters of application should be typewritten individually.

Below are guides to follow in writing your letter of application:

1. Be certain to include your full address above the date of your letter.
2. Address the letter appropriately. If you are responding to a classified advertisement that provides a return box only, you should use the address given and the salutation should be *Ladies and Gentlemen.*

   If you have learned about a position through your high school placement office or through a friend, you will be given the name of the firm and perhaps the name of the person in charge of employment. If a person's name is given, address your letter in this manner:

   Mr. Thomas L. Leeper, Personnel Manager
   The Azzaro Corporation
   3689 Wilson Street
   Atlanta, GA   30315

   The salutation should be *Dear Mr. Leeper:*

P E R S O N A L   D A T A   S H E E T

NAME: Helen B. Korstange

ADDRESS: 461 Clinton Avenue
              Wichita, KS 67208

TELEPHONE: (316) 561-4561

DATE OF BIRTH: March 17, 19--

PLACE OF BIRTH: Wichita, Kansas

PHYSICAL CONDITION: Excellent

EDUCATION:

Will graduate from Central High School, June 4, 19--

Business courses completed:

    Typewriting (50 words a minute)
    Office Machines (operate printing calculator,
        adding machines, transcribing machines, and
        duplicating machines)
    Office procedures (knowledge of procedures
        for handling mail, files, and records for
        purchasing, sales, and inventory departments;
        knowledge of telephone techniques and
        receptionsit duties)

EXTRACURRICULAR ACTIVITIES:

    Class Secretary during Sophomore year
    Vice-President of Future Business Leaders of
        America
    Reporter for the Spot Light, the high school
        newspaper

EXPERIENCE:

    Part-time clerk at central desk of Wichita City
        Library, Summer, 19--
    Typist for Hammell and Scherman, Attorneys at
        Law, Summers of 19-- and 19--

REFERENCES:

    Mrs. T. G. Birmingham, Head Librarian, Wichita
        City Library, 461 Pine Lane, Wichita 67211,
        Telephone: 391-3167

    Mr. Benjamin F. Scherman, Attorney at Law,
        Denney Building, 47 Monroe Avenue, Wichita 67210
        Telephone: 391-4569

    Ms. Janice Mouser, Chairperson, Business Education
        Department, Central High School, Wichita 67209,
        Telephone: 369-7871

Illus. 16-13   Personal data sheet

---

461 Clinton Avenue
Wichita, Kansas
May 24, 19--

Mr. Frederick C. Moore
Personnel Director
Constitution Life Insurance Company
209 West Fourth Street
Wichita, KS 67209

Dear Mr. Moore

Miss Dorothy Fowler, one of your employees who attended Central
High School with me, told me that there will be an opening in
your word processing center on June 14. I would like to apply
for the position.

As I have indicated on my enclosed data sheet, I have completed
a number of high school courses that have prepared me for an
entry-level office position, including office machines, clerical
office procedures, and of course typewriting. For two summers
I worked as a typist at a local law firm, and for one summer
I was a part-time clerk at the public library.

May I be interviewed for the clerk/typist position which you
are seeking to fill? I am available any weekday after 3:30
when my school day finishes.

                                    Sincerely yours

                                    Helen B. Korstange

                                    Helen B. Korstange

Enclosure

Illus. 16-14   Letter of Application

3. State your interest in the first paragraph.

> The clerk/typist position which you advertised in <u>The Atlanta Times</u> on Monday, June 3, is of interest to me.

or

> Miss Cathie Royer, the Placement Counselor at Greenville High School, has suggested that I apply for the clerk/typist position which is available in your firm.

4. In the second paragraph, highlight the main points of your education and experience. You might write:

> As you will note from the enclosed data sheet, I will graduate from Central High School in June. While in high school I successfully completed several business courses, including typewriting, office machines, and clerical office procedures. I have also held two summer jobs where I have had opportunities to use my business skills and abilities.

5. In the final paragraph of your application letter, you will want to indicate your desire for a personal interview as well as the times when you are available.

> I would be happy to visit your office to be interviewed for the clerk/typist position which you seek to fill. I complete my school day at three each afternoon and would be free to come to your office any afternoon after that time.

6. The complimentary close may be a simple *Sincerely yours* or *Yours very truly*, depending upon your salutation (see page 83). Be sure to sign your name and indicate the enclosure.

If you apply for a job through an agency, you will generally go to the firm for an interview. No letter of application will be necessary. In such a case, you will find it helpful to have a copy of your personal data sheet with you, for the details on it will be useful in filling in an application form.

Follow-up of an Application Letter

anticipated: expected

Most companies that ask persons interested in a position to write to them will respond quickly to all applicants. However, there are times when the number of interested persons is greater than anticipated and the task of answering letters of application may take several weeks. If you have not heard from a company to which you wrote in response to an advertisement, it is appropriate to write a brief letter after two weeks in which you state that you wrote earlier and that you hope to hear from the company.

If you write a company seeking a job when you had no information about the need of the company for employees, you can expect to hear from the company. However, you should allow at least three weeks for a response. If you don't receive a letter or telephone call, it is generally an indication that workers with your skills are not needed. It is usually not fruitful to follow up with another inquiry. However, if you are especially interested in the company, you could write a second brief letter and en-close another copy of your data sheet. Your chances of getting a response are slight, but there is always the possibility that your first letter was misplaced or misdirected and the second one will arrive at a time when the company needs persons with your skills and interests.

fruitful:
beneficial, productive

REVIEWING IMPORTANT POINTS

1. How does a personal data sheet differ from a letter of application?
2. What are the typical sections of a personal data sheet?
3. For what reason might an employer be interested in your extracur-ricular activities?
4. Who is generally best able to provide information about your schol-arship?
5. Is it necessary for every copy of your personal data sheet to be an original typewritten copy? Discuss.
6. What must you be sure to include in a letter of application?
7. How should your letters of application be prepared?
8. Is "To Whom it May Concern" a good salutation for a letter of appli-cation? Discuss.
9. If you type your name on your letter of application, is there any need for your signature?
10. Is there ever a situation when you might write a second letter to a company in which you would like to work? Explain.

MAKING IMPORTANT DECISIONS

1. Garry Tompkins was preparing a personal data sheet. He had been told by his high school teacher that he should list references. He couldn't see the need for references, since he didn't believe anyone really knew him very well. He also didn't think a company would waste time checking on him. He felt that if a company wanted to hire him, it would hire him without references. Therefore, he didn't list any in his data sheet. What do you think of Garry's decision?
2. When Francine Gibbs began to think whom she might list on her personal data sheet as references, she recalled that she had had

some volunteer work experience. She had spent many of her free hours in August, September, and October working in the office of a local politician who was running for the U.S. House of Representatives. She got to know the politician very well, and he commented on how well she could handle office work. Francine wondered if she should ask the politician if she could list his name as a reference. What do you think Francine should do?

LEARNING TO WORK WITH OTHERS

Roger Davis answered an advertisement of a local company that was hiring office workers. In its advertisement the company stated that only applicants who had the required qualifications would receive a reply. Roger mailed his letter on Monday afternoon and did not receive a response by the end of the week. On Friday afternoon he called the personnel office and said, "I wrote your company a letter on Monday. I know that I have the qualifications needed for the positions you have open, but I haven't heard from you. May I come in for an interview on Monday?"

What do you think of Roger's handling of this situation?

IMPROVING LANGUAGE SKILLS

Suffixes are word endings that change the spelling of base words. Common suffixes include -ing, -ly, -ily, -ally, -ness, -able, -ible.

On a separate sheet of paper correctly spell each of the following words, using the suffix indicated.

Add -ing to each of the following:

- bargain
- change
- charge
- accept

Add -ly, -ily, or -ally to each of the following:

- probable
- usual
- frequent
- realistic

Add -ness to each of the following:

- neat
- happy
- ready
- clean
- fit

Add -able or -ible to each of the following:

- change
- depend
- prevent
- manage
- defense

IMPROVING ARITHMETIC SKILLS

Some clerical tests that companies give to applicants require the application of arithmetic skill to job-like tasks. Below you are given the inventory at the end of the year and the inventory at the beginning of the year for each of the items in stock as well as the purchases, or additions to stock, made during the year. For each item, calculate how much was used during the year.

ITEM	Stock January 1, 19—	Stock December 31, 19—	Used
TNW 4531	$1,432.45	$781.23	
GWT 561	321.45	754.24	
GWT 563	452.50	325.68	
GWT 569	213.50	145.00	
DNW 432	543.25	450.25	
DNW 433	450.00	300.00	
DNW 567	320.90	290.00	
DNW 578	100.45	156.00	
CWT 567	89.50	98.00	
CWT 573	451.50	215.00	

The purchases made during the year included:

TNW 4531	$800.49	DNW 433	$600.50
GWT 561	$1,345.50	DNW 567	$450.69
GWT 563	$789.90	DNW 578	$356.75
GWT 569	$420.00	CWT 567	$125.50
DNW 432	$350.00	CWT 573	$535.25

DEMONSTRATING OFFICE SKILLS

1. Prepare a personal data sheet, using Illus. 16-13, page 637, as a model. Type an original and a carbon.
2. Type a letter of application in response to an advertisement in a local paper. Indicate in your letter that you are enclosing a personal data sheet.

Part 4

Your First Job and Beyond

Phillip Jessen was approaching the building where he was to begin his first day of work as a clerk/typist. He had been hired for his job shortly before his high school graduation about a month ago. He liked the way in which the personnel staff handled his interview and the general atmosphere of the offices as he was introduced to his supervisor shortly after he was hired. He knew he had a great deal to learn; at the same time, he felt sure that his study of office procedures in high school had given him the basic understandings and skills that he would soon use. He entered the building and said good morning to the receptionist. His full-time work experience was about to begin!

Your Adjustment to Work

You have received a general introduction to the work of the office and to procedures that are typical in many organizations. However, as you know, organizations differ in the kinds of work they perform and in the manner in which employees carry through the directives of their executives. Therefore, the procedures you may use for a particular task will differ from the general ones you know. Do not let this disturb you. Organizations have reasons for their particular procedures and, as you learn these reasons, you will understand what is to be accomplished.

Because organizations differ from each other, they do not expect beginners to know exactly how to perform their job on their first day of work. Many organizations provide job orientation sessions for new employees. Some organizations have formal orientation sessions; others assume that the person under whom you will work will provide informal orientation to the company and your job.

directives:
official instructions or orders

orientation:
process of acquainting with surroundings and environment

Formal Orientation

While there are various methods of formal orientation of new employees, a popular method is to plan for new employees to meet together for the first day at work. During this day new employees are introduced to the company and to the department in which each will work. Here is a schedule for a group of new high school graduates who began office positions in a large company on July 1.

Illus. 16-15

As a new office worker you may be given a brief tour of the company's facilities.

9:00 to 10:30   Meeting in Conference Room — 5th Floor
1. Greetings from the Vice-President of Operations, Ms. Jayne Ashton
2. Discussion of the work of the organization and the overall staff, by Personnel Director, Mr. Alfonso Bartelli
3. Film showing the range of activities of the firm throughout the world

10:30 to 10:50   Coffee with the President, Mr. T. W. Perez

10:50 to 12:00   Discussion of company organization and how the work flows through the organization, by Mr. Stanley Fenwick and Ms. Delores Phillips, of the Personnel Department

12:00 to 1:30   Lunch in company cafeteria, newcomers seated with experienced co-workers; tour of main office; discussion of neighborhood resources

1:30 to 2:30   Questions and discussion in Conference Room

2:30 to 5:00   Orientation in department where employed, plus departmental coffee; introduction to specific tasks of new job

On the second day the new employees report to their job locations at 9:00 a.m. After two weeks all new employees are called together for a one-hour session. At this session they are encouraged to ask questions about the company's policies and operations.

Informal Orientation

Most small companies and some medium and large companies make no formal arrangements for orientation. Usually a supervisor introduces and guides the new employee so that company policies and job procedures are learned in a reasonable time. The new employee usually reports to the supervisor at the regular hour for beginning work each day and is given details about the work that is to be done. Here is a portion of one supervisor's comments made to a new clerk in a central records department:

"Sue, we are happy to welcome you. I hope you will like working here. First, I want you to meet the other five clerks in this department. (At this point, Sue walks with the supervisor to the work stations of the five and is introduced to each.)

I think the easiest way to understand the work you are to do is for me to give you some specific jobs, explain them, and then let you do them. As soon as you have a question, just let me know. I am here to help you; so please don't hesitate to ask questions."

In this company the new employees are scheduled for a brief meeting with someone in the personnel office who discusses the company's policies and benefits. Also, the supervisor is responsible for explaining the coffee break and lunch arrangements for the department.

Illus. 16-17

On your first day you will be introduced to your co-workers.

Expectations of Supervisors

The cost of doing the paperwork of an organization is watched carefully by company executives. Executives try to keep these costs, like *all* costs, to a minimum. Executives want their employees to enjoy their work, but they also want them to be worthy of the salaries they receive. Supervisors are the persons responsible for maintaining an **environment** that encourages workers to do their work diligently and pleasurably.

environment: surroundings

There are many ways that supervisors will observe you to learn what help you need and to enable them to make recommendations for salary increases and promotions. Among the considerations of supervisors are these:

1. Your punctuality in the morning and in returning from coffee breaks and lunch periods.
2. Your attention and accuracy in doing your work.
3. Your accomplishments each day. (Do you hold up others because you fail to finish your part of a task?)
4. Your response to extra demands during emergencies.
5. Your general attitude toward your work.

Supervisors realize that people should work comfortably and at a reasonable **pace**. There may be times, however, when you will be expected to increase your pace; but, as a general rule, the number of employees assigned to a task can do the job efficiently on a normal workday. Companies try to minimize periods of pressure as well as periods of insufficient work.

pace: rate of movement or progress

Reviewing Your Own Performance

As a beginning office worker, you will find that paying attention to how well you do your own work will help you improve your performance. Some of the questions you can raise about your own performance are these:

1. Am I always on time — in the morning, after coffee breaks, after lunch?
2. Am I keeping up with the quantity of work I am expected to do?
3. Am I doing all tasks right the first time and checking my work?
4. Am I working at a reasonably fast pace?
5. Do I understand well what I am doing?

You will find that as you learn your job your performance will improve and you will work with more skill and confidence. Your attention to doing a good job will result in your doing the kind of work supervisors appreciate.

Educational Opportunities

With your high school education completed, you will have basic preparation for many office positions. You will learn much as you work and think about your job. Developments in every job give you a chance to learn something new.

In addition to the knowledge that you acquire through your job, you may have chances to take courses or attend workshops that are sponsored by your company, professional organizations in the community, adult education centers, or colleges. You should carefully consider any announcements that you see and enroll in those courses that you think will be valuable to your work or to you personally.

Many communities have evening programs in adult education centers and in community colleges that may be of value to you. Many office workers, for example, enroll in community college programs on a part-time basis. A student who completes the full two-year program in a community college earns an associate degree, which may be an A.A. (Associate in Arts, A.S. (Associate in Science), or A.A.S. (Associate in Applied Science). The degree earned depends on the program studied. Many four-year colleges accept the credits earned in the community college, so that a person may transfer to a four-year college after two years of work at the community college level. That person can then earn a bachelor's degree. Many business people have earned bachelor's degrees at night while working during the day. Both community colleges and four-year colleges offer evening courses in all business areas, including accounting, office skills, data processing, and management.

Many companies encourage employees to further their education by offering tuition reimbursement. These plans vary, with some providing full tuition for all courses taken and passed; in other cases, the company refunds only a portion of the tuition for the courses passed. While some companies make refunds only for courses that relate to the work the employee is doing, other companies make refunds for all college-level studies completed satisfactorily by employees.

Consider furthering your education. In our rapidly changing society, you may find that going to college is a rewarding way of keeping yourself aware of the world in which you live and work.

Promotional Opportunities

During this course you have learned about many jobs that are available to beginning workers with little or no experience. You have realized that these jobs are foundations for better positions. Every organization needs people who are willing and able to assume more responsibility. There are many levels of responsibility in every organization. People do not move up from the low levels to the high levels automatically. Personnel staff members are constantly **assessing** the talents and potential abilities of employees to discover who are most likely to meet the demands of higher level jobs.

assessing: determining the value of

Promotions in the Same Type of Work

Some clerical positions demand more experience and skill than others. Hence, clerical positions are often ranked or graded according to the complexity of the work and the amount of responsibility the job entails. Illustration 16-18 describes the skills required for a Grade III clerk/typist in the offices of one state government.

Persons who become competent in beginning positions and show signs of possessing the abilities needed in higher level jobs will earn promotions.

Promotions in Other Areas of Work

Transfers are often made from one type of work to another when there are common aspects of the work in the two departments. The abilities that supervisors value highly for promotions are the following:

Clerk-Typist III	Same requirements as for Clerk I and Clerk II, plus
	Considerable knowledge of modern office practices, procedures, and equipment
	Considerable knowledge of English, spelling, and arithmetic
	Working knowledge of the principles of office management and supervision and of standard record maintenance procedures
	Ability to maintain complex clerical records and to prepare reports from various statistical or accounting information
	Ability to carry out routine administrative and supervisory detail independently and conduct correspondence without review
	Ability to understand and follow moderately complex oral and written directions
	Ability to plan, assign, and coordinate the work of a moderate-size clerical staff
	Ability to instruct and train clerical subordinates effectively
	Ability to develop, lay out, and install clerical procedures from general instructions
	A high degree of clerical aptitude and general intelligence as evidenced by a passing grade in a practical written test
	Ability to type accurately from plain copy at the rate of 40 words a minute as evidenced by a passing grade in a typing performance test

Source: *Missouri Personnel Division*
117 East Dunklin Street
Jefferson City, MO 65101

1. Ability to be responsible for the accuracy of your own work.
2. Ability to take initiative and make decisions.
3. Ability to work with others and supervise their work.
4. Ability to learn new procedures, and to absorb new techniques and new information.
5. Ability to improve upon the procedures that you have used.

Many employees have earned promotions because of their success in doing their jobs. Here are two instances.

Ralph Jansky was hired as a receptionist/typist in a busy private employment agency when he graduated from high school six years ago. He liked the two partners who owned the business. The agency was well-organized and every employee, as well as every person who came seeking assistance in finding a job was respected. Shortly after he began his job, Ralph decided to take some courses in a local community college. He enjoyed his studies so much that he enrolled in an associate degree program. He completed that program recently and has transferred to a four-year college into a bachelor's degree program. In the meantime, his responsibilities in the office have changed several times. Now he is a full-time interviewer of all persons seeking management positions. When Ralph was asked what prepared him for this full-time professional job, he commented: "I think my preparation began when I studied office procedures in high school and learned how important it was to be friendly to people and to truly enjoy helping others. In my very first job as a receptionist, ! found that I enjoyed talking with the clients and helping them obtain the information they sought. I guess because I enjoyed knowing people, I easily remembered everything they told me, which made it very easy to follow up when they called the office or came back for a second interview."

Joy Vincent is now a supervisor in the accounting department. Her first job when she graduated from high school five years ago was as a clerk in the same accounting office. She liked this large insurance company and found the company offered her many opportunities. She enrolled in an evening college program in accounting. She continues to go to college and hopes to complete the requirements for a bachelor's degree. After she had been with the company about a year she was promoted to a junior accounting clerk, and later she became an accountant. She has been a supervisor for almost a year. The personnel director believes that there are more promotions ahead for this fine employee.

Outlook for Clerical Employment

A considerable proportion of the labor force is employed in clerical occupations. In 1974, for example, there were almost 86 million workers employed in the United States. During that year, one out of every six employees was classified as a "clerical worker." Approximately 42 million workers were in the white-collar category, with four out of ten of them considered "clerical workers." The projections to 1985 for employment in the United States indicate an increase of 33 percent in "clerical workers." Projections for some positions are shown below, along with the number of workers in each category in the year 1974.

Clerical Occupation[1]	Number Employed in 1974	Projected Average Annual Openings 1974–1985
Bank clerks	517,000	54,000
Bookkeeping workers	1,700,000	121,000
Cashiers	1,110,000	97,000
Computer operating personnel	500,000	27,500
File clerks	275,000	25,000
Office machine operators	170,000	12,800
Receptionists	460,000	57,500
Shipping clerks	465,000	20,500
Stenographers and secretaries	3,300,000	439,000
Stock clerks	490,000	26,000
Typists	1,000,000	125,000

[1]United States Department of Labor, *Occupational Outlook Quarterly*, Volume 20, Number 1 (Spring, 1976).

Your Future in the Office

Today's business office is undergoing many changes. Some predictions include far greater use of computers as well as marked basic changes in handling paperwork. Microfilm, automatic retrieval, and teletypewriters have been introduced into many offices. These innovations are likely to become commonplace in the future.

innovations:
new ideas, methods, or devices

You are prepared not only for your first job but for learning new tasks. You have been introduced to basic skills and problem-solving methods that will be useful in different kinds of offices. If you do your job with an awareness of how it relates to what is going on in the office around you, you will develop the skills to cope with the innovations that are introduced into your own work.

REVIEWING IMPORTANT POINTS

1. Do companies expect beginning workers to know how to do all the tasks they will have to do on their jobs? Why?
2. What is the purpose of a formal orientation session?
3. How does informal orientation differ from formal orientation?
4. What do supervisors observe about the work of beginners?
5. How does asking questions about your own performance help you improve your work?
6. What kind of degree can be earned at a community college?
7. Why do companies encourage employees to study?
8. Are there promotional opportunities for typists? Discuss.
9. Is initiative an important attribute for promotion? Discuss.
10. What is the meaning of the figures shown on page 649 under the heading "Projected Average Annual Openings 1974–1985?

MAKING IMPORTANT DECISIONS

Gail began working for a large company as a typist early in June shortly after she graduated from high school. In August, she received a memorandum from the Personnel Department describing a program of tuition payment for courses taken at one of the local colleges. The memorandum suggested that anyone interested in learning more about the program should meet in the conference room during the coffee break next Tuesday. Gail didn't think she should be wasting her time going to night courses. She was a high school graduate and she met all the requirements for her job. She tossed the memorandum in the waste basket. What do you think of Gail's judgment? What would you have done?

LEARNING TO WORK WITH OTHERS

Robert Weeks is a new accounting clerk in a large accounting office. One day, shortly after he began working, a fellow clerk told him "I've been watching you. You work too hard. Why are you killing yourself on this job? The work will be here long after you're gone. You ought to slow down. Why are you such an eager beaver — do you think you'll get a promotion?"

What do you think Robert should say to his fellow worker?

IMPROVING LANGUAGE SKILLS

Knowing the meaning of prefixes can aid you in adding words to your vocabulary. The definitions of some common prefixes are:

ab — away; from; off; under
con, com, col — together; with; jointly
contra — counter to; against
dis — opposite to; absence of
fore — beforehand; ahead of; previous to
mis — opposite of; lack of; wrong
pre — in front of; before
trans — across; beyond

Below is a list of words that contain the prefixes above. On a separate sheet of paper write or type a sentence using each of these words correctly. Refer to your dictionary if you need help working out the meaning of a word.

1. absolve
2. abstract
3. collateral
4. compact
5. compassion
6. compressed
7. concur
8. condominium
9. contradiction
10. contraposition
11. disadvantage
12. disservice
13. forecast
14. foresee
15. miscount
16. misfile
17. preconvention
18. predetermine
19. transatlantic
20. transmission

IMPROVING ARITHMETIC SKILLS

Clerical tests that applicants for jobs take often include arithmetic reasoning problems. Here are some typical questions you may have to answer. On a separate sheet of paper record the figures needed to compute your answers.

1. What is the total cost of the following items: 6 storage boxes for 3" by 5" cards at $2.60 each, 12 magazine files at 95 cents each, 6 pads of paper at 79 cents each, and 500 envelopes at $1.59 per hundred?
2. What is the sales tax on a purchase of $496.56 if the tax rate is 7 percent?
3. How much interest is earned in one year on an account of $1,540.50 if the interest rate is 7.25 percent?
4. An employee who was earning $135.00 per week was promoted to a job with a salary of $150.00 per week. What is the employee's percentage of increase?
5. If the price of admission to a museum increased 60 percent during the past year and the current admission is $2, what was the price of admission a year ago?

DEMONSTRATING OFFICE SKILLS

1. Assume that you are interested in studying on a part-time basis after you complete your high school studies and begin working full-time. What are the schools and colleges in your community, or within commuting distance of your community, where you could study on a part-time, evening basis? Make a list of such educational institutions and briefly discuss what kinds of courses you could take at each of these institutions.
2. Write a brief essay, approximately 600 words, in which you describe your present attitude toward promotional opportunities — how important they are to you as you think about beginning full-time work, what you believe it means to be promotable, and what you believe the most appropriate view of future jobs is for you at this moment.

IMPROVING OFFICE SKILLS (Optional)

As you think about future opportunities to study, either full-time or part-time, what do you believe are the subjects that would be of greatest value if you were interested in continuing to work in the business world? Write a brief essay in which you answer this question.

If, at this moment, you don't believe you have a long-term interest in working in business, discuss in a brief essay the field of work that is most appealing to you and what you think you should study in order to enter that field.

ALL★STAR
sporting goods company

Simulated Office Activities

An Orientation

The units in this textbook provide information and exercises to assist you in understanding the key tasks of office workers. Office tasks aren't done in isolation. You have already seen that many office tasks are inter-related because you have regularly used knowledge acquired in earlier units as a basis for understanding later units. Indeed, the office worker combines in each assignment many skills and understandings.

The Simulated Office Activities provided in the *Supplies Inventory* will give you a clearer understanding of how office tasks are interrelated. They will also provide you with an opportunity to plan your work, to make decisions, and to follow the instructions of an employer in a realis-tic setting. Each of the four Simulated Office Activities will require from two or three hours to complete. All are performed in the same office. Your goal is to complete the assignments just as if you were actually employed in the office and responsible to your employer for your own work. Your teacher may assign one Simulated Office Activity at a time, after completing a block of units in the textbook, or all four Simulated Office Activities at the same time, as a major project at the end of the course.

You will find that you have had experience with all of the tasks you are asked to complete. However, you will have to make decisions that go beyond just completing a single assignment. For example, one of your primary decisions will be to determine the order in which you will do a number of tasks based on the importance of each task. You will also have to make decisions about how to arrange materials and what supplies to use. Your decisions in each case will be guided by your knowledge of office procedures.

All-Star Sporting Goods Company   **653**

Your Office Position

You are employed as an office worker for the general manager of the ALL-STAR SPORTING GOODS COMPANY, 5002 Boulder Avenue, Denver, CO 80231. This large retail store carries a wide variety of all-seasons sporting goods for men and women.

Mr. Clark Newsom, the general manager for whom you are working, is responsible for coordinating all store departments so that they work smoothly and effectively together. Mr. Newsom counts on you to be accurate and thorough in your work. You represent Mr. Newsom and ALL-STAR to the public whenever you answer the telephone or greet callers. Mr. Newsom's ability to carry out his responsibilities, and hence the success of the business as a whole, will be affected by how efficiently and diligently you perform your office tasks. As you handle your various office jobs, you will become acquainted with the business activities of this interesting company.

Supplies

Many of the supplies you will need for the four Simulated Office Activities are provided in your *Supplies Inventory*. Others are easily obtained supplies which you will furnish yourself.

Supplies Provided

The following supplies, included in the Supplies Inventory, are required to complete the Simulated Activities.

Simulated Office Activity I:	3 All-Star Sporting Goods Company letterheads
	2 interoffice memo forms
Simulated Office Activity II:	1 All-Star Sporting Goods Company letterhead
	8 memo of call forms
	16 file folder labels
Simulated Office Activity III:	2 purchase requisition forms
	2 interoffice memo forms
	1 register of incoming mail form
Simulated Office Activity IV:	2 All-Star Sporting Goods Company letterheads
	2 interoffice memo forms

Additional Supplies

You will have to furnish the following supplies:

Simulated Office Activity I:

2	sheets plain paper
6	sheets onionskin paper
3	No. 10 envelopes
2	sheets carbon paper
1	folder labeled "For Your Action"
1	folder labeled "To Be Filed"

Simulated Office Activity II:

3½	sheets plain paper
2	sheets onionskin paper
1	No. 10 envelope
1	sheet carbon paper
1	folder labeled "For Your Action"
1	folder labeled "To Be Filed"

Simulated Office Activity III:

34	5" × 3" cards
1	spirit master
1	sheet carbon paper
1	folder labeled "For Your Action"
1	folder labeled "To Be Filed"

Simulated Office Activity IV:

2	sheets plain paper
2	sheets onionskin paper
2	No. 10 envelopes
1	sheet carbon paper
1	folder labeled "For Your Action"
1	folder labeled "To Be Filed"

Each page of supplies in the *Supplies Inventory* is marked with the Simulated Office Activity for which it is to be used. All supplies that are alike, however — for example, all letterheads — are grouped together in the Simulated Office Activities supplies section of the *Supplies Inventory*. You will have to decide on the type of supply you will need to complete each assignment. Make sure it relates to the Simulated Office Activity you are working on and remove it from the *Supplies Inventory*. Extra supplies are included for most items.

General Procedures

Each of the four Simulated Office Activities takes place on one day in the office. At the beginning of each day, Mr. Newsom gives you a number of business papers which you will use to complete your assignments. These papers may be outgoing letters or memos which you are to type, forms which you are to complete, or other kinds of business papers. These business papers are found in the Supplies Inventory and are labeled to match the Simulated Office Activity you are working on.

Each Simulated Office Activity includes realistic instructions. However, this does not mean that all instructions will be complete. You are to assume that any instructions not provided should be considered standard instructions which you understand from your study of the textbook.

To make the experience as realistic as possible, approach the activities just as you would your work at the beginning of a regular day on a real job. Follow these basic procedures:

1. Locate the business papers for the Simulated Office Activity you are to complete. Remember that the papers are labeled to match the Activity. Remove the business papers from the workbook, separating them at the perforation marks.

2. Read each business paper carefully, including all handwritten instructions. You will have to decide which job to complete first, second, third, etc., based on how soon you are told it is needed. After reading each paper carefully, decide the order in which you will complete the jobs and sort the papers into three stacks as follows:

   a. *RUSH*. All items which must be completed immediately; all items that must be completed so that further action can be taken by someone else in the immediate future; all items which must be sent out in the morning mail; all telephone messages.

   b. *ASAP (As Soon As Possible)*. All items which must be done today but which do not require immediate attention; items marked "take care of today," or "needed by end of today."

   c. *AYC (At Your Convenience)*. All other items which do not require *RUSH* or *ASAP* handling. These are routine assignments which are done when all other tasks are completed, or items on which action need not be taken until some time in the future.

3. After sorting the papers by priority, complete the Summary Form which you removed from the *Supplies Inventory* along with the business papers. Indicate in the appropriate blanks on the form which business papers you placed in each priority category by recording the circled job number that appears on each business paper. Later, when you have finished all the jobs in the Simulated Office Activity, you

will attach the Summary Form to the completed jobs and submit them to your teacher for evaluation.

4. After filling in the Summary Form, place the business papers in one stack with the *RUSH* items on top and the *AYC* items on the bottom. You are now ready to start the tasks beginning with the *RUSH* items.

5. Before processing a paper, read it a second time. Look at the circled job number on the business paper and find this job number in the list of instructions for the Simulated Office Activity on which you are working. Read the instructions carefully. Some of the instructions for a task may be given on the business paper itself. If all the instructions are not given, you must decide how to proceed based on what you have learned in your study of the textbook. Unless you are directed otherwise, refer to the textbook anytime you need to review specific procedures.

6. Secure the supplies you need to complete the job from the *Supplies Inventory* and from those you furnished. For each job make a carbon copy on onionskin paper unless you are instructed otherwise.

7. Use letterheads and prepare envelopes for all letters typed. Mr. Newsom prefers the modified block style letter with open punctuation and paragraph indentions. His name and title are typed as:

Clark Newsom
General Manager

8. After you finish a job, check it carefully. The responsible office worker strives to present the employer with work that is error-free. After you have completed and checked the job, type your name at the top unless you are directed otherwise by your teacher. Attach the business paper relating to each job to the back of the original you typed and place them in the "For Your Action" folder. Place the carbon copy of the completed job in the "To Be Filed" folder.

9. When you have completed all the jobs in a Simulated Office Activity:

   a. Remove the completed jobs from the "For Your Action" folder.
   b. Arrange the jobs in the order in which you completed them.
   c. Attach the Summary Form you completed earlier to the finished jobs.
   d. Put the completed jobs and the Summary Form back into the "For Your Action" folder and then give the folder to your teacher for evaluation.

After your work has been checked, the folder will be returned to you for use in the next Simulated Office Activity. (You may place the completed assignments returned to you by your teacher in another folder if you desire.)

You are now ready to begin work on the Simulated Office Activities. Good luck!

Appendix A

Grammar

Grammar is important in speaking and writing. Knowing the rules of grammar is necessary if you are to carry out your responsibilities confidently.

Grammar is the study of the words of a language, but particularly the study of the relationship of those words to one another. Words are subdivided into nine classifications that are known as parts of speech.

I. Nouns	VI. Adverbs
II. Pronouns	VII. Prepositions
III. Adjectives	VIII. Conjunctions
IV. Articles	IX. Interjections
V. Verbs	

I. Nouns

A noun is a word that names

A. A person (Winston Churchill)
B. A place (Palm Beach)
C. A thing (cake)
D. A quality (honesty)
E. An action (dancing)
F. An idea (liberty)

Proper Noun. A proper noun names a particular being or thing. It is always capitalized.

Thomas Edison, California, Statute of Liberty

Common Noun. A common noun names any member of a class of beings or things.

woman (women), light (lights), flower (flowers)

Collective Noun. A collective noun is a common noun that names a group.

company, committee, family, group, team

II. Pronouns

A pronoun is a word that is used instead of and that refers to a noun.

Pronoun	used instead of	Noun
he		John
she		Marilyn
they		jury

Personal Pronouns and Their Antecedents. A personal pronoun is a pronoun that shows by its form whether it represents the

A. Speaker (first person)
B. Person spoken to (second person)
C. Person spoken of (third person)

An antecedent is a noun that is referred to by a pronoun. (In all examples below, the antecedent is shown by one underline and the pronoun by two underlines.)

The singer took his stereo onto the plane.

His (the pronoun) refers to *singer* (the noun). *Singer* is therefore the antecedent of *his*.

The pronoun must be in agreement with its antecedent in person, number, and gender. There are several types of antecedents that require particular attention.

1. When two or more singular antecedents of a pronoun are connected by *and*, the pronoun must be plural.

   The clerk and the mail boy received their checks.

   If, however, the antecedents are merely different names for the same person or thing, the pronoun must be singular.

   The well-known businessman and public servant has received his award.

2. When two or more singular antecedents of a pronoun are connected by *or* or *nor*, the pronoun must be singular.

   Either Joyce or Linda must bring her notebook.

   If one of the antecedents is plural, it should be placed last, and the pronoun should be plural.

   Neither the general manager nor his assistants realized that they had so little time.

3. If the antecedent of a pronoun is a collective noun that expresses unity, the pronoun must be singular.

   The committee quickly reached its decision.

If the collective noun refers to the individuals or parts that make up a group, however, the pronoun of which it is the antecedent must be plural.

> The class brought their own lunches.

4. The number of an antecedent is not changed when it is followed by such connectives as *in addition to* and *as well as*.

> The boy, as well as his brothers, did his duty.

5. Since there is no third person, singular number, common gender pronoun, the masculine he, his, or him is generally used when the antecedent requires such a pronoun.

> Each office worker must do his best.

The issue of deciding whether to use a feminine or masculine pronoun is sometimes avoided by using a plural pronoun.

> All office workers must do their best.

When it is especially important to be accurate, both masculine and feminine pronouns may be used.

> Every employee should be careful about his or her personal appearance.

Relative Pronouns. A relative pronoun is one that joins a subordinate clause to its antecedent. *Who, which, what,* and *that* are the relative pronouns.

> Typists *who* know grammar are valuable.

The relative pronoun *who* joins its antecedent *secretaries* to the subordinate clause *know grammar*.

Some compound relative pronouns are *whoever, whichever,* and *whatever*; they differ from regular relative pronouns in that they contain their antecedents.

Relative pronouns present two problems:

1. Using the correct relative pronoun with reference to persons and things — for example, *who* refers to persons and, sometimes, to highly trained animals; *which* refers to animals or things; *that* refers to persons, animals, or things.

2. Using correct case form.

> *Who* and *whoever* are in the nominative case and are used when a relative pronoun is the subject of a subordinate clause.

> Mr. Johnson is a man *who* can do the job.

Whose is in the possessive case and is used to show ownership.

Whose hat is this?

Whom and *whomever* are in the objective case and are used when a relative pronoun is the object of a verb or preposition.

Grace is the girl *whom* we are addressing.

The Pronoun after *Be*. The same case may be used after the verb *be* in any of its forms *(am, are, is, was, were, be, being, have been)* as appears before it. This is usually the nominative case. When the object of a transitive verb, however, precedes the infinitive *to be*, the objective case must follow it.

It was *she* (not *her*).
If I were *he* (not *him*).
Did you expect those children to be *them* (not *they*)?

III. Adjectives

An adjective is a word that is used to modify a noun or a pronoun. There are two types of adjectives:

A. A *descriptive* adjective names some quality of or describes the person or object expressed by the noun or pronoun that it modifies.

pretty flower, *large* house, *white* dress

B. A *definitive* adjective points out or expresses the number or quantity of the object named by the noun or referred to by the pronoun.

eight people, *this* book, *that* desk, *ten* pages

Proper Adjectives. Proper adjectives are those derived from proper nouns, and they are always capitalized.

French language, *American* interests

Comparison of Adjectives. Comparison is the expression of an adjective to indicate an increasing or decreasing degree of quality, quantity, or manner. There are three degrees of comparison:

1. The *positive degree* is expressed by the simple form of the adjective.

light, pretty

2. The *comparative degree* is used to compare two objects. The comparative degree of almost all adjectives of *one* syllable, and

of a few of two syllables, is formed by the addition of *r* or *er* to the simple form.

lighter, prettier

The comparative degree of most adjectives of *two* or more syllables is formed by the placing of *more* or *less* before the simple form of the adjective.

more beautiful, *less* useful

3. The *superlative degree* is used to compare *three* or more objects. The superlative degree of most adjectives of one syllable, and some of two syllables, is formed by the addition of *est* to the simple form.

lightest, prettiest

The superlative degree of most adjectives of two or more syllables is formed by the placing of *most* or *least* before the simple form of the adjective.

most satisfactory, *least* attractive

Some adjectives are compared irregularly. The following are a few:

Positive	Comparative	Superlative
good	better	best
much	more	most
little	less	least
bad	worse	worst

IV. Articles

The, *a*, and *an* are articles.

A. *The* is a *definite* article because it refers to a particular person or thing in a class.

The manager read *the* application.

B. *A* and *an* are *indefinite* articles because they refer to persons or things in general. *An* is used before nouns that start with a vowel sound.

a person, *an* application, *an* honor

V. Verbs

A verb is a word that shows action or state of being of the subject. There are two classifications of verbs:

A. A *transitive verb* is one that requires an object to complete its meaning. The object may be a noun or a pronoun and it *must* be in the objective case. The object is used to complete the meaning of the verb.

To determine the object of a transitive verb, ask *What?* or *Whom?* after the verb.

> He *reported* the accident (Reported what? the accident).

B. An *intransitive verb* does *not* require an object to complete its meaning.

> The light *shines*. The boy *ran*.

Many verbs may be used both as transitive and intransitive verbs. For example, in the sentence, "The boy ran," *ran* is an intransitive verb requiring no object.

The verb *ran* may, however, be used as a transitive verb: for example, The boy *ran* a race. Here *race* is the object of the verb *ran*, and the verb becomes transitive.

Some verbs, however, may be used correctly only as intransitive verbs. *Sit*, *lie*, and *rise* are examples of verbs that are always intransitive verbs since they permit no object; while *set*, *lay*, and *raise* are examples of verbs that are always transitive because they require an object to complete their meaning.

Voice of Verbs. Voice indicates whether the subject of the verb is (1) the doer of the action or (2) the receiver of the action that is expressed by the verb.

A verb in the *active voice* identifies the subject as the doer of the action.

> The new stenographer *typed* the letter.

A verb in the *passive voice* identifies the subject as the receiver of the action.

> The letter *was typed* by the new stenographer.

Any transitive verb may be used in either the active or the passive voice.

In the independent clauses of a compound sentence or in a series of related statements, verbs of the same voice should be used. This is known as *parallel construction*.

> (Wrong) The letter *was dictated* by the executive and the secretary *transcribed* it.
> (Right) The executive *dictated* the letter and the secretary *transcribed* it.

Tense. Tense expresses the time of the action of a verb. There are three primary tenses:

1. The *present tense* of a verb is used to denote the present time. It is used in expressing a general truth or that which is customary. The present tense is also used to describe in a more vivid way what took place in past time. This is known as the *historical present*.

> George Washington *crosses* the Delaware and immediately *attacks* Trenton.

2. The *past tense* indicates past time.

> We *shipped* your order yesterday.

3. The *future tense* indicates that which will take place in the future. The future tense is expressed by the use of *shall* or *will* with the present form of the verb.

> I *shall go* early. You *will arrive* on time.
> She *will come* in at eight o'clock.

Frequent errors are made in the use of *will* and *shall*. The future tense may be used to express simple futurity or to express determination or promise. Simple futurity is denoted by the use of *shall* with the first person, and *will* with the second and the third persons.

> I *shall be* happy to see you when you arrive.
> He *will be* home early.

If determination or promise is to be expressed, the rule for futurity is reversed. Use *will* with a first person subject, *shall* with a second or third person subject.

> I *will be* there without fail.
> You *shall* certainly *go*.
> They *shall return* tomorrow.

In asking questions, use *shall* when the subject is in the first person (I, we).

> *Shall* we go?

When the subject is in the second or third person, either *shall* or *will* may be used, depending upon which form is expected in the answer.

> *Will* you write the letter? (Answer expected: I *will* write the letter.)
> *Shall* you miss your friends when you move? (Answer expected: I *shall* miss my friends.)

In addition to the primary tenses, there are three verb phrases, known as the perfect tenses, that represent completed action or being.

1. The *present perfect* tense denotes an action or an event completed at the present time. It is formed by the placing of *have* or *has* before the perfect participle.

I *have read* several chapters.
He *has studied* his French.

2. The *past perfect* tense indicates an action or an event completed at or before a stated past time. It is formed by the placing of *had* before the perfect participle.

> They *had completed* the picture by the time dinner was served.
> I *had assumed* you would come by plane before we received your letter.

3. The *future perfect* tense indicates that an action or an event will be completed at or before a stated future time. It is formed by the placing of *shall have* or *will have* before the perfect participle.

> I *shall have gone* before you arrive.
> He *will have arrived* home before you can get there.

Whether *shall have* or *will have* is used depends upon the basic rules for the use of *shall* or *will*.

Mood. Mood is that property of a verb that indicates the manner in which the action or state of being is expressed.

1. The *indicative mood* is used in asserting something as a fact or in asking a question.

> She reads well.
> Where is the book?

2. The *imperative mood* is used in expressing a command, a request, or an entreaty.

> Bring me my coat, please.
> Sit up!

3. The *subjunctive mood* is used in expressing a doubt, a wish, or a condition contrary to reality.

(a) A condition contrary to *present* reality is expressed with *were*, not *was*.

> (Wrong) If I *was* tall, I could reach the book.
>   If Ann *was* going, you could go along.
> (Right) If I *were* tall, I could reach the book.
>   If Ann *were* going, you could go along.

(b) A condition contrary to *past* reality is expressed by *had been*.

> If the plane *had been* on time, this might not have happened.

Agreement of Verb and Subject. A verb must agree with its subject in person and number. The verb *to be* has person and number forms: *I am, you are, he is, we are, you are,* and *they are; I was, you were, he was, we were, you were,* and *they were*. Other verbs have only one expression for all number and person forms.

When the subject is in the third person, singular number, a verb or an auxiliary (helping verb) in the present or the present perfect tense must end in *s*.

> Mr. White *dictates* very slowly.
> Miss Stewart *has* been his secretary for a long time.

A very common error is the use of a singular verb with a plural subject, or a plural verb with a singular subject.

1. When the verb and the subject are separate in the sentence, the verb must agree with its subject. A common error is to make the verb agree with the word near it rather than with the real subject.

   > (Wrong) The *activity* of the board at its weekly meetings *are* always interesting.
   > (Right) The *activity* of the board at its weekly meetings *is* always interesting.

2. If the subject is plural in form but singular in meaning, a singular verb is required.

   > The news *has* been good.

3. Two or more singular subjects connected by *or* or *nor* require a singular verb.

   > Neither Kurt nor Bill *is* at the office.

4. When two or more subjects connected by *or* or *nor* differ in number, the plural subject is placed nearest the verb and the verb made plural.

   > Neither the vice-president nor the executives have that bulletin.

   When two or more subjects connected by *or* or *nor* differ in person, the verb must agree with the subject that is nearest to it.

   > Either you or I *am* at fault.

   It is frequently better to rephrase the sentence so as to use a verb with each subject.

   > Either you *are* at fault or I *am*.

5. Two or more singular subjects connected by *and* require a plural verb.

The typewriter and the adding machine *are* both in need of repair.

6. When the subjects connected by *and* refer to the same person, a singular verb must be used.

   The great novelist and playwright *is* on his way home.

7. When the subjects connected by *and* represent one idea or are closely connected in thought, a singular verb should be used.

   Ice cream and cake *is* a popular dessert.

8. When either or both subjects connected by *and* are preceded by *each, every, many a*, etc., a singular verb is required.

   Each stock clerk and supervisor *is* expected to work late on the inventory.

9. When one of two subjects is in the positive and the other in the negative, the verb agrees with the one in the positive.

   The teacher, and not the students, *is* planning to attend.

10. The number of a subject is not affected by words connected to it by *as well as, and also, in addition to*, etc.

    Mother, as well as the rest of the family, *is* expecting to go.

11. When a collective noun expresses unity, a singular verb is used.

    The jury *is* asking that a point be clarified.

Contractions. Contractions may be used in informal communications.

In writing contractions, remember that *don't* the contraction of *do not*, is plural and is used with plural nouns and the pronouns *I, we, you*, and *they. Doesn't*, the contraction of *does not*, is singular and is used with singular nouns and the pronouns *he, she*, and *it*.

   It *doesn't* bother them much, but I *don't* like it.

Infinitives. An infinitive is expressed by placing the word *to* before a verb: *to be, to walk, to talk, to cry*. The infinitive may be used:

1. As a subject.

   To run takes energy.

2. As an adjective.

   The place *to go* is Colorado.

3. As a predicate noun.

   To jog is *to exercise.*

4. As a direct object.

Mary likes *to sing*.

5. As an adverb.

Jack waited *to leave* with me.

Participles. A participle is a verb form used as an adjective and having the double function of verb and adjective. There are three forms of the participle:

1. The *present participle* is formed by the addition of *ing* to the simple form of the verb. It expresses action as being in progress, usually at the same time as some other action. It is used as an adjective and at the same time retains some of the properties of a verb.

   The clerk *counting* the money is new here.

   In this sentence *counting* is an adjective modifying the noun *clerk*; it also has the property of a verb in that it takes the object *money*.

2. The *past participle* expresses action prior to that of the governing verb. It is used as an adjective and is usually formed by the addition of *d* or *ed* to the present tense of the verb.

   The machine *used* by the secretary was defective.
   The teacher, *interrupted* by the students, did not complete her grading.

3. The *perfect participle* is formed by the combination of *being*, *having*, or *having been* with some other participle.

   Having written the letters, she was free to go.

   In the preceding sentence the perfect participle *having written* modifies the subject of the sentence *she*.

   A common error is that of putting at the beginning of a sentence a participial phrase that does not modify the subject. This is referred to as *dangling* participle.

   (Wrong) Having completed the statement, it was time to file the letters.
   (Right) Having completed the statement, she found it was time to file the letters.

VI. Adverbs

An adverb is a word used to modify a verb, an adjective, or another adverb.

A. An adverb modifies a verb by answering the questions *how? when?* or *where?*

> She walked *lightly*.
> He arrived *early*.
> The report is *here*.

B. An adverb modifies adjectives and other adverbs by expressing degree *(how much? how little?)* or by answering the question *in what manner?*

> The clerk will file *more* often.
> She spoke *less* clearly than before.
> He was mechanically precise.
> Julia was painfully aware of the problem.

Comparison of Adverbs. Like adjectives, adverbs are compared to show degree.

1. A few adverbs are compared by the addition of *er* or *est* to the positive form of the adverb.

   > *soon, sooner, soonest; slow, slower, slowest*

2. Some adverbs are compared irregularly.

   > *well, better, best*

3. Most adverbs, however, are compared by the use of *more* or *most* and *less* or *least* with the simple (positive) form of the adverb.

   > *more* brightly, *most* often; *less* lightly, *least* likely

Placing the Adverb. Ordinarily an adverb follows the verb it modifies, but it may precede it. It should be placed where its meaning is most clearly shown. *Only, merely*, and *also*, which are sometimes adverbs and sometimes adjectives, give the most trouble in placing, since they may convey very different meanings in different positions in a sentence.

> *Only* I saw him.   I saw *only* him.
> I *only* saw him.   I saw him *only*.

Other Rules for Adverbs. There are a few errors frequently made in the use of adverbs.

1. *Very* or *too* should generally not be used to modify participles directly.

   > (Wrong) Her work was very improved.
   > (Right)   Her work was very much improved.

2. *Too*, which is an adverb that means *also* or *more than enough*, should be spelled correctly and not confused with *to* or *two*.

   > By *two* o'clock she had *too* much work *to* do.

3. *Well* is usually an adverb. In speaking of health, however, *well* is used as an adjective. Be careful not to use *good* as an adverb in place of *well*.

    (Wrong) He does his work *good*.
              I don't feel very *good*.
    (Right)   He does his work *well*.
              I don't feel very *well*.

4. *Very* is an adverb of degree, while *real* is an adjective of quality. Do not use *real* in place of *very*.

    (Wrong) He had a *real* beautiful office.
    (Right)   He had a *very* beautiful office.

5. Adverbs of manner, those ending in *ly*, are frequently confused with adjectives derived from the same root. Adverbs of manner modify verbs that express action.

    She sings *sweetly*. (Adverb)
    Her singing is *sweet*. (Adjective)

6. *Not* is an adverb used to express negation; it should not be used in combination with other negatives.

    (Wrong) The clerk will *not* wait for *nobody*.
    (Right)   The clerk will *not* wait for *anybody*.
    (Right)   The clerk will wait for *nobody*.

VII. Prepositions

A preposition connects a noun or a pronoun with some other element of the sentence and shows the relationship between them. The noun or pronoun that follows the preposition is its object.

There are two kinds of prepositions:

A. Simple — *to, for, at, through of*
B. Compound — *into, in spite of, instead of, in regard to, on account of, because of, according to, out of, as to.*

Prepositional Phrases. A group of words made up of a preposition and its object, together with any words used to modify the object, is called a *prepositional phrase*. The object of a preposition may be determined by asking *whom* or *what* after the preposition; what the prepositional phrase modifies may be determined by asking *what* or *who* before the preposition.

Prepositional phrases, like adjectives and adverbs, should be placed as close as possible to the words they modify to make the sentence as clear as possible.

Choice of Prepositions. Many errors are made in the use of prepositions because some words demand certain prepositions; for example *angry with* is used in reference to persons, and *angry at* is used in reference to things, animals, or situations. Some of the most common situations in which prepositions are misused are given below.

1. *Into* should be used after a verb that indicates the motion of a person or a thing from one place to another. *In* is used after a verb expressing the idea of rest or, in some cases, motion within a certain place

   The girl went *into* the classroom.
   The clerk is *in* the filing department.

2. *Between* should be used only in reference to two persons or objects. *Among* should be used when referring to three or more persons or objects.

   The two boys divided the work *between* them.
   Gifts were distributed *among* the children.

3. Do not use unnecessary prepositions.

   (Wrong) The wastebasket is *in under* the desk. Where is it *at?*
   (Right) The wastebasket is *under* the desk. Where is it?

4. Do not omit prepositions that are needed to make sentences grammatically correct. Avoid telegraphic style in letters.

   (Wrong) Mr. Finley will arrive North Station 11:00 Sunday.
   (Right) Mr. Finley will arrive at the North Station at 11:00 a.m. Sunday.

VIII. Conjunctions

A conjunction is a word used to connect words, phrases, or clauses. There are three kinds of conjunctions:

A. A *coordinate conjunction* connects words or clauses of the same grammatical relation or construction, neither being dependent upon the other for its meaning.

   You *and* I are elected.
   Their father is out of town, *and* their sister is on a vacation.

B. A *subordinate conjunction* connects a subordinate clause with some word in the principal clause upon which it is dependent for its meaning.

   The man left hurriedly *since* he was late.

C. *Correlative conjunctions* are conjunctions that are used in pairs, the first introducing and the second connecting the elements. They must be placed just before the elements that they introduce or connect.

(Wrong) I will *either* meet you in Boston *or* Washington.
I will meet you *either* in Boston *or* Washington.
(Right) I will meet you in *either* Boston *or* Washington.
I will meet you *either* in Boston *or* in Washington.

Or should only be used with *either*, *nor* with *neither*. They are used in reference to two things only.

(Wrong) *Either* Bob, Jack, *or* Don will pitch today's game.
Neither the superintendent, the principal, *nor* the teachers agreed with him.
Neither Jack *or* Don will pitch today's game.

(Right) Bob, Jack, *or* Don will pitch today's game.
The superintendent, the principal, *and* the teachers disagreed with him.
None of them — the superintendent, the principal, the teachers — agreed with him.
Neither Jack *nor* Don will pitch today's game.

Some cautions concerning the use of conjunctions follow.

1. Conjunctions should not be used in place of some other part of speech.

   (Wrong) Seldom *or* ever should such an example be used.
   You should try *and* improve your speech.
   (Right) Seldom *if* ever should such an example be used.
   You should try *to* improve your speech.

2. A clause, which is a part of a sentence containing a subject and a predicate, having meaning in itself, is connected to the other parts of the sentence by either a conjunction or a relative pronoun. A phrase, which contains no verb and has no meaning by itself, is introduced by a preposition, participle, or infinitive, but not by a conjunction.

   The project cannot be completed *without* your help.
   (*Without* is a preposition introducing a phrase.)
   The project cannot be completed *unless* you help us.
   (*Unless* is a conjunction introducing a clause.)

3. *Except* and *without* are prepositions and should not be used in place of *unless*, which is a conjunction.

   (Wrong) You will not master shorthand *except* you concentrate.
   (Right) You will not master shorthand *unless* you concentrate.

4. *Like* is not a conjunction and should never be used in place of the conjunction *as*.

(Wrong) She walks *like* you do.
(Right) She walks *as* you do.

IX. Interjections

Interjections are exclamatory words or phrases used in a sentence for emphasis or to indicate feeling. They have no grammatical connection with the rest of the sentence, and are set off by a comma or an exclamation mark.

Oh, so you saw it?
Ouch! that hurt.

Grammar Reference Books. Although many questions concerning grammar can be answered by using a good dictionary, you should have available a standard reference book on English grammar.

In Appendix H you will find a list of recommended books. A ready reference on grammar will help you produce better letters and reports for your employer.

Appendix B
Punctuation

Punctuation is used to make more forceful and to indicate more clearly the relationship of written thoughts. Punctuation is the written substitute for the changes in voice, the pauses, and the gestures that are used in oral expression.

The excessive use of punctuation marks is not good form. The importance of using punctuation accurately, however, is illustrated daily by the serious errors that may be found in office correspondence.

You will need to know the correct punctuation of business letters and reports. Although you are not expected to be an authority on punctuation, you should be familiar with the most important rules.

General guidelines for spacing after punctuation marks are:

1. One space is left after punctuation marks within a sentence with the exception of the colon.
2. Two spaces are left after colons and all punctuation marks at the ends of sentences.
3. No spaces are left between two marks of punctuation when they are used together.

Rules for punctuation are given alphabetically in this appendix.

Apostrophe (')

The apostrophe is used

1. To form possessives. There are several rules that govern the formation of the possessive case of words, depending on the final letter or syllable of the word and whether the word is singular or plural. There are no spaces before or after an apostrophe that is part of a word. A few important rules to follow are listed below.

    (a) The possessive of singular and plural common and proper nouns not ending with the *s* or *z* sound (excepting *ce*) is usually formed by the addition of an apostrophe and *s* to the singular form.

| typist's desk | men's coats |
| Shaw's plays | Lawrence's mail |

(b) The possessive of a singular noun ending in *s* is formed by adding an apostrophe and *s* if the *s* is to be pronounced as an extra syllable. If not, add only the apostrophe.

| waitress's | politeness' |
| class's | species' |

(c) The possessive of plural common nouns ending in *s* is formed by the addition of only an apostrophe.

| boys' shirts | players' uniforms |
| committee's reports | |

(d) The possessive of a one-syllable proper noun ending in an *s* or *z* sound is generally formed by the addition of an apostrophe and *s*, although in newspapers addition of only the apostrophe is frequently seen.

| Burns's poems | Marx's ideas |
| Liz's book | |

(e) The possessive of proper nouns of more than one syllable ending in an *s* or *z* sound (excepting *ce*) is formed by the addition of an apostrophe only.

| Essex' papers | Adams' chronicle |
| Burroughs' house | |

(f) The possessive of a compound noun is formed by the addition of an apostrophe or an apostrophe and *s* [according to Rules (a), (b), (c) and (d)] to its final syllable.

mother-in-law's visit
City of Detroit's council
letter carrier's route
passers-by's expressions

(g) The possessive of a series of names connected by a conjunction showing joint ownership is indicated by an apostrophe or an apostrophe and *s* to the last name.

Simon and Walter's garage
Adams and Anderson's firm

(h) If joint ownership does not exist in a series of names, the possessive case is formed by the addition of an apostrophe or apostrophe and *s* to each proper name in the series.

Macy's and Hayne's stores
Jack's, Joe's, and Bill's gloves

(i) The possessive of abbreviated words is formed by adding an apostrophe and *s* to the last letter of the abbreviation.

YMCA's membership
the X's function
the Mr.'s position in the heading
the OK's presence

(j) The apostrophe is never used to form the possessive of pronouns.

his   yours
hers

2. To show the omission of letters (in a contraction) or the omission of figures.

don't (for *do not*)   Class of '78 (for *1978*)
it's (for *it is*)

3. To form the plurals of figures, letters, signs, and words.

If you have no 6's, use 9's turned upside down.
Her *v*'s and *u*'s and *T*'s and *F*'s are too much alike.
The +'s and −'s denote whether the sentences were correct or not.
There were too many *and*'s and *the*'s in the essay.

4. To form the past tense of arbitrarily coined verbs; it is followed by a *d*.

She OK'd the copy.
He X'd out three lines.

Asterisk (*)

The asterisk is sometimes used instead of a raised number to refer to a footnote.

Mr. Martin used the reports* as a reference.

---

*The reports are from the Mackenzie Case.

Brackets [ ]

Brackets are used

1. To enclose a correction, an addition, or a comment which a writer inserts in matter he is quoting.

"In 1942 [a typographical error for 1492] Columbus discovered America."

2. To enclose the term *sic*, Latin for *thus*, to show that a misspelling or some other error appeared in the original and is not an error by the one quoting.

In applying for the job he wrote, "I am very good in athletics [*sic*], and I can teach mathmatics [*sic*]."

3. When it is necessary to place a parenthesis within another parenthesis; but in general, such complicated usages should be avoided.

   At 3:30 p.m. (the time agreed upon at the conference [see John Coleman's letter of April 9]) the announcement of the new salary agreement was made to the news media.

Colon (:)

The colon is used

1. To introduce formally a word, a list, a statement, or a question; a series of statements or questions; or a long quotation.

   The book had many good points: it contained an interesting story; it contained humor; it was well illustrated.

2. Between hours and minutes whenever they are expressed in figures.

   8:30 a.m.   1:45 p.m.

3. After salutations in some styles of business letters:

   Dear Sir: Ladies and Gentlemen:
   Dear Mrs. Jones:

Comma (,)

The comma is the most frequently used form of punctuation; therefore, errors in its use are frequent. The comma is used

1. To set off a subordinate clause preceding a main clause.

   When the bell rings, you may leave.

2. To set off a nonrestrictive phrase or subordinate clause. (A phrase or a clause is nonrestrictive if the main clause in the sentence expresses a complete thought when the nonrestrictive phrase or clause is omitted.)

   My doctor, who is now on vacation, will prepare the report next week.

3. To separate long coordinate clauses that are joined by the conjunctions *and*, *but*, *for*, *neither*, *nor*, and *or*. The comma precedes the conjunction.

   He worked far into the night, for the deadline was noon the next day.

4. To set off phrases or expressions at the beginning of a sentence when they are loosely connected with the rest of the sentence.

Nevertheless, we feel the way you do about it.

5. To separate words, phrases, or clauses in a series. Most writers include a comma before the last item in the series.

The group now has no meeting place, no supplies, and no money.
They told us when they heard it, where they heard it, and from whom they heard it.

6. To separate two or more adjectives if they both precede or follow the noun they modify, provided each adjective alone modifies the noun. If an adjective modifies a combination of a noun and another adjective, however, no comma is used between the two adjectives.

An old, shaggy, forlorn-looking dog came limping out to greet us.
Happy young people come here frequently.

7. To set off words and phrases used in apposition.

My cousin, the doctor in the family, has a practice in Syracuse.

8. To set off parenthetical words, clauses, or phrases.

Tomorrow, on the other hand, business will be much better.

9. To set off words in direct address.

Children, we must get ready for the party.

10. To set off the words *yes* and *no* when used in sentences.

Yes, you may go now.
Frankly, no, I don't care.

11. To set off the name of a state when it is used with a city.

They lived in Denver, Colorado, for many years.

12. To separate the day of the month from the year and to set off the year when used with the month.

The project must be completed by August 20, 1978, at the latest.

13. To set off a mild interjection.

Ah, he surely enjoyed that story.

14. To set off a participial expression used as an adjective.

Smiling pleasantly, she entered the office.

15. To separate unrelated numbers.

   In 1960, 25 new students enrolled.

16. To divide a number of four or more digits into groups of three, counting from right to left. Do not space after the comma.

   1,567,039

17. To set off phrases that denote residence or position.

   Professor William Smith, of Harvard, will speak.

18. To indicate the omission of a word or words readily understood from the context.

   In June the book sales amounted to $523; in July, to $781.

19. Before a short, informal, direct quotation.

   The employer asked, "Have you transcribed those letters?"

Dash (—)

The dash is formed in typewriting by the striking of two hyphens without a space preceding or following them. The dash is used

1. To indicate a change in the sense or construction of a sentence.

   Hemingway, Wolfe, Green — these are my favorites.

2. Instead of a comma to emphasize or to guard against confusing the reader.

   The laborer is worthy of his hire — if his labor is.
   If — and only if — we go, the day will be complete.

3. To precede a reference.

   No, the heart that has truly loved never forgets. — Moore.

Diagonal (/)

The diagonal is used

1. Between two words with no spaces around it. The diagonal indicates that either or both of the words may be used in the sentence.

   You may write the report and/or prepare a notebook.

2. Between two numbers with no spaces around it to express a fraction.

   The height is 2/3 of the width.

Ellipsis (. . .)

The ellipsis is used

1. To show that words have been omitted from the beginning or middle of a sentence. An ellipsis is three periods, each separated by one space. There is one blank space before the first period and one after the last period.

   Original statement: Mary typed and proofread the report.
   Mary . . . proofread the report.

2. To show that a statement is unfinished or dies away. A period is placed at the end of the sentence after an ellipsis.

   Mary typed and proofread . . . .

Exclamation Point (!)

The exclamation point, like the period, represents a full stop. It is used at the end of a thought expressing strong emotion or command. The thought may be represented by a complete sentence, a phrase, or a word.

   Aha! We caught you this time!

Hyphen (-)

The hyphen is used

1. To divide a word between syllables at the end of a line.

   The traffic near my sister's apartment was heavy yesterday afternoon.

2. To show compound words

   She has a new wash-and-wear blouse.

Parentheses ( )

Parentheses are used

1. To enclose figures or letters that mark a series of enumerated elements.

   She wanted three things: (1) a promotion, (2) a salary increase, and (3) more responsibility.

2. To enclose figures verifying a number which is written in words.

   twenty (20) dollars
   twenty dollars ($20)

3. To enclose material that is indirectly related to the main thought of a sentence.

> We shall postpone (at least for the present) a decision.

4. To enclose matter introduced as an explanation.

> The answer (see page 200) is puzzling.

The rules covering the use of other marks of punctuation with parentheses are:

1. If needed in the sentence, a comma or dash that normally precedes a parenthetic element is transferred to follow the closing parenthesis.

> He sent a belated, though clever (and somewhat personal), greeting card.

2. Punctuation at the end of a parenthetic expression *precedes* the parenthesis if it applies to the parenthetic material only; it *follows* the parenthesis if it applies to the sentence as a whole.

> When she heard him (he shouted, "Who goes there?"), she was surprised.
> (See the discussion on page 78.)
> This experiment has interesting results (see Table I).

Period (.)

The period is used

1. After complete declarative or imperative sentences.

> Today we shall study the use of the period.

2. After initials in a name.

> H. L. Andrews

3. Within an abbreviation. Do not space after these periods.

> a.m., e.g., i.e.

4. After most abbreviations:

> pres., lb., et al.

The following are some exceptions:

> (a) Mme (Madame), Mlle (Mademoiselle)
> (b) IOU, c/o, OK, SOS, A1
> (c) Chemical symbols: H_2O, Zn, Pb
> (d) Office and agencies of the federal government: SEC, FBI, FCC

5. In decimal numbers, and between dollars and cents when expressed in figures, and after the abbreviations *s*, and *d*, for shilling and pence. Do not space after a period that is used as a decimal point.

> 3.45, $16.13, 13s., 7d.

Question Mark (?)

The question mark is used

1. After a direct question, but not after an indirect question.

> Are you ready?
> He asked what caused the fire.

It is not necessary to use a question mark after a polite request.

> Will you please let us know your decision at once.

2. To indicate uncertainty.

> The applicant was born in 1952(?).

3. After each question in a series if special emphasis is desired. When it is used in this way, it takes the place of the comma; and each element begins with a small letter.

> Where is my pen? my notebook? my file?

Quotation Marks (" ")

Quotation marks are used

1. To enclose direct quotations. Single quotation marks are used to enclose a quotation within a quotation.

> The director said, "I hope you are familar with this play."
> She said, "Unkind as it may be, I can't help saying 'I told you so' to her."

2. To enclose the titles of articles, lectures, reports, etc., and the titles of subdivisions of publications (that is, the titles of parts, chapters, etc.). The titles of books and magazines are not enclosed in quotation marks, but underscored or typed in all capital letters.

> She thought the chapter "Producing Mailable Transcripts" was helpful.

3. To enclose unusual, peculiar, or slang terms.

> Her "five o'clocks" were famous.
> When they saw us, they "flipped."

4. To enclose words used in some special sense, or words to which attention is directed in order to make a meaning clear.

> He said "yes," not "guess."
> The term "title by possession" is often used.

5. To enclose the titles of short poems, songs, and television and radio shows.

> "Fog" (poem)
> "Yesterday" (song)
> "All in the Family" (TV show)
> "David Brinkley's Journal" (radio show)

6. When consecutive paragraphs of the same work are quoted, at the beginning of each paragraph but at the end of only the last paragraph.

Quoted Matter. When quoted matter appears within a letter, an article, or a report, it is advisable that it be indicated as a quotation. This may be done in three ways:

1. The material may be indented from the regular margins on the left and right.
2. It may be underscored throughout.
3. It may be enclosed in quotation marks.

Sometimes the quoted matter is both indented and enclosed in quotation marks. The practice of using quotation marks is the most widely used.

A long quotation is single-spaced, even though the rest of the copy is double-spaced.

Quotation Marks with Other Marks of Punctuation. At the end of quoted material, a quotation mark and another mark of punctuation are often used together. The rules governing the order of these marks are not entirely logical; but since they are well established and generally accepted, you should follow them.

1. A period or a comma should precede the quotation mark even though it may not be a part of the quotation.

> "I saw you," he said, "when you left."

2. A semicolon or colon should follow the closing quotation mark, even when it is a part of the quotation.

> Mary, Ruth, and John visited that "house of antiques"; and the "antiques" were very unusual.
> We can say one thing about his "story": it is true.

3. Other marks of punctuation should precede the closing quotation mark if they apply to the quotation only, and should

follow the mark if they apply to the sentence as a whole and not just to the quotation.

> She asked, "Will you go?"
> Did you read the article "Better Sales Letters"?

Semicolon (;)

The semicolon is used

1. In a compound sentence between closely related clauses that are not joined by a conjunction.

> That is good taste; it suggests discretion.

2. In a compound sentence if either clause contains subclauses or long phrases requiring commas.

> Since the weather was rainy and windy, she grew cold; but she continued on her journey.

3. Before such words and abbreviations as *e.g., i.e., viz., for example, namely,* and *to wit* when they introduce a long list of items. A comma precedes the list.

> Some pairs of words are bothersome to students; for example, affect and effect, loose and lose, sit and set.

4. Between elements in a listing when there are commas within the elements.

> James Craig, Newport High; William Parker, Forest Hills High; and Ken Caldwell, Jefferson High were the winners.

5. Before connectives when such words introduce sentences, principal clauses, or an abrupt change in thought. (The comma follows the connective when used in this manner only if the connective is to be emphasized.) Some of these connectives are *accordingly, consequently, hence, however, in fact, moreover, nevertheless, therefore, thus, whereas, yet.*

> It is February; therefore, we have many holidays.

Underscore (Italics)

A typist can emphasize an important word, phrase, or sentence in typewritten material several ways. The kind of copy and the purpose for which it is being typed determine to some extent the emphasis that should be indicated.

In typewriting, underscoring takes the place of printed italics and is the method most often used to give prominence to a word or group of words. Emphasis is also achieved by typing in red in the midst of copy typed in black or blue, and by making characters darker by typing over them several times.

In addition to emphasizing a word or words, the underscore (italics) should be used

1. To refer to a word or letter taken out of its context.

   Always dot your i's, and cross your t's.
   Do not write and and the slantwise across the line.

2. To designate a foreign word not yet anglicized.

   Her faux pas was noticeable.

3. To indicate titles of plays, motion pictures, musical composi-tions, paintings, art objects, books, pamphlets, newspapers, and magazines. (Parts of these, such as chapters in a book or article in a magazine or newspaper, are designated by quota-tion marks.)

   Have you seen My Fair Lady?
   El Greco's View of Toledo was on display at the museum.
   We also saw Rodin's The Thinker.
   She found Unit 8, "Meeting the Public," in Secretarial Office Pro-cedures very helpful.
   The Wall Street Journal contains a regular feature entitled "Wash-ington Wire."

4. To designate the names of ships, airplanes, and spacecraft.

   U.S.N.S. Nautilus
   Lindbergh's Spirit of St. Louis
   Apollo 15

Appendix C
Word Choice and Spelling

An office worker cannot afford to be indifferent to words, but must constantly be concerned with their spelling, meaning, and appropriateness. Continuous vigilance is necessary to insure that misspelled words and words that do not convey precisely the meaning intended do not slip by in proofreading copy. An office worker who does not choose words carefully soon becomes guilty of poor communication skills.

A dictionary is a regularly used reference in every office. Become acquainted with your dictionary. Learn to understand all abbreviations that are used. Your dictionary will dispel uncertainties about proper spelling and meanings of words.

Good Usage

To convey messages precisely, it is important that you use words that conform to current good usage. *Colloquialisms*, which are words and phrases that are acceptable in informal conversations and sometimes in letters, are not considered good usage in formal business correspondence. *Provincialisms*, which are terms that are used informally in particular areas of the country, are also to be avoided in formal communications. *Archaic* and *obsolete* words, which are words that were once standard, are no longer in fashion and should be avoided.

Below is a list of *colloquialisms* that should be avoided in business communications.

Incorrect in Formal Writing	*Correct in Formal Writing*
all-round (adj.)	generally serviceable
around	about, nearly
back of, in back of	behind, at the back of
bit	a short time, a little while
calculate	think, plan, expect
cute	clever, amusing
enthuse	enthusiastic
get hold of	to learn, to master
have got to	must, have to

Incorrect in Formal Writing	Correct in Formal Writing
lots of, a great deal of	many, much
most	almost, nearly
not a one	not one
off of	off
over with	finished, done
quite some time	a long time
show up	arrive
stand for	allow, stand

Some *provincialisms* which may fail to convey meaning when used outside a local area, and which should be avoided, are shown below.

Use	Rather than
declare, maintain	allow
raise	rear
short distance	piece
think, suppose, guess	reckon
want to come in	want in
you	you all
intend to	is fixing to

Words That Are Pronounced Alike

Words that are pronounced alike but differ in meaning are called *homonyms*. These words are often confusing and require close attention to the meaning of the sentence so that the correct word is used.

Some examples of homonyms are:

aid, aide	hoard, horde
aisle, isle	incite, insight
allowed, aloud	knew, new
altar, alter	lead, led
bare, bear	plain, plane
base, bass	right, write
berth, birth	role, roll
brake, break	stationary, stationery
creak, creek	through, threw
fair, fare	ware, wear, where

Words That Are Not Pronounced Alike

Many words that are very close in spelling are *not* pronounced alike. These words are frequently confused in use simply because they look alike when written or sound similar to the ear. Words of this type are listed below. Can you distinguish the meaning and pronunciation of each?

accept, except	content, contest
adapt, adept, adopt	council, counsel
addition, edition	formerly, formally
affect, effect	local, locale
all ways, always	moral, morale
allusion, illusion	personal, personnel
ascent, assent	test, text

Compound Words

In the regular routine of daily business, one class of words that gives considerable trouble is made up of compound words. Compound words fall into three groups: hyphenated compounds, single-word compounds, and two-word compounds.

There are a few rules that will assist you in becoming familar with certain groups of compound words that use the hyphen.

1. A hyphen is always used in a compound number.

   twenty-one, fifty-eight

2. A hyphen is used between the numerator and the denominator of a fraction written in words except when one of the elements already contains a hyphen. A fraction used as a noun requires no hyphen.

four-fifths share	forty-one hundredths
two-thirds interest	forty one-hundredths
one half of the total	
two fifths of the class	

3. A hyphen is used between two or more words when the words serve as a single adjective *before* a noun. In applying this rule you must be careful that the words are not a series of independent adjectives. The exception to the rule is that proper nouns made up of two or more words are not hyphenated when used as adjectives.

   a well-liked boy, *but* a boy well liked
   a fresh-water fish, *but* a fish from fresh water
   a New England dinner, a New Jersey product
   a large black horse; a deep, clear pool

4. Groups of three or more words used as a single word are usually hyphenated.

   four-in-hand, well-to-do, sister-in-law, up-to-date

5. A hyphen is used after a prefix

   (a) when the prefix is joined to a proper noun

   pro-Republican, anti-Christian

(b) to prevent confusion between some verbs and compounds

re-form (meaning to form again)
re-sign (meaning to sign again)

(c) to prevent an awkward piling up of consonants

bell-like, well-loved

(d) to separate double vowels that might be mispronounced as one sound

de-emphasize, re-ink

When *any, every, no,* and *some* are combined with other words, the compound is a single word: *anything, everyone, nowhere, somehow.* Sometimes, however, the parts of the compound expression are written as separate words: *no one, every one.*

Compound words change form. Some become single-word compounds through constant use; at some time in the past most were hyphenated compounds. The following compound words occur frequently.

Hyphenated Compounds

by-line	do-it-yourself
by-product	self-confidence
cross-reference	vice-president

Single-Word Compounds

billboard	network
bondholder	nevertheless
bookkeeper	northeast
bylaws	notwithstanding
checkbook	outgoing
guesswork	overdue
handwriting	overhead
headline	payday
headquarters	payroll
henceforth	policyholder
hereafter	postcard
laborsaving	postmarked
letterhead	takeoff
meantime	trademark
middlemen	viewpoint

Two-Word Compounds

account book	income tax
bank note	parcel post
card index	price list
cash account	trade union
civil service	vice versa

Plural Forms of Nouns

Some nouns exist in only the plural form (*annals, news, thanks*), and other nouns are the same in both the singular and the plural forms (*deer, corps, chassis*). Still other nouns are irregular in form (*man, men; child, children; foot, feet*). Generally speaking, however, the plural of a noun is formed by adding *s* to the singular form.

The following rules are helpful in the formation of plural nouns.

1. Form the plurals of nouns ending with *y* preceded by a consonant by dropping the *y* and adding *ies*. When the *y* is preceded by a vowel, add *s* only.

lady, ladies	alley, alleys
salary, salaries	tally, tallies
story, stories	turkey, turkeys

2. Form the plural of a hyphenated compound noun by changing the principal word of the compound from singular to plural. The principal word of a compound is not always the last word.

   sisters-in-law, cross-purposes, passers-by

3. Form the plural of a single-word compound by adding *s* to the end of the word.

   cupfuls, viewpoints, headquarters

4. The plurals of some words of foreign origin are formed in accordance with the rules of the language from which they are derived.

axis, axes	datum, data
alumnus, alumni	alumna, alumnae

5. A few words of foreign origin have both foreign and English plural forms. In some cases, one form is preferred over the other (*strata* instead of *stratums*); while in other cases both forms are considered equally acceptable (*indexes* and *indices, memorandums* and *memoranda*). Consult a dictionary for the preferred usage of plural words of foreign origin.

6. Two persons bearing the same name and title may be referred to in the following manner: *The Messrs. Haviland, The Misses McKenzie, The Doctors Butler,* or *The Mr. Havilands, The Miss McKenzies, The Doctor Butlers.* In formal and business language, the plural form of the title is preferred.

7. The plural of a letter, a noun-coinage, or of a word as a word is formed by the addition of an apostrophe and *s*.

p's and *q*'s	Her *I-don't-care*'s were . . .
the *and*'s	too many *that*'s

8. The plurals of proper nouns that have more than one syllable and end with an "s" or "z" sound, are formed by adding just an apostrophe.

> The Curtises' home . . .
> The Mullins' dog . . .

9. The plurals of nouns ending in *o* vary individually; some take *s* and others *es*.

> motto, mottoes   piano, pianos
> potato, potatoes   folio, folios

Word Division

Frequently a word must be divided at the end of a line in order to keep the right margin even. Words should be divided only between syllables. In case of doubt, consult a dictionary. The following rules apply to typewritten copy.

1. When a final consonant preceded by a single vowel is doubled before addition of a suffix, divide the word between the two consonants (prefer-*r*ing, program-*m*ing).

2. A single-letter syllable at the beginning or the end of a word should not be separated from the remainder of the word (*above* not *a-bove*).

3. A two-letter syllable at the end of a word should not be separated from the rest of the word (*calmly* not *calm-ly*).

4. A syllable that does not contain a vowel should not be separated from the rest of the word (*coundn't* not *could-n't*).

5. Hyphenated words should be divided only at the hyphens (*follow-up* not *fol-low-up*).

6. A four-letter word should not be divided; it is seldom permissible to divide five- or six-letter words (*into* not *in-to*), (*camel* not *cam-el*), (*never* not *nev-er*).

7. When a word containing three or more syllables is to be divided at a one-letter syllable, the one-letter syllable should be written on the first line rather than on the second line (*maga-zine* not *mag-azine*).

8. When a word is to be divided at a point where two vowels that are pronounced separately come together, these vowels should be divided into separate syllables (*continu-ation* not *continua-tion*).

9. Compound words are preferably divided between the elements of the compound (*turn-over* not *turno-ver*).

10. Proper names should not be divided; and titles, initials, or degrees should not be separated from names (*President* not *Pres-ident*).

11. Avoid dividing words at the end of more than two successive lines, at the end of a page, or at the end of the last complete line of a paragraph.

12. Avoid awkward or misleading divisions that may cause difficulty in reading (*carry-ing* not *car-rying*).

13. When the single-letter syllable *a, i,* or *u* is followed by *ble, bly, cle,* or *cal,* do not separate the single-letter syllable and the suffix (*agree-able* not *agreea-ble*).

14. Avoid the division of figures and abbreviations, the parts of an address or date. If it is necessary to separate an address, keep together the number and street name, the city and ZIP Code.

2143 Market Street	*not*	2143 Market Street

In separating a date, leave the day with the month.

March 3, 19--	*not*	March 3, 19--

Spelling

Learning to spell correctly requires becoming so familiar with words that you use again and again that you are able to spell them without giving special thought to them. It also means that you should continue to question how you have spelled a word until you are *absolutely* sure of its accuracy. A dictionary will be an important aid in determining whether what you guessed as the right spelling is indeed right. If you find that certain words cause you difficulty frequently, you should make a list of them and take some time to study them so that in the future you will have no uncertainty about them.

Below are some spelling rules that will guide you in determining the correct spelling of many words.

1. Use the vowel combination *ie* rather than *ei* whenever it is pronounced like *ee* and occurs after any letters except *c*.

belief	grievance
chief	lien
expedient	relieve
field	reprieve
frieze	siege

Use *ei* after *c*.

ceiling	perceive
conceive	receipt
deceive	receive

Exceptions:

either	seize
neither	leisure

2. A final *e* is usually dropped before a suffix beginning with a vowel, unless doing so would change the pronounciation or meaning of the word.

bride, bridal	hope, hoping
force, forcible	manage, managing
college, collegiate	subdue, subduing

Exceptions:

dye, dyeing
change, changeable
courage, courageous

3. The final *e* is usually retained before a suffix beginning with a consonant.

lone, lonely	hate, hateful
move, movement	pale, paleness

Exceptions:

judge, judgment	argue, argument

4. Before the suffix *ing, ie* is changed to *y*.

die, dying	lie, lying

5. A final double consonant is retained before a suffix.

will, willful	odd, oddly
ebb, ebbing	

6. Usually the final consonant is doubled in words of one syllable, or words ending in a single consonant preceded by a single vowel with the accent on the last syllable, before a suffix beginning with a vowel.

occur, occurred	refer, referring
begin, beginning	plan, planned

Exceptions:

fix, fixed	refer, reference

7. The final *y* preceded by a consonant is usually changed to *i* before a suffix not beginning with *i*.

worry, worried   happy, happiness

Exceptions:

shy, shyness   beauty, beauteous

8. The final *y* preceded by a vowel is usually retained before any suffix or the letter *s*.

annoy, annoyance   buy, buyer
delay, delayed   pay, payable
journey, journeys   attorney, attorneys

9. The final *l* is always single in words ending in *ful*.

careful   hopeful
doubtful   regretful

10. Only one word ends in *sede* — *supersede*; only three words end in *ceed* — *exceed, proceed, succeed*; all other words having this sound end in *cede* — *concede, intercede, precede, secede*.

11. When *i* and *e* come together in the same syllable, generally *i* is used before *e*.

Commonly Used Business Words That Are Often Misspelled

accept	definite	immediately	quantity
accommodate	description	its	questionnaire
across	develop		
affect	difference	judgment	really
all right	disappoint	lose	receive
already			recommend
among	eligible	necessary	reference
analysis	embarrass	noticeable	referred
appearance	endeavor		
arrangement	equipped	occasion	
	especially	occurred	separate
	except	opportunity	similar
beginning	existence	original	stationery
benefited	experience		
business	explanation	paid	their
		pamphlet	too
		personnel	
canceled (cancelled)	foreign	possession	undoubtedly
coming	fourth	practically	using
committee		preferred	
confident	government	principal	volume
conscientious	grammar	privilege	
convenience		probably	whether
criticism	height	proceed	writing

694   Appendix C

Appendix D
Abbreviations

Abbreviations are shortened forms of words or phrases that provide a means of conserving space. With the extensive use of computers and related equipment, the need for using abbreviations has grown. The use of abbreviations is guided by custom and equipment restrictions. A general rule that continues to be followed is that abbreviations are used sparingly in correspondence. Abbreviations are common, however, in the typing of forms, such as invoices and statements, where space is limited.

Abbreviations of Proper Names

For proper names these are generally accepted rules.

1. A person's family name should never be abbreviated. Given names may be represented by initials, but it is desirable for others to conform to a person's own style or signature. For example, if a person signs his name *Henry F. Grimm*, it is good form for others to write his name that way, rather than *H. R. Grimm*. As a general rule, given names such as *Charles* or *William* should not be abbreviated to *Chas.* or *Wm.*, unless the person uses the abbreviation so consistently that it is obviously the spelling preferred.

2. Names of cities, with the exception of those containing the word *Saint* (*St.*), should not be abbreviated.

3. Names of states and territories should be spelled out, except in lists, tabular matter, footnotes, bibliographies, and indexes. In such cases the standard abbreviations listed below should be used. The United States Postal Service has authorized the two-letter all-capital abbreviations listed on the next page for use *only* with ZIP CODES.

Abbreviations in the Body of a Letter

The shortening of words in the body of a letter can convey a lack of care and time in presenting an attractive, thoughtful message. One should not write: The advt. can be supplied for your dept. @ 50¢ per p.

State or Territory	Standard Abbreviation	ZIP Code Abbreviation	State or Territory	Standard Abbreviation	ZIP Code Abbreviation
Alabama	Ala.	AL	Missouri	Mo.	MO
Alaska	*	AK	Montana	Mont.	MT
Arizona	Ariz.	AZ	Nebraska	Nebr.	NE
Arkansas	Ark.	AR	Nevada	Nev.	NV
California	Calif.	CA	New Hampshire	N.H.	NH
Canal Zone	C.Z.	CZ	New Jersey	N.J.	NJ
Colorado	Colo.	CO	New Mexico	N.Mex.	NM
Connecticut	Conn.	CT	New York	N.Y.	NY
Delaware	Del.	DE	North Carolina	N.C.	NC
District of Columbia	D.C.	DC	North Dakota	N.Dak.	ND
Florida	Fla.	FL	Ohio	*	OH
Georgia	Ga.	GA	Oklahoma	Okla.	OK
Guam	*	GU	Oregon	Oreg.	OR
Hawaii	*	HI	Pennsylvania	Pa.	PA
Idaho	*	ID	Puerto Rico	P.R.	PR
Illinois	Ill.	IL	Rhode Island	R.I.	RI
Indiana	Ind.	IN	South Carolina	S.C.	SC
Iowa	*	IA	South Dakota	S.Dak.	SD
Kansas	Kans.	KS	Tennessee	Tenn.	TN
Kentucky	Ky.	KY	Texas	Tex.	TX
Louisiana	La.	LA	Utah	*	UT
Maine	*	ME	Vermont	Vt.	VT
Maryland	Md.	MD	Virginia	Va.	VA
Massachusetts	Mass.	MA	Virgin Islands	V.I.	VI
Michigan	Mich.	MI	Washington	Wash.	WA
Minnesota	Minn.	MN	West Virginia	W.Va.	WV
Mississippi	Miss.	MS	Wisconsin	Wis.	WI
			Wyoming	Wyo.	WY

*No standard abbreviation

It would be better to write: The advertisement can be supplied for your department at the rate of 50 cents per page.

Abbreviations may be used in the body of a letter when they have become commonly recognized symbols, such as SEC, FTC, CIO, and YMCA. If, however, a letter is written to someone who may not understand an abbreviation, it is better to spell it out in the first sentence of its use so that the reader understands the term when it appears thereafter in abbreviated form. For example, the complete term *Securities and Exchange Commission* may be used first; then, in subsequent references, the abbreviation SEC may be used if the document is not a formal one.

Frequently used abbreviations are listed in the dictionary. Each field of work has developed specialized abbreviations, and office workers learn these when they begin work in a new office.

Periods in Abbreviations

Periods are dropped from an abbreviation when it is commonly recognized and does not require the periods for clarity. NBC, SEC, and FTC, for example, are written without periods and without spaces between the letters. The omission of a period in some abbreviations, however, might be confusing. For example, without the periods, *in.* for *inch* might be mistaken for the preposition; *a.m.* for *morning* might be confused with the verb form. If, in order to avoid confusion, periods are used with an abbreviation, such as *a.m.*, they should be used in *p.m.* in order to maintain a consistent style.

Abbreviations with Numbers

The abbreviations *st, d,* and *th* should not follow a date when the date comes after the month.

> He leaves for London on August 21.

The abbreviations *st, d,* and *th* should follow the date when the date is given before the month. Do not use a period after the abbreviation *st, d,* and *th*.

> He was planning to leave on the 21st of August.
> Mr. Smith went to Los Angeles on the 3d of July.

In enumerations, it is better to write *first, second, third* rather than *1st, 2d, 3d*.

Diagonal Lines in Abbreviations

The use of the diagonal signifies the omission of such words as *per, of, to, upon*. In abbreviated forms that include a diagonal the period is not usually used, as in *B/L*. The period is sometimes retained, however, in three- or four-word combinations, as *lb./sq. ft.*

Plurals of Abbreviations

The plural form of most abbreviations is made by adding *s* to the singular form, but many abbreviations have only one form for both singular and plural. Several single-letter abbreviations are made plural by doubling the letter.

> chgs., lbs.
> ft., in., oz., deg., cwt.
> pp. (pages), ll. (lines)

Plurals of capitalized abbreviations may be formed simply by adding a small *s*. Apostrophe and *s* may be added to form the plurals of abbreviations composed of letters (capital and small), signs, and symbols. There is no single rule, however, that completely governs all cases that may arise.

> YMCAs, a.m.s, IOU's, P's, Q's, 6's, FOB's, OK's, #s

Coined Verbs

Often an abbreviation is used as a verb in informal correspondence. To make the necessary change, an apostrophe may be added with *d, s,* or *ing* according to the use of the abbreviation.

> OK'd

Possessives of Abbreviations

Generally the singular possessive is formed by adding the apostrophe and *s,* as in *Jr.'s, RR's, Sr.'s, SOS's.*

The plural possessive is formed by adding an apostrophe to abbreviations whose plural forms end in *s,* as in *Jrs.', Drs.'.*

Appendix E

Titles, Capitalization, and Numbers

Titles

The use of titles is governed by customs that are accepted by the people of a given society. Every office worker should learn the correct titles of the persons with whom she or he associates. There is one principle for the use of titles in oral communication that should always be remembered: *Never use a title alone.* For example, a person who holds a Ph.D. should never be addressed as just *Doctor*. The proper address is *Doctor Jones*. Current practice governing the use of titles in writing follows.

Birthright Titles. The title of *Mr., Ms., Mrs.,* or *Miss* is customary for adults who have no other title.

Mr. is used before the name of a man who has no other title. *Messrs.,* the abbreviation of *Messieurs* (French for gentlemen), is the plural of *Mr.*

Ms. is used before the name of a woman when her marital status is unknown or when the person has shown a preference for *Ms.* as a term of address.

Mrs. is a title used by many married women and widows. A married woman may prefer to be addressed by her husband's name, as in *Mrs. John Brown,* or by her legal name, as in *Mrs. Helen Brown.* A widow, likewise, may use her deceased husband's name or her own name, whichever she prefers. When *Mrs.* is applied to two or more married women, the title *Mesdames,* or its abbreviation, *Mmes.,* is used, as in *Mmes. Clark, Wright* and *Grant.*

Miss is frequently used before the name of an unmarried woman or girl. *Misses* is the plural of *Miss,* as in the *Misses Alice Henderson* and *Dorothy Jones.*

Doctor. *Dr.* is the title of a person who holds any of the various doctors' degrees. It is usually abbreviated. When two doctors are being addressed, the word *Doctors* or the abbreviation *Drs.* may be used.

Reverend. This title is properly carried by a minister, priest, or rector. The abbreviation *Rev.* is commonly used, although it is considered better usage to write the word in full. More than one Reverend may be addressed as *Reverend Messrs.* or the repetition of the word *Reverend* before each name.

Abbreviated Titles Following Personal Names. *Senior* and *Junior*, terms used to distinguish a father and son of exactly the same name, are written after the name as the abbreviations *Sr.* and *Jr.* The abbreviation is capitalized, followed by a period, and is usually separated from the name by a comma. *Second* and *Third*, which distinguish members of the same family or close relatives whose names are identical, are indicated by the abbreviations *2d* and *3d*, or by the Roman numerals, *II* and *III*. The former style is now more common. Note that these abbreviations are not followed by a period, but they may be separated from the name by a comma.

The abbreviation *Esq.* is used after a gentleman's name in England but is rarely seen in this country. When it is used, the title *Mr.* is omitted.

Double Titles. A person's name may be written with two titles, one before the name and one after, only if the two titles distinguish the person in different ways. Different abbreviations which stand for the same title should not be used together. For example, it is correct to say Rev. H. C. Samuel, Ph.D., but not Dr. H.C. Samuel, Ph.D.

Mr., Ms., Mrs., Miss, and Dr. are dropped whenever another title is used. Thus, you would write Megan Mountain, M.A., never Ms. Megan Mountain, M.A.

Titles in Addresses and Salutations. Except for *Mr., Ms., Mrs.* and *Dr.*, all titles used in the address and salutations of letters are better written in full. Abbreviations, however, are not uncommon. Whenever you are in doubt, type the title in full. No one will be offended by seeing his or her title in full.

The correct titles and salutations to be used for federal and state officials, members of religious organizations, school officials, and individuals are given in Appendix F.

Capitalization

A good dictionary is the best source for determining proper capitalization. A person who must refer to the dictionary for the most elementary information of this type, however, wastes much time. Therefore, a working knowledge of the principles of capitalization adds to the office worker's efficiency and effectiveness.

One of the purposes of capitalization is to designate the names or titles of specific things, positions, or persons. Overuse of capitalization, however, tends to detract from the effectiveness of the writing.

The most common rules of capitalization are:

1. Every sentence begins with a capital letter.
2. The pronoun *I* and the interjection *O* are always capitalized.

3. The salutation and the first word of the complimentary close of a letter begin with capitals.
4. The days of the week, holidays, and the months of the year are capitalized.
5. All important words in the titles of the main agencies of a government begin with capital letters.
6. Direct quotations begin with a capital letter.

Business Titles and Positions. Titles are capitalized when they immediately precede or follow individual names and are directly related to them, or when they refer to specific persons.

> President W. L. Matthews will speak.
> Mr. R. Hubert McGraw, Jr., Vice-President, Investors Corporation
> Mrs. Samantha Jones is Executive Secretary and Treasurer of Hammet Co.

Business titles are not capitalized when they do not refer to specific persons.

> Three men have been president of this company.
> A treasurer will be elected at the meeting tomorrow.

Geographic Names. Names of countries, cities, rivers, bays, mountains, islands, commonly recognized names given to regions of countries, and sections of cities are capitalized.

> Ohio River, Pacific Ocean, Union County, Harlem, the Great Plains, the Mississippi Valley

A geographic term such as *river, ocean, county, city*, and *street* that is not a part of the name but is used before the name, or a geographic term that is used in the plural, should not be capitalized.

> the river Danube
> county of Hamilton
> the city of San Diego
> the Atlantic and Pacific Oceans
> at the corner of Grant and Lee streets

Points of the compass designating specific geographic sections of the country are capitalized.

> the South, the Midwest, and the Northwest

Points of the compass used to indicate direction are not capitalized.

> South Dakota is south of North Dakota.
> The wind is coming from the west.

A noun that refers to the inhabitants of a particular part of the country is capitalized.

> Westerners, a Southerner, a New Englander

Proper names denoting political divisions are always capitalized.

British Empire, Ward 13, Platt Township, the Papal States

Words before Figures. With the exception of *page, line,* and *verse,* words used in connection with figures in typewritten references are usually capitalized. It is important that one rule be followed consistently. If the word *figure* is capitalized when followed by a number in one place, it should be capitalized in all other places in the text.

Chapter XV	line 3
Figure 8	page iii

Individual Names. All units in the full name of an individual are capitalized, except some surname prefixes such as *von, du, van,* and *je,* which are capitalized or left lower case according to the practice of the individual. When a part of a surname begins a sentence or when a surname is not preceded by a given name within a sentence, however, it is always capitalized.

Vincent van Gogh *but* Van Gogh
George Louis du Maurier *but* Du Maurier

Hyphenated Words. In general, there are three rules that govern the capitalization of the parts of a hyphenated word.

1. If both parts of a hyphenated word would ordinarily be capitalized when written alone, then both parts should be capitalized in the hyphenated word.

   Senate-House debate
   Spanish-American War

2. In a heading or title, it is permissible to capitalize the parts of a compound word to conform to a general style.

   Forty-Second Street   Mid-January Sale

3. In straight text material, the way in which a word is used determines the part of the compound that should be capitalized.

Thirty-first Street	anti-Nazi
mid-January	pro-British
Treasurer-elect	French-speaking
ex-President	pre-Pueblo

Headings and Titles of Articles and Reports. Only the first word and important words in headings or titles — nouns, pronouns, verbs, adverbs, and adjectives — are capitalized. Short, unimportant words are not capitalized. Examples of such words are the conjunctions *and, but,* and *or;* the articles *a, an,* and *the;* and the prepositions *of, in, to,* and *but.*

If the word needs to be stressed, however, it may be capitalized. Frequently long prepositions such as *between, after, before*, and *among* are capitalized.

Numbers

Numbers can be written as figures or as words. Although figures are used almost exclusively in business forms, both figures and words are used in letters and other types of transcripts that are written in sentence and paragraph form. If there are two or more ways in which an amount can be expressed, it is usually written in the way that requires the fewest words. A number such as 1,300 is written as *thirteen hundred* rather than *one thousand three hundred*. The following rules specify proper practice in writing numbers.

Numbers at the Beginning of a Sentence. A number that begins a sentence should be spelled out, even though other numbers are expressed in figures in the same sentence. It is wise, therefore, to avoid beginning a sentence with a large number that is cumbersome in words.

Amounts of Money. Amounts of money, except in legal documents, should be written in figures. Amounts less than one dollar are written in figures with the word *cents* following. In writing even sums of money, the decimal and ciphers are omitted.

> We enclose our check for $21.75.
> He paid 22 cents for the paper.
> He will pay $125 for the painting.

Cardinal Numbers. Numbers from one to ten are spelled out unless such numbers are used with others above ten. In business, figures are commonly used for all numbers except those which begin a sentence.

> We have 50 employees
> There will be eight in the group
> We have 8 secretaries in our group of 295 employees.

Dates. Except in legal or formal writing, the day of the month and the year are usually written in figures. When a date appears in the body of a letter, the year is customarily omitted if it is the same as that which appears in the date line. It is necessary to use *st, d,* or *th* in dates only when the day is written before or is separated from the month.

> the 3d of June
> in July, either the 3d or 4th

Streets. It is good form to use words for street numbers that are ten or less; figures should be used for street numbers above ten. When the name of the street is a number that is written in figures, it is separated from the number of the building by a dash. If the street name is preceded by one of the words *South, North, East,* or *West,* that word should not be abbreviated.

Tenth Street
72 — 125 Street   72 Fifth Avenue
19 West 115 Street   173rd Street

Time of Day. The abbreviations *p.m.* and *a.m.* should be written in small letters and should be used only with figures. The hour is spelled in full when *o'clock* is used. Do not use *p.m.* or *a.m.* to designate noon or midnight.

School starts at 8:30 a.m.
He will leave the office at four o'clock.
12 midnight, 12 noon

Measurements. Practically all measurements are written in figures.

Size 7½ AA Shoe   12-gal. bottle

Fractions and Decimals. Common fractions appearing alone are spelled out in ordinary reading matter. Mixed numbers are written as figures. Decimals are always expressed in figures.

Miscellaneous Usage. Sessions of Congress and the identifying numbers of various military bodies, political divisions, and dynasties are always written in words.

the Thirty-sixth Congress   Sixteenth Infantry
Thirteenth Ward

The result of a ballot is written in figures.

The count was 34 in favor of the motion, 36 against it.

Page, chapter, section, and footnote numbers are always written in figures.

pp. 45–67   Section 7
[2]Hawley, J.   Chapter 9

When two numbers immediately follow each other, it is better that the smaller one be spelled out and the larger one be expressed in figures.

125 two-cent stamps   Five 100-dollar bills

Unrelated groups of figures that come together should be separated by commas. Hundreds should be divided from thousands by a comma except in dates, policy numbers, street numbers, and telephone numbers.

In 1970, 417,296 gallons were sold.
The policy number is 73288.

Appendix F

Special Forms of Address, Salutations, and Complimentary Closings

Appendix F lists the correct forms of address with appropriate salutations and complimentary closings for the following special groups:

United States Government officials
Diplomatic representatives
State and local government officials
Members of religious organizations
School officials
Individuals

The correct forms of address for envelopes and letters are shown at the left. Open punctuation is used in addresses. The appropriate salutations and complimentary closings are given in the order of decreasing formality.

United States Government Officials

Address	Salutation	Complimentary Closing
The President of the United States		
The President The White House Washington, DC 20500	Sir, Madam Mr. President Madam President Dear Mr. President Dear Madam President	Respectfully yours Very truly yours
The Vice-President of the United States		
The Vice-President United States Senate Washington, DC 20510	Sir, Madam Dear Sir, Dear Madam Mr. Vice-president Madam Vice-president Dear Mr. Vice-president Dear Madam Vice-president	Respectfully yours Very truly yours Sincerely yours
The Chief Justice of the United States		
The Chief Justice The Supreme Court of the United States Washington, DC 20543	Sir, Madam Mr. Chief Justice Madam Chief Justice Dear Mr. Chief Justice Dear Madam Chief Justice	Respectfully yours Very truly yours Sincerely yours

Associate Justice of the Supreme Court

Mr. Justice (Name)
Ms., Mrs., Miss Justice (Name)
The Supreme Court of the
   United States
Washington, DC 20543

Sir, Madam
Mr. Justice, Madam Justice
Dear Mr. Justice
Dear Madam Justice

Very truly yours
Sincerely yours

The Speaker of the House

The Honorable (Name)
Speaker of the House of
   Representatives
Washington, DC 20515

Sir, Madam
Dear Sir, Dear Madam
Dear Mr. Speaker
Dear Madam Speaker

Very truly yours
Sincerely yours

Member of the Cabinet

The Honorable (Name)
Secretary of (Office)
Washington, DC 20515

Sir, Madam
Dear Sir, Dear Madam
Dear Mr. Secretary
Dear Madam Secretary

Very truly yours
Sincerely yours

Senator

The Honorable (Name)
The United States Senate
Washington, DC 20520

Sir, Madam
Dear Sir, Dear Madam
Dear Senator
Dear Senator (Name)

Very truly yours
Sincerely yours

Representative

The Honorable (Name)
The House of Representatives
Washington, DC 20515

Sir, Madam
Dear Sir, Dear Madam
Dear Representative (Name)
Dear Congressman (Name)
Dear Congresswoman (Name)

Very truly yours
Sincerely yours

Head of a Government Bureau

The Honorable (Name), Chairperson
Commission of Fine Arts
Interior Building
18th and C Streets, N.W.
Washington, DC 20240

Sir, Madam
Dear Sir, Dear Madam
Dear Commissioner
Dear Mr. (name)
Dear Ms., Mrs., Miss (Name)

Very truly yours
Sincerely yours

Diplomatic Representatives

American Ambassador

The Honorable (Name)
American Ambassador
(Foreign City, Country)

Sir, Madam
Dear Mr. Ambassador
Dear Madam Ambassador
Dear Ambassador (Name)

Very truly yours
Sincerely yours

American Minister

The Honorable (Name)
American Minister
London, England

Sir, Madam
Dear Mr. Minister
Dear Madam Minister
Dear Mr. (Name)
Dear Ms., Mrs., Miss (Name)

Very truly yours
Sincerely yours

American Consul General, Chargé d'Affaires, Consul or Vice Consul

(Name), Esq. (male only)
Ms., Mrs., Miss (Name)
United States Embassy
Bonn, West Germany

Sir, Madam
Dear Mr. (Name)
Dear Ms., Mrs., Miss (Name)

Very truly yours
Sincerely yours

Secretary-General of the United Nations

His or Her Excellency (Name)
Secretary-General of the United
    Nations
New York, NY 10017

Your Excellency
Sir, Madam
Mr. Secretary-General
Madam Secretary-General

Very truly yours
Sincerely yours

United States Representative to the United Nations

His or Her Excellency (Name)
Ambassador Extraordinary and
    Plenipotentiary Permanent
    Representative to the United
    Nations
New York, NY 10017

Your Excellency
Sir, Madam
Dear Mr. Ambassador
Dear Madam Ambassador

Very truly yours
Sincerely yours

Ambassador to the United States

His or Her Excellency (Name)
Canadian Ambassador to the
    United States
1746 Massachusetts Avenue, N.W.
Washington, DC 20036

Your Excellency
Sir, Madam
Dear Mr. Ambassador
Dear Madam Ambassador

Very truly yours
Sincerely yours

State and Local Government Officials

His or Her Excellency, the
    Governor of New York
The Executive Chamber, Capitol
Albany, NY 12224

Governor
Sir, Madam
Dear Governor
Dear Governor (Name)

Respectfully yours
Very truly yours
Sincerely yours

Attorney General

The Honorable (Name)
Attorney General of Connecticut
State Capitol
Hartford, CT 06115

Sir, Madam
Dear Mr. Attorney General
Dear Madam Attorney General
Dear Mr. (Name)
Dear Ms., Mrs., Miss (Name)

Very truly yours
Sincerely yours

State Senator

The Honorable (Name)
State Capitol Building
Trenton, NJ 08625

Sir, Madam
Dear Sir, Dear Madam
Dear Senator (Name)

Very truly yours
Sincerely yours

State Representative

The Honorable (Name)
The State Assembly
Albany, NY 1224

Sir, Madam
Dear Sir, Dear Madam
Dear Representative (Name)
Dear Mr. (Name)
Dear Ms., Mrs., Miss (Name)

Very truly yours
Sincerely yours

Mayor

The Honorable (Name)
Mayor of the City of Chicago
City Hall
Chicago, IL 60602

Sir, Madam
Dear Sir, Dear Madam
Dear Mr. Mayor
Dear Madam Mayor
Dear Mayor (Name)

Very truly yours
Sincerely yours

School Officials

President of a University or College

(Name), President
Teachers College
Columbia University
525 West 120th Street
New York, NY 10027

Dear Sir, Dear Madam
Dear President (Name)
Dear Dr. (Name)

Very truly yours
Sincerely yours

Dean of a College

(Name), Dean
School of Education
New York University
Washington Square East
New York, NY 10003

Dear Sir, Dear Madam
Dear Dean (Name)
Dear Dr. (Name)

Very truly yours
Sincerely yours

Professor of a College or University

(Name)
Professor of Business Administration
Indiana University
Bloomington, IN 47401

Dear Sir, Dear Madam
Dear Professor (Name)
Dear Dr. (Name)

Very truly yours
Sincerely yours

Superintendent of Schools

Superintendent (Name)
Tupper Lake Central Schools
Tupper Lake, NY 12986

Dear Sir, Dear Madam
Dear Superintendent (Name)
Dear Mr. (Name)
Dear Ms., Mrs., Miss (Name)

Very truly yours
Sincerely yours

Principal of a School

(Name, Principal
Alexander Hamilton High School
Elizabeth, NJ 07202

Dear Sir, Dear Madam
Dear Mr. (Name)
Dear Ms., Mrs., Miss (Name)

Very truly yours
Sincerely yours

One (Man)

Mr. (Name)
65 South Water Street
Chicago, IL 60601

Dear Mr. (Name)

Sincerely yours

One (Woman)

Ms., Mrs., Miss (Name)
2606 Kanuga Road
Hendersonville, NC 28739

Dear Ms., Mrs., Miss (Name)

Sincerely yours

More than One (Women)

Ms. (Name) and Ms. (Name)
Mmes. (Name) and (Name)
Misses (Name) and (Name)

Ladies

Very truly yours

More than One (Men)

Mssrs. (Name) and (Name)

Gentlemen

Very truly yours

Physician

(Name), M.D. or Dr. (Name)
274 Main Street
Springfield, MA 01105

Dear Dr. (Name)

Very truly yours
Sincerely yours

Attorney

Mr. (Name)
Ms., Mrs., Miss (Name)
Attorney at Law
One Pondfield Road
Bronxville, NY 10708

Dear Mr. (Name)
Dear Ms., Mrs., Miss. (Name)

Very truly yours
Sincerely yours

Appendix G
Systems of Measurement

There are two commonly used methods of measurement. One, the *English*, or *imperial*, system, is used in the United States; the other is the *metric* system which is used in most parts of the world. In the English system the units used for measuring lengths are inches, feet, yards, and miles. The basic measuring unit for distance in the metric system is the meter. The metric system is a decimal system, which means that you can convert from one measuring unit to another merely by moving a decimal point. For example: 10 decimeters = 1 meter. By moving the decimal point one place to the left, you have converted decimeters into meters.

Lengths

English System	Metric System	Equivalencies
12 inches = 1 foot	10 millimeters = 1 centimeter	1 inch = 2.540 centimeters
3 feet = 1 yard	10 centimeters = 1 decimeter	1 foot = 30.48 centimeters
5,280 feet = 1 mile	10 decimeters = 1 meter	39.37 inches = 1 meter
	10 meters = 1 decameter	1 mile = 1.609 kilometers
	10 decameters = 1 hectometer	
	10 hectometers = 1 kilometer	

Weights

English System	Metric System	Equivalencies
16 ounces = 1 pound	10 milligrams = 1 centigram	1 ounce = 28.35 grams
100 pounds = 1 hundredweight	10 centigrams = 1 decigram	1 pound = 453.6 grams
2,000 pounds = 1 ton	10 decigrams = 1 gram	1 ton = 907.2 kilograms
	10 grams = 1 decagram	
	10 decagrams = 1 hectogram	
	10 hectrograms = 1 kilogram	

English System	Metric System	Equivalencies
Dry Measure:	**Dry and Liquid Measure:**	Dry Measure:
2 pints = 1 quart	10 milliliters = centiliter	1 pint = 0.550 liters
8 quarts = 1 peck	10 centiliters = 1 deciliter	1 quart = 1.101 liters
4 pecks = 1 bushel	10 deciliters = 1 liter	1 peck = 8.809 liters
	10 liters = 1 decaliter	1 bushel = 35.238 liters
Liquid Measure:	10 decaliters = 1 hectoliter	Liquid Measure:
2 pints = 1 quart	10 hectoliters = 1 kiloliter	1 pint = 0.473 liters
4 quarts = 1 gallon		1 quart = 0.946 liters
		1 gallon = 3.785 liters

Metric Systems of Measurement

Appendix H

Reference Books

Every office worker should have at least three reference books available for immediate use: a desk-size dictionary, a secretarial handbook, and a telephone directory.

Dictionaries

If you are to carry out your office assignments efficiently and accurately, you should have a modern desk-size dictionary at your desk. You will find it valuable for verifying the spelling, syllabication, and proper usage of words as you transcribe your employer's dictation. It contains not only the pronunciation and derivation of words but also the meaning of foreign expressions and standard abbreviations, the names of places and notable people, and other essential information.

If a desk-size dictionary is not readily available, you should invest in a paperback pocket-size one. Pocket dictionaries generally contain definitions; guides to correct spelling and pronunciation; lists of synonyms and antonyms; commonly used abbreviations, foreign words and phrases; and population figures for the United States and Canada.

Office Reference Books

The secretary's handbook is a compact, thoroughly indexed reference book. It includes a wide range of secretarial procedures. It is an authoritative source of information on such topics as proper grammatical construction, plural and possessive forms, pronunciation and punctuation, and the correct writing of numbers in letters and reports. It can be a great help in deciding, for example, where to place the *subject line* in a business letter, whether to place the apostrophe before or after the letter *s* in *women's salaries*, and when to capitalize directions in geographic areas such as on the *East Coast* or in *western Montana*.

Some popular office reference books are:

Doris, Lillian, and Bessie May Miller. *Complete Secretary's Handbook*, 3d ed. Englewood Cliffs, N.J.: Prentice-Hall, Inc., 1970.

House, Clifford R., and Apollonia M. Koebele. *Reference Manual for Office Personnel*, 5th ed. Cincinnati: South-Western Publishing Co., 1970.

Hutchinson, Lois Irene. *Standard Handbook for Secretaries*, 8th ed. New York City: McGraw-Hill, Inc., 1969.

Telephone Directories

The most frequently consulted reference book in any office is the telephone directory. It is used not only to find the telephone numbers of listed subscribers but also to verify the spelling of their names and the correctness of their addresses. The Yellow Pages, or classified section of a telephone directory, may also serve as a buyer's guide because the names, addresses, and telephone numbers of business subscribers are listed under their product or service.

A small booklet supplied by the telephone company, designed for use as a personal telephone directory, can save considerable telephoning time. On alphabetically arranged pages it provides spaces for writing the names, addresses, area codes, and telephone numbers of frequently called local and out-of-town telephones.

Writing References

The content and format of all types of business communications can be improved if appropriate reference books are consulted.

Business Communications. A recommended reference book for the writing of business letters and other communications of a business nature is:

Wolf, Morris P., and Robert R. Aurner. *Effective Communication in Business*, 6th ed. Cincinnati: South-Western Publishing Co., 1974.

Business Reports. Manuals and style books are available to serve as references on how to present papers and reports. Two widely used manuals and a style book are listed below.

A Manual of Style. The University of Chicago. 12th ed., rev. Chicago: University of Chicago Press, 1969.

United States Government Printing Office Style Manual, rev. ed. Washington: U.S. Government Printing Office, 1973.

Perrin, Porter G. *Writer's Guide and Index to English*, 5th ed., Glenview, Illinois: Scott, Foresman and Company, 1972.

Business Speeches. A wide variety of reference books may be consulted to provide the prospective speaker or master of ceremonies at a business function with words, phrases, ideas, and quotations that will enhance and enliven a presentation. Some of these follow.

Bartlett, John. *Familiar Quotations*, 14th ed. Secaucus, N.J.: Citadel Press, 1971.

Fernald, James C. *Funk & Wagnalls Standard Handbook of Synonyms, Antonyms, and Prepositions*, rev. ed. New York City: Wilfred Funk, Inc., 1947.

Stevenson, Burton E. *Home Book of Quotations*, rev. ed. New York City: Dodd, Mead & Company, 1967.

Roget's Thesaurus of English Words and Phrases. New York City: World Pub., 1970.

Webster's New Dictionary of Synonyms. Springfield, Mass.: G & C. Merriam Company, 1973.

Specific References

Reference books in all fields from many different sources, ranging from the *American Library Association Catalog* to the *Zweng Aviation Dictionary*, are listed and annotated in a single volume, the *Guide to Reference Books*. To determine what, if any, reference books are available on a specific subject, consult this guide:

Winchell, Constance M. *Guide to Reference Books*, 8th ed. Chicago: American Library Association, 1967.

Specific information on business and related subjects may be obtained from many reference books. The information includes statistics on all major industries, directories of all large corporations, biographies of notable people, and factual information on a wide variety of business topics. The examples that follow are arranged alphabetically by subjects.

Accounting The standard handbook in which leading authorities cover the major divisions of accounting is:

Wixon, Rufus, *et. al. Accountants' Handbook*, 5th ed. New York City: The Ronald Press Company, 1970.

Almanacs. Published annually, there are four widely used and comprehensive American almanacs of miscellaneous information.

Information Please Almanac. New York City: Simon & Schuster, Inc.

New York Times Encyclopedic Almanac. New York City: Book and Educational Division, The New York Times Company.

Reader's Digest Almanac and Yearbook. Pleasantville, New York: The Reader's Digest Association, Inc.

World Almanac and Book of Facts. New York City: Doubleday & Company, Inc.

Banks. The Bankers Blue Book, one of the leading bank directories published semiannually with monthly supplements, is:

Rand-McNally Bankers Directory. Chicago: Rand-McNally & Company.

Biographical Information. Revised and reissued every two years, the best known and generally the most useful biographical dictionary, with full biographical sketches of approximately 73,000 notable living American men and women, is:

Who's Who in America. Chicago: Marquis-Who's Who, Inc.

Books. A complete list of all available books, new and old, including hardcovers, paperbacks, trade books, textbooks, and juvenile books is published annually with full ordering information in the following volumes:

Books in Print. Authors, Vol. I, New York City: R. R. Bowker Company.
Books in Print. Titles and Publishers, Vol. II, New York City: R. R. Bowker Company.
Subject Guide to Books in Print. A to J, Vol. I, New York City: R. R. Bowker Company.
Subject Guide to Books in Print. K to Z, Vol. II, New York City: R. R. Bowker Company.

A world list of books in the English language is published annually with monthly supplements in the following:

Cumulative Book Index. New York City: The H. W. Wilson Company.

Business Libraries. A reference book that should be consulted to be sure that the business library is used efficiently and that no available source of business information has been overlooked is:

Johnson, H. Webster. *How to Use the Business Library*, 4th ed. Cincinnati: South-Western Publishing Co., 1972.

City Directories. City directories are compiled, published, and sold commercially for most of the cities of the United States and Canada. Each directory contains the names, the addresses, and the occupations of all individuals residing in a community. It usually contains a street directory and a map of the city.

City Officials. A directory of city officials is usually published annually for each large city. The *City of New York Official Directory*, for example, lists all branches of the city government, the courts, and the state and federal government agencies with offices in New York City. It contains an index of the names of all executives listed in the directory.

> *The City of New York Official Directory.* Room 2213 Municipal Building, New York, NY 10007.

Colleges. A widely used college guide gives the entrance requirements, accreditation, and other factual information about more than 2,800 American colleges and universities. The guide also contains related information about junior colleges, community colleges, and technical institutes.

> Lovejoy, Clarence I. *Lovejoy's College Guide*, 12th ed. New York: Simon and Schuster, Inc., 1974.

A comparative guide to American colleges analyzes every accredited four-year college in the United States. It provides a basis for college selection with data on admission requirements, academic opportunities offered by the institution, special programs, faculty qualifications, and enrollment figures.

> Cass, James, and Max Birnbaum. *Comparative Guide to American Colleges*, 7th ed. New York City: Harper and Row, Publishers, 1975.

Junior Colleges. Information about the recognized, nonprofit junior colleges in the United States, the Canal Zone, and Puerto Rico is published by the American Council on Education. Information for each college includes: admission and graduate requirements, enrollment, curricula offered, calendar, staff, student aid, graduates, foreign students, library, publications, finances, buildings and grounds, history, control, and administrative officers.

> Gleazer, Edmund J. Jr. (ed.). *American Junior Colleges*, 8th ed. Washington: American Council on Education, 1971.

Congress. A directory containing the names, addresses, and brief biographies of all congressmen and chief executives of the federal government is issued annually. In it are also listed the members of all congressional committees, the executives of all departments and agencies of the federal government, and all diplomatic representatives.

> *Congressional Directory.* Superintendent of Documents, U.S. Government Printing Office. Washington, DC 20402.

Corporations. A complete national directory of executive personnel in approximately 28,000 companies engaged in all branches of business and industry is published in *Poor's Register of Corporations, Directors, and Executives.* Each company listing includes the names and addresses of all officers, directors, and other executive personnel; the number of employees and the approximate annual sales; and all products and services of the company in order of their importance.

The register is sold commercially and is not available in most public and high school libraries.

> *Standard and Poor's Register of Corporations, Directors, and Executives.* Standard & Poor's Corporation. New York, NY 10014.

Credit Ratings. Credit ratings and credit reports are distributed for retail, wholesale, and manufacturing companies. While the reports are not available to the general public, they may be obtained by annual subscription.

> *Dun & Bradstreet Ratings and Reports.* Dun & Bradstreet, Inc. New York, NY 10007.

Encyclopedias. Encyclopedias provide authoritative information on a great number of subjects in concise and convenient form. Because no other single reference book can offer so extensive a survey of universal knowledge, it is often wise to start an inquiry with an encyclopedia. Two encyclopedias are:

> *Encyclopedia Britannica* (30 volumes). 15th ed. Chicago: Encyclopedia Britannica, Inc., 1974.
> *Encyclopedia Americana* (30 volumes). New York: Grolier Incorporated, 1975.

A compact single-volume general encyclopedia available for instant reference with concise articles on places, persons, and subjects is published in hardcover and paper editions.

> *Columbia Viking Desk Encyclopedia*, 3d ed. New York: The Viking Press, Inc., 1968.

Etiquette. Business and social etiquette is covered in a number of books on etiquette but the two most prominent authors are:

> Post, Elizabeth L. *Emily Post's Etiquette*, 12th ed. New York: Funk & Wagnalls, Inc., 1968.
> Vanderbilt, Amy. *Amy Vanderbilt's Etiquette*. Garden City, New York: Doubleday & Company, Inc., 1972

Geographic Information. Atlases and gazetteers are reference sources for all kinds of geographical information. An atlas is a book of maps with supporting geographical, statistical and population figures for each area. Such a book may be an atlas of the world, of a country, of a state, of a county, or of a city. Two of the atlases frequently used in business offices are given on the following page.

Rand McNally New Cosmopolitan World Atlas, rev. ed. Chicago:
   Rand McNally & Company, 1975.
Hammond's Contemporary World Atlas New Census Edition: Garden
   City, New York: Doubleday & Company, Inc., 1971.

A gazetteer is a geographical dictionary giving, in alphabetic order,
the names and descriptions of towns, villages, cities, rivers, mountains,
and countries with pronunciations and related historical and geographical information. One of the most comprehensive gazetteers with information about all important places in the world and all incorporated
cities, towns, and villages in the United States and Canada with popula-
tions of 1,500 or more is:

Webster's New Geographical Dictionary, rev. ed. Springfield,
   Mass.: G. & C. Merriam Company, 1972.

Law. A three-volume law directory, published annually, with a complete list of the lawyers in the United States and Canada given in Volumes I and II and digests of the laws of the states in the United States
and the provinces of Canada in Volume III is available.

Martindale-Hubbell Law Directory. Summit, N.J.: Martindale-
   Hubbell, Inc.

Magazine Articles. Articles in a selected number of periodicals are
indexed according to author, title, and subject. They are listed in an annual publication with monthly supplements that are available in all
public libraries.

Readers' Guide to Periodical Literature. New York: The H. W.
   Wilson Company.

Manufacturers. A list of almost all American manufacturers with a
classification of their products, trade names, and brands is published annually by the Thomas Publishing Company.

Thomas Register. New York: Thomas Publishing Company.

Medicine. A register of legally qualified physicians of the United
States and Canada with related medical biographies and a list of approved medical schools and hospitals is published every two years.

American Medical Directory. Chicago: American Medical
   Association.

Newspaper Articles. All items and reports printed in the *New York
Times* are briefly summarized, indexed, and cross-referenced by subject
and name. They are listed alphabetically with the date, page, and column
of publication.

New York Times Index. New York: The New York Times
   Company.

Postal Information. A complete listing of the postal services in the United States, with detailed regulations and procedures covering these services and up-to-date postal rates, is given in this publication:

Postal Service Manual. Superintendent of Documents, U.S. Government Printing Office. Washington, DC 20402.

A directory of ZIP Codes for the entire United States is available:

The National ZIP Code Directory. Superintendent of Documents, U.S. Government Printing Office. Washington, DC 20402.

Shipping Information. Shipments are frequently made by means other than parcel post — by rail, truck, bus, ship, and, more frequently, by air express. A complete shipper's guide containing rates and routings for parcel post, express, and freight shipments is published in separate editions for different parts of the country. This guide also includes information concerning Canadian and foreign parcel post.

Leonard's Guide. New York: G. R. Leonard & Company, Inc.

A complete list of all post offices, railroad stations, shipping lines, and freight receiving stations is published.

*Bullinger's Postal Shipper's Guide for the United States, Canada, and
   Newfoundland*. Bullinger's Guides, Inc., Westwood, New Jersey.

Travel Information. Travel information is available in many forms of guide books, bulletins, and directories.

Guides. Approximately 20,000 accommodations and restaurants in the United States are rated in the paperback editions of the *Mobil Travel Guides* by Simon & Schuster, Inc., New York. The guides also list the outstanding historical, educational, and scenic points of interest throughout the country. Regional guide books are revised and reprinted annually.

Bulletins. Travel bulletins may be obtained from all travel agencies. Two of the better known agencies with offices in all the principal cities of the world are *Thomas Cook & Son* and the *American Express Company*.

Directories. The most frequently consulted directory which annually lists hotels and motels approved by the American Hotel Association with their respective rates, accommodations, and plans of operation is:

Hotel & Motel Red Book. New York: American Hotel Association
   Directory Corporation.

Overseas Guides. A popular overseas guide is:

Fodor's Europe, 1976. New York: David McKay Co., Inc.

Index

data processing, electronic:
  common machine language, 428
  computer tapes and disks, 363
  magnetic ink character recognition (MICR), 428
  optical scanning, 429
  program, 421
  random access, 447
  retrieval, 363
  role in business, 420–421
  role of office worker in, 362
  software, 421
  tabulating (punched) cards, 362–363
data processing, integrated, 428
data processing cycle:
  flow chart, 426
  flow chart symbols, 426
  hardware, 425
  input of data, 425
  origin of data, 424
  output of data, 425–426
  processing of data, 425
  source documents, 424
date line in a letter, 79
dates:
  in legal papers, 166
  written out, 703
decimal point placement:
  in division, 58
  in multiplication, 55–56
decimals:
  converting fractions to, 60
  expressed in writing, 704
deed, defined, 170–171
denominator, 58
denominator, least common, 59
deposits:
  procedure for making, 571–573
  slips for, 572–573
deposit slips:
  identifying checks on, 572
  information needed on, 572
diagonal, 679
dictating, 113–114
  see also word processing systems
dictating equipment, 117
diction, see word choice
dictionaries, 712
dictionary, reading a, 33–35
difference, 54
direct dialing, 228
direct distance dialing, 220–221
direct imaging, 470
directories:
  city, 715
  telephone, 713
  trade, 550, 508
discount, defined, 61
discounts:
  cash, 502
  quantity, 502
  trade, 502
distributive firms, inventories in, 526–527
division, 57–58, 60
domestic mail service, see mail service, domestic
drawer labels, 304

duplicating machines, see fluid duplication; offest duplication; stencil duplication
duplicating processes, 454

E

EDP, 414
educational opportunities, for office workers, 464–647
electronic data processing, see data processing, electronic
electronic display calculator, 434
electronic printing calculator, 434
electrostatic photocopier, 456
elevator files, 358
ellipsis, 680
employee's earnings record, 599
Employee's Withholding Exemption Certificate (W-4 Form), 596–597
employment agencies, 614
employment opportunities:
  beginning positions, 610
  civil service announcements, 616
  classified advertisements, 614–616
  direct inquiry to organization, 616
  employment agencies, 614
  location of work place, 613
  outlook for clerical employment, 644
  school guidance office, 614
  sizes of organizations, 611–612
  types of organizations, 610–611
enclosure notations in a letter, 86
English (imperial) system of measurement, 710–711
enunication, 195
envelopes:
  business reply, 102
  chain feeding of, 396–397
  checking before mailing, 386–387
  folding and inserting letters into, 381–382
  interoffice, 102–103
  kept with incoming letters, 371–372
  precanceled, 383–384
  sealing, 382–383
  sizes of, 100
  stamped, 384
  typing, 100–103
  window, 101–102
erasing, see correcting errors in typed copy
exclamation point, 632, 680
Express and Parcel Post Comparative Rate Guide, 405
express mail, 406

F

federal employment, 616
federal income tax, deducted from pay, 596–597
files:
  card, 353–358

card tickler, 329
central, 256
elevator, 358
follow-up, for purchasing orders, 510
lateral, 298
random, 358
rotary, 357
shelf, 298–299
vertical, 297
filing:
  as basic office skill, 6
  defined, 256
  importance of, 256–257
filing equipment, see files; filing supplies
filing procedures:
  arranging materials in folders, 317
  coding, 312–314, 338
  collecting papers, 310
  cross-referencing, 287, 338
  efficiency in, 317–319
  indexing, 312, 338
  inspecting, 311, 338
  placing records in files, 317
  release mark, 311
  sorting, 315–316, 338
filing rules for names of organizations, see alphabetic indexing for business firms and other organizations
filing rules for personal names, see alphabetic indexing for individuals
filing supplies:
  accessories, 305
  drawer lables, 304
  folder labels, 303
  folders, 299, 301–303
  guides, 299, 300–301
filing systems:
  alphabetic name, 257
  alphabetic subject, 257
  alpha-numeric, 343–344
  chronological, 258
  combination subject and name, 338
  compared, 348
  developing, 364
  geographic, 257, 344–347
  numeric, 258, 338–344
  "office-made"
  subject, 335–338
  tab positions for guides and folders, 304–305
financial duties, of office worker, 8
financial reports:
  balance sheet
  carbon copies of, 159
  checking accuracy of calculations in, 154
  final draft of, 159
  guidelines for typing, 154–158
  importance of, 152
  income statement, 153
  proofreading, 158–159
  studying previous reports, 153–154
first-class mail, 387